Barcelona

timeout.com/barcelona

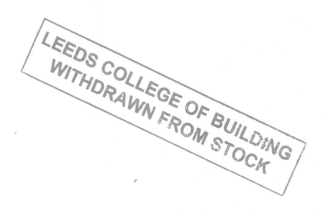

Published by Time Out Guides Ltd, a wholly owned subsidiary of Time Out Group Ltd.
Time Out and the Time Out logo are trademarks of Time Out Group Ltd.

© **Time Out Group Ltd 2005**
Previous editions 1996, 1998, 2000, 2001, 2002, 2003, 2004.

10 9 8 7 6 5 4 3 2 1

This edition first published in Great Britain in 2005 by Ebury
Ebury is a division of The Random House Group Ltd,
20 Vauxhall Bridge Road, London SW1V 2SA

Random House Australia Pty Limited, 20 Alfred Street, Milsons Point, Sydney, New South Wales 2061, Australia
Random House New Zealand Limited, 18 Poland Road, Glenfield, Auckland 10, New Zealand
Random House South Africa (Pty) Limited, Endulini, 5A Jubilee Road, Parktown 2193, South Africa

Random House UK Limited Reg. No. 954009

Distributed in USA by Publishers Group West
1700 Fourth Street, Berkeley, California 94710

Distributed in Canada by Penguin Canada Ltd
10 Alcorn Avenue, Toronto, Ontario, Canada M4V 3B2

For further distribution details, see www.timeout.com

ISBN 1-904978-35-5

A CIP catalogue record for this book is available from the British Library

Colour reprographics by Icon, Crowne House, 56-58 Southwark Street, London SE1 1UN

Printed and bound in Germany by Appl
Papers used by Ebury Press are natural, recyclable products made from wood grown in sustainable forests

Time Out Guides Limited
Universal House
251 Tottenham Court Road
London W1T 7AB
Tel + 44 (0)20 7813 3000
Fax + 44 (0)20 7813 6001
Email guides@timeout.com
www.timeout.com

Editorial

Editor Sally Davies
Deputy Editors Will Fulford-Jones, Ros Sales
Listings Editors Alix Leveugle, Alex Phillips
Proofreader Tamsin Shelton
Indexer Jonathan Cox

Editorial/Managing Director Peter Fiennes
Series Editor Ruth Jarvis
Deputy Series Editor Lesley McCave
Business Manager Gareth Garner
Guides Co-ordinator Holly Pick
Accountant Sarah Bostock

Design

Art Director Mandy Martin
Deputy Art Director Scott Moore
Senior Designer Tracey Ridgewell
Designer Oliver Knight
Junior Designer Chrissy Mouncey
Digital Imaging Dan Conway
Ad Make-up Charlotte Blythe

Picture Desk

Picture Editor Jael Marschner
Deputy Picture Editor Tracey Kerrigan
Picture Researchers Monica Roche, Helen McFarland

Advertising

Sales Director Mark Phillips
International Sales Manager Ross Canadé
International Sales Executive Simon Davies
Advertising Sales (Barcelona) Creative Media Group
Advertising Assistant Lucy Butler

Marketing

Marketing Director Mandy Martinez
Marketing & Publicity Manager, US Rosella Albanese

Production

Production Director Mark Lamond
Production Controller Samantha Furniss

Time Out Group

Chairman Tony Elliott
Managing Director Mike Hardwick
Group Financial Director Richard Waterlow
Group Commercial Director Lesley Gill
Group Marketing Director Christine Cort
Group General Manager Nichola Coulthard
Group Circulation Director Jim Heinemann
Group Art Director John Oakey
Online Managing Director David Pepper
Group Production Director Steve Proctor
Group IT Director Simon Chappell

Contributors

Introduction Sally Davies. **History** Nick Rider, Jason Garner (*Barna in books: Cervantes, Derail in anger* Dani Campi). **Barcelona Today** Andrew Losowsky (*Voting with your ass* Jonathan Bennett). **Architecture** Nick Rider, Dani Campi. **God's Own Architect** Gijs van Hensbergen. **Where to Stay** Alix Leveugle, Tara Stevens. **Sightseeing** Sally Davies, Nadia Feddo, Alex Leith, John O'Donovan (*Barna in books* Dani Campi; *Flashpoints* Jason Garner; *No more bull* Sarah Couli). **Restaurants** Sally Davies (*Eating on the Go* Dani Campi; *Casas regionales* Tara Stevens). **Cafés, Tapas & Bars** Sally Davies (*Strange brews, No shrinking Violeta* Andrew Losowsky). **Shops & Services** Nadia Feddo, Alix Leveugle. **Festivals & Events** Nadia Feddo (*Urban tribes: Castellers* Alex Leith). **Children** Nadia Feddo. **Film** Jonathan Bennett (*Stars above the silver screen* Sally Davies). **Galleries** Alex Phillips. **Gay & Lesbian** Quim Pujol (*Sitges* Dexter Lee). **Music & Nightlife** Kirsten Foster, Guillermo González (*Chips with everything* Andrew Losowsky). **Performing Arts** Classical Music & Opera Jonathan Bennett; Theatre & Dance Tamzin Townsend. **Sport & Fitness** Alex Leith. **Trips Out of Town** Sally Davies, Alex Leith (*What's the time, Mr Wolf?, Tales of the city* Sally Davies; *Rolling out the barrels* Alex Johnson). **Directory** Alix Leveugle.

Maps Mapworld (71 Blandy Road, Henley on Thames, Oxon, RG9 1QB) and JS Graphics (john@jsgraphics.co.uk).

Photography Matei Glass, except pages 10, 26 AISA; pages 16, 24 AKG; page 17 Art Archives; page 18 Col. Rossend Casanova; page 24 Alamy; page 25 Bridgeman Art Library; page 92 AP; page 135 Sally Davies; page 265 Miquel Taverna Homs/Avui Música; page 269 David Ruano.

The Editor would like to thank all the contributors, Alfonso Blanco, Clementina Milà, Gemma Giménez, George Cowdery, Lluis Bosch, Manel Baena, Montse Pozo, Sarah Guy and especially John O'Donovan.

Contents

Introduction	6	Galleries	234
		Gay & Lesbian	238
In Context	**9**	Music & Nightlife	246
		Performing Arts	262
History	10	Sport & Fitness	271
Barcelona Today	31		
Architecture	35		
God's Own Architect	45	**Trips Out of Town**	**277**
		Getting Started	278
Where to Stay	**49**	Around Barcelona	279
		Tarragona & the Costa Daurada	283
Where to Stay	50	*Map: Tarragona*	283
		Girona & the Costa Brava	290
Sightseeing	**81**	*Map: Girona*	290
		Vic to the Pyrenees	298
Introduction	82		
Barri Gòtic	86	**Directory**	**303**
Raval	97		
Sant Pere & the Born	103	Getting Around	304
Barceloneta & the Ports	110	Resources A-Z	308
Montjuïc	115	Spanish Vocabulary	323
The Eixample	122	Catalan Vocabulary	324
Gràcia & Other Districts	131	Further Reference	325
		Index	326
Eat, Drink, Shop	**143**	Advertisers' Index	332
Restaurants	144		
Cafés, Tapas & Bars	173	**Maps**	**333**
Shops & Services	189		
		Trips Out of Town	334
Arts & Entertainment	**215**	Around Barcelona	335
		Barcelona Areas	336
Festivals & Events	216	Street Maps	337
Children	225	Street Index	346
Film	230	RENFE Local Trains	349
		Metro	350

Introduction

Unassailable proof that what doesn't kill you makes you stronger, Barcelona over the centuries has been buffeted by invading forces, fleeced by trade restrictions and strangled by autocratic central governments – and every time has bounced back prouder and more audacious. After the 'grey years', the interminable period between the end of the civil war and Franco's dying breath, there was a huge zest for change, to move on to a new era. It stoked the desire to transform the city itself, while the Olympic bid and then the Games themselves provided extra incentive, not to mention cash.

The finest architects and urban planners were persuaded to take part in this vision. The axis upon which the project spun was the idea to 'turn Barcelona around' to face the sea, creating whole swathes of beach from virtual wasteland. Ugly high-rises flung up during the Franco regime were pulled down, derelict blocks razed to provide open spaces and parkland, and world-class artists and sculptors – Roy Lichtenstein, James Turrell, Claes Oldenburg and Eduardo Chillida among them — commissioned to brighten up street corners. Along with the creation of the new Barcelona in bricks and mortar went the promotion of Barcelona-as-concept, a seductive cocktail of architecture, imagination, tradition, style, nightlife and primary colours.

Helped, in large part, by the legacy of Gaudí and his Modernista contemporaries, which provided the city with a unique foundation both architecturally and in spirit, this was perhaps the most spectacular, and certainly the most deliberate, of Barcelona's reinventions; it succeeded in large part because this image of creativity and vivacity simply fitted well with an idea of the city already held by many of its citizens. Thrown into the mix were the core values of nationalist pride and a delight in traditional ways, from dancing the *sardana* in front of the cathedral, to wheeling out the *papier mâché* giants at the first hint of a celebration. Barcelona's love of eccentricity had already brought about a wealth of quirky museums (such as those devoted to shoes, perfume, sewers, funeral carriages and mechanical toys), to which more were added. Its handsome but grimy façades were buffed up, its streets renamed and its churches restored. It was as if the drab decades had been just a collective bad dream.

The glittering, buoyant result, according to every poll worth its clipboard, is the most popular city in Europe today.

ABOUT THE TIME OUT CITY GUIDES

The *Time Out Barcelona Guide* is one of an expanding series of Time Out City Guides, now numbering more than 45, produced by the people behind London and New York's successful listings magazines. Our guides are all written and updated by resident experts who have striven to provide you with all the most up-to-date information you'll need to explore the city or read up on its background, whether you're a local or a first-time visitor. The guide contains detailed practical information, plus features that focus on unique aspects of the city.

THE LOWDOWN ON THE LISTINGS

Above all, we have tried to make this book as useful as possible. Addresses, telephone numbers, websites, transport information, opening times, admission prices and credit card details are included in our listings. And, as far as possible, we've given details of facilities, services and events, all checked and correct at the time we went to press. However, owners and managers can change their arrangements at any time, and often do. Many small shops and businesses in Barcelona do not keep precise opening hours and may close earlier or later than stated here. Similarly, arts programmes are often finalised very late, and liable to change. We would advise you whenever possible to phone ahead and check opening times, ticket prices and other particulars. While every effort has been made to ensure the accuracy of this guide, the publishers cannot accept responsibility for any errors it may contain.

PRICES AND PAYMENT

The prices given in this guide should be treated as guidelines, not gospel. If they vary wildly from those we've quoted, please write and let us know. We aim to give the best and most up-to-date advice, so we always want to know when you've been badly treated or overcharged. Wherever possible we have factored in the sales tax (IVA), which many restaurants and hotels leave out of their advertised rates.

We have listed prices in euros (€) throughout, and we have noted whether venues take credit cards, but have only listed the major cards – American Express (**AmEx**), Diners Club (**DC**), MasterCard (**MC**), Visa (**V**). Many businesses will also accept other cards, including **JCB**. Some shops, restaurants and attractions take travellers' cheques.

THE LIE OF THE LAND

We have divided the city into areas – simplified, for convenience, from the full complexity of Barcelona's geography – and the relevant area name is given with each venue listed in this guide. Wherever possible, a map reference is provided for every venue listed, indicating the page and grid reference for where it can be found in the street maps at the back of the book.

TELEPHONE NUMBERS

It is necessary to dial provincial area codes with all the numbers in Spain, even for local calls. Hence all normal Barcelona numbers begin 93, whether you're calling from inside or outside the city. From abroad, you must dial 34 (the international dialling code for Spain) followed by the number given in the book – which includes the initial 93. For more information on telephones and codes, *see p319.*

ESSENTIAL INFORMATION

For all the practical information you might need for visiting Barcelona, including emergency phone numbers and details of local transport, turn to the **Directory** chapter at the back of the guide. It starts on page 303.

LANGUAGE

Barcelona is a bilingual city; street signs, tourist information and menus can be in either Catalan or Spanish, and this is reflected in the guide. We have tried to use whichever is more commonly used or appropriate in each case.

MAPS

The map section of the book includes some overviews of the greater Barcelona area and its neighbourhoods; detailed street maps of the Eixample, the Raval, Gràcia and other districts, and a large-scale map of the Old City, with a

comprehensive street index, a map of the entire region for planning trips out of town and maps of the local rail and metro networks. The maps start on page 333.

LET US KNOW WHAT YOU THINK

We hope you enjoy the *Time Out Barcelona Guide*, and we'd like to know what you think of it. We welcome tips for places that you consider we should include in future editions and take note of your criticism of our choices. There's a reader's reply card at the back of this book for your feedback – or you can email us at guides@timeout.com.

There is an online version of this book, along with guides to over 45 other international cities, at **www.timeout.com**.

In Context

History	**10**
Barcelona Today	**31**
Architecture	**35**
God's Own Architect	**45**

Features

Walk on Roman remains	12
Barna in books Cervantes	18
Failed utopias	23
Derail in anger	26
Voting with your ass	32
You lookin' at me?	39
Sexing up the skyline	42
Don't miss Gaudí creations	46

Wilfred the Hairy. *See p11.*

History

The Catalonia story.

While cultural, political and social diversity flourish in today's Barcelona, it has not always been that way. For long periods of its history, the city was the victim of attempts by governments in Madrid to absorb Catalonia within a centralised unified Spanish state. Under several leaders, notably Philip V in the 17th century and Franco in the 20th, these attempts resulted in a policy aimed at stamping out any vestige of Catalan culture or independence. However, the region always re-emerged stronger, more vibrant and with a heightened desire to show the world its distinctive character, both socially and culturally. The results are visible in the city's numerous museums and monuments, the diversity of its architecture and the scope and variety of its cultural and artistic lives. It might always be reinventing itself, but Barcelona constantly has an eye on its past.

IN THE BEGINNING

The Romans founded Barcelona in about 15 BC on the Mons Taber, a small hill between two streams that provided a good view of the Mediterranean, and which today is crowned by a cathedral. At the time, the plain around it was sparsely inhabited by the Laetani, an agrarian Iberian people who produced grain and honey, and gathered oysters. Then called Barcino, the town was smaller than Tarraco (Tarragona), the capital of the Roman province of Hispania Citerior, but it had the only harbour between there and Narbonne.

Like virtually every other Roman new town in Europe, Barcino was a fortified rectangle with a crossroads at its centre (where the Plaça Sant Jaume is today). It was also a decidedly unimportant provincial town, but the rich plain provided it with a produce garden and the sea gave it an incipient maritime trade. It acquired a Jewish community soon after its foundation and became associated with Christian martyrs, most particularly Santa Eulàlia, Barcelona's first patron saint. Eulàlia was supposedly executed at the end of the third century via a series of revolting tortures that included being rolled naked in a sealed barrel full of glass shards down the alley now called Baixada (descent) de Santa Eulàlia (*see p91*, **Fingered**).

The people of Barcino accepted Christianity in AD 312, together with the rest of the Roman Empire, which by then was under growing threat of invasion. In response, the town's rough defences were replaced with massive stone walls in the fourth century, many sections of which can still be seen today. It was these ramparts that ensured Barcelona's continuity, making the stronghold desirable to later warlords.

Nonetheless, defences like these could not prevent the empire's disintegration. In 415 Barcelona, as it became known, briefly became capital of the kingdom of the Visigoths, under their chieftain Ataülf. They soon moved on southwards to extend their control over the whole of the Iberian peninsula, and for the next 400 years the town was a neglected backwater. The Muslims swept across the peninsula after 711, crushing Goth resistance; they made little attempt to settle Catalonia, but much of the Christian population retreated into the Pyrenees, the first Catalan heartland.

Then, at the end of the eighth century, the Franks drove south, against the Muslims, from across the mountains. In 801 Charlemagne's son, Louis the Pious, took Barcelona and made it a bastion of the Marca Hispanica (Spanish March), which was the southern buffer of his father's empire. This gave Catalonia a trans-Pyrenean origin entirely different from that of the other Christian states in Spain; equally, it is for this reason that the closest relative of the Catalan language is Provençal, not Castilian.

When the Frankish princes returned to their main business further north, loyal counts were left behind to rule sections of the Catalan lands. At the end of the ninth century one of them, Count Guifré el Pilós ('Wilfred the Hairy'), managed to gain control over several of these Catalan counties from his base in Ripoll. By uniting them under his rule he laid the basis for a future Catalan state, founding the dynasty of the Counts of Barcelona that reigned in an unbroken line until 1410. His successors made Barcelona their capital, setting the seal on the city's future.

As a founding patriarch, Wilfred is the stuff of legends, not least of which is that he was the creator of the Catalan flag. The story goes that he was fighting the Saracens alongside his lord, the Frankish emperor, when he was severely wounded. In recognition of Wilfred's heroism, the emperor dipped his fingers into his friend's blood and ran them down the Count's golden shield; thus, the Quatre Barres, four bars of red on a yellow background, also known as La Senyera. Recorded facts make this story highly unlikely, but whatever its origins, the four-stripe symbol was first recorded on the tomb of Count Ramon Berenguer II from 1082, making it

the oldest national flag in Europe. What is not known is exactly in what way Wilfred was so notably hairy.

A century after Wilfred, in 985, a Muslim army attacked and sacked Barcelona. The hirsute count's great-grandson, Count Borrell II, requested aid from his theoretical feudal lord, the Frankish king. He received no reply, and so repudiated all Frankish sovereignty over Catalonia. From then on, although the name was not yet in use, Catalonia was effectively independent, and the Counts of Barcelona were free to forge its destiny.

LAYING THE FOUNDATIONS

In the first century of the new millennium, Catalonia was consolidated as a political entity, and entered an age of cultural richness. This was the great era of Catalan Romanesque art, with the building of the magnificent monasteries and the churches of northern Catalonia, such as Sant Pere de Rodes near Figueres, and the painting of the glorious murals now housed in the Museu Nacional on Montjuïc. There was also a flowering of scholarship, reflecting Catalan contacts with northern Europe and with Islamic and Carolingian cultures. In Barcelona, shipbuilding and trade in grain and wine all grew, and a new trade developed in textiles. The city expanded both inside its old Roman walls and outside them, with *vilanoves* (new towns) appearing at Sant Pere and La Ribera.

Catalonia also gained more territory from the Muslims to the south, beyond the Penedès, and – either through marriage or with Arab booty – large areas of what is now southern France. The most significant marriage, however, occurred in 1137, when Ramon Berenguer IV (1131-62) wed Petronella, heir to the throne of Aragon. In the long term, the marriage bound Catalonia into Iberia. The uniting of the two dynasties created a powerful entity known as the Crown of Aragon: each element retained its separate institutions, and was ruled by monarchs known as the Count-Kings. Since Aragon was already a kingdom, it was given precedence and its name was often used to refer to the state, but the language used in the court was Catalan and the centre of government remained in Barcelona.

Ramon Berenguer IV also extended Catalan territory to its current frontiers in the Ebro valley. At the beginning of the next century, however, the dynasty lost virtually all its land north of the Pyrenees to France, when Count-King Pere I 'the Catholic' was killed at the battle of Muret in 1213. This proved a blessing in disguise. In future years, the Catalan-Aragonese state became oriented decisively towards the Mediterranean and the south, and was able to embark on two centuries of imperialism that would be equalled in vigour only by Barcelona's burgeoning commercial enterprise.

THE EMPIRE GROWS

Pere I's successor was the most expansionist of the Count-Kings. Jaume I 'the Conqueror' (1213-76) abandoned any idea of further adventures in Provence and joined the campaign against the Muslims to the south, taking Mallorca in 1229, Ibiza in 1235 and, at greater cost, Valencia in 1238 (he made it another separate kingdom, the third part of the Crown of Aragon). Barcelona became the centre of an empire that spanned across the Mediterranean.

The city grew tremendously. In the middle of the 13th century Jaume I ordered the building of a second wall along the line of the Rambla and roughly encircling the area between there and the modern Parc de la Ciutadella, thus bringing La Ribera and the other *vilanoves* within the city.

He also gave Barcelona a form of representative self-government in 1274: the Consell de Cent, a council of 100 chosen citizens, an institution that would last for more than 400 years. In Catalonia as a whole, royal powers were strictly limited by a parliament, the Corts, with a permanent standing committee known as the Generalitat.

The Count-Kings commanded a powerful fleet and a mercenary army centred on the Almogàvers, irregular warriors who had been hardened in the endless battles with the Muslims on the Catalan frontier. The Almogàvers were themselves feared equally by Christians and Muslims as they travelled the Mediterranean conquering, plundering and enslaving in the name of God and the Crown of Aragon.

In 1282 Pere II 'the Great' sent his armies into Sicily; Catalan domination over the island would last for nearly 150 years. The Catalan empire reached its greatest strength under Jaume II 'the Just' (1291-1327). Corsica (1323)

Walk on Roman remains

Duration: 45 minutes.

In 15 BC Roman soldiers established a colony on a small hill called the **Mons Taber**, which later was to become the settlement of **Barcino**. Medieval Barcelona and all subsequent buildings in the Barri Gòtic were constructed on top of the site; over the last century many a local resident has set out to remodel a bathroom and turned up a lump of ancient masonry.

Barcino has also had an unappreciated impact on the two millennia of life that followed its beginnings. Many of Barcelona's most familiar streets – C/Hospital, even Passeig de Gràcia – follow the line of Roman roads, and the best way to get an idea of the Roman town is to walk the line of its walls. Along the way sit all kinds of Roman remains, poking out from where they were reused or constructed over by medieval builders and those that followed them.

A logical place to start a walk is at **C/Paradís**, between the cathedral and Plaça Sant Jaume, where a round millstone is set into the paving to mark what was believed to be the precise centre of the Mons Taber. It's here that you'll find the remains of the **Temple Romà d'Augusti** (*see p95*). Where C/Paradís meets the Plaça Sant Jaume was where Barcino's two main thoroughfares once met; the road on the left, **C/Llibreteria**, began life as the **Cardus Maximus**, the main road to Rome. Just off this road is the Plaça

del Rei and the extraordinary **Museu d'Història de la Ciutat**, below which you can visit the largest underground excavation of a Roman site in Europe.

Rejoining C/Llibreteria, turn left at **C/Tapineria** to reach **Plaça Ramon Berenguer el Gran** and the largest surviving stretch of ancient wall, incorporated into the medieval Palau Reial. Continue along Tapineria, where you'll find many sections of Roman building, to **Avda de la Catedral**. The massive twin-drum gate on C/Bisbe, while often retouched, has not changed in its basic shape, at least at the base, since it was the main gate of the Roman town. To its left you can see fragments of an aqueduct, and at its front Joan Brossa's bronze letters, spelling out 'Barcino'. If you take a detour up C/Capellans to **C/Duran i Bas**, you can see another four arches of an aqueduct; heading left and straight over the Avda Portal de l'Àngel is the Roman necropolis in **Plaça Vila de Madrid**, with the tombs clearly visible. In accordance with Roman custom, these had to be outside the city walls.

Returning to the cathedral, turn right into **C/Palla**. A little way along sits a large chunk of Roman wall, only discovered in the 1980s when a building was demolished. Palla runs into **C/Banys Nous**; at No.16 sits a centre for disabled children, inside which is a piece of wall with a relief of legs and feet (phone ahead for a viewing time; 93 318 14 81).

and Sardinia (1324) were added to the Crown of Aragon, although the latter would never submit to Catalan rule and would from then on be a constant focus of revolt.

THE GOLDEN AGE

The Crown of Aragon was often at war with Arab rulers, but its capital flourished through commerce with every part of the Mediterranean, Christian and Muslim. Catalan ships also sailed into the Atlantic, to England and Flanders, their ventures actively supported by the Count-Kings and burghers of Barcelona and regulated by the first-ever code of maritime law, known as the *Llibre del Consolat de Mar* (written 1258-72). By the late 13th century around 130 consulates ringed the Mediterranean, engaged in a complex system of trade.

Not surprisingly, this age of power and prestige was also the great era of building in medieval Barcelona. The Count-Kings' imperial conquests may have been ephemeral, but their talent for permanence in building can still be seen today. Between 1290 and 1340, the construction of most of Barcelona's best-known Gothic buildings was initiated. Religious edifices such as the cathedral, Santa Maria del Mar and Santa Maria del Pi were matched by civil buildings such as the Saló de Tinell and the Llotja, the old market and the stock exchange. As a result, Barcelona contains the most important collection of historic Gothic civil architecture anywhere in Europe.

The ships of the Catalan navy were built in the monumental Drassanes (shipyards), begun by Pere II and completed under Pere III, in 1378. In 1359 Pere III also built the third, final city wall along the line of the modern Paral·lel, Ronda Sant Pau and Ronda Sant Antoni. This gave the 'old city' of Barcelona its definitive shape. La Ribera, 'the waterfront', was the centre of trade and industry in the 14th-century

At No.4 is **La Granja** (*see p175*), a lovely old café with yet another stretch of Roman wall at the back; beyond this is the junction with **C/Call**, the other end of the Cardus, and so the opposite side of the Roman town from Llibreteria-Tapineria. The staff of the clothes wholesalers at C/Call 1 are also used to people wandering in to examine their piece of Roman tower. Carry on across C/Ferran and down **C/Avinyó**, the next continuation of the perimeter. Two sides of the cave-like dining room at the back of **El Gallo Kiriko**, the Pakistani restaurant at No.19, are actually formed by portions of the Roman wall.

From **C/Milans**, turn left on to **C/Gignás**. Near the junction with **C/Regomir** are remains of the fourth sea gate of the town, which would have faced the beach, and the Roman shipyard. Take a detour up C/Regomir to visit one of the most important relics of Barcino, the **Pati Llimona** (*see p91*); then, continue walking up **C/Correu Vell**, where there are more fragments of wall, to reach one of the most impressive relics of Roman Barcelona in the small, shady **Plaça Traginers**: a Roman tower and one corner of the ancient wall, in a remarkable state of preservation despite having had a medieval house built on top of it. Finally, turn up **C/Sots-Tinent Navarro**, which boasts a massive stretch of Roman rampart, to end the walk at Plaça de l'Àngel.

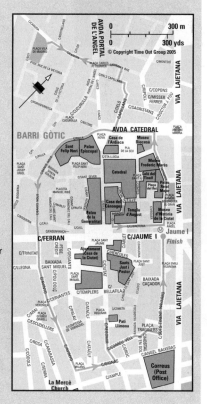

city. Just inland, the Carrer Montcada was where newly enriched merchants displayed their wealth in opulent Gothic palaces. All around were the workers of the various craft guilds, grouped together in their own streets.

The Catalan Golden Age was also an era of cultural greatness. Catalonia was one of the first areas in Europe to use its vernacular language, as well as Latin, in written form and as a language of culture. The oldest written texts in Catalan are the *Homilies d'Organyà*, 12th-century translations from the Bible. The court and the aristocracy seem very early to have attained an unusual level of literacy: Jaume I even wrote an autobiography, the *Llibre dels Feits* or 'Book of Deeds', in which he recounted his achievements and conquests.

Incipient Catalan literature was given a vital thrust by Ramon Llull (1235-1316). After a debauched youth, he experienced a series of religious visions and became the first man in post-Roman Europe to write philosophy in a vernacular language. Steeped in Arabic and Hebrew writings, Llull brought together Christian, Islamic, Jewish and classical ideas, and wrote a vast amount on other subjects – from theories of chivalry to poetry and visionary tales, in doing so effectively creating Catalan as a literary language. Catalan translations were undertaken from Greek and Latin. Chroniclers such as Ramon Muntaner recorded the exploits of Count-Kings and Almogàvers; in 1490, in the twilight of the Golden Age, the Valencian Joanot Martorell published *Tirant lo Blanc*, a bawdy adventure widely considered the first European novel.

REVOLT AND COLLAPSE

The extraordinary prosperity of the medieval period did not last. The Count-Kings had over-extended Barcelona's resources, and over-invested in far-off ports. By 1400 the effort to maintain their conquests by force, especially Sardinia, had exhausted the spirit and the coffers of the Catalan imperialist drive. The Black Death, which arrived in the 1340s, also had a devastating impact on Catalonia, intensifying the bitterness of social conflicts between the aristocracy, the merchants, the peasants and the urban poor.

In 1410, Martí I 'the Humane' died without an heir, bringing to an end the line of Counts of Barcelona unbroken since Wilfred the Hairy. The Crown of Aragon was passed to a member of a Castilian noble family, the Trastámaras: Fernando de Antequera (1410-16). In the 1460s, the effects of war and catastrophic famine led to a sudden collapse into violent and destructive civil war and peasant revolt. The population was depleted to such an extent that Barcelona

would not regain the numbers it had had in 1400 (40,000) until the 18th century.

In 1469 an important union for Spain initiated a woeful period in Barcelona's history; dubbed by some Catalan historians the Decadència, it eventually led to the end of Catalonia as a separate entity. In that year, Ferdinand of Aragon (1479-1516) married Isabella of Castile (1476-1506) and so united the different Spanish kingdoms, even though they would retain their separate institutions for another two centuries.

EAST OF EDEN

As Catalonia's fortunes had declined, so those of Castile to the west had risen. In 1492 Granada, the last Muslim foothold in Spain, was conquered; Isabella decreed the expulsion of all Jews from Castile and Aragon; and, most famously, Columbus discovered America.

It was Castile's seafaring orientation towards the Atlantic, as opposed to the Mediterranean, that confirmed Catalonia's decline. The discovery of the New World was a disaster for Catalan commerce: trade shifted decisively away from the Mediterranean, and Catalans were officially barred from participating in the exploitation of the new empire until the 1770s. The weight of Castile within the monarchy was increased, and it soon became the clear seat of government.

In 1516 the Spanish crown passed to the House of Habsburg, in the shape of Ferdinand and Isabella's grandson, Holy Roman Emperor Charles V. His son, Philip II of Spain, established Madrid as the capital of all of his dominions in 1561. Catalonia was managed by viceroys, and the power of its institutions increasingly restricted, with a down-at-heel aristocracy and a meagre cultural life.

GRIM REAPERS

While Castilian Spain went through its 'Golden Century', Catalonia was left on the margins. However, worse was to come in the following century with the two national revolts, both heroic defeats that have since acquired a role in central Catalan mythology.

The problem for the Spanish monarchy was that Castile was an absolute monarchy and thus could be taxed at will, but in the former Aragonese territories, and especially Catalonia, royal authority kept coming up against a mass of local rights and privileges. As the Habsburgs' empire became bogged down in endless wars and expenses that not even American gold could meet, the Count-Duke of Olivares, the formidable great minister of King Philip IV (1621-65), resolved to extract more money and troops from the non-Castilian dominions of the crown. The Catalans, however, felt they were taxed quite enough already.

Ferdinand of Aragon. *See p15.*

Anjou, as King Philip V of Spain (1700-46). However, the alternative candidate, the Archduke Charles of Austria, promised that he would restore the traditional rights of the former Aragonese territories, and won their allegiance. He also had the support, in his fight against France, of Britain, Holland and Austria.

But Catalonia had backed the wrong horse. In 1713, Britain and the Dutch made a separate peace with France and withdrew their aid, leaving the Catalans stranded with no possibility of victory. After a 13-month siege in which every citizen was called to arms, Barcelona fell to the French and Spanish armies on 11 September 1714. The most heroic defeat of all, the date marked the most decisive political reverse in Barcelona's history, and is now commemorated as Catalan National Day, the Diada. Some of Barcelona's resisters were buried next to the church of Santa Maria del Mar in the Born in the Fossar de les Moreres (Mulberry Graveyard), now a memorial.

> **'Barcelona was rebellious, liberal, republican and free-thinking; utopian groups proliferated.'**

In 1715, Philip V issued his decree of Nova Planta, abolishing all the remaining separate institutions of the Crown of Aragon and so, in effect, creating 'Spain' as a single, unitary state. Large-scale 'Castilianisation' of the country was initiated, and Castilian replaced the Catalan language in all official documents. In Barcelona, extra measures were taken to keep the city under control. The crumbling medieval walls and the castle on Montjuïc were refurbished with new ramparts, and a massive new citadel was built on the eastern side of the old city, where the Parc de la Ciutadella is today. To make space, thousands were expelled from La Ribera and forcibly rehoused in the Barceloneta, Barcelona's first-ever planned housing scheme, with its barrack-like street plan unmistakably provided by French military engineers. The citadel became the most hated symbol of the city's subordination.

RETAIL THERAPY

Politically subjugated and without a significant native ruling class, Catalonia nevertheless revived in the 18th century. Shipping picked up again, and in the last years of the 18th century Barcelona had a booming export trade to the New World in wines and spirits from Catalan vineyards, and textiles, wool and silk. In 1780, a merchant called Erasme de Gómina opened Barcelona's first true factory, a hand-powered

In 1640, a mass of peasants, later dubbed Els Segadors (the Reapers), gathered on the Rambla in Barcelona, outside the Porta Ferrissa (Iron Gate) in the second wall. The peasants rioted against royal authority, surged into the city and murdered the viceroy, the Marquès de Santa Coloma. This began the general uprising known as the Guerra dels Segadors, or the 'Reapers' War'. The authorities of the Generalitat, led by its president Pau Claris, were fearful of the violence of the poor; lacking the confidence to declare Catalonia independent, they appealed for protection from Louis XIII of France. French armies, however, were unable to defend Catalonia adequately, and in 1652 a destitute Barcelona capitulated to the equally exhausted army of Philip IV. In 1659 France and Spain made peace with a treaty that gave the Catalan territory of Roussillon, around Perpignan, to France. After the revolt, Philip IV and his ministers were magnanimous, allowing the Catalans to retain what was left of their institutions despite their disloyalty.

THE REIGN IN SPAIN

Fifty years on came the second of the great national rebellions: the War of the Spanish Succession. In 1700, Charles II of Spain died without an heir, and Castile accepted the grandson of Louis XIV of France, Philip of weaving mill in C/Riera Alta with 800 workers. In the next decade, Catalan trade with Spanish America quadrupled; Barcelona's population had grown from 30,000 in 1720 to around 100,000 by the end of the century.

The prosperity was reflected in a new wave of building in the city. Neo-classical mansions appeared, notably on C/Ample and La Rambla, but the greatest transformation was in La Rambla itself. Until the 1770s, it had been no more than a dusty, dry riverbed where country people came to sell their produce, lined on the Raval side mostly with giant religious houses and on the other with Jaume I's second wall. In 1775, the Captain-General, the Marqués de la Mina, embarked on an ambitious scheme to demolish the wall and turn the Rambla into a paved promenade. Beyond the Rambla, the previously semi-rural Raval was swiftly becoming densely populated.

Barcelona's expansion was briefly slowed by the French invasion of 1808. Napoleon sought to appeal to Catalans by offering them national recognition within his empire, but was met with curiously little response. After six years of turmoil, Barcelona's growing business class resumed its many projects in 1814, with the restoration of the Bourbon monarchy in the shape of Ferdinand VII.

GETTING UP STEAM

On his restoration, Ferdinand VII (1808-33) attempted to reinstate the absolute monarchy of his youth and reimpose his authority over Spain's American colonies, but failed to do either. On his death he was succeeded by his three-year-old daughter Isabel II (1833-68), but the throne was also claimed by his brother Carlos, who was strongly backed by the most reactionary sectors in the country.

To defend Isabel's rights, the Regent, Ferdinand's widow Queen María Cristina, was obliged to seek the support of liberals, and so granted a very limited form of constitution. Thus began Spain's Carlist Wars, which had a powerful impact in conservative rural Catalonia, where Don Carlos's faction won a considerable following, in part because of its support for traditional local rights and customs.

While this see-saw struggle went on around the country, a liberal-minded local administration in Barcelona, freed from subordination to the military, was able to engage in some city planning, opening up the soon-to-be fashionable C/Ferran and Plaça Sant Jaume in the 1820s and later adding the Plaça Reial. A fundamental change came in 1836, when the government in Madrid decreed the Desamortización (or the 'disentailment') of Spain's monasteries. In Barcelona, where

convents and religious houses still took up great sections of the Raval and the Rambla, a huge area was freed for development. The Rambla took on the appearance it roughly retains today, while the Raval, the main district for new industry in a Barcelona still contained within its walls, filled up with tenements and textile mills several storeys high.

In 1832, the first steam-driven factory in Spain was built on C/Tallers, sparking resistance from hand-spinners and weavers. Most of the city's factories were still relatively small, however, and the Catalan manufacturers were aware that they were at a disadvantage in competing with the industries of Britain and other countries to the north. Complicating matters further, they didn't even have the city to themselves. Not only did the anti-industrial Carlists threaten from the countryside, but Barcelona soon became a centre of radical ideas. Its people were notably rebellious, and liberal, republican, free-thinking and even utopian socialist groups proliferated between sporadic bursts of repression. In 1842 a liberal revolt, the Jamancia, took over Barcelona, and barricades went up around the city. This would be the last occasion on which Barcelona was bombarded from the castle on Montjuïc, as the army struggled to regain control.

Charles V. *See p15.*

Barna in books Cervantes

Think of *Don Quixote* and the image that usually comes to mind is of the wide-open, windmill-flecked spaces of La Mancha. However, it's less well known that Barcelona plays a central role in Cervantes's 'novel of novels'. This year, Spain celebrates the 400th anniversary of the publication of the first part of *Don Quixote*, an event that's to be celebrated in Barcelona with various exhibitions and events.

Barcelona at the dawn of the 17th century is the setting for the final stage in Don Quixote's long adventures. Upon his arrival in the city, accompanied by the ever-faithful Sancho, he sees the sea for the first time and realises he can go no further. There, on the beach at Barceloneta, Don Quixote finally meets his match: where sunbathers today enjoy a beer or a massage, the Don is defeated by his nemesis, the Caballero de la Blanca Luna, a humiliation that signals the end of his knightly delusions.

The symbolism of the sea aside, Cervantes chose to end his story in Barcelona because in the early 17th century, as it is today, Barcelona was the publishing capital of Spain. It is in Barcelona that Don Quixote comes face to face with his fame: walking along the C/Call, he enters a bookshop and finds the story of his life printed in various apocryphal editions. Many citizens greet him with incredulity, accusing him of merely pretending to be the famous knight, transforming him instantly into the fictional character that – in a sense – he has always aspired to be (part of what Borges called 'the strange game of ambiguities', which continues to fascinate literary theorists to this day).

But there is another, more personal, reason why Cervantes chose Barcelona to play such an important role in his story: the writer himself spent time in Barcelona on the run from his creditors, living in a house at Passeig de Colom 2. Cervantes arrived in a Barcelona that had seen better days, having spent the previous century steadily losing power and influence to Madrid. Critics have commented that the Barcelona-set chapters of *Don Quixote* (nos.61-65) contain more violence and death than the preceding 60 chapters combined; indicative, perhaps, of the climate of insecurity in the city, which was suffering frequent raids by Moorish pirates from the sea and the activities of lawless brigands on its outskirts.

However, to Cervantes in the summer of 1610, Barcelona was 'the flower of all cities': a place which, to Cervantes as well as to many other Spanish writers throughout history, represented a cosmopolitan haven and a place of unparalleled intellectual freedoms. Reading Don Quixote's impressions of Barcelona as he enters the city on St John's Day in 1614, one gets a glimpse of a city that survives to this day: 'A home to foreigners, a refuge to the poor... unique in position and in beauty.'

By this time, the Catalan language had been relegated to secondary status, spoken in every street but rarely written or used in cultured discourse. Then, in 1833, Bonaventura Carles Aribau published his *Oda a la Pàtria*, a romantic eulogy in Catalan of the country, its language and its past. The poem had an extraordinary impact and is still traditionally credited with initiating the Renaixença (rebirth) of Catalan heritage and culture. The year 1848 was a high point for Barcelona and Catalonia, with the inauguration of the first railway in Spain, from Barcelona to Mataró, and the opening of the Liceu opera house.

SETTING AN EIXAMPLE

The optimism of Barcelona's new middle class was counterpointed by two persistent obstacles: the weakness of the Spanish economy as a whole, and the instability of their own society, which was reflected in atrocious labour relations. No consideration was given to the manpower behind the industrial surge: the underpaid, overworked men, women and children who lived in appalling conditions in high-rise slums within the cramped city. In 1855 the first general strike took place in Barcelona. The Captain-General, Zapatero, inaugurating a long cycle of conflict, refused to permit any workers' organisations to function, and bloodily suppressed all resistance.

One response to the city's problems that had almost universal support in Barcelona was the demolition of the city walls, which had imposed a stifling restriction on its growth. For years, however, the Spanish state refused to relinquish its hold on the city. To find space, larger factories were established in villages around Barcelona, such as Sants and Poblenou, and in 1854 permission finally came for the demolition of the citadel and the walls. The work began with enthusiastic popular participation, crowds of volunteers joining in at weekends. Barcelona at last broke out of the space it had occupied since the 14th century and spread outward into its new *eixample* (extension), to a controversial new plan by Ildefons Cerdà.

In 1868 Isabel II, once a symbol of liberalism, was overthrown by a progressive revolt. During the six years of upheaval that followed, power in Madrid would be held by the provisional government, a constitutional monarchy under an Italian prince and later a federal republic. However, workers were free to organise; in 1868 Giuseppe Fanelli brought the first anarchist ideas, and two years later, the first Spanish workers' congress took place in Barcelona. The radical forces were divided between many squabbling factions, while the established classes of society felt increasingly threatened

and called for the restoration of order. The Republic proclaimed in 1873 was unable to establish its authority, and succumbed to a military coup less than a year later.

IF YOU BUILD IT, THEY WILL COME

In 1874 the Bourbon dynasty was restored to the Spanish throne in the person of Alfonso XII, son of Isabel II. Workers' organisations were again suppressed. The middle classes, however, felt their confidence renewed. The 1870s saw a frenzied boom in stock speculation, known as the *febre d'or* (gold fever), and the real take-off of building in the Eixample. From the 1880s Modernisme became the preferred style of the new district, the perfect expression for the confidence and impetus of the industrial class. The first modern Catalanist political movement was founded by Valentí Almirall.

Barcelona felt it needed to show the world all that it had achieved, and that it was more than just a 'second city'. In 1885 a promoter named Eugenio Serrano de Casanova proposed to the city council the holding of an international exhibition, such as had been held successfully in London, Paris and Vienna. Serrano was a highly dubious character who eventually made off with large amounts of public funds, but by the time this became clear the city fathers had fully committed themselves to the event.

The Universal Exhibition of 1888 was used as a pretext for the final conversion of the Ciutadella into a park. Giant efforts had to be made to get everything ready in time, a feat that led the mayor, Francesc Rius i Taulet, to exclaim that 'the Catalan people are the yankees of Europe'. The first of Barcelona's three great efforts to demonstrate its status to the world, the 1888 Exhibition signified the consecration of the Modernista style, the end of provincial, dowdy Barcelona and its establishment as a modern-day city on the international map.

THE CITY OF THE NEW CENTURY

The 1888 Exhibition left Barcelona with huge debts, a new look and plenty of reasons to believe in itself as a paradigm of progress. The Catalan Renaixença continued, and acquired a more political tone. In 1892 the Bases de Manresa were drawn up, a draft plan for Catalan autonomy. Middle-class opinion gradually became more sympathetic to political Catalanism.

A truly decisive moment came in 1898, when the underlying weakness of the Spanish state was made plain over the superficial prosperity of the first years of the Bourbon restoration. It was then that Spain was forced into a short war with the United States, in which it lost its remaining empire in Cuba, the Philippines and

If you are looking for the heart
of the city in this guide,
you have found it.

Opening late autumn 2005

GRAND HOTEL
CENTRAL
BARCELONA

Via Laietana 30, 08003 Barcelona · Tel. No. 00 34 933 104 363 · grandhotelcentral.com

Puerto Rico. Industrialists were horrified at losing the lucrative Cuban market, and despaired of the ability of the state ever to reform itself. Many swung behind a conservative nationalist movement: the Lliga Regionalista (Regionalist League), founded in 1901 and led by Enric Prat de la Riba and the politician-financier Francesc Cambó, promised both national revival and modern, efficient government. At the same time, however, Barcelona continued to grow, fuelling Catalanist optimism. The city officially incorporated most of the surrounding smaller communities in 1897, reaching a population of over half a million, and in 1907 initiated the 'internal reform' of the Old City by creating the Via Laietana, which cut right through it.

Catalan letters were thriving. The Institut d'Estudis Catalans (Institute of Catalan Studies) was founded in 1906, and Pompeu Fabra set out to create the first Catalan dictionary. Above all, Barcelona had a vibrant artistic community, centred on Modernisme, consisting of great architects and established painters such as Rusiñol and Casas, but also the penniless bohemians who gathered round them, among them a young Picasso.

The bohemians were drawn to the increasingly wild nightlife of the Raval, where cabarets, bars and brothels multiplied at the end of the 19th century. Located around the cabarets, though, were the poorest of the working classes, for whom conditions had only continued to decline: Barcelona had some of the worst overcrowding and highest mortality rates in Europe. Local philanthropists called for something to be done, but Barcelona was more associated with revolutionary politics and violence than with peaceful social reform. Rebellion among the working classes pre-dated the arrival of anarchism; the Catholic church was the frequent target of the mobs in the 19th century, protesting against its collusion with the authorities and the control it exercised over the day-to-day life of the poorer classes.

In 1893 more than 20 people were killed in a series of anarchist terrorist attacks, which included the notorious throwing of a bomb into the wealthy audience at the Liceu. The perpetrators acted alone, but the authorities seized the opportunity to round up the usual suspects – local anarchists and radicals – several of whom, known as the 'Martyrs of Montjuïc', were later tortured and executed in the castle above the city. One retaliation came in 1906, when a Catalan anarchist tried to kill King Alfonso XIII on his wedding day.

Anarchism was still only in a fledgling stage among workers in the 1900s. However, rebellious attitudes, along with growing republican sentiment and a fierce hatred of the Catholic Church, united the underclasses and led them to take to the barricades. The Setmana Tràgica (Tragic Week) of 1909 began as a protest against the conscription of troops for the colonial war in Morocco, but degenerated into a general riot, with the destruction of churches by excited mobs. Suspected culprits were summarily executed, as was the anarchist educationalist Francesc Ferrer, who was accused of 'moral responsibility' even though he wasn't even in Barcelona at the time.

These events dented the optimism of the Catalanists of the Lliga. However, in 1914 they secured from Madrid the Mancomunitat, or administrative union, of the four Catalan provinces, the first joint government of any kind in Catalonia in 200 years. Its first president was Prat de la Riba, who would be succeeded on his death in 1917 by the architect Puig i Cadafalch. However, the Lliga's plans for an orderly Catalonia were to be obstructed by a further surge in social tensions.

CHAMPAGNE AND SOCIALISTS

Spain's neutral status during World War I gave a huge boost to the Spanish, and especially Catalan, economy. Exports soared as Catalonia's manufacturers made millions supplying uniforms to the French army. Barcelona's industry was at last able to diversify from textiles into engineering, chemicals and other more modern sectors.

Barcelona also became the most amenable place of refuge for anyone in Europe who wanted to avoid the war. Its international refugee community included artists Sonia and Robert Delaunay, Francis Picabia, Marie Laurencin and Albert Gleizes, but it was also a bolt-hole for all kinds of low-life from around Europe. The Raval area was soon dubbed the Barrio Chino ('Chinatown'), definitively identifying it as an area of sin and perdition.

Some of the regular patrons of the lavish new cabarets were industrialists; many of the war profits were spent immediately in very conspicuous consumption. The war also set off massive inflation, driving people in their thousands from rural Spain into the big cities. Barcelona doubled in size in 20 years to become the largest city in Spain, and also the fulcrum of Spanish politics. Workers' wages, meanwhile, had lost half their real value.

The chief channel of protest in Barcelona was the anarchist workers' union, the Confederación Nacional del Trabajo (CNT), constituted in 1910, which gained half a million members in Catalonia by 1919. The CNT and the socialist Union General de Trabajadores (UGT) launched a joint general strike in 1917, roughly co-ordinated with a campaign by the Lliga and other liberal politicians for political reform. However, the politicians soon withdrew at the prospect of serious social unrest. Inflation continued to intensify, and in 1919 Barcelona was paralysed for more than two months by a CNT general strike over union recognition. Employers refused to recognise the CNT and the most intransigent among them hired gunmen to get rid of union leaders. Union activists replied in kind, and virtual guerrilla warfare developed between the CNT, the employers and the state. More than 800 people were killed on the city's streets over five years.

In 1923, in response both to the chaos in the city and a crisis in the war in Morocco, the Captain-General of Barcelona, Miguel Primo de Rivera, staged a coup and established a military dictatorship under King Alfonso XIII. The CNT, was already exhausted, and was suppressed. Conservative Catalanists, longing for an end to disorder and the revolutionary threat, initially supported the coup, but were rewarded by the abolition of the Mancomunitat and a vindictive campaign by the Primo regime against the Catalan language and national symbols.

This, however, achieved the opposite of the desired effect, helping to radicalise and popularise Catalan nationalism. After the terrible struggles of the previous years, the 1920s were actually a time of notable prosperity for many in Barcelona, as some of the wealth recently accumulated filtered through the economy. It was also, though, a highly politicised society, in which new magazines and forums for discussion – despite the restrictions of the dictatorship – found a ready audience.

A prime motor of Barcelona's prosperity in the 1920s was the International Exhibition of 1929, the second of the city's great showcase events. It had been proposed by Cambó and Catalan business groups, but Primo de Rivera saw that it could also serve as a propaganda event for his regime. A huge number of public projects were undertaken in association with the main event, including the post office in Via Laietana, the Estació de França and Barcelona's first metro line, from Plaça Catalunya to Plaça d'Espanya. Thousands of migrant workers came from southern Spain to build them, many living in decrepit housing or shanty towns on the city fringes. By 1930 Barcelona was very different from the place it had been in 1910; it contained more than a million people, and its urban sprawl had crossed into neighbouring towns such as Hospitalet and Santa Coloma.

For the Exhibition itself, Montjuïc and Plaça d'Espanya were comprehensively redeveloped, with grand halls by Puig i Cadafalch and other local architects in the style of the Catalan neo-

classical movement Noucentisme, a backward-looking reaction to the excesses of Modernisme. They contrasted strikingly, though, with the German pavilion by Ludwig Mies van der Rohe (the Pavelló Barcelona), which emphatically announced the trend toward rationalism.

THE REPUBLIC SUPPRESSED

Despite the Exhibition's success, Primo de Rivera resigned in January 1930, exhausted. The king appointed another soldier, General Berenguer, as prime minister, with the mission of restoring stability. The dictatorship, though, had fatally discredited the old regime, and a protest movement spread across Catalonia against the monarchy. In early 1931 Berenguer called local elections as a first step towards a restoration of constitutional rule. The outcome was a complete surprise, for republicans were elected in all of Spain's cities. Ecstatic crowds poured into the streets, and Alfonso XIII abdicated. The Second Spanish Republic was proclaimed on 14 April 1931.

The Republic arrived amid real euphoria; especially in Catalonia, where it was associated with hopes for both social change and national reaffirmation. The clear winner of the elections in the country had been the Esquerra Republicana, a leftist Catalanist group led by Francesc Macià. A raffish, elderly figure, Macià was one of the first politicians in Spain to win genuine affection from ordinary people. He declared Catalonia to be an independent republic within an Iberian federation of states, but later agreed to accept autonomy within the Spanish Republic.

The Generalitat was re-established as a government that would, potentially, acquire wide powers. All aspects of Catalan culture were then in expansion, and a popular press in Catalan achieved a wide readership. Barcelona was also a small but notable centre of the avant-garde. Miró and Dalí had already made their mark in painting; under the Republic, the Amics de l'Art Nou (ADLAN, Friends of New Art) group worked to promote contemporary art, while the GATCPAC architectural collective sought to work with the new authorities to bring rationalist architecture to Barcelona.

In Madrid, the Republic's first government was a coalition of republicans and socialists led by Manuel Azaña, its overriding goal to modernise Spanish society through liberal-democratic reforms. However, as social tensions intensified, the coalition collapsed, and a conservative republican party, with support from the traditional Spanish right, secured power shortly after new elections in 1933. For Catalonia, the prospect of a return to right-wing rule prompted fears that it would immediately

Failed utopias

Monturiol's submarine.

In 1847 a small group of Barcelona's republicans gathered together to publish a new journal, *La Fraternidad*. Led by Narcis Monturiol, the group also included Ramón Martí i Alsina, who would become a successful painter; Josep Anselm Clavé, the father of Catalan choral societies; and a young Ildefons Cerdà, who went on to become the architect of the Eixample. The newspaper publicised the views of the French utopian socialist Étienne Cabet.

Cabet's grand plan was for a new society that he called Icaria, isolated from the corrupt and unjust society of the time. In this utopia, everything would be shared, with each member contributing according to his abilities and receiving according to his needs. Cabet went as far as designing the architectural layout of his new world, based on scientific method and egalitarian principles. Cerdà based his schemes for what became the Eixample on Cabet's designs, and Barcelona would be similarly divided into equal sectors, each with its own school, church nursery, almshouse and public space. The Eixample would be everything the old Barcelona was

not: spacious, green and clean. That said, the project was, at best, only partly successful (*see p37*).

In 1847 Cabet bought a large expanse of land in northern Texas, which he earmarked as the perfect location of his Icaria. The experiment proved a total disaster; faced with starvation, the volunteers – who included a young Catalan doctor called Joan Rovira, a representative of the *Fraternidad* group – were forced to abandon their paradise after only a few months. His illusions shattered, and in the presence of his wife and newborn child who had come to join him, Rovira put a gun to his head and killed himself.

The *Fraternidad* group had been dispersed by the authorities in 1848, with many members forced into exile in France. Six years later, revolution broke out on the streets of Barcelona; although the revolt was soon quashed, repression once again became the dominating force. The old Icarians sought different avenues for their revolutionary ideals: Clavé sought to unite the working class movement through song in his choral societies; Cerdà hoped his urban designs would create a better world; and Monturiol hoped to transform society through science and dedicated himself to inventing a prototype submarine with the plan to 'continue revolutionary politics by underwater means'. Monturiol hoped that his new creation would discover minerals or foods that might help cure the problems of the known world above.

Incredibly, Monturiol did invent and build two prototypes of his submarine, named the *Ictíneo* ('fish boat' in Greek), and went on to organise a number of successful trips around the port in which friends and the intrepid were offered the opportunity to see the world from deep under the sea's surface. The submarine raised great interest among the public, who helped sponsor its manufacture, but failed to attract business interest, perhaps in part because of suspicion from potential investors at Monturiol's socialist views and revolutionary friends. Eventually, the project went bankrupt, and the submarine was seized and sold as scrap metal. However, there's a full scale reconstruction of *Ictíneo* in the *plaça* which bears its name, just beside the port where it made its only underwater voyages.

Spanish Civil War. *See p27.*

abrogate the Generalitat's hard-won powers. On 6 October 1934, while a general strike was launched against the central government in Asturias and some other parts of Spain, Lluís Companys, leader of the Generalitat since Macià's death the previous year, declared Catalonia independent. The 'uprising', however, turned out to be something of a farce: the Generalitat had no means of resisting the army, and the new 'Catalan Republic' was rapidly suppressed. The Generalitat was suspended and its leaders imprisoned.

'Far from the front, Barcelona was the chief centre of the revolution.'

Over the following year, fascism seemed to become a real threat for the left, as political positions became polarised. Then, in February 1936, elections were won by the Popular Front of the left across the country. The Generalitat was reinstated, and in Catalonia the next few months were peaceful. In the rest of Spain, though, tensions were close to bursting point; right-wing politicians, refusing to accept the loss of power, talked openly of the need for the military to intervene. In July, the 1929 stadium on Montjuïc was to be the site of the Popular Olympics, a leftist alternative to the Olympics of that year in Nazi Germany. On 18 July, the day of their inauguration, army generals launched a coup against the Republic and its left-wing governments, expecting no resistance.

UP IN ARMS

In Barcelona, militants from the unions and leftist parties, on alert for weeks, suddenly poured into the streets to oppose the troops in fierce fighting. Over the course of 19 July, the military were gradually worn down, and finally surrendered in the Hotel Colón on Plaça Catalunya (by the corner with Passeig de Gràcia, the site of which is now occupied by the Radio Nacional de España building). Opinions have always differed as to who could claim most credit for this remarkable popular victory: workers' militants have claimed it was the 'people in arms' who defeated the army, while others stress the importance of the police remaining loyal to the Generalitat throughout the struggle. A likely answer is that they actually encouraged each other.

Tension released, the city was taken over by the revolution. People's militias of the CNT, different Marxist parties and other left-wing factions marched off to Aragon, led by streetfighters such as the anarchists Durruti and García Oliver, to continue the battle. The

Derail in anger

On 7 June 1926 an old man was struck down by a tram on the corner of Gran Via and C/Bailén. Apart from an old crucifix, his pockets were empty and his shabby clothes were held together by safety pins. Assuming he was just an unfortunate tramp who hadn't paid attention while crossing the road, the police took him to the Santa Creu paupers' hospital in the Barrio Chino, where he died three days later. The old man was Antoni Gaudí and the tram was one of the hundreds that criss-crossed the city at the time.

The story of Barcelona's tram network has long been accompanied by controversy, defined by accidents, political intrigue and general unrest. The trams made what many assumed to be their final journeys in the city in 1971. However, the city fathers' search for 'greener' methods of public transport, which coincided with the Forum of Cultures eco-fest, resulted in the tram network making a comeback in 2004. Today, two private companies run trams from one end of the city to the other.

But we're getting ahead of ourselves a little. The first tram line in Barcelona opened on 27 June 1872, an elegant horse-drawn carriage that made stately progress up La Rambla from Drassanes to Gràcia. This new medium of transport, provided by the English Barcelona Tramways Company, soon provoked the ire of residents, who complained that the tickets were too expensive and the route was designed to serve the needs of the bourgeoisie, who used the service to travel to their holiday homes in Sarrià. The first trams were replaced by steam-driven engines in 1877 and electric trams 22 years later, but continued to provoke anger among many citizens, who reacted to accidents by burning carriages or pulling up the tracks. But as the 'tank', as the vehicle was nicknamed, was replaced by the 'sardine can', new lines proliferated and prices fell. The tram soon established itself in the city as a popular form of transport; in 1929, it transported more than 250 million passengers a year in 800 vehicles.

The tram workers' union, controlled by the anarchist CNT, became a focus for the workers' revolution of 1936, which transformed the city following the outbreak of the Civil War. The trams were collectivised, effectively handing control to the workers, who took the unanimous decision to raise their wages by 1,000 per cent while cutting ticket prices by half. The authoritarian position of the ticket inspector, seen as highly suspect to the anarchists' egalitarian sensibilities, was abolished, leaving local residents to begin the long-standing (and still popular) Barcelona tradition of fare-dodging.

Back then, the trams were painted in the black and red of the anarchist flag, which was swiftly converted to a more politically neutral yellow following the arrival of Franco's forces in the city. (Barcelona's taxi cabs still sport that colour.) The new, improved, shiny trams of 2005, however, have been painted a different colour to reflect the caring face of corporate public transport in the 21st century: green...

army rising had failed in Spain's major cities but won footholds in Castile, Aragon and the south, although in the heady atmosphere of Barcelona in July 1936 it was often assumed that their resistance could not last long, and that the people's victory was near inevitable.

Far from the front, Barcelona was the chief centre of the revolution in republican Spain, the only truly proletarian city. Its middle class avoided the streets, where, as Orwell recorded in his *Homage to Catalonia*, everyone you saw wore workers' clothing. Barcelona became a magnet for leftists from around the world, drawing writers André Malraux, Hemingway and Octavio Paz. All kinds of industries and public services were collectivised, including cinemas, the phone system and food distribution. Ad hoc 'control patrols' of the revolutionary militias roamed the streets supposedly checking for suspected right-wing agents and sometimes carrying out summary executions, a practice that was condemned by many leftist leaders.

The alliance between the different left-wing groups was unstable and riddled with tensions. The communists, who had some extra leverage because the Soviet Union was the only country prepared to give the Spanish Republic arms, demanded the integration of these loosely organised militias into a conventional army under a strong central authority. The following months saw continual political infighting between the discontented CNT, the radical-Marxist party Partit Obrer d'Unificació Marxista (POUM), and the communists. Co-operation broke down totally in May 1937, when republican and communist troops seized the telephone building in Plaça Catalunya (on the corner of Portal de l'Àngel) from a CNT committee, sparking off the confused war-within-the-civil-war witnessed by Orwell from the roof of the Teatre Poliorama. A temporary agreement was patched up, but shortly afterwards the POUM was banned, and the CNT excluded from power. A new republican central government was formed under Dr Juan Negrín, a socialist allied to the communists.

After that, the war gradually became more of a conventional conflict. This did little, however, to improve the Republic's position, for the nationalists under General Francisco Franco and their German and Italian allies had been continually gaining ground throughout it all. Madrid was under siege, and the capital of the Republic was moved to Valencia, and then to Barcelona, in November 1937.

Catalonia received thousands of refugees, as food shortages and the lack of armaments ground down morale. Barcelona also had the sad distinction of being the first major city in

Europe to be subjected to sustained intensive bombing – to an extent that has rarely been appreciated – with heavy raids throughout 1938, especially by Italian bombers based in Mallorca. The Basque Country and Asturias had already fallen to Franco, and in March 1938 his troops reached the Mediterranean near Castellón, cutting the main Republican zone in two. The Republic had one last throw of the dice, in the Battle of the Ebro in summer 1938, when for months the Popular Army struggled to retake control of the river. After that, the Republic was exhausted. Barcelona fell to the Francoist army on 26 January 1939. Half a million refugees fled to France, to be interned in barbed-wire camps along the beaches.

THE FRANCO YEARS

In Catalonia, the Franco regime was iron-fisted and especially vengeful. Thousands of Catalan republicans and leftists were executed, among them Generalitat president Lluís Companys; exile and deportation were the fate of thousands more. Publishing, teaching and any other public cultural expression in Catalan, including even speaking it in the street, were prohibited, and every Catalanist monument in the city was dismantled. All independent political activity was suspended, and the entire political and cultural development of the country during the previous century and a half was brought to an abrupt halt.

The epic nature of the Spanish Civil War is known worldwide; more present in the collective memory of Barcelona, though, is the long *posguerra* or post-war period, which lasted for nearly two decades after 1939. During those years, the city was impoverished, and food and electricity were rationed; it would not regain its prior standard of living until the mid 1950s. Nevertheless, migrants in flight from the still more brutal poverty of the south flowed into the city, occupying precarious shanty towns around Montjuïc and other areas in the outskirts. Reconstruction work on the nearly 2,000 buildings destroyed by bombing was slow, and the regime built little during its first few years other than monumental showpieces and the vulgarly ornate basilica on top of Tibidabo, which was said to have been erected to expiate Barcelona's 'sinful' role during the war.

Some underground political movements were able to operate: the anarchist Sabaté brothers carried on their own small-scale urban guerrilla campaign, and 1951 saw the last gasp of the pre-war labour movement in a general tram strike. Some Catalan high culture was tolerated, and the young Antoni Tàpies held his first exhibition in 1949. For many people, though, the only remaining focus of any collective excitement was Barcelona football club, which took on an extraordinary importance at this time, above all in its twice-yearly meetings with the 'team of the regime', Real Madrid.

As a fascist survivor, the Franco regime was subject to a UN embargo after World War II. Years of international isolation and attempted self-sufficiency came to an end in 1953, when the USA and the Vatican saw to it that this anti-communist state was at least partially re-admitted to the western fold. Even a limited opening to the outside world meant that foreign money finally began to enter the country, and the regime relaxed some control over its population. In 1959 the Plan de Estabilización (Stabilisation Plan), drawn up by Catholic technocrats of the Opus Dei, brought Spain definitively within the western economy, throwing its doors wide open to tourism and foreign investment. After years of austerity, tourist income at last brought the Europe-wide 1960s boom to Spain and set off change at an extraordinary pace.

Two years earlier, in 1957, José María de Porcioles was appointed mayor of Barcelona, a post he would retain until 1973. Porcioles has since been regarded as the personification of the damage inflicted on the city by the Franco regime during its 1960s boom, and was accused of covering it with drab high-rises and road schemes without any concern for its character. Many valuable historic buildings, such as the grand cafés of the Plaça Catalunya, were torn down to make way for bland modern business blocks, and minimal attention was paid to collective amenities.

After the years of repression and the years of development, 1966 marked the beginning of what became known as *tardofranquisme*, 'late Francoism'. Having made its opening to the outside world, the regime was losing its grip, and labour, youth and student movements began to emerge from beneath the shroud of repression. Nevertheless, the Franco regime never hesitated to show its strength. Strikes and demonstrations were dealt with savagely, and just months before the dictator's death the last person to be executed in Spain by the traditional method of the garrotte, a Catalan anarchist named Puig Antich, went to his death in Barcelona. In 1973, however, Franco's closest follower, Admiral Carrero Blanco, was assassinated by a bomb planted by the Basque terrorist group ETA, leaving no one to guard over the core values of the regime. Change was in the air.

GENERALISIMO TO GENERALITAT
When Franco died on 20 November 1975, the people of Barcelona took to the streets in celebration; by evening, there was not a bottle

of cava left in the city. But no one knew quite what would happen next. The Bourbon monarchy was restored under King Juan Carlos, but his attitudes and intentions were not clear. In 1976 he charged a little-known Francoist bureaucrat, Adolfo Suárez, prime minister, with leading the country to democracy.

The first years of Spain's 'transition' were difficult. Nationalist and other demonstrations continued to be repressed by the police with considerable brutality, and far-right groups threatened less open violence. However, political parties were legalised, and June 1977 saw the first democratic elections since 1936. They were won across Spain by Suárez's own new party, the Union de Centro Democratico (UCD), and in Catalonia by a mixture of socialists, communists and nationalists.

It was, again, not clear how Suárez expected to deal with the demands of Catalonia, but shortly after the elections he surprised everyone by going to visit the president of the Generalitat in exile, a veteran pre-Civil War politician, Josep Tarradellas. His office was the only institution of the old Republic to be so recognised, perhaps because Suárez astutely identified in the old man a fellow conservative. Tarradellas was invited to return as provisional president of a restored Generalitat, and arrived amid huge crowds in October 1977.

The following year, the first free council elections since 1936 were held in Barcelona. They were won by the Socialist Party, with Narcís Serra as mayor. The party has retained control of the council ever since. In 1980, elections to the restored Generalitat were won by Jordi Pujol and his party, Convergència i Unió, who held power for the next 23 years.

CITY OF DESIGN
Inseparable from the restoration of democracy was a complete change in the city's atmosphere after 1975. New freedoms – in culture, sexuality and work – were explored, and newly released energies expressed in a multitude of ways. Barcelona soon began to look different too, as the inherent dowdiness of the Franco years was swept away by a new Catalan style for the new Catalonia: postmodern, high-tech, punkish, comic strip, minimalist and tautly fashionable. For a time, street culture was highly politicised, but simultaneously it was also increasingly hedonistic. In the 1980s, design mania struck the city, a product of unbottled energies and a rebirth of Barcelona's artistic, artisan and architectural traditions.

This emphasis on a slick, fresh style first began underground, but it was soon taken up by public authorities, and above all the Ajuntament, as a part of its drive to reverse the policies of the regime. The highly educated technocrats in the socialist city administration began, slowly at first, to 'recover' the city from its neglected state, and in doing so enlisted the elite of the Catalan intellectual and artistic community in their support. No one epitomises this more than Oriol Bohigas, the architect and writer who was long the city's head of culture and chief planner. A programme of urban renewal was initiated, beginning with the open spaces, public art and low-level initiatives, such as the campaign in which hundreds of historic façades were given an overdue facelift.

> **'More than just a sports event, the Games were to be the third great effort to cast aside suggestions of second-city status.'**

This ambitious, emphatically modern approach to urban problems acquired much greater focus after Barcelona's bid to host the 1992 Olympic Games was accepted, in 1986. Far more than just a sports event, the Games were to be Barcelona's third great effort to cast aside suggestions of second-city status and show the world its wares. The exhibitions of 1888 and 1929 had seen developments in the Ciutadella and on and around Montjuïc; the Olympics provided an opening for work on a citywide scale. Taking advantage of the public and private investment the Games would attract, Barcelona planned an all-new orientation of itself toward the sea, in a programme of urban renovation of a scope unseen in Europe since the years of reconstruction after World War II.

Inseparable from all this was Pasqual Maragall, mayor of Barcelona from 1982 to 1997, a tireless 'Mr Barcelona' who appeared in every possible forum to expound his vision of the role of cities, and intervened personally to set the guidelines for projects or secure the participation of major international architects. In the process, Barcelona, a byword for modern blight only a few years before, was turned into a reference point in urban affairs. Maragall also established a personal popularity well beyond that of his Catalan Socialist Party (PSC).

ENDGAMES

The Games were finally held in July and August 1992 and universally hailed as an outstanding success. Barcelona and Catalonia rode out Spain's post-1992 recession better than any other part of the country. The Ajuntament announced still more large-scale projects, such as the old Port and the Raval. Pasqual Maragall, however,

was to stand down amid general surprise in 1997, after winning a fifth term. He was succeeded as mayor by his then little-known deputy, Joan Clos, who has held on to the Ajuntament ever since. Maragall, meanwhile, sought to work his electoral magic beyond the city limits by becoming the socialist candidate for president of the Generalitat in the 1999 elections. He would not succeed, as once again Pujol was to triumph, thanks in no small part to his several years of successful horse-trading with the then minority PP central government.

In 2001 Pujol finally announced, two years in advance, that he would not be standing for another term, and named his then deputy, Artur Mas, as his chosen successor. When new regional elections finally came round on 16 November 2003, though, the results defied all predictions. Maragall, media frontrunner for months, seemed once again to have been disappointed, as the PSC won a few more votes than Convergència, but also gained fewer seats in the Catalan parliament. For a short while it appeared Mas had triumphed, until it became clear that the real winners of the night, taking seats off both the 'majors', were previously fringe left-wing parties: the 'eco-communists' of the ICV and, above all, Esquerra Republicana (ERC). The ERC is directly descended from the old Esquerra of the 1930s, and it all but doubled its vote, so that in some areas as much as one-fifth of voters supported a party that, at least theoretically, is in favour of total or partial Catalan independence, and which rejects the Spanish monarchy.

A month of wrangling followed, until it was announced that the PSC had agreed to form a left-wing coalition with the ERC and ICV, bringing Convergència's apparently eternal hold on local power to an end. Maragall would finally get the Generalitat, but only in return for a commitment to push strongly for a new Autonomy Statute, an idea that the Madrid government immediately condemned, and one that since he came to power, Maragall has shown relatively little enthusiasm in pursuing.

A few months later, in March 2004, the general elections were to shake up the political scene yet again. The results mirrored those in Catalonia six months earlier, with the triumphant PSOE (Spanish Socialist Workers' Party) being forced to form a coalition government with the ERC and Izquierda Unida (the nationwide version of ICV). With the socialists dependent on the votes of the Catalan nationalists in both the Generalitat and the national government, the future promises to be interesting. More surprises are all but guaranteed; along with, eventually, some very tough decisions.

Barcelona Today

Waving the red flag while welcoming the blue-chip.

It was supposed to be the year that the world would sit up and take notice of Barcelona. However, hardly anyone outside Catalonia was even aware of the Universal Forum of Cultures 2004. The Forum was designed as an attempt to revive something of the Olympic spirit that had revolutionised the city in 1992. However, few people left the exhibitions and concerts feeling culturally revitalised or invigorated by an event that cost a cool €3 billion to stage.

Despite a seemingly endless stream of whizz-bang audio-visual extravaganzas warning of the speed at which languages disappear and preaching about the importance of clean water, the sole popular exhibit at the Forum was the one at which the local government set out its construction plans for the future of the city. Apt, really: for all the event's talk of issues both national and global, the expensive conference facilities left behind by the event were, for most, what it was really about. With future plans also raising interest – a major new train station and a new Frank Gehry building in La Sagrera, plus the pretentiously named redevelopment 22@ in Poblenou – the Forum was just one component in the expansion of the city.

PRICED OUT OF THE MARKET

Sit down with any *barceloní* for more than five minutes, and the conversation will soon turn to the price of flats and the difficulty of buying one. As the city grows and the old centre is renovated, the cost of a half-decent flat within central Barcelona has risen more than 60 per cent in the last few years. Rents aren't far behind, more than doubling in less than a decade and putting them beyond the reach of most young couples on the lookout for independence. Many are opting to move to the peripheries: the urban sprawl of the huge satellite town L'Hospitalet, for example, or the bucolic calm of La Floresta, only 20 minutes by train from Plaça Catalunya.

Meanwhile, vast shopping centres have sprung up in the suburbs, putting pressure on smaller shops in town and challenging the traditional notion of the Catalans as a nation of *botiguers* (shopkeepers). On central streets such as C/Ferran, old cafés are being replaced with fast-food chains, Irish pubs and even Starbucks, all catering for the tourists who now arrive en masse. The new bête noir of Barcelona's residents is *'el especulador'*: the real estate entrepreneur who buys entire buildings

Voting with your ass

the rescue with stoicism and steadfastness. Yes, Catalonia has long had an indigenous and aspirational beast of its own, one fit to bear the hopes and desires of the Catalan nation. Trot forward the ass.

Better still, the fortunes of the indigenous Catalan donkey (or *guarà*) mirror those of Catalonia itself: prolific in bygone eras, almost eradicated during Franco's years and now making a comeback (by the 1970s, a population of thousands had dwindled to around 30 but is now up to 350 and rising).

As a national symbol, the bull is unbeatable: strong, sleek, aggressive and noble, a rippling, testosterone-filled package of elegance and beauty. This is all fine if you're Spanish and can appropriate these virtues for yourself (while also subjecting your beloved symbol to cruel and unusual practices in the bullring every Sunday afternoon). But if you reject Spain as your nation, as many Catalan nationalists do, you also must reject the bull as a totem of your identity.

But then what do you stick on the back of your car in order to show your national allegiance? Vigorous drivers from the rest of Spain have a black silhouette of a bull, a small echo of the Osborne bulls that guard the nation's highways and psyches, standing out against unmistakeably Hispanic landscapes to remind drivers not so much to drink more brandy (the link these days is tenuous, to say the least) but to be more Spanish. But the Catalans want to be less Spanish. Some of them don't want to be Spanish at all. So out goes the bull and in comes... the what? What symbol sufficiently reflects the qualities and aspirations of an entire nation while, at the same time, maintaining a link to the region?

A rhinoceros, a kind of armoured bull equipped with nose-mounted, anti-bull weaponry, would be ideal, except that it's not indigenous to Catalonia. The bear would have been perfect had it not been hunted to extinction on both sides of the Pyrenees. Fortunately, a solution is at hand, trotting to

Consequently, when Banyoles-based designers Jaume Sala and Àlex Ferreiro started, under their own initiative, to produce donkey stickers to replace bulls, they galloped off the shelves as Catalans voted with their wallets. So, too, did less widely accepted, more symbolic images: an ass mounting a bull, for example, and the reverse in retaliation.

The Catalan Lliga Anticolonial, however, had other ideas. A bull is a symbol of fierce pride and an ass is a symbol of submission, they responded. How to reflect the quiet fortitude and grace of the Catalans, known for eschewing the pomp and bombast of their Castilian cousins, and to simultaneously sneak in a nifty play on words? The cat, perhaps. It so very nearly works, but the cat, in Catalan, is *gat*. Enter, then, the *catigat*.

This stocky, cartoonish feline is now seen on around ten per cent of Catalan bumpers, vying for second-division supremacy with the *rat-penat* ('bat' – the Valencian response to the issue, chosen, curiously, for its 'unfettered flight, silence and wisdom' in the face of Spanish machismo) and even the locust, after a plague of them descended on the Costa Brava. But it's still the classic donkey that leads the way. Thousands of Catalan cars have been adorned with a sticker of this fine beast: strong, reliable, plodding but indefatigable, faithful if a little dull. An excellent symbol, some have said, for the Catalans themselves.

in the centre of town, empties them of their unprofitable, rent-paying long-term residents and sells them at an exorbitant sum, often to people from outside Spain who'll pay an inflated asking price. Support for the old local tradition of squatting has now taken on a new resonance, and is now seen as cheerleading a rare poke in the eye for the ambitious property developers.

Still, while life in the centre of Barcelona has changed substantially over the last few years, it's arguably changed less than in comparable European cities. Thanks to intervention by the council's famously hands-on urban planning authority – rent-protected flats in the centre for young people in any major new development (though not enough, scream detractors), a moratorium on the granting of licences for larger shops – Barcelona has remained a city with a centre in which people actually want to live. If only they could afford it.

NOT FROM ROUND HERE?

In the 1960s Barcelona's population swelled by nearly 50 per cent, as hundreds of thousands of immigrants arrived from the poorer areas of Spain to work in the city's booming industries. Locals looked down on these new arrivals; the offensive epithet *charnego* (derived from *'nocharnego'*, or 'someone who wanders the street at night') was invented to describe them. An ethnic class system sprang up, dividing pure-bred Catalans from the Spaniards who poured their drinks, drove their taxis and worked in their factories. The children of these immigrants now make up a substantial proportion of the population and are themselves Catalans, albeit with strong roots in other parts of Spain. Increasingly confident of their role within a new Catalan society, they're at the forefront of a cultural scene where *mestizaje*, the Spanish word for cultural and ethnic mix, is the new cool. It's a trend typified by the wildly popular rumba-flamenco-hip hop fusion bands such as Ojos de Brujo or Manu Chao, heard everywhere.

Similarly, the Raval, still an economically depressed area filled with North African immigrants, is now the coolest part of town. It has even spawned its own CD: the *Raval Sessions*, a compilation of local acts that mixes North African rhythms and fast Spanish lyrics. However, multiculturalism is a concept that sometimes sits uneasily in a small country that's intensely proud of its local traditions and has spent centuries defending them from the Spanish big brother next door. Some *catalanistes* have begun to voice concern that after the huge strides made since the end of the dictatorship, the 'normalisation' and promotion of Catalan as Barcelona's official language is in danger of taking a step back.

Immigrant populations have more than trebled in three years in fringe areas of the city such as Nou Barris and Sant Marti. By far the biggest group to arrive over the last few years are Ecuadoreans, closely followed by other Latin Americans and North Africans. Most use Spanish as their lingua franca; while subsidised Catalan lessons are available from the regional government (the Generalitat), those entering the low-wage service industry argue, not without good reason, that they don't need to learn the more obscure language, and would rather spend their time trying to earn money.

'A multiracial Barcelona is emerging without any real headaches.'

That said, although a few old Catalan men still mutter under their breath about foreigners (by which they also mean 'Spaniards', a term that refers only to non-Catalans), a multiracial Barcelona is emerging without any real headaches. The major battle, particularly for both North and sub-Saharan Africans, is in the struggle for legal residency papers. Both national and regional governments are trying to make the process easier, but a workable solution has yet to be reached. Still the most common crime in the city is to be '*sin papeles*', an illegal immigrant.

EXPLOSIVE CHANGES

On 11 March 2004 a series of bombs planted by Islamic fundamentalists exploded during the rush hour on Madrid trains, killing more than 200 people. The reaction in Barcelona was one of shock and grief. For those who witnessed the local mourning, there was no doubt that, for all the calls for Catalan independence and oft-expressed distrust of the capital, there is an inviolable connection between the two cities. And yet the marches organised by the right-wing Partido Popular (the PP, then the party in power) 'in support of the Spanish constitution' were interpreted locally both as a way of mourning the dead and reminding Madrid that the constitution needed examination. The country's leaders may have envisioned a nationwide march to unite the country, but the banners in Via Laietana reminded them that their Catalan subjects, for all their grief, were having none of it.

The PP then made a hideous miscalculation in the aftermath of the bomb, which occurred just three days before the general election, when they attempted to blame Basque separatists for the tragedy, apparently in order to deflect further criticism of its pro-Iraq War stance. The night before the election, crowds gathered outside the local headquarters of the governing

PP all over the country to register their protests at the government's apparent attempts to cover up the truth. The demonstrations were organised ad hoc via text message and email; right-wing conspiracy theorists claimed it was a deliberate attempt by Grupo Prisa, a Barcelona-based left-wing media group, to subvert the political process. Whoever was behind it, the next day's results left little room for argument: socialist leader José Luis Rodríguez Zapatero had turned certain defeat, according to pre-bombing polls, into a clear margin of victory.

Zapatero's election was very good news for the Catalanists, whose attempts to renegotiate the national constitution in order to get more autonomy had received little sympathy from the PP and its leader, José María Aznar. During the government changeover period, which in Spain is a month (shredding that many documents is a slow process, explain the cynics), some schools began teaching more pro-Catalan syllabuses. Zapatero had promised such freedom in his manifesto, and some local teachers didn't want to wait and see if he'd make good on his word.

It had been a different story five months earlier. Amid a generally gloomy resignation to the PP's re-election, Catalan politics had taken a lurch to the radical left when the ERC (the Republican Left of Catalonia, a Catalan nationalist party) doubled its representation in the local parliament. The party is led by unpredictable firebrand Josep Carod Rovira, who lists 'collecting "do not disturb" signs from hotels' as one of his hobbies. If indeed he does hoard them, he certainly doesn't heed them.

Ever since his party had the deciding vote in choosing Socialist Party leader and ex-Barcelona mayor Pasqual Maragall as President of Catalonia, Carod has made his presence felt in the coalition with a succession of inflammatory statements against Madrid.

More so than ever, discussions are taking place about autonomy from Madrid in affairs such as tax, sporting representation and the possibility of introducing Catalan as an official EU language. Prime Minister Zapatero has thus far remained sanguine, talking to all parties and then emerging with encouraging words but few concrete solutions. It remains to be seen how long the nationalists will remain patient.

In October 2004, *catalanistes* got very excited about roller hockey: along with speed-skating, korfball and women's indoor five-a-side soccer, it's one of the very few sports to allow Catalonia to compete as a separate team. A professional Catalan side destroyed an amateur English one in the final of the World B Cup in Macau, watched by Maragall (in the official box) and Carod (from the stands). The victory was seen as a significant metaphor for an emerging Catalonia, but a month later, Catalonia's provisional national status in the sport was revoked, a decision that appeared to have been influenced by some fierce Spanish lobbying. As a result, Carod then called for a boycott against Madrid's 2012 Olympic bid, though he later changed his mind.

SMALL CONCERNS

Meanwhile, the municipal government (the Ajuntament) has been quietly preoccupied with a number of 'quality of life' initiatives: getting rid of litter, closing squats, stopping after-hours parties and clamping down on noise, dog shit and (human) alfresco peeing. More comical have been attempts to stop buskers who aren't very good: one Sunday afternoon, two police vans, several police cars, four motorbikes and dozens of policemen descended on Ciutadella Park, brandishing official orders to stop people playing the bongos. Buskers now officially need to audition for a licence, and to book pitches in the Old City. Still, so the argument goes, if these are the most important issues the Ajuntament can find, then things must be all right.

Nor is the city doing too badly on the world stage. A recent *Newsweek* article referred to the 'Barcelona Model', a phenomenon being studied by urban planners everywhere. The city has apparently mastered the art of mixing urban spaces with private money, and hosting big-scale events that help cover the costs of construction. It's what Mayor Joan Clos calls 'a successful city operating in a free market'. Left-wing pragmatism with some big business sponsorship seems to be Barcelona's new order.

La Pedrera. *See p40.*

Architecture

Building Barcelona.

Successful urban architecture takes inspiration, good planning and civic pride, mixed with strong municipal authorities. All are qualities that have been abundant at different times in Barcelona's history. A direct line can be drawn between the elegant civil Gothic constructions of the Old City, built by rich, independently minded merchants, to the rational late 19th-century street network of the Eixample, to the grand urban redevelopment projects that preceded the 1992 Olympic Games. These three periods left an indelible mark on the city, tearing down and reinventing whole districts in a process that reflected the creative and entrepreneurial energy of its inhabitants and the use of grand architectural projects as a means of expressing a local identity.

Architecture is sometimes regarded as Catalonia's greatest contribution to the history of art. Indeed, there are few cities in the world that boast as many examples of architectural flair as Barcelona; no fewer than five of its buildings have now been designated as UNESCO World Heritage sites, more than either Paris or Florence can boast. Catalan craftsmen have been famed since the Middle Ages for their use of fine materials and skilled finishings, and Catalan architects have been both artists and innovators: traditional Catalan brick vaulting techniques were the basis of visionary structural innovations that allowed later architects to span larger spaces and build higher structures. Contemporary Catalan architects have inherited the international prestige of their forebears; the work of artists such as Ricard Bofill, Oriol Bohigas or the late Enric Miralles can be seen in a number of major cities around the world.

Unlike many European cities, Barcelona has never rested on its architectural laurels or tried to preserve its old buildings as relics. Contemporary buildings are often daringly constructed alongside or even within old ones, and a mix of old and new is a prime characteristic of some of the most successful recent projects seen in Barcelona, which all goes to create a thoroughly modern city firmly rooted in its

▶ For more on the architecture of Antoni Gaudí, *see pp45-48,* **God's Own Architect**.

Sant Pau del Camp.

architectural heritage. The importance of architecture is also reflected in public attitudes: Barcelona's citizens take a keen interest in their buildings. A range of architectural guides is available, some in English, and informative leaflets on building styles are also provided (in English) at tourist offices (*see p321*).

ROMAN TO GOTHIC

The Roman citadel of Barcino was founded on the hill of Mons Taber, just behind the cathedral, which to this day remains the religious and civic heart of the city. It left an important legacy in the fourth-century city wall, fragments of which are visible at many points around the Old City. Barcelona's next occupiers, the Visigoths, left little, although a trio of fine Visigothic churches survives in nearby Terrassa. When the Catalan state began to form under the Counts of Barcelona from the ninth century, its dominant architecture was massive, simple Romanesque. In the Pyrenean valleys, there are hundreds of fine Romanesque buildings, notably at **Sant Pere de Rodes**, **Ripoll**, **Sant Joan de les Abadesses** and **Besalú**. There is, however, little in Barcelona.

On the right-hand side of the cathedral, looking at the main façade, is the 13th-century **chapel of Santa Llúcia**, incorporated into the later building; tucked away near Plaça Catalunya is the **church of Santa Anna**; and in La Ribera sits the **Capella d'en Marcús**, a tiny travellers' chapel. The city's greatest Romanesque monument, however, is the beautifully plain 12th-century church and cloister of **Sant Pau del Camp**, built as part of a larger monastery.

By the 13th century Barcelona was the capital of a trading empire, and was growing rapidly. The settlements – called *ravals* or *vilanoves* – that had sprung up outside the Roman walls were brought within the city by the building of Jaume I's second set of walls, which extended west to the Rambla. This commercial growth and political eminence formed the background to the great flowering of Catalan Gothic, with the construction of many of the city's most important civic and religious buildings. The **cathedral** was begun in 1298, in place of an 11th-century building. Work began on the **Ajuntament** (Casa de la Ciutat) and **Palau de la Generalitat** – later subject to extensive alteration – in 1372 and 1403 respectively. Major additions were made to the **Palau Reial** of the Catalan-Aragonese kings, especially the **Saló del Tinell** of 1359-62. The great hall of the Llotja was finished in 1380-92. Many of Barcelona's finest buildings were built or completed in these years, in the midst of the crisis that followed the Black Death.

Catalan Gothic has characteristics that distinguish it from northern, classic Gothic. It is simpler, and gives more prominence to solid, plain walls between towers and columns, rather than the empty spaces between intricate flying buttresses that were trademarks of the great French cathedrals. This means that the Catalan buildings appear much more massive. In façades, as much emphasis is given to horizontals as to verticals; octagonal towers end in cornices and flat roofs, not spires. Decorative intricacies are mainly confined to windows, portals, arches and gargoyles. Many churches have no aisles but only a single nave, the classic example of this being the beautiful **Santa Maria del Pi** in Plaça del Pi, built between 1322 and 1453. This style has ever since provided the historic benchmark for Catalan architecture. It is simple and robust, yet elegant and practical. Innovative, sophisticated techniques were developed: the use of transverse arches supporting timber roofs allowed the spanning of great halls uninterrupted by columns, a system used in the **Saló del Tinell**. Designed by Pere III's court architect Guillem Carbonell, it has some fo the largest pure masonry arches in Europe, the elegance and sheer scale of which give the space tremendous splendour. The **Drassanes**, built from 1378 as the royal shipyards (and now the **Museu Marítim**), is really just a very beautiful shed, but its enormous parallel aisles make this one of the most imposing spaces in the city.

La Ribera, the Vilanova del Mar, was the commercial centre of the city, and gained the magnificent masterpiece of Catalan Gothic, **Santa Maria del Mar**, built 1329-84. Its superb proportions are based on a series of squares imposed on one another, with three aisles of almost equal height. The interior is quite staggering in its austerity.

The architecture of medieval Barcelona, at least that of its noble and merchant residences, can be seen at its best in the line of palaces along **Carrer Montcada**, next to Santa Maria. Built by the city's merchant elite at the height of their confidence and wealth, they conform to a very Mediterranean style of urban palace, and make maximum use of space. A plain exterior faces the street, with heavy doors opening into an imposing patio, on one side of which a grand external staircase leads to the main rooms on the first floor (*planta noble*), which often have elegant open loggias.

MARKING TIME

By the beginning of the 16th century, political and economic decline meant that there were far fewer patrons for new buildings in the city. A good deal was built in the next 300 years, but rarely in any distinctively Catalan style; as a result, these structures have often been disregarded. In the 1550s the **Palau del Lloctinent** was built for the royal viceroys on one side of Plaça del Rei, while in 1596 the present main façade was added to the **Generalitat**, in an Italian Renaissance style.

The Church also built lavishly around this time. Of the baroque convents and churches along La Rambla, the **Betlem** (1680-1729), at the corner of C/Carme, is the most important survivor. Later baroque churches include **Sant Felip Neri** (1721-52) and **La Mercè** (1765-75).

Another addition, after the siege of Barcelona in 1714, was new military architecture, since the city was encased in ramparts and fortresses. Examples remaining include the **Castell de Montjuïc**, the buildings in the **Ciutadella**, and the **Barceloneta**.

A more positive 18th-century alteration was the conversion of La Rambla into a paved promenade, a project that began in 1775 with the demolition of Jaume I's second wall. Neo-classical palaces were built alongside: **La Virreina** and the **Palau Moja** (at the corner of C/Portaferrisa) both date from the 1770s. Also from that time, but in a less classical style, is the **Gremial dels Velers** (Candlemakers' Guild) at Via Laietana 50, with its two-coloured stucco decoration.

> ## 'Cerdà's plan was closely related to visionary rationalist ideas of its time.'

However, it wasn't until the closure of the monasteries in the 1820s and '30s that major rebuilding on the Rambla could really begin. Most of the first constructions that replaced them were still in international, neo-classical styles. The site that is now the **Mercat de la Boqueria** was first remodelled in 1836-40 as Plaça Sant Josep to a design by Francesc Daniel Molina, based on the English Regency style of John Nash. It's actually buried beneath the 1870s market building, but its Doric colonnade can still be detected. Molina also designed the **Plaça Reial**, begun in 1848. Other fine examples from the same era are the colonnaded **Porxos d'en Xifré**, blocks built in 1836 opposite the Llotja on Passeig Isabel II, by the Port Vell.

BIRTH OF THE MODERN CITY

In the 1850s Barcelona was able to expand physically, with the demolition of the walls, and psychologically, with economic expansion and the cultural reawakening of the Catalan Renaixença. And from the off, one could see in operation one of the characteristics of modern Barcelona: audacious planning. The city would eventually spread outwards and be connected up to Gràcia and other outlying towns through the great grid of the **Eixample**, designed by **Ildefons Cerdà** (1815-75). An engineer by trade, Cerdà was a radical influenced by utopian socialist ideas, and concerned with the poor condition of workers' housing in the Old City.

With its love of straight lines and grids, Cerdà's plan was closely related to visionary rationalist ideas of its time, as was the idea of placing two of its main avenues along a geographic parallel and a meridian. Cerdà's central aim was to alleviate overpopulation

Santa Maria del Mar. *See p.37.*

while encouraging social equality by using quadrangular blocks of a standard size, with strict building controls to ensure that they were built only on two sides, to a limited height, and with a garden. Each district would be of 20 blocks, with all community necessities. In the event, however, this idealised use of space was rarely achieved, private developers regarding Cerdà's restrictions as pointless interference. Buildings exceeded planned heights, and all the blocks from Plaça Catalunya to the Diagonal were enclosed. Even the planned gardens failed to withstand the onslaught of construction.

However, the development of the Eixample did see the refinement of a specific type of building: the apartment block, with giant flats on the *principal* floor (first above the ground), often with large glassed-in galleries for the drawing room, and small flats above. In time, the interplay between the Eixample's straight lines and the disorderly tangle of the older city became an essential part of the city's identity.

MODERNISME

Art nouveau was the leading influence in the decorative arts in Europe and the US between 1890 and 1914. Here, its influence merged with the cultural and political movement of the Catalan Renaixença to produce what became known as Modernisme (used here in Catalan to avoid confusion with 'modernism' in English, which refers to 20th-century functional styles).

For all of Catalonia's many traditions in building and the arts, no style is as synonymous with it as Modernisme. This is in part due to the enormous modern popularity of its most famous proponent, Gaudí, and to its mix of unrestrained decoration, eccentric unpredictability, dedicated craftsmanship and solid practicality. Modernisme can also be seen as matching certain archetypes of Catalan character, as a passionately nationalist expression that made use of Catalan traditions of design and craftwork. Artists strove to revalue the best of Catalan art, showing enormous interest in the Romanesque and Gothic of the Catalan Golden Age; Domènech i Muntaner, for example, combined iron frame construction with distinctive brick Catalan styles from the Middle Ages, regarding them as an 'expression of the Catalan earth'.

All art nouveau had a tendency to look both past and future, combining a love of decoration with new industrial techniques and materials; so it was in Catalonia. Even as they constructed a nostalgic vision of the Catalan motherland, Modernista architects plunged into experiments with the newest technology. Encouraged by wealthy patrons, they designed works made of iron and glass, introduced electricity, water and gas piping to building plans, were the first to tile bathroom and kitchen walls, made a point of allowing extensive natural light and fresh air into all rooms, and toyed with the most advanced, revolutionary expressionism.

Catalan Modernista creativity was at its peak from 1888 to 1908. The Eixample is the style's display case, with the greatest concentration of art nouveau in Europe, but Modernista buildings can be found in innumerable other locations: in streets behind the Avda Paral·lel and villas on Tibidabo, in shop interiors and dark hallways, in country town halls and in the cava cellars of the Penedès.

International interest in Gaudí often eclipses the fact that there were many other remarkable architects and designers working at that time. Indeed, Modernisme was much more than an architectural style: the movement also included painters such as **Ramon Casas**, **Santiago Rusiñol** and **Isidre Nonell**, sculptors such as **Josep Llimona**, **Miquel Blay** and **Eusebi Arnau**, and furniture makers like the superb Mallorcan, **Gaspar Homar**. Much more than any other form of art nouveau, it extended into literature, thought and music, marking a whole generation of Catalan writers, poets, composers and philosophers. Although it was in architecture that it found its most splendid

You lookin' at me?

On a stroll through the Barri Gòtic, you might get the uncomfortable sensation that beastly eyes are following you. Take a look up at the looming walls and you will see a diabolical medieval bestiary that has fascinated the city's residents for generations.

Gargoyles were the medieval builder's answer to the perennial problem of what to do with the water that collects on roofs. The statuettes were installed on the buttresses of cathedrals and palaces and connected to the roof's gutters by channels, allowing the water to come out of their mouths. Of course, their function was symbolic too: these snarling monsters were protectors, designed to give the evil eye to diabolical spirits. Among the outlandish figures seen on C/Bisbe are a man being eaten alive by snakes and a leering monk on the side of the Palau de la Generalitat, unicorns and other mythical creatures protecting the cathedral, and what can only be described as Maradona's medieval twin, looking down at passers-by from the heights of the Casa de Canonges.

Gargoyles (or, more accurately, the 'grotesques', their non-functional counterparts) made a comeback in Barcelona in the 19th century; along with many other aspects of Gothic architecture, they were picked up by Gaudí and other Modernistes. Some buildings on Passeig de Gràcia sport their own beastly guardians, including the Casa Amatller's neo-Gothic fantasy next to the Casa Batlló; a building which, in itself, could be seen as one huge grotesque, with its elephant-foot columns, ridged dragon back of a roof and shimmering reptilian scales.

The medieval tradition appealed to Gaudí's sense of the importance of symbolism. Much

of his work contains nods to the mythical creatures of the past, including the repeated dragon motifs on his gates and the bats sitting on his lamp-posts along Passeig de Gràcia. The Sagrada Família is a naturally perfect place for the tradition of the grotesque to make its last shout, and the statuary that adorns the Passion façade includes, among the figures of Christ and Gaudí, a cockerel, a snake and a dog. That said, the style here is more Disney than *The Lord of the Rings*.

Sagrada Familia.

expression, Modernisme was an artistic movement in the fullest sense of the word, and, in Catalonia, took on a nationalistic element.

Seen as the genius of the Modernista movement, **Antoni Gaudí i Cornet** was really a one-off, an unclassifiable figure. His work was a product of the social and cultural context of the time, but also of his own unique perception of the world, together with a deep patriotic devotion to anything Catalan.

Gaudí worked first as assistant to Josep Fontseré in the 1870s on the building of the **Parc de la Ciutadella**; the gates and fountain are attributed to him. Around the same time he also designed the lamp-posts in the **Plaça Reial**, but his first major commission was for **Casa Vicens** in Gràcia, built between 1883 and 1888. An orientalist fantasy, the building is structurally quite conventional, but Gaudí's control of the use of surface material already stands out in the neo-Moorish decoration, multicoloured tiling and superbly elaborate ironwork on the gates. Gaudí's **Col·legi de les Teresianes** convent school (1888-9) is more restrained, but the clarity and fluidity of the building, with its simple finishes and use of light, is very appealing.

In 1878, Gaudí met Eusebi Güell, heir to one of the largest industrial fortunes in Catalonia. The pair shared many ideas on religion,

philanthropy and the socially redemptive role of architecture, and Gaudí produced several buildings for Güell. Among them were the **Palau Güell** (1886-8), a darkly impressive, historicist building that firmly established his reputation, and the crypt at **Colònia Güell** outside Barcelona, one of his most structurally experimental and surprising buildings.

In 1883 Gaudí became involved in the design of the **Sagrada Familia**, begun the previous year. A profoundly religious conservative Catholic, part of his obsession with the building came from a belief that it would help redeem Barcelona from the sins of secularism and the modern era. From 1908 until his death in 1926 he worked on no other projects.

The Sagrada Familia became the testing ground for Gaudí's ideas on structure and form, although he would live to see the completion of only the crypt, apse and nativity façade, with its representation of 30 species of plants. As his work matured he abandoned historicism and developed free-flowing, sinuous expressionist forms. His boyhood interest in nature began to take over from more architectural references, and what had previously provided external decorative motifs became the inspiration for the actual structure of his buildings.

In his greatest years, Gaudí combined other commissions with his cathedral; **La Pedrera**, begun in 1905, was his most complete project. The building has an aquatic feel about it: the balconies resemble seaweed, and the undulating façade the sea, or rocks washed by it. Interior patios are in blues and greens, and the roof resembles an imaginary landscape inhabited by mysterious figures. The **Casa Batlló**, on the other side of Passeig de Gràcia, was an existing building that Gaudí remodelled in 1905-7; the roof looks like a reptilian creature perched high above the street. The symbolism of the façade is the source of endless speculation. Some link it to the myth of St George and the dragon; others maintain it is a celebration of carnival, with its harlequin hat roof, its wrought-iron balcony 'masks' and the cascading, confetti-like tiles. This last element was an essential contribution of **Josep Maria Jujol**, who many believe was even more skilled than his master as a mosaicist.

Gaudí's fascination with natural forms found full expression in the **Park Güell** (1900-14), where he blurred the distinction between natural and artificial forms in a series of colonnades winding up the hill. These paths lead up to the large central terrace projecting over a hall; a forest of distorted Doric columns planned as the marketplace for Güell's proposed 'garden city'. The terrace benches are covered in some of the finest examples of *trencadís* (broken mosaic work), again mostly by Jujol.

Modernista architecture received a vital, decisive boost around the turn of the 19th century from the **Universal Exhibition of 1888**. The most important buildings for the show were planned by the famed **Lluís Domènech i Montaner** (1850-1923), who was then far more prominent than Gaudí as a propagandist for Modernisme in all its forms, and much more of a classic Modernista architect. Domènech was one of the first Modernista architects to develop the idea of the 'total work', working closely with large teams of craftsmen and designers on every aspect of a building. Not in vain was he dubbed 'the great orchestra conductor' by his many admirers.

Most of the Exhibition buildings no longer exist, but one that does is the **Castell dels Tres Dragons** in the Ciutadella park, designed as the Exhibition restaurant and now the **Museu de Zoologia**. It already demonstrated many key features of Modernista style: the use of structural ironwork allowed greater freedom in the creation of openings, arches and windows; and plain brick, instead of the stucco usually applied to most buildings, was used in an exuberantly decorative manner.

Domènech's greatest creations are the **Hospital de Sant Pau**, built as small 'pavilions' within a garden to avoid the usual effect of a monolithic hospital, and the fabulous **Palau de la Música Catalana**, an extraordinary display of outrageous decoration. He also left quite a few impressive constructions in Reus, near Tarragona, notably the ornate mansions **Casa Navàs** and **Casa Rull**, as well as the spectacular pavilions of the **Institut Pere Mata**, a psychiatric hospital and forerunner of the Hospital de Sant Pau.

Third in the trio of leading Modernista architects was **Josep Puig i Cadafalch** (1867-1957), who showed a neo-Gothic influence in such buildings as the **Casa de les Punxes** (or the 'House of Spikes', officially the **Casa Terrades**) in the Diagonal, combined with many traditional Catalan touches. Nearby on Passeig de Sant Joan, at No.108, is another of his masterpieces: the **Casa Macaya**, its inner courtyard inspired by the medieval palaces of C/Montcada. Puig was responsible for some of the best industrial architecture of the time, an area in which Modernisme excelled: the Fundació La Caixa's cultural centre recently moved from Casa Macaya to another of Puig i Cadafalch's striking creations, the **Fábrica Casaramona** at Montjuïc, built as a textile mill, and outside Barcelona he designed the extraordinary **Caves Codorníu** wine

Sexing up the skyline

In 2004, speaking at an event to celebrate the achievements of the recently closed Fòrum, Mayor Joan Clos announced that Barcelona was about to enter 'a new architectural cycle'. In other words, the city is about to be turned upside down yet again as various architectural giants flex their creative muscles and vie to create the most spectacular part of the Barcelona of the future. Since Norman Foster and Richard Meier left their marks on Barcelona in the 1990s, the city has had no trouble in attracting big-name architects to take on signature projects, and the buildings currently going up in Barcelona are no exception. This new wave will leave the city with a series of impressive high-rise constructions, a symptom both of the extreme lack of space in Barcelona and the city planners' penchant for being on the cutting edge of new architectural trends, based this time on the vogue for 'deconstructed skyscrapers'.

First up is Jean Nouvel's frighteningly phallic new addition. His 142-metre (466-foot) office building, the **Torre Agbar** in the Plaça de les Glòries, is a space-age ovoid, clothed in an aluminium and glass covering that reflects different tonalities of colour depending on how sunlight strikes it. Nouvel claims his design pays homage to the mountains of Montserrat but, inevitably, the city's residents have come up with a cheekier moniker for this thrusting, tumescent tower. Not to be outdone, Enric Miralles has placed another unlikely skyscraper on the beachfront: his fragmented monolith, the **Edifici de Gas**

Natural, promises to be the late architect's most enduring legacy to the city of his birth.

Perhaps the most eagerly awaited project for the city is Frank Gehry's plan for the area around the new station for the high-speed train link at **La Sagrera**; or, as the mayor calls it in typical Clos-speak, the 'City of Transport'. The area will consist of five towers of different heights covered in metal and glass, which twist upon themselves to create that feeling of movement and lightness that makes Gehry's buildings so distinctive. In fact, with a nod to Gehry's world-famous building in Bilbao, the Sagrera project has been dubbed 'Barcelona's Guggenheim'; it's hoped that it will completely regenerate a previously depressing area of town by joining the Rambla d'11 Setembre with the Rambla del Prim.

The building revolution will also tackle some painful historical thorns in the side of Barcelona, including the redesign of the Plaça de les Glòries. This *plaça*, an urban nightmare where three major roads collide in a traffic-hell wasteland, is infamous as the antithesis of Cerdà's human-friendly design for the rest of the Eixample. The regeneration will channel much of that traffic through tunnels, and will include a new **Design Museum** created by MBM architects (Oriol Bohigas's model for the projected museum resembles a huge industrial stapler waiting for a giant hand). Zaha Hadid, one of contemporary architecture's hottest properties, will also be represented with her **Plaça de les Arts**, a vast cinema complex and public square.

cellars. His best-known work, however, is the **Casa Amatller**, between Domènech's **Casa Lleó Morera** and Gaudí's **Casa Batlló** in the **Manzana de la Discòrdia**.

The style caught on with extraordinary vigour all over Catalonia, and some of the most engaging architects are really not very well known internationally. Impressive apartment blocks and mansions were built in the Eixample by **Joan Rubió i Bellver** (Casa Golferichs, Gran Via 491), **Salvador Valeri** (Casa Comalat, Avda Diagonal 442) and **Josep Vilaseca**. North of Barcelona is La Garriga, Catalonia's Baden-Baden, where **MJ Raspall** built exuberant summer houses for the rich and fashionable families of the time; there are also some dainty Modernista residences in towns along the coast such as Canet and Arenys de Mar. Some of the finest Modernista industrial architecture is in Terrassa, designed by the municipal architect **Lluís Moncunill** (1868-1931), while another local architect, **Cèsar Martinell**, built co-operative cellars that are true 'wine cathedrals' in Falset, Gandesa and many other towns in southern Catalonia.

THE 20TH CENTURY

By the 1910s Modernisme had become too extreme for the Barcelona middle classes; Gaudí's later buildings, indeed, were met with derision. The new 'proper' style for Catalan architecture was Noucentisme, which stressed the importance of classical proportions. However, it failed to produce anything of much note: the main buildings that survive are those of the 1929 Exhibition, Barcelona's next 'big event' that served as the excuse for the bizarre, neo-baroque **Palau Nacional**. The Exhibition also brought the city one of the most important buildings of the century: Ludwig Mies van der Rohe's German Pavilion, the **Pavelló Barcelona**, rebuilt near its original location in 1986. Its impact at the time was extraordinary; even today, it seems modern in its challenge to the conventional ideas of space.

Mies van der Rohe had a strong influence on the main new trend in Catalan architecture of the 1930s, which, reacting against Modernisme and nearly all earlier Catalan styles, was quite emphatically functionalist. Its leading figures were **Josep Lluís Sert** and the **GATCPAC** collective (Group of Catalan Architects and Technicians for the Progress of Contemporary Architecture), who struggled to introduce the ideas of their friend Le Corbusier and of the International Style to local developers. Under the Republic, Sert built a sanatorium off C/Tallers, and the **Casa Bloc**, a workers' housing project at Passeig Torres i Bages 91-105 in Sant Andreu. In collaboration with

Mies van der Rohe's **Pavelló Barcelona**.

Le Corbusier, the GATCPAC also produced a plan for the radical redesign of the whole of Barcelona as a 'functional city', the **Pla Macià** of 1933-4; drawings for the scheme present a Barcelona that looks more like a Soviet-era new town in Siberia, and few regret that it never got off the drawing board. In 1937 Sert also built the Spanish Republic's pavilion for that year's Paris Exhibition, since rebuilt in Barcelona as the **Pavelló de la República** in the Vall d'Hebron. His finest work, however, came much later in the shape of the **Fundació Joan Miró**, built in the 1970s after he had spent many years in exile in the United States.

BARCELONA'S NEW STYLE

The Franco years had an enormous impact on the city. As the economy expanded at breakneck pace in the 1960s, Barcelona received a massive influx of migrants, in a context of unchecked property speculation and of minimal planning controls; the city became ringed by a chaotic mass of high-rise suburbs. Another legacy of the era are some ostentatiously tall office blocks, especially on the Diagonal and around Plaça Francesc Macià.

When an all-new democratic city administration took over the reins of Barcelona at the end of the 1970s there was a great deal for it to do. A generation of Catalan architects had been chafing at Francoist restrictions for years. However, the tone set early on, above all by Barcelona's ubiquitous chief planner Oriol Bohigas – who has continued to design individual buildings as part of the MBM partnership with Josep Martorell and David Mackay – was one of 'architectural realism', with a powerful combination of imagination and practicality.

'Barcelona placed itself at the forefront of international urban design.'

Budgets were limited, so it was decided that resources should initially be concentrated not on buildings but on the gaps between them: public spaces, a string of fresh, modern parks and squares, many of which were to incorporate original artwork. From this beginning, Barcelona placed itself at the forefront of international urban design.

Barcelona's renewal programme took on a far more ambitious shape with the award of the 1992 Olympics, helped by a booming economy in the late 1980s. The third and most spectacular of the city's great events, the Barcelona Games were intended to be stylish and innovative, but most of all were designed to provide a focus for a sweeping renovation of the city, with emblematic new buildings and infrastructure projects linked by clear strategic planning.

The three main Olympic sites – **Vila Olímpica**, **Montjuïc** and **Vall d'Hebron** – are quite different. The Vila Olímpica had the most comprehensive masterplan: drawn up by Bohigas and MBM themselves, it sought to extend Cerdà's grid down to the seafront. The main project on Montjuïc was to be the transformation of the 1929 stadium, but there is also Arata Isozaki's **Palau Sant Jordi** and its space-frame roof. Vall d'Hebron is the least successful of the three sites, but Esteve Bonell's **Velòdrom** is one of the finest (and earliest) of the sports buildings, built in 1984 before the Olympic bid had succeeded.

Not content with all the projects completed by 1992, the city continued to expand through the '90s; one major scheme followed another. Post-1992, the main focus of activity shifted to the **Raval** and the **Port Vell** (old port), and then more recently to the Diagonal-Mar area in the north of the city. Many of the striking buildings here are by local architects, among them Helio Piñón and Albert Viaplana. Their work combines fluid, elegant lines with a strikingly modern use of materials, from the controversial 1983 **Plaça dels Països Catalans** through transformations of historic

buildings such as the Casa de la Caritat, now the **Centre de Cultura Contemporània**, and all-new projects like **Maremàgnum** in the Port.

Other important contributions in the post-Olympic remodelling of Barcelona were made by foreign architects: notable examples include Richard Meier's bold white **MACBA**, and Norman Foster's **Torre de Collserola** on Tibidabo, which has become an emblem for Barcelona's skyline. Recently, two venerable buildings have been extensively remodelled in the service of the city's residents: the last stage of Gae Aulenti's interior redesign of the **Palau Nacional** on Montjuïc has been finished after 14 years to create the new **Museu Nacional d'Art de Catalunya** (see p119), and the CosmoCaixa building in Tibidabo (see p137), which again converts a 19th-century hospice into a spectacular exhibition space, this time as home to the new science museum. Also undergoing a major facelift, after decades lying as an abandoned shell, the Moorish-style arches of the Las Arenas bullring are being converted by Richard Rogers into a big and futuristic shopping and leisure centre due to open in 2005.

In the economic climate of the 21st century, architectural projects are increasingly circumscribed by commercial imperatives, sometimes causing tensions between the traditions of Barcelona urban architecture, the real needs of a city of this size and projection and the globalisation of commerce. The huge changes to the cityscape linked to the Fòrum Universal de les Cultures 2004 are a case in point. The area at the mouth of the Besòs river, near where Avda Diagonal meets the sea, was transformed for the occasion, most notably by the construction of a glittering triangular building, the **Edifici Fòrum**, designed by Herzog and de Meuron of Tate Modern fame. Nearby, the late Catalan architect Enric Miralles, best known for the Scottish Parliament building, created a fiercely modern and rather soulless park, the **Parc Diagonal-Mar**.

Whether or not this fourth stage in the re-imagining of Barcelona can be linked back to those previous outbursts of Barcelona's architectural creativity in the service of urban planning is debatable. While the value of many of these buildings is unquestionable, some see the dark hand of big business behind the latest developments and dismiss the new expansions connected to the Forum as more about making money than about making art. On the other hand, others defend this new, pragmatic approach to remodelling the city as another example of Barcelona's thousand-year-old capacity to reinvent itself in the search to create a city that is both a stunning town to look at and a comfortable place to live.

Park Güell.
See p48.

God's Own Architect

Antoni Gaudí: a visionary radical, building for religion.

Over the last century or so, the public images of architect Antoni Gaudí and the city of Barcelona have virtually blended into one. Crazy paving and splintered shards of tile, surrealist distortions marching across rooftops like wounded golems, kaleidoscopic explosions of garish colour: the city has almost grown to be defined by the creations of its most famous architectural son. Images of Gaudí's buildings are commonly used by television companies and publishing firms as shorthand for the city's exoticism; a handful have become local icons. Gaudí's buildings have transformed Barcelona into a virtual pilgrimage site: while some come to pray at the feet of the high priest of kitsch, others come to commune directly with buildings pinned by many as masterpieces but by others as mere freak shows. Who's right?

On the surface, Gaudí can appear simply to be a shameless showman, an attention-grabbing

eccentric. But behind the raw energy and audacious daring is an innate sense of design, pulling the apparent craziness together in unexpected fashion. Without it, the buildings might have survived, but they surely wouldn't have endured. Like the city in which he worked, Gaudí initially seduces us with myriad first impressions that help to foster the illusion that nothing is ever more than skin-deep. But, of course, there's more to both Gaudí and Barcelona than that.

IN PURSUIT OF A QUARRY

To discover the flesh and bones that underpin a Gaudí structure, there's no better place to start than **La Pedrera** ('the quarry'), the generally accepted nickname for the **Casa Milà** (*see p129*) on the Passeig de Gràcia. Perhaps more than any other Gaudí building, this rocky behemoth demonstrates perfectly that behind the showman lay a skilled and radical engineer.

Unlike almost all his architectural rivals, Gaudí came from *menestral* (artisan) stock, and was reared among the working-class craftsmen of Catalonia. Born in 1852 in provincial Reus (now about two hours south of Barcelona by train), his early inspirations were not other architects but his boilermaker father's dexterity in creating three-dimensional space, and what he later called 'the great book of nature'. From early on in his life and career, Gaudí could think just as comfortably with his hands as with his head.

These twin skills are visible at La Pedrera. Now owned by the Caixa Catalunya, the structure offers a perfect introduction to the unique and strange Gaudinian world. Built originally between 1906 and 1909 as a luxury apartment block – with, incidentally, the first drive-in garage in the world – its undulating forms echo the swell of the Mediterranean and the rocky crags of the nearby Collserola hills.

A century ago, La Pedrera qualified as enormously avant-garde: newspapers of the time were filled with cartoons of the building, which some nicknamed a 'Zeppelin hangar'. Even today, it still appears curious. However, up in the interpretation centre, Gaudí's rationale is explained with a collection of models, plans, drawings and scaled-down versions of his structural 'toys'. No aspect of Gaudí's life and career is more deceptively simple than the architect's revolutionary idea that gravity and God, working hand in hand, could shape the way we build. Take a chain, hold it in two hands, invert its natural swaggy shape with a mirror and, lo and behold, you have a catenary arch, one of nature's most resistant and structurally efficient shapes. Above your head, brick arches fan out gracefully and echo poignantly what you have just seen played out in front of you.

Climb the spiral staircase and head out on to the roof, and you enter a fairytale landscape of sci-fi chimneys and playful towers. Initially spirit-lifting, they grow increasingly disturbing with reflection, like other-worldly centurions. This is Gaudí the profound Catholic at work: even the wealthiest tenants needed firm moral guidance, he thought, perhaps more than most. Like the building's formerly privileged residents, stealing a few moments of peace and quiet up on the roof, we're caught there in a kind of purgatory, trapped between heaven and the everyday 'hell' that is the street below.

With Gaudí, everything has the potential for spiritual meaning. However, his buildings could also be fantastically practical. Go back down to the recently restored 'Pis' – the Catalan for flat – and marvel at how the naturally lit organic spaces flow smoothly from one end to the next. There is just one dividing line, the kitchen's sliding doors, separating the worlds of service and noisy children from the bourgeois parents' plumped-up cushions and the serious demands of social intercourse and hard-headed business. In the office, the framed stock and share certificates speak plainly of the Catalan gift for business that underpins this appetite for fancy. Gaudí was such a product of his time and place that it's impossible to imagine his works being conceived and completed in any other era.

HIS MASTER'S CHOICE

Gaudí's rise as an architect went hand in hand with Catalonia's growing sense of its own identity. The 'Renaixença', a literary and artistic movement that promoted all things Catalan, needed an appropriate and defining architecture. Gaudí was on hand to create it, providing Catalonia's politicians and ruling élite with just the kind of buildings they needed: made from expensive materials, such as onyx,

---

Don't miss — Gaudí creations

Casa Batlló
The reptilian town-house on the Passeig de Gràcia (*see p48*).

Colònia Güell
Another of Güell and Gaudí's utopian ideas for a garden city, never finished but worth visiting for its extraordinary crypt (*see p48*).

Palau Güell
Beyond the striking Gothic features is a wonderful interior, sadly closed to the public until late 2006 (*see p48*).

Park Güell
An incomplete, tantalising vision of Gaudí's ideal world (*see p48*).

La Pedrera
Gaudí's most successful combination of imagination and radical architectural innovation (*see p45*).

La Sagrada Familia
Modernisme's most eccentric, ambitious monument, overwhelming and overpowering (*see p48*).

Casa Batlló. *See p48.*

La Pedrera. *See p45.*

Casa Batlló. *See p48.*

Park Güell. *See p48.*

Sagrada Familia. *See p48.*

Park Güell.

a sacred Catalan space: wander the length of the serpentine bench, covered with a riotous explosion of trencadis (broken tiles), and look out for the secret graffiti scratched in by Gaudí as invocations to the Virgin Mary and as prayers to God. Gaudí even lived here for a time; indeed, his former house is now open as a museum, and offers a privileged view of his furniture and his Spartan, profoundly religious lifestyle.

'There is something monstrous, almost megalomaniacal, about the level of ambition.'

Other Gaudí buildings dot the city, some more spectacularly than others. The undulating marine life surface of **Casa Batlló** (see p123) is best seen, floodlit, at night. The wonderful restaurant at the **Casa Calvet** (see p161) affords visitors the opportunity to taste fine Catalan cuisine while admiring the simplicity and practicality of an industrial space. The **Dragon Gate** at **Pedralbes** (see p137) is a masterpiece of ironwork, while the **Col·legi de les Teresianes** (see p137) shows off Gaudí's powers of invention using just the humble brick. But over them all, visible from the Park Güell, stand the dramatic spires of Gaudí's expiatory temple, the **Sagrada Família** (see p129).

The temple, started in 1882, and now planned for completion some time around 2030, was Gaudí's life's work. But don't be fooled by the entrance: the Darth Vader sculptures date from the 1970s on. Around the far side at the Nativity façade, and down in the basement museum, we encounter the real Gaudí. There is something monstrous, almost megalomaniacal, about the level of ambition. The scale overwhelms, but the sheer creative range *overpowers*. Gaudí hoped here to illustrate the whole of Catalan Creation and the Catholic faith. Plaster casts of human bodies, chloroformed chickens, fishing boats, stars, octopuses, palms and Christmas trees melt together in a concert of stone. It is extraordinarily dramatic, a piece of unashamed religious theatre.

However, it's not Gaudí's greatest architectural achievement; at least, not quite. For that, you need to take a short ride (15 kilometres/9.5 miles or so) out to Santa Coloma de Cervelló, and the crypt at **Colònia Güell** (see p282). All of Gaudí's genius is distilled into this enchanting symphony built from rubble, discarded tiles, overburnt brick and rough-hewn stone. It's an exquisite sight.
● *Gijs van Hensbergen is the author of* Gaudí *(Harper Collins) and* Guernica: The Biography of a Twentieth-Century Icon *(Bloomsbury).*

tortoiseshell and exquisite cast bronze, and with a design that artfully triggered 'imperial' echoes while mixing the Ruskinian obsession with craft and the decadent perfume of the fin de siècle. No building offers as enticing a window on to this world as the **Palau Güell** (see p102), a masterpiece also notable for the fact that when Gaudí started building the palace in 1886, he found, in the shape of Don Eusebi Güell, his patron for life.

The Palau Güell was placed symbolically at the crossroads of two very distinct worlds, just a stone's throw from La Rambla and the exclusive Liceu opera house. On the street, absinthe, prostitution, criminality and urban decay prevailed. But behind the closed gates of the Palau, the pungent smell of incense, associated as always with the religiously observant *haute monde*, fugged the air.

Shuttered windows prevented the young Güell children from peering across the street at the brothels, drinking dens, regular fights and the teenage Picasso up to his harmless pranks. Little has changed since its construction; the palace still has a heavy morbid atmosphere. It's more uplifting to see what the patron and his architect achieved together when they left the Palau's oppressive atmosphere and emerged into the open air: specifically, at **Park Güell** (see p133), high above Barcelona in the Collserola hills.

Built between 1900 and 1904 as a private development for luxury housing, it's simply one of the most delightful gardens you'll ever find. But embedded in the fabric of this city retreat, its landscape shaped by mosaic dragons, rubble-built road bridges and grottoes, is a serious message, which Gaudí and Güell hoped might be transmitted to all who visited. The gardens were regarded by both men as

Where to Stay

Where to Stay   50

Features

The best Hotels   51
Hot suites   56
Star bars   71
The fairest of them all   74

Where to Stay

Don't make your bed, just lie in it.

Hotel Pulitzer. *See p69.*

As Barcelona has moved steadily up through the ranks of popular European destinations, so it's added more and more top-class hotel accommodation. However, it's the three- and four star section of the market that's really been skyrocketing, begging the question as to whether Barcelona can really fill so many hotel rooms. Many of the more upmarket places have slashed their prices of late in order to put pressure on the mid-range hotels; be sure to check online for preferential rates before you book. One good side effect of this rise in the quality of accommodation has been the trickledown effect it's had on once dull and dreary operations; newly renovated *pensiones* have added internet access and other flourishes.

It's still quite difficult to find a room in Barcelona outside the winter months, especially in mid-range to budget establishments. Booking in advance – by at least two weeks, and more in summer – is strongly advised, at least in those places where it's possible: many of the cheaper hotels won't accept reservations. Don't be surprised if a hotel requires you to guarantee your booking with credit card details or a deposit; whether or not you've provided either, it's always worth calling a few days before your arrival to reconfirm the booking (get it in writing if you can; many readers have reported problems), and to check the cancellation policy. Often you will lose at least the first night.

To be sure of getting a room with natural light or a view, ask for an outside room (*habitación exterior*), which will usually face the street. Many of Barcelona's buildings are built around a central patio or airshaft, and the inside rooms (*habitación interior*) around them can be quite gloomy, albeit quieter. However, in some cases, these inward-facing rooms look on to large, open-air patios or gardens, which have the benefit of being quiet and having a view; we have tried to mention these hotels in the listings where possible.

Theft is a problem in some places, especially in lower-end establishments, but occasionally also in luxury ones. If you're sleeping cheap, you might want to travel with a padlock to lock your door, or at least lock up your bags. As a rule of thumb, check to see if youth hostel rooms have lockers if you're sharing with other people. Use hotel safes where possible.

STAR RATINGS AND PRICES

Accommodation in Catalonia is divided into two official categories: hotels (H) and *pensiones* (P). To be a hotel (star-rated one to five), a place must have en suite bathrooms in every room. Ratings are based on physical attributes rather than levels of service; often the only difference between a three- and a four-star hotel is the presence of a meeting room. *Pensiones*, usually cheaper and often family-run, are star-rated one or two, and are not required to have en suite bathrooms (though many do). Some *pensiones* are called *hostales*, but, confusingly, are not youth hostels; those are known as *albergues*.

For a double room, expect to pay €40-€65 for a budget *pensión*, €60-€160 for a mid-range spot and from €160 to more than €450 for a top-of-the-range hotel. However, prices can vary considerably depending on the time of year; always check for special deals. All bills are subject to seven per cent IVA (value added tax) on top of the basic price; this is not normally included in the advertised rate, but we have factored it into the prices we have given. Breakfast is not included unless stated.

Booking agencies

Barcelona On-Line

Gran Via de les Corts Catalanes 662, Eixample (93 343 79 93/fax 93 317 11 55/www.barcelona-on-line.es). Metro Passeig de Gràcia. **Open** 9am-7pm Mon-Fri; 9am-2pm Sat. **Map** p342 D5.
This booking agency can book hostel or hotel rooms and private apartments online, over the phone or at its office. Staff are multilingual and the service is free, but there's a fee if you cancel less than 48 hours before arrival. You'll also need to make a prepayment for apartment reservations.

Europerator

93 451 03 32/fax 93 451 14 89/www.barcelona-accommodation.net. **Open** 9.30am-2pm, 4.30-7.30pm Mon-Fri; 9.30am-2pm Sat. **Credit** AmEx, MC, V.
Europerator is a room-search service that deals with hotels and *pensiones*, along with apartments, aparthotels and rooms in private houses. The multilingual staff will waive booking fees or commission for *Time Out* readers, so make sure to mention it. Paypal online payments are accepted.

Viajes Iberia

Vestibule, Sants railway station (93 491 44 63/fax 93 491 35 32/www.viajesiberia.com). Metro Sants Estació. **Open** 9am-9pm Mon-Fri; 9am-2pm Sat, Sun. **Credit** AmEx, DC, MC, V. **Map** p341 A4.

This agency can book a room at many of Barcelona's hotels and some *pensiones*. You'll be charged a fee of €3 per reservation, and will need to pay a deposit. **Other locations**: throughout the city.

Barri Gòtic & La Rambla

While La Rambla is handy for sights and is a focal point for visitors, it retains precious little authenticity; hotels here can be both noisy and overpriced. Head into the Gòtic for more reasonable alternatives, but bear in mind that old buildings in narrow medieval streets can mean that rooms often do not enjoy much light.

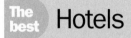 **Hotels**

For cut-price cool

Get a glimpse of Barcelona's trademark minimalist style without breaking the bank at **Hotel Actual** (*see p70*), **Hotel Banys Orientals** (*see p63*) and **Hotel Constanza** (*see p70*). Even the thriftiest of interior design buffs will get their kicks at the green and groovy **Hostal Gat Xino** (*see p59*).

For romantic retreats

Lovebirds nest at **Hotel Duques de Cardona** (*see p64*) or revel in the **Hotel Neri**'s sensual extravagranza (*see p53*). **Hotel Axel** (*see p65*) is the hotspot for starry-eyed gay couples. And you don't need to be flush to whisper sweet nothings in a gorgeous setting, with **Hostal Girona** (*see p74*) on the scene.

For group gatherings

Three (or four) isn't a crowd at **Pensió 2000** (*see p63*), **Hostal Orleans** (*see p63*) or **Citadines** (*see p79*).

For pampering and preening

Steal away to the dizzying heights of unadulterated luxury at **Hotel Arts**' (*see p63*) new 42nd-floor spa or the mountain-top mud therapies, beauty treatments and massages at **Gran Hotel La Florida** (*see p77*).

For making waves

Pools don't get much more glamorous than those at **Gran Hotel La Florida** (*see p77*) or **Hotel Majestic** (*see p69*). While the dipping pools at **Hotel Jazz** (*see p67*) and **Hotel Ambassador** (*see p59*) are an oasis of cool in the downtown heat, serious swimmers get some lengths in at the **Podium** (*see p69*).

Expensive

Hotel Colón

Avda Catedral 7 (93 301 14 04/fax 93 317 29 15/
www.hotelcolon.es). Metro Jaume I or Urquinaona.
Rates €107-€198 single; €139.10-€310.30 double;
€374.50 suite. **Credit** AmEx, MC, V. **Map** p344 B2.
With its chintzy furnishings, thick carpets and walls
bedecked in bright floral prints, the Colón is not the
most spruce or the most trendy hotel in town, but
it's eminently dependable. Its matchless location, on
the square in front of the cathedral, is best enjoyed
in the rooms that overlook the magnificent Gothic
edifice, some of which have a large private balcony.
Bar. Internet (dataport, wireless). Restaurant. Room
service. TV (pay movies).
Other locations: Hotel Regencia Colón
C/Sacristans 13, Barri Gòtic (93 318 98 58).

Hotel Le Meridien Barcelona

La Rambla 111 (93 318 62 00/fax 93 301 77 76/
barcelona.lemeridien.com). Metro Catalunya or Liceu.
Rates €417.30-€470.80 single/double; €535-€2,140
suite. **Credit** AmEx, MC, V. **Map** p344 A2.
An elegant and genteel hotel, Le Meridien is famed
for having the best and dearest suites in town, and
draws an accordingly star-studded clientele. Despite
its size (it has 212 rooms), it manages to retain an air
of intimacy thanks to its helpful, friendly staff.
Renovations due to be completed in spring 2005 will
add wood floors and leather furnishings throughout,
along with Egyptian cotton bedlinen, rain showers
and plasma-screen TVs. All rooms are soundproofed
and the best look out over La Rambla. Additional
facilities include a new fitness centre.
Bar. Disabled-adapted rooms (4). Internet (high
speed). Non-smoking floors (2). Parking (€20/day).
Restaurant. Room service. TV.

Hotel Neri

C/Sant Sever 5 (93 304 06 55/fax 93 304 03 37/
www.hotelneri.com). Metro Jaume I or Liceu. **Rates**
€230.10-€329.60 single/double; €267.50-€384.20
suite. **Credit** AmEx, DC, MC, V. **Map** p345 B3.
This gorgeous boutique hotel, located in a former
18th-century palace, has even the most seasoned
travellers swooning. The lobby, which teams flag-
stone floors and wooden beams with funky designer
fixtures, luscious red velvet and lashings of gold leaf,
gives a taste of what's to come in the 22 sumptuous
rooms, where neutral tones, natural materials and
rustic finishes (untreated wood and unpolished marble) stand in stylishly orchestrated contrast with
bolts of lavish satins and velvets, sharp design and
high-tech perks (hi-fis, plasma-screen TVs).
Bar. Disabled-adapted room. Internet (wireless). Non-
smoking rooms (10). Restaurant. Room service. TV
(pay movies).

Hotel Nouvel

C/Santa Anna 20 (93 301 82 74/fax 93 301 83 70/
www.hotelnouvel.com). Metro Catalunya. **Rates** (incl
breakfast) €105.90-€123.60 single; €171.20-€222.60
double. **Credit** MC, V. **Map** p342 D5.

Opened in 1917, the Nouvel has bags of old-world
charm. Guestrooms don't quite live up to the lobby,
which features carriage lanterns, ornately embossed
ceilings and curved wooden fittings. But they are
airy, comfortable and decorated in a neutral classic
style, with spacious, well-equipped bathrooms. A
few preserve the original tiled floors. The seven
recently renovated rooms on the top floor are the
brightest and most luxurious.
Non-smoking rooms (7). Restaurant. TV.

H10 Racó del Pi

C/Pi 7 (93 342 61 90/fax 93 342 61 91/www.h10.
es). Metro Liceu. **Rates** €177.60 single; €206.50
double. **Credit** AmEx, MC, V. **Map** p344 B2.
Part of the H10 chain, the Raco del Pi offers spacious
rooms with parquet floors, handsome terracotta-
tiled bathrooms and an elegant glass conservatory
on the ground floor. It can be a bargain out of season, when rates can be substantially cheaper than
those given here. Check the website for details.
Bar. Disabled-adapted room. Internet (dataport,
shared terminal). Non-smoking rooms (9). TV.
Other locations: H10 Catalunya Plaza Plaça
Catalunya 7, Eixample (93 317 71 71); and throughout
the city.

Hotel Rivoli Ramblas

La Rambla 128 (93 481 76 76/fax 93 317 50 53/
www.rivolihotels.com). Metro Catalunya or Liceu.
Rates €233.30 single; €278.20-€339.20 double; €413-
€771.50 suite. **Credit** AmEx, MC, V. **Map** p344 A2.
The peaceful Rivoli is a world apart from the bustle
outside. The rooms are comfortable and classy, with
soundproofed windows blocking out most of the
noise in the rooms facing La Rambla. The Blue Moon
cocktail bar is a slick place to start or end an evening,
and if you can't quite face heading to the beach,
guests can use the rooftop pool and terrace across
the street at the Hotel Ambassador (*see p59*).
Bar. Disabled-adapted rooms (4). Gym. Non-smoking
rooms (20). Parking (€17.70/day). Restaurant. Room
service. TV (pay movies).

Mid-range

Hostal Jardí

Plaça Sant Josep Oriol 1 (93 301 59 00/fax 93 342
57 33). Metro Liceu. **Rates** €68-€83 single; €83
double. **Credit** AmEx, DC, MC, V. **Map** p345 A3.
The Hostal Jardi offers spartan accommodation but
an excellent location in the Barri Gòtic. The decor is
rather clinical (avoid, especially, the dark *interior*
rooms), but they are clean, and all have en suite bathrooms. The best, well worth the extra expense, have
balconies overlooking the pretty *plaça*.
TV.

Hotel Barcelona House

C/Escudellers 19 (93 301 82 95/fax 93 412 41 29/
www.hotelbarcelonahouse.com). Metro Drassanes.
Rates (incl breakfast) €32-€50.30 single; €57.80-
€81.40 double; €88.80-€103.80 triple. **Credit** DC,
MC, V. **Map** p345 A3-B3.

Grab an occasional bargain at the **Hotel Racó del Pi**. *See p53.*

This 67-room hotel, popular with bright young things, toys with full-on retro kitsch while dipping into modern styling. There are three types of accommodation: recently redecorated 'comfort' rooms, which boast air-conditioning, parquet floors and a blue and yellow colour scheme; passably shabby 'standard' rooms; and the camp 'charme' rooms, with pink walls, floral bedspreads and rococo bedheads. Eccentric staff fit in with the hotel's split personality. A connecting door allows free entrance to Café Royale (*see p247*) until midnight.
TV (some rooms).

Duc de la Victòria

C/Duc de la Victòria 15 (93 270 34 10/fax 93 412 77 47/www.nh-hotels.com). Metro Catalunya. **Rates** €116.80-€139.70 single/double. **Credit** AmEx, DC, MC, V. **Map** p344 B2.
The trusty NH chain has high standards of comfort and service, and this good value downtown member of the family is no exception. The 160 rooms, with parquet floors and a blue and beige colour scheme, are safe but unexciting. But the location on a quiet street a stone's throw from La Rambla is unbeatable. *Disabled-adapted rooms (2). Internet (dataport). Non-smoking floor. Restaurant (lunch only). Room service. TV (pay movies).*

Hotel Oriente

La Rambla 45-47 (93 302 25 58/fax 93 412 38 19/ www.husa.es). Metro Liceu. **Rates** €115.60-€129.50 single; €143.40-€162.70 double; €171.20-€202.30 triple. **Credit** AmEx, DC, MC, V. **Map** p345 A3.

It may have been inaugurated as Barcelona's first ever 'grand hotel' in 1842, but the Oriente has been a fairly ordinary spot for a number of years. However, a recent full-scale renovation has brightened things up considerably. All bedrooms now have pale wood floors, minimalist design and sleek electrical gadgetry, in striking contrast to the ritzy olde worlde ballroom and dining room. Sadly, no amount of renovation can do away with the noise that floods up from La Rambla; it is highly recommended that light sleepers should ask for a room at the back of the hotel, or pack earplugs.
Bar (Mar-Oct only). TV.

Budget

Hostal Fontanella

Via Laietana 71, 2° (tel/fax 93 317 59 43/www. hostalfontanella.com). Metro Urquinaona. **Rates** €35.30-€42.80 single; €53.50-€72.80 double; €66.90-€91 triple. **Credit** AmEx, DC, MC, V. **Map** p337 B1.
Unremarkable – aside from a splendid Modernista lift – but more than adequate, this 11-room *hostal* has got enough chintz, lace and dried flowers to give Laura Ashley a serious run for her money. The downside of the central location on the thoroughfare bordering the Born, the Barri Gòtic and the Eixample is that outward-facing rooms are abuzz with the sound of traffic. However, it's a clean and comfortable place to stay, and double-glazing is apparently being installed around early 2005.
TV.

Hostal Lausanne

Avda Portal de l'Àngel 24, 1º 1ª (93 302 11 39).
Metro Catalunya. **Rates** €25 single; €45-€50 double;
€75-€80 triple. **No credit cards**. **Map** p344 B2.
Situated on one of downtown Barcelona's busiest
shopping streets, this *hostal* occupies the first floor
of a fine old building. Of the 17 basic rooms, two have
en suite bathrooms. Furniture is dated, but it's a friendly and safe place, with a fun backpacker vibe. The
street is as quiet at night as it is busy during the day.
TV room.

Hostal Maldà

C/Pi 5, 1º 1ª (93 317 30 02). Metro Liceu. **Rates**
€10-€15 single; €28-€35 double; €45 triple. **No**
credit cards. **Map** p344 B2.
Once you've found the entrance (inside a shopping
arcade), negotiated several flights of stairs (there's
no lift), and discovered that this *hostal* harbours a
startling number of rooms (around 30) in the architectural equivalent of Mary Poppins' handbag, you'll
likely find that you're not alone in the lobby. That's
because no bookings are taken at this exceedingly

Hot suites

Gran Hotel La Florida

See p63.
The top-flight Gran Hotel La Florida attracts TV
stars and pop princesses to its mountain-top
lair; Kylie Minogue, Lenny Kravitz, Harrison
Ford and Calista Flockhart have all swanned
around these ramparts recently. Eight of
the hotel's 22 suites are designed by
internationally acclaimed artists and
architects. Rebecca Horn's Tower Suite
has a chill-out zone in a turret that gives
360-degree views; the Japanese Imperial
Suite by Dale Keller has hanging gardens
and a jacuzzi; and for lovers of wide open
spaces the Great Presidential Suite by

Cristina Macava has acres of marble, arched
floor-to-ceiling windows and stupendous
views to the Med.

Hotel Arts

See p63.
For model spotting, you can't beat the Arts,
where guests have a good chance of running
into Kate, Jade and Cindy in the slick Club
Lounge. Suite 101 (*pictured*) is the favoured
pad, with views over the beach and the city;
two-storey apartments offer every luxury, from
butler service and complex techno gadgets to
pre-prepared baths for gentlemen (cigars and
cognac) and ladies (champagne and roses).

Hotel Majestic

See p69.
The Majestic gets top points for royalty:
Spain's Queen Sofía, King Constantine and
Queen Anne-Marie of Greece have all checked
in over the years, along with Norah Jones,
John Galliano and Joan Miró. The best suite
is the newly opened penthouse, with a vast
private terrace complete with soft, squidgy
sun loungers and a rolling hot tub. Bonus
treats include use of a SMART roadster
cabriolet, an open bar, 24-hour room service
and a daily fix of champagne and canapés.
All on the house.

Hotel Neri

See p53.
Housed in an 18th-century palace, the
city's flashiest boutique hotel gets full marks
for Gothic glamour, with slate-grey stone walls
offset by scarlet couches. John Malkovich
spent two weeks here for the opening of his
play *Hysteria* in September 2004, staying
in the deluxe suite. The suite's crammed
with sumptuous materials in forest greens
and golds, plush velvet drapes and satin
bedspreads, with a silver and blood-red
bathroom giving it a vampish finish.

Style on a budget at the **Hostal Gat Xino**. *See p59.*

popular backpackers' haunt. Some of the rooms are small and gloomy, and only one has (very basic) en suite facilities, but at these ridiculous prices, you weren't expecting any frills, right?
TV room.

Hostal Noya

La Rambla 133, 1° (93 301 48 31). Metro Catalunya. **Rates** €20-€24 single; €30-€35 double. **No credit cards. Map** p344 A2.
This cheerful cheapo has a smiling *mamá* on hand to greet you, fake ferns in the doorways and handsome old tiles on the floor. The lone bathroom is white, weathered and worn, and can get busy since it's shared between 12 rooms (there is a separate WC), but all bedrooms do have their own sinks.
Other locations: **Pensión Bienestar** C/Quintana 3, Barri Gòtic (93 318 72 83).

Hostal Parisien

La Rambla 114 (tel/fax 93 301 62 83). Metro Liceu. **Rates** €22-€24 single; €40-€60 double; €60-€75 triple. **No credit cards. Map** p344 A2.
Hostal Parisien is a passable budget option right on the noisy main drag. Tall ceilings add a sense of space to otherwise smallish rooms; two have en suite bathrooms, while another two have a private shower. Say hello to Fede the parrot, a long-established fixture who acts as a screeching welcoming committee. Dopey but friendly staff attend to an international blend of largely student travellers. Bookings are not usually taken at peak holiday times.
TV room.

Hostal Rembrandt

C/Portaferrissa 23, pral 1ª (tel/fax 93 318 10 11/ hostrembrandt1000@yahoo.es). Metro Liceu. **Rates** €28 single; €45-€60 double; €65-€75 triple. **Credit** MC, V. **Map** p344 B2.
A charming 15-room *hostal*: fairly stylish (for the price) with lots of wood panelling and soft lighting. An added bonus is the pretty interior courtyard, which makes for a pleasant chill-out zone/eating area. Rooms out front can be a little noisy.
TV.

Hotel Toledano

La Rambla 138, 4° (93 301 08 72/fax 93 412 31 42/ www.hoteltoledano.com). Metro Catalunya. **Rates** €34.30-€38.50 single; €52.50-€63.20 double; €80.30 triple; €89.90 quadruple. **Credit** AmEx, DC, MC, V. **Map** p344 A2.
All 17 rooms here are spotless and some have air-conditioning, but whether you end up with acres of space or just up from a broom cupboard is a lottery. Some rooms have balconies, with the occasional glimpse of the cathedral. Service is friendly, and free internet access and a book exchange system are nice touches. There are 11 more basic rooms in the *pensión* upstairs (same number). Booking is essential.
Internet (shared terminal, wireless). TV: TV room.

Pensión Hostal Mari-Luz

C/Palau 4 (phone/fax 93 317 34 63/pensionmariluz @menta.net). Metro Jaume I or Liceu. **Rates** €40-€46 double; €14-€18/person 4-6-person rooms. **Credit** AmEx, DC, MC, V. **Map** p345 B3.

You'll have to climb several flights of a grand stone staircase to reach the Mari-Luz, but the effort is well worth it for the smiling service and the homey atmosphere. Stripped wood doors and old floor tiles add character to the otherwise plain but quiet rooms, some of which face a plant-filled inner courtyard. There are dorms as well as double and triple rooms (no.4 and no.6 have good en suite bathrooms).
Other locations: Pensión Fernando C/Ferran 31, Barri Gòtic (93 301 79 93).

Pensión Portugal

C/Josep Anselm Clavé 27 (tel/fax 93 342 60 61/www. pensionportugal.com). Metro Drassanes. **Rates** €25-€35 single; €50-€65 double; €80 triple. **Credit** MC, V. **Map** p342 D6.
A basic budget *pensión* from the people behind the Hostal-Residencia Ramos (*see p60*). Air-con in all rooms is a welcome perk in this price range; while furnishings are sparse and worn, the place is clean. The spacious rooms are gradually being repainted in a rainbow of colours. Staff are cheery, and the overall atmosphere is young and fun.
TV.

Pensión Segre

C/Simó Oller 1, 1º (93 315 07 09). Metro Drassanes. **Rates** €20 single; €35-€45 double. **No credit cards. Map** p345 B4.
A kitsch and friendly, first-floor *pensión* (no lift). The rooms are comfortable enough; some have private bathrooms, and there's a small functional lounge. A bonus is the fairly tranquil street and the fact that you're spitting distance from the Port Vell.
TV room.

Residencia Victòria

C/Comtal 9, 1º 1ª (93 318 07 60/93 317 45 97/ victoria@atriumhotels.com). Metro Catalunya. **Rates** €29 single; €39-€42 double; €55 triple. **No credit cards. Map** p344 B2.
This spacious and peaceful *pensión* is on the second floor (no lift). Rooms are basic, clean and light, with sinks but no en suite bathrooms. Extras include communal cooking and washing facilities, and a cute outdoor terrace. Friendly service keeps a steady stream of folks coming back, so make sure to book in advance. Rooms must be paid for upfront, in cash.
TV room.

Raval

The Raval is the grungier neighbour of the Barri Gòtic, but recent regeneration means it's also the coolest *barrio* for bars and restaurants.

Expensive

Hotel Ambassador

C/Pintor Fortuny 13 (93 342 61 80/fax 93 302 79 77/www.rivolihotels.com). Metro Catalunya. **Rates** €233.30-€259 single; €278.20-€339.20 double; €413-€771.50 suite. **Credit** AmEx, MC, V. **Map** p342 C5.

The four-star Ambassador slipped into obscurity after the '92 Olympics. Odd; it's one of the nicest hotels in the area. It's been refurbished lately, with a heady blend of water features, gold paint and smoked glass, a glittering colossus of a chandelier and a free-standing Modernista bar dominating the lounge area. Rooms are sleek and comfortable; there's also a pool and a jacuzzi on the rooftop.
Bar. Disabled-adapted rooms (4). Gym. Internet (dataport: some rooms, shared terminal). Non-smoking floor. Parking (€18.20/day). Pool (outdoor). Restaurant. Room service. TV (pay movies).

Mid-range

Casa Camper

C/Elisabets 11 (93 342 62 80 /fax 93 342 75 60/ www.casacamper.com). Metro Catalunya. **Rates** incl breakfast & snack €187.30-€219.40 single; €203.30-€240.80 double; €208.70-€262.20 suite. **Credit** AmEx, DC, MC, V. **Map** p344 A2.
Another of the Mallorcan footwear giant's diversification ventures (next door to its restaurant, FoodBall, *see p153*), was only just opening its sliding doors at the time of writing, but promises to be a holistic concept-fest of a boutique hotel where Mediterranean peasant (*camper* in Mallorquín) simplicity is to meet contemporary cool. Funky style credentials are courtesy of Vinçon (*see p197*) Frederic Amat's interior design; hi-tech features (plasma TVs, DVDs, CD players) and quirky touches (a healthy snack and breakfast included, hammocks, specially designed bicycles) are underscored by functionality and environmental awareness.
Business centre. Disabled: adapted room. Internet (wireless). No smoking. TV (pay movies, DVD).

Hostal Gat Raval

C/Joaquin Costa 44, 2ª (93 481 66 70/fax 93 342 66 97/www.gataccommodation.com). Metro Universitat. **Rates** €35.30-€41.70 single; €51.50-€76 double. **Credit** AmEx, MC, V. **Map** p342 C5.
Gat Raval embodies everything that 21st-century budget accommodation should be: smart, clean and funky, with bright, sunshiney rooms that each boast a work by a local artist. Some have balconies while others have views of the MACBA. The only downside is that nearly all bathrooms are communal (though very clean).
Internet (pay terminal). TV.
Other locations: Hostal Gat Xino C/Hospital 155 (93 324 88 33).

Hostal Gat Xino

C/Hospital 155 (93 324 88 33/www.gataccomm odation.com). Metro Sant Antoni. **Rates** (incl breakfast) €64.20-€74.90 single; €96.30 double; €128.40 4-person suite. **Credit** AmEx, MC, V. **Map** p342 C6.
The 'Gats' are pioneers of a new way to stay: inexpensive, modern places that combine the polish of a classy boutique hotel with the practicality and price of a B&B. Added extras in the newest member of

Hotel Axel. *See p65.*

the family include a bright, breezy breakfast room with apple-green polka dot walls, a wood-decked patio and a sprawling roof terrace, its fate yet undecided. There's more bright green and sober black in the bedrooms (all en suite) with comfortable beds, crisp white linen and flat-screen TVs. The best rooms have small terraces of their own.
Internet (pay terminal). TV.
Other locations: Hotel Gat Raval C/Joaquín Costa 44, Raval (93 481 66 70).

Hostal-Residencia Ramos

C/Hospital 36 (93 302 07 23/fax 93 302 04 30/ www.hostalramos.com). Metro Liceu. **Rates** €35-€45 single; €60 double; €90 triple. **Credit** MC, V.
Map p345 A3.
This family-run *hostal* offers one of the best deals in the Raval. There's no air-conditioning, but plenty of windows and balconies keep it cool. Rooms (all en suite) are basic, but light and airy. The best rooms have balconies on to the *plaça*, though, not for the faint-hearted, they can get quite noisy.
TV.

Hotel España

C/Sant Pau 9-11 (93 318 17 58/fax 93 317 11 34/ www.hotelespanya.com). Metro Liceu. **Rates** (incl breakfast) €50-€66 single; €98 double; €130 triple.
Credit AmEx, DC, MC, V. **Map** p345 A3.
The lower floors at this Modernista landmark were designed by Domènech i Montaner in 1902. The main restaurant is decorated with floral tiling and elaborate woodwork; the larger dining room beyond it features extravagant murals of river nymphs by Ramon Casas. The bedrooms might disappoint after

all this grandeur, but they have been considerably improved of late. All are en suite, and the nicest rooms open on to a bright interior patio.
Disabled-adapted rooms (2). Restaurant. TV room. TV.

Hotel Gaudí

C/Nou de la Rambla 12 (93 317 90 32/fax 93 412 26 36/www.hotelgaudi.es). Metro Liceu. **Rates** (incl breakfast) €107 single; €144.50 double; €187.50 triple; €214 quadruple. **Credit** AmEx, DC, MC, V.
Map p345 A3.
In a nod to the great architect (the Palau Güell is right opposite), the Hotel Gaudí has a replica of the palace's roof in the lobby, but you can feast your eyes on the real thing if you book into one of the upper rooms with a small terrace. Rooms are cool and comfortable, and all have good-sized bathrooms.
Disabled-adapted rooms (2). Gym. Internet (pay terminal). Parking (€15/day). Room service. TV.

Hotel Mesón Castilla

C/Valldonzella 5 (93 318 21 82/fax 93 412 40 20/ www.mesoncastilla.com). Metro Universitat. **Rates** (incl breakfast) €101.70 single; €130.60-€144.50 double; €171.20 triple. **Credit** AmEx, DC, MC, V.
Map p344 A1.
This chocolate-box hotel opened in 1952; before then, it was a private house belonging to an aristocratic Catalan family. Public areas are full of antiques and curious artworks, but the rooms are fairly uniform, with cosy soft furnishings to contrast with the tiled floors. The best have tranquil terraces, with a delightful plant-packed one off the breakfast room.
Parking (€20/day). TV.

With its buff, sandstone walls and huge, arched windows looking on to the *plaça*, not to mention the pink marble lobby filled with forest-green furniture, this imposing hotel is the most handsome in the Raval and the oldest in Barcelona. Housed in the former convent of St Augustine, it was converted into a hotel in 1840; what might once have been bare-boned saintliness has been replaced with creature comforts. Rooms are nice, but there's no soundproofing.
Bar. Disabled-adapted rooms (2). Internet (shared terminal). Restaurant (dinner only). TV.

Budget

Hostal La Palmera

C/Jerusalem 30 (93 317 09 97/fax 93 342 41 36). Metro Liceu. **Rates** (incl breakfast) €35-€37.50 single; €45-€59 double. **Credit** V. **Map** p344 A2.
The best rooms in this basic *hostal* have balconies that look over La Boqueria market. Despite the daytime bustle and the fact that many of the Raval's funkiest bars are right on the doorstep, it's surprisingly quiet at night. The decor is unremarkable, but the rooms are light, airy and spotless.

Hostal La Terrassa

C/Junta de Comerç 11 (93 302 51 74/fax 93 301 21 88). Metro Liceu. **Rates** €22 single; €34-€40 double; €54 triple; €68 quadruple. **Credit** DC, MC, V. **Map** p345 A3.
Clean, friendly and, above all, cheap, La Terrassa is a typical first-floor (no lift) backpackers' joint; it's also the top spot, apparently, for travelling skateboarders. There's no air-con but rooms have fans, it's kid-friendly, and there's a scruffy terrace out back for soaking up the sun and making new friends over a cold beer.

Hostal Opera

C/Sant Pau 20 (93 318 82 01/www.hostalopera.com). Metro Liceu. **Rates** €38 single; €58 double; €83 triple. **Credit** MC, V. **Map** p345 A3.
This *pensión* is situated right beside the Liceu opera house, just off La Rambla. All the renovated rooms have plenty of natural light, private bathrooms, central heating and air-con. Those at the back of the hotel are the nicest and the quietest, so book early.
Disabled-adapted rooms (3). Internet (pay terminal). TV room.

Hosteria Grau

C/Ramelleres 27 (93 301 81 35/fax 93 317 68 25/www.hostalgrau.com). Metro Catalunya. **Rates** €30-€42.80 single; €48.70-€70.10 double; €65.80-€88.30 triple; €74.90-€139.10 apartment. **Credit** AmEx, DC, MC, V. **Map** p344 A1.
This charming, family-run *hostal* oozes character, with a tiled spiral staircase and fabulous 1970s-style communal areas. The open fireplace is a luxury if you visit in the winter. Rooms are basic, comfortable and fairly quiet. If you're after self-catering, the family also has apartments that are available for rent.
Bar. Internet (pay terminal). TV room.

Hotel Peninsular

C/Sant Pau 34-36 (93 302 31 38/fax 93 412 36 99). Metro Liceu. **Rates** (incl breakfast) €50 single; €70 double; €85 triple; €110 quadruple. **Credit** MC, V. **Map** p345 A3.
This colonial-style hotel is housed in a building that once belonged to Augustinian monks and spans several floors (no lift), with a breakfast cafeteria on ground level. The handsome, fern-filled interior patio is great for writing postcards, but the rooms have seen better days; if you opt for a cheaper room, with communal bathroom, expect the basics.
TV room.

Hotel Principal

C/Junta de Comerç 8 (93 318 89 74/fax 93 412 08 19/www.hotelprincipal.es). Metro Liceu. **Rates** €65-€120 single; €70-€160 double. **Credit** AmEx, DC, MC, V. **Map** p345 A3.
The Principal distinguishes itself by the ornate furniture in its 120 renovated rooms, all of which have good bathrooms, and its sunny, communal roof terrace. Bedrooms are comfortable with the odd piece of very chintzy furniture. The best are those facing the street (all with balconies), though a couple of late-opening bars nearby can make them noisy.
Disabled-adapted rooms (3). Internet (shared terminal). No smoking. TV.

Hotel Sant Agustí

Plaça Sant Agusti 3 (93 318 16 58/fax 93 317 29 28/www.hotelsa.com). Metro Liceu. **Rates** (incl breakfast) €85.50-€107 single; €96-€142.50 double; €128-€170 triple. **Credit** AmEx, DC, MC, V. **Map** p345 A3.

Sant Pere & the Born

Rich in sights, restaurants, bars and shops, and also boasting one of the city's finest parks, this is also one of the trendier, more gentrified areas. Prices are high and tourists are everywhere.

Mid-range

Banys Orientals

C/Argenteria 37 (93 268 84 60/fax 93 268 84 61/ www.hotelbanysorientals.com). Metro Jaume I. **Rates** (incl breakfast) €85.60-€96.30 single; €101.70 double. **Credit** AmEx, DC, MC, V. **Map** p345 B3.
Opened in 2002 to great acclaim, this hotel remains one of the best deals in town. It exudes cool, from its location at the heart of the Born to the deeply stylish shades-of-grey minimalism of its rooms, and nice touches such as complimentary mineral water on the landings. The main debit is the smallish size of some of the double rooms. Plans to create a luxurious new service by tapping into the eponymous thermal baths that lie underneath the hotel are in the proverbial pipeline. More definite and eagerly anticipated is the opening, at the start of 2005, of nearby apartments with a similar look and hotel services.
Disabled-adapted room. Internet (high-speed). Restaurant. TV.

Hotel Catalonia Princesa

C/Rec Comtal 16-18 (93 268 86 00/fax 93 268 84 91/www.hoteles-catalonia.es). Metro Arc de Triomf. **Rates** €101.70-€171.20 single; €123.10-€184.10 double. **Credit** AmEx, DC, MC, V. **Map** p344 C2.
This old, pretty building, a former textile factory, has been tastefully converted, with a sunny atrium plunging down the middle. All 90 rooms have parquet floors, smart fittings and abundant natural light; spacious bathrooms are a cushy extra. The lower down you are in the building, the bigger your balcony, but avoid ground-floor rooms, as they look right on to the street. While the hotel is pleasantly located on a small street close to the park, the immediate area has its share of bag-snatchers.
Bar. Disabled-adapted rooms (3). Internet (dataport, wireless). Restaurant. Room service. TV.

Budget

Hostal Orleans

Avda Marquès de l'Argentera 13 (93 319 73 82/ fax 93 319 22 19/www.hostalorleans.com). Metro Barceloneta. **Rates** €24-€39 single; €45-€55 double; €55-€68 triple; €80 quadruple. **Credit** AmEx, DC, MC, V. **Map** p343 E6.
This unspectacular but dependable *hostal* on a traffic-filled avenue has 18 refurbished rooms, most of which have en suite bathrooms and air-con. Given the standards of comfort and cleanliness, the competitive rates don't leave much room for argument. Spacious quadruple rooms are a steal for groups. *TV.*

Pensió 2000

C/Sant Pere Més Alt 6, 1º (93 310 74 66/fax 93 319 42 52/www.pensio2000.com). Metro Urquinaona. **Rates** €38.50-€49.20 single; €48.20-€65.90 double; €19.30 3rd person; €16.10 4th person. **Credit** MC, V. **Map** p344 B2.
Friendly owners Manuela and Orlando run one of Barcelona's most endearing and best value *pensiones* in a charming old building opposite the Palau de la Música. Only two of its six bright and airy rooms are en suite, but the communal facilities are sparkling. With tall windows, buttercup-yellow walls and a lounge peppered with books and toys, it's a cheery sunbeam of a place, with a warm, relaxed atmosphere. The big rooms also make it a good bet for families.

Pensión Francia

C/Rera Palau 4 (93 319 03 76). Metro Barceloneta. **Rates** €26.80 single; €40.60-€58.90 double; €53.50-€64.20 triple. **Credit** AmEx, DC, MC, V. **Map** p345 C4.
The only frills here are on the bedspreads: many of the 18 simple, spotless rooms are very small and some singles feel especially cramped. Some have a shower, sink and toilet; others have one or more of these facilities outside the room. On the plus side, staff are amiable and the location, just off a lively square, is excellent. Rooms are spread over two upper floors; there's no lift. *TV.*

Ports & shoreline

Aside from the Sea Point youth hostel (*see p80*), Barcelona's only seaside lodgings are at the Hotel Arts, though this may change soon.

Expensive

Hotel Arts

C/Marina 19-21 (93 221 10 00/fax 93 221 10 70/www.ritzcarlton.com). Metro Ciutadella-Vila Olímpica. **Rates** €390-€813 double; €508-€1,926 suite; €1,284-€2,568 apartment; €10,700 royal suite. **Credit** AmEx, DC, MC, V. **Map** p343 F7.
To celebrate its tenth anniversary, the 44-storey, Ritz-Carlton-owned Arts has spruced up all of its rooms, and continues to score top marks for service. Plush robes, Bang & Olufsen CD players, sea views and a 'Club' floor for VIPs are just some of the hedonistic perks awaiting guests. Even seasoned travellers are dazzled by the personal service, art-filled hallways and the city's only beachfront pool, overlooking Frank Gehry's bronze fish sculpture. The luxury duplex apartments have round-the-clock butlers and chef services, and a spa facility should have opened on the 42nd floor by the time this guide comes out.
Bar. Business centre. Disabled-adapted rooms (4). Gym. Internet (high speed). Non-smoking floors (20). Parking (€37.50/day). Pool (outdoor). Restaurants (4). Room service. Spa. TV (DVD: some rooms).

Where to Stay

Grand Marina Hotel

*Edificio World Trade Center, Moll de Barcelona (93
603 90 00/fax 93 603 90 90/www.grandmarinahotel.
com). Metro Drassanes.* **Rates** €187.30-€428 single/
double; €374.50-€1,712 suite. **Credit** AmEx, DC, MC,
V. **Map** p342 C7.

For business travellers, this five-star hotel in the
World Trade Center at the end of the pier in the
Port Vell could hardly be more convenient, but its
location – within easy reach of the Old City, yet isolated from its chaos – is also excellent for tourists.
All the 235 rooms are spacious, with minimalist furnishings, jacuzzis and views over the sea or city.
Facilities include a rooftop gym and pool, an elegant
piano bar and a restaurant.

*Bar. Business centre. Disabled-adapted rooms (4).
Gym. Internet (shared terminal, web TV, wireless).
Non-smoking floor. Parking (€23/day). Pool (outdoor).
Restaurants. Room service. Spa. TV (DVD, music).*

Hotel Duquesa de Cardona

*Passeig Colom 12 (93 268 90 90/fax 93 268
29 31/www.hduquesadecardona.com). Metro
Drassanes or Jaume I.* **Rates** €198 single;
€235.40 double; €369.20 suite. **Credit** AmEx,
DC, MC, V. **Map** p342 D6.

This elegantly restored 16th-century palace is furnished with natural materials – wood, leather and
stone – complemented by a soft colour scheme that
reflects the original paintwork. Cosy bedrooms
make it ideal for a romantic stay, and if guests can't
quite face the ten-minute walk to the beach, they can
opt to take the lift to the wood-decked roof terrace
to sunbathe, cool off in the pool and take in some
amazing views. The arcaded restaurant serves a
menu of modern Catalan dishes.

*Business centre. Disabled-adapted room. Internet
(high speed). Non-smoking floor. Pool (outdoor).
Restaurant. Room service. TV.*

Budget

Marina Folch

*C/Mar 16, pral (93 310 37 09/fax 93 310 53 27).
Metro Barceloneta.* **Rates** €40 single; €60 double.
Credit AmEx, DC, MC, V. **Map** p342 D7.

Given the dearth of budget accommodation near the
sea, this small family-run *hostal* is a welcome find
in the Barceloneta *barrio*. Simple but clean and comfortable, it has ten rooms, all of which are painted in
bright, breezy blues, have plenty of space and offer
private bathrooms.

TV.

Poble Sec

A quiet, leafy residential area between
Montjuïc mountain and the Avda Paral·lel.
While it may seem out of the way, most parts
of Poble Sec are within reasonable walking
distance of the Rambla, and even closer to the
bars and restaurants of the Raval.

Mid-range

Hotel Nuevo Triunfo

*C/Cabanes 34 (93 442 59 33/fax 93 443 21 10/
www.hotelnuevotriunfo.com). Metro Paral·lel.* **Rates**
€73 single; €103 double; €115-€130 triple. **Credit**
MC, V. **Map** p342 C6.

Neat as a pin, with 40 fresh, bright and spotless
rooms, this pleasant if somewhat bland hotel is
located in a peaceful street at the foot of Montjuïc.
The four best rooms counteract the austerity of the
sparse, modern fittings with plant-filled terraces.

Disabled-adapted room. Internet (pay terminal). TV.

Budget

Hostal Restaurante Oliveta

*C/Poeta Cabanyes 18 (93 329 23 16/july206@
hotmail.com). Metro Paral·lel.* **Rates** €25-€35 single;
€45-€55 double; €65 triple; €80 quadruple. **Credit**
MC, V. **Map** p341 B6.

These six diminutive and basic rooms, tucked away
above a family-run bar-restaurant, are all modern
and fresh, but renovation is nevertheless on the cards
for 2005. Bonuses include air-con in all rooms and 24-
hour service from the bar downstairs (more a sleepy
little watering hole than a rip-roaring nightspot).
Only two of the rooms have en suite bathrooms, but
communal facilities are squeaky clean. Expect a
small surcharge if you pay by credit card.

Bar. Restaurant.

Hotel Omm. *See p69.*

Eixample

Architecture aficionados, shopaholics and lovers of ornate paving stones get their kicks on the broad leafy boulevards of the Eixample. Some of Barcelona's trendiest hotels – among them the **Prestige** (*see p70*), the **Axel** (*see below*) and the **Omm** (*see p69*) – are located in the neighbourhood.

Expensive

Hotel Astoria

C/Paris 203 (93 209 83 11/fax 93 202 30 08/ www.derbyhotels.es). Metro Diagonal. **Rates** €128.40-€181.90 single; €142.30-€200.10 double; €236.50 duplex. **Credit** AmEx, DC, MC, V. **Map** p338 C4.

Built in 1954 and renovated in the '90s, the 117 rooms here are undergoing a radical facelift; by mid 2005, all should sport a slick new look, though vintage features will be preserved. The classic lobby's domed ceiling is supported by columns and adorned with frescoed dolphins, while the bar is all marble floors, chandeliers and chesterfield sofas. There's also a delightful room featuring an antique pool table and vintage posters. Other revamp plans include a rooftop pool.

Bar. Gym. Internet (dataport, wireless). Non-smoking rooms (25). Parking (€19.25/day). Restaurant (lunch only). Room service. TV.

Hotel Atrium Palace

Gran Via de les Corts Catalanes 656 (93 342 80 00/fax 93 342 80 01/www.hotel-atriumpalace.com). Metro Passeig de Gràcia. **Rates** €97-€204 single; €107-€214 double; €267.50-€321 suite. **Credit** AmEx, DC, MC, V. **Map** p342 D-E5.

Housed in an attractive old building, this is a modern, light-filled and cutting-edge hotel with an unstuffy atmosphere unusual in places this smart. Rooms, done in a minimalist attire of creams and browns, narrowly sidestep sterility thanks to plenty of wood and token fresh flowers. Gadget fiends will love the special safes in which to stash and charge your laptop all at once, web TV and remote-controlled beds in the suites. Budget airline-style pricing strategies mean that rates are lower the earlier you book and, unusually, drop on weekdays. Check the website.

Business centre. Disabled-adapted rooms (2). Gym. Internet (dataport, web TV, wireless). Non-smoking rooms (15). Pool (indoor). Restaurant. TV (music, pay movies).

Other locations: **Hotel Millenni** Ronda Sant Pau 14, Poble Sec (93 441 41 77); **Hotel Splendid** Muntaner 2, Eixample (93 451 21 42); and throughout the city.

Hotel Axel

C/Aribau 33 (93 323 93 93/fax 93 323 93 94/ www.hotelaxel.com). Metro Universitat. **Rates** €96.30-€181.90 single; €144.50-€230.10 double; €283.60-€321 suite. **Credit** AmEx, DC, MC, V. **Map** p342 C5.

Behind a fetching Modernista façade is a funky boutique hotel, mainly intended as a place for discerning gays (but everyone's welcome). The slinky lobby and restaurant set the scene, but bedrooms are lighter on the senses, with ivory walls, bleached flooring and the odd splash of colour. Functional modular furniture plays second fiddle to the king-size beds; plasma-screen TVs and hi-fis keep technophiles happy. 'Superior' rooms have stained-glass gallery balconies and hydro-massage bathtubs. The rooftop is where it's all happening, with a little nook, a jacuzzi, a bar and a relaxing sundeck. The library has information on Barcelona; there's even an on-site designer clothes store.
Bar. Business centre. Disabled-adapted rooms (2). Gym. Internet (wireless). Non-smoking floor. Pool (outdoor). Restaurant. Room service. TV.

Hotel Balmes

C/Mallorca 216 (93 451 19 14/fax 93 451 00 49/ www.derbyhotels.es). Metro Passeig de Gràcia. **Rates** €137-€192.60 single; €152-€214 double; €260 duplex. **Credit** AmEx, DC, MC, V. **Map** p338 C4.
The star feature of this well-groomed three-star is its lush patio-garden, which boasts a cute pool, a handful of tables and a discreet bar. Displays of African art, some duplex rooms and plant-filled interior patios are charismatic signature touches of the Claris family (*see below* Hotel Claris). However, the chic but slightly outmoded rooms can be quite small and beds err on the short side.
Bar. Internet (dataport, shared terminal, wireless). Non-smoking rooms (25). Parking (€16/day). Pool (outdoor). Restaurant (lunch only). Room service. TV.

Hotel Catalonia Berna

C/Roger de Llúria 60 (93 272 00 50/fax 93 272 00 58/www.hoteles-catalonia.es). Metro Girona or Passeig de Gràcia. **Rates** €139.10 single; €180.90 double. **Credit** AmEx, DC, MC, V. **Map** p338 D4.
The Catalonia group has a policy of restoring historical buildings into modern hotels; Berna is no exception, with an eye-catching exterior designed in 1864 by Josep Cerdà. The Italian artist Raffaelo Beltramini painted the façade, whose brightly coloured allegorical figures represent Nature, Art and Science. The swish, modern interior is another world, however. Some of the rooms are on the small side, but they are sleekly appointed throughout.
Bar. Disabled-adapted rooms (4). Internet (wireless). Parking (€16.10/day). Restaurant. Room service. TV.

Hotel Claris

C/Pau Claris 150 (93 487 62 62/fax 93 215 79 70/ www.derbyhotels.es). Metro Passeig de Gràcia. **Rates** €261.10-€369.20 single; €288.90-€409.80 double; €483.70 suite; €558.60-€1,043.30 duplex. **Credit** AmEx, DC, MC, V. **Map** p338 D4.
With its neo-classical exterior, plush antique furniture, eclectic art collection (the Claris holds the largest private collection of Egyptian art in Spain) and sleek steel and glass fixtures, it's little wonder that many consider this Barcelona's finest hotel. In the bedrooms, antique artworks and chesterfield

sofas sit alongside elegant modern installations, while Warhol prints liven up the East 47 restaurant. Sidle past the glorious rooftop pool and solarium to the bar, where a DJ will soundtrack your cocktail.
Business centre. Car park (€19.30/day). Disabled-adapted rooms (4). Gym. Internet (wireless). Non-smoking floor. Pool (outdoor). Restaurants. Room service. TV.

Hotel Condes de Barcelona

Passeig de Gràcia 73-75 (93 445 00 00/ fax 93 445 32 32/www.condesdebarcelona.com). Metro Passeig de Gràcia. **Rates** €208.70-€347.80 single/double; €508.30 suite. **Credit** AmEx, DC, MC, V. **Map** p338 D4.
Made up of two buildings that face each other on C/Mallorca at the intersection of Passeig de Gràcia, the family-owned Condes has a split personality. The building on the north side occupies a 19th-century palace and has recently been given a facelift; a plush dipping pool sits on the roof, where the terrace offers evening dining and jazz. In the newer building, rooms on the seventh floor have terraces and a bird's-eye view of La Pedrera. Lodgings range from comfortable standard rooms to themed suites with extras such as jacuzzis. Both offer 'romantic weekend' packages, including champagne, theatre tickets, gourmet lunch boxes and airport transfers.
Bar. Disabled-adapted rooms (2). Gym. Internet (dataport, web TV, wireless). Non-smoking floors (2). Parking (€16.60/day). Pool (outdoor). Restaurant. Room service. TV (music, pay movies).

Hotel Inglaterra

C/Pelai 14 (93 505 11 00/fax 93 505 11 09/www. hotel-inglaterra.com). Metro Universitat. **Rates** €106-€230.10 single; €198-€278.20 double; €149.80-€353.10 triple. **Credit** AmEx, DC, MC, V. **Map** p344 A1.
With over 75 years in the business, the Inglaterra is one of the original 'designer' hotels and is surprisingly peaceful considering the hubbub of shoppers on the street outside. With blond wood hallways, and neat, minimalist bedrooms with meditative Japanese characters sunk into the walls, it's a simple and elegant place. Star features include a leafy roof terrace and a comfortable living room and cafeteria. Guests may use the pool at the Majestic (*see p69*), the Inglaterra's sister hotel.
Bar. Disabled-adapted room. Internet (dataport, wireless). Restaurant. Room service. TV (pay movies).

Hotel Jazz

C/Pelai 3 (93 552 96 96/97/www.nnhotels.es). Metro Catalunya. **Rates** €133.80-€192.60 single; €155.20-€214 double; €203.30-€262.20 triple; €267.50 suite. **Credit** AmEx, DC, MC, V. **Map** p344 A1.
Rooms at the Jazz are decked out in neutral greys, beiges and black, softened with parquet floors, and spiced up with dapper pinstripe cushions and splashes of funky colour. Beds are roomy and bathrooms are super-sleek, with cool, polished black tiles. The latest technology comes naturally to this newbie, which boasts flat-screen TVs and wireless internet. A rooftop pool and sundeck top things off.

Bar. Business centre. Disabled-adapted rooms (4). *Non-smoking floor. Internet (high speed, wireless). Pool (outdoor). TV.*
Other locations: Hotel Barcelona Universal Avda Paral·lel 76-78, Poble Sec (93 567 74 47); and throughout the city.

Hotel Majestic
Passeig de Gràcia 68 (93 488 17 17/fax 93 488 18 80/www.hotelmajestic.es). Metro Passeig de Gràcia. **Rates** €374.50-€470.80 single/double; €535-€1,819 suite; €2,675 apartment. **Credit** AmEx, DC, MC, V. **Map** p338 D4.
The Majestic has positioned itself among the front-runners of Barcelona's swishest hotels. Behind a neo-classical façade lies a panoply of perks, such as a service that allows you to print a selection of the day's newspapers from all over the world from the comfort of the lobby. Its crowning achievement is the new ninth floor, which boasts an apartment and a sumptuous 'Sagrada Família' suite with a private outdoor jacuzzi. Mere mortals can enjoy the highlife in the rooftop pool and gym, which offer stunning views over the city, though the opulent guestrooms, decorated with classical flair, are impressive. The Drolma restaurant is one of the finest in the city.
Bars (2). Business centre. Disabled-adapted rooms (4). Gym. Internet (wireless). Non-smoking floors (2). Parking (€16.05/day). Pool (outdoor). Restaurant. Room service. TV (pay movies).

Hotel Omm
C/Rosselló 265 (93 445 40 00/fax 93 445 40 04/ www.hotelomm.com). Metro Diagonal. **Rates** €208.70-€374.50 single/double; €535 suite. **Credit** AmEx, DC, MC, V. **Map** p338 D4.
The hottest new hotel in town, the Omm is part space-age movie set, part feng shui lounge, offering everything the world's beautiful people could possibly need for a slick metropolitan getaway. The open-plan lobby is perfect for people-watching, while the newly installed rooftop plunge pool offers fabulous views of Gaudí's landmark buildings. Bedrooms are super-stylish with cool, natural materials, two bathrooms and every gadget imaginable, from high-tech illumination to state-of-the-art hi-fis. A spa is due to open in 2005. *See p161* for Moo, the hotel restaurant.
Bar. Disabled-adapted rooms (2). Internet (high speed, wireless). Pool (outdoor). Restaurant. Room service. TV.

Hotel Onix Rambla Catalunya
Rambla Catalunya 24 (93 342 79 80/fax 93 342 51 52/www.hotelsonix.com). Metro Catalunya or Passeig de Gràcia. **Rates** €110.20-€192.60 single; €120.90-€203.30 double; €160.50-€246.10 triple. **Credit** AmEx, DC, MC, V. **Map** p342 D5.
This new and seamlessly elegant hotel has a rooftop pool and views of the Collserola hills. Bedrooms have retained some original features, among them floor-to-ceiling windows, and are fairly plush. Elsewhere, the only things to break the starkness are a few well-chosen works of modern art.

Hotel Condes de Barcelona. *See p67.*

Bar. Disabled-adapted room. Gym. Internet (dataport). Non-smoking rooms (4). Parking (€13/day). Pool (outdoor). Room service. TV.
Other locations: Onix Fira (*see p77*).

Hotel Podium
C/Bailén 4-6 (93 265 02 02/reservations 91 398 44 00/fax 93 265 05 06/www.nh-hotels.com). Metro Arc de Triomf. **Rates** €165.90-€215.10 single; €215.10-€257.90 double; €514.70 suite. **Credit** AmEx, DC, MC, V. **Map** p343 E5.
Attractively located behind an early 20th-century façade but essentially a business hotel, the Podium is worth checking for discounts at weekends and other off-peak times. The rooms are smart and comfortably equipped (with Playstations!); the rooftop fun-land includes a bar and, unusually, a pool big enough for swimming as opposed to just dipping.
Bar. Business centre. Disabled-adapted rooms (5). Gym. Internet (wireless). Non-smoking rooms (20). Parking (€14.70/day). Pool (outdoor). Restaurant. Room service. TV (pay movies).

Hotel Pulitzer
C/Bergara 8 (93 481 67 67/fax 93 481 64 64/www. hotelpulitzer.es). Metro Catalunya. **Rates** €160.50-€192.60 single; €192.60-€272.90 double. **Credit** AmEx, DC, MC, V. **Map** p344 A1.
An unprepossessing façade reveals an impressive lobby stuffed with white leather sofas, a reading area overflowing with glossy picture books, a swanky bar and a restaurant. The rooftop terrace is

a fab spot for a sundowner and makes up in squishy loungers, scented candles and tropical plants what it lacks in a view. The rooms themselves are not terribly spacious, but are sumptuously decorated with cool elephant-grey marble (*very* now), fat fluffy pillows and kinky leather trim.

Bar. Disabled-adapted rooms (5). Internet (dataport). Non-smoking floors (3). Restaurant. Room service. TV.

Prestige Paseo de Gràcia

Passeig de Gràcia 62 (93 272 41 80/fax 93 272 41 81/www.prestigepaseodegracia.com). Metro Passeig de Gràcia. **Rates** €245-€333 single/double; €526.50 junior suite. **Credit** AmEx, DC, MC, V. **Map** p338 D4.

The Prestige was born when architect Josep Juanpere took a 1930s building and revamped it with funky oriental-inspired minimalist design and Japanese gardens. Work in perks such as Bang & Olufsen plasma-screen TVs, intelligent lighting systems, free minibars and even umbrellas in every room (as well as the usual bathrobes et al), add the effortlessly handsome 'Zeroom' lounge-bar-library, where expert concierges are constantly on hand, and you get Barcelona's ultimate designer boutique hotel. If you can't bear to leave it all behind, you can even buy a copy of one of the designer fixtures (all are on sale) to take home.

Bar. Disabled-adapted room. Internet (dataport, wireless). Non-smoking rooms (4). Room service. TV.
Other locations: Prestige Congress Pedrosa B 9-11, Hospitalet de Llobregat (93 267 18 00).

Ritz Hotel

Gran Via de les Corts Catalanes 668 (93 318 52 00/ fax 93 318 01 48/www.ritzbcn.com). Metro Passeig de Gràcia. **Rates** €406.40-€540.40 single/double; €508.30-€2,600 suite. **Credit** AmEx, DC, MC, V. **Map** p342 D5.

In its heyday, the Ritz was peopled by the likes of Frank Sinatra, Ava Gardner and Salvador Dalí, who famously had a horse brought up to his room. It's looking a little the worse for wear these days, but it remains the grande dame of Barcelona's hotels; a bastion of old-school luxury, it sparkles with gilded edges and teardrop chandeliers. Features include open fireplaces, mosaic 'Roman baths' and four-poster beds. The brand new junior suites are sleek and modern, for those who find this kind of grandeur oppressive. Chef Romain Fornell, the youngest ever to be awarded a Michelin star, heads up the kitchen.
Bar. Business centre. Gym. Internet (web TV, wireless). Non-smoking floors (3). Restaurant. Room service. Spa. TV (DVD, music, pay movies).

Mid-range

Hostal d'Uxelles

Gran Via de les Corts Catalanes 688, pral (93 265 25 60/fax 93 232 85 67/www.hoteluxelles.com). Metro Tetuán. **Rates** €64.20 single; €80.25 double; €105.90 triple; €144.50 quadruple. **Credit** AmEx, MC, V. **Map** p343 E5.

A delightfully pretty *hostal*, and a steal at the price. The angels above reception are a hint of what's to come: pine floors or Modernista tiles, cream walls with gilt-framed mirrors, antique furnishings and bright, Andaluz-tiled bathrooms (all en suite). Pastel colours rule and plush drapes hang romantically above the bedsteads. The best rooms have plant-filled balconies with tables and chairs. The second wing, which echoes the first in ambience and decor, is housed in a building down the road.
TV.
Other locations: Hostal d'Uxelles 2 Gran Via de les Corts Catalanes 667, entl 2ª (same number).

Hostal Goya Principal

C/Pau Claris 74, 1º (93 302 25 65/fax 93 412 04 35/www.hostalgoya.com). Metro Urquinaona. **Rates** €32.10-€37.45 single; €53.50-€88.30 double. **Credit** MC, V. **Map** p342 D5.

Its renovations now completed, this *hostal* represents excellent value. Upstairs guests have use of a light and airy communal TV room with vast sofas and sleek palms, as well as a terrace. Bedrooms are done out in luscious chocolates and creams, with comfy beds, chunky duvets and scatter cushions. Bathrooms have a real Habitat feel – no bad thing – and on the whole, the Goya Principal puts other *hostals* of its ilk to shame.
TV room.

Hotel Actual

C/Rosselló 238 (93 552 05 50/fax 93 552 05 55/ www.hotelactual.com). Metro Diagonal. **Rates** €138 single; €152 double. **Credit** AmEx, DC, MC, V. **Map** p338 D4.

The 29 simple yet elegant rooms at this minimalist boutique hotel live up to expectations set in motion by its bright, stylish, cream and chocolate-brown lobby. Dark wood fittings are complemented by crisp white sheets, velvet curtains and slate-grey bathrooms. Eight new suites overlooking Passeig de Gràcia are planned for 2005.
Car park (€19.30/day). Disabled-adapted room. Internet (high speed). Room service. TV.

Hotel Constanza

C/Bruc 33 (93 270 19 10/fax 93 317 40 24/www. hotelconstanza.com). Metro Urquinaona. **Rates** €107-€117.70 single; €128.40 double; €160.50 triple. **Credit** AmEx, MC, V. **Map** p343 D5.

Here's a rarity: a seriously stylish, boutique hotel that doesn't cost the earth. The lobby of the Hotel Constanza looks a bit like the chill-out lounge of an exclusive nightclub, with boxy, white sofas, lots of dark wood and Japanese silk screens painted with giant white lilies separating the breakfast room from the main area. Upstairs, wine-coloured corridors lead to sumptuous bedrooms, with dark wood and leather furnishings, huge pillows and quality cotton sheets. The bathrooms are just as chic as the bedrooms and go overboard on the toiletries. Those at the back are quietest, and some of them have their own private terraces.
Internet (dataport). TV.

Star bars

Stuck in a windowless *pensión* with only the queue for the communal bathroom by way of social interaction? Well, if you can't afford the rack rates at Barcelona's more luxurious lodgings, a Martini or a glass of cava at one of the city's swankiest hotels can add a much-needed sprinkle of glamour to a weekend away.

Smack bang in the centre of the Barri Gòtic, the bar at the **Hotel Neri** (*see p53*) gives on to the eerily evocative Plaça Felip Neri. The pockmarked victim of a tragic bomb strike during the Civil War, the square retains a spookily quiet ambience, making it perfect for morning coffee, afternoon tea and, of course, pre-dinner drinks. Around Plaça Catalunya, a rash of new hotels offers several far splashier meeting places than the overcrowded, cool-in-the-'80s Café Zurich. In 2005 hip *barcelonins* hang at the **Pulitzer** (*pictured; see also p69*) for white leather sofas, modern art and Sunday morning Bloody Marys (it's very LA, darlings) or the **Hotel Jazz** (*see p67*) for some rather more understated boozing.

In the lower Eixample, the **Axel** (*see p65*) is a darkened, moody affair, good for illicit love trysts. You don't have to be gay to hang out here, but it helps. Higher up the Eixample grid, the bar at the **Hotel Omm** (*see p69*) is a wine-lovers' heaven, with 550 wines and cavas on its list. And yes, there are more designer sofas and Côstes-style music for stylish lounging. More upbeat is Arola at the **Hotel Arts** (*see p63*) on the seashore. This posh surfers' bar is great for pre-clubbing cocktails (Club Catwalk is a mere totter away across the street) and offers backside views of Frank Gehry's glittering fish, not to mention the Med.

For sheer class, however, you can't beat having a drink at the **Gran Hotel La Florida** (*see p77*), perched high above the city at the top of Tibidabo. The bar terraces tumble down the hillside amid scented gardens, the views of the Lilliputian city and the endless blue sea are extraordinary and the exertion of getting there is well worth it for the reward of marvelling, if just for a moment, at how the other half use their expense accounts.

Hotel Ginebra

Rambla Catalunya 1, 3° 1ª (93 317 10 63/fax 93 317 55 65/hotelginebra@telefonica.net). Metro Catalunya. **Rates** €45 single; €75 double; €85 triple. **Credit** DC, MC, V. **Map** p344 B1.

The 12 rooms in this dusky old *hostal* are very reasonable, with old-fashioned floral decor and ample en suite bathrooms, but it's the ultra-central location on Plaça Catalunya that's the real crowd-puller. Eight rooms have balconies looking over the city's hub, but sliding shutters inside the windows keep the din to a low buzz.
TV.

Hotel Gran Via

Gran Via de les Corts Catalanes 642 (93 318 19 00/fax 93 318 99 97/www.nnhotels.es). Metro Passeig de Gràcia. **Rates** €80.25-€107 single; €133.75 double; €176.55 triple; €208.65 quadruple. **Credit** AmEx, DC, MC, V. **Map** p342 D5.

The faded splendour of this old mansion, built in 1870 and converted into a hotel in 1936, has a certain faded charm. The paint is beginning to chip, and the rooms are on the Spartan side, but they are ample and furnished with antiques. On the plus side it does boast a pretty garden, and the lobby is quite astounding with its looming columns, yawning arches and buckets of gilt. Decor is old-fashioned, though more 1970s than 1870s.
Disabled-adapted rooms (2). Internet (pay terminal). TV.

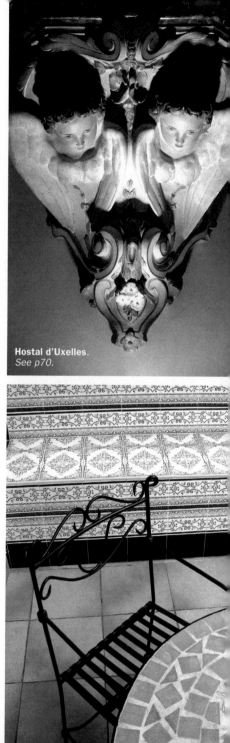

Hostal d'Uxelles.
See p70.

Budget

Hostal Central Barcelona

C/Diputació 346, pral 2ª (93 245 19 81/fax 93 231 83 07/www.hostalcentralbarcelona.com). Metro Tetuán. **Rates** €27.90-€42.80 single; €42.80-€68.50 double; €80.30-€96.30 triple; €26.80-€32.10/person 4-6-person suite. **Credit** DC, MC, V. **Map** p343 E5.

These 13 rooms, spread over two floors of an old Modernista building, have kept their original tiling and high ceilings, but are kitted out with air-con and double-glazing, keeping out the roar of the traffic. Most have en suite facilities, but the modern glass-brick cubicles in some eat up bedroom space. Walls painted in a wide palette, from duck-egg blue to daffodil yellow, jolly things up. Clean and friendly, this is a bargain for budget travellers. Buses to Ryanair flights in Girona leave from nearby.
No smoking.

Hostal Eden

C/Balmes 55, pral 1ª (93 454 73 63/fax 93 452 66 21/www.hostaleden.net). Metro Passeig de Gràcia. **Rates** €35-€45 single; €50-€65 double; €60-€75 triple; €70-€85 quadruple. **Credit** AmEx, MC, V. **Map** p338 D4.

The name is an exaggeration, but this warm and relaxed 32-room *pensión* does have its perks, chiefly free internet access and a sunny patio. Specify your room on booking; the best have corner baths, and Nos.114 and 115, at the rear, are quiet and have large

The fairest of them all

After years shrouded in scaffolding, and nearly a century after it was originally fashioned, the ornate marble façade that once earned the **Casa Fuster** its reputation as the city's most expensive abode is back on show. Not only that, but the stunning interior has also been painstakingly restored. Nestled at the upper end of the city's most distinguished boulevard, Barcelona's first 'five-star deluxe landmark' hotel's top-notch installations make for a luxurious stay; but its cachet ultimately resides in its history.

After marrying the Marquès of Alella's daughter in 1905, Majorcan high society gentleman Mariano Fuster commissioned the illustrious Modernista architect Lluís Domènech i Montaner (of Palau de la Música fame) to design them a home in Barcelona. Completed in 1911, the magnificent edifice was to be his last project. The Fuster family left the house in the early 1920s, but it has retained their name through spells as the home of renowned Catalan poet Salvador Espriu, and as boutiques, a chic café and a cinema. In the early 1960s it was acquired by a local electrical company, which was keen to tear it down. A public outcry saved it and it was bought by the Hoteles Center chain, which pledged to restore it to its former splendour.

Just as art nouveau, of which Modernisme is the Catalan manifestation, looked both backwards to traditional craftsmanship

and decorative arts and forwards to new techniques and materials, so the Casa Fuster has teamed its scrupulous renovation with 21st-century luxury. The 96 opulent rooms have sleek, modern designs, cutting-edge technology and original architectural features. Suites have king-size beds and wrought-iron

windows overlooking the patio. Room 103 is dark but good-sized and quirky, with a sprawling bathroom behind sliding doors. Other rooms can be a bit cramped and noise travels between them. No lift. *Internet (2 shared terminals). TV.*

Hostal Girona

C/Girona 24, 1º 1ª (93 265 02 59/fax 93 265 85 32/ www.hostalgirona.com). Metro Urquinaona. **Rates** €30-€40.70 single; €58.90-€66.40 double. **Credit** DC, MC, V. **Map** p344 C1.
This gem of a *hostal* is filled with antiques, chandeliers and oriental rugs. Simple rooms follow suit, with tall windows, pretty paintwork (gilt detail on the ceiling roses) and tiled floors. It's worth splashing out on rooms in the refurbished wing, with en suite bathrooms, although rooms in the older wing are equally charming and some have en suite showers. Brighter, outward-facing rooms have small balconies overlooking C/Girona or bigger balconies on to a huge and quiet patio. Gorgeous and good value. *TV.*

Hostal de Ribagorza

C/Trafalgar 39 (tel/fax 93 319 19 68/www.hostal ribagorza.com). Metro Urquinaona. **Rates** €45-€60 double; €50-€65 triple. **Credit** MC, V. **Map** p344 C2.
Pedro and his mother give this lacy one-floor *hostal* a homely feeling, with flowers and plants, a cosy lounge and conversation on tap. Modernista elements jazz up the 11 simple rooms, four of which have en suite bathrooms. Most of them face on to a big avenue and can consequently be noisy. (*Interior* rooms are quiet but devoid of charm.) Room 106 has a light-filled gallery. *TV.*

Hostal San Remo

C/Ausiàs Marc 19, 1º 2ª (93 302 19 89/fax 93 301 07 74/www.hostalsanremo.com). Metro Urquinaona. **Rates** €37 single; €58-€62 double. **Credit** MC, V. **Map** p344 C1.
Staying in this bright, neat, peaceful apartment feels a bit like staying with an amenable relative. Friendly owner Rosa and her fluffy white dog live

detail. From the exquisite leather upholstery of the restaurant chairs to the doorbells in the suites and the breakfast hall's spectacular mosaic floor, every element is part of a finely tuned whole, where the furniture and interior design are as prized as the architecture. What could not be restored has been duplicated, and original techniques used where possible.

These features come into their own in the ground-floor Café Vienés, which boasts its own pedigree as one of the city's most fashionable meeting places in the 1940s. Less faithful to original design than to contemporary luxuries is the swish roof terrace, featuring a gym, Swedish showers, a sauna, an open-air dipping pool, a bar and a handful of discreetly scattered tables. Panoramic views put it all in context, with a plunging perspective down Passeig de Gràcia, the city's finest Modernista stage.

balconies, while all rooms feature flat-screen TVs and remote-controlled lighting. The ultra-plush bathrooms have period tiling alongside hydro-massage bathtubs and power showers.

True to the spirit of the 'total work' that Domènech i Montaner pioneered, the refurbishment has tended to every minor

Casa Fuster

Passeig de Gràcia 132 (93 255 30 00/ fax 93 255 30 02/www.hotelescenter.es). Metro Diagonal. **Rates** €385.20-€481.50 single/double; €556.40 junior suite; €1,337.50-€1,872.50 suite. **Credit** AmEx, DC, MC, V. **Map** p338 D3.
Bar. Business centre. Disabled-adapted rooms (5). Gym. Non-smoking floor (1). Internet (high speed). Pool (outdoor). Restaurant. Room service. TV (pay movies).

on site and take good care of guests. All seven rooms are equipped with air-conditioning, blue and white-striped bedspreads and modern wooden furniture; five have en suite bathrooms and most have a little balcony and double-glazing. *TV.*

Residencia Australia

Ronda Universitat 11, 4° 1ª (93 317 41 77/fax 93 317 07 01/www.residenciaustralia.com). Metro Universitat. **Rates** €30 single; €48-€70 double; €15 extra bed. **Credit** MC, V. **Map** p344 A1.
Maria, the owner of Residencia Australia, fled Franco's Spain to Australia in the 1950s, and returned after the Generalisimo's death to carry on the family business and open this small, friendly, home-from-home *pensión*. There are just four cute rooms (one en suite); all are cosy and clean and simply done. There's a minimum two-night stay. The family also has an apartment nearby that can be booked if rooms are full.
Internet (shared terminal). TV (some rooms).

Gràcia

One of Barcelona's most peaceful and charismatic *barrios* lies off the beaten tourist track. Its narrow streets and leafy squares have a villagey feel, but there are plenty of decent restaurants, shops and nightlife. It's a five- to ten-minute metro ride to the town centre.

Expensive

See also above **The fairest of them all**.

Mid-range

Hotel Confort

Travessera de Gràcia 72 (93 238 68 28/fax 93 238 73 29/www.mediumhoteles.com). Metro Diagonal or Fontana. **Rates** €107-€128.40 single; €123.10-€154.10 double. **Credit** AmEx, DC, MC, V. **Map** p338 D3.

Opened in 2001, the Confort still feels shiny and new, and is light-years ahead of other two-star establishments, with 36 simple but smart modern bedrooms with curvy light wood furnishings and gleaming marble bathrooms. All the rooms get lots of light, thanks to several interior patios. There's a bright dining room and lounge, with a large leafy terrace that makes a lovely setting for a sunny summer breakfast or a cool drink on a balmy night.
Disabled-adapted room. Internet (dataport, pay terminal). TV.
Other locations: Hotel Monegal C/Pelai 62, Eixample (93 302 65 66); and throughout the city.

Budget

Acropolis Guest House
C/Verdi 254 (tel/fax 93 284 81 87/www.acropolis. o-f.com). Metro Lesseps. **Rates** €25-€35 single; €40-€50 double; €54-€70 triple. **No credit cards.** **Map** p339 E3.
Broken flowerpots and jumble-sale furniture scattered about the gardens and balconies, semi-exposed brick walls, retro chandeliers and nightlights, rampant bougainvillea over the gate... the Acropolis is indeed a different beast. Some rooms are en suite and three share a huge balcony, though that's nothing compared to the attic room's roof terrace and sweeping views. Providing you're not expecting hotel services and don't mind being slightly out-of-the-way, the schlep up the steep hill is worth every minute.
No smoking. TV room.

Sants

Although the Plaça de Espanya and the Parc Joan Miró have their charms, the only reason to stay in Sants is to catch an early train. Most visitors are here on business, and need to be near the *fira* (trade fair) facilities. Rates here drop at weekends and other off-peak business seasons. It's a ten- to 15-minute metro ride to town.

Expensive

Hotel Catalonia Barcelona Plaza
Plaça d'Espanya 6-8 (93 426 26 00/fax 93 426 04 00/www.hoteles-catalonia.es). Metro Espanya. **Rates** €145.50-€224.70 single; €183-€259 double. **Credit** AmEx, DC, MC, V. **Map** p341 A5.
This monolithic business hotel has 338 rooms spread over 11 floors, and a range of services including an on-site bank and travel agency. The standard rooms are grey-carpeted feats of blandness, though they're highly comfortable and very well equipped. Those on the C/Tarragona side overlook the conversion of the Arenas bullring into a shopping mall, the noise from which isn't fully shut out in the lower rooms. There are stunning panoramic views from the vantage point of the rooftop pool, even in winter, when it dons a glass cover and is heated.

Bar. Business centre. Disabled-adapted rooms (4). Gym. Internet (wireless). Parking (€16.05/day). Pool (outdoor). Restaurant. Room service. TV (pay movies).

Mid-range

Hotel Onix Fira
C/Llançà 30 (93 426 00 87/fax 93 426 19 81/www. hotelsonix.com). Metro Espanya. **Rates** €87.80-€131.60 single; €98.44-€163.70 double; €125.20-€199 triple. **Credit** AmEx, DC, MC, V. **Map** p341 B5.
With grey marble floors and inoffensive salmon bedspreads, these 80 rooms have the sterile lustre of the business hotel about them, but are smart and fully equipped. The best have views over the sparse greenery of the Parc Joan Miró while others overlook the sluggish (and noisy) building work on the Arenas bullring. The roof is a welcome surprise, with two wooden sundecks pleasantly garnished with greenery and a munchkin-sized pool.
Bar. Disabled-adapted rooms (2). Internet (dataport, wireless). Parking (€13). Pool (outdoor, summer only). Room service. TV.

Budget

Hostal Sofía
Avda Roma 1-3, entl (93 419 50 40/fax 93 430 69 43). Metro Sants Estaciò. **Rates** €35 single; €40-€50 double; €50-€60 triple. **Credit** DC, MC, V. **Map** p341 B4.
These 17 basic rooms just across the busy roundabout from the city's main station are a sound budget option if an early train or quick stopover forces you to spend the night. Some have en suite bathrooms. As the *hostal* is on the first floor and traffic is fierce, outward-facing rooms are usually noisy.
TV (some rooms).

Zona Alta

Staying in the city's uptown neighbourhoods is handy if you're on business or fancy a taste of secluded residential chic.

Expensive

Gran Hotel La Florida
Carretera de Vallvidrera al Tibidabo 83-93 (93 259 30 00/fax 93 259 30 01/www.hotellaflorida.com). **Rates** €331.70-€626 single/double; €695.50-€1,605 suite. **Credit** AmEx, DC, MC, V.
From 1925, when it opened, through to the 1950s, this was Barcelona's best hotel, frequented by royalty and film stars. After a long renovation, it reopened in 2003, with lavish suites, private terraces and gardens, a five-star restaurant, an outdoor nightclub in summer and a spa. Perched atop Tibidabo, La Florida offers bracing walks in the hills and breathtaking 360-degree views, which culminate in the jaw-dropping infinity pool (with a

heated indoor part for winter dips). Getting a cab to take you back from town at night can be tricky: there's a free shuttle service but it only runs until 8pm in summer, and earlier in winter. Check the website for discounts.

Bar. Business centre. Disabled-adapted rooms (2). Gym. Internet (high speed, wireless). Non-smoking floor. Parking (€19.30/day). Pool (outdoor/indoor). Restaurant. Room service. Spa. TV (pay movies).

Mid-range

Hotel Guillermo Tell

C/Guillem Tell 49 (93 415 40 00/fax 93 217 34 65/ www.hotelguillermotell.com). Metro Fontana/FGC Plaça Molina. **Rates** €74.90-€160.50 single; €94.20-€179.80 double; €127.30-€242.90 suite; €33.20-€63.20 extra bed. **Credit** AmEx, DC, MC, V. **Map** p338 D2.
A neat little uptown three-star with 61 trim, comfortable and generally spacious rooms classically decked out in ecru and sky-blue stripes. Located on the periphery of the Zona Alta, it's only a ten-minute walk to Gràcia's abundant shops, restaurants and bars and a short metro ride to the city centre.
Car park (€14/day). Disabled-adapted rooms (2). Internet (wireless). TV.

Petit Hotel

C/Laforja 67, 1° 2ª (93 202 36 63/fax 93 202 34 95/www.petit-hotel.net). FGC Muntaner. **Rates** (incl breakfast) €69.60-€71.70 single; €85.60-€99.50 double; €31 extra bed adult, €24.60 under-12s.
Credit AmEx, DC, MC, V. **Map** p338 C3.
Located in the smart neighbourhood of Sant Gervasi, this charming and convivial B&B has four neat, fresh-feeling bedrooms set around a softly lit lounge. Although only one of the rooms is en suite, the others share two large, immaculate modern bathrooms; and there are plans to give them all private facilities in the course of 2005. There's also a homely kitchen where the owners, Rosa and Leo, are always happy to chat and provide insider information on the city. Breakfast is served all day from 8.30am.
Internet (pay terminal). TV.

Citadines

La Rambla 122 (93 270 11 11/fax 93 412 74 21/ www.citadines.com). Metro Catalunya. **Rates** €145-€170 1-2-person studio); €230-€250 1-4-person apartment; €18-€27 cleaning. **Credit** AmEx, DC, MC, V. **Map** p342 D5.
What the Citadines lacks in character, it makes up for in convenience. This gleaming apartment block is situated in a prime location, offering 115 smartly renovated studios and 16 one-bedroom apartments (all sleep four). It's ideal for longer business trips, groups or families. One weekly clean is included in the price; there's an option to pay extra for the daily cleaning service. Breakfast is served in a cafeteria on the first floor, which looks out over La Rambla.
Disabled-adapted rooms (4). Parking (€20/day). TV.

Hispanos Siete Suiza

C/Sicilia 255, Eixample (93 208 20 51/fax 93 208 20 52/www.hispanos7suiza.com. Metro Sagrada Familia. **Rates** (apartments, incl breakfast) €128.40-€192.60 1-2 people; €160.50-€224.70 3 people; €192.60-€256.80 4 people; €385.20 up to 6 people.
Credit AmEx, DC, MC, V. **Map** p339 E4.
Lovers of vintage automobiles will get a real kick out of the Hispanos Siete Suiza, named for the seven lovingly restored pre-war motors that take up much of the lobby. Mostly, though, the vibe is more home sweet home, albeit a luxury one: the 19 elegant and spacious apartments each have a kitchen and sitting area with parquet floors, a terrace and two bedrooms. All profits go to the cancer research foundation that runs the hotel. It also has a good restaurant called La Cupola.
Bar. Disabled-adapted room. Internet (dataport). Parking (€13/day). Restaurant. Room service. TV.

In the last few years, a rash of agencies and websites offering short-term room and apartment rental has appeared. Some companies rent out their own apartments, while others act as intermediaries between apartment owners and visitors, taking a cut of the rents.

When renting, it pays to use a little common sense. Check the small print (payment methods, deposits, cancellation fees, etc) and exactly what is included in the price (cleaning, towels

Petit Hotel.

and so on) before booking. Note that apartments offered for rental tend to be very small.

Apart from the places listed below, check out www.inside-bcn.com, www.barcelonaliving. com, www.oh-barcelona.com, www.rentaflatin barcelona.com, www.friendlyrentals.com, www. 1st-barcelona.com, www.flatsbydays.com, www. barcelonabeachapartments.com and the gay-operated www.outlet4spain.com. www.habit servei.com can also find rooms in shared flats.

For student and youth services and websites that can take reservations for hostels, see p318.

Youth hostels

For student and youth services and websites that can take reservations for hostels, see p318.

Alberg Mare de Déu de Montserrat

Passeig de la Mare de Déu del Coll 41-51, Gràcia (93 210 51 51/fax 93 210 07 98/www.tujuca.com). Metro Vallcarca. **Open** *Reception* 8am-3pm, 4.30-11pm daily. **Rates** (incl breakfast) €16.20-€18.50 under-25s; €19.60-€21.90 over-25s; €2/per person/stay sheets. **Credit** AmEx, DC, MC,V.
Central it isn't, but this handsome Trinity Towers-style hostel does boast an architectural edge over the average. It's located in a magnificent building that has been a private mansion, hospital and orphanage over the years. Many of the original details in the form of Modernista tilework, whimsical plaster carvings and stained-glass windows have been retained, not to mention lovely gardens. IYHF cards are required for anyone wishing to stay.
Parking (free). Disabled-adapted room. Internet (pay terminals). Kitchen. Laundry facilities. No smoking. Restaurant. TV room.

Barcelona Mar Youth Hostel

C/Sant Pau 80, Raval (93 324 85 30/fax 93 324 85 31/www.barcelonamar.com). Metro Paral.lel. **Open** 24hrs daily. **Rates** (incl breakfast) €15.50-€23; €2.50 per person/stay sheets. **Credit** AmEx, MC, V. **Map** p342 C6.
Clean and no-nonsense, the Barcelona Mar is cheap as chips, with pleasant communal areas, sparkling washrooms and handy on-site facilities. There are no individual rooms, only dorms stacked with bunk beds; in a token nod to privacy, all can be cordoned off by powder-blue drapes.
Bicycle rental. Disabled-adapted room. Internet (pay terminals). Laundry. Lockers (free). No smoking. TV room.

Center Ramblas Youth Hostel

C/Hospital 63, Raval (93 412 40 69/fax 93 317 17 04/www.center-ramblas.com). Metro Liceu. **Open** 24hrs daily. **Rates** (incl breakfast) €16.20-€18.50 under-25s; €19.60-€21.90 over-25s; €2 per person/stay sheets/towels; €3 per person/stay sheets & towels. **No credit cards. Map** p344 A2.
Similar to the above with handy extras like free internet access, communal fridge, microwave, safes and individual lockers for each guest, this super-friendly *hostal* has 201 beds in all, in dorms that sleep three to ten. It's a good place to meet up with

other young travellers, but beds sell out fast, so reserve your space at least two weeks in advance.
Disabled-adapted room. Internet (shared terminal). Lockers (free). No smoking. TV room.

Gothic Point

C/Vigatans 5, Born (93 268 78 08/fax 93 310 77 55/www.gothicpoint.com). Metro Jaume I. **Open** 24hrs daily. **Rates** (incl breakfast) €17-€22.50 per person; €1.80 per person/night sheets/blankets/towels. **Credit** DC, MC, V. **Map** p345 B3.
Paper lanterns and brightly painted wall murals give this friendly hostel a faintly Asian feel familiar to anyone who's done the backpacker route. Dorms (six to 14 beds) are a bit cramped and although an undersheet and pillowcase are provided, anything else must be rented. There are washing machines and dryers, a microwave and fridge. Beach bums should stay at sister hostel Sea Point on the seafront.
Disabled-adapted room. Internet (shared terminal). Lockers (€1.20). No smoking. TV room.
Other locations: Sea Point Plaça del Mar 1-4, Barceloneta (93 224 70 75); **La Ciutat Albergue Residencia** Alegre de Dalt 66, Zona Alta (93 213 03 00).

Itaca Alberg-Hostel

C/Ripoll 21, Barri Gòtic (93 301 97 51/www.itaca hostel.com). Metro Catalunya or Urquinaona. **Open** *Reception* 7am-4am daily. **Rates** (incl sheets) €19 dormitory; €48 twin. **No credit cards. Map** p344 B2.
A laid-back place where you can take time out from the travel circuit and recharge your batteries. Sited on a quiet street a stone's throw from the cathedral, its swirling murals, squishy sofas and lobby music give it a homely atmosphere; there's also a communal kitchen, a small breakfast room and shelves of books and games. Its 33 beds are in five cheerful and airy dorms, all with balconies. Bathrooms are clean.
Dining room. Internet (pay terminal). Kitchen. Lockers (free). No smoking.

Campsites

For more information on campsites not far from the city, get the *Catalunya Campings* book from tourist offices (*see p321*) or bookshops, or check www.barcelonaturisme.com

Estrella de Mar

Autovia de Castelldefels km 16.7, Castelldefels (93 633 07 84/fax 93 633 03 707/www.campingestrella demar.com). **Open** *Reception* 9am-2pm, 4-7pm daily. *Campsite* 7.30am-midnight daily. **Rates** €4.70/person; €3.40 under-10s. €4.70 tent/caravan/car; €8.85 motorhome; €4 electricity connection. **Credit** MC, V.

Camping Masnou

Carretera N2, km 633, El Masnou, Outer Limits (tel/fax 93 555 15 03). **Open** *Reception* Oct-May 9am-noon, 3-7pm daily. June-Sept 8am-10pm daily. *Campsite* 7am-11.30pm daily. **Rates** €5.35/person; €4.30 2-10s; free under-2s; €5.35 car/caravan/electricity. **Credit** MC, V.

Sightseeing

Introduction	**82**
Barri Gòtic	**86**
Raval	**97**
Sant Pere & the Born	**103**
Barceloneta & the Ports	**110**
Montjuïc	**115**
The Eixample	**122**
Gràcia & Other Districts	**131**

Features

Three days in Barcelona	83
Squaring up	88
Fingered	91
Barna in books Orwell	92
Flashpoints Plaça Salvador Segui	97
Barna in books Genet	102
Flashpoints C/Canvis Nous	107
Walk on Medieval trading	108
Walking on the beaches	111
Making waves	112
No more bull	116
Walk on Modernisme	124
Rambling free	128
Flashpoints Plaça Rius i Taulet	134
Urban tribes Okupas	139

Introduction

Getting the hang of Barcelona's *barrios*.

Most visitors to Barcelona head first to the Old City, a maze of meandering streets, alleys and squares, where Gothic churches nestle next to lofty palaces, and ancient fountains trickle in quiet *plaças*. Beyond lie the architectural glories of Gaudí and the Modernistas, the long stretch of beach, the hills of Montjuïc and Tibidabo, and parts of the city with a wholly different feel, untouched by the hand of tourism.

Cutting straight through the Old City are La Rambla and Via Laietana. **La Rambla**, once a seasonal riverbed that formed the western limit of the 13th-century city, is now a tree-lined boulevard dividing the **Barri Gòtic** from the **Raval**, and is best strolled on a quiet Sunday morning. The nocturnal hugger-mugger of drunks, cutpurses and prostitutes, although not completely without attraction, is redolent of the city's unkempt years as a hard-edged port. Via Laietana, driven through in the 19th century to bring light and air to the slums, is the boundary between the Barri Gòtic and **Sant Pere** and the achingly trendy **Born**. Between these two thoroughfares is the **Plaça Sant Jaume**, the heart of the city ever since it was the centre of

the Roman fort from which Barcelona grew. Now it is home to two bastions of government, the **Ajuntament** (City Hall) and the **Generalitat** (the regional government).

With the demolition of the medieval walls in 1854, the open fields beyond the choleric city were a blank canvas for urban planners, architects and sculptors. The **Eixample** (literally, the 'expansion'), with its gridiron layout, is a showcase for the greatest works of Modernisme, including the **Sagrada Família**, **La Pedrera** and the **Hospital Sant Pau**. When the only traffic was the clip-clopping of the horse and cart, these whimsical flights of architectural fancy must have been still more impressive; nowadays the Eixample can be noisy and polluted, as almost every road carries four lanes of traffic. Beyond lies the **Park Güell**, with Gaudí's emblematic dragon, and *barrios* such as **Gràcia**, **Sants** and **Sarrià**, once independent towns that were swallowed up into the expanding city.

Barcelona is not a violent city, but bag-snatching and pickpocketing are rife. Leave whatever you can in your hotel, and be especially wary of anyone trying to clean something off your shoulder or sell you a posy. Those wanting to swap a coin for one from your country are also wont to empty out your wallet.

GETTING AROUND

The Old City is wonderfully compact and can be crossed on foot in about 20 minutes. A fun and eco-friendly way to get around it (and to head to the beach) is to hire a bright yellow **Trixi** rickshaw. Running noon to 8pm, April to September, and costing €1.50 per person/kilometre, they can be hailed on the street, or booked on (mobile) 677 732 773/www.trixi.com. The public transport system, including a recently inaugurated tram network, serves every part of the city and is cheap and efficient.

Discount schemes

As well as the schemes described below, a ticket on the Bus Turístic (see p85) also includes a book of coupons valid for admittance to many of the city's museums and attractions.

Articket

Rate €17.
The Articket gives free entry to six major museums and art galleries (one visit each over three months): **Fundació Miró** (see p118), **MACBA** (see p101), the **MNAC** (see p119), **Espai Gaudí-La Pedrera** (see p129), the **Fundació Tàpies** (see p125) and the **CCCB** (see p99). The ticket is available from participating venues, tourist offices (see p321), via Tel-entrada (see p214) and branches of Caixa Catalunya.

Barcelona Card

Rates *1 day* €17; €14 concessions. *2 days* €20; €17 concessions. *3 days* €23; €20 concessions. *4 days* €25; €22 concessions. *5 days* €27; €24 concessions. One to five days of unlimited transport on the metro and buses, as well as discounts on the airport bus and cable cars, reduced entry to a wide variety of museums and attractions, along with discounts at dozens of restaurants, bars and shops. The card is sold at the airport, tourist offices (see p321), **L'Aquàrium** (see p226), **Casa Batlló** (see p123), the **Monument a Colom** (see p111), Sants railway station, Estació Nord bus station and at branches of El Corte Inglés (see p191).

Montjuïc Card

Information 93 289 28 30. **Rates** €20; €10 concessions.
A great way to take advantage of the park is with this one-day card, which offers free use of the Tren Montjuïc and cable car, bike rental, access to the Jardi Botànic and the Bernat Picornell swimming pool and admittance to the Poble Espanyol and Montjuïc museums. It also lets you choose a show at the Ciutat del Teatre theatre complex. Find it at the Font del Gat information centre on Montjuïc, tourist offices and via ServiCaixa (see p214).

Three days in Barcelona

You could of course eschew the sights altogether and follow our **walks** on *p12*, *p108* and *p124* for the essence of the city. Or you could hop on either of the **tourist buses** (see *p85*) and let the sights come to you. But if you must fill two photo albums when you get home, here's how.

DAY ONE

Start with a stroll down **La Rambla**. Cut in to the **Plaça Reial**, admire Gaudí's lamp-posts and from there head to the heart of the **Barri Gòtic** and the **cathedral**. Crossing the Via Laietana takes you to the **Palau de la Música Catalana**, with its fantastic façade. From here head down into the Born proper, and perhaps tuck into some lunchtime tapas outside the majestic **Santa Maria del Mar**. From here it's a skip and a hop to the **Museu Picasso**. If you've any energy left, wander down to the **Port Vell**, **Barceloneta** and the **beach**, with its seafront restaurants.

DAY TWO

Head up the **Passeig de Gràcia** to admire the masterpieces of the **Manzana de la Discòrdia**. Further up is Gaudí's **La Pedrera**, with its Modernista apartment and strange and beautiful roofscape. Backtrack slightly to catch a direct metro to Gaudí's most legendary work, the **Sagrada Família**. The Avda Gaudí has several places to grab a *bocadillo*, after which you could drop in to the stunning **Hospital Sant Pau**. From here hop in a cab (or a tourist bus) to the beautiful colours of Gaudí's **Park Güell**. The 24 bus will get you back in time for dinner.

DAY THREE

Venture into the Raval to see the **MACBA** and the nearby **CCCB**. Walk to the Ronda Sant Antoni to take a 55 bus up to **Montjuïc** and the **Fundació Miró**, which is also a good spot for lunch. From here you can walk to the **Olympic stadium** and then to the nearby **Jardí Botànic** for leafy tranquillity and spectacular views. Walk back past the Miró to get to the **cable car**, which will take you on a vertiginous ride to the **Port Vell** and the myriad seafood restaurants along Passeig Joan de Borbó.

Sightseeing

Ruta del Modernisme

Centre del Modernisme, Casa Amatller, Passeig de Gràcia 41, Eixample (93 488 01 39/www.bcn.es). Metro Passeig de Gràcia. **Open** 10am-7pm Mon-Sat; 10am-2pm Sun. **Rates** €12; €5 concessions. **No credit cards. Map** p340 D5.

Recently doubled in size to take in 111 Modernista buildings in Barcelona and other Catalan towns, this is not so much a route as a ticket, which includes a guidebook and entitles the holder to discounts of between 15% and 50% on entry to many of the buildings. There are four suggested itineraries and the ticket is valid for 30 days. Profits go towards conservation of the buildings.

Ruta del Disseny

www.rutadisseny.com

Again, not a route, but a guide to the city's 100 best designed buildings, as chosen by experts such as Oriol Bohigas and Javier Mariscal. It's divided into four categories: bars, restaurants, shops, buildings and urban spaces. The guidebook (containing a map) is available at tourist offices, or there is a comprehensive website.

Tours

By bike

Barcelona by Bicycle

Un Cotxe Menys, C/Esparteria 3, Born (93 268 21 05/www.bicicletabarcelona.com). Metro Barceloneta. **Open** 10am-7pm Mon-Sat; 10am-2pm Sun (call ahead for bike hire outside these times). **Tours** *Jan, Feb* 11am daily. *Mar-Dec* 11am, 4.30pm Mon, Wed, Fri; 11am, 7.30pm Tue, Thur, Sat; 11am Sun. **Rates** *Tours* €22 incl guide & bike rental. *Hire* €5 1hr; €11 half-day; €15 1 day; €65 1wk. **No credit cards. Map** p345 C3-4.

Individuals or small groups don't need to book, but can simply meet in Plaça Sant Jaume for a three-hour tour of the city in English. Booking is required for a tailor-made tour, and the meeting point is C/Esparteria 3. Ordinary bike hire is also available.

Fat Tire Bike Tours

C/Escudellers 48 (93 301 36 12/www.fattirebike tours.com). Metro Drassanes. **Tours** *Mar-mid Apr* 12.30pm daily. *Mid Apr-July* 11.30am & 4.30pm daily. *Aug* 4pm daily. *Sept-mid Dec* 12.30pm daily. **Rates** *Tours* €22. *Hire* €7 3hrs; €10 6hrs. **No credit cards. Map** p345 A3.

Booking isn't necessary, although there are discounts for pre-arranged groups. Tours meet at the Monument a Colom (*see p111*) and last for four and a half hours, taking in the Old City, Sagrada Família, Ciutadella park and the beach.

By bus

Barcelona Tours

93 317 64 54. **Tours** 9am-8pm daily. Approx every 15-20mins Nov-May; approx every 8-10mins June-Oct. **Tickets** *1 day* €17; €10 concessions. *2 days* €20; €13 concessions. Free under-4s. Available on board bus. **No credit cards.**

A decent recorded commentary on the sights, via headphones, and fewer passengers are the advantages to these bright orange buses. It takes around three hours to cover the large tour circuit if you don't break the journey. The disadvantages are that tours are not as frequent as those of rivals Bus Turístic, and there are no discounts offered to attractions.

Bus Turístic

Tours *Apr-Oct* 9am-9pm daily; approx every 6-10mins. *Nov-Mar* 9am-7pm daily; approx every 30mins. **Tickets** *1 day* €17; €10 concessions. *2 days* €21; €13 concessions. Free under-4s. Available from tourist offices or on board bus. **No credit cards.**

Bus Turístic (white and blue, splashed with colourful images of the sights) runs two circular routes, both passing through Plaça Catalunya: the northern (red) route passes La Pedrera, Sagrada Família, Park Güell, the tram stop to Tibidabo and Pedralbes; the southern (blue) route takes in Montjuïc, Port Vell, Vila Olímpica and the Barri Gòtic. Both are one-way. Ticket holders get discount vouchers for a range of attractions.

On foot

The **Travel Bar** (C/Boqueria 27, 93 342 52 52) organises pub/club crawls on Tuesday, Thursday and Saturday at 9.30pm for €18.

Barcelona Walking Tours

807 117 222. **Tours** *Gothic* 10am (English), noon (Catalan/Spanish) Sat, Sun. *Picasso* 10.30am (English), 11.30am (Catalan/Spanish) Sat, Sun. **Tickets** *Gothic* €8.50; €3 concessions. *Picasso* €10.50; €6 concessions; €8.50; €3 concessions 1st Sun of mth. **No credit cards. Map** p344 B1.

Tours start in the underground tourist office in Plaça Catalunya. The Gothic tour concentrates on the history and buildings of the Old City, while the Picasso visits the artist's haunts and ends with a visit to the Picasso Museum (entry is included in the price). Tours take around 90 minutes, excluding the trip to the museum. Reservations are advised.

My Favourite Things

Mobile 637 265 405/678 542 753/www.myft.net.

Walking tours of the city (€25-€30) that delve into unusual nooks and crannies. The routes, based on different themes such as architecture and food, include a tour of the Eixample and an explanation of how the flowering of Modernisme shaped the Catalan identity. Phone or check out the funky website for details.

Saboroso

Mobile 667 770 492/www.saboroso.com.

A friendly company run by knowledgeable British food-lovers, offering tailor-made gastronomic tours of Barcelona, as well as trips to vineyards in the Penedès and the Priorat.

Sightseeing

Barri Gòtic

Ancient Barcelona unveiled.

Maps p344-p345

The part of the Old City between Via Laietana
and La Rambla, the Barri Gòtic is the best-
preserved medieval quarter in Europe, dotted
with some astounding Roman remains. Neither
as glacially cool as the Born or as bohemian as
the Raval, it's nonetheless an essential port of
call. Save for the dramatic destruction of a huge
part of the medieval core for the construction
of C/Jaume I and C/Ferran (1849-53) and Via
Laietana (1909), its ancient splendour has
survived the last 500 years or so virtually intact.

For the last 2,000 years, the heart of the city
has been Plaça Sant Jaume, where the main
Roman axes – the *cardo maximus*, where C/Call
becomes C/Llibreteria and later C/Carders, and
the *decumanus maximus*, now called C/Bisbe
and C/Ciutat – used to run. At the crossroads
of these streets, dominating the forum, was the
Temple of Augustus, four columns of which
can still be seen (*see p95*) in C/Pietat. The
square now contains the municipal government
(**Ajuntament**; *see p88*) and Catalan regional
government (**Palau de la Generalitat**; *see
p93*) buildings, which stand opposite each
other. They have not always done so: the square
was only opened up in 1824, when a church was
demolished. Soon after, the stolid neo-classical
façade was added to the Ajuntament.

The façade of the Generalitat (1598-1602), on
the other hand, is one of the few Renaissance
buildings in the city. This architectural dearth
can be explained by a terrible series of wars
that lasted from about 1460 to 1715. The greater
part of both buildings, however, was built in the
early 15th century, and both of their original
main entrances open on to what was once the
decumanus maximus at the side, that of the
Generalitat (1416-18) being particularly fine.

On this street is one of the most photographed
features of the Barri Gòtic, the **bridge** across
C/Bisbe from the Generalitat. It's actually a
pastiche from 1928, when the idea of the locale
as a 'Gothic Quarter' took off. Other alterations
from the same period include the decorations
on the **Casa dels Canonges** (a former set of
canons' residences, and now Generalitat offices),
on the other side of the bridge.

Many buildings around here represent
history written in stone. In C/Santa Llúcia, in
front of the cathedral, is **Casa de l'Ardiaca**;
originally a 15th-century residence for the

Plaça Vila de Madrid. *See p87*.

archdeacon (*ardiaca*), is has a superb tiled patio.
It was renovated recently and houses the city
archives, but in a previous renovation in the
1870s, it acquired its curious letterbox showing
swallows and a tortoise. Designed by Domènech
i Montaner, it's believed by some to symbolise
the contrast between the 'swiftness of justice
and the law's delay'; others, more prosaically,
think it to be a reflection on the postal service.

On the other side of Plaça Nova is the
Col·legi d'Arquitectes, the architects'
association. It's mainly of interest for its sand-
blasted mural of Catalan folk scenes, designed
by Picasso while in self-imposed exile in the
1950s and executed by other artists. Behind
its atypical style is a story that when Picasso
heard that Miró was also being considered, he
responded dismissively that he could easily 'do
a Miró'. In front of the cathedral, on the right as
you come out, is the **Museu Diocesà**, housing
religious art (*see p91*); around the side of the
cathedral, meanwhile, is the little-visited but
fascinating **Museu Frederic Marès** (*see p93*).

Further along is the 16th-century **Palau del
Lloctinent** (Palace of the Lieutenant, or, here,
'Viceroy'); currently undergoing restoration, it

once housed the archive of the Crown of Aragon. It was also the local headquarters for the Spanish Inquisition, from where the unfortunates were carted off to the Passeig del Born to be burnt. The building was once part of the former royal palace (**Palau Reial**), and has another exit to the medieval palace square, the well preserved **Plaça del Rei**. The complex houses the **Museu d'Història de la Ciutat** (*see p92*) and includes some of Barcelona's most historically important buildings: the **chapel of Santa Àgata** and the 16th-century watchtower (**Mirador del Rei Martí**). Parts of the palace are said to date back to the tenth century, and there have been many remarkable additions to it since, notably the 14th-century Saló del Tinell, a medieval banqueting hall that is a definitive work of Catalan Gothic. It is here that Ferdinand and Isabella are said to have received Columbus on his return from America.

The narrow streets centred on C/Call once housed a rich Jewish ghetto (*call*). At the corner of C/Sant Domènec del Call and C/Marlet is the medieval **synagogue**, now restored and open to the public (*see p93*). At C/Marlet 1 is a 12th-century inscription from a long-demolished house. Hebrew inscriptions can be seen on stones in the eastern wall of the **Plaça Sant Iu**, across from the cathedral, and at ankle level in the south-west corner of the Plaça del Rei.

Near the centre of the *call* is the beautiful little **Plaça Sant Felip Neri** and its fine baroque church, whose damaged façade is the result of an Italian bombing raid during the Civil War. Over 200 were killed, many of them refugee children who had gathered to go on a Sunday outing. This square is another 20th-century invention; the shoemakers' guild building (now housing the **Museu del Calçat**, for which *see p91*) was moved here in 1943 to make way for the Avda de la Catedral, while the nearby tinkers' guild was moved earlier last century when Via Laietana was driven through the district. Close by are the leafily attractive **Plaça del Pi** and **Plaça Sant Josep Oriol**, where there are great pavement bars and artisanal weekend markets. The squares are separated by **Santa Maria del Pi**, one of Barcelona's most distinguished – but least visited – Gothic churches, with a magnificent rose window and spacious single nave. Opposite is the 17th-century neo-classical retailers' guildhall, with colourful sgraffiti added the following century.

Despite the expansion of Barcelona into the Eixample, the old centre has remained a hub of cultural, social and political life. In C/Montsió, a narrow street off Portal de l'Àngel, is the **Els Quatre Gats** café (*see p174*), legendary haunt of Picasso and other artists and bohemians, in a wonderful Modernista building designed by

Puig i Cadafalch. Between C/Portaferrissa and Plaça del Pi lies **C/Petritxol**, one of the most charming streets of the Barri Gòtic, known for its traditional *granges* offering coffee and cakes, and also housing the **Sala Parés** (*see p235*), the city's oldest art gallery; Rusiñol, Casas and the young Picasso all exhibited here. On the other side of C/Portaferrissa, heading up C/Bot, is the newly done-up **Plaça Vila de Madrid**, where there are the excavated remains of a Roman necropolis, and a rare expanse of city-centre grass. Between here and the Plaça Catalunya is the marvellous little Romanesque **church of Santa Anna**, begun in 1141 and containing an exquisite 14th-century cloister.

Back on the seaward side of the Barri Gòtic, if you walk from Plaça Sant Jaume up C/Ciutat, to the left of the Ajuntament, and turn down the narrow alley of C/Hércules, you'll come to **Plaça Sant Just**, a fascinating old square with a recently restored Gothic water fountain from 1367 and the **church of Sants Just i Pastor**, built in the 14th century on the site of a chapel founded by Charlemagne's son Louis 'the Pious', and now looking rather unloved inside.

The once wealthy area between here and the port became more rundown throughout the 20th century. It has a different atmosphere from the northern part of the Barri Gòtic: shabbier and with less prosperous shops. The city authorities made huge efforts to change this, particularly in the 1990s, when new squares were opened up: **Plaça George Orwell** on C/Escudellers,

Ajuntament. *See p88.*

Sightseeing

Squaring up

Plaça Reial.

Palmed and dangerous

Plaça Reial. This neo-classical square, built in 1846 and with iron lamp-posts later added by a young Gaudí, is all faded grandeur. The palm-shaded interior is a magnet for daytime drinkers and night-time pickpockets, but it's a place you can't ignore for long.
When to go: For early morning coffee at one of the terrace cafés.

Rose-tinted

Plaça del Pi. Dominated by the façade of Barcelona's most underrated church, with its vast rose window and its baboon gargoyles, is the discerning coffee drinker's hangout.
When to go: Every Thursday there's an artisan market of organic cheeses, sausages and cakes.

Red square

Plaça Sant Jaume. Is and always has been the administrative centre of the city, flanked by its two political institutions, the neo-classical Ajuntament (the City Hall, south side) and the Renaissance Generalitat (seat of the regional government), both now in socialist hands. This is where *barcelonins* go to demonstrate and to celebrate, or simply to talk politics, football or the state of their investments.
When to go: In December, to visit the life-sized nativity scene.

Big Brother's watching

Plaça George Orwell. Barcelona's homage to Eric Blair was, ironically, the first place in the city to have 24-hour CCTV cameras. Nicknamed 'Plaça Trippy', it's become a home from home for all sorts of lowlife and hustlers. Leandre Cristòfol's surrealist statue somehow sums the whole place up.
When to go: During daylight hours.

known as the 'Plaça del Trippy' by the youthful crowd that hangs out there and the subject of much heated debate when CCTV was recently introduced (the irony of which was lost on no one), and **Plaça Joaquim Xirau**, off La Rambla. Another tactic was the siting of parts of the Universitat Pompeu Fabra on the lower Rambla. Just above is the area's heart: **Plaça Reial**, known for its bars and cheap hotels, and a popular spot for a drink or an outdoor meal (provided you don't mind the odd drunk and are prepared to keep an eye on your bags). An addition from the 1840s, the *plaça* has the **Tres Gràcies** fountain in the centre and **lamp-posts** designed by the young Gaudí. It's the only work he ever did for the city council.

The grand porticoes of some of the buildings around the **church of La Mercè**, once the merchants' mansions, stand as testament to the former wealth of the area before the building of the Eixample. The **Plaça de la Mercè** itself was only created in 1982, with the destruction of the houses that used to stand here; the 19th-century fountain was moved here from the port. There are also a dwindling number of lively *tascas* (small traditional tapas bars) on C/Mercè. Beyond C/Ample and the Mercè, you emerge from narrow alleys or the pretty **Plaça Duc de Medinaceli** on to the **Passeig de Colom**, where a few shipping offices and ships' chandlers still recall the dockside atmosphere of decades gone by. Monolithic on Passeig de Colom is the **Capitanía General**, the army headquarters whose façade has the dubious distinction of being the one construction in Barcelona directly attributable to the dictatorship of Primo de Rivera.

Ajuntament (City Hall)

Plaça Sant Jaume (93 402 70 00/special visits 93 402 73 64/www.bcn.es). Metro Liceu or Jaume I. **Open** *Office* 8.30am-2.30pm Mon-Fri. *Visits* 10am-1.30pm Sun. **Admission** free. **Map** p345 B3.

Just do it

Plaça Sant Just. Filled on summer nights by the chairs and tables of the Cafè de l'Acadèmia, this charming square boasts Barcelona's oldest fountain. Dating from 1367, it features three cherubs with pursed lips, forever in the shadow of the church's impressive belltower.

When to go: Plaça Sant Just is best visited on the first Thursday of the month, when there's a little food market.

Hole in the wall

Plaça de Sant Felip Neri. Gaudí was on his way from a visit to the church in Plaça de Sant Felip Neri in 1928 when he was run over by a tram. Ten years later two Italian bombs landed in the square, killing around 70 children and 140 adults, leaving hundreds of shrapnel marks in the wall (still visible to this day), and no doubt disturbing the peace of those buried in the city's old medieval cemetery underneath. Now the tinkle of a fountain is all the noise there is.

When to go: Early evening.

King of squares

Plaça del Rei. The buildings of the former palace complex combine to give an almost MC Escher-like perspective that fills it with art students trying to capture its angles. This is where Ferdinand and Isabella are

Plaça de Sant Felip Neri.

said to have received Columbus to hear the news that Galicia wasn't after all the end of the world.

When to go: For a concert during the Mercè festival in September (*see p222*).

The centrepiece and oldest part of the Casa de la Ciutat is the stately 15th-century Saló de Cent, flanked by the semicircular Saló de la Reina Regent, where council meetings are still held, and the Saló de Cròniques, spectacularly painted with murals by Josep Maria Sert. The Catalan Gothic old entrance on C/Ciutat contrasts with the dull neo-classical façade (1830-47) on the main entrance. On Sundays there are guided tours (in several different languages) every 20 minutes.

Cathedral

Pla de la Seu (93 315 15 54). Metro Jaume I.
Open *Combined ticket* 1.30-4.30pm daily. *Church* 8am-12.45pm, 5-7.30pm Mon-Fri; 8am-12.45pm, 5-6pm Sat; 8-9am, 5-6pm Sun. *Cloister* 9am-12.30pm, 5-7pm daily. *Museum* 10am-1pm, 5.15-7pm daily.
Admission *Combined ticket* €4. *Church & cloister* free. *Museum* €1. *Lift to roof* €2. *Choir* €1.50.
No credit cards. Map p345 B3.
Construction of the present-day cathedral, based on a three-naved basilica that once stood on the site of the Roman forum, began in 1298 and ended with the addition of the neo-Gothic façade at the end of the 19th century. The building is predominantly Gothic, save for the Romanesque chapel of Santa Llúcia to the right of the main façade. Aside from the glorious, light-filled cloister, it is a slightly forbidding place, but contains many images, paintings and sculptures, and an intricately carved choir built in the 1390s. The cathedral museum, in the 17th-century chapter house, has paintings and sculptures, including works by the Gothic masters Jaume Huguet, Bernat Martorell and Bartolomé Bermejo. Santa Eulàlia, patron saint of Barcelona, lies in the dramatically lit crypt in an alabaster tomb carved with scenes from her martyrdom (*see p91* **Fingered**). To one side, there's a lift to the roof; take it for a magnificent view of the Old City. A combined ticket (*visita especial*) has a special timetable intended to keep tourists and worshippers from bothering one another. During the afternoons, ticketholders have the run of the cloister, church, choir and lift, and can enter some chapels and take photographs (normally prohibited).

c

Cultural information for citizens

Direct customer care

Cultural information point in Barcelona

Rambla de Santa Mònica, 7

Cultural activities
Museums
Exhibitions
Theatre and dance
Music
Popular culture

and lots more in...
http://cultura.gencat.net

Generalitat de Catalunya
Departament de Cultura

Centre Cívic Pati Llimona

C/Regomir 3 (93 268 47 00). Metro Jaume I.
Open 9am-2pm, 4.30-8.30pm Mon-Fri; 10am-2pm,
4-8pm Sat. **Exhibitions** 9am-2pm, 4.30-10pm
Mon-Fri; 10am-2pm, 4-8pm Sat. Closed Aug.
Admission free. **Map** p345 B3.
A building incorporating part of a round tower that
dates from the first Roman settlement with later
Roman baths and a 15th-century residence. The
excavated foundations are visible from the street
behind glass. It is now used as a civic centre, and
stages frequent photography exhibitions.

Museu del Calçat (Shoe Museum)

*Plaça Sant Felip Neri 5 (93 301 45 33). Metro Jaume
I.* **Open** 11am-2pm Tue-Sun. **Admission** €2.50;
free under-7s. **No credit cards. Map** p345 B3.
A tiny, offbeat museum of the type Barcelona does
so well, and one of only three in the world, this
footwear museum details the cobbler's craft from

Roman times to the present day. Embroidered
slippers from the Arabic world, 17th-century
musketeers' boots and delicately hand-painted 18th-
century party shoes are all highlights, along with
what is, according to the *Guinness Book of World
Records*, the the biggest shoe in the world.

Museu Diocesà

*Avda de la Catedral 4 (93 315 22 13). Metro Jaume
I.* **Open** 10am-2pm, 5-8pm Tue-Sat; 11am-2pm Sun.
Admission €4; €2 concessions; free under-10s.
Credit (shop only) MC, V. **Map** p344 B2.
A hotchpotch of religious art punctuated with occasional exhibitions on unrelated themes, the Diocesan
Museum is worthwhile for its 14th-century alabaster
virgins, altarpieces by Bernat Martorell and wonderful Romanesque murals. The building itself is
interesting, and includes the Pia Almoina, a former
almshouse, stuck on to a Renaissance canon's residence, which in turn was built inside a Roman tower.

Sightseeing

Fingered

Barcelona has two patron saints: Mercè,
who is celebrated with a week-long festival in
September (*see p222*), and the young Eulàlia
(known affectionately as Laia), who has come
to be the children's saint, with festivities on
her day on 12 February (*see p224*) geared
towards the wee ones. The daughter
of an aristocractic family in Sarrià,
she was known for her charitable
works and her fearlessness.
　The legend goes that, during
the final persecution of
Diocletian in 303, the young
Eulàlia went to see the
governor of Barcelona,
Dacian, to take issue with
him over his cruelty to
the Christian community.
Dacian was so enraged
with the temerity of this
13-year-old upstart that he
sentenced her to as many
gruesome punishments as she
had years. Readers of a gentler
disposition should look away now.
Her flesh was torn with hooks; she
was lashed; she was put inside a barrel
filled with broken glass and nails and rolled
down a slope (today, the Baixada de Santa
Eulàlia, behind the cathedral); she was
placed in a box with hungry fleas; her wounds
were sprinkled with boiling oil; and, finally,
she was nailed to a cross in what is now the
Plaça del Pedró in the Raval. She bore all
these tortures in silence.

Her body remained buried beneath the
basilica of Santa Maria del Mar until a ninth-
century bishop decided she should be moved
to the cathedral. A procession of the great
and the good set off from the church amid
much ceremony until they reached the city
gates, when the coffin bearers ground
to a halt, their load suddenly too
heavy to bear.
　The bishop entreated
the faithful to pray, fearing
trouble ahead. No sooner
had they bowed their heads
than an angel descended,
pointing accusingly at one
of the canons. The guilty
priest fell to his knees
and confessed that he
had taken the saint's
finger as a relic. The digit
reunited with its owner,
the procession was able to
continue on its way, and Laia
was buried in the crypt of the
cathedral, where her tomb can
still be visited.
　The city gates were renamed Puerta de
Santa Eulàlia until the city walls came down,
and the square named Plaça de l'Àngel;
it still takes the same name even today.
The copper sculpture of the angel that was
erected in the square can now be seen in
the Museu d'Història de la Ciutat (*see p92*),
while a small reproduction sits in a niche on
the north side of the square.

Barna in books Orwell

George Orwell thought he had found paradise in Barcelona, but he almost ended up in hell. *Homage to Catalonia*, Orwell's account of his time in Spain, begins and ends in Barcelona, opening with the writer's arrival in a city in the throes of an egalitarian revolution and ending with his farcical escape to France, just as that revolution had begun to devour its children.

As an idealistic, Eton-educated Englishman, Orwell was struck by the atmosphere on his arrival in Barcelona in 1936, where it seemed that class differences had been wiped out at a stroke. He describes being lectured by a hotel manager for attempting to tip the lift boy and wrote a poem dedicated to a fraternal encounter at the Lenin Barracks on Plaça d'Espanya, when an Italian soldier with 'a crystal spirit' embraced him wordlessly.

When he turned up at the recruiting station of the left-wing, anti-Stalinist POUM (Workers' Party of Marxist Unity) brigade, Orwell cut an unlikely figure. The tall, well-spoken journalist, carrying size 12 shoes around his neck, stuck out amid the poor labourers and Catalan boys volunteering to fight the fascists. Before leaving for the front, Orwell sat in a café on La Rambla, and watched a city where all signs of wealth and ostentation had been replaced with a revolutionary spirit that filled him with joy. But he had no idea of the fractious, sectarian rivalries that were bubbling underneath the surface.

Orwell returned to the city after a deeply frustrating stint on the Aragonese front to find a very different city. He stayed at the Hotel Continental at the south-east corner of Plaça Catalunya; he watched from the window as the various left-wing factions tried to take control of the huge Telephone Exchange building (now owned by Telefónica). Orwell rejoined his POUM comrades in May 1937 and spent three days on the roof of the Teatre Poliorama (La Rambla 15), staring out a Civil Guard position on the roof of the Café Moka opposite; an ersatz copy of the café now sits on the site. Orwell survived on sardines and oranges, desperately unhappy about the situation in Barcelona and keen to return to the fighting at the front. But his love of an early morning cigarette attracted the unwanted attentions of a sniper's bullet; and Orwell was shot through the neck.

Recovering at the Maurin sanatorium in the suburbs of Barcelona, Orwell was unaware that a warrant had been issued for his arrest after a report had classified him as 'a confirmed Trotskyite'. Awaiting official papers from the British consulate that would allow him to leave safely, Orwell slept rough in the city's backstreets at night and posed as a moneyed English tourist during the day, narrowly avoiding the fate that awaited many of his POUM comrades.

Orwell left Barcelona defiantly angry, his ideals severely tested. However, as he states in his book, the whole dreadful experience had given him 'not less, but more belief in the decency of human beings'. Whatever else Orwell took away from his time in Barcelona, he had learned a hard lesson in the workings of totalitarianism, without which he would never have written his classics *Animal Farm* and *1984*.

Museu d'Història de la Ciutat

Plaça del Rei 1 (93 315 11 11/www.museuhistoria. bcn.es). Metro Jaume I. **Open** *June-Sept* 10am-8pm Tue-Sat; 10am-3pm Sun. *Oct-May* 10am-2pm, 4-8pm Tue-Sat; 10am-3pm Sun. **Guided tours** by appointment. **Admission** *Permanent exhibitions* €4; €2.50 concessions; free under-16s. *Temporary exhibitions* varies. *Both* free 4-8pm 1st Sat of mth. **No credit cards. Map** p345 B3.

The Casa Padellàs, a merchant's palace dating from 1498, was another of the buildings that had to be moved from its original location in 1930 to make way for Via Laietana. During excavations of the plot, extensive Roman remains lying under the Plaça del Rei were unearthed, including streets, villas and storage vats for oil and wine. The excavations continued until 1960; today, the whole underground labyrinth, as far as the cathedral, can be visited as part of the City History Museum. The admission fee also gives you access to the Santa Àgata chapel – with its 15th-century altarpiece by Jaume Huguet, one of the greatest Catalan painters in medieval times – and the Saló del Tinell, at least when there's no temporary exhibition. This majestic room (1370) began life as the seat of the Catalan parliament and was converted in the 18th century into a heavy baroque church, which was dismantled in 1934. The Rei Martí watchtower is still closed to the public while it awaits reinforcement.

Throughout 2005, there will be an exhibition on the tearing down of the medieval city walls in 1854, and, as part of the Year of the Book festivities, a look at the descriptions of Barcelona in *Don Quixote* (Mar-Oct). Tickets for the museum are also valid for the monastery at Pedralbes (*see p138*) and the Museu Verdaguer (*see p135*).

Museu Frederic Marès

Plaça Sant Iu 5-6 (93 310 58 00/www.museumares. bcn.es). Metro Jaume I. **Open** 10am-7pm Tue-Sat; 10am-3pm Sun. **Admission** €3 concessions; free under-16s. Free 3-7pm Wed, 1st Sun of mth. **Guided tours** noon Sun. **Credit** (shop only) AmEx, MC, V. **Map** p345 B3.

Despairing of his lack of space, obsessive hoarder, kleptomaniac and sculptor Frederic Marès cut a deal with the Ajuntament: he would donate his extraordinary collections to the city, if, in return, the city would find an appropriate building in which to house both them and him. The result is one of the city's most charming museums, where the number of pieces makes labelling impossible (Marès disapproved of displays that demonstrated a value hierarchy) and where the mind behind the collections is as fascinating as the exhibits themselves.

The ground floor contains an array of Romanesque crucifixes, virgins and saints, while the first floor takes sculpture up to the 20th century. The basement contains remains from ecclesiastical buildings dating back to Roman times: capitals, tombs, gargoyles, stone window frames and entire church portals, exquisitely carved. On the second floor is the 'Gentleman's Room', stuffed to the gunwhales with walking sticks, key fobs, smoking equipment, matchboxes and opera glasses, while the charming 'Ladies' Room' contains fans, sewing scissors, nutcrackers and perfume flasks. Also on the second floor is a new room devoted to photography, and Marès's study and library, now filled with sculptures (many of them his own). An exhibition on classical sculpture and its uses in later interior design, façades and gardens will take place from May to July 2005; from December 2005 to spring 2006, there'll be a look at the history of paper theatres in Catalonia.

Note: not all floors are open daily. The first floor is open on Wednesdays, Fridays and Sundays, and the second and third are open on Tuesdays, Thursdays and Saturdays. Tickets are valid for two days.

Palau de la Generalitat

Plaça Sant Jaume (93 402 46 17/www.gencat.net). Metro Liceu or Jaume I. **Guided tours** every 30mins 10.30am-1.30pm 2nd & 4th Sun of mth; also 9.30am-1pm, 4-7pm Mon, Fri by appointment. **Admission** free. **Map** p345 B3.

Like the Ajuntament, the Generalitat has a Gothic side entrance on C/Bisbe, with a beautiful relief of St George (Sant Jordi), patron saint of Catalonia, made by Pere Johan in 1418. Inside, the finest features are the first-floor Pati de Tarongers ('Orange Tree Patio'), which was to become the model for many patios in Barcelona, and the magnificent chapel of Sant Jordi of 1432-4, the masterpiece of Catalan architect Marc Safont. The Generalitat is traditionally open to the public on Sant Jordi (23 April), when its patios are spectacularly decorated with red roses and queues are huge. It normally also opens on 11 September (Catalan National Day) and 24 September (La Mercè).

Sinagoga Shlomo Ben Adret

C/Marlet 5 (93 317 07 90/www.calldebarcelona.org). Metro Jaume I or Liceu. **Open** 11am-2.30pm, 4-7.30pm Tue-Sun; 11am-2.30pm Sun. **Admission** free (€2 donation encouraged). **Map** p345 B3.

It's only in the last few years that historians have come to agree that the small basement in the building at C/Marlet 5 was the synagogue of the main *call*. The front of the building, slightly skewing the street,

Palau de la Generalitat.

fulfils religious requirements by which the façade has to face Jerusalem; the two windows at knee height allow light to enter from that direction.

Temple Romà d'Augusti

C/Paradis 10 (93 315 11 11). Metro Jaume I.
Open 10am-2pm, 4-8pm Tue-Sat; 10am-3pm Sun. **Admission** free. **Map** p342 D5.
The Centre Excursionista de Catalunya (a hiking club) contains four fluted Corinthian columns that formed the rear corner of the Temple of Augustus, built in the first century BC as the hub of the town's forum. Opening hours can vary.

La Rambla

It used to be said that every true Barcelona citizen was obliged to walk down the mile-long Rambla at least once a day. Today, many locals have become weary of the place, tired of its tawdry souvenir shops and of elbowing through crowds of tourists, but the boulevard remains one of Barcelona's essential attractions. The multitude of human statues, fortune tellers, card sharps, puppeteers, dancers and musicians might be infuriating to anyone late for work, but for those with a ringside seat at a pavement café, it's not far short of pure theatre.

The name derives from *ramla*, an Arabic word for sand; originally, this was a seasonal riverbed, running along the western edge of the 13th-century city. From the Middle Ages to the baroque era, many churches and convents were built along here, some of which have given their names to sections of it: as one descends from Plaça Catalunya, it is successively called Rambla de Canaletes, Rambla dels Estudis (or dels Ocells), Rambla de Sant Josep (or de les Flors), Rambla dels Caputxins and Rambla de Santa Mònica. For this reason, many people refer to it in the plural, as Les Rambles.

The Rambla also served as the meeting ground for city and country dwellers, for on the far side of these church buildings lay the still scarcely built-up Raval, 'the city outside the walls', and rural Catalonia. At the **fountain** on the corner with C/Portaferrissa, colourful tiles depict the city gateway that once stood here (*porta ferrissa* means 'iron gate'). The space by the gates became a natural marketplace; from these beginnings sprang **La Boqueria**, now the largest market in Europe.

The Rambla took on its recognisable present form between approximately 1770 and 1860. The second city wall came down in 1775, and the Rambla was paved and turned into a boulevard. But the avenue only acquired its definitive shape after the closure of the monasteries in the 1830s, which made swathes of land available for new building. No longer on the city's edge, the Rambla became a wide path through its heart.

As well as having five names, the Rambla is divided into territories. The first part – at the top, by Plaça Catalunya – has long belonged, by unwritten agreement, to groups of men perpetually engaged in a *tertulia*, a classic Iberian half-conversation, half-argument about anything from politics to football. The **Font de Canaletes** drinking fountain is beside them; if you drink from it, goes the legend, you'll return to Barcelona. Here, too, is where Barça fans converge in order to celebrate their increasingly frequent triumphs.

Next comes perhaps the best-loved section of the boulevard, known as **Rambla de les Flors** for its line of magnificent flower stalls, open into the night. To the right is the **Palau de la Virreina** exhibition and cultural information centre (*see p96*), and the superb Boqueria market. A little further is the **Pla de l'Os** (or **Pla de la Boqueria**), centrepoint of the Rambla, with a pavement **mosaic** created in 1976 by Joan Miró. On the left, where more streets run off into the Barri Gòtic, is the extraordinary **Bruno Quadros** building (1883), with umbrellas on the wall and a Chinese dragon protruding over the street.

The lower half of the Rambla is initially more restrained, flowing between the sober façade of the **Liceu** opera house and the more *fin-de-siècle* (architecturally and atmospherically) **Cafè de l'Opera** (*see p174*), Barcelona's second most famous café after the Zurich. On the right is C/Nou de la Rambla (where you'll find Gaudí's neo-Gothic **Palau Güell**, closed to the public until late 2006); the promenade then widens into the **Rambla de Santa Mònica**. The area has long been popular among prostitutes; although clean-up efforts have reduced its visibility, and while renovations (including the 1980s addition of an arts centre, the **Centre d'Art Santa Mònica**) have done much to dilute the seediness of the area, single males walking at night can expect to be approached. Across the street are the unintentionally hilarious **Museu de Cera** (Wax Museum; *see p226*) and, at weekends, stalls selling bric-a-brac and craftwork. Then it's a short skip to the port, and the **Monument a Colom** (*see p113*).

Centre d'Art Santa Mònica

La Rambla 7 (93 316 28 10/www.cultura.gencat.net/ casm). Metro Drassanes. **Open** 11am-8pm Tue-Sat; 11am-3pm Sun. **Admission** usually free. **Map** p345 A4.
The cloister and tower of the convent of Santa Mònica (1626) were turned into this exhibition space in 1988, with recent alterations allowing for more space. There'll be around 20 shows from local and international artists in 2005, including work from Portuguese photographer Helena Almeida and young Canadian Marcel Dzama. Of particular

Sightseeing

interest will be the explorations by Spanish artists and identical twins, MP and MP Rosado, into questions of individuality and difference.

Museu de l'Eròtica

La Rambla 96 bis (93 318 98 65/www.erotica-museu.com). Metro Liceu. **Open** *June-Sept* 10am-midnight daily. *Oct-May* 11am-9pm daily. **Admission** €7.50; €6.50 concessions. **Credit** AmEx, MC, V. **Map** p345 A3.

Let down by some horrendous airbrushed paintings of the maidens and serpents school, the Erotica Museum does contain some genuine rarities. These include Japanese drawings, 19th-century engravings by German Peter Fendi and compelling photos of brothels in Barcelona's Barrio Chino in the decadent 1930s. Other curiosities include S&M apparatus and simulated erotic phone lines, but the Eròtica is something of an embarrassment for a city with true connoisseurship for the bawdy.

Palau de la Virreina

La Rambla 99 (93 301 77 75/www.bcn.es/cultura). Metro Liceu. **Open** 10am-8pm Mon-Sat; 11am-3pm Sun. **Admission** €1-€3; 50¢-€1.50 concessions; free under-16s. **No credit cards. Map** p344 A2.

This classical palace, with baroque features, takes its name from the widow of an unpopular former viceroy of Peru, who commissioned it and lived in it after its completion in the 1770s. The Virreina houses the city cultural department, and has information on events and shows, but also boasts strong programming in its two distinct exhibition spaces. Upstairs is dedicated to one-off exhibitions, with the smaller downstairs gallery focused on historical and contemporary photography. This will feature, from March to May 2005, a collection of photographs of Barcelona from 1950 to 1970 by Eugeni Forcano. From March to June, the upstairs space will show the work of clothing designer Antonio Miró.

La Rambla. *See p95.*

Raval

Ghetto fabulous.

There are streets here that the Barcelona City Council doesn't want you to see. From La Rambla, signposts for **MACBA** (*see p101*) carefully guide visitors along the gentrified 'tourist corridors' of C/Tallers and C/Bonsuccès to a bourgeois bohemian's playground of cafés, galleries and boutiques. Elsewhere, the city's sponge has yet to cleanse this defiantly tough working-class area that doubles as Barcelona's inner city red-light district. That said, as long as you leave your mink coat at home and are not too rattled by the odd hooker or junkie, a visit to this vibrant neighbourhood can be enjoyable. Just as there are few major sights, there are correspondingly few tourists.

Some of the Raval's most rundown streets have become immigrant ghettos. The intense cultural fusion is exemplified by 08001, a collective of some 20 musicians named after the Raval's postcode. Their *mestissa* sound of raï, dub, flamenco and reggae forms the perfect soundtrack for a stroll here, past shops selling everything from halal meat to Pakistani eyebrow-threading and Bollywood videos.

Ever on the margins, Raval (*arrabal* in Spanish) is a generic word adapted from the Arabic *ar-rabad*, meaning 'outside the walls'. When a defensive wall was built down the north side of La Rambla in the 13th century, the area now sandwiched between Avda Paral·lel and La Rambla was a sparsely populated green belt of garden plots. Over the centuries, the land absorbed the functional spillover from the city in the form of monasteries, religious hospitals, prisons and virtually any noxious industry that citizens didn't want on their doorstep. When industrialisation arrived in the 18th century, it became Barcelona's working-class district.

This was also the area of town where the most land was available; more emerged after liberal governments dissolved the monasteries in 1836 and early industries, mainly the textile mills, mushroomed. Some of the bleak buildings known as *cases-fàbriques* (residential factories) can still be seen here; among them is the **Can Ricart** textile factory on C/Sant Oleguer, now being converted into a sports centre.

Workers lived in crowded slums devoid of ventilation or running water, and malnutrition, TB, scrofula and typhus kept the average life expectancy to 40 years. It's no coincidence that the city's sanatoriums, orphanages and hospitals were based here. Then known to most people as the Quinto or 'Fifth District', the area was also where the underclasses forged the centre of revolutionary Barcelona, a breeding

Flashpoints

Plaça Salvador Seguí

As a child, Salvador Seguí sold sugared sweets in the bars and cafés of the Barrio Chino, which gained him the nickname of '*Noi del Sucre*' ('Sugar Boy'). Self-educated, the young Seguí was a constant presence in debates on philosophy, culture and politics held regularly in the bars of the Raval, famed as much for his oratory skills as for his flamboyant fashion sense. He quickly rose to prominence in the anarchist trade union, the Confederación Nacional del Trabajo (CNT).

Seguí was a moderate anarchist who opposed the terrorism favoured by extremist and revolutionary sections of the CNT that hoped to use the strikes as a prelude to revolution. He argued that anarchism was 'not only an arm to overthrow the state, but a means to build a new, better and more just society'. However, his moderate views were his undoing. On Sunday 10 March 1923, Seguí was shot dead on the corner of C/Sant Rafael, the most eminent of the 464 victims killed in the gun warfare waged between employers and unions from 1918 to 1923. The Employers' Federation hoped that his death would allow more extremist elements to take control of the CNT, and so it proved: the intense violence of summer 1923 provided the justification for a military coup in September, and for the subsequent ban on the CNT. When many streets took on new titles after Franco's death, a small square just a few steps from where he died was renamed Plaça Salvador Seguí.

Gat rides in the Raval.

resistance to this type of gentrification is strong, and the project has been hampered by business owners refusing to vacate their premises. One demonstration culminated in the burning of an effigy of Puig's putative hotel.

Current efforts to fill the rather empty new *rambla* include licences for new clubs and bars, Botero's deliciously bulging *Gat* (Cat) sculpture and an ethnic Saturday street market, **Món Raval**. The market's multicultural nature reflects the number of immigrants living in the Raval (mainly Pakistanis, North Africans and Filipinos), who were originally attracted by the lower cost of housing. The facelift has raised the prices, though, and as the immigrants, often young men sleeping ten to a room, are squeezed out, a wealthier community of arty western expats has moved in, scattering the area with galleries, boutiques and cafés. C/Doctor Dou is now virtually a whole street of galleries, C/Ferlandina is packed solid with boho cafés, and the old industrial spaces along C/Riereta now serve as studios to over 40 artists.

Upper Raval

The Upper Raval has never had such a louche reputation as the Lower Raval; indeed, in recent years, a plethora of late-night bars, galleries and restaurants has made it one of Barcelona's hippest places. It's not all new, though: the section between C/Carme and Plaça Catalunya was the focus of cultural rejuvenation in 1979.

The epicentre of the Upper Raval is the Plaça dels Àngels, where the 16th-century **Convent dels Àngels** houses both the **FAD** design institute and a gigantic almshouse, the **Casa de la Caritat**, that's since been converted into a cultural complex housing the **MACBA** (*see p101*) and the **CCCB** (*see p99*). When the clean, high-culture MACBA opened in 1995, it seemed to embody everything the Raval was not, and was initially mocked as an isolated and isolating social experiment. But over the years, the square and surrounding streets have filled with restaurants, boutiques and galleries; the university students who flock here have changed the character of the place.

Below here is the first part of the Raval to take on an urban character, a triangle bordered by C/Hospita, C/Carme and La Rambla. C/Hospita and C/Carme meet at the Plaça Pedró, where the tiny Romanesque chapel of **Sant Llàtzer** sits. From La Rambla, the area is accessed along either street or through the **Boqueria** market, itself the site of the Sant Josep monastery until the sale of church lands led to its destruction in the 1830s. Behind the Boqueria is the **Antic Hospital de la Santa Creu** (*see p99*), which took in the city's sick

ground for anarchists and other radicals. Innumerable riots and revolts began here; entire streets became no-go areas after dark.

Heroin's arrival in the late 1970s caused extra problems; the semi-tolerated petty criminality became more threatening and affected the tourist trade. Spurred on by the approaching 1992 Olympics, the authorities made a clean sweep of the Chino (Lower Raval). Whole blocks with associations to drugs or prostitution were demolished, and many of the displaced families were transferred to housing estates on the edge of town, out of sight and out of mind.

A sports centre, a new police station and office blocks were constructed, and some streets were pedestrianised. But the most dramatic plan was to create a '*Raval obert al cel*' ('Raval open to the sky'), the most tangible result of which is the sweeping, palm-lined Rambla del Raval. Completed in 2000, it's a continuation of the Avda Drassanes, an earlier attempt to 'open up' the Raval in the 1960s. Nearly five blocks have vanished in its wake; more will soon fall, to allow a planned perpendicular extension to the Ronda de Sant Pau over municipal land that once held the Folch i Torres swimming pools (and before that, a women's prison).

All this work will provide better access to the next grand project: **L'Illa de la Rambla del Raval**, a mega-complex halfway up the new *rambla* that will contain offices, protected housing, shops and the Filmoteca. It's hoped that the star of the show, a luxury hotel by Pere Puig, will provide the area with a glittering new landmark. If it ever gets started, that is. Local

from the 15th century until 1926; it now houses Catalonia's main library and the headquarters of the Institute of Catalan Studies, and **La Capella**, an attractive exhibition space. C/Carme is capped at the Rambla end by the 18th-century **church of Betlem** (Bethlehem) with its serpentine pillars and geometrically patterned façade. Its name features on many shop signs nearby; older residents still refer to this part of the Raval as Betlem.

Antic Hospital de la Santa Creu & La Capella

C/Carme 47-C/Hospital 56 (no phone). Metro Liceu. **Open** 9am-8pm Mon-Fri; 9am-2pm Sat. *La Capella (93 442 71 71)* noon-2pm, 4-8pm Tue-Sat; 11am-2pm Sun. **Admission** free. **Map** p344 A2.

There was a hospital on this site as early as 1024, but in the 15th century it expanded to centralise all the city's hospitals and sanatoriums (with the exception of the Santa Margarida leper colony, which remained outside the city walls). By the 1920s it was hopelessly overstretched and its medical facilities moved uptown to the Hospital Sant Pau. One of the last patients was Gaudí, who died here in 1926; it was also here that Picasso painted one of his first important pictures, *Dead Woman* (1903).

Renovated in 2001, the buildings are some of the most majestic in the city, combining a 15th-century Gothic core with baroque and classical additions. They're now given over to cultural institutions, among them the Massana Arts School, Catalonia's main library, the Institute of Catalan Studies and the Royal Academy of Medicine. Highlights include a neo-classical lecture theatre complete with revolving marble dissection table, and the entrance hall of the Casa de Convalescència, tiled with lovely baroque ceramic murals telling the story of Sant Pau (St Paul); one features an artery-squirting decapitation scene. La Capella, the hospital chapel, was rescued from a sad fate as a warehouse and sensitively converted to an exhibition space for contemporary art. The beautifully shady colonnaded courtyard is a popular spot for reading or eating lunch.

CCCB (Centre de Cultura Contemporània de Barcelona)

C/Montalegre 5 (93 306 41 00/www.cccb.org). Metro Catalunya. **Open** *Mid June-mid Sept* 11am-8pm Tue-Sat; 11am-3pm Sun. *Mid Sept-mid June* 11am-2pm, 4-8pm Tue, Thur, Fri; 11am-8pm Wed, Sat; 11am-7pm Sun. **Admission** *1 exhibition* €4; €3 concessions & Wed. *2 exhibitions* €5.50; €4 concessions & Wed. Free under-16s. **Credit** MC, V. **Map** p344 A1.

Spain's largest cultural centre was opened in 1994 at the huge Casa de la Caritat, built in 1802 on the site of a medieval monastery to serve as the city's main workhouse. The massive façade and part of the courtyard remain from the original building; the rest was rebuilt in dramatic contrast, all tilting glass and steel, by architects Piñón and Viaplana, in what could be seen as an echo of their Maremàgnum shopping centre (*see p191*). As a centre for contemporary culture, it picks up whatever falls through the cracks elsewhere: urban culture, early 20th-century art and festivals such as a May season of Asian cinema, Dies de Dansa (*see p220*) and Sónar (*see p219*).

The CCCB's exhibitions tend to favour production values over content. Running from February to May 2005, *Paris and the Surrealists* covers the time of the surrealist revolution from 1919 to 1966 with over 300 paintings, films, writing and *objets trouvés*. *The West Seen from the East* (May to September)

Antic Hospital.

Sightseeing

Articket BCN

Visit **6** art centres in Barcelona for **17€** ~~38€~~

Museu Nacional d'Art de Catalunya

Museu d'Art Contemporani de Barcelona

Fundació Joan Miró

Fundació Antoni Tàpies

Centre de Cultura Contemporània de Barcelona

Fundació Caixa Catalunya

Ticket valid for three months
www.telentrada.com
From abroad (+34) 93 326 29 48
Ticket offices at the art centers.

www.articketbcn.com

TEL·ENTRADA
902 10 12 12
CAIXA CATALUNYA

examines historical perceptions of the West through the paintings, cinema, maps and other objects of various Eastern countries; Catalan literature from the Franco years is the subject of *Literature in Exile* from September to January 2006, and in the autumn there's an exhibition of the work of film-makers Victór Erice and Abbas Kiarostami.

MACBA (Museu d'Art Contemporani de Barcelona)

Plaça dels Àngels 1 (93 412 08 10/www.macba.es). Metro Catalunya. **Open** *June-Sept* 11am-8pm Mon, Wed-Fri; 10am-8pm Sat; 10am-3pm Sun. *Oct-May* 11am-7.30pm Mon, Wed-Fri; 10am-8pm Sat; 10am-3pm Sun. **Guided tours** (Catalan/Spanish) 6pm Wed, Sat; noon Sun. **Admission** *Museum* €5.50; €4 concessions. *Temporary exhibitions* €4; €3 concessions. *Combined ticket* €7; €5.50 concessions. **Credit** MC, V. **Map** p344 A1.

The MACBA was mocked as a triumph of style over substance when it opened in 1995, and it was noted that visitors spent more time photographing Richard Meier's Persil-bright building than they did looking at the paltry exhibits. A decade on, the place has fattened up its holdings considerably, but the wow factor of the triple-level transitional atrium and zigzag ramps still overshadows most of the shows, which are often heavily political in concept and occasionally radical to the point of inaccessibility. If you can't or won't see the socio-political implications of, say, a roomful of beach balls, the MACBA may leave you cold. It's not overly harsh to suggest that the only really great work of art here is the building itself.

The holdings cover the last 50 years; although there's no permanent collection as such, some of these works are usually on display. The earlier pieces are strong on Spanish expressionists such as Saura and Tàpies (of whom director Manuel Borja-Villel is an ardent fan), alongside Dubuffet, and Basque sculptors Jorge Oteiza and Eduardo Chillida. Works from the last 40 years are more global, with the likes of Beuys, Basquiat and Penk; the contemporary Spanish collection includes Catalan painting (Ferran García Sevilla, Miquel Barceló) and sculpture (Sergi Aguilar, Susana Solano).

Temporary shows due to run in the first half of 2005 include *Disagreements: On Art, Politics and the Public Sphere in Spain* (until May), and *10 Blocks Around My House* (May to August), a retrospective of the work of Francis Alÿs that's based around the square in Mexico City in which he lives. *Stanley Brouwn 1960-2005* (June to September) is the first Spanish show for this minimalist conceptual artist; those exhibiting in the autumn include multimedia artist Robert Whitman, Actionist painter Günter Brus and photographer Jo Spence.

Lower Raval

The lower half of the Raval, from C/Hospital downwards, is generally referred to as the **Barrio Chino** ('Barri Xino' in Catalan). The nickname was coined in the 1920s by a journalist comparing it to San Francisco's Chinatown, and referred to its underworld feel rather than to any Chinese population. In those days, drifters filled the bars and cheap *hostals* along streets such as Nou de la Rambla, where there were high-class cabarets and brothels for the rich and cheap porn pits for the poor. Many writers revelled in the sleaze: for insights, read Genet's *Thief's Journal* (1949), André Pieyre de Mandiargues' *The Margin* (1967) and

The 200-year-old almshouse that houses the **CCCB**. *See p99.*

Sightseeing

Barna in books Genet

Jean Genet's novelistic memoir, *A Thief's Journal*, describes the author's days as a beggar and prostitute in the Barrio Chino. Although some romanticise his early life, the book acquiring a sheen of seedy glamour as an existentialist hymn to living on the edge, *A Thief's Journal* is really a depressing account of Genet's struggle to survive in abject poverty.

Genet ended up in Barcelona after drifting around the Mediterranean, following his escape from the French Foreign Legion. By 1932, the Depression had hit southern Spain hard, forcing hundreds of thousands of Andalucians to abandon their villages. Many of these vagrants ended up in Barcelona and formed a huge, poverty-stricken underclass, in which Genet found himself at home.

At the time, the Mediterranean seaport of Barcelona was a natural magnet to petty thieves, ne'er-do-wells and hangers-on of all descriptions. Genet describes soliciting on the corners of C/Carme and C/Mediodia, begging scraps of food from the housewives shopping on the Parallel, sleeping in a *pensión* in what is now the Plaça Jean Genet, and sharing his bed with 'six other vagrants', including his lover Salvador and a one-armed pimp named Stilitano. The author describes himself as 'a louse, and conscious of being one', during this era. After ripping off his friends and having one too many run-ins with the local constabulary, he was reluctantly forced to move on to his next port of call.

Twenty years later, Genet was a celebrity, an icon of cool in 1950s Paris, fêted by the likes of Sartre and Cocteau. But in some ways, he had never left the backstreets of the Barrio Chino. Genet's poetic depiction of Barcelona is of a place that both trapped him and liberated his fantasies, a long way from the cold realities of the Parisian orphanage in which he had been raised. It is said that *The Balcony*, his masterpiece of absurdist theatre in which a bizarre whorehouse becomes an analogy for a sick society, was based on a famous Barcelona establishment that offered more than mere sex: it also gave clients the opportunity to act out their most cherished fantasies. One popular room recreated a sleeping carriage on the Orient Express, complete with a vibrating bed and images of passing towns through the fake windows.

Nowadays, a surprising amount of the beggars in the centre of Barcelona are, like Genet, young Europeans searching for their own fantasies. But looking at them – the wasted expressions in their eyes, the string-led dogs and empty McDonald's cups by their sides – it's hard to recognise the 'sordid grandeur' that Genet claims he found on the streets of Barcelona in the 1930s.

Raval-born Manuel Vázquez Montalbán's series of Carvalho detective books. (The latter author died in 2003, but is commemorated by a plaque at C/Botella 11, where he was born.) Recent explorations of the Chino have been more hard-hitting, such as José Luís Guerín's excellent film *Work in Progress* (2001).

C/Nou de la Rambla, the area's main street, is home to Gaudí's first major project: **Palau Güell** at No.3-5, built for his patron, Eusebi Güell. A fortress-like edifice shoehorned into a narrow six-storey sliver, it was an extension of Güell's parents' house (now a hotel) on La Rambla; it's closed for renovation until the end of 2006. Nearby, in C/Sant Pau, is a Modernista landmark, Domènech i Montaner's **Hotel España** (*see p60*), and at the end of the street sits the Romanesque tenth-century church of **Sant Pau del Camp** (*see below*). Iberian remains dating to 200 BC have been found next to the edifice, marking it as one of the oldest parts of the city. At the lower end of the area were the **Drassanes** (shipyards), now home to the **Museu Marítim**. Along the Paral·lel side of this Gothic building lies the only large section of Barcelona's 14th-century city wall.

Sant Pau del Camp

C/Sant Pau 101 (93 441 00 01). Metro Paral.lel. **Open** *Visits* noon-1pm; 7.30-8.30pm Mon-Fri. *Mass* 8pm Sat; noon Sun. **Admission** €1. **Map** p342 C6. The name, St Paul in the Field, reflects a time when the Raval was still countryside. Archaeologists date the construction of this little Romanesque church back 1,000 years; indeed, the date carved on the church's most prestigious headstone – that of Count Guifré II Borell, son of Wilfred the Hairy and inheritor of all Barcelona and Girona – is 912AD.

The church's impressive façade includes sculptures of fantastical flora and fauna along with human grotesques. The tiny cloister features some extraordinary Visigoth capitals and triple-lobed arches. Restored after stints as a school in 1842, an army barracks from 1855 to 1890 and a bomb site in the Civil War, it's now a national monument.

Sant Pere & the Born

Dedicated to followers of fashion.

Parc de la Ciutadella.
See p108.

Maps p344-p345

If any district epitomises Barcelona's celebrated combination of historical treasures and ever-cool attitude, it's the Born. The most uptown area of downtown, it mixes chapels and shoe shops with enviable élan and now boasts some of the highest property prices in the city. Neighbouring Sant Pere is a little scuzzier and less self-important, but it's poised to catch up with the Born in 2005 when its new centrepiece, a market and broad avenue, is finally ready.

Both districts together are still sometimes referred to as La Ribera ('the waterfront'), a name that recalls the time before permanent quays were built, when the shoreline reached much further inland. Originally contained, like the Barri Gòtic, within the second, 13th-century city wall, it's one of the most engaging districts of the Old City. In Barcelona's Golden Age, from the 12th century onwards, La Ribera was the favourite residential area of the city's merchant elite, as well as the principal centre of commerce and trade.

The area is demarcated to the east by the **Parc de la Ciutadella** (*see p108*), and to the west by Via Laietana, both the product of historic acts of urban vandalism. The first came after the 1714 siege, when the victors, acting on

the orders of Philip V, destroyed 1,000 houses, hospitals and monasteries to construct the fortress of the Ciutadella (Citadel). The second occurred when the Via Laietana was struck through the district in 1907, in line with the theory of 'ventilating' unsanitary city districts by driving wide avenues through them. Within La Ribera, Sant Pere and the Born are divided by C/Princesa, running between the Parc de la Ciutadella and the **Plaça de l'Àngel** (once called the Plaça del Blat, or 'wheat square'), the commercial and popular heart of the city where all grain was traded. The area north of C/Princesa is centred around the monastery of **Sant Pere de les Puelles**, which still stands, if greatly altered, in Plaça de Sant Pere. For centuries this was Barcelona's main centre of textile production; to this day, streets such as Sant Pere Més Baix and Sant Pere Més Alt contain many textile wholesalers and retailers.

The area may be medieval in origin, but its finest monument is also one of the most extraordinary works of Modernisme – the **Palau de la Música Catalana** (*see p107*), facing C/Sant Pere Més Alt. Less noticed on the same street is a curious feature, the **Passatge de les Manufactures**, a 19th-century arcade between C/Sant Pere Més Alt and C/Ortigosa.

Palau de la Música Catalana. *See p107.*

Sant Pere is currently undergoing dramatic renovation, with the gradual opening up of a continuation of the Avda Francesc Cambó, which will eventually swing around to meet with C/Allada-Vermell, a wide street formed when a block was demolished in 1994. The district's market, **Mercat de Santa Caterina,** is one of Barcelona's oldest, and is being rebuilt to a design by the late Enric Miralles (who also famously designed the Scottish Parliament), and remains of the medieval **Santa Caterina convent** will be shown behind glass at one end. At the time of writing the undulating mosaic roof was complete, but the market isn't due to open until spring 2005. In the meantime its stallholders have been relocated along Passeig Lluís Companys, by the park. Another convent nearby is the **Convent de Sant Agustí,** now a civic centre, on C/Comerç. The entrance contains *Deuce Coop,* a magical 'light sculpture' by James Turrell, which was commissioned by the Ajuntament in the 1980s and is turned on after dark.

Where C/Carders meets C/Montcada is the Placeta d'en Marcús, with a small chapel, the 12th-century **Capella d'en Marcús,** built as part of an inn. It was founded by Bernat Marcús, who is said to have organised Europe's first postal service. It was from this chapel, then outside the city wall, that his riders set off for the north, and it also provided a refuge for them and other travellers who arrived after the city gates had closed for the night.

From this tiny square **C/Montcada,** one of the unmissable streets of old Barcelona, leads into the Born. It is lined with a succession of

medieval merchants' mansions, the greatest of which house a variety of museums, including the **Museu Tèxtil** (*see p107*), the **Museu Barbier-Mueller** (*see p105*) of pre-Columbian art and, above all, the **Museu Picasso** (*see p105*). In 1148 land ceded to Guillem Ramon de Montcada became the site for the construction of this street, where the opulence of the many merchant-princes of the time is still very visible. The streets nearby were filled with workshops supplying anything the inhabitants needed, and these trades are commemorated in the names of many of the streets (*see p108* **Walk on: Medieval trading**).

'Born' originally meant 'joust' or 'list', and in the Middle Ages and for many centuries thereafter the neighbourhood's main artery, the **Passeig del Born,** was the centre for the city's festivals, processions, tournaments, carnivals and the burning of heretics by the Inquisition. At one end of the square is the old **Born market,** a magnificent 1870s wrought-iron structure that used to be Barcelona's main wholesale food market. It closed in the 1970s, and the market was transferred elsewhere. Plans to turn it into a library were thwarted by the discovery of perfectly preserved medieval remains. The foundations of buildings razed by Philip V's troops were found to contain hundreds of objects, some domestic and some, like rusty bombs, suggesting the traumas of the period. A viewing platform, with useful diagrams and notes, has been erected on C/Fusina, and ultimately the remains will be incorporated into a cultural centre and museum, although progress seems painfully slow.

At the other end of the Passeig from the market stands the greatest of all Catalan Gothic buildings, the spectacular basilica of **Santa Maria del Mar** (*see p109*). On one side of it, a square was opened in 1989 on the site where it is believed the last defenders of the city were executed after the Barcelona fell to the Spanish army in 1714. Called the **Fossar de les Moreres** (the 'Mulberry Graveyard'), the square is inscribed with patriotic poetry, and nationalist demonstrations converge here every year on Catalan National Day, 11 September. The 'eternal flame' sculpture is a more recent, and less popular, addition.

From here narrow streets lead to the **Plaça de les Olles** or the grand **Pla del Palau** and another symbol of La Ribera, **La Llotja** (the 'exchange'). Its neo-classical outer shell was added in the 18th century, but its core is a superb 1380s Gothic hall, sadly closed to the public, save for occasional functions organised through the Chamber of Commerce. Until the exchange moved to the Passeig de Gràcia in 1994, this was the oldest continuously functioning stock exchange in Europe.

Metrònom

C/Fusina 9 (93 268 42 98/www.metronom-bcn.org). Metro Arc de Triomf or Jaume I. Open 11am-2pm, 5-8pm Tue-Sat. Closed Aug. **Map** p345 C3.

After stunning renovation of its Modernista stained-glass skylights and iron columns, this former warehouse won a FAD award when it opened as a gallery in 1984. Exhibitions focus on photography and multimedia installations, but there is also space for choreography, electronic music, online projects and magazines through the MetrònomLab. The Phonos Foundation presents its musical creations every spring and autumn and Metrònom hosts an experimental music festival every winter. In June and July 2005 art collective 22A presents *Body Thieves*, alongside photography from Katherine Mayer.

Museu Barbier-Mueller d'Art Precolombí

C/Montcada 14 (93 310 45 16/www.barbier-mueller. ch). Metro Jaume I. Open 10am-6pm Tue-Sat; 10am-3pm Sun. **Admission** €3; €1.50 concessions; free under-16s. Free 1st Sun of mth. **Credit** (shop only) AmEx, MC, V. **Map** p345 C3.

Located in the 15th-century Palau Nadal, this world-class collection of pre-Columbian art was ceded to Barcelona in 1996 by the Barbier-Mueller museum in Geneva. The frequently changing selection of masks, textiles, jewellery and sculpture includes pieces dating from as far back as the second millennium BC to the early 16th century (showing just how loosely the term 'pre-Columbian' can be used). The Barcelona holdings focus solely on the Americas, representing most of the styles from the ancient cultures of Meso-America, Central America, Andean America and the Amazon region. From April to September 2005 there'll be a monographic exhibition on South American art from the museum holdings, including pieces from the Nazca, Moche and Inca civilisations.

Museu de Ciències Naturals de la Ciutadella

Passeig Picasso, Parc de la Ciutadella (93 319 69 12/www.bcn.es/museuciencies). Metro Arc de Triomf. **Open** 10am-2pm Tue, Wed, Fri-Sun; 10am-6pm Thur. **Admission** *All exhibitions & Jardí Botànic* €4; €2 concessions. *Museums only* €3; €1.50 concessions. *Temporary exhibitions* €3.50; €1.50 concessions. Free under-12s. Free 1st Sun of mth. **No credit cards. Map** p343 E6.

The Natural History Museum now comprises the zoology and geology museums in the Parc de la Ciutadella. Both suffer from old-school presentation: dusty glass cases filled with moth-eaten stuffed animals and serried rows of rocks. The zoology museum is redeemed by its location in the Castell dels Tres Dragons, built by Domènech i Montaner as the café-restaurant for the 1888 Exhibition, and by its interesting temporary exhibitions – as part of the Year of the Book, the Mythology of Dinosaurs (June 2005-April 2006) looks at the depiction of dinosaurs in science fiction, comics and cinema and includes models of both real dinosaurs and cultural icons such as Godzilla. Also in 2005 the museum celebrates its 125th anniversary (making it the oldest public museum in Barcelona) and a year-long exhibition celebrates the life and personal collection of its founder, Francesc Martorell. The geology part is for aficionados only, with a dry display of minerals, painstakingly classified, alongside explanations of geological phenomena found in Catalonia. More interesting is the selection from the museum's collection of 300,000 fossils, many found locally. A combined ticket now also grants entrance to the Jardí Botànic on Montjuïc (*see p118*).

Museu Picasso

C/Montcada 15-23 (93 319 63 10/www.museu picasso.bcn.es). Metro Jaume I. **Open** (last ticket 30mins before closing) 10am-8pm Tue-Sat; 10am-3pm Sun. **Admission** *Permanent collection only* €5; €2.50 concessions. *With temporary exhibition* €8; €4.70 concessions; free under-16s. Free (museum only) 1st Sun of mth. **Credit** (shop only) AmEx, MC, V. **Map** p345 C3.

As the Picasso Museum grew from its beginnings in the Palau Aguilar in 1963 to encompass a row of medieval mansions, the spread was felt to be somewhat disjointed. In 2003 a complete overhaul of the space corrected its many flaws, and created more room. The main entrance is now at the Palau Meca, and the exit at the Palau Aguilar. By no means an overview of the artist's work, the Museu Picasso is rather a record of the vital formative years that the young Picasso spent nearby at La Llotja art school (where his father taught), and later hanging out with Catalonia's *fin-de-siècle* avant-garde. The culmination of Picasso's early genius in *Les Demoiselles d'Avignon* (1907) and the first cubist paintings from the time (many of them done in Catalonia), as well as

Sightseeing (vertical side tab)

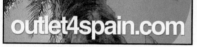

GO
AND
SEE!

Guided tour

PRICES
8€ **Individual**
7€ **Groups** (minimum of 25 members)

VISITING TIMES
Weekdays and weekends:
10 am - 3.30 pm
The visiting times may be altered or cancelled, depending on availibility of the concert hall.

INFORMATION
Palau de la Música Catalana
c./ de Sant Francesc de Paula 2
08003 Barcelona
Tel. 93 295 72 00 · Fax. 93 295 72 10
www.palaumusica.org

PALAU DE LA MÚSICA CATALANA
BARCELONA

his collage and sculpture, are all completely absent. The founding of the museum is down to a key figure in Picasso's life, his friend and secretary Jaume Sabartés, who donated his own collection for the purpose. Tribute is paid with a room dedicated to Picasso's portraits of him (best known is the Blue Period painting of Sabartés's wearing a white ruff), and Sabartés's own doodlings. The seamless presentation of Picasso's development from 1890 to 1904, from deft pre-adolescent portraits to sketchy landscapes to the intense innovations of his Blue Period, is unbeatable, then it leaps to a gallery of mature cubist paintings from 1917. The pièce de résistance is the complete series of 57 canvases based on Velázquez's famous *Las Meninas*, donated by Picasso himself, and now stretching through three rooms. The display later ends with a wonderful collection of ceramics donated by his widow. Temporary exhibitions are held under the magnificent coffered ceiling of the Palau Finestres, and in 2005 will include a retrospective of radical abstractionist Jean Hélion from March to June, and, in autumn, a collection of over 50 books illustrated by Picasso, in conjunction with the Year of the Book.

Museu Tèxtil

C/Montcada 12 (93 319 76 03/www.museutextil.bcn.es). Metro Jaume I. **Open** 10am-6pm Tue-Sat; 10am-3pm Sun. **Admission** *Combined admission with Museu de les Arts Decoratives & Museu de Ceràmica* €3.50; €2 concessions; free under-16s. Free 1st Sun of mth. **Credit** (shop only) AmEx, DC, MC, V. **Map** p345 C3.

The displays of the Textile and Clothing Museum occupy two adjacent buildings, the Palau Nadal and Palau dels Marquesos de Lló; the latter retains some of its 13th-century wooden ceilings. Items include medieval Hispano-Arab textiles, liturgical vestments and the city's lace and embroidery collection. The real highlight is the historic fashions – from baroque to 20th-century – that collector Manuel Rocamora donated in the 1960s, one of the finest collections of its type anywhere. Recent important donations include one from Spanish designer Cristóbal Balenciaga, famous for the 1958 baby doll dress and pill-box hat. The museum shop is a great place to pick up presents, and there's a wonderful café in the courtyard. At an unspecified date in the future, the museum is to move to a new Museu de Disseny (Design Museum) in the Plaça de les Glòries.

Museu de la Xocolata

C/Comerç 36 (93 268 78 78). Metro Jaume I. **Open** 10am-7pm Mon, Wed-Sat; 10am-3pm Sun. **Admission** €3.80; €3.20 concessions; free under -7s. **Credit** MC, V.

Chocoholics of all ages will enjoy this small collection of *mones* (chocolate sculptures). Made by Barcelona's master *pastissers* for the annual Easter competition, the *mones* range from models of the Sagrada Família and Montserrat to scenes from *Finding Nemo* or *Ben-Hur*. Inevitably, this is not a collection that ages well: photos have replaced most of the older sculptures and those that are not in glass

cases bear the ravages of hands-on appreciation from the museum's smaller visitors. A brief history of chocolate is pepped up with audio-visual displays and the odd touch-screen computer but the busiest area is the glass-fronted cookery workshop with classes for all ages and levels. That, and the irresistible chocolate shop.

Palau de la Música Catalana

C/Sant Francesc de Paula 2 (93 295 72 00/www.palaumusica.org). Metro Urquinaona. **Open** *Box office* 10am-9pm Mon-Sat. **Guided tours** 10am-3.30pm daily. **Admission** €8; €7 concessions. **Credit** (minimum €20) MC, V. **Map** p344 B-C2.

The façade of Domènech i Montaner's Modernista concert hall, with its bare brick, busts and mosaic friezes representing Catalan musical traditions and composers, is impressive enough, but it is surpassed

Sightseeing

Flashpoints

C/Canvis Nous (map p345 B4).

On the evening of Sunday 7 June 1895, the Corpus Christi parade, including ecclesiastical, military and civil authorities, had almost reached the church of Santa Maria del Mar when a bomb was thrown into the procession, in the C/Canvis Nous, killing six people and injuring 42. Religious authorities, in league with the state and the military, accused anyone of vaguely liberal or anticlerical ideas of having been accomplices to the act. Some 400 people were subsequently arrested.

A military trial was finally held in December, behind closed doors. It lasted just four days. Confessions had been extracted by the most gruesome torture in the dungeons of Montjuïc Castle: at least one prisoner had been killed and others sent mad. The defence lawyer of one man committed suicide on hearing the preposterous verdict. Eight men were sentenced to death and over 50 others were given prison sentences.

News of the torture and police excesses against the anarchists and free thinkers spread rapidly throughout Europe. In retaliation for the 'Montjuïc Processes' an Italian anarchist, Michele Angiolillo, would later kill the Spanish President Antonio Cánovas. It was never discovered who was responsible for the bombing: many claimed that the fact that the bomb was thrown at the rear of the procession, killing ordinary people, suggested a police plot, organised with the intention of justifying the later repression.

by the building's staggering interior. Decoration erupts everywhere: the ceiling centrepiece is of multicoloured stained glass; 18 half-mosaic, half-relief figures representing the musical muses appear out of the back of the stage; and on one side, massive Wagnerian carved horses ride out to accompany a bust of Beethoven. The old Palau has been bursting under the pressure of the musical activity going on inside it, and an extension and renovation project by Oscar Tusquets in the 1980s is being followed by yet more alterations by the same architect. The ugly church next door has been knocked down to make way for the extension of the façade, a subterranean concert hall and a new entrance.

Guided tours are available in English, Catalan or Spanish every 30 minutes or so. They begin with a rather tedious video, which can make the remaining tour a bit rushed. Be sure to ask plenty of questions, particularly if there's something you really want to know – the guides are very knowledgeable, but usually they concentrate mainly on the triumphs of the renovation unless drawn out by customers. If you have a chance, an infinitely preferable way to see the hall is by catching a concert (see p263).

Parc de la Ciutadella

Passeig Picasso (no phone). Metro Arc de Triomf or Barceloneta. **Open** 10am-sunset daily. **Map** p343 E6.
In 1869, when General Prim announced that the area taken up by the loathed Bourbon citadel could be reclaimed for public use, the city's joy was boundless. Soon the park was to become the site of the 1888 Exhibition; Domènech i Montaner's Castell de Tres Dragons at the entrance served as the cafeteria, while the Arc de Triomf to the north formed the main entrance. Prim is honoured with a large equestrian statue at the south end.

Surprisingly extensive, the park also contains a host of attractions: the zoo, the Natural History Museum, a boating lake and an array of imaginative statuary. The giant mammoth, at the far side of the boating lake, is a huge hit with kids, as is the group of leaping gazelles. Beside the lake is the *Cascade*, an ornamental fountain on which the young Gaudí worked as assistant to Josep Fontseré, the architect of the park. Not to be missed are Fontseré's Umbracle (literally, 'shade house'), which was built in the 1880s with a cast-iron structure reminiscent of his Mercat del Born on C/Comerç and then later

Walk on Medieval trading

Duration: 45 minutes.
From **Plaça de l'Àngel**, site of the Plaça del Blat, the grain market, cross Via Laietana to **C/Bòria**, a name that probably means 'outskirts' or 'suburbs', since it was outside the original city. C/Bòria continues into the evocative little **Plaça de la Llana**, the old centre of wool (*llana*) trading in the city, now an animated meeting place for the Dominican Republic community. Alleys to the left were associated with food trades: **C/Mercaders** ('traders', probably in grain), **C/Oli** ('olive oil') just off it, and **C/Semoleres**, where semolina was made. To the right on Bòria is **C/Pou de la Cadena** ('well with a chain'), a reminder that water was essential for textile working.

After Plaça de la Llana the Roman road's name becomes **C/Corders** ('ropemakers'), and then **C/Carders** ('carders' or combers of wool). Where the name changes there is a tiny square, Placeta Marcús, with an even smaller Romanesque chapel, the **Capella d'en Marcús**, built in the early 12th century.

The chapel was built to give shelter to travellers who arrived after the city gates had closed for the night. Bernat Marcús, who paid for it, is also said to have organised the first postal service in Europe, and it was from here that his riders would set off north. If you carry on a little way along C/Carders, you arrive at the **Plaça Sant Agustí Vell**, where the

architecture can be dated as far back as the Middle Ages. Just off it, **C/Basses de Sant Pere** leads away to the left where you'll find a 14th-century house.

Retrace your steps down C/Carders, then turn left into **C/Blanqueria** ('bleaching'). Here wool was washed before being spun. At **C/Assaonadors** ('tanners'), turn right. At the end of this street, behind the Marcús chapel, is a statue of John the Baptist, patron saint of the tanners' guild.

Now you are at the top of **C/Montcada**, one of Barcelona's great museum centres and a beautiful street in itself. The first of the line of medieval merchants' palaces you reach after crossing C/Princesa is the **Palau Berenguer d'Aguilar**, home of the **Museu Picasso**, which has also taken over four more palaces. Opposite is one of the finest and largest palaces, the **Palau dels Marquesos de Lió**, now the **Museu Tèxtil**, with a fine café. To the right is the milliners' street **C/Sombrerers**; opposite it is Barcelona's narrowest street, **C/Mosques** ('flies'), not even wide enough for an adult to lie across, and now closed off with an iron gate because too many people were pissing in it at night. C/Montcada ends at **Passeig del Born**, a hub of the city's trading for 400 years.

Turn left, and on the left is **C/Flassaders** ('blanket makers'), and to the right **C/Rec**, restored to provide a pocket of tropical forest within the city, and the elegant Hivernacle ('winter garden'), which has a fine café, L'Hivernacle (see p180). Outside on the Passeig Picasso is Antoni Tàpies's A Picasso, a giant cubist monument to the artist.

Sala Montcada

C/Montcada 14 (93 310 06 99/www.fundacio.la caixa.es/salamontcada). Metro Jaume I. **Open** 11am-3pm, 4-8pm Tue-Sat; 11am-3pm Sun. **Admission** free. **Map** p345 C3.

This is a diminutive contemporary arts outpost of the CaixaForum (see p117), and is equally as ground-breaking in its own right. Each year three different curators develop excellent mixed programmes of Spanish and international artists. In 2005 this includes The Day Before – Star System, a selection of photographs by Renaud Auguste-Dormeuil (April-June) and multimedia exhibitions from David Bestué and Blanca Casa Brullet (June-July).

Santa Maria del Mar

Plaça de Santa Maria (93 310 23 90). Metro Jaume I. **Open** 9am-1.30pm, 4.30-8pm Mon-Sat; 10am-1.30pm, 4.30-8pm Sun. **Admission** free. **Map** p345 C3.

This graceful basilica, named after Mary in her role as patroness of sailors, was built on the site of a small church known as Santa Maria del Arenys (sand), for its position close to the sea. It was actually built remarkably quickly for a medieval building, and was entirely constructed between 1329 and 1384, with an unusual unity of style for structures from that period. Inside, two rows of slim, perfectly proportioned columns soar up to fan vaults, creating a wonderful atmosphere of space and a sense of peace. There's also some superb stained glass, especially in the form of the great 15th-century rose window above the main door. The original window, built only slightly earlier, fell down during an earthquake, killing 25 people and injuring dozens more.

It's perhaps thanks to the group of anti-clerical anarchists who set this magnificent church ablaze in 1936 that its superb features can be appreciated – without the wooden baroque images that clutter so many Spanish churches, the simplicity of its lines can emerge. The incongruous modern window at the other end was a 1997 addition, belatedly celebrating the Olympics. Try and catch a concert here if you can; particularly stirring are Handel's Messiah at Christmas and the Requiem at Easter.

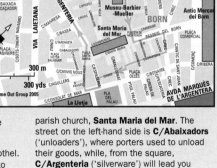

the old irrigation canal. Go down Rec to turn right into **C/Esparteria**, where espart (hemp) was woven. Turnings off it include **C/Calders**, where smelting furnaces would have been found, and **C/Formatgeria**, where one would have gone for cheese. After that is **C/Vidrieria**, where glass was stored and sold. Esparteria runs into C/Ases, which crosses **C/Malcuinat** ('badly cooked'). Turn left into **C/Espaseria** ('sword-making') to emerge out of ancient alleys on to the open space of Pla del Palau. Turn right, and then right again into **C/Canvis Vells** (or 'old exchange'). A tiny street to the left, **C/Panses**, has an archway above it, with an ancient stone carving of a face over the second floor. This face, called a carabassa, indicated the location of a legalised brothel.

At the end of Canvis Vells you come to **Plaça Santa Maria** and the Born's superb

parish church, **Santa Maria del Mar**. The street on the left-hand side is **C/Abaixadors** ('unloaders'), where porters used to unload their goods, while, from the square, **C/Argenteria** ('silverware') will lead you back to the Plaça de l'Àngel.

Barceloneta & the Ports

The shoreline gets shipshape.

Port Vell

It took a crack of the Olympic whip to get the planners working on the city coastline but Barcelona has been furiously swabbing its decks ever since. Over the last 15 years Port Vell (the 'Old Port') has changed beyond recognition from an industrial dockyard to a palm-fringed paradigm of urban integration, attracting over 16 million visitors a year.

The clean-up has extended to the whole seven kilometres (four miles) of city seashore, which, by the end of 2005, will be a virtually continuous strip of modern construction: new docks, beaches, marinas, hotels, the Diagonal-Mar area, conference centres and cruise and ferry harbours will be joined by Ricard Bofill's Nova Bocana harbour development with its new maritime esplanade and sail-shaped luxury hotel.

The first wharves were built in the Middle Ages when Barcelona was on its way to becoming the dominant power in the Western Mediterranean. The immense Drassanes Reials (Royal Shipyards), now housing the **Museu Marítim** (*see p112* **Making waves**), bear witness to the sovereignty of the Catalan navy,

and the city became a military centre and the hub of trading routes between Africa and the rest of Europe. The city's power was dealt a blow when Columbus sailed west and found what he thought was the East; soon the Atlantic became the important trade route and Barcelona went into recession. Prosperity returned in the 19th century when it became the base for the Spanish industrial revolution.

Despite putting the city out of business, Columbus was commemorated in 1888 with the **Monument a Colom** (*see p113*), a statue inspired by Nelson's Column, complete with four majestic lions. Consistent with the great discoverer's errant sense of direction, his pointing finger is not directed west to the Americas at all, but eastwards, to Mallorca. He might just turn out to have the last laugh, however, if current Spanish DNA investigations can back claims that he came from Genova in Mallorca rather than Genoa in Italy. A cynic might suggest that he is pointing in bemusement at the **World Trade Center**, a hulking, ship-shaped construction built on a jetty in 1999 to house offices and a five-star hotel. Or he could be pointing at the **Moll d'Espanya**, an artificial island linked to land by the undulating Rambla de Mar footbridge housing the **Maremàgnum** mall (*see p191*), an **IMAX** cinema (*see p232*) and the **aquarium** (*see p226*).

Take a lift up through the centre of **Columbus's column** to check out the view from the top, or jump aboard the rickety **cable car** (*transbordador aeri*). Below, the **catamaran** and the **Golondrinas** pleasure boats begin their excursions out to sea (for both, *see below*). To the right, beyond the busy ferry and cruise ports, is the grandly named **Porta d'Europa**, the longest drawbridge in Europe, which curtains off the vast container port. Andreu Alfaro's enormous *Onas* (*Waves*) cheers up the gridlocked roundabout of Plaça de la Carbonera, where a grim basin of coal commemorates where the steamboats once refuelled.

To Columbus's left you can see the newly refurbished **Moll de la Fusta** (literally 'wood wharf') boulevard, built after the city sea walls were demolished in 1878. The wooden pergolas, one of which is topped by Mariscal's much-loved fibreglass *Gamba* (*Prawn*), are all that remain of some ill-fated restaurants and bars.

Walking on the beaches

Let it all hang out
Platja de Sant Sebastià
Isolated by the swimming pools behind it and the building works of the new breakwater to its side, this isolated stretch of sand is the unofficial nudist beach and the hangout of assorted windsurfers, daytime dope smokers and any other eccentrics happy to swap an uninspiring background of industrial rubble for a bit more space. It's bound to change beyond recognition when the Bofill hotel complex is completed.

A bit of a Goa
Platja de Sant Miquel
A city beach if ever there was one – in the summer the streets of Barceloneta empty a constant flow of sunbathers out on to this narrow belt of sand. It's a great place for people-watching, with a high proportion of tattoos and dreadlocks: at night from May to October the *xiringuitos* (beach shacks) pump out garage and house music and revellers linger on the beach drinking beer until sunset.

Pebble dash
Platja de Barceloneta
This is a grubby family-oriented beach with slightly thinner crowds (as it's a bit of a walk from the metro station and the sand gets painfully pebbly where the sea breaks). Nearby are handy restaurants, nightclubs (including the hugely hip CDLC, *see p256*, and the vulgar Baja Beach Club, *see p250* **Chips with everything**), and spaces for tables where wizened old men play topless dominoes. Boats from the sailing school gingerly tack this way and that just out beyond the line of yellow buoys.

Having a ball
Platja de Nova Icària
The first beach after the Port Olímpic and well served by Ciutadella-Vila Olímpica metro station, this wide stretch has a suburban feel to it after Barceloneta. Sheltered by the marina, the water is calm, if crowded in the summer by a nondescript mixture of local and *guiri* (foreign) yoof throwing balls and playing beach tennis. Three volleyball courts ensure a constant backdrop of whoops and high fives.

Rough stuff
Platja de Bogatell
A long and slightly narrower stretch of beach, this strip is less sheltered than Nova Icària, and so has rougher seas and, on the most stormy days, sand banked up into walls. The *chiringuito* in the wider stretch of the beach further north puts torches and deckchairs out at night from May to October.

Let it all hang out II
Platja de Mar Bella
The official nudist beach, this stretch is protected from prying eyes by sand dunes, and flanked by the hip bar-restaurant Base Nautica (where clothes are encouraged). Afternoons here are punctuated by yelps of triumph and pain from skateboarders, skaters and BMXers on the popular half-pipe behind.

A beach too far
Platja de Nova Mar Bella
Backed by a car park and a forest of high-rise residential blocks, this short but quiet stretch at the end of the line is largely used by local families and those who enjoy the techno music perpetually blasting out of the *xiringuito*.

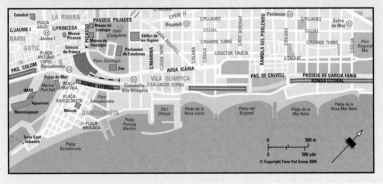

Making waves

It only lasted for four hours, but the Battle of Lepanto on 7 October 1571 was one of the most decisive sea battles in history and the biggest naval engagement anywhere since the Battle of Actium in 30 BC.

Fighting to prevent the Ottoman empire from turning the Mediterranean into a Muslim lake, Don Juan de Austria commanded the Holy League, made up of Spanish, Venetian and papal ships along with vessels from a number of Italian states. They were closely matched by Ali Pasha's vast Ottoman fleet. As sails were inappropriate for close combat, each galley was rowed by up to 35 banks of eight galley slaves – usually convicts, prisoners of war or unfortunate victims of press-ganging.

At noon they clashed in the waters at the mouth of the Gulf of Patras off the Greek port of Lepanto. By all accounts, Don Juan was a master strategist and he finally managed to out-manoeuvre the Turks by performing a sudden 90-degree turn, pinning them like butterflies against the coast. When the smoke cleared at around 4pm the Turkish fleet had been broken, around 15,000 Turks were slain or captured and 12,000 Christian galley slaves were liberated.

The victors also suffered heavy losses and among the wounded was the young Cervantes, who permanently lost the use of his left hand after a bullet wound, earning the nickname *El Manco de Lepanto* ('the one-handed one of Lepanto' – it's snappier in Spanish). He later worked this experience (and his five-year stint as a slave after being kidnapped by Barbary pirates) into his masterpiece *Don Quixote*.

Though this victory did not accomplish all that was hoped for, since the Turks appeared the very next year with a brand new fleet, it was the first great defeat of the infidels at sea and ended the myth of their naval invincibility. Control of the Mediterranean was key, and the Christian victory marked the beginning of the Ottoman Empire's decline.

A full-scale replica of Don Juan de Austria's royal galley is the mainstay of the collection at the **Museu Marítim**, complete with a ghostly crew of galley slaves projected on to the rowing banks. The original ship was built in these very same shipyards, one of the finest examples of civil Gothic architecture in Spain and a monument to Barcelona's

importance in Mediterranean naval history. With the aid of an in-depth audio guide, the absorbing range of maps, nautical instruments, multimedia displays and models show you how shipbuilding and navigation techniques have developed over the years. A small supplement allows you access to the three-masted *Santa Eulàlia* schooner docked in the Moll de la Fusta. Temporary exhibitions in 2005 include, from June to September, a look at Cervantes' adventures at sea, and *Don Quixote*'s adventures in Barcelona.

Museu Marítim

Avda de les Drassanes (93 342 99 29/ www.diba.es/mmaritim). Metro Drassanes. **Open** 10am-7pm daily. **Admission** €5.40; €2.70 concessions; free under-7s. *Temporary exhibitions varies. Combined ticket with Las Golondrinas* (35mins) €6.60; €4-€5.10 concessions; free under-4s. (1hr 30mins) €10.10; €5.70-€7.70 concessions; free under-4s. **Credit** MC, V. Map p345 A4.

Seafront shopping: **Maremàgnum**. *See p110.*

Roy Lichtenstein's pop art ***Barcelona Head***
signposts the marina with its endless lines of
yachts and the **Palau de Mar**, a converted
port warehouse that now houses the **Museu
d'Història de Catalunya** (*see below*).

Catamaran Orsom

*Portal de la Pau, Port de Barcelona (93 441 05 37/
www.barcelona-orsom.com). Metro Drassanes.*
Sailings (approx 1hr 20mins) *Mar-Oct* noon-8pm
3-4 sailings daily. All sailings subject to weather
conditions. **Tickets** €12; €6-€9 concessions; free
under-4s. *Jazz cruises* €14; €7-€10 concessions.
No credit cards. Map p342 D7.

Departing from the jetty by the Monument a Colom,
this 23-metre (75ft) catamaran chugs up to 80 sea-
farers round the Nova Bocana harbour development,
before unfurling its sails and peacefully gliding
across the bay. There are 8pm jazz cruises from June
to September or, if you don't want to fight for the
trampoline sun deck, the catamaran can also be
chartered for private trips along the Costa Brava.

Las Golondrinas

*Moll de Drassanes (93 442 31 06/www.lasgolondrinas.
com). Metro Drassanes.* **Drassanes to breakwater
& return** (35mins) *Jan-Mar, Nov, Dec* 11am-2pm
Mon-Fri; 11.45am-7pm Sat, Sun. *Apr-June, Oct* 11am-
6pm Mon-Fri; 11.45am-7pm Sat, Sun. *July-Sept*
11.45am-7.30pm daily. **Tickets** €3.80; €1.90
concessions; free under-4s. **Drassanes to Port
Olímpic & return** (1hr 30mins) *Jan-Mar, Nov, Dec*
11.30am, 1.30pm Mon-Fri; 11.30am, 1.30pm, 4.30pm
Sat, Sun. *Apr-June, Oct* 11.30am, 1.30pm, 4.30pm
Mon-Fri; 11.30am, 1.30pm, 4.30pm, 6.30pm Sat, Sun.

July-Sept 11.30am, 1.30pm, 4.30pm, 6.30pm, 8.30pm
daily. **Tickets** €9.20; €4-€6.50 concessions; free
under-4s. **Credit** MC, V. **Map** p342 C7.

For over 115 years the 'swallow boats' have chugged
around the harbour, giving passengers a bosun's-
eye view of Barcelona's rapidly changing seascape.
The fleet is made up of three double-decker pleasure
boats and two glass-bottomed catamarans, moored
next to the Orsom catamaran (*see above*). Boats leave
around every 40 minutes for the shorter trip.

Monument a Colom

*Plaça Portal de la Pau (93 302 52 24). Metro
Drassanes.* **Open** *Oct-May* 10am-6.30pm daily.
June-Sept 9am-8.30pm daily. **Admission** €2;
€1.30 concessions; free under-4s. **No credit
cards. Map** p345 A4.

The end of La Rambla is marked by the Columbus
monument, designed for the 1888 Great Exhibition.
A tiny lift takes you up inside the column to a
circular viewing bay for a panoramic view of city and
port. Claustrophobes and vertigo sufferers should
stay away; the slight sway is particularly unnerving.

Museu d'Història de Catalunya

*Plaça Pau Vila 3 (93 225 47 00/www.mhcat.net).
Metro Barceloneta.* **Open** 10am-7pm Tue, Thur-Sat;
10am-8pm Wed; 10am-2.30pm Sun. **Admission** €3;
€2.10 concessions; free under-7s. Free to all 1st Sun
of mth. **Credit** (shop only) MC, V. **Map** p345 C4.

Located in a lavishly converted 19th-century port
warehouse, the Museum of Catalan History's com-
pass spans the Paleolithic era right up to Jordi
Pujol's proclamation as President of the Generalitat
in 1980. With very little in the way of original artefacts, it is more a virtual chronology of the region's
past revealed through two floors of text, photos,
film, animated models and reproductions of everything from a medieval shoemaker's shop to a 1960s
bar (complete with table football). Hands-on activities such as trying to lift a knight's armour or irri-
gating lettuces with a Moorish water wheel add a
little pzazz to the rather dry early history but the
later section covering the 18th century to the present
day (on the third floor) is noticeably denser and more
colourful. Every section has a decent introduction in
English, but the reception desk will loan a copy of
the in-depth museum guide free of charge. Upstairs
there's a café with terrace and an unbeatable view.

Transbordador Aeri

*Torre de Sant Sebastià, Barceloneta (93 441 48 20).
Metro Barceloneta. Also Torre de Jaume I, Port Vell,
to Ctra Miramar, Montjuïc. Metro Drassanes.* **Open**
Mid June-mid Sept 10.45am-7.15pm daily. *Mid Sept-
mid June* 10.30am-5.45pm daily. **Tickets** €7.50
single; €9 return; free under-3s. **No credit cards.
Map** p342 C/D7.

Take the lift up the Sant Sebastià tower at the very
far end of Passeig Joan de Borbó or the Jaume I tower
in front of the World Trade Center to jump on one
of the battered old cable cars. To ensure a clear view,
try to avoid mid-morning and mid-afternoon, when
you'll be jostling for window space.

Barceloneta

In their hurry to get to the beach, most visitors charge straight down the restaurant-lined boulevard of Passeig Joan de Borbó, stopping no longer than it takes to wolf a paella. Yet behind this façade of elegant buildings overlooking the yacht marina lies a robust maritime quarter with huge charm and a turbulent history.

Barceloneta ('Little Barcelona') was born of necessity. When the old maritime *barrio* of La Ribera was demolished in 1714 to make way for the hated citadel (*see p16*), thousands were left homeless and without compensation. It was not until 1753 that the new district of Barceloneta was created and the homeless refugees made do with makeshift slums on the beach for nearly 40 years. Military engineer Prosper Verboom maximised the potential of the triangle of reclaimed marshland with narrow rows of cheap worker housing set around a parade ground (now the market square). The two-storey houses became home to fishermen and sailors, and soon became so overcrowded that they were split in half and later quartered. These famous *quarts de casa* (quarter houses) typically measured no more than 30 square metres (323 sqare feet), had no running water until the 1960s and often held families of ten or more. Most were later built up to six or more levels, but even today, three-tier bunk beds are not uncommon and in the summer months the street becomes an extended living room, with armchairs and TVs out on the pavement. This partly explains Barceloneta's exceptionally full street life and the district is famous for its colourful local celebrations.

Now crowded with sunbathers, it's hard to believe that Barceloneta's beach was once a filthy Hell's Bathroom of sewage, heavy industry and warehouses. Any usable parts of the narrow grey beach were clogged up with private swimming baths and beach shacks (*xiringuitos*) that served seafood on trestle tables set up on the sand. Once the 1992 Olympics opened Barcelona's eyes to the vast commercial potential of its shoreline, the beaches were swiftly cleared and filled with tons of golden sand, imported palm trees, drainage systems, flood lighting and landscaped promenades.

Since the beach clean-up, Barceloneta has enjoyed a much higher profile and current redevelopment includes a new market, university housing and Enric Miralles' towering Gas Natural headquarters, covered in mirrored glass to resemble rocks emerging from the waters of the Mediterranean. The area has also been the beneficiary of a quite staggering amount of sculpture, particularly around the Port Vell.

Lothar Baumgarten's **Rosa dels Vents** has the names of Catalan sea winds embedded in the pavement, and, at the other end of Passeig Joan de Borbó is Juan Muñoz's disturbing sculpture of five caged figures known as **Una habitació on sempre plou** (*A Room Where it Always Rains*). Behind this somewhat gloomy piece is the city's popular municipal **swimming pool** (*see p276*) newly marked by the soaring figures of Alfredo Lanz's **Homenatge a la Natació** (*Homage to Swimming*) to mark the 2003 World Swimming Championships held in Barcelona.

Nearby, the Port still preserves a small fishing area with the clock tower which gives its name to the wharf – Moll del Rellotge ('clock wharf'). Further down, the road leads to the Nova Bocana development, which will soon be dominated by Ricard Bofill's tall sail-shaped hotel. If you head left at the end of Passeig Joan de Borbó, you'll reach Barceloneta beach and Rebecca Horn's tower of rusty cubes, **Estel Ferit** (*Wounded Star*) that pays homage to the much-missed *xiringuitos*. The Passeig Marítim esplanade runs north from here, and is a popular hangout for in-line skaters, locals walking off their Sunday paella and outpatients from the enviably positioned Hospital del Mar. At its far end are Frank Gehry's shimmering copper **Fish**, the U-shaped biomedical research park and the twin skyscrapers of the exoskeletal Hotel Arts and the Torre Mapfre, which form an imposing gateway to the Port Olímpic.

Vila Olímpica

In the two years preceding the 1992 Olympics, the 'Olympic Village' was transformed from an industrial wasteland into a model neighbourhood, using a team of 30 prize-winning architects and based on Cerdà's Eixample grid (*see p122*). With accommodation for 15,000 athletes, parks, a metro stop, a multiplex cinema, four beaches and a leisure marina, it constituted a suburban idyll.

The result is a spacious and comfortable neighbourhood but the lack of cafés and shops leaves it devoid of Mediterranean charm and bustle, unless you count the weekend skaters and cyclists. Most social activity takes place in the seafront Port Olímpic, home to docked sailboats, restaurants, beaches, a large casino, and a waterfront strip of cheesy nightclubs and theme pubs catering to the stags and hens. Wide empty boulevards lend themselves well to large-scale sculpture and landmark pieces include a jagged pergola on Avda Icària by Enric Miralles and Carme Pinós, in memory of the ripped up industrial railway tracks, and Antoni Llena's abstract *David i Goliat* in the Parc de les Cascades.

Sightseeing

Montjuïc

The magic mountain.

Though it wasn't always thus, Montjuïc is the city's Xanadu, a pleasure ground of gardens, museums and galleries, perfect for a leafy stroll with majestic views over the city. Calatrava's Olympic needle and the other buildings of the 1992 Games are scattered over the landward side, while facing the sea is the lighthouse and the enormous cemetery. A reminder of the city's violent past lurks on top of it all, scarcely visible from below: the squat and heavily fortified Castell de Montjuïc, a place of dark memories for the city's older citizens.

The mists of time cover the etymology of Montjuïc, but an educated guess is that 'juïc' comes from the old Catalan word meaning Jewish. It was here that the medieval Jewish community buried their dead; some of the excavated headstones are now kept in the **Museu Militar** (*see p120*). Other headstones with their Hebraic inscriptions can be seen in the walls of the 16th-century Palau de Lloctinent, just to the east of the cathedral; following the expulsion of all Jews from Spain by Ferdinand and Isabella in 1492, the cemetery was plundered and the stone reused.

The 17th-century fortress was rebuilt in its current form after Philip V's troops broke the siege of Barcelona in 1714. From its vantage point overlooking the city, the central government was able to impose its will on the unruly populace until the death of Franco. From here, in 1842, the city was bombed to repress an uprising against the government's policies. Here many republicans were executed after the Civil War, including Generalitat President Lluís Companys, who was killed in 1940, victim No.2,761 of Franco's firing squads in Catalonia. However, the government of José Luis Zapatero ceded formal ownership of the castle to the city of Barcelona in 2004, and approved a law that allows for the pardon of Civil War victims.

The 1929 Exhibition (*see p22*) was the first attempt to turn the hill into a leisure area. Then in the 1940s thousands of immigrant workers from the rest of Spain settled on the hill. Some squatted in precarious shacks, while others rented brick and plaster sheds laid out along improvised streets that covered the hillside, then virtually treeless. These *barraques* thrived until the last few stragglers moved out in the 1970s. Energetic visitors can follow the same steep routes these residents once took home,

Fundació Joan Miró. See p118.

straight up C/Nou de la Rambla or C/Margarit in Poble Sec: the stairway at the top leaves you just a short distance from the **Fundació Joan Miró** (*see p118*) and the Olympic stadium area.

The long axis from **Plaça d'Espanya** is still the most popular access to the park, with the climb now eased by a sequence of open-air escalators. In the centre of Plaça d'Espanya itself is a monument designed by Josep Maria Jujol (who created the wrought-iron balconies on La Pedrera) with representations of the rivers Ebre, Tagus and Guadalquivir. The Las Arenas bullring, in a neo-Mudéjar style, is currently being remade into a shopping and leisure centre by architect Richard Rogers. On the other side of the square, two Venetian-style towers announce the beginning of the **Fira**, the trade show area, with pavilions from 1929 and newer buildings used for conventions and congresses. Further up, the rebuilt Mies van der Rohe **Pavelló Barcelona**, a modernist classic, contrasts sharply with the neo-classical

No more bull

With the disused bullring Las Arenas preparing for a future as a leisure complex, animal rights campaigners have been given hope of seeing an end to bullfighting in Barcelona. A long-running campaign in Catalonia to ban what is largely regarded as a Spanish sport reached a climax in 2004 when the council declared Barcelona an 'anti-bullfighting city'. The symbolic vote has been hailed as the first true representation of how *barcelonins* feel about bullfighting, and the result sparked a debate that begged the question: not how moral, but how *Catalan*, is bullfighting?

A loud minority of aficionados reacted to the vote with the 'tradition' argument. Historians have noted that the violent anti-clerical uprising in 1835 was triggered by a bad fight. Catalans in Ceret, over the French border, seal the relationship between their mother region and bullfighting by dancing the *sardana* on the death of the fifth bull, traditionally during the July fights. And the Catalan matador Mario Cabre, who took time out from the slaughter to write poetry and act, is quoted as having said: 'I am a bullfighter and a Catalan, which is equivalent to being a bullfighter two times over.'

Catalonia, however, also has a history of opposition to bullfighting, which has traditionally been under-reported. In particular, animal rights became an important issue within Barcelona's thriving anarchist movement before the Civil War. Vegetarianism had already been adopted by the most austere anarchists and, at the time of the General Strike, an increasing number of activists rejected meat along with fascism, committed to an ideology that cruelty and exploitation of man or beast had no place in an anarchist society. In *Homage to Catalonia*, George Orwell observed that during the Spanish Civil War, 'Even in Barcelona there were hardly any bullfights nowadays; for some reason all the best matadors were fascists.'

At Las Arenas, the last bull met its fate in the 1970s. The ubiquitous Sir Richard Rogers is overseeing the mammoth transformation project, to be completed in 2006, which will give the building a facelift while restoring the existing bullring and filling it with shops and offices. The vision encompasses a 'piazza in the sky', a giant roof terrace that will allow for alfresco events and offer panoramic views over Barcelona.

structures nearby. Across the street, Puig i Cadafalch's Modernista factory has been converted into the excellent **CaixaForum** cultural centre (*see below*). Further up the hill is the bizarre **Poble Espanyol** (*see p121*), a model village also designed in 1929 especially to showcase Spanish crafts and architecture.

Presiding over it all is the bombastic **Palau Nacional**, originally built as a 'temporary exhibition' for the expo, and now home to the **Museu Nacional d'Art de Catalunya** (*see p119*), housing Catalan art from the last millennium and recently reopened after a lengthy refurbishment. At night, the entire setting is illuminated by a water-and-light spectacular, the **Font Màgica**, still operating with its complex original mechanisms (*see p118*). Other nearby buildings erected for the 1929 expo have been converted into the **Museu d'Arqueologia de Catalunya** (*see p118*) and the **Ciutat del Teatre** (theatre city) complex. From the same period are the nearby **Teatre Grec** (Greek theatre), used for summer concerts during the Grec festival, and the beautifully restored **Jardins Laribal**, designed by French landscape architect JCN Forestier. At the top of this garden is the **Font del Gat** information centre. The **Museu Etnològic**, a typical 1970s construction, sits just below it (*see p119*).

If walking isn't your thing, another way up the hill is via the **funicular railway**, integrated with the city's metro system, leaving from the Paral·lel station. The **Telefèric** cable car, which usually links this station to the **castle**, is being extended down to the port and will be closed until the end of 2006. A more circuitous way up is by the **Transbordador Aeri** cable car across the harbour to **Miramar**. But bear in mind that at Miramar work on a five-star hotel has dug up the road in front and turned a peaceful spot with an unmatchable view across the city into a temporary building site.

Montjuïc's **Anella Olímpica** (Olympic Ring) is a convergence of diverse constructions all laid out for the 1992 Olympic Games. The **Estadi Olímpic** (home to the city's 'second' football team, Espanyol, until they move to Cornellà in 2006), although entirely new, was built within the façade of a 1929 stadium by a design team led by Federico Correa and Alfonso Milà. The horse sculptures are copies of the originals by Pau Gargallo. Next to it is the most original and attractive of the Olympic facilities, Arata Isozaki's **Palau Sant Jordi** indoor arena, whose undulating façade evoking Gaudí, and a high-tech interior featuring a transparent roof. It now regularly serves as a venue for concerts and other events. In the hard, white *plaça* in front rises Santiago Calatrava's remarkable, Brancusi-inspired **communications tower**.

Across the square is the city's best swimming pool, the **Piscina Bernat Picornell** (*see also p276*), while further down is the INEFC physical education institute, by architect Ricard Bofill. Walk across the road and you look over a cliff on to a rugby pitch and an equestrian area, where children can take pony rides. The cliff itself is a favourite hangout for rock-climbers.

The many parks and gardens include the **Jardins Mossèn Costa i Llobera** (*see p118*), which abound in tropical plants, but particularly cacti, just below Miramar, on the steep flank nearest the port. Not far above are the **Jardins del Mirador**, from where there is a spectacular view over the harbour. These gardens are also the starting point for a new path for pedestrians and cyclists, running precariously below the castle, and leading to a magical outdoor café, **La Caseta del Migdia** (*see p185*). One of the newest parks is the nearby **Jardins de Joan Brossa**, featuring humorous, hands-on contraptions where children can manipulate water-courses and do creative adventure sports. Walk down towards the funicular station and you will reach the **Jardins Cinto Verdaguer**, with a quiet pond, water lilies and grassy slopes. All these gardens play an adjunct role to the creative biospheres of the **Jardí Botànic**, just above the Olympic stadium, exquisitely designed and finally maturing into an important scientific collection (*see p118*).

CaixaForum

Casaramona, Avda Marquès de Comillas 6-8 (93 476 86 00/www.fundacio.lacaixa.es). Metro Espanya. **Open** 10am-8pm Tue-Sun. **Admission** free. **Credit** (shop only) AmEx, DC, MC, V. **Map** p341 A5.

Puig i Cadafalch designed the creative brickwork of this former mattress factory in 1911. It spent most of the last century in a sorry state, acting briefly as a police barracks and then falling into dereliction. Fundació La Caixa, the charitable arm of Catalonia's largest savings bank, bought it and gave it a huge rebuild. The brick factory was supported while the ground below was excavated to house an entrance plaza by Arata Isozaki (who designed the Palau Sant Jordi on the other side of the hill), a Sol LeWitt mural, a 350-seat auditorium, bookshop and library. In addition to the smaller permanent contemporary art collection, upstairs there are three impressive spaces for temporary exhibitions.

To celebrate the foundation's 20th anniversary in 2005, there will be an exhibition of previously unshown works (*A Vision of the Future*) from February to May. From March to June *Turner and Venice* will display more than 100 of the artist's paintings from Tate Britain, then from June to September, *The Bauhaus Has Fun* looks at parties and everyday life in the school, bringing together 150 photographers and drawings by some of its most famous alumni, Klee and Kandinsky among them.

Cementiri del Sud-oest

C/Mare de Déu de Port, 54-58 (93 484 17 00).
Bus 38. **Open** 8am-6pm daily. **Admission** free.
This enormous necropolis, perched at the side of the motorway out of town, serves as a daily reminder to commuters of their own mortality. It has housed the city's dead since 1883, originally placing them in four sections: one for Catholics, one for Protestants, one for non-Christians and a fourth for abortions. It now stretches over the entire south-west corner of the mountain, with family tombs stacked five or six storeys high. Many, especially those belonging to the gypsy community, are a riot of colour and flowers. The Fossar de la Pedrera memorial park remembers those fallen from the International Brigades and the Catalan martyrs from the Civil War. There is also a Holocaust memorial, and a pantheon to former Generalitat President Lluís Companys.

Font Màgica de Montjuïc

Plaça d'Espanya (93 316 10 00/www.bcn.es/fonts).
Metro Espanya. **Fountain** *May-Sept* 8pm-midnight Thur-Sun; music every 30mins 9.30pm-midnight. *Oct-Apr* 7-9pm Fri, Sat; music every 30mins 7-9pm. **Map** p341 A5.
Still using its original art deco waterworks, the 'magic fountain' works its wonders with 3,600 pieces of tubing and over 4,500 light bulbs. Summer evenings after nightfall see the multiple founts swell and dance to various hits ranging from Sting to the *1812 Overture*, showing off its kaleidoscope of pastel colours, while searchlights play in a giant fan pattern over the palace dome.

Fundació Joan Miró

Parc de Montjuïc (93 329 19 08/www.bcn.fjmiro.es).
Metro Paral·lel, then Funicular de Montjuïc/61 bus.
Open *July-Sept* 10am-8pm Tue, Wed, Fri, Sat; 10am-9.30pm Thur; 10am-2.30pm Sun. *Oct-June* 10am-7pm Tue, Wed, Fri, Sat; 10am-9.30pm Thur; 10am-2.30pm Sun. **Guided tours** 11.30pm Sat, Sun. **Admission** *All exhibitions* €7.20; €5 concessions. *Temporary exhibitions* €4; €3 concessions. Free under-14s.
Credit MC, V. **Map** p341 B6.
Josep Lluís Sert, who spent the years of the dictatorship as Dean of Architecture at Harvard University, designed one of the world's great museum buildings on his return. Approachable, light and airy, these white walls and arches house a collection of more than 225 paintings, 150 sculptures and all of Miró's graphic work, plus some 5,000 drawings. The permanent collection, highlighting Miró's trademark use of primary colours and simplified organic forms symbolising stars, the moon, birds and women, occupies the second half of the space. On the way to the sculpture gallery is Alexander Calder's lovely reconstructed *Mercury Fountain*, originally seen at the Spanish Republic's Pavilion at the 1937 Paris Fair. In other works, Miró is shown as a cubist (*Street in Pedralbes*, 1917), naïve (*Portrait of a Young Girl*, 1919) or surrealist (*Man and Woman in Front of a Pile of Excrement*, 1935). Downstairs are works donated to the museum by 20th-century artists. In the upper galleries large, black-outlined paintings from the final period precede a room of works with political themes.

In 2005 temporary shows include a retrospective of Sert's work and an exhibition of contemporary Japanese artists. The Espai 13 in the basement features young contemporary artists. Outside is a pleasant sculpture garden with fine work by some contemporary Catalan artists.

Galeria Olímpica

Estadi Olímpic, Parc de Montjuïc (93 426 06 60/ www.fundaciobarcelonaolimpica.es). Metro Espanya/bus all routes to Plaça d'Espanya.
Open *Apr-Sept* 10am-2pm, 4-7pm Mon-Fri. *Oct-Mar* (by appointment) 10am-1pm, 4-6pm Mon-Fri. **Admission** €2.70; €2.40-€1.50 concessions. **Credit** AmEx, MC, V. **Map** p341 A6.
Of fairly limited interest, this is a hotchpotch of imagery and paraphernalia commemorating the 1992 Olympics, including costumes from the opening ceremony and the ubiquitous mascot Cobi.

Jardí Botànic

C/Doctor Font i Quer (93 426 49 35). Metro Espanya. **Open** *Apr-June, Sept* 10am-5pm Mon-Fri; 10am-8pm Sat, Sun. *July, Aug* 10am-8pm daily. *Oct-Mar* 10am-5pm daily. **Admission** €4; €2 concessions; free under-16s. Free last Sun of mth. **No credit cards.** **Map** p341 A6-7.
This botanic garden was opened in 1999, with the idea of collecting plants from seven global regions with a climate similar to that of the Western Mediterranean. The result is highly impressive. Everything about the futuristic design, from the angular concrete pathways to the raw sheet steel banking (and including even the design of the bins), is the complete antithesis of the more naturalistic, Jekyll-inspired gardens of England. It is meticulously kept, with all plants being tagged in Latin, Catalan, Spanish and English along with their date of planting, and has the added advantage of wonderful views across the city. There is a small space housing occasional temporary exhibitions.

Jardins Mossèn Costa i Llobera

Ctra de Miramar 1. Metro Drassanes or Paral·lel.
Open 10am-sunset daily. **Admission** free.
Map p341 B7.
The port side of Montjuïc is protected from the cold north wind, creating a microclimate two degrees warmer than the rest of the city, which is perfect for 800 species of the world's cactus. It is said to be the most complete collection of its type in Europe. Along with the botanic curiosities, there is a Josep Viladomat bronze of a young girl making lace, which is four times life-size.

Museu d'Arqueologia de Catalunya

Passeig de Santa Madrona 39-41 (93 423 21 49/56 01/www.mac.es). Metro Poble Sec. **Open** 9.30am-7pm Tue-Sat; 10am-2.30pm Sun. **Admission** €2.40; €1.80 concessions; free under-16s. **Credit** (shop only) MC, V. **Map** p341 B6.

Jardí Botanic.
See p118.

The time frame for this archaeological collection starts with the Palaeolithic period, and there are relics of Greek, Punic, Roman and Visigoth colonisers, up to the early Middle Ages. A massive Roman sarcophagus is carved with scenes of the rape of Persephone, and an immense statue of Aesculapius, the god of medicine, towers over one room. A few galleries are dedicated to the Mallorcan Talayotic cave culture, and there is a very good display on the Iberians, the pre-Hellenic, pre-Roman inhabitants of south-eastern Spain. An Iberian skull with a nail driven through it effectively demonstrates a typical method of execution from that time. The display ends with the marvellous, jewel-studded headpiece of a Visigoth king. One of the best-loved pieces, inevitably, is an alarmingly erect Priapus, found during building work in Sants in 1848 and kept under wraps 'for moral reasons' until 1986.

Museu Etnològic

Passeig de Santa Madrona s/n (93 424 68 07/ www.museuetnologic.bcn.es). Metro Poble Sec. **Open** 10am-7pm Tue, Thur; 10am-2pm Wed, Fri-Sun. **Admission** €3; €1.50 concessions; free under-16s, over-65s. **No credit cards**. **Map** p341 A6.

The ethnology museum has recently been renovated and expanded, in order to simultaneously display more pieces from its vast collections of artefacts. The basement storage room has now been spruced up and opened to the public, and makes for an enjoyable wander through glass-fronted cabinets, stuffed with all manner of objects from all over the world.

Of the displays upstairs, most outstanding are the Moroccan, Japanese and Philippine holdings, though there are also some interesting pre-Columbian finds. The attempts to arrange the pieces in thematically interesting ways, however, are not altogether successful, and a potentially fascinating exhibition entitled 'Taboos' transpires to be a rather limp look at nudity in different cultures.

MNAC (Museu Nacional d'Art de Catalunya)

Palau Nacional, Parc de Montjuïc (93 622 03 76/ www.mnac.es). Metro Espanya. **Open** 10am-7pm Tue-Sat; 10am-2.30pm Sun. **Admission** *Permanent exhibitions* €8.50; €5.95 concessions. *Temporary exhibitions* varies. *Combined entrance with Poble Espanyol* €10.40. Free under-7s. Free 1st Thur of mth. **Credit** MC, V. **Map** p341 A6.

After a renovation that overran even the most pessimistic estimates of time and expense, the MNAC has reopened with another floor open to the public, doubling its size. It has now absorbed that part of the Thyssen-Bornemisza collection that was previously kept in the convent in Pedralbes, along with the mainly Modernista holdings from the former Museum of Modern Art in Ciutadella park, and now houses a dizzying overview of Catalan art from the 12th to 20th centuries, with a fine photography section, coins and the bequest of Francesc Cambó.

The highlight of the museum, however, is still the Romanesque collection. As art historians realised that scores of solitary tenth-century churches in the

Poble Espanyol. *See p121.*

Pyrenees were falling into ruin – and with them were going extraordinary Romanesque mural paintings that had served to instruct doubting villagers in the basics of the faith – the laborious task was begun of removing murals intact from church apses. The display here features 21 mural sections in loose chronological order. The artworks are set into freestanding wood supports or in reconstructed church interiors. One highlight is the tremendous *Crist de Taüll*, from the 12th-century church of Sant Climent de Taüll. Even 'graffiti' scratchings (probably by monks) of animals, crosses and labyrinths have been preserved.

The Gothic collection is also excellent, and starts with some late 13th-century frescoes that were discovered in 1961 and 1997 when two palaces in the city were being renovated. There are carvings and paintings from Catalonia churches, including works of the indisputable Catalan masters of the Golden Age, Bernat Martorell and Jaume Huguet. The highlight of the Thyssen collection is Fra Angelico's *Madonna of Humility* (c1430s), while the Cambó bequest contains some stunning old masters – works by Titian, Rubens and El Greco among them.

Museu Militar

Castell de Montjuïc, Ctra de Montjuïc 66 (93 329 86 13). Metro Paral·lel, then funicular & cable car. **Open** *Apr-Oct* 9.30am-8pm Tue-Sun. *Nov-Mar* 9.30am-6pm Tue-Fri; 9.30am-7pm Sat, Sun. **Admission** €2.50; €1-€1.25 concessions; free under-7s. **No credit cards. Map** p341 B7.

The Military Museum occupies the 17th-century fortress overlooking the city, which was used to bombard rather than protect Barcelona in past conflicts and as a prison and place of execution, the castle has strong repressive associations. The holdings here include armour, swords and lances; muskets (beautiful Moroccan *moukhala*), rifles and pistols; and menacing crossbows. Other highlights include 23,000 lead soldiers representing a Spanish division of the 1920s. Oddly, a display of Jewish tombstones from the mountain's desecrated medieval cemetery is the only direct reminder of death within its thick walls. There are plans to turn this into a Peace Museum in the future.

Pavelló Mies van der Rohe

Avda Marquès de Comillas (93 423 40 16/ www.miesbcn.com). Metro Espanya. **Open** 10am-8pm daily. **Admission** €3.50; €2 concessions; free under-18s. **Credit** (shop only) MC, V. **Map** p341 A5.

Mies van der Rohe built the Pavelló Alemany (German Pavilion) for the 1929 Exhibition not as a gallery, but as a simple reception space, sparsely furnished by his trademark 'Barcelona Chair'. The pavilion was a founding monument of modern rationalist architecture, with its flowing floor plan and a revolutionary use of materials. Though the original was demolished after the Exhibition, a fine replica was built on the same site in 1986, the simplicity of its design setting off the warm tones of the marble and expressive Georg Kolbe sculpture in the pond.

Poble Espanyol

Avda Marquès de Comillas (93 325 78 66/ www.poble-espanyol.com). Metro Espanya. **Open** 9am-8pm Mon; 9am-2am Tue-Thur; 9am-4am Fri, Sat; 9am-midnight Sun. **Admission** €7.50; €4-€5 concessions; €14 family ticket; free under-7s. **Credit** AmEx, MC, V. **Map** p341 A5.

Another legacy of the 1929 Exhibition, this time an enclosed area showing examples of traditional architecture from every region in Spain. A Castilian square leads to an Andalucían church, then on to village houses from Aragon, and so on. There are numerous bars and restaurants (including vegetarian), and 60-plus shops. Many are workshops in which craftspeople make and sell Spanish folk artefacts, such as ceramics, embroidery, fans, metalwork and candles. Some of the work is quite attractive, some tacky, and prices are generally high. Outside, street performers recreate bits of Catalan and Spanish folklore; there are children's shows and the 'Barcelona Experience', an audiovisual presentation (available in English). The Poble is unmistakably aimed at tourists, but it has been working to raise its cultural profile, as with the Fundació Fran Daurel collection of contemporary art and the recent opening of a quality gallery of Iberian arts and crafts.

Telefèric de Montjuïc

Estació Funicular, Avda Miramar (93 443 08 59/ www.tmd.net). Metro Paral·lel, then funicular. **Map** p341 B6.

The Telefèric, and its four-person cable cars, is closed for renovations until summer 2006, after which it will extend down to the port. In the meantime there is a replacement bus service (11am-7.15pm daily, every 15mins) running from the funicular to the castle.

Tren Montjuïc

Plaça d'Espanya (information 93 415 60 20). Metro Espanya. **Open** *Apr-mid June, 1st 2wks Sept* 10am-8.30pm Sat, Sun. *Mid June-Aug* 10am-8pm daily. Closed mid Sept-Mar. **Frequency** every 30mins daily. **Tickets** *All-day* €3.20; €2-€2.55 concessions. **No credit cards. Map** p341 A/B5.

Not a train but an open trolley pulled by a truck that goes up Montjuïc to Miramar, passing all the hilltop sights along the way.

Poble Sec & Paral·lel

Poble Sec, the name of the neighbourhood between Montjuïc and the Avda Paral·lel, means 'dry village', which is explained by the fact that it was 1894 before the thousands of poor workers or the *barri* who lived on the flanks of the hill celebrated the installation of the area's first water fountain (which is still standing in C/Margarit).

The name Avda Paral·lel derives from the fact that it coincides exactly with 41° 44' latitude north, one of Ildefons Cerdà's more

eccentric conceits. The avenue was the prime centre of Barcelona nightlife – often called the city's 'Montmartre' – in the first half of the 20th century, and was full of theatres, nightclubs and music halls. A statue on the corner with C/Nou de la Rambla commemorates Raquel Meller, a legendary star of the street who went on to equal celebrity around the world. She now stands outside Barcelona's notorious live-porn venue, the Bagdad. Apart from this, most of its cabarets have disappeared, although there are still theatres and cinemas along the Paral·lel. A real end of an era came in 1997 when El Molino, the most celebrated of the avenue's traditional, vulgar old music halls, suddenly shut up shop. It seemed to symbolise the change that had come to the neighbourhood.

Today, Poble Sec is a friendly, working class area of quiet, relaxed streets and leafy squares. On the stretch of the Paral·lel opposite the city walls three tall chimneys stand amid modern office blocks. They are all that remain of the Anglo-Canadian-owned power station known locally as *La Canadença* ('The Canadian'). This was the centre of the city's largest general strike, in 1919. Beside the chimneys an open space has been created and dubbed the **Parc de les Tres Xemeneies** (Park of the Three Chimneys). It is now particularly popular with skateboarders and Pakistani expat cricketers.

Towards the Paral·lel are some distinguished Modernista buildings, which local legend has maintained were built for *artistas* from the nude cabarets by their rich sugar daddies. At C/Tapioles 12 is a beautiful, narrow wooden Modernista door with particularly lovely writhing ironwork, while at C/Elkano 4 is **La Casa de les Rajoles**, which is known for its peculiar mosaic façade. Incongruous in such a central area is the small neighbourhood of single family dwellings with quaint gardens, off the upper reaches of C/Margarit, which is worth seeing solely for the juxtaposition.

Refugi Antiaeri del Poble Sec

C/Nou de la Rambla 175 (93 319 02 22). Metro Paral·lel. **Open** (guided tour & by appointment only) 11am. 1st Sat of mth. *Call to book* 10am-2pm Mon-Fri; 4-6pm Tue, Thur. **Admission** €3.20; free under-7s. **Meeting place** Biblioteca Francesc Boix, C/Blai 34. **Map** p341 B6.

About 1,500 Barcelona civilians were killed during the vicious air bombings of the Civil War, a fact that the government long silenced. As Poble Sec particularly suffered the effects of bombing, a large air-raid shelter was built partially into the mountain at the top of C/Nou de la Rambla; one of some 1,200 in the entire city. Recently rediscovered, and converted into a museum, it is worth a visit. The guided tour takes 90 minutes.

The Eixample

The discreet charm of the bourgeois *barrio*.

Plaça Catalunya, the hub of the city, links the old medieval quarter to the vast, grid-patterned Eixample ('enlargement'). Largely built in the late 19th century, it's a gold mine of elegant palaces and swanky shops, and the spiritual centre of bourgeois Barcelona. This huge area is bisected by the **Passeig de Gràcia**, one of Europe's most sophisticated shopping streets. It's the highlight of the **Quadrat D'Or** (Golden District), a square mile between C/Muntaner and C/Roger de Flor that contains 150 protected buildings, many of them Modernista gems. It's just a pity about the traffic, which courses through the area like blood through veins.

The Eixample was Europe's first expansive work of urban planning, necessitated by the chronic overcrowding of old Barcelona, which by the 1850s had become rife with cholera and crime, hemmed in by its much-hated city walls. It was eventually decided that the walls must come down, whereupon the Ajuntament held a competition to build an ambitious new urban zone in the open land outside them. It was won by municipal architect Antoni Rovira i Trias, whose popular fan-shaped design can be seen at the foot of the statue of him in the Gràcia *plaça* that bears his name. The Madrid government, however, vetoed the plan, instead choosing the work of Ildefons Cerdà, a military engineer.

Cerdà's plan, reflecting the rationalist mindset of the era, was for a grid of uniform blocks stretching from Montjuïc to the Besòs river, criss-crossed by two diagonal highways, Avda Diagonal and Avda de la Meridiana, and meeting at Plaça de les Glòries, which was to become the new hub of the modernised city. The ideas were utopian: each block was to be built on only two sides, just two or three storeys high, and the remainder of the space was to contain gardens, their leafy extremes joining at the crossroads and forming a quarter of a bigger park. Of course, when it came to the practical business of filling the grid (which never became as extensive as planned), many of the engineer's stipulations were ignored by developers. A concrete orchard of gardenless, fortress-like, six- or seven-storey blocks grew up instead.

Fortunately, the period of construction coincided with Barcelona's golden age of architecture: the city's flourishing bourgeoisie employed architects such as Gaudí, Puig i Cadafalch and Domènech i Muntaner to build them ever more elegant and daring townhouses in an orgy of avant-garde one-upmanship. The result is extraordinary but maddeningly difficult to negotiate on foot; the lack of open spaces and over-abundance of traffic lights can, at times, give you the uncanny feeling that you're caught up inside an enormous industrial waffle iron. The Ajuntament, however, is gradually attempting to make the area more liveable: in 1985, it set up the ProEixample, a project that aims to claim back some of the courtyards proposed in Cerdà's plans so that everybody living in the area should be able to find an open space within 200 metres (650 feet) of their home. Two of the better examples are the palm-fringed mini beach around the **Torre de les Aigües** water tower (C/Llúria 56) and the patio at **Passatge Permanyer** (C/Pau Claris 120).

The overland railway that once ran down C/Balmes has traditionally been the dividing line through the middle of the Eixample. The fashionable **Dreta** ('Right') contains the most distinguished Modernista architecture, the main museums and the shopping avenues. The **Esquerra** ('Left'), meanwhile, was built slightly later; it contains some great markets and some less well known Modernista sights.

The Dreta

Trees, ceramic benches and idle ramblers make the **Passeig de Gràcia** feel like a calmer Champs Elysées. The Eixample's central artery, it's notable for its magnificent wrought-iron **lamp-posts** by Pere Falqués and for its **pavement**, hexagonal slabs decorated with intertwining nautilus shells and starfish. First designed for the patio of Gaudí's **Casa Batlló** (*see p123*), they were repeated in his aquatic-looking apartment block **La Pedrera** (*see p129*) before covering the whole boulevard.

The Passeig de Gràcia has always been the Eixample's most desirable address, and is thus where you'll find Modernisme's most flamboyant townhouses. For a primer, head to the block known as **Manzana de Discòrdia**, which boasts buildings designed by the era's three great architects. Its name is a pun on *manzana*, which in Spanish means both 'block' and 'apple', and alludes to the fatal choice of Paris when judging which of a group of divine beauties would win the golden Apple of Discord.

If the volume of camera-toting admirers is anything to go by, the fairest of these Modernista lovelies is undoubtedly Gaudí's **Casa Batlló**, permanently illuminated by flashbulbs. The runners-up are Domènech i Montaner's **Casa Lleó Morera**, a decadently melting wedding cake (partially defaced during the architecturally delinquent Franco era) on the corner of C/Consell de Cent at No.35, and Puig i Cadafalch's **Casa Amatller** (No.41). Built for a chocolate baron, the latter has a stepped Flemish pediment covered in shiny ceramics that look good enough to eat, and a gallery of medieval grotesques sculpted by Eusebi Arnau. It also houses the **Centre de Modernisme**, which organises the Ruta del Modernisme (*see p85*).

Other buildings on the Passeig de Gràcia hit parade also impress. The **Casa Casas** (No.96) was once home to Ramon Casas, one of the city's greatest painters, and now houses design emporium Vinçon. The first floor of the building has a Modernista interior; there's also a patio overlooking La Pedrera's rear façade. In addition, Enric Sagnier's neo-Gothic **Cases Pons i Pascual** (Nos.2-4) is worth a look, while the **Casa Vídua Marfà** (No.66) has one of the most breathtakingly sumptuous entrance halls in the Eixample.

The other great building of the Modernisme movement is, of course, the towering mass of the **Sagrada Familia** (*see p129*). Whether you love it or hate it, and George Orwell called it 'one of the most hideous buildings in the world', it has become the city's emblem and *sine qua non* of Barcelona tourist itineraries. A less famous masterpiece bookends the northerly extreme of the Avda Gaudí in the shape of Domènech i Montaner's **Hospital de Sant Pau**. A few blocks further south, there's more welcome space in the **Parc de l'Estació del Nord** and, over C/Marina, one of Barcelona's weirdest museums, the creepy **Museu de Carrosses Fúnebres** (*see p127*).

The streets above the Diagonal are mainly residential and mostly built after 1910, but with some striking Modernista buildings such as Puig i Cadafalch's 1901 **Palau Macaya** at Passeig de Sant Joan 108. Other buildings of interest include the charming, tiled **Mercat de la Concepció** on C/Aragó, designed by Rovira i Trias. Over to the right is the egg-topped **Plaça de Braus Monumental**, but the city's last active bullring is now mainly frequented by tour buses from the Costa Brava; out of season, it hosts alternative animal abuse in the form of tatty travelling circuses. Just off the main drag is what is considered to be Modernisme's first ever building, designed by Domènech i Muntaner, now housing the **Fundació Antoni**

Gaudí's **Casa Batlló**.

Tàpies. The area is rich in museums: over the other side, is the **Museu Egipci de Barcelona**, next door to the eclectic art collection in the **Fundació Francisco Godia**.

Casa Batlló

Passeig de Gràcia 43 (93 216 03 06/www.casabatllo. es). Metro Passeig de Gràcia. **Open** 9am-8pm daily. **Admission** *Apartment only* €10; €8 concessions; free under-6s. *Complete visit* €16; €12.80 concessions; free under-6s. **Credit** DC, MC, V. **Map** p338 D4.
There's no more telling example of Gaudí's pre-eminence over his Modernista contemporaries than the Casa Batlló, sitting in the same block as masterworks by his two closest rivals, Puig i Cadafalch

Walk on Modernisme

its spiky turrets and gables. Look out for the individual entrances and staircases built for each of the family's three daughters.

Turn down C/Girona and then right on to C/Mallorca to see Barenys i Gambús' fantasy **Casa Dolors Xiró** at No.302, followed by two Domènech i Montaner masterpieces: the **Casa Josep Thomas** (No.291), now home to the BD Design emporium (see p192), and the **Palau Ramón de Montaner** (No.278), which now houses government offices.

Double back a few steps and turn downhill on to C/Roger de Llúria. On the corner at No.80 is Fossas i Martinez's spike-topped **Casa Villanueva** and, just opposite at No.82, striking columns of stained-glass windows decorate Granell i Manresa's **Casa Jaume Forn**. Just a few steps further down C/Roger de Llúria, the **Queviures Murrià** grocery (No.85) retains original decoration by painter Ramón Casas and, on the right at No.74, is the lovely stained-glass and floral decoration of the **Farmàcia Argelaguet**, one of many Modernista pharmacies in the area.

Retrace your steps up to the corner again, and turn right onto C/València. Continue along for three blocks, and at No.339 is a stunning corner building by Gallissà i Soqué: the **Casa Manuel Llopis i Bofill**. The façade is a blend of red brick and white sgraffito to Gaudí's collaborator, Josep Maria Jujol, while the neo-Mudéjar turrets, ceramics and keyhole shapes take their inspiration from the Alhambra.

Backtrack a block and turn left on C/Girona. At No.86 is the **Casa Isabel Pomar**, Rubió i Bellver's eccentric sliver of a building that squeezes in a neo-Gothic pinnacle, lively red brickwork and a staggered gallery window on the first floor. This contrasts with the spacious feel of Viñolas i Llosas' **Casa Jacinta Ruiz** (No.54). Glass galleries are a characteristic feature of Modernista houses, but here the jutting windows form the pivot for the design and give a three-dimensional effect. Further

Duration: 1 hour 30 minutes.

The tour begins with the splendid **Casa Comalat** by Valeri i Pupurull, which has the unusual distinction of two façades. The front (Avda Diagonal 442) has 12 voluptuously curvy stone balconies complete with whiplash wrought-iron railings, while the more radical back façade (C/Còrsega 316) is a colourful harlequin effect with curiously bulging green-shuttered balconies. Almost opposite on Avda Diagonal is Puig i Cadafalch's sombre **Palau Baró de Quadras** (No.373) and his **Casa Terrades** (Nos.416-20), known colloquially as La Casa de les Punxes ('House of Spikes') for

and Domènech i Muntaner. Opinions differ on what the building's remarkable façade represents, most particularly its polychrome shimmering walls, its sinister skeletal balconies and its humpbacked scaley roof. Some say it's the spirit of carnival, others a Costa Brava cove. However, the most popular theory, which takes into account the architect's patriotic feelings, is that it depicts Sant Jordi and the dragon: the cross on top is the knight's lance, the

roof is the back of the beast, and the balconies below are the skulls and bones of its hapless victims. The building was constructed for textile tycoon Josep Batlló between 1902 and 1906, and the chance to explore inside (at a cost) offers the best opportunity of understanding how Gaudí, sometimes considered the lord of the bombastic and overblown, was really the master of tiny details, from the ingenious ventilation in the doors to the amazing natural light down, turn right on Gran Via, to another extravagant Modernista pharmacy, **Farmàcia Vilardell**, and Salvat i Espasa's elegant **Casa Ramon Oller** (No.658).

From there, turn left down C/Pau Claris and left again on to C/Casp. At No.22, **Casa Llorenç Camprubí**, Ruiz i Casamitjana's intricate stonework is a delight, but the real treasure lies a little further along at No.48. Gaudí's **Casa Calvet** may look somewhat conventional for the master, but closer study reveals characteristic touches: the columns framing the door and gallery allude to the bobbins used in the owner's textile factory, while the intricate wrought iron depicts a mass of funghi surrounded by stone flowers. The corbel underneath the gallery interweaves the coat of arms of Catalonia with Calvet's

La Casa de les Punxes.

initial 'C'. Should you peek inside at the excellent restaurant (*see p161*), lift the massive crucifix door-knockers to see the squashed bugs (a symbol of evil) beneath.

Turn right down C/Girona on to C/Ausiàs Marc, one of the most notable streets of the Quadrat d'Or. At Nos.37-9 are the **Cases Tomàs Roger** by prominent Modernista architect, Enric Sagnier, combining graceful arches with beautifully restored sgraffito. At No.31 is the **Farmàcia Nordbeck**, with a dark wood and stained-glass exterior. The last stop before reaching Plaça Urquinaona is the **Casa Manuel Felip** (No.20), designed by a little-known architect, Fernández i Janot, with sumptuous stonework and slender galleries connecting the first two floors.

reflecting off the azure walls of the inner courtyard and the way in which the brass window handles are curved so as to fit precisely the shape of a hand. For the Year of Gaudí in 2003, an apartment within was opened to the public, as, more recently, were the attic and roof terrace: the whitewashed arched rooms of the top floor, originally used for washing and hanging clothes, are among the master's most atmospheric spaces.

Fundació Antoni Tàpies

C/Aragó 255 (93 487 03 15/www.fundaciotapies. org). Metro Passeig de Gràcia. **Open** 10am-8pm Tue-Sun. **Admission** €4.20; €2.10 concessions; free under-16s. **Credit** (over €6) MC, V. **Map** p338 D4. Antoni Tàpies, Barcelona's most celebrated living artist, set up the Tàpies Foundation in this, the former Muntaner i Simon publishing house in 1984, dedicating it to the study and appreciation of

Two more good reasons to spend some tim
in Barcelona...

Learn to speak Spanish or learn
to teach English in one of Spain's longes
established and most prestigious language school

contemporary art. He promptly crowned the building with a glorious tangle of aluminium piping and ragged metal netting (*Núvol i Cadira*, or *Cloud and Chair*), a typically contentious act by an artist whose work, a selection of which is on permanent display on the top floor of the gallery, has caused controversy since he burst on the scene in the '60s. 'Give the organic its rights,' he proclaimed, and thus devoted his time to making the seemingly insignificant significant, using materials such as mud, string, rags and cardboard to build his rarely pretty but always striking works. The lower two floors of the building are dedicated to temporary exhibitions of contemporary artists: Fernando Bryce will show from April to July 2005, and Pedro G Romero from September to November.

Fundació Francisco Godia

C/Valencia 284 pral (93 272 31 80/www.fundacion fgodia.org). Metro Passeig de Gràcia. **Open** 10am-8pm Mon, Wed-Sun. Closed Aug. **Admission** €4.50; €2.10 concessions; free under-5s. *Combined ticket with Museu Egipci* €8.50; €6.50 concessions. **Credit** (shop only) MC, V. **Map** p338 D4.

Godia's first love was motor-racing: he was a Formula 1 driver for Maserati in the 1950s. His second, though, was art, which is how this private museum has come to house an interesting selection of medieval religious art, historic Spanish ceramics and modern painting. Highlights include Alejo de Vahía's medieval *Pietà* and a baroque masterpiece by Lucio Giordano, along with some outstanding Romanesque sculptures, and 19th-century oil paintings by Joaquín Sorolla and Ramón Casas. The modern collection has works by Miró, Julio González, Tàpies and Manolo Hugué. Temporary exhibitions in 2005 include a display of Modernista drawings (March to June) and a collection of privately owned Catalan ceramics (October to January 2006).

Hospital de la Santa Creu i Sant Pau

C/Sant Antoni Maria Claret 167 (93 291 90 00/ www.santpau.es). Metro Hospital de Sant Pau. **Map** p339 F4.

White-coated doctors mingle with recovering patients and camera-wielding tourists in the green and pleasant grounds of Domènech i Muntaner's 'garden city' of a hospital, a collection of 18 pavilions abundantly adorned with the medieval flourishes that characterise the architect's style. The hospital, composed of 18 pavilions and connected by an underground tunnel system, spreads over nine blocks in the north-east corner of the Eixample, a short walk from the madding crowds at the Sagrada Familia. It is set at a 45° angle from the rest of Ildefons Cerdà's grid system, so as to catch more sun: Domènech i Muntaner built the hospital very much with its patients in mind, convinced that aesthetic harmony and pleasant surroundings were good for the health. Unfortunately, the old buildings don't entirely suit the exigencies of modern medicine: by 2006, all patient care will be phased out and

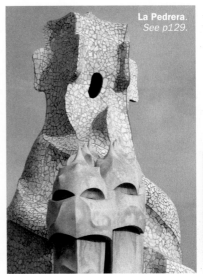

La Pedrera.
See p129.

See p129.

moved to the Nou Sant Pau, a recently inaugurated blocky white monstrosity of a building on the north side of the hospital grounds, leaving the old complex to be used entirely for educational and research purposes. The public has free access to the grounds; guided tours (€4.20) are offered on Saturdays and Sundays between 10am and 2pm, or can be arranged during the week by calling 93 488 20 78.

Museu de Carrosses Fúnebres

C/Sancho de Avila 2 (93 484 17 10). Metro Marina. **Open** 10am-1pm, 4-6pm Mon-Fri; 10am-1pm Sat, Sun (wknds call to check). **Admission** free. **Map** p343 F5.

Ask at the reception desk of the Ajuntament's funeral service and, eventually, a security guard will take you down to a perfectly silent and splendidly shuddersome basement housing the world's biggest collection of funeral carriages and hearses dating from the 18th century to the 1950s. There are ornate baroque carriages and more functional Landaus and Berlins, and a rather wonderful '50s silver Buick. The white carriages were designed for children and virgins, and there's a windowless black-velour mourning carriage for the forlorn mistress. The vehicles are manned by ghoulish dummies dressed in period gear whose eyes follow you around the room, making you glad of that security guard.

Museu del Perfum

Passeig de Gràcia 39 (93 216 01 21/www.museodel perfume.com). Metro Passeig de Gràcia. **Open** 10.30am-1.30pm, 4.30-8pm Mon-Fri; 11am-2pm Sat. **Admission** €5; €3 concessions. **Map** p338 D4.

In the back room of the Regia perfumery sits this collection of nearly 5,000 scent bottles, cosmetic flasks and related objects. The collection is divided

Rambling free

La Rambla is certainly Barcelona's most famous street. Thanks to the influx of street entertainers, drunken stag parties, hookers and pickpockets, it can also be its most depressing. However, Barcelona has several other promenades, modelled on La Rambla, which do a rather better job at serving their local communities.

Rambla de Catalunya

The pedestrianised section of Rambla de Catalunya, stretching from Gran Via to Diagonal, is in effect a continuation of La Rambla, but without a human statue in sight and with several good spots in which to enjoy an alfresco drink or tapa. Sheltered by pretty lime trees and lined by high-priced shops, this is where Barcelona's bourgeoisie have long come to stroll, see and be seen; though crossed by nine busy roads, it's the most pleasant way to walk from the Old City to Gràcia. While the buildings can't compete with the Modernista architecture of Passeig de Gràcia, there's plenty to admire: check out Casas Juncadella and Fargas, at Nos.33 and 47, by the prolific Enric Sagnier, and Puig i Cadafalch's Casa Serra at No.126, sadly blighted by the functional '80s monstrosity alongside it. Make sure you catch the bronze statues by Josep Granyer that top and tail the *rambla*: a thinking man's bull at the bottom, and a cheeky-looking giraffe at the top.

Rambla del Raval

The epicentre of what was long known as the 'Barrio Chino' (the red light district, a dangerous area of cheap prostitution and rampant drug-dealing) was pulled down in the '90s. It eventually became Barcelona's latest *rambla*, the Rambla del Raval, completed in 2000 and now a multicultural meeting place picking up momentum year after year. Barcelona's widest pedestrian walkway, it's lined with palm trees and kebab shops, and inhabited by a mixture of cricket-playing Pakistanis and young hipsters on their way to or from the many bars and restaurants around. One permanent resident, as of 2002, is Fernando Botero's *Gat*, a fat bronze cat that acts as a climbing frame for children in the daytime and a leaning post for alfresco drinkers by night. At weekends, there's a New Age street market, 'Món Raval' ('Raval World'), with stalls selling a varied mixture of clothes, music and food. What is currently a building site on the east side of the *rambla* will soon be home to the Generalitat's new Filmoteca.

Rambla de Poblenou

An early-evening walk up the city's second-oldest *rambla*, completed in 1866, is a step back in time and a reminder of how important public space is for a community. It couldn't be much further removed from the hassle and bustle of its city-centre counterpart: ancient denizens of the *barrio* chat on benches, couples stroll hand in hand or sit at pavement cafés sipping beer, and just about everybody gathers at the legendary El Tio Ché (No.46, 93 309 18 72) for its *horchata* (tiger nut milk). Lined by Modernista buildings (see the façades at Nos.51, 63, 72 and 102) and tourist-free, the Rambla is quintessentially Catalan. Appropriately enough, its most dramatic statue (at the top end) is a memorial to Josep Trueta, a pioneering surgeon who fled to Oxford during the Civil War and from there did much to promote the Catalan cause in the Anglo-Saxon world, most impressively in his English-language classic, *The Spirit of Catalonia*.

into two parts. One shows all manner of unguent vases and essence jars in chronological order, from a tube of black eye make-up from pre-dynastic Egypt to Edwardian atomisers and a prized double flask pouch that belonged to Marie Antoinette. The second section exhibits perfumery brands such as Guerlain and Dior; some are in rare bottles, among them a garish Dalí creation for Schiaparelli and a set of rather disturbing golliwog flasks for Vigny.

Museu Egipci de Barcelona

C/Valencia 284 (93 488 01 88/www.fundclos.com). *Metro Passeig de Gràcia.* **Open** 10am-8pm Mon-Sat; 10am-2pm Sun. **Admission** *Museum* €5.50; €4.50 concessions; free under-5s. *Combined ticket with Fundació Godia* €8.50; €6.50 concessions. **Discounts** BC. **Credit** AmEx, MC, V. **Map** p338 D4.
Two floors showcase a well-chosen collection spanning 3,000 years of Nile-drenched culture. Exhibits include religious statuary, such as the massive baboon heads used to decorate temples, everyday copper mirrors or alabaster headrests, and oddly moving infant sarcophagi. Outstanding pieces include some painstakingly matched fragments from the Sixth Dynasty Tomb of Iny, a bronze statuette of the goddess Osiris breastfeeding her son Horus, and mummified cats, baby crocodiles and falcons. Another highlight is a 5,000-year-old bed, which still looks comfortable enough to sleep in. On Friday and Saturday nights, there are dramatic reconstructions of popular themes such as the mummification ritual or the life of Cleopatra, for which reservations are essential. The museum is owned by renowned Egyptologist Jordi Clos, and entrance is waived for guests at his Hotel Claris (*see p67*).

Parc de l'Estació del Nord

C/Nàpols (no phone). Metro Arc de Triomf. **Open** 10am-sunset daily. **Admission** free. **Map** p343 E/F5/6.
Otherwise known as Parc Sol i Ombra ('Sun and Shadow'), this slightly shabby space is perked up by three pieces of land art in glazed blue ceramic by New York sculptor Beverley Pepper. Along with a pair of incongruous white stone entrance walls, *Espiral Arbrat* (*Tree Spiral*) is a spiral bench set under the cool shade of lime-flower trees and *Cel Caigut* (*Fallen Sky*) is a 7m (23ft) high ridge rising from the grass, while the tiles recall Gaudí's *trencadís* technique.

La Pedrera (Casa Milà)

Passeig de Gràcia 92-C/Provença 261-5 (93 484 59 00/www.caixacatalunya.es). Metro Diagonal. **Open** 10am-8pm daily. **Admission** €7; €3.50 concessions; free under-12s. **Guided tours** (in English) 4pm Mon-Fri. **Credit** MC, V. **Map** p338 D4.
The last secular building designed by Antoni Gaudí, the Casa Milà (popularly known as La Pedrera, 'the stone quarry') is a stupendous and daring feat of architecture, the culmination of the architect's experimental attempts to recreate natural forms with bricks and mortar (not to mention ceramics and even

smashed-up cava bottles). It looks like it might have been washed up on the shore, its marine feel complemented by Jujol's tangled balconies, doors of twisted kelp ribbon, sea-foamy ceilings and interior patios as blue as a mermaid's cave. When it was completed in 1912, it was so far ahead of its time that the woman who financed it as her dream home, Roser Segimon, became the laughing stock of the city. Its rippling façade, bereft of straight lines, led local painter Santiago Rusiñol to quip that a snake would be a better pet than a dog for the inhabitants of the building. But La Pedrera has become one of Barcelona's best loved buildings, and is adored by architects for its extraordinary structure: it is supported entirely by pillars, without a single master wall, allowing the vast asymmetrical windows of the façade to invite in great swathes of natural light.
There are three exhibition spaces. The first-floor art gallery hosts free exhibitions of eminent artists: from March to June 2005 there's a look at different representations of *Don Quixote*, followed by a show on decadence in art (July to October) and a major Rembrandt exhibition (November to February 2006). Upstairs is dedicated to a finer appreciation of the building's architect: you can visit a reconstructed Modernista flat on the fourth floor, with a sumptuous bedroom suite by Gaspar Homar, while the attic, framed by parabolic arches worthy of a Gothic cathedral, holds a museum dedicated to an insightful overview of Gaudí's career. Informative titbit-filled guided tours in English are run daily at 4pm. Best of all is the chance to stroll on the roof of the building amid its *trencadís*-covered ventilation shafts: their heads are shaped like the helmets of medieval knights, which led the poet Pere Gimferrer to dub the spot 'the garden of warriors'.

Sagrada Família

C/Mallorca 401 (93 207 30 31/www.sagradafamilia. org). Metro Sagrada Família. **Open** Apr-Sept 9am-8pm daily. Oct-Mar 9am-6pm daily. **Admission** €8; €5 concessions; €3 7-10 years; free under-6s. Lift to spires €2. **Credit** (shop only) MC, V. **Map** p337 F4.
The Temple Expiatori de la Sagrada Família is both Europe's most fascinating building site and Barcelona's most emblematic structure. At times breathtaking, at other times grotesque, it deserves the hubbub of superlatives that floats around it, though not all are positive. George Orwell berated the 1930s anarchists for 'showing bad taste by not blowing it up'. They did, however, manage to set fire to Gaudí's intricate plans and models for the building; ongoing work is a matter of some conjecture and controversy, with the finishing date of 2020 looking increasingly optimistic. The church's first mass is scheduled for Sant Josep's day (March 19th) 2007, 125 years after its foundation stone was laid.
Gaudí, buried beneath the nave, dedicated over 40 years to the project, the last 14 exclusively, and the crypt, the apse and the Nativity façade, completed in his lifetime, are the most beautiful elements of the church. The latter, facing C/Marina, looks at first

Sightseeing

glance as though some careless giant has poured candle wax over a Gothic cathedral, but closer inspection shows every protuberance to be an intricate sculpture of flora, fauna or human figure, combining to form an astonishingly moving stone tapestry depicting scenes from Christ's life. The other completed façade, the Passion that faces C/Sardenya, is more austere, with vast diagonal columns in the shape of bones and haunting sculptures by Josep Maria Subirachs. Japanese sculptor Etsuro Sotoo has chosen to adhere more faithfully to Gaudí's intentions, and has fashioned six more modest musicians at the rear of the temple, as well as the exuberantly coloured bowls of fruit to the left of the Nativity façade.

An estimated five million tourists visit the Sagrada Familia each year, two million of them paying the entrance fee. A ticket allows them to wander through the interior of the church, a marvellous forest of vast columns laid out in the style of the great Gothic cathedrals with a multi-aisled central nave crossed by a transept. The central columns are fashioned of porphyry, perhaps the only natural element capable of supporting the church's projected great dome that's destined to rise 170 metres into Barcelona's skyline, which will make the Sagrada Familia once again the highest building in the city.

A ticket also gives visitors access to the museum in the basement, offering insight into the history of the construction, original models for sculptural work and the chance to watch the current sculptors working at their plaster-cast models through a large window. But the highlight of any trip is a vertiginous hike up one of the towers (you can also take a lift), which affords unprecedented views through archers' windows.

The Esquerra

The left side of the Eixample was always a lot less fashionable than the right, and eventually became the setting for the sort of city services the bourgeoisie didn't want ruining the upmarket tone of their new neighbourhood. A huge slaughterhouse was built at the eastern edge of the area (and was only knocked down in 1979, when it was replaced by the **Parc Joan Miró**). Also here are the busy **Hospital Clínic**, an ugly, functional building that covers two blocks between C/Corsega and C/Provença; on C/Entença, a little further out, is the grim, star-shaped **La Model** prison, due to be relocated out of town and replaced by subsidised houses and offices in 2005 after an impressive 101 years of service. The huge **Escola Industrial** on C/Comte d'Urgel, formerly a Can Batlló textile factory, was redesigned in 1909 as a centre to teach workers the methods used in the burgeoning textile industry.

Not all the civic buildings are so grim. The central **Universitat de Barcelona** building on Plaça Universitat, completed in 1872, is an elegant construction with a pleasant cloister-like garden. Two markets bustle with locals rather than tourists: the **Ninot**, by the hospital, and the **Mercat de Sant Antoni**, on the edge of the Raval, which turns into a second-hand book market on Sunday mornings. Also, as the positioning of the Quadrat d'Or recognises, the Esquerra contains a number of Modernista jewels, such as the **Casa Boada** (C/Enric Granados 106) and the **Casa Golferichs** (Gran Via 191) built in 1901 by Joan Rubio i Bellver, one of Gaudí's main collaborators. Beyond the hospital, the Esquerra leads to **Plaça Francesc Macià**, centre of the city's business district and a gateway to the Zona Alta.

Parc Joan Miró (Parc de l'Escorxador)

C/Tarragona (no phone). Metro Tarragona or Espanya. **Open** 10am-sunset daily. **Map** p341 B4/5. The demolition of the old slaughterhouse provided some much-needed urban parkland, although there's precious little greenery here. The rows of stubby *palmera* trees and grim cement lakes are dominated by a library and Miró's towering phallic sculpture *Dona i Ocell* (*Woman and Bird*).

Sagrada Familia. *See p129.*

Gràcia & Other Districts

Includes two of Gaudí's greatest achievements, and much more besides.

Tramvia Blau. *See p140.*

The rigid blocks of the Eixample, planned in 1850 to fill the open fields between the Old City and the thriving town of Gràcia, physically joined the two conurbations. Barcelona's success had rendered Gracia's nominal independence irrelevant by 1897; amid howls of protest from its populace, the town was annexed. Dissent has been a recurring feature in Gràcia's history: streets boast names such as Llibertat, Revolució and Fraternitat, and for the 64 years before the Civil War, there was a satirical political magazine called *La Campana de Gràcia*, named for the famous bell in Plaça Rius i Taulet (*see p134* **Flashpoints**).

The political activity came from the effects of rapid industrial expansion. This was a mere village in 1821, centred around the 17th-century convent of Santa Maria de Gràcia and with just 2,608 inhabitants. By the time of annexation, however, the population had risen to 61,935, making it the ninth largest town in Spain and a real hotbed of Catalanism, republicanism and anarchism. Today, few vestiges of radicalism remain: sure, the *okupa* squatter movement inhabits a relatively high number of buildings

in the area, but the middle class population has been waging a campaign to dislodge them with some success.

Nowadays, the *barrio* is a favourite hangout of the city's bohemians. There are many workshops and studios here, and the numerous small, unpretentious bars are frequented by artists, designers and students. However, it really comes into its own for a few days each August, when its famous *festa major* grips the entire city (*see p220*). The streets are festooned with startlingly original homemade decorations and all of Barcelona turns up in a party mood. Open-air meals are laid on for the residents of Gràcia, and entertainment is laid on for everybody: from street parties for the old-timers singing along to *habaneros* (shanties) to amusements for the resident squatters who get to pogo to punk bands.

Of Gràcia's many squares, **Plaça de la Virreina** is perhaps the most relaxing spot, silvered by the chairs and tables of bar terraces, and overlooked by Sant Joan church. **Plaça del Sol** is busier: home to half a dozen bars and restaurants, it's the main focus of the drinking

For science, read *ciència*; for *ciència*, see **CosmoCaixa**. *See p137.*

crowd. Other favourites include **Plaça Rius i Taulet**, dominated by the 33-metre (108-foot) bell tower; the leafy **Plaça Rovira** (with a bronze statue of the neighbourhood's pensive planner, Antoni Rovira i Trias, sitting on a bench, his rejected plan for the Eixample at his feet); the rather rougher **Plaça del Diamant**, the setting for the Mercè Rodoreda novel *The Time of the Doves* (and with a peculiar sculpture to prove as much); and **Plaça John Lennon**, where the Liverpudlian singer is remembered with a huge model of the *Give Peace a Chance* single.

Much of Gràcia was built in the heyday of Modernisme, something evident in the splendid main drag, the C/Gran de Gràcia. Many of the buildings are rich in nature-inspired curves and fancy façades, but the finest example is Lluís Domènech i Muntaner's **Casa Fuster** at No.2, newly reopened as a luxury hotel (*see p74* **The fairest of them all**). Gaudí's disciple Francesc Berenguer was responsible for much of the civic architecture, most notably the **Mercat de la Llibertat** (Barcelona's oldest covered market, but, dating back to before the annexation, it is decorated with the coat of arms of the independent Gràcia) and the old **Casa de la Vila** (Town Hall) in Plaça Rius i Taulet.

However, the district's most overwhelming Modernista gem is one of Gaudí's earliest and most fascinating works, the **Casa Vicens** of 1883-8, hidden away in C/Carolines. The building is a private residence and thus not open to visitors, but the castellated red brickwork and colourful tiled exterior with Indian and Mudéjar influences should not be missed; notice, too, the spiky wrought-iron leaves on the gates. And one of Gaudí's last works, the stunning **Park Güell**, is a walk away, across the busy Travessera de Dalt and up the hill. It's well worth the effort: not only for the architecture, but for the magnificent view of Barcelona and the sea.

Fundació Foto Colectània

C/Julián Romea 6, D2 (93 217 16 26/ www.colectania.es). FGC Gràcia. **Open** 5-8.30pm Mon; 11am-2pm, 5-8.30pm Tue-Sat. Closed Aug. **Map** p338 D3.
Dedicated to the promotion of photography collecting, this private photography foundation promotes collections of other important galleries and museums. Major Spanish and Portuguese photographers from the 1950s are also shown.

Park Güell

C/Olot (Casa-Museu Gaudí 93 219 38 11). Metro Lesseps/bus 24, 25. **Open** *Park* 10am-sunset daily. *Museum* Apr-Sept 10am-7.45pm daily. Oct-Mar 10am-5.45pm daily. **Admission** *Museum* €4; €3 concessions; free under-9s. **Credit** (shop only) MC, V. **Map** p339 E2.

Gaudí's brief for this spectacular project was to emulate the English garden cities so admired by his patron Eusebi Güell (hence the spelling of 'park'): to lay out a self-contained suburb for the wealthy, but also to design the public areas. The original plan was for the plots to be sold off and the properties themselves subsequently designed by other architects. The idea never took off – perhaps because it was too far from the city, perhaps because it was too radical an idea – and the Güell family donated the park to the city in 1922.

It is a real fairytale place; the fantastical exuberance of Gaudí's imagination is breathtaking even today. The two gatehouses were based on designs the architect made earlier for the opera *Hansel and Gretel*, one of them featuring a red and white mushroom for a roof. From here, walk up a splendid staircase flanked by multicoloured battlements, past the iconic mosaic dragon, to what would have been the marketplace. Here, 100 palm-shaped pillars hold up a roof, reminiscent of the hypostyle hall at Luxor. On top of this structure is the esplanade, a circular concourse surrounded by undulating benches decorated with shattered tiles. (It's a technique called *trencadís*, actually perfected by Gaudí's overshadowed but talented assistant Josep Maria Jujol.) Like all Gaudí works, these seats are by no means a case of design over function, and are as comfortable as park benches come.

The park itself is magical, with twisted rough stone columns supporting curving colonnades or merging with the natural structure of the hillside. Gaudí lived for a time in one of the two houses built on the site (which was, in fact, designed by his student Berenguer). It's now the Casa-Museu Gaudí; guided tours, some in English, are given. The best way to get to the park is on the 24 bus; if you go via Lesseps metro, be prepared for a steep uphill walk.

Sants

For many arriving by bus or train, Estació de Sants is their first sight of Barcelona. Most take one look at the forbidding **Plaça dels Països Catalans**, which looks like it was designed with skateboard tricks in mind, and get the hell out of the area. It's perhaps not the most picturesque part of town – and be warned, the station is particularly popular among the city's bag-snatchers – but for those with time to spare, it's worth a few hours' investigation for historic if not aesthetic reasons.

Sants was originally built to service those who arrived after the town gates had shut at 9pm, with inns and blacksmiths there to cater for latecomers. In the 19th century, though, it became the industrial motor of the city. Giant textile factories such as the **Vapor Vell** (which is now a library), **L'Espanya Industrial** (now a futuristic park) and **Can Batlló** (still a workplace) helped create the bourgeois wealth

Sightseeing

that the likes of Eusebi Güell spent on the Modernista dream homes that still grace more salubrious areas of the city. The inequality did not go unnoticed. The *barrio* has been a hotbed of industrial action: the first general strike in Catalonia broke out here in 1856, only to be violently put down by the infamous General Zapatero (known as the 'Tiger of Catalonia'). The left-wing nationalist ERC party, which now shares power in the Generalitat, was founded here in 1931, at C/Cros 9.

Nearby **Plaça de Sants**, with Jorge Castillo's *Ciclista* statue, is the hub of the district, right in the middle of the C/Sants high street. Also worth checking out are the showy Modernista buildings at Nos.12, 130, 145 and 151, all designed by local architect Modest Feu. However, the more humble workers' flats nearby in the narrow streets off C/Premià are more typical of this very working class area. From there, C/Creu Coberta, an old Roman road once known as the Cami d'Espanya, 'the road to Spain', runs to Plaça d'Espanya.

Flashpoints

Plaça Rius i Taulet (map p338 D3).

This little square, or more specifically its impressive belltower, has been synonymous with resistance since La Revolta de les Quintes in 1870. On 4 April of that year, the government announced a decision to reintroduce the *quintes* (military draft), reneging on a previous promise. Public response was swift and fierce, most particularly in Sants and Gràcia, both still separate towns at the time. In the Plaça Rius i Taulet, 300 women stormed the town hall in protest, looting the building and then burning the call-up lists and other documents in a massive fire in the *plaça*.

The revolt lasted a full week, during which time the bell (*campana*) of the clock tower continued to chime, calling people from surrounding towns to join the revolt. The army, which bombarded the town day and night, finally entered Gràcia on 9 April and violently ransacked the town, destroying houses and businesses and taking 30 people to the Plaça del Sol to be executed. Soon afterwards, the tale of the bell entered the popular mythology of the area, and the long-running satirical magazine *La Campana de Gràcia* was named in its honour.

Parc de l'Espanya Industrial

Passeig de Antoni (no phone). Metro Sants-Estació. **Open** 10am-sunset daily. **Map** p341 A4.

In the 1970s the owners of the old textile factory announced their intention to use the land to build blocks of flats. The neighbourhood, though, put its collective foot down and insisted on a park, which was eventually built in 1985. The result is a puzzling space, designed by Basque Luis Peña Ganchegui, with ten watchtowers looking over a boating lake with a statue of Neptune in the middle, flanked by a stretch of mud used mainly for walking dogs. By the entrance kids can climb over Andrés Nagel's *Drac,* a massive and sinister black dragon.

Les Corts

Row after row of apartment blocks now obscure any trace of the rustic origins of Les Corts (literally, 'cowsheds' or 'pigsties'), as the village itself was swallowed up by Barcelona in the late 19th century. But search and you will find **Plaça de la Concòrdia**, a quiet square dominated by a 40-metre (131-foot) bell tower. This is an anachronistic oasis housing the civic centre Can Deu, formerly a farmhouse and now home to a great bar that hosts jazz acts every other Thursday. The area is much better known, though, for what happens every other weekend, when tens of thousands pour in to watch FC Barcelona, whose **Nou Camp** (*see below*) takes up much of the west of the *barrio*. At night, the area is the haunt of transvestite prostitutes and their kerb-crawling clients.

Nou Camp – FC Barcelona

Nou Camp, Avda Aristides Maillol, access 9, Les Corts (93 496 36 00/08/www.fcbarcelona.com). Metro Collblanc or Palau Reial. **Open** 10am-6.30pm Mon-Sat; 10am-2pm Sun. **Admission** €5.30; €3.70 concessions; free under-5s. *Guided tour* €9.50; €6.60 concessions. **Credit** (shop only) MC, V. **Map** p337 A3.

The Nou Camp, where FC Barcelona have played since 1957, is one of football's great stadiums, a vast cauldron of a ground that holds 98,000 spectators. That's a lot of noise when they're doing well, and an awful lot of silence when they aren't. If you can't get there on matchday (and you can usually pick up tickets if you try) but love the team, it's worth visiting the club museum. A guided tour of the stadium takes you though the players' tunnel to the dugouts and then, via the away team's changing room, on to the President's box, where there is a replica of the European Cup, which the team won at Wembley in 1992. The museum commemorates those glory years, making much of the days when the likes of Kubala, Cruyff, Maradona, Koeman and Lineker trod the hallowed turf, with pictures, video clips and souvenirs spanning the century that has passed since the Swiss business executive Johan Gamper first founded the club. *See also p271.*

Jardins de Cervantes. *See p137.*

Tibidabo & Collserola

During his temptation of Christ, the devil took him to the top of a mountain and offered him all before him, with the words '*tibi dabo*' (Latin for 'To thee I will give'). This gave rise to the name of the dominant peak of the Collserola massif, with its sweeping views of the whole of the Barcelona conurbation stretching out to the sea: quite a tempting offer, given the present-day price of the city's real estate. The ugly, neo-Gothic **Sagrat Cor** temple crowning the peak has become one of the city's most recognisable landmarks; it's clearly visible for miles around. At weekends, thousands head to the top of the hill in order to whoop and scream at the **funfair**. Nowadays the only one in Barcelona, it's been running since 1921 and has changed little since (*see p226*) are creaky and old-fashioned, but very quaint. Within the funfair is the **Museu d'Automates**, a fine collection of fairground coin-operated machines from the early 20th century.

Getting up to the top on the clanking old **Tramvia Blau** (Blue Tram; *see p140*) and then the **funicular railway** (*see below*) is part of the fun; Plaça Doctor Andreu between the two is a great place for an alfresco drink. For the best view of the city, either take a lift up the needle of Norman Foster's communications tower, the **Torre de Collserola** (*see p137*), or up to the *mirador* at the feet of Christ atop the Sagrat Cor.

The vast **Parc de Collserola** is more a series of forested hills than a park; its shady paths through holm oaks and pines open out to spectacular views. It's most easily reached by FGC train on the Terrassa-Sabadell line from Plaça Catalunya or Passeig de Gràcia, getting off at **Baixador de Vallvidrera** station. A ten-minute walk from the station up into the woods (there's an information board just outside the station) will take you to the **Vil·la Joana**, an old *masia* covered in bougainvillea and containing the **Museu Verdaguer** (93 204 78 05, open by appointment Tue-Fri, 10am-2pm Sat, Sun, admission free) dedicated to 19th-century Catalan poet Jacint Verdaguer, who used this as his summer home. Just beyond the Vil·la Joana is the park's **information centre** (93 280 35 52, open 9.30am-3pm daily), which has basic maps for free and more detailed maps for sale. Almost all the information is in Catalan, but staff are very helpful. There's also a snack bar and an exhibition area.

Funicular de Tibidabo

Plaça Doctor Andreu to Plaça Tibidabo (93 211 79 42). FGC Avda Tibidabo, then Tramvia Blau.
Open As funfair (*see p223*), but starting 30mins earlier. **Tickets** *Single* €2; €1.50 concessions. *Return* €3; €2 concessions. **No credit cards**.
This art deco vehicle offers occasional glimpses of the city below as it winds through the pine forests up to the summit. The service has been running since 1901, but only according to a complicated timetable. If it's not running, take the FGC line from

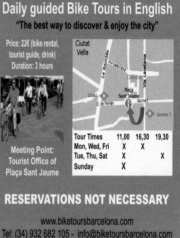

Plaça Catalunya to Peu del Funicular, get the funicular up to Vallvidrera Superior, and then catch the 111 bus to Tibidabo (a process not half as complicated as it sounds). Alternatively, it's nearly an hour's (mostly pleasant) hike up from Plaça Doctor Andreu for those who are feeling energetic.

Torre de Collserola

Ctra de Vallvidrera al Tibidabo (93 406 93 54/ www.torredecollserola.es). FCG Peu Funicular, then funicular. **Open** *Apr-May, Nov-Mar* 11am-2.30pm, 3.30-7pm Wed-Fri; 11am-7pm Sat, Sun. *June-Aug* 11am-2.30pm, 3.30-8pm Wed-Fri; 11am-8pm Sat, Sun. *Sept* 11am-2.30pm, 3.30-7pm Wed-Fri; 11am-8pm Sat, Sun. *Oct* 11am-2.30pm, 3.30-6pm Wed-Fri; 11am-7pm Sat, Sun. **Admission** €4.80; €3.40-€4 concessions; free under-7s. **Credit** AmEx, MC, V.

Five minutes' walk from the Sagrat Cor is its main rival as Barcelona's most visible landmark, Norman Foster's communication tower, built in 1992 to transmit images of the Olympics around the world. Visible from just about everywhere in the city and always flashing at night, the tower is loved and hated in equal measure. Those who don't suffer from vertigo attest to the stunning views of Barcelona and the Mediterranean from the top.

Zona Alta

Zona Alta (the 'upper zone', or, simply, 'uptown') is the name given collectively to a series of smart neighbourhoods, including **Sant Gervasi**, **Sarrià**, **Pedralbes** and **Putxet**, that stretch out across the lower reaches of the Collserola hills. The handful of tourist sights around here includes the **Palau Reial**, with its lovely gardens and its brace of museums, the **Museu de Ceràmica** and **Museu de les Arts Decoratives**; the **CosmoCaixa** science museum; and the remarkable **Pedralbes Monastery**, well worth a visit despite the fact that its selection of religious paintings from the **Thyssen-Bornemisza collection** have recently been moved to the revamped MNAC, for which *see p119*). The centre of Sarrià and the streets of old Pedralbes around the monastery still retain an appreciable flavour of the sleepy country towns these once were.

For many downtown residents, the Zona Alta is a favourite place to relax in the parks and gardens that wind into the hills. At the end of Avda Diagonal, next to the functional Zona Universitària (university district), is the **Jardins de Cervantes**, with its 11,000 rose bushes, the striking *Dos Rombs* sculpture by Andreu Alfaro and, during the week, legions of picnicking students. From the park, a turn back along the Diagonal towards Plaça Maria Cristina and Plaça Francesc Macià will take you to Barcelona's main business and shopping district. Here is the small **Turó Parc**, a semiformal garden good for writing postcards amid

inspirational plaques of poetry. The **Jardins de la Tamarita**, at the foot of Avda Tibidabo, is a pleasant dog-free oasis with a playground, while further up at the top of the tramline is the little-known **Parc de la Font de Racó**, full of shady pine and eucalyptus trees. A fair walk to the north-east, an old quarry has been converted into a swimming pool, the **Parc de la Creueta del Coll**.

Gaudí fans are rewarded by a trip up to the **Pavellons de la Finca Güell** at Avda Pedralbes 15; its extraordinary and rather frightening wrought-iron gate features a dragon into whose gaping mouth the foolhardy can fit their heads. Once inside the gardens, via the main gate on Avda Diagonal, look for a delightful fountain by the master. Across near Putxet is his relatively sober **Col·legi de les Teresianes** (C/Ganduxer 85-105), while up towards Tibidabo, just off Plaça Bonanova, rises his remarkable Gothic-influenced **Torre Figueres** or **Bellesguard**.

CosmoCaixa

C/Teodor Roviralta 47-51 (93 212 60 50/www. fundacio.lacaixa.es). Bus 60/FGC Avda Tibidabo, then Tramvia Blau (see p140). **Open** 10am-8pm Tue-Sun. **Admission** €3; €2 concessions; free under-3s. *Planetarium* €2; €1.50 concessions. **Credit** AmEx, DC, MC, V.

The long-awaited revamp of the Fundació La Caixa's science museum and planetarium, to create the biggest in Europe, has been only partially successful. First off, its size is somewhat misleading: apart from a couple of new (and, admittedly, important) spaces – the Flooded Forest, a reproduction of a corner of Amazonia complete with flora and fauna, and the Geological Wall – the collection has not been proportionally expanded to fit the new building. A glass-enclosed spiral ramp runs down an impressive six floors, but actually represents quite a long walk to reach the main collection five floors down.

It is here that temporary exhibitions are housed, too. Until October 2005 the impressively intact skeletons of six iguanodon dinosaurs, on loan from the Belgian government, will continue to crouch menacingly. From here, it's on to the Matter Room, which covers 'inert', 'living', 'intelligent' and then 'civilised' matter: in other words, natural history. However, for all the fanfare made by the museum about taking exhibits out of glass cases and making scientific theories accessible, many of the displays still look very dated. Written explanations are often impenetrable, containing phrases such as 'time is macroscopically irreversible,' and making complex those concepts that previously seemed simple.

On the plus side, the installations for children are better than ever: the Bubble Planetarium pleases kids aged 3-8, and the wonderful Clik (ages 3-6) and Flash (ages 7-9) introduces children to science through games. Toca Toca! ('Touch Touch') educates children on which animals and plants are safe

Gaudí's **Casa Vicens**.
See p133.

and which to avoid. And one of the real highlights, for kids and adults, is still the hugely entertaining sound telescope outside on the Plaça de la Ciència.

Monestir de Pedralbes

Baixada del Monestir 9 (93 280 14 34). FGC Reina Elisenda. **Open** 10am-2pm Tue-Sun. **Admission** *Monastery* €4; €2.50 concessions; free under-12s. Free 1st Sun of mth. **Credit** (shop only) AmEx, DC, MC, V. **Map** p337 A1.

In 1326 the widowed Queen Elisenda of Montcada used her inheritance to buy this land and build a convent for the 'Poor Clare' order of nuns, which she soon joined. The result is a jewel of Gothic architecture, with an understated single-nave church with fine stained-glass windows and a beautiful three-storey 14th-century cloister. The place was out of bounds to the general public until 1983 when the nuns, a closed order, opened it up as a museum in the mornings (they escape to a nearby annexe).

The site offers a fascinating insight into life in a medieval convent, taking you through its well-preserved kitchens, pharmacy and refectory with its huge vaulted ceiling. To one side is the tiny chapel of Sant Miquel, with striking murals dating to 1343 by Ferrer Bassa, a Catalan painter and student of Giotto. In the former dormitory next to the cloister, where part of the Thyssen art collection once hung, is a selection of hitherto undisplayed objects belonging to the nuns. Among them are illuminated books, furniture and other objects reflecting the artistic and religious life of the community.

Museu de Ceràmica
& Museu de les Arts Decoratives

Palau Reial de Pedralbes, Avda Diagonal 686 (93 280 16 21/www.museuceramica.bcn.es/www.museu artsdecoratives.bcn.es). Metro Palau Reial. **Open** 10am-6pm Tue-Sat; 10am-3pm Sun. **Admission** *Combined admission with Museu Tèxtil* €3.50; €2 concessions; free under-16s. Free 1st Sun of mth. **No credit cards. Map** p337 A2.

These two collections – accessible, along with the Textile Museum, on the same ticket – are housed in the august Palau Reial; originally designed for the family of Eusebi Güell, Gaudí's patron, it was later used as a royal palace. The Museum of Decorative Arts is informative and fun, and looks at the different styles informing the design of artefacts in Europe since the Middle Ages, from Romanesque to art deco and beyond. A second section is devoted to post-war Catalan design of objects as diverse as urinals and man-sized inflatable pens.

The Ceramics Museum is equally fascinating, showing how Moorish ceramic techniques from the 13th century were developed after the Reconquista with the addition of colours (especially blue and yellow) in centres such as Manises (in Valencia) and Barcelona. Two 18th-century murals are of sociological interest: one, *La Xocolatada*, shows the bourgeoisie at a garden party, while the other, by the same artist, depicts the working classes at a bull-fight in the Plaza Mayor in Madrid. Upstairs is a

Urban tribes Okupas

Description *Esquàters* (squatters) with an elevated political conscience and a distinctive sense of style built around dreadlocks and stripy leggings.

Natural habitat Abandoned houses, factories and even police stations are fair game. Larger spaces are turned into fully fledged social centres. The old La Hamsa factory in Sants, which closed down in August 2004, had a library, projection rooms, art workshops and a children's swimming pool, and was also used for theatre, concerts and assemblies during transport and postal strikes.

Grooming Accessories for the wannabes: mangy dog, piercings, bongos. Accessories for the real thing: mangy dog, piercings, manual entitled *How to Build Your Own Septic Tank*.

Distinctive behaviour Spelling. The proliferation of Ks and Xs in Basque, the language of the original *okupa* movement, is taken on as a symbol of rebellion. Hence, *ocupa* is spelled *okupa* and *¿Qué pasa?* becomes *¿K pasa?*.

Evolution Barcelona has become Spain's *okupa* capital, ahead of traditional strongholds such as Euskadi (the Basque country) and Andalucía.

Take me to your leader Don't you mean dealer?

Endangered species? Even though 2004 saw over 20 evictions, Barcelona still has around 150 occupied buildings housing 1,000 people, many in and around the Gràcia area.

Any survivors? Hanging on by a hair, Gràcia's Kasa de la Muntanya (Avda Santuari Sant Josep de la Muntanya 33, www.nodo50.org/kasadelamuntanya) is *okupa* HQ. The building was originally the police station for Gaudí's failed housing estate of Park Güell; the Güell family and the *okupas* are currently locked in a protracted court battle over the property.

Can I join in? Only if you don't mind sharing a biotoilet with 15 other people and attend at least two demonstrations a week.

Do say '*¿K pasa?*'

Don't say 'Come on. Let's go grab a skinny latte in my SUV.'

section showing 20th-century ceramics, including a room dedicated to Miró and Picasso. The two museums, along with the Textile Museum and several smaller collections, are to be merged in the future in a Museu de Disseny (Design Museum) as part of the cultural overhaul of the Plaça de les Glòries.

Parc de la Creueta del Coll

C/Mare de Déu del Coll (no phone). Metro Penitents.
Open 10am-sunset daily. **Admission** free.
Created from a quarry in 1987 by Josep Matorell and David Mackay, the team that went on to design the Vila Olímpica, this park boasts a sizeable swimming pool complete with a 'desert island' and an interesting sculpture by Eduardo Chillida: a 50-ton lump of curly granite suspended on cables, called *In Praise of Water*. Three people were injured by this flying work of art in 1998 when the cables snapped: view from a safe distance.

Tramvia Blau

Avda Tibidabo (Plaça Kennedy) to Plaça Doctor Andreu (93 318 70 74/www.tramvia.org/tramvia blau). FGC Avda Tibidabo. **Open** *Mid June-mid Sept* 10am-8pm daily. *Mid Sept-mid June* 10am-6pm Sat. **Frequency** 20mins. **Tickets** €2.10 single; €3.10 return. **No credit cards.**

Barcelonins and tourists have been clanking 1,225m (4,000ft) up Avda Tibidabo in the 'blue trams' since 1902. In the winter months, when the tram only operates on weekends, a rather more prosaic bus takes you up (or you can walk it in 15 minutes).

Poblenou & beyond

Poblenou has been many things in its time: a farming community, a fishing port, the site of heavy industry factories and a trendy post-industrial suburb. Now it's also a burgeoning technology and business district, snappily tagged '22@'. Many of the factories around here closed down in the 1960s; these days, buildings that have not already been torn down or converted into office blocks are used as schools, civic centres, workshops, open spaces or, increasingly, coveted lofts.

The main drag, the pedestrianised **Rambla de Poblenou**, dating from 1886, is a much better place for a relaxing stroll than its busy central counterpart, and gives this still villagey area a heart. Meanwhile, a bone's throw away, the city's oldest and most atmospheric

Pont de Calatrava. *See p141.*

cemetery, the **Cementiri de l'Est**, shows that most *barcelonins* spend their death as they did their life: cooped up in large high-rise blocks. Some were able to afford roomier tombs, many of which were built at the height of the romantic-Gothic craze at the turn of the 19th century. A leaflet or larger guide (€15) sold at the entrance suggests a route around 30 of the more interesting monuments.

Nearby, **Plaça de les Glòries** finally seems ready to fulfil its destiny. The creator of the Eixample, Ildefons Cerdà, hoped that the square would become the new centre of the city, believing his grid-pattern blocks would spread much further north than they did and shift the emphasis of the city from west to east. Instead, it became little more than a glorified roundabout on the way out of town. Now, with the hugely phallic **Torre Agbar** to landmark the area from afar, the *plaça* has become the gateway to Diagonal-Mar, and the new infrastructure being built around the Fòrum 2004.

The tower, designed by the French architect Jean Nouvel and owned by the Catalan water board, has been a bold and controversial project. A concrete skyscraper with a domed head surrounded by a glass façade, it's not unlike London's famed 'Gherkin'. Nouvel says it's been designed to reflect the Catalan mentality: the concrete represents stability and severity, the glass openness and transparency. At 144 metres (472 feet), it's Barcelona's third highest building (behind the two Olympic towers) and contains no fewer than 4,400 multiform windows. Remarkably, it will have no air-conditioning: the windows will let the breeze do the job. Nouvel claims Gaudí as the inspiration for the multicoloured skin of a building that has already captured the public imagination and come to dominate the district.

One breath of fresh air in the rather stagnant area north of here is the **Parc del Clot**, and just beyond it, the **Plaça de Valentí Almirall**, with the old town hall of Sant Martí and a 17th-century building that used to be the Hospital de Sant Joan de Malta, somewhat at odds with the buildings that have mushroomed around them. Further north, up C/Sagrera, the entrance to a former giant truck factory now leads to the charming **Parc de la Pegaso**. The area also has a fine piece of recent architecture, the supremely elegant **Pont de Calatrava** bridge. Designed by Santiago Calatrava, it links to Poblenou via C/Bac de Roda.

Diagonal-Mar

Many detractors of the **Fòrum**, the six-month cultural symposium held in 2004, felt that its real purpose was to regenerate this post-industrial wasteland. Certainly, a large element of its legacy are the enormous conference halls and hotels that will hopefully draw many wealthy business clients into the city, together with a scarcely believable increase in real estate values.

If you're approaching from the city, the first sign of this resurgent *barrio* is **Parc de Diagonal-Mar**, containing an angular lake decorated with scores of curling aluminium tubes and vast Gaudían flower pots. Designed by Enric Miralles (of Scottish Parliament fame), the park may not be to most *barcelonins'* taste, but the local seagull population has found it to be an excellent roosting spot. Just over the road from here is the Diagonal-Mar shopping centre, a woefully undervisited three-storey mall of high street chains, and the grand Hotel Princesa, a triangular skyscraper designed by architect-designer-artist-local hero Oscar Tusquets.

The **Edifici Fòrum**, a striking blue triangular construction by Herzog and de Meuron (responsible for London's Tate Modern), is the centrepiece of the €3 billion redevelopment. The remainder of the money was spent on the solar panels, marina, new beach and the **Illa Pangea**, an island 60 metres (197 feet) from the shore, reachable only by swimming. It's all a far cry from the local residential neighbourhood, **Sant Adrià de Besòs**, a poor district of tower blocks that includes the notorious La Mina neighbourhood, a hotbed of drug-related crime. It's hoped that the new development will help regenerate the area, best known for its Feria de Abril celebrations in April (*see p217*), the Andalucían community's version of the more famous annual celebrations in Seville. There's also a fine *festa major* in **Badalona**, just up the coast, in May, in which a large effigy of a devil is burned on the beach in a shower of whoops and fireworks.

Horta & around

Horta, to the far west of the blue metro line, is a picturesque little village that still remains aloof from the city that swallowed it up in 1904. Originally a collection of farms (its name means 'market garden'), the *barrio* is still peppered with old farmhouses, such as **Can Mariner** on C/Horta, dating back to 1050, and the medieval **Can Cortada** at the end of C/Campoamor, now a huge restaurant in beautiful grounds. An abundant water supply also made Horta the place where much of Barcelona's laundry got done: a whole community of *bugaderes* (washerwomen) lived and worked in the lovely C/Aiguafreda, where you can still see their wells and open-air stone washtubs.

To the south, joined to Gràcia by Avda Mare de Déu de Montserrat, the steep-sided neighbourhood of **Guinardó**, with its steps and escalators, consists mainly of two big parks. **Parc del Guinardó**, a huge space designed in 1917 (making it Barcelona's third oldest park) full of eucalyptus and cypress trees, is a relaxing place to escape. The smaller **Parc de les Aigües** shelters the neo-Arabic **Casa de les Altures** from 1890, Barcelona's most eccentrically beautiful council building.

The **Vall d'Hebron** is a leafy area located just above Horta in the Collserola foothills, in which formerly private estates have been put to public use; among them are the château-like **Palauet de les Heures**, now a university building. The area was one of the city's four major venues for the Olympics and is rich in sporting facilities, including public football pitches, tennis courts, and cycling and archery facilities at the **Velòdrom**. Around these venues there are a number of striking examples of street sculpture, including Claes Oldenberg's *Matches* and Joan Brossa's *Visual Poem* (in the shape of the letter 'A'). The area also conceals the rationalist **Pavelló de la República** and the zany **Parc del Laberint**, dating back to 1791 and surrounded by a modern park. More modern still is the **Ciutat Sanitària**, Catalonia's largest hospital; a good proportion of *barcelonins* first saw the light of day here.

Parc del Laberint

C/Germans Desvalls, Passeig Vall d'Hebron (no phone). Metro Mundet. **Open** 10am-sunset daily. **Admission** €2; €1.20 concessions Mon, Tue, Thur-Sat; free under-6s, over-65s. Free Wed, Sun.

In 1791 the Desvalls family, owners of this marvellously leafy estate, hired Italian architect Domenico Begutti to design scenic gardens set around a cypress maze, with a romantic stream and a waterfall. The mansion may be gone (replaced with a 19th-century Arabic-influenced building), but the gardens are remarkably intact, shaded in the summer by oaks, laurels and an ancient sequoia. Best of all, the maze, an ingenious puzzle that still intrigues those brave enough to try it, is also still in use. Nearby stone tables provide a handy picnic site. On paying days, last entry is one hour before sunset.

Pavelló de la República

Avda Cardenal Vidal y Barraquer (93 428 54 57). Metro Montbau. **Open** 9am-8pm Mon-Fri. **Admission** free.

This austerely functionalist building now houses an interesting university library specialising in materials from the Spanish Civil War and the clandestine republican movement that operated continually during Franco's dictatorship. The structure was built in 1992 as a facsimile of the emblematic rationalist pavilion of the Spanish Republic, designed by Josep Lluís Sert for the Paris Exhibition in 1937 and

later to hold Picasso's *Guernica*. It makes for an interesting juxtaposition with Oldenberg's pop art *Matches* across the street.

The outer limits

L'Hospitalet de Llobregat lies beyond Sants, completely integrated within the city's transport system but nevertheless a distinct municipality with its own very strong sense of separateness. Many of its inhabitants have Andalucian roots and this is Catalonia's main centre for flamenco (and not of the polka-dot-dress variety): there are many flamenco *peñas* (social clubs), bars and restaurants with a strong Andalucian flavour. The area also boasts a rich cultural life, with good productions at the **Teatre Joventut** (C/Joventut 10, 93 448 12 10) and excellent art exhibitions at the **Tecla Sala Centre**.

Sant Andreu is another vast residential district in the north-east of the city, and was once a major industrial zone. Apart from the Gaudí-designed floor mosaic in the **Sant Pacià church** on C/Monges, there's little reason to venture here, unless you have a historical interest in Josep Lluis Sert's rationalist **Casa Bloc**, which were originally workers' residences from the brief republican era. A recently installed wine press in Plaça Xandri recalls Sant Andreu's pre-industrial rural past.

The name of **Nou Barris**, on the other side of the Avda Meridiana, translates as 'nine neighbourhoods', but it is actually a collection of 11 former hamlets. The council has compensated for the area's poor housing (many tower blocks were built in the area in the 1950s and have fallen into disrepair) with the construction of public facilities such as the **Can Dragó**, a sports centre incorporating the biggest swimming pool in the city, and a **Parc Central**. The district is centred on the roundabout at Plaça Llucmajor, which also holds Josep Viladomat's bold *La República*, a female nude holding aloft a sprig of laurel as a symbol of freedom. The renovation of the nearby **Seu de Nou Barris** town hall has brightened up an area that badly needed it, although it's not quite a tourist draw.

Tecla Sala Centre Cultural

Avda Josep Tarradellas 44, Hospitalet de Llobregat (93 338 57 71/www.l-h.es/ccteclasala). Metro La Torrassa. **Open** 11am-2pm, 5-8pm Tue-Sat; 11am-2pm Sun. **Admission** free.

Tecla Sala is an old textile factory now housing a number of cultural concerns, including a vast library and this excellent gallery, which exhibits an eclectic mixture of national and international artists. For 2005, there are scheduled exhibitions of the work of artists from L'Hospitalet and photographs by José Manuel Aizpurúa.

Eat, Drink, Shop

Restaurants	**144**
Cafés, Tapas & Bars	**173**
Shops & Services	**189**

Features

The best Restaurants	145
Casas regionales	151
Menu glossary	154
Eating on the go	166
The best Places	173
Strange brews	181
No shrinking Violeta	187
The best Shops	189
Urban tribes Pijos	194
Buying the flag	199
Retail road map	205
Barcelona sucks	206

Restaurants

It's getting better all the time.

Les Quinze Nits: choose carefully, and it'll be well worth the wait. *See p146.*

It's taken Spanish cuisine an age to get over its image problem but it seems to be finally on its way. To be fair, the bad press that Spanish restaurants have had from foreigners until recently was down, in large part, to ignorance or cultural inflexibility. The oft-heard complaint of the northern tourist regarding the lack of vegetables fails to take into account that they're served first, in order that the meat may be better appreciated. Ironically, this then gives rise to another complaint when a mere plate of vegetables is presented as a starter. 'My water wasn't chilled!' is another moan, but Spaniards often find water more palatable at room temperature. And so on, and on.

Yet as the traditional Spanish ways of preparing and eating food are beginning to gain in popularity beyond its own shores, a new generation of chefs over here is working overtime to promote a pan-global minimalist form of fusion. Designed, presumably, for well-off, jetsetting anorexics, the style is most often attributed to Ferran Adrià and his legendary restaurant **El Bulli** (*see p171*), though little of

it benefits from anything like his genius. Meanwhile, authentic international cuisine is still hard to find. Local resistance to spices and the difficulty of sourcing key ingredients mean that it's difficult to find good Indian, Chinese or Italian food. The good news is that there are a greater number of Middle Eastern and Japanese restaurants, and a growing number of Latin American places. Most of the ethnic variety is to be found in Gràcia.

WHAT HAPPENS WHEN

Lunch starts around 2pm and goes on until roughly 3.30pm or 4pm; dinner is served from 9pm until 11.30pm or midnight. Some restaurants open earlier in the evening, but arriving before 9.30pm or even 10pm generally means you'll be dining alone or in the company of foreign tourists. Reserving a table is usually a good idea: not only on Friday and Saturday nights, but also on Sunday evenings and Monday lunchtimes, when few restaurants are open. Many also close for lengthy holidays, including about a week over Easter, two or three weeks in August or early September, and often the first week in January. We have listed closures of more than a week where possible, but restaurants are fickle, particularly on the issue of summer holidays, so call to check.

PRICES AND PAYMENT
Eating out in Barcelona is not as cheap as it used to be, but low mark-ups on wines keep the cost relatively reasonable for northern Europeans and Americans. All but the most upmarket restaurants are required by law to serve an economical fixed-price *menú del dia* (*menú* is not to be confused with the menu, which is *la carta*) at lunchtime; this usually consists of a starter, main course, dessert, bread and something to drink. The idea is to provide cheaper meals for the workers, but while these menus can be real bargains, they're not by any means a taster menu or a showcase for the chef's greatest hits; rather, they're a healthier version of what in other countries might amount to a snatched lunchtime sandwich.

Laws governing the issue of prices are routinely flouted, but, legally, menus must declare if the seven per cent IVA (VAT) is included in prices or not (it rarely is), and also if there is a cover charge (generally expressed as a charge for bread). Catalans, and the Spanish in general, tend to tip very little, but tourists let their conscience decide.

Barri Gòtic

Cafè de l'Acadèmia
C/Lledó 1 (93 319 82 53). Metro Jaume I. **Open** 9am-noon, 1.30-4pm, 8.45-11.30pm Mon-Fri. Closed Aug. **Main courses** €12.85-€17.10. *Set lunch* €8.56-€13.40 Mon-Fri. **Credit** AmEx, MC, V. **Map** p345 B3.
The tables outside on the shady little Plaça Sant Just are some of the most sought-after in the city, especially at night time. By day, however, it's a slightly different proposition, rammed as it is with besuited workers from the nearby city hall, and with a set lunch that offers no choices. Nonetheless, the regular menu of creative Catalan classics offers superb value and has had no need to change its direction over the years; expect to find a home-made pasta (try shrimp and garlic), creamy risotto with duck foie, guineafowl with a tiny tarte tatin and lots of duck.

Can Culleretes
C/Quintana 5 (93 317 30 22). Metro Liceu. **Open** 1.30-4pm, 9-11pm Tue-Sat; 1.30-4pm Sun. Closed July. **Main courses** €7-€10. *Set lunch* €15. **Credit** MC, V. **Map** p345 A3.
The rambling dining rooms at the wonderfully named 'House of Teaspoons' have been packing 'em in since 1786, and they show no signs of slowing down. The secret to the restaurant's longevity is a straightforward one: honest, hearty cooking and

decent wine at the lowest possible prices. Under huge oil paintings and a thousand signed black and white photos, diners munch sticky boar stew, pork with prunes and dates, goose with apples, partridge escabeche and superbly fresh seafood.

Los Caracoles
C/Escudellers 14 (93 302 31 85). Metro Liceu. **Open** 1pm-midnight daily. **Main courses** €8-€12. **Credit** AmEx, DC, MC, V. **Map** p345 B3.
Venerated by the sort of people who take pictures of their food, Los Caracoles functions far better as a sight than a place to eat, its endless series of low-ceilinged, characterful dining rooms adorned with heavy beams, pretty tiling and ancient fittings. The trick is to order conservatively: the food is acceptably unexceptional and not the real reason you're here. Stick with one of the chickens twirling outside on a spit, and avoid the fish dishes and eponymous snails, which come in a tomatoey gloop fizzing with e-numbers. The pricing is somewhat creative.

The best Restaurants

For eating under the stars
Cafè de l'Acadèmia (*see left*); Can Travi Nou (*see p171*); Els Pescadors (*see p171*).

For eating under the sun
Agua (*see p167*); Bestial (*see p169*); Lupino (*see p153*); El Suquet de l'Almirall (*see p169*).

For hanging with the cool crowd
Astoria (*see p159*); Arola (*see p167*); Comerç 24 (*see p157*); Lupino (*see p153*); Noti (*see p161*); Re-Pla (*see p158*).

For eating for nearly nothing
Can Culleretes (*see left*); L'Econòmic (*see p157*); Elisabets (*see p150*); Mesón David (*see p153*); La Paradeta (*see p158*); Pollo Rico (*see p153*); Les Quinze Nits (*see p146*).

For taking a date
Biblioteca (*see p149*); El Cafetí (*see p150*); El Pebre Blau (*see p158*); Silenus (*see p153*).

For taking your mum
Casa Calvet (*see p161*); El Gran Café (*see p146*); El Cafetí (*see p150*); Octubre (*see p165*); Pla de la Garsa (*see p158*); Set Portes (*see p169*).

For a taste of heaven
Cinc Sentits (*see p161*); Gaig (*see p161*); Windsor (*see p162*).

El Gran Café

C/Avinyó 9 (93 318 79 86). Metro Liceu. **Open**
1-4pm, 7.30pm-12.30am daily. **Main courses**
€13.50-€16.05. *Set lunch* €11.80 Mon-Fri. **Credit**
AmEx, DC, MC, V. **Map** p345 B3.
El Gran Café blends a smart 1940s Parisian
brasserie look with a crowd-pleasing menu. It covers all bases, from Catalan classic (*esqueixada* or
xató salad) to modish Mediterranean (goose with
mango chutney, skewered monkfish with king
prawns), all adapted to the Anglo-Saxon palate (two
veg with the main course, butter pats for the bread
roll). Puddings and wines follow the same lines; on
weekdays, there's a good set lunch.

Mastroqué

*C/Codols 29 (93 301 79 42). Metro Drassanes
or Jaume I.* **Open** 8.30pm-1am Thur-Sat. Closed
3wks Aug. **Main courses** €9-€10. **Credit** MC, V.
Map p345 B4.
Based on a list of smallish dishes *per picar* (to share),
Mastroqué offers a sophisticated array of French-
influenced *platillos*, including duck magret, potato
and apple timbale, aubergine 'caviar' and foie gras.
It's somewhat off the beaten track, down a dark and
narrow alley, but all the more welcoming for that.

Mercè Vins

C/Amargós 1 (93 302 60 56). Metro Urquinaona.
Open 8am-5pm Mon-Thur; 8am-5pm, 8.30pm-
midnight Fri. **Set lunch** €8.50 Mon-Fri. **Credit** V.
Map p344 B2.

FoodBall.
See p150.

With its green beams, buttercup walls and fresh
flowers, few places are as cosy and welcoming as
Mercè Vins. In the morning it functions as a breakfast bar, before moving on to serve a set lunch, while
on Friday nights it dishes up *pica-pica* plates of ham
and cheese, with generous rounds of bread rubbed
with tomato. The standard of cooking on the lunch
deals can vary quite a bit, but occasionally a pumpkin soup or inventive salad might appear, before
sausages with garlicky sautéed potatoes. Dessert
regulars are flat, sweet *coca* bread (with a glass of
muscatel), chocolate flan and figgy pudding.

Mesón Jesús

*C/Cecs de la Boqueria 4 (93 317 46 98). Metro
Jaume I or Liceu.* **Open** 1-4pm, 8-11pm Mon-Fri.
Closed Aug-early Sept. **Main courses** €7.45-€12.85.
Set lunch €8.50 Mon-Fri. *Set dinner* €12.50 Mon-Fri.
Credit MC, V. **Map** p345 A3.
The atmosphere here is authentically Castilian, with
gingham tablecloths, oak barrels, cart wheels and
pitchforks hung around the walls, while the waitresses are incessantly cheerful with their largely
non-Spanish-speaking clientele, and especially oblig-
ing when it comes to looking after children. The
menu is limited and never changes to boot, but the
dishes are reliably good and inexpensive to boot: get
the sautéed green beans with ham to start, then try
the superb grilled prawns or a tasty fish stew.

Els Quatre Gats

*C/Montsió 3 (93 302 41 40/www.4gats.com). Metro
Catalunya.* **Open** 1pm-1am daily. **Main courses**
€15.10-€19.10. *Set lunch* €11.75. **Credit** AmEx, DC,
MC, V. **Map** p344 B2.
This Modernista classic, once frequented by Picasso
and various other luminaries of the period, nowadays caters mainly to tourists. Sadly, the almost
inevitable consequence of such a change of clientele
is higher prices, so-so food and, worst of all, house
musicians. However, it's still dazzling in its design;
if you want to avoid the worst excesses of touristi-
fication, come along at lunchtime for a reasonably
priced and respectably varied *menú* and spare yourself *Bésame Mucho* in the process.

Les Quinze Nits

Plaça Reial 6 (93 317 30 75). Metro Liceu. **Open**
1-3.45pm, 8.30-11.30pm daily. **Main courses** €6.45-
€9.65. *Set lunch* €7.30 Mon-Fri. **Credit** AmEx, MC,
V. **Map** p345 A3.
Combining fast-food speed and prices with tablecloths, potted palms and soft lighting has made this
chain a legend in its own lunchtime. Waiting in line
is a pain, but, for many, the rock-bottom prices fully
justify the inconvenience. The turnover is brisk, as
squadrons of harried waiters serve up good salads
and local favourites such as meatballs with squid in
black ink, grilled bream with asparagus, *botifarra*
and beans, and *crema catalana*. But do choose carefully: the quality of the steaks is variable and the
paella can taste mass-produced.
Other locations: La Fonda C/Escudellers 10
(93 301 75 15); and throughout the city.

Whether for a casual lunch or a late-night drink, **Elisabets** is queen of the Raval. *See p150.*

El Salón

C/Hostal d'en Sol 6-8 (93 315 21 59). Metro Jaume I.
Open 8.30pm-midnight Mon-Sat. Closed 2wks Aug.
Main courses €10.70-€15. *Set dinner* €21.40 Mon-Sat. **Credit** AmEx, MC, V. **Map** p345 B4.

The only problem with this convivial little restaurant, with its air of stylish bohemia, are the chest-height tables. (And that's Nordic chest-height, not Mediterranean.) The food, however, is superb, as varied as it is accomplished: seafood bisque shares billing with lamb tagine, burritos, duck magret with ginger, and blackcurrant crumble. It can be hard to get a table, but the same people run nearby Ginger (*see p175*), if similarly delectable tapas will suffice. A bar and a couple of sofas ensure there's a full house for a long time after the kitchen closes.

Taxidermista

Plaça Reial 8 (93 412 45 36). Metro Liceu. **Open** 1.30-4pm, 8.30-12.30am Tue-Sun. Closed 3wks Jan. **Main courses** €11.80-€16. *Set lunch* €8.45-€16.50 Tue-Fri. **Credit** AmEx, DC, MC, V. **Map** p345 A3.

When this place was a taxidermist's, Dalí famously ordered from it 200,000 ants, a tiger, a lion and a rhinoceros, the latter wheeled into the Plaça Reial so Dalí could be photographed sitting on top. Those who leave here stuffed nowadays are generally tourists, though, unusually, this hasn't affected standards, which remain reasonably high. À la carte offerings include foie gras with quince jelly and a sherry reduction, langoustine ravioli with seafood sauce, steak tartare, and some slightly misjudged fusion elements, such as wok-fried spaghetti with vegetables. The lunch *menú* is excellent.

International

La Locanda

C/Doctor Joaquim Pou 4 (93 317 46 09). Metro Jaume I or Urquinaona. **Open** 1.15-4.30pm, 8.15pm-midnight Tue-Sun. Closed 3wks Aug. **Main courses** €8.70-€16.05. **Credit** MC, V. **Map** p344 B2.

This cosy restaurant serves up fresh, good quality Italian food amid potted palms and the odd mural of Roman gods. The pizzas – divided into red (with tomato), white (with three cheeses) and calzone – continue the Classical theme: Vulcan (salami), Apollo (egg and parmesan) or Gladiator (a fey combination of ricotta and mascarpone). There's a solid selection of classic salads, pastas, gnocchi, focaccia and risottos, and an all-Italian wine list.

Matsuri

Plaça Regomir 1 (93 268 15 35). Metro Jaume I. **Open** 1.30-3.30pm, 8.30-11.30pm Mon-Thur; 1.30-3.30pm, 8.30pm-midnight Fri; 8.30pm-midnight Sat. **Main courses** €7.50-€10.70. **Credit** MC, V. **Map** p345 B3.

Slowly, the city's Asian restaurants increase in number and quality. Matsuri is more convincing than most, with a perfectly executed look – trickling fountain, dark shades of terracotta and amber, wooden carvings and wall-hung candles – that's saved from cliché by the occidental lounge soundtrack. Reasonably priced tom yam soup, sushi, pad Thai and other South-east Asian favourites top the list; less predictable choices include a zingy mango and prawn salad dressed with lime and chilli, and a rich, earthy red curry with chicken and aubergine.

taxidermista...cafè restaurant
Plaça Reial 8   08002 Barcelona   tel. 93 412 45 36

El Paraguayo

C/Parc 1 (93 302 14 41). Metro Drassanes. **Open**
1-4pm, 8pm-midnight Tue-Sun. **Main courses** €10-
€12. **Credit** AmEx, DC, MC, V. **Map** p345 A4.
The pleasures are exclusively carnal at this warm,
wood-panelled little steakhouse, brightened with
Colombian paintings of buxom madams and their
dapper admirers. The cuts of beef are quite different to those in the north and complicated to trans-
late, but to try a range of *vacío, entraña, bife de
cuadril, churrasco* and so on, the lunchtime tasting
menu isn't a bad idea at €14 (and will serve two people), while the €33 T-bone feeds up to four. Baked
potatoes are the standard side dish, but beyond that,
El Paraguayo is, like most South American restaurants, an unwitting pioneer of the Atkins diet.

Peimong

C/Templers 6-10 (93 318 28 73). Metro Jaume I.
Open 1-4.30pm, 8-11.30pm Tue-Sun. **Main courses**
€7.50-€8.60. **Credit** MC, V. **Map** p345 B3.
With its tapestries of Macchu Pichu and plastic flowers, Peimong wins no prizes for design, but makes
up for its rather unforgiving and overlit interior with
some tasty little South American dishes. Start with
a Pisco Sour and a dish of big fat yucca chips, or
maybe some stuffed corn tamales, and then move on
to *ceviche, pato en aji* (a hunk of duck with a spicy
sauce and rice) or the satisfying *lomo saltado,* pork
fried with onions, tomatoes and coriander.

Shunka

C/Sagristans 5 (93 412 49 91). Metro Jaume I.
Open 1.30-3.30pm, 8.30-11.30pm Mon-Fri; 2-4pm,
8.30-11.30pm Sat, Sun. **Main courses** €8.50-€15. *Set
lunch* €13.50 Mon-Fri. **Credit** MC, V. **Map** p344 B2.
Although it has been increasingly compromised by
its own success, Shunka is still one of the better
Japanese restaurants in town, a favourite haunt of
superchef Ferran Adrià. Reserve a table for the
sumo-sized set lunch of rich miso soup, a leafy salad
topped with salmon and punchy vinegar and teriyaki dressing, followed by vegetable and shrimp tempura and six pieces of maki and extremely good
nigiri sushi. The best seats in the house are up at the
counter, in front of the performing chefs.

Tokyo

C/Comtal 20 (93 317 61 80). Metro Catalunya.
Open 1.30-4pm, 8-11pm Mon-Sat. **Main courses**
€9.65-€11.80. *Set lunch* €13.90 Mon-Thur. **Credit**
DC, MC, V. **Map** p344 B2.
Resist the suggestion that is no *menú,* for this is the
way to eat here. A zingy little salad is followed by a
mountain of prawn and vegetable tempura and a
platter of maki rolls, nigiri and a bowl of miso soup.
It's a simple, cosy space, cleverly divided with slat-
ted wooden partitions, with a reassuring Japanese
presence. À la carte, the speciality is edomae (hand-
rolled nigiri sushi), but the meat and veg sukiyaki
cooked at your table is also good. Check out Javier
Mariscal's grateful signed drawing of Cobi (the
Olympic mascot) dressed as a Japanese chef.

La Verònica

C/Avinyó 30 (93 412 11 22). Metro Liceu. **Open**
7.30pm-12.30am Mon-Thur; 7.30pm-1am Fri;
12.30pm-1am Sat, Sun. Closed 2wks Feb, 2wks
Aug. **Main courses** €9.65-€10.70. **Credit** MC, V.
Map p345 B3.
With plate-glass windows and a high-exposure terrace, this bright orange, gay-friendly pizzeria makes
the perfect posing gallery. The pizzas are as thin and
well dressed as the clientele, with trendy toppings
such as apple and gorgonzola along with the usual
classics. Designer salads of rocket and ginger or
parsnip, cucumber and poppy seeds take care of the
vegetation and puddings are competent pan-EU
standards of tiramisu, cheesecake and brownies.

Vegetarian

Juicy Jones

*C/Cardenal Casañas 7 (93 302 43 30). Metro
Liceu.* **Open** noon-midnight daily. **Main courses**
€5-€8. *Set lunch* €7.75 Mon-Fri. **No credit cards.**
Map p345 A3.
Wake up and smell the tofu at this Danish-owned
juice bar, where all the food, with the exception of
the honey in the soy milkshakes, is completely
vegan. A staff of international backpackers serve
the bargain all-day menu amid retina-wrenching
graffiti and thumping eurotrance. If rice and couscous are too filling, try a baguette of roast beetroot,
dill, apple and nuts, or a salad of ginger, noodles,
tofu and beansprouts. For nibbles to accompany
organic wines and beers, there are tapas or freshly
baked fruitcake and hazelnut cookies.

Raval

Ánima

C/Angels 6 (93 342 49 12). Metro Liceu. **Open**
1-4pm, 9pm-midnight Mon-Sat. **Main courses**
€10-€12. *Set lunch* €9 Mon-Fri. **Credit** MC, V.
Map p344 A2.
Mediterranean food is served in a sharp-edged space
with a thoughtfully positioned mirror allowing curious diners to watch the chefs at their work. A jumble of sautéed wild mushrooms, and rocket salad
with crispy pear are tasty, and sea bass with crab
bisque a smooth follow-up. Unfortunately, the puddings sound better than they taste: apple crumble is
actually a patty of apple, banana and crushed
almonds, and pumpkin cake with peppermint ice-
cream is just weird. Hit or miss, then, but mostly hit.

Biblioteca

C/Junta de Comerç 28 (93 412 62 21). Metro Liceu.
Open 1-4pm, 9pm-midnight Tue-Sat. Closed 2wks
Aug. **Main courses** €12.90-€13.90. *Set lunch* €9.65
Tue-Fri. **Credit** AmEx, MC, V. **Map** p345 A3.
A very zen-like space with a minimalist cream decor,
Biblioteca is all about food. Food and books about
food, that is. From Bocuse to Bourdain, all are for
sale, and their various influences collide in some

Eat, Drink, Shop

Re-Pla. See p158.

increasingly rare, jam sessions. Apart from a little fusion confusion (Thai curry with nachos; cajun chicken with mash; curried sausage with baked apple, and all manner of things with yucca chips) the food's not half bad for the price, but the service could look a little livelier.

Drassanes

Museu Marítim, Avda Drassanes (93 317 52 56). *Metro Drassanes.* **Open** 1-4pm Mon-Wed; 1-4pm, 9pm-midnight Thur-Sat. **Main courses** €9-€14. *Set lunch* €10.70 Mon-Fri. **Credit** AmEx, DC, MC, V. **Map** p345 A4.

Dwarfed by the lofty 14th-century arches of the former shipyard (*drassanes*, in Catalan), now housing the Maritime Museum, local office workers fill the tables here at lunchtime for the good value set menu. The quality can be variable, but at its best, it's unbeatable, with Catalan classics such as *botifarra* sausage with wild mushrooms appearing alongside grilled fish and pasta. Going à la carte, the dishes traverse the globe, from wok-fried prawns and vegetables on yakisoba noodles, to duck magret with sour apple sauce or Thai curry.

Elisabets

C/Elisabets 2-4 (93 317 58 26). Metro Catalunya. **Open** 1-4pm, 9-11pm Mon-Sat. Closed 3wks Aug. **Main courses** *Set lunch* €7.60 Mon-Fri. *Set dinner* €10-€12 Fri. **No credit cards**. **Map** p344 A2.

Also open in the mornings for breakfast, and late at night for drinking at the bar, Elisabets maintains a sociable local feel, despite the recent gentrification of its street with the opening of various boutiques. Dinner, which is served only on Fridays, is actually a selection of tapas; at other times, only the set lunch or myriad *bocadillos* are served. The lunch deal is terrific value, however, with osso buco, vegetable and chickpea stew, baked cod with garlic and parsley and roast pork knuckle all making regular appearances on the menu.

Las Fernández

C/Carretes 11 (93 443 2043). Metro Paral·lel. **Open** 9pm-1.30am Tue-Fri; 9pm-1am Sat, Sun. **Main courses** €6.45-€8.55. **Credit** AmEx, DC, MC, V. **Map** p342 C6.

Las Fernández's inviting entrance, a bright, pillarbox red, is a beacon of welcoming cheer on one of Barcelona's more insalubrious streets. Inside, the three Fernández sisters have created a light and unpretentious bar-restaurant that specialises in wine and food from their native León. Alongside *cecina* (dried venison), gammon and sausages from the region you'll find lighter, Mediterranean dishes and some generous salads: smoked salmon with mustard and dill, pasta filled with wild mushrooms, and sardines with a citrus escabeche, for example.

FoodBall

C/Elisabets 9 (93 270 13 63). Metro Catalunya. **Open** noon-11pm daily. **Main courses** €1.65/ball. **Credit** MC, V. **Map** p344 A2.

occasionally sublime cooking. Beetroot gazpacho with live clams and quail's egg is a dense riot of flavour, and endive salad with poached egg and *romesco* wafers is superb. Mains aren't quite as head-spinning, but are nevertheless accomplished. The set lunch menu offers a more basic fare of pasta dishes and creative salads, and an excellent wine list contains a crisp and reasonably priced Martivilli if the heavyweights don't appeal.

El Cafetí

C/Hospital 99 (end of passage) (93 329 24 19/www. *elcafeti.com). Metro Liceu.* **Open** 1.30-3.30pm, 8.30-11.30pm Tue-Sat; 1.30-3.30pm Sun. Closed 2wks Aug. **Main courses** €9.70-€12.90. *Set lunch* €9 Tue-Sat. **Credit** AmEx, DC, MC, V. **Map** p342 C6.

This discreet little *noucentista* gem has the feel of a Victorian parlour, all lace curtains, polished mahogany sideboards, gleaming brass and dried flower arrangements. The house speciality is paella in its many forms, but don't miss the *pica-pica* starters: the clams *a la marinera* are superb. Steak tartar and *xató* salad are also good, and there's a great lunchtime *menú*, but El Cafetí's fish often sees a little too much of the frying pan. Otherwise, it's a great place for dinner *à deux*.

Dos Trece

C/Carme 40 (93 301 73 06). Metro Liceu. **Open** 1.30-4pm, 9pm-midnight Tue-Sun. **Main courses** €7-€15. *Set lunch* €9 Tue-Sat. **Credit** AmEx, DC, MC, V. **Map** p344 A2.

Is it a bar? Is it a restaurant? Is it a nightclub? Where's my salad? Dos Trece caters to everyone from hangover victims, with its brunch on Sunday, to musos and their friends, with occasional, though

Casas regionales

For a whistle-stop tour of Spain, soaking up the flavour and ambience of different regions without ever actually leaving this one, Barcelona's numerous *casas regionales* are the way to go. These cultural centres and clubhouses provide a taste of home for nationals who have left their own corners of the peninsula behind, playing host to various activities, folkloric performances and member dinners, as well as providing replicas of the cafés and bars back home.

Often, the *casas regionales* are among the best places in town to try authentic regional cooking. Take, for example, the comfortably cosy **Casa de Andalucía** (Via Laietana 59 pral, 93 318 61 38) with its splashy tilework and dolls' house sized, green-painted tables and chairs. It's a friendly place in which to chow down on *pescadito frito* and hearty peasant fare of fried eggs and *chorizo*. The roof terrace goes all out to imitate the *plazas* of the Pueblos Blancos in the summer, while the small theatre hosts flamenco classes and performances year round.

In the eye of the Born, the **Centre Cultural Euskal Etxea** (Placeta Montcada 1-3, 93 310 22 00) is a dark, cosy bar boasting the best *pintxos* this side of San Sebastian; half boiled eggs topped with giant prawns and unctuous mayonnaise; tender octopus sprinkled with paprika served on wooden dishes; and hunks of smokey Idiazabal cheese topped with *membrillo* (quince paste). If you want to get really integrated, come here for Euskera classes, and learn to play the country's hobbit-like musical intruments: the *txalapara* (a wooden block that's beaten with drumsticks) and *trikitixa* (a small accordion).

The bright, modern **Casa de la Rioja** (C/ Peu de la Creu 8-10, 93 443 33 63) offers a wealth of knowledge about this little-explored region. The library is excellent and stocks everything you need to know about *casas rurales* (country inns and guesthouses) and suggested itineraries. The menu runs through a solid repertoire of traditional and new Rioja cuisine: starters include a deeply satisfying

array of dishes like anchovies marinated in rosemary and pine nuts, scrambled eggs with spicy *chistorra* sausage, and baby broad beans with ham and cuttlefish. A big shout out, too, for the juicy T-bone steaks that go for 32 a kilo, but could feed a family of four.

And so on to the nearby **Espai Mallorca** (C/Carme 55, 93 442 91 93), a cultural centre for all the Balearic islands. The bookshop doubles as a small publisher and stocks an extensive range of guidebooks, maps, poetry and novels about the islands as well as some glossy coffee-table tomes. It also has a small delicatessen where aficionados can get their fix of *hierbas* (a menthol-green coloured digestif made from mountain herbs), Binassalem wine, olive oils and capers. The café, though not strictly Mallorcan in theme, offers delicious home-made cakes and quiches as well as local cheeses, charcuterie and cakes such as *ensaimadas* (delicious sugar-dusted spiral pastries eaten for breakfast on the island).

Galicia is nowadays much appreciated for its superlative seafood, the richness of its meats and the creaminess of its cheeses. The **Casa Gallega** (C/Rambla Capuchinos 35-37 1º, 93 301 28 92) reflects the hospitality of the motherland and is one of the few eateries on La Rambla that is worth a stop, offering a fine selection of regional specialities from *empanadas* (pasties) to *percebes* (goose-neck barnacles) as well as a selection of the region's highly acclaimed white wines. A well-chilled Albariño with a heap of shellfish here is as good as it gets.

Eat, Drink, Shop

Camper shoes has joined forces with Marti Guixé, the Catalan food designer, to create a new and very bizarre catering concept. First off, the food is presented in, yes, balls. Spherical patties of rice holding chicken, mushrooms, seaweed and tofu. Dense globes of carob and dates. Then there's the space – tiered concrete strewn with raffia pads and facing a TV screen where goldfish glide and waves crash on the shore, while earnest murals extol the virtues of ethnic diversity and organic food ('Revolution begins in the vegetable patch'). Payment with cowrie shells must surely be just around the corner.

Lupino

C/Carme 33 (93 412 36 97). Metro Liceu. **Open** 1-4pm, 9pm-midnight Mon-Thur, Sun; 1-4pm, 9pm-1am Fri, Sat. **Main courses** €8.56-€12.85. *Set lunch* €10 Mon-Fri; €12 Sat, Sun. **Credit** MC, V. **Map** p344 A2.

Lupino opened a couple of years ago with what was then a new retro-futuristic look. Unfortunately, nothing dates so fast as futurism and now what was once unique can be seen pretty much everywhere else. Its navy panelling, yellow flight cases and soft coloured lighting are ageing fairly well, however, though its designer showiness and oh-so-cool cocktail bar haven't attracted the hoped-for supermodels. Rather, you'll find here an unpretentious crowd, chowing down on the surprisingly honest food: *trinxat Cerdanya* (like bubble and squeak, with bacon), chicken kebabs, roast lamb and so on.

Mama Café

C/Doctor Dou 10 (93 301 29 40). Metro Catalunya or Liceu. **Open** 1-4pm, 8pm-midnight Mon-Sat. **Main courses** €9.65-€11.75. *Set lunch* €7 Mon-Fri. **Credit** AmEx, MC, V. **Map** p344 A2.

A wildly diverse crowd is attracted to the good, fresh food and low-key new age vibe of the Mama Café; dreadlocks settle in next to blue rinses for melon gazpacho, venison tataki with caramelised black grapes and chestnut purée, wok-fried vegetables with smoked tofu or monkfish and some truly scrumptious desserts. The deep colours and relaxing music make it an easy place to sit back and stay a while.

Mesón David

C/Carretas 63 (93 441 59 34). Metro Paral·lel. **Open** 1-4.30pm, 8-11.45pm Mon, Tue, Thur-Sun. Closed Aug. **Main courses** €6-€7.50. *Set lunch* €7. **Credit** AmEx, MC, V. **Map** p342 C6.

Rough and ready, noisy, chaotic a lot of fun, Mesón David is also one of the cheapest restaurants in Barcelona. Be prepared to share a table and expect plenty of banter with the staff as you pore over a list of mainly Galician dishes: *caldo gallego* (cabbage broth) or fish soup to start, followed by *lechazo* (a vast hunk of roast pork), *trucha navarra* (trout stuffed with cured ham and cheese) or just a hefty steak. Of the excellent desserts, the almond *tarta de Santiago* battles for supremacy with the quarter of fresh baby pineapple doused in Cointreau.

Pla dels Àngels

C/Ferlandina 23 (93 329 40 47). Metro Universitat. **Open** 1.30-4pm, 9-11.30pm Mon-Thur, Sun; 1.30-4pm, 9pm-midnight Fri, Sat. **Main courses** €12.85-€16.05. *Set lunch* €5.35 Mon-Fri. **Credit** DC, MC, V. **Map** p342 C5.

Beautifully designed, in keeping with its position opposite the MACBA, Pla dels Àngels is a kaleidoscopic riot of colours, a look that also translates to its menu (glued to a wine bottle, no less). Salads might include mango, yoghurt and mint oil, or radicchio, serrano ham and roast peppers, followed by a short list of pasta and gnocchi and a couple of meat dishes. 'Delirium tremens' is the richest of chocolate fantasies, while the cheap-as-chips set lunch includes two courses and a glass of wine.

Pollo Rico

C/Sant Pau 31 (93 441 31 84/www.polloricosl.com). Metro Liceu. **Open** 10am-1am Mon, Tue, Thur-Sat, Sun. **Main courses** €6-€8. *Set lunch* €6.60 Mon, Tue, Thur-Sat. **No credit cards.** **Map** p345 A3.

A Raval institution, the 'Tasty Chicken' has the best rotisserie fowl in the city twirling away in its windows. Picnickers can take away a golden-skinned quarter for just €3 while local characters and tourists all troop upstairs for heartier portions, litre jugs of wicked sangria, or the €3 plate of *botifarra* and beans. The only downsides are the supermarket lighting and the droopy, greasy chips.

Silenus

C/Àngels 8 (93 302 26 80). Metro Liceu. **Open** 1.30-4pm, 8.45pm-11.30am Mon-Thur; 1.30-4pm, 8.45pm-12.30am Fri, Sat. **Main courses** €15-€19.25. *Set lunch* €11 Mon-Fri; €16 Sat. **Credit** AmEx, DC, MC, V. **Map** p344 A2.

Run by arty types for arty types, Silenus works hard to create and maintain its air of scuffed elegance, with carefully chipped and stained walls whereon the ghost of a clock is projected and the faded leaves of a book float up on high. The food, too, is artistically presented (although the omnipresence of poppy seeds becomes quite funny by the time you start picking them from the ice-cream); never more so than with the lunchtime tasting menu, which allows a tiny portion of everything on the menu, from French onion soup to a flavoursome haricot bean stew and entrecôte with mashed potatoes.

Zarabanda

C/Ferlandina 55 (mobile 653 169 539). Metro Sant Antoni. **Open** 7pm-1am Mon-Sat. Closed 2wks Aug. **Main courses** €5.50-€6.50. **No credit cards.** **Map** p324 C5.

Probably the only place in town to have a shared bowl of nachos as its signature dish, Zarabanda attracts a fair few students, looking for somewhere more comfortable than a bar but cheaper than a restaurant. Its cosy vibe is nudged along with low lighting, creative paintwork and the much sought-after sofa space; the food is decent and good value, particularly the salads and crêpes. Occasional flamenco, jazz and even electro take over the tiny stage.

Eat, Drink, Shop

Menu glossary

Essential terminology

Catalan	Spanish	
una cullera	una cuchara	a spoon
una forquilla	un tenedor	a fork
un ganivet	un cuchillo	a knife
una ampolla de	una botella de	a bottle of
una altra	otra	another (one)
més	más	more
pa	pan	bread
oli d'oliva	aceite de oliva	olive oil
sal i pebre	sal y pimienta	salt and pepper
amanida	ensalada	salad
truita	tortilla	omelette
(note: **truita** can also mean trout)		
la nota	la cuenta	the bill
un cendrer	un cenicero	an ashtray
vi negre/	vino tinto/	red/rosé/
rosat/blanc	rosado/ blanco	white wine
bon profit	aproveche	Enjoy your meal
sóc	soy	I'm a…
vegetarià/ana	vegetariano/a	vegetarian
diabètic/a	diabético/a	diabetic

Cooking terms

a la brasa	a la brasa	char-grilled
a la graella/ planxa	a la plancha	grilled on a hot metal plate
a la romana	a la romana	fried in batter
al forn	al horno	baked
al vapor	al vapor	steamed
fregit	frito	fried
rostit	asado	roast
ben fet	bien hecho	well done
a punt	medio hecho	medium
poc fet	poco hecho	rare

Carn i aviram/Carne y aves/ Meat & poultry

ànec	pato	duck
bou	buey	beef
cabrit	cabrito	kid
conill	conejo	rabbit
embotits	embotidos	cold cuts
fetge	higado	liver
gall dindi	pavo	turkey
garrí	cochinillo	suckling pig
guatlla	codorniz	quail
llebre	liebre	hare
llengua	lengua	tongue
llom	lomo	loin (usually pork)
oca	oca	goose
ous	huevos	eggs
perdiu	perdiz	partridge
pernil (serrà)	jamón serrano	dry-cured ham
pernil dolç	jamón york	cooked ham
peus de porc	manos de cerdo	pigs' trotters
pichón	colomí	pigeon
pintada	gallina de Guinea	guinea fowl
pollastre	pollo	chicken
porc	cerdo	pork
porc senglar	jabalí	wild boar
vedella	ternera	veal
xai/be	cordero	lamb

Peix i marisc/Pescado y mariscos/Fish & seafood

anxoves	anchoas	anchovies
bacallà	bacalao	salt cod
besuc	besugo	sea bream
caballa	verat	mackerel
calamarsos	calamares	squid
cloïsses	almejas	clams
cranc	cangrejo	crab
escamarlans	cigalas	crayfish
escopinyes	berberechos	cockles

International

Fil Manila

C/Ramelleres 3 (93 318 64 87). Metro Catalunya. **Open** 11.30am-4.30pm, 8-11.30pm daily. Closed Tue Nov-Feb. **Main courses** €5.90-€6.50. **No credit cards. Map** p344 A2.

There's practically a dish for every one of the 7,000 or so Philippine islands on this epic menu. Malay, Chinese and Spanish influences all contribute to the classic flavours of sour fish soup, *pancit* (noodles), chicken and pork adobo, fried *lumpia* (crispy veg-etable or meat rolls) or a *halo-halo* dessert of fruits, crushed ice and milk. The bamboo-lined decor does-n't try too hard to be exotic and the faithful patron-age of local Filipinos augurs well for the food's authenticity. As for the food spicy if you want as the natives would eat it.

Moti Mahal

C/Sant Pau 103 (93 329 32 52/www.motimahal bcn.com). Metro Liceu. **Open** noon-4pm, 8pm-midnight daily. **Main courses** €7-€9. *Set lunch* €8.25 Mon-Fri. **Credit** AmEx, DC, MC, V. **Map** p342 C6.

carxofes	alcachofas	artichokes
ceba	cebolla	onion
cigrons	garbanzos	chickpeas
col	col	cabbage
enciam	lechuga	lettuce
endivies	endivias	chicory
espinacs	espinacas	spinach
mongetes blanques	judías blancas	haricot beans
mongetes verdes	judías verdes	French beans
pastanagues	zanahorias	carrot
patates	patatas	potatoes
pebrots	pimientos	peppers
pèsols	guisantes	peas
porros	puerros	leek
tomàquets	tomates	tomatoes
xampinyons	champiñones	mushrooms

espardenyes	espardeñas	sea cucumbers
gambes	gambas	prawns
llagosta	langosta	spiny lobster
llagostins	langostinos	langoustines
llamàntol	bogavante	lobster
llenguado	lenguado	sole
llobarro	lubina	sea bass
lluç	merluza	hake
moll	salmonete	red mullet
musclos	mejillones	mussels
navalles	navajas	razor clams
percebes	percebes	barnacles
pop	pulpo	octopus
rap	rape	monkfish
rèmol	rodaballo	turbot
salmó	salmón	salmon
sardines	sardinas	sardines
sípia	sepia	squid
tallarines	tallarinas	wedge clams
tonyina	atún	tuna
truita	trucha	trout

(note: **truita** can also mean an omelette)

Postres/Postres/Desserts

flam	flan	crème caramel
formatge	queso	cheese
gelat	helado	ice-cream
música	música	dried fruit and nuts, served with muscatel
pastís	pastel	cake
tarta	tarta	tart

Fruïta/Fruta/Fruit

figues	higos	figs
gerds	frambuesas	raspberries
maduixes	fresas	strawberries
pera	pera	pear
pinya	piña	pineapple
plàtan	plátano	banana
poma	manzana	apple
préssec	melocotón	peach
prunes	ciruelas	plums
raïm	uvas	grapes
taronja	naranja	orange

Verdures/Legumbres/Vegetables

albergínia	berenjena	aubergine
all	ajo	garlic
alvocat	aguacate	avocado
bolets	setas	wild mushrooms
carbassós	calabacines	courgette

While it might be true that Indian food still has a long way to go before turning Spain into the culinary outpost of the subcontinent that Britain has become, this bright and noisy curry house, with Germolene pink walls and reasonable selection, is a respectable member of the vanguard. Specialities include tandoori and a richly flavoured range of vegetable dishes served in little brass tureens, most notable among them the creamy dahl *makhni* and the *bhindi* (okra). Make it clear if you want it hot (*picante*): the default setting is mild, even for a vindaloo, in order to keep local palates sweet.

Vegetarian

Organic

C/Junta de Comerç 1 (93 301 0902). Metro Liceu.
Open 12.30-5pm, 8pm-midnight. **Main courses**
€7-€12.50. *Set lunch* €8 Mon-Fri; €10.95 Sat; €12
Sun. **Credit** AmEx, MC, V. **Map** p345 A3.
The last word in refectory chic, Organic is better designed and lighter in spirit (its motto: 'Don't panic, it's organic!') than the vast majority of the city's vegetarian restaurants. The friendly and attentive staff will usher you inside, seat you and give you a run-

Eat, Drink, Shop

down on meal options: an all-you-can-eat salad bar, a combined salad bar and main course, or the full whammy – salad, soup, main course and dessert (set lunches above). Listen for the bell and collect your plate when ready. Beware the little extras (such as drinks), which hitch up the prices a fair bit.

Sésamo

C/Sant Antoni Abat 52 (93 441 64 11). Metro Sant Antoni. **Open** 1-3.30pm Mon; 1-3.30pm, 8.30-11.30pm Wed-Sun. **Main courses** €9-€11. *Set lunch* €8.75 Mon, Wed-Sat. **Credit** MC, V. **Map** p342 C5.
Another veggie restaurant not to take itself too seriously (yoga ads, but no whale song), Sésamo offers a creative bunch of dishes in a cosy, buzzing back room. Salad with risotto and a drink is quite a bargain at €6.50, or try cucumber rolls stuffed with smoked tofu and mashed pine nuts, crunchy polenta with baked pumpkin, gorgonzola and radicchio, or spicy curry served in popadom baskets with dahl and wild rice. Vegan dishes include a tasty meze selection.

Sant Pere & the Born

Bar Salvador

C/Canvis Nous 8 (93 310 10 41). Metro Jaume I or Barceloneta. **Open** 9am-4pm Mon-Fri. **Main courses** €3.50-€5. **Credit** MC, V. **Map** p345 B4.
Providing breakfast and lunch for the workers, this unalloyed little gem also pulls in the local literati and their friends, who sit in large animated groups passing aloft glass *porrones* of beer. Daily changing mains might include a sticky pork knuckle with fiery *all i oli*, duck with haricot beans or sardines in garlic and parsley, all nestling alongside fat, crisp potato wedges. As well as nearly free house red from the barrel, a bottle of excellent Gotim Bru is a staggeringly low €9.75.

Cal Pep

Plaça de les Olles 8 (93 310 79 61). Metro Barceloneta. **Open** 8-11.45pm Mon; 1.30-4pm, 8-11.45pm Tue-Sat. Closed Aug. **Main courses** €15-€20. **Credit** AmEx, DC, MC, V. **Map** p344 C4.
As much tapas bar as restaurant, Cal Pep is always packed: get here early for the coveted seats at the front and a bit more elbow room. There is a cosy dining room at the back, but it's a shame to miss the show. The affable Pep will take the order, steering the neophytes towards the *trifásico* – a mélange of fried whitebait, squid rings and shrimp, all lightly battered. Other favourites are the exquisite little *tallarines* (wedge clams), and *botifarra* sausage with beans. Then, squeeze in four shot glasses of foam – coconut with rum, coffee, *crema catalana* and lemon – as a light and scrumptious pudding.

Comerç 24

C/Comerç 24 (93 319 21 02). Metro Arc de Triomf. **Open** 1.30-3.30pm, 8.30pm-midnight Mon-Sat. **Main courses** €10.70-€19.25. **Credit** AmEx, MC, V. **Map** p345 C3.

One of the acknowledged masters of Catalan new wave cuisine, Carles Abellan was, inevitably, a disciple of Ferran Adrià in the kitchens of El Bulli (*see p171*), but nowadays ploughs his own, highly successful furrow in this urbane and sexy restaurant. A selection of tiny playful dishes changes seasonally, but might include a 'Kinder egg' (lined with truffle); tuna sashimi and seaweed on a wafer-thin pizza crust; a fun take on the *bikini* (a cheese and ham toastie); or a densely flavoured fish *suquet*. Order a selection in the shape of the '*menú festival*' to understand Catalonia's food revolution a little better.

L'Econòmic

Plaça Sant Agustí Vell 13 (93 319 64 94). Metro Arc de Triomf. **Open** 12.30-4.30pm Mon-Fri. Closed Aug. **Main courses** €5-€7.50. *Set lunch* €8.30 Mon-Fri. **No credit cards**. **Map** p344 C2.
In some restaurants, you're there to eat; others you visit simply to refuel. While L'Econòmic sidles into the latter category, the dining room is very charming: deep and narrow, lined with colourful tiles and oil paintings. The cheapest lunch deal around covers vegetable or fish soup, broad beans with ham and lettuce hearts with tuna to start, followed by unadorned fried pork or minute steak, lemon chicken, cod croquettes or fried hake. Getting hold of a table after 2pm is something of an ordeal.

Hofmann

C/Argenteria 74-78 (93 319 58 89/www.hofmann-bcn.com). Metro Jaume I. **Open** 1.30-3.15pm, 9-11.15pm Mon-Fri. Closed Aug. **Main courses** €26.75-€28.90. *Set lunch* €31.20. **Credit** AmEx, DC, MC, V. **Map** p345 C3.
Said to be the best cookery school in the world after the Cordon Bleu, Hofmann puts its pupils to good use in its top-class restaurant. A succession of small dining rooms include a light-filled atrium, and another decorated in deep reds, orange and green; all are adorned with plants and dramatic flower arrangements. The affordable set lunch menu might start with a truffle salad, followed by bream wrapped in bacon or carré of lamb with mustard sauce, but the puddings are the real high point. Artful constructions such as a jam jar and lid made of sugar and filled with red fruits, or a tarte tatin in a spun-sugar 'cage', are as delicious as they are clever.

Mundial Bar

Plaça Sant Agustí Vell 1 (93 319 90 56). Metro Arc de Triomf or Jaume I. **Open** 11am-4pm, 8.30-11.30pm Tue-Fri; noon-4pm, 8.30pm-midnight Sat; noon-3.30pm Sun. Closed 2wks Aug. **Main courses** €9-€15. **Credit** MC, V. **Map** p344 C2.
Since 1925 this family establishment has been dishing up no-frills platters of seafood, cheeses and the odd slice of cured meat. Colourful tiles and a marble trough of a bar add charm to basic decor, but it's not as cheap as it looks. People come for the steaming piles of fresh razor clams, shrimp, oysters, fiddler crabs and the like, but there's plenty of tinned produce, so check the bar displays to see which is which.

Eat, Drink, Shop

La Paradeta

C/Comercial 7 (93 268 19 39). Metro Arc de Triomf or Jaume I. **Open** 8-11.30pm Tue-Fri; 1-4pm, 8pm-midnight Sat; 1-4pm Sun. **Main courses** €5-€7. **No credit cards. Map** p345 C4.

Superb seafood, served refectory style. Choose from glistening mounds of clams, mussels, squid, spider crabs and whatever else the boats have brought in, let them know how you'd like it cooked (grilled, steamed or a la marinera), pick a sauce (Marie Rose, spicy local *romesco*, *all i oli* or onion with tuna), buy a drink and wait for your number to be called. A great – and cheap – experience for anyone not too grand to clear their own plate.

El Pebre Blau

C/Banys Vells 21 (93 319 13 08). Metro Jaume I. **Open** 8.30pm-midnight daily. **Main courses** €8.55-€16.05. **Credit** MC, V. **Map** p345 C3.

A breathless gastronomic globetrot: Turkish lamb kebabs, Moroccan tagines, Indian curries, Greek salads and Mexican moles. The salad selection alone covers ten different countries. Stone floors and arches are warmed by buttery yellow lighting, and Born socialites wearing overly interesting spectacle frames nibble at goat's cheese timbale with caramelised endives or peruse a large section entitled 'All we can do with a duck'; options include sautéeing its livers with sherry and apples or dousing it with banana, chocolate, yucca and ginger. **Other locations: L'Ou Com Balla** C/Banys Vells 20, Born (93 310 53 78).

Pla de la Garsa

C/Assaonadors 13 (93 315 24 13). Metro Jaume I. **Open** 8pm-1am daily. **Main courses** €6.50-€10. **Credit** AmEx, MC, V. **Map** p345 C3.

The owner of Pla de la Garsa has graced his 16th-century dairy with a wrought-iron spiral staircase, painted mirrors and rustic tiling, but the food's delicious, too. The exellent wine list complements fabulous pâtés, confit of duck thighs, sausages and Catalan goat's cheeses. Of the various taster menus (minimum two people), the €19 variety might include flat *coca* bread with *alboronia* (ratatouille); croquettes of courgette, beer and sea urchin; almogrote cheese; garum terrine, and lamb *botifarra*.

Re-Pla

C/Montcada 2 (93 268 30 03). Metro Jaume I. **Open** 9pm-midnight Mon-Thur, Sun; 9pm-1am Fri, Sat. **Main courses** €16.05-€23.55. **Credit** MC, V. **Map** p345 C3.

This newer branch of Pla in the Barri Gòtic is preferable to its big brother: it serves a similar assortment of hip Asian-Mediterranean fusion, but hasn't been around long enough to pack in the crowds. The wildly varied menu might include anything from a sushi platter to ostrich with green asparagus, honey and grilled mango slices. Veggie options are clearly marked and desserts rich and creative. For once, the lighting is low and the artwork easy on the eye. **Other locations: Pla** C/Bellafila 5, Barri Gòtic (93 412 65 52).

Taberna Santa Maria

C/Abaixadors 10 (93 310 30 96). Metro Jaume I. **Open** 1-4pm Mon, Sun; 1-4pm, 9pm-midnight Tue-Fri; 1-4pm, 10pm-1am Sat. **Main courses** €12.50-€18. *Set lunch* €7.50-€14 Mon-Fri. **Credit** AmEx, DC, MC, V. **Map** p345 B4.

An olde Castilian tavern straight from central casting, with bare bricks, Gothic arches and heavy iron chandeliers. The menu is in keeping, with a long, long list of *carnes a la brasa*, as well as boards of cheese and ham. Various good lunch deals involve thick soups (*caldo gallego* is a winner, with pork and cabbage), and maybe peppers stuffed with hake or roast pork knuckle (*codillo*) to follow. Puddings run the usual gamut of eggy comfort food. The real surprise is the wine list, which includes some top-notch bottles from La Rioja and Ribera del Duero.

International

Bunga Raya

C/Assaonadors 7 (93 319 31 69). Metro Jaume I. **Open** 8pm-midnight Tue-Sun. **Main courses** €8-€10. **No credit cards. Map** p345 C3.

Expats flock to the tiny, bamboo-lined 'Hibiscus Flower' for the excellent Malaysian taster menu: a pile of coconut rice with curried squid rings, beef rendang, fried peanuts with coconut shavings, spicy pineapple, marinated beansprout salad, chicken and beef satay, and a bowl of chicken curry. Other good dishes include curried anchovies and a chokingly spicy shrimp tom yam soup; avoid the uninspired vegetable dishes and puds. There's an airier room upstairs, but what you gain in space, you lose in waiter attentiveness. On a first visit, we recommend you order the tasting menu for €12.95.

La Cua Curta

C/Carassa s/n (93 310 00 15). Metro Jaume I. **Open** 8.30pm-midnight Tue-Thur, Sun; 8.30pm-1.30am Fri, Sat. **Main courses** €11.75-€13.90. **Credit** AmEx, DC, MC, V. **Map** p345 C3.

Having tired of mullets and swingers' bars, the retro-obsessed of Barcelona have turned their attention to the quietly thriving fondue restaurants. Yes, it's hip to dip once again, but *Abigail's Party* this is not: quaintly Gallic with its etched mirrors and lacy embroidered lampshades, La Cua Curta is a refined affair, where only the menus glued to record sleeves evoke anything but the 1920s. Start with a generous salad before tackling one of the dozen variations on the emmenthal and gruyère theme, and stay off the water if you intend digesting the cheese.

Dionisus

Avda Marquès de Argentera 27 (93 268 24 72). Metro Ciutadella. **Open** 1.30-4pm, 8pm-midnight Mon-Thur; 1.30-4pm, 8pm-12.30am Fri-Sun. **Main courses** €7.50-€9. *Set lunch* €9 Mon-Fri. *Set dinner* €19.65 Mon-Fri. **Credit** MC, V. **Map** p345 C4.

Bottles of golden retsina filter the light like stained glass on to the Aegean blue walls at this excellent Greek restaurant. Filled pittas are served at the bar and on the parkside terrace tables, while inside, diners go for the set lunch. À la carters should split a huge *pikilia megali* of houmous, *dolmadakia* (stuffed vine leaves), feta, tsatsiki and taramasalata, followed by *souvlaki* (skewers) of steak and seafood and lemon-roast potatoes. And if there's any space, finish off with halva or Greek yoghurt with honey. **Other locations:** C/Torrent de l'Olla 144, Gràcia (93 237 34 17); C/Comte d'Urgell 90, Eixample (93 451 54 17).

Habana Vieja

C/Banys Vells 2 (93 268 25 04). Metro Jaume I. **Open** 1.30-3.30pm, 8.30-11.30pm Mon-Sat. **Main courses** €8.60-€12.90. **Credit** AmEx, DC, MC, V. **Map** p345 C3.

A tiny, laid-back Cuban restaurant, with plenty of *son* and rumba to get the evening going. The sharp taste of limes in the Mojitos and Caipirinhas complement the love-it-or-hate-it parade of Havana cuisine, which involves lots of meat, stodge and frying pans. Rice and beans accompany tender *ropa vieja* (shredded chilli beef), fried yucca with *mojo cubano* (garlic sauce), banana or *malanga* fritters (a taro-like root vegetable) with fresh guava for dessert. The prices seem quite high for this sort of food, but the portions are big enough to share.

Al Passatore

Pla del Palau 8 (93 319 78 51). Metro Barceloneta. **Open** 1pm-12.30am Mon-Wed; 1pm-1am Thur-Sun. **Main courses** €8-€13. **Credit** MC, V. **Map** p345 C4.

No Gianni-come-lately, this chain – now with eight branches – completely dominates the market for budget Italian food. The service is entirely charmless but nowhere is faster: within ten minutes of ordering there's a pizza the size of a tractor tyre on your plate. Cooked in an authentic Neapolitan wood-fired oven, they come in a whopping 40 varieties and not one of them costs over €11. Unfortunately, the rest of the food can be mediocre, with limp, watery salads and cheap cuts of meat. **Other locations:** throughout the city.

Eixample

Alkimia

C/Indústria 79 (93 207 61 15). Metro Sagrada Família. **Open** 1.30-3.30pm, 9-11pm Mon-Fri; 9-11pm Sat. Closed 3wks Aug. **Main courses** €21.40-€26.75. **Credit** AmEx, DC, MC, V. **Map** p339 E3.

It came as no surprise to Alkimia's regulars when it was recently awarded a Michelin star (as a consequence of which, reservations are now all but essential). A great way to explore is the gourmet menu, with four savoury courses, including complex dishes playing with Spanish classics – deconstructed gazpacho, wild rice with crayfish, oxtail stew with mash, strips of tuna on a bed of foamed mustard – and a couple of desserts. An excellent wine cellar adds to the experience, as does impeccable service and a gracefully modern dining room.

Astoria

C/Paris 193 (93 414 47 99). Metro Hospital Clínic. **Open** 9pm-midnight Tue-Sat. Closed Aug. **Main courses** €8-€14. **Credit** AmEx, DC, MC, V. **Map** p338 C3.

Party like it's 1985 in this stunning converted theatre, kitted out in red and blue neon and plush black upholstery. The tables overlook the dancefloor from

Cinc Sentits. *See p161.*

Eat, Drink, Shop

the glassed-in upper dress circle, and there's no danger of getting yourself too stuffed for a boogie: the Thumbelina portions are designed to maintain the cubist bone structures of the model/hairdresser clientele. What there is, though, is delectable: mango and tiger prawn salad, lobster claws on green beans, steak tartar, or médaillons of prime, pan-fried sirloin. All are a worthy precursor to the hot chocolate soufflé or sweet-and-sour truffles.

Casa Calvet

C/Casp 48 (93 412 40 12). Metro Urquinaona. **Open** 1-3.30pm, 8.30-11pm Mon-Sat. **Main courses** €20.50-€25.70. **Credit** AmEx, DC, MC, V. **Map** p344 C1.

The loafer's guide to sightseeing would surely have Casa Calvet at the top of the list: this is a place where you can sample stellar cuisine and appreciate the master of Modernisme at once. One of Gaudí's more understated buildings from the outside, Casa Calvet has an interior full of glorious detail in the carpentry, stained glass and tiles. The food is up to par, with surprising combinations almost always hitting the mark: squab with puréed pumpkin, risotto of duck confit and truffle with yoghurt ice-cream, and smoked foie gras with mango sauce. The puddings are supremely good, particularly the pine nut tart with foamed *crema catalana*, and the cheeseboard contains some unexpected finds.

Cata 1.81

C/València 181 (93 323 68 18). Metro Hospital Clínic or Passeig de Gràcia. **Open** 6pm-midnight Mon-Thur; 6pm-1am Fri, Sat. Closed last 3wks Aug. **Main courses** €11.80-€15. **Credit** AmEx, DC, MC, V. **Map** p338 C4.

Until recently, the emphasis at Cata 1.81 was on the encyclopaedic wine list (a *cata* is a tasting measure), with food as an accompaniment, but there's been a shift in direction. Now, a modest wine list complements a range of *platillos*, small dishes designed to be shared, and which might contain pigs' trotters with figs, walnuts and honey ice-cream (a surefire way to convert the squeamish); salt cod with three peppers covered in fine pasta; and fried or tuna teriyaki with caramelised watermelon. The only downside is that the menus are exclusively in Catalan and the waiting staff are often too rushed to be of much assistance to the hapless tourist.

Cinc Sentits

C/Aribau 58 (93 323 94 90/www.cincsentits.com). Metro Passeig de Gràcia or Universitat. **Open** 1.30-3.30pm Mon; 1.30-3.30pm, 8.30-11pm Tue-Sat. **Main courses** €17-€21.50. **Credit** AmEx, MC, V. **Map** p342 C5.

Opened in 2004, the 'Five Senses' is creating quite a buzz in Barcelona gastronomic circles, and it's easy to see why. Globally sourced ingredients, from Danish beef to Australian river salt, have been placed together in uplifting combinations, cooked with meticulous precision and served in elegant but unstuffy surroundings. Lamb cutlets with a porcini

crust are inspired, but the slow-braised pork belly on gingerbread balanced with bitter escarole and walnut dressing is simply superb. To finish, a sour apple sorbet prepares the palate for a dense maple 'quesada' (think cheesecake then raise expectations by the power of ten) and the suggested wine pairings are impeccable throughout.

Gaig

Hotel Cram, C/Aragó 214 (93 429 10 17). Metro Passeig de Gràcia. **Open** 1.30-3.30pm, 9-11pm Mon-Sat. **Main courses** €26.75-€32.10. **Credit** AmEx, DC, MC, V. **Map** p338 C4.

Recently displaced from its long-term (for over 130 years, in fact) home in Horta after structural problems, Gaig has lost none of its shine in the process of moving. Carles Gaig's cooking never fails to thrill, from the crayfish tempura *amuse-gueule*, served with a dip of creamed leek salted with a piece of pancetta, through to a shot glass holding layers of tangy lemon syrup, *crema catalana* mousse, caramel ice-cream and topped with burnt sugar (to be eaten by plunging the spoon all the way down), every dish is as surprising and perfectly composed as the last. If you treat yourself to only one top-class restaurant while in Barcelona, then let it be this one.

Moo

C/Rosselló 265 (93 445 40 00). Metro Diagonal. **Open** 1.30-4pm, 8.30-11pm daily. **Main courses** (half portions) €16.05-€21.40. **Credit** AmEx, DC, MC, V. **Map** p338 D4.

As desirable as the rooms at the Hotel Omm (*see p69*) are the tables in its restaurant, Moo. The superbly inventive cooking is overseen by Catalan chef Joan Roca and designed as 'half portions'; all the better to experience the full range, from sea bass with lemongrass to exquisite suckling pig with a sharp Granny Smith purée. Wines (from a list of 500) are suggested to go with every course, and many dishes are built around them. Finish, for example, with 'Sauternes', the wine's bouquet perfectly rendered in mango ice-cream, saffron custard and grapefruit jelly. Service is exemplary.

Noti

C/Roger de Llúria 35 (93 342 66 73). Metro Passeig de Gràcia or Urquinaona. **Open** 1.30-4pm, 8.30pm-midnight Mon-Fri; 8.30pm-midnight Sat. **Main courses** €19.25-€23.55. *Set lunch* €18.20 Mon-Fri. **Credit** AmEx, DC, MC, V. **Map** p342 D5.

At the very cutting edge of the vanguard, Noti is at once wildly glamorous and deadly serious about its food. Centrally positioned tables surrounded by reflective glass and gold panelling make celebrity-spotting a natural hazard, but the myriad other reasons for coming here include a rich and aromatic fish soup with velvety rouille; lobster carpaccio with crispy seaweed; smoky hunks of seared tuna; and a succulent lamb brochette with spiced couscous and spring vegetables. Modern jazz gives way to house as the night progresses and the restaurant transforms into a bar for the city's most gorgeous.

Eat, Drink, Shop

Principal

*C/Provença 286 (93 272 0845). FGC Provença/
Metro Diagonal.* **Open** 1.30-4pm; 8.30-11pm Mon-
Thur, Sun; 1.30-4pm; 8.30pm-midnight Fri, Sat.
Closed 1wk Aug. **Main courses** €16-€26.50. *Set
lunch* €21.40 Mon-Fri. **Credit** AmEx, DC, MC, V.
Map p338 C4.

Another hit from the Tragaluz empire (*see right*),
albeit at the swisher end of the scale. The immaculate shades-of-grey interior contrasts with the
Modernista excesses of the building itself. There are
various dining rooms, most reserved for large
groups and opulent wedding celebrations making
for distracted and less-than-helpful staff. The food,
though, is accomplished, and covers all the bases
from light, fresh fusion (tuna sashimi with avocado
and mozzarella) to old-school Catalan with bells on
(venison with quince chutney). Look out for a stunning Marqués de Vargas Rioja on the wine list.

Semproniana

*C/Rosselló 148 (93 453 18 20). Metro Hospital
Clínic.* **Open** 1.30-4pm, 9-11.30pm Mon-Thur; 1.30-
4pm, 9pm-midnight Fri, Sat. **Main courses** €14.75-
€17. *Set lunch* €17.15. **Credit** V. **Map** p338 C4.

The Old Curiosity Shop meets Tate Modern at this
incredibly popular former printing house, wallpapered with old leaflets and book pages. The combination of antique furniture with arty mobiles made
out of tortured kitchen utensils is as offbeat as the
food: turbot with passion fruit and *escopinyes* (cockles); an all-white 'monochrome of cod and chickpeas';
a green salad that comes with a mad scientist's test-
tube rack of 14 different aerosol dressings.

Tragaluz

*Ptge de la Concepció 5 (93 487 01 96). Metro
Diagonal.* **Open** 1.30-4pm, 8.30pm-midnight Mon-
Wed, Sun; 1.30-4pm, 8.30pm-1am Thur-Sat. **Main
courses** €21.40-€24.60. *Set lunch* €21.40 Mon-Fri.
Credit AmEx, DC, MC, V. **Map** p338 D4.

The flagship for this extraordinarily successful
group of restaurants – including Agua (*see p167*),
Bestial (*see p169*) and Principal (*see left*) – has
weathered the city's culinary revolution and is still
covering new ground in Mediterranean creativity.
Prices have risen and the wine mark-up is hard to
swallow, but there's no faulting tuna tataki with a
cardamom wafer and a ratatouille-like *pisto*; monkfish tail in a sweet tomato *sofrito* with black olive
oil; and braised oxtail with cabbage. Finish with
cherry consommé or a thin tart of chocolate.
Other locations: throughout the city.

Windsor

C/Còrsega 286 (93 415 84 83). Metro Diagonal.
Open 1.15-4pm, 8.30-11pm Mon-Fri; 8.30-11pm Sat.
Closed Aug. **Main courses** €20.30-€22.40. **Credit**
AmEx, DC, MC, V. **Map** p338 D4.

Let down slightly by a smart but drab dining room
and a preponderance of British and American businessmen, Windsor nevertheless serves some of the
most creative and uplifting food around. Start with
an *amuse-gueule* of a tomato reduction with pistachio; warm up with wild mushroom cannel in truffle sauce or a divine foie gras on thin slices of fruit
cake; and peak with a dense, earthy dish of cod on
black lentils followed by a foamed *crema catalana*.
Then come down to earth with the bill.

Noti bene. *See p161.*

International

Thai Lounge

*C/València 205 (93 454 90 32). Metro Passeig de
Gràcia.* **Open** 1.30-3.30pm, 8.30-11.30pm Mon-Thur,
Sun; 1.30-3.30pm, 8.30pm-12.30am Fri, Sat. **Main
courses** €9.65-€12.85. *Set meal* €25.70 Mon-Fri.
Credit MC, V. **Map** p338 D4.
With a restrained tone, atmospheric lighting and
plenty of teak, Thai Lounge doesn't go too far down
the ethnic tat route, with only an occasional garlanded Buddha to remind diners of the food on offer.
There's also a set meal for those thrown by the
menu, including a selection of starters, *kai pad met
mamuang* (chicken sautéed with cashew nuts and
vegetables), yellow beef curry, red prawn curry, pad
Thai and perfumed rice. It's worth asking for extra
spice; otherwise, it can all seem slightly bland.

Ty-Bihan

*Ptge Lluís Pellicer 13 (93 410 90 02). Metro Hospital
Clínic.* **Open** 1.30-3.30pm Mon; 1.30-3.30pm, 8.30-
11.30pm Tue-Fri; 8.30-11.30pm Sat. **Main courses**
€6-€8.50. *Set lunch* €9.50 Mon-Fri. **Credit** MC, V.
Map p338 C3.
Functioning both as crêperie and Breton cultural centre, Ty-Bihan has chosen a sharp look over wheat
sheaves and pitchforks. A long list of sweet and
savoury galettes (crêpes made with buckwheat flour)
are followed up with scrumptious little blinis – try
them smothered in strawberry jam and cream – and
crêpes suzettes in a pool of flaming Grand Marnier.
The Petite menu takes care of *les enfants*, while a
bowl of Breton cider takes care of the grown-ups.

Gràcia

Blanc i Negre

C/Matilde 2 (93 217 09 83). Metro Fontana. **Open**
8pm-midnight Tue-Thur, Sun; 8pm-1am Fri, Sat.
Closed 2wks Aug. **Main courses** €8.60-€17. **Credit**
AmEx, DC, MC, V. **Map** p338 D3.
The name refers not only to the stark black and
white design, but also to the impressive wine list (*vi
negre*, in Catalan, is red wine), put together by
British wine importer Rafael de Haan. The food is
no less hip than the aesthetic, and has an eye to
every current vogue: it comes as small *platillos*,
whimsically named ('3,000 metres high' turns out to
be a turbot dish dreamed up by the chef while on a
plane), which combines sweet with savoury (venison with chestnut compôte and peanut brittle) and
shows plenty of Asian influences.

Botafumeiro

C/Gran de Gràcia 81 (93 218 42 30). Metro Fontana.
Open 1pm-1am daily. **Main courses** €18.50-€27.80.
Credit AmEx, DC, MC, V. **Map** p338 D3.
Love it or hate it (and the size, the racket and the
overwhelmingly *arriviste* diners mean no one leaves
undecided), there's no denying Botafumeiro's success, and its dozens of tables are rarely empty for
any period of time. The speciality is Galician seafood
in every shape and form, served with military precision by the fleet of nautically clad waiters. The turbot with clams is excellent; at the other end of the
scale, cod with chickpeas isn't half bad either. Non-
fish-eaters have a reasonable choice of typically
Galician numbers to choose from, including a rich
caldo gallego (cabbage and pork broth) and *lacón con
grelos* (gammon with turnip tops).

Envalira

Plaça del Sol 13 (93 218 58 13). Metro Fontana.
Open 1.30-4pm, 9pm-midnight Tue-Sat; 1.30-5pm
Sun. Closed Aug. **Main courses** €10-€12.50.
Credit AmEx, MC, V. **Map** p338 D3.
Old-school Spain lives on as penguin-suited waiters
solemnly hand out brown PVC menus at plastic
teak-effect tables under austere lighting. It's worth
it for the food: as traditionally brown as the decor,
it runs the full gamut of hefty Iberian classics. Start
with fish soups or lentils and go on to paellas, roast
meats and seafood stews, followed by serious, own-
made *crema catalana* or *tarta de Santiago*. Arrive
early for the leather banquettes at the front.

Folquer

*C/Torrent de l'Olla 3 (93 217 43 95). Metro
Diagonal or Verdaguer.* **Open** 1-4pm, 9-11.30pm
Mon-Fri; 9-11.30pm Sat. Closed 3wks Aug. **Set
meal** €23.55-€34.25. **Set lunch** €9.50-€12.
Credit AmEx, DC, MC, V. **Map** p338 D3.
For anyone not artsy or Catalan (or, preferably,
both), walking into Folquer feels a little like an intru-
sion. However, filled as it is with an animated, close
clientele, it's ultimately a welcoming space, with daffodil yellow wood panelling and huge and splashy

hello sushi
food, drink & lounge

...In the historic centre of Barcelona you can enjoy award-winning sushi and hot dishes of traditional Japonese cuisine. We invite you to try our thematic midday and evening menus based on Mediterranean & Japonese fusion specially prepared with fresh products from the Boqueria market. Here you can also have a drink in an urban atmosphere with a Zen touch...

open
Tuesday to Sunday
12:30pm to 16:30pm
20:00pm to 01:00pm

tel.93 412 08 30
Junta de Comerc st. 1
metro Liceu-Raval

www.hello-sushi.com

artworks. The inventive food is well executed and reasonably priced, never more so than in the various lunch deals: the 'executive' is a sturdy main, such as entrecôte, with a salad, pudding and wine for €11, while the normal *menú* is cheaper and still creative, with a gourmet hamburger and wild mushrooms, or *suquet de pop* (octopus stew).

Jean Luc Figueras

C/Santa Teresa 10 (93 415 28 77). Metro Diagonal. **Open** 1.30-3pm, 8.30-11.30pm Mon-Sat. **Main courses** €40.65-€46. **Credit** AmEx, DC, MC, V. **Map** p338 D4.

Spend it like Beckham at this superb Michelin-starred restaurant in the palatial old atelier of fashion deity Balenciaga. Designer handbags rest on tiny tapestry stools, while their owners tuck into silver spoonfuls of Figueras's innovative Catalan-French cuisine. The menu might include fresh foie on fig bread with a reduction of anisette and ratafia, fried prawn and ginger pasta in mango and mustard sauce, or sea bass with cod and black pudding. Desserts, such as parfait of peanuts and the caramelised banana with milk chocolate sorbet, are sumptuous blends of temperature and texture.

Laurak

C/Granada del Penedès 14-16 (93 218 71 65). FGC Gràcia. **Open** 1-4pm, 9-11.30pm Mon-Sat. **Main courses** €26.75-€32.10. **Credit** AmEx, DC, MC, V. **Map** p338 D3.

When Basques aren't eating or forming new gastronomic societies, they're opening restaurants, and sleek, elegant Laurak, liveliest at lunchtime, is one of the finest. Living up to Basque cuisine's reputation, dishes include a heavenly salad of tender pigs' trotters with octopus, caramelised suckling pig with pistachio mousse or a *porrusalda* (cod, potato and leek soup) deconstructed into foams, slices and swirls. The indecisive should try the five-course traditional menu or even the seven-dish taster.

Octubre

C/Julián Romea 18 (93 218 25 18). FGC Gràcia or metro Diagonal. **Open** 1.30-3.30pm, 9-11pm Mon-Fri; 9-11pm Sat. Closed Aug. **Main courses** €8.55-€10.70. **Credit** MC, V. **Map** p338 D3.

Time stands still in this quiet little spot, with its quaint old-fashioned decor, swathes of lace and brown table-linen. Time often stands still, in fact, between placing an order and receiving any food, but it's all part of Octubre's sleepy charm; also contributing is a roll call of reasonably priced, mainly Catalan dishes. Beef in mustard sauce is excellent and the wild mushroom risotto, while not outstanding, is fine for the price. The puddings vary a fair bit, but Octubre is more about atmosphere.

Ot

C/Torres 25 (93 284 77 52). Metro Diagonal or Verdaguer. **Open** 2-3.30pm, 9-10.30pm Mon-Fri; 9-10.30pm Sat. Closed 3wks Aug. **Main courses** *Set lunch* €36.90. *Set meal* €51.35. **Credit** MC, V. **Map** p339 E3.

It's all the little extras that make the Ot experience so memorable: an olive oil tasting to start; a shot glass of warm cauliflower soup speckled with herring eggs as an *amuse-bouche*; the sweet and sour layers of coconut and hibiscus flower foam that accompany the coffee. The assured cooking comes from a surprisingly young team, working within colourful intimate environs. There's no à la carte menu, just a couple of set-price parades of dainty dishes. But these are very safe hands in which to leave yourself; when they say chocolate soufflé needs basil ice-cream, by Jove, they're right.

International

Cantina Machito

C/Torrijos 47 (93 217 34 14). Metro Fontana or Joanic. **Open** 1-4pm, 7pm-12.30am daily. **Main courses** €6.50-€8.50. **Credit** MC, V. **Map** p339 E3.

One of life's perpetual mysteries is whether Mexican desserts are any good or not, given that no one has ever had any room left to actually try one. Here, for example, 'your starter for ten' takes on a whole new meaning with the tasty but completely unfinishable *orden de tacos*, while mains largely comprise *enmoladas* or *enchiladas* the size of wine bottles, beached like whales next to a sea of thick mole sauce. Talking of wine, it's worth noting that the mark-up on Raimat is almost negligible here, while for beer fans there's Coronita or dark, malty Negra Modelo. The tequila shots and Margaritas go without saying.

Emu

C/Guilleries 17 (93 218 45 02). Metro Fontana. **Open** 1-4pm, 7pm-2am Mon-Thur; 1-4pm, 7-3am Fri, Sat. **Main courses** €10. **No credit cards.** **Map** p338 D3.

Run by two Australians and known locally as a Thai restaurant, Emu is actually, well, Australian, meaning that its pad Thai and red curry are complemented by Malaysian beef rendang, Vietnamese spring rolls with spicy peanut sauce and a very convincing but thoroughly occidental Caesar salad. The wine list, too, is largely antipodean, with some smooth robust reds and fruity whites also available by the glass. There are only seven tables, so you need to get there early or book ahead.

Himali

C/Milà i Fontanals 68 (93 285 15 68). Metro Joanic. **Open** noon-4pm, 8pm-midnight Tue-Sun. **Main courses** €7-€9. *Set lunch* €7. **Credit** AmEx, MC, V. **Map** p339 E3.

Cocking a snook at the town's many mediocre Indian restaurants, Barcelona's first Nepalese eaterie has become a real hit. Faced with an alien and mostly impenetrable menu, the set meals are tempting, but not the best option: press the waiters for recommendations or try *mugliaco kukhura* (barbecued butter chicken in creamy tomato sauce) or *khasi masala tarkari* (baked spicy lamb). Meat cooked in the tandoori oven (*txulo*) is also worth a try, and there are plenty of vegetarian options available.

Eating on the go

To the Spanish, whose two-hour lunch break is sacred and for whom the midday meal (never eaten before 2pm) remains the most important repast of the day, fast food remains anathema. However, cheap flights and the phenomenon of weekend tourism have meant that Barcelona now offers all manner of quick-fix food options for people in too much of a hurry to eat sitting down. It might be depressing to see McRestaurants in places that once housed elegant old tapas bars, but visitors to the city can still find traditional alternatives for a quick snack while taking in the sights. The Catalans have never been lovers of mobile cuisine, but food is such a central part of their culture that there are natural exceptions to the rule.

One of these exceptions is a *churro*, a deep-fried stick of batter covered in sugar and served in paper cones. *Churrerías* are found all over town, selling various versions of *churros*: covered in chocolate or filled with cream are options for those with a serious cholesterol death wish. In other parts of Spain, *churros* are usually eaten dipped in hot chocolate as an afternoon snack, or with coffee for breakfast, but the Catalans prefer their *churros* to go.

Various festivals, too, have street food associated with them. At the end of September, in the run up to All Saints' Day (the day after Hallowe'en for the heathens),

the streets of Barcelona fill up with temporary stalls, exuding the smell of roast chestnuts (*castanyes*) and sweet potatoes (*moniatos*) and attracting passers-by to the irresistible heat of their braziers. At Barcelona's biggest street party, Sant Joan on 24 June, revellers tuck in to huge slabs of *coca*, a crispy sweet pastry flavoured with aniseed and washed down with copious amounts of cava. It is easy to confuse this dish, commonly known as *Coca de Sant Joan*, with the savoury version of *coca*, a kind of flat bread made with olive oil sold in many bakeries around town. This delicious snack, which resembles a thin slice of pizza, is usually covered in sweet onions, peppers and aubergines or, during carnival in February, sardines. It's one of the great undiscovered triumphs of Catalan cuisine.

However, the king of the meal on the go in Barcelona remains the humble and timeless *bocadillo*: essentially, a baguette rubbed with fresh tomatoes and olive oil with a pinch of salt, and filled with a huge variety of fillings, from ham and cheese to aubergine tortilla or grilled pork fillets with melted cheese and onions. At the football match, for a snack in the park or just to fill up the hole in between meals, the Catalan sandwich is a masterpiece of quick, filling and delicious snack technology. Almost every bar serves these hunger-busters; they beat a soggy hamburger any day of the week.

Mesopotamia

C/Verdi 65 (93 237 15 63). Metro Fontana.
Open 8.30-11pm Tue-Thur; 8.30pm-midnight Fri,
Sat. Closed 2wks Apr. **Main courses** €12.75.
Set dinner €25.70 daily. **No credit cards**.
Map p339 D3.
The policy at Barcelona's only Iraqi restaurant is to
have everything on the menu at the same price, so
that the cost won't hold anybody back from ordering what they want. The menu is based on Arab
'staff of life' foods, such as yoghurt and rice. Best
value is the enormous taster menu, which includes
great Lebanese wines, a variety of dips for your
riqaq bread, bulgur wheat with aromatic roast meats
and vegetables, sticky baclawa and Arabic teas.
Also good are the potato croquettes stuffed with
minced meat, almonds and dried fruit.

San Kil

*C/Legalitat 22 (93 284 41 79). Metro Fontana or
Joanic.* **Open** 1-4pm, 8.30pm-midnight Mon-Sat.
Closed 2wks Aug. **Main courses** €10-€16.
Credit MC, V. **Map** p339 E3.
If you've never eaten Korean food before, it pays to
gen up before you head to this bright and Spartan
restaurant. *Panch'an* is the ideal starter: four little
dishes containing vegetable appetisers, one of which
will be tangy *kimch'i* (fermented cabbage with chilli).
Then try mouth-watering *pulgogi* (beef served siz-
zling at the table and eaten rolled into lettuce leaves)
and maybe *pibimbap*, rice with vegetables (and occasionally meat) topped with a fried egg. Just as you're
finishing with a shot of *soju* rice wine, the Korean
telly sparks up and it's time to move on.

Shojiro

C/Ros de Olano 11 (93 415 65 48). Metro Fontana.
Open 1.30-3.30pm, 8.30-11pm, 9-11.30pm
Tue-Sat. Closed 2wks Apr, 2wks Aug. **Main
courses** *Set lunch* €15.75 (all incl) Mon-Sat.
Set dinner €40.66 (only food). **Credit** DC, MC, V.
Map p338 D3.
The food is a curious but successful mix of Catalan
and Japanese, but so is the decor, original 'mosaic'
flooring and dark green paintwork setting off a clean
feng-shuied look and monochrome prints. There are
only set meals (unusually, water, wine, coffee and
tax are all included), starting with an *amuse-bouche*,
then offering sushi with strips of nori, sticky rice and
salad, or courgette soup with pancetta as a starter,
then salmon teriyaki or spring chicken confit with a
potato dauphinoise as mains. Puddings might
include a refreshing own-made apple ice-cream.

Barceloneta & the Ports

Agua

*Passeig Maritim 30 (93 225 12 72). Metro
Barceloneta.* **Open** 1.30-4pm, 8.30pm-midnight
Mon-Thur; 1.30-4pm, 8.30pm-1am Fri; 1.30-5pm,
8.30pm-1am Sat; 1.30-5pm, 8.30pm-midnight Sun.
Main courses €12.85-€16. **Credit** AmEx, MC, V.
Map p343 F7.

Jean Luc Figueras. *See p165.*

Let down somewhat by an avoidable front-of-house
chaos, Agua is otherwise one of the freshest, most
relaxed places to eat in the city, with a large terrace
smack on the beach and a sunny interior filled with
animated regular diners. The menu rarely changes,
but visitors never tire of the competently executed
monkfish tail with *sofregit*, the risotto with partridge, and fresh pasta with juicy prawns. Scrummy
puddings include marron glacé mousse and sour
apple sorbet. The wine mark-up is quite high for
such reasonably priced food; a couple of notable
exceptions are white Creu de Lavit or red Añares.

Arola

*Hotel Arts, C/Marina 19-21, Port Olímpic (93 483
80 90). Metro Ciutadella-Vila Olímpica.* **Open** 1-
3.30pm, 8.30-11pm Wed, Sun; 2-4pm, 8.30-11.30pm
Thur-Sat. **Main courses** €26.75-€32.10. **Credit**
AmEx, DC, MC, V. **Map** p343 F7.
Culinary wunderkind Sergi Arola flies over from his
Michelin-starred Madrid restaurant once a week to
oversee this new venture in the elegant Hotel Arts
(*see p63*). With a menu based around the Catalan concept of *pica-pica* (food to share), Arola takes traditional favourites and adds his own deft touch:
sardines come smoked, and patatas bravas resemble
maki rolls, tiny hollowed out cylinders of potato filled
with chilli sauce. Before becoming a chef Arola was
a musician and has placed music central stage:
there's a DJ every night, and funk and other retro
sounds play during the day.

Can Maño

C/Baluard 12 (93 319 30 82). Metro Barceloneta.
Open noon-4pm, 8-11pm Mon-Fri; noon-4pm Sat.
Main courses €4-€6. **No credit cards**.
Map p343 E7.

With a roaring telly, fruit machines and tables so cramped the waiters have to frisbee the food at you, this neighbourhood caff is a local institution, catering principally to hungry local workers. The huge portions of market-fresh cuttlefish, red mullet or bream usually come with chips, although you can request fried tomatoes or aubergine (if you can keep the waiter's attention that long). Arrive early.

Can Solé
C/Sant Carles 4 (93 221 50 12). Metro Barceloneta. **Open** 1.30-4pm, 8-11pm Tue-Sat; 1.30-4pm Sun. Closed 2wks Aug. **Main courses** €19.25-€22.50. **Credit** AmEx, DC, MC, V. **Map** p343 E7.
Located in an old fisherman's cottage, this lavishly tiled restaurant has been serving its traditional harbourside food for over a century. Regulars, usually of port-quaffing age themselves, tuck into plates of shrimp, wild mackerel, stewed lobster and superb paellas cooked almost under their noses in the bustling open kitchen. The decor is elegant yet not overboard, with photos of former fans like Santiago Rusiñol and Joan Miró, but the occasionally lackadaisical service can take the edge off the charm.

Set Portes
Passeig d'Isabel II 14 (93 319 30 33). Metro Barceloneta. **Open** 1pm-1am daily. **Main courses** €17.35-€19.25. **Credit** AmEx, DC, MC, V. **Map** p345 C4.
The 'Seven Doors' open on to as many dining salons, all kitted out in elegant 19th-century decor. Long-aproned waiters bring regional dishes, served in

enormous portions, including a stewy fish *zarzuela* with half a lobster, a different paella daily (shellfish, for example, or with rabbit and snails), and a wide array of fresh seafood or heavier dishes such as herbed black bean stew with pork sausage and *orujo* sorbet to finish. Reservations are only available for certain tables (two to three days in advance is recommended); without one, expect a long wait outside.

El Suquet de l'Almirall
Passeig Joan de Borbó 65 (93 221 62 33). Metro Barceloneta. **Open** 1-4pm, 9-11pm Tue-Sat; 1-4pm Sun. Closed 2wks Aug. **Main courses** €13.90-€16.05. **Credit** MC, V. **Map** p342 D7.
One of the famous beachfront *chiringuitos* that was moved and refurbished in time for the '92 Olympics, El Suquet remains a friendly family concern despite the smart decor and mid-scale business lunchers. Fishy favourites range from *xató* salad to *arròs negre* and a variety of set menus, including the 'blind' selection of tapas, a gargantuan taster menu and, most popular, the *pica-pica*, which includes roast red peppers with anchovies, a bowl of steamed cockles and clams, and a heap of *fideuà* with lobster.

International

Bestial
C/Ramón Trias Fargas 2-4 (93 224 04 07). Metro Barceloneta. **Open** 1.30-4pm, 8.30pm-midnight Mon-Wed; 1.30-5pm, 8.30pm-1am Thur-Sat. **Main courses** €8-€15. *Set lunch* €16 Mon-Fri. **Credit** AmEx, DC, MC, V. **Map** p343 F7.

Sun, sea and *cerveza* at **Agua**.
See p167.

Vivanda.

Its tiered wooden decking and ancient olive trees making it the most elegant restaurant on this stretch of beach, Bestial is a peerless spot for alfresco seaside dining. The interior design manages to match the splendour of the exterior, with black-clad waiters sashaying along sleek runways holding their trays high, for all the world like models in Milan or Paris; at weekends, coloured lights play over the tables as a DJ takes to the decks. The food is modern Italian: dainty mini-pizzas, rocket salads with Parma ham and a lightly poached egg, tuna with black olive risotto and all the puddings you'd expect.

Montjuïc & Poble Sec

El Foc

C/Blasco de Garay 8 (93 442 22 53). Metro Paral·lel or Poble Sec. **Open** 8pm-midnight Mon-Sat; 1.30-5pm, 8pm-midnight Sun. Closed 2wks Aug. **Main courses** €10-€15. **Credit** AmEx, MC, V. **Map** p341 B6.
An inviting restaurant with bare-bricked walls, hessian table runners and an expansive owner. As well as British cuisine at its protean best – salmon with mash, leeks and crunchy bacon; beef and Guinness casserole; roast beef and Yorkshire pud; pork with tarragon and mushrooms – Mediterranean zest is added with a foamed pea, mint and basil soup, sprightly salads and stuffed roast peppers with goat's cheese and couscous, all of it excellent and keenly priced. There is only house wine, and little in the way of desserts, but it's all too easy to fill up beforehand on the superb own-made onion bread.

La Font del Gat

Passeig Santa Madrona 28 (93 289 04 04). Funicular Parc Montjuïc/bus 55. **Open** 1-4pm Tue-Sun. **Main courses** €10.70-€19.30. Set lunch €10.70. **Credit** MC, DC, V. **Map** p341 A6.

A new and much-needed watering hole perched high on Montjuïc between the Miró and ethnological museums. A small and informal-looking restaurant, it has a surprisingly sophisticated menu: ravioli with truffles and wild mushrooms, for example, and foie gras with Modena caramel. However, most come for the set lunch: start with egg scrambled with Catalan sausage and peppers or a salad, follow it with baked cod or chicken with pine nuts and basil, and finish with fruit or simple dessert. Tables outside attract a surcharge, but enjoy a fantastic view of the city.

La Tomaquera

C/Margarit 58 (no phone). Metro Poble Sec. **Open** 1.30-3.45pm, 8.30-10.45pm Tue-Sat. Closed Aug. **Main courses** €7.20-€13. **No credit cards**. **Map** p341 E6.
Like a curmudgeonly but beloved old uncle, La Tomaquera grows more popular as it grows more obstreperous. It's bright and loud, its waiters are brusque, there's no booking, there's only house wine (and no soft drinks), there's only grilled meat served with weapons-grade all i oli (unless you count the snails) and no, you can't pay with Visa. And if you don't like it, you can go elsewhere. But nobody does.

International

La Bella Napoli

C/Margarit 14 (93 442 50 56). Metro Paral·lel. **Open** 1.30-4pm, 8.30pm-midnight Tue-Sun. **Main courses** €7.50-€12. **Credit** DC, MC, V. **Map** p341 B6.
It's been renovated with a sleeker, more modern look, but La Bella Napoli was never a Chianti-in-a-basket kinda place to begin with. Welcoming Neapolitan waiters can talk you through the long, long list of antipasti and pasta dishes, though you can't go wrong with the crispy baked pizzas.

Portions are generous and everything is fresh, bar the dull ice-cream desserts; you'll have to ask for the own-made cheesecake and tiramisu. Even for those with reservations, the queue can snake out of the door.

Horta & Poblenou

Can Travi Nou

C/Jorge Manrique (93 428 03 01). Metro Horta or Montbau. **Open** 1.30-4pm, 8.30pm-midnight Mon-Sat; 1.30-4pm Sun. **Main courses** €15-€21.40. **Credit** AmEx, DC, MC, V.
This ancient farmhouse, clad in electric violet bougainvillea and perched high above the city, offers wonderfully rustic dining rooms with log fires in winter. In summer, the action moves out to a covered terrace in a bosky, candlelit garden. The food is hearty, traditional Catalan cuisine, though it's a little expensive for what it is, and suffers from the sheer volume being churned out of the kitchen. Puddings are better, and come with a *porrón* (a glass jug with a drinking spout) of *muscatel*. But the Can Travi Nou experience is really all about location, location, location.

Els Pescadors

Plaça Prim 1 (93 225 20 18). Metro Poblenou. **Open** 1-3.45pm, 8.30pm-midnight daily. **Main courses** €25.70-€32.10. **Credit** AmEx, DC, MC, V.
Smartly dressed members of the Catalan bourgeoisie sit at large, luxuriously laid terrace tables or in one of the two elegant dining rooms to enjoy some of the most imaginatively prepared seafood to be had in the city. The house speciality is succulently fresh cod, in dishes such as 'green' paella with *kokotxas* (tender throat flesh) or cod with garlic mousseline, while starters include the likes of sautéed green asparagus with foie gras or creamy leek soup with rock mussels. Service is impeccable, as are desserts.

Zona Alta

La Venta

Plaça Doctor Andreu (93 212 64 55). FGC Avda Tibidabo, then Tramvia Blau. **Open** 1.30-3.15pm, 9-11.15pm Mon-Sat. **Main courses** €21.40-€23.50. **Credit** AmEx, DC, MC, V.
Perched high above the city mayhem, La Venta's Moorish-influenced interior plays second fiddle to the terrace for every season: shaded by day and uncovered by night in the summer, sealed and warmed with a wood-burning stove during winter. Complex starters include lentil and spider crab salad; sea urchins au gratin (a must), and langoustine ravioli, filled with leek and foie mousse. Simpler, but high quality mains run from rack of lamb to delicate monkfish in filo pastry with pesto. A mille-feuille of red fruits wraps things up nicely.

Vivanda

C/Major de Sarrià 134 (93 205 47 17). Metro FGC Reina Elisenda. **Open** 9-11.30pm Mon; 1.30-3.30pm, 9-11.30pm Tue-Sat. **Main courses** €15-€19.30. *Set lunch* €11.80 Tue-Fri. **Credit** DC, MC, V. **Map** p337 B1.
As if the peaceful, bosky garden, dappled with sunlight, weren't reason enough to come here, the waiters are completely charming and the chefs skilled. In keeping with the look of the place, starters are a light and healthy bunch, with crisp salads and baby vegetables, but mains are more traditionally Catalan and thus more filling. Oxtail is stuffed with cured duck with shallot 'jam', or there are more straightforward choices of pork with mustard sauce, hake, sea bass, bonito and, bizarrely, ostrich. Try the own-made pistachio ice-cream for a lighter finish.

Out of town

El Bulli

Cala Montjoi (972 15 04 57/www.elbulli.com). By car A7 or N11 north (7km/4.5 miles from Roses)/by train RENFE from Sants or Passeig de Gràcia to Figueres, then bus to Roses, then taxi. **Open** *Apr-June* 8-10pm Wed-Sun. *June-Sept* 8-10pm daily. Closed Oct-Apr. **Set dinner** €160. **Credit** AmEx, DC, MC, V.
Darling of the Sunday papers, El Bulli is possibly the most talked about restaurant in the world today; thus, it merits a mention here, despite its location up on the Costa Brava. There's only a *degustación*, and diners must arrive by 8.30pm if they're to finish the 34 or so – that's not a misprint – courses by midnight. Dinner here is an extraordinary experience, occasionally exalted and frequently frustrating, where the diners are cossetted guinea pigs, their reactions scanned by the chef Ferran Adrià and his maître d'. Raw quail's yolk in caramelised gold leaf, sautéed rabbit brains with a truffled cigar of veal marrowbone, edible cling film peppered with trout's eggs… every dish is as much food for the mind as the stomach. Love it or hate it, €160 will never again be this memorably spent.

Eat, Drink, Shop

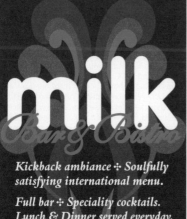

Cafés, Tapas & Bars

Coffee, a *caña*, conversation: join Barcelona's café culture.

Had anybody asked him, Napoleon might well have described the Spanish as a nation of barkeepers. His canny brother Joseph, plonked on the Spanish throne from 1808 to 1813, had as his only real policy scything cuts on alcohol taxes, a move that won him the nickname Pepe Botella (Joe Bottle) and much-needed public support. The proliferation of cafés and bars, however, says less about Spaniards' love of alcohol than their love of social ritual. The Spanish do not drink to get drunk. Drinking accompanies food, reflection or good company; starting, perhaps, with a thoughtful shot of anis with a morning coffee and ending with '*la penúltima*', the final drink of the night with friends (*última* is never uttered, and to do so would be bad luck), with all manner of snifters in between.

BEER BEFORE WINE

Generally, if you ask for a *caña*, you'll be given a draught beer; usually around half a (UK) pint, though some places also serve *jarras*, closer to a pint. Ask for a *cerveza*, meanwhile, and you'll be given a bottle. Damm beer is ubiquitous in Catalonia, with Estrella, a strong lager, the most popular variety. Damm also produces an even stronger lager (Voll Damm) and a dark one (Bock Damm). Shandy (*clara*) is popular, untouched by the stigma it has in the UK.

Among wines, Rioja is well known, but there are many excellent wines from other regions in the north of Spain, such as the Penedès in Catalonia, Navarra or El Duero. Most wine drunk here is red (*tinto/negre*), but Galicia produces good whites, including a slightly sparkling and very refreshing wine called *vino turbio*. The Basques have a similar, clearer wine called Txacoli and, of course, Catalonia has its many cavas, running from *semi-sec* ('half-dry', but actually pretty sweet) to *brut nature* (very dry). Well-known Catalan brands such as Freixenet or Codorníu are much cheaper here.

CAFFEINE KICKS

Spanish coffee is very strong and generally excellent. The three basic types are *café solo* (*cafè sol* in Catalan, also known simply as '*café*'), a small strong black coffee; *cortado/tallat*, the same but with a little milk; and *café con leche/cafè amb llet*, the same with more milk. Cappuccino has yet to catch on; whipped cream as a substitute for foam is not unheard of. Then there's *café americano* (a tall black

coffee diluted with more water), and spiked coffee: a *carajillo*, which is a short, black coffee with a liberal dash of brandy. If you want another type of liqueur, you have to specify, such as *carajillo de ron* (rum) or *carajillo de whisky*. A *trifásico* is a *carajillo* with a layer of milk. Decaffeinated coffee (*descafeinado*) is widely available, but specify for it *de máquina* (from the machine) unless you want Nescafé. Decaff is popular in Spain and very good.

Tea, on the other hand, is pretty poor. If you can't live without it, ask for cold milk on the side ('*leche fría aparte*') or run the risk of getting a glass of hot milk and a teabag. Basic herbal teas, such as chamomile (*manzanilla*), limeflower (*tila*) and mint (*menta*), are common.

ETIQUETTE

Except in very busy bars or when sitting outside, you won't usually be required to pay until you leave. If you have trouble attracting

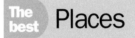

The best **Places**

For breakfast
Arc Café (*see p174*); **La Fianna** (*see p180*) and **Xocoa** (*see p175*).

For tapas
La Cova Fumada (*see p184*); **Mam i Teca** (*see p178*); **Quimet i Quimet** (*see p185*) and **Taller de Tapas** (*see p175*).

For authenticity
Bar Celta (*see p175*); **Granja M Viader** (*see p177*); **Marsella** (*see p179*) and **El Portalón** (*see p175*).

For chilling
L'Antic Teatre (*see p180*); **Iposa** (*see p178*) and **Spiritual Café** (*see p179*).

For a great view
La Caseta del Migdia (*see p185*); **Merbeyé** (*see p188*) and **La Miranda del Museu** (*see p184*).

For sitting in the sun
Bar Colombo (*see p184*); **Daguiri** (*see p184*); **Taller de Tapas** (*see p175*) and **Têxtil Cafè** (*see p180*).

Eat, Drink, Shop

Xocoa. *See p175.*

a waiter's attention, a loud but polite '*oiga*' or, in Catalan, '*escolti*', is perfectly acceptable. Tipping is not obligatory, but it's customary to leave a few coins if you've been served at a table. On the vexed question of throwing detritus on the floor (cigarette ends, paper napkins, olive pits and so on), it's safest to keep an eye on what the locals are doing.

Barri Gòtic

Cafés

Arc Café
C/Carabassa 19 (93 302 52 04/www.arccafe.com). Metro Drassanes or Jaume I. **Open** 10am-1am Mon-Thur; 10am-2am Fri; 11am-2am Sat; 11am-1am Sun. **Credit** AmEx, DC, MC, V. **Map** p345 B4.
A sunny and convivial café popular with expats: it's a veritable Babel of languages. The winning strategy is in predicting exactly what the foreigners might be missing, from eggs and bacon in the mornings to a Thai curry (properly spicy) or a slice of cheesecake in the afternoons. Night-times are a more local affair.

Café de l'Opera
La Rambla 74 (93 317 75 85). Metro Liceu. **Open** 8.30am-2.15am Mon-Thur, Sun; 8.30am-2.45am Fri, Sat. **No credit cards. Map** p345 A3.
Cast-iron pillars, etched mirrors and bucolic murals create an air of fading grandeur now incongruous among the fast-food joints and tawdry souvenir shops. A reasonable selection of tapas is served by attentive bow-tied waiters to a largely tourist clientele. Given the atmosphere (and the opposition), there's no better place for a coffee on La Rambla.

La Clandestina
Baixada Viladecols 2 (93 319 05 33). Metro Jaume I. **Open** 10am-10pm Mon-Thur; 10am-midnight Fri, Sat; 11am-10pm Sun. **No credit cards. Map** p345 B3.
Turn in at the sign of the hanging kettle for a mellow, new age tea house with breakfasts, homemade cakes and a huge range of teas – including masala chai, lotus flower, or cherry and redcurrant – along with an impressive array of fresh fruit juices and lassis. The trapeze hanging from the ceiling is occasionally swung into action.

La Granja
C/Banys Nous 4 (93 302 69 75). Metro Liceu. **Open** *Sept-July* 9.30am-2pm, 4-9pm Mon-Fri; 9.30am-2pm, 5-9pm Sat; 5-10pm Sun. *Aug* 9.30am-2.30pm, 6.30-9pm Mon-Sat; 6.30-10pm Sun. Closed 2wks Aug. **No credit cards. Map** p345 B3.
There are a number of these old *granjes* (milk bars, often specialising in hot chocolate) around town, but this is one of the loveliest, with handsome antique fittings and its very own section of Roman wall at the back. You can stand your spoon in the chocolate, and it won't be to all tastes. However, the spicy version with chilli or the mocha espresso will set you up for a hard day's shopping.

Els Quatre Gats
C/Montsió 3 bis (93 302 41 40). Metro Catalunya. **Open** 9am-2am daily. **Credit** AmEx, DC, MC, V. **Map** p344 B2.
Housed in a gorgeous building designed in 1897 by Puig i Cadafalch, Els Quatre Gats was once the hangout of the city's finest artists, including Pablo Picasso, who held his first exhibition here, and Modernistes Santiago Rusiñol and Ramon Casas,

who painted pictures for the place. The food served in the adjoining restaurant could be better, but the setting certainly couldn't.

Schilling

C/Ferran 23 (93 317 67 87). Metro Liceu. **Open** *Sept-July* 10am-2.15am Mon-Sat; noon-2.15am Sun. *Aug* 5pm-2.15am daily. **Credit** (over €12) MC, V. **Map** p345 A3.

Spacious and utterly elegant, with a particularly large gay clientele, Schilling is no longer as fashionable as it once was, although the supercilious waiters appear not to have realised. Nonetheless, it's an unbeatable place for meeting up, and the window seats remain the city's No.1 spot for budding travel writers to scribble in their journals.

Xocoa

C/Petritxol 11 (93 301 11 97/www.xocoa-bcn.com). Metro Liceu. **Open** 9am-9pm Mon-Sat; 9am-2pm, 4-9.30pm Sun. **Credit** MC, V. **Map** p344 A2.

Chocoholics stand drooling at the windows of this buzzing little café and its sister shop next door, while inside, ladies take a break from shopping to pick at scrumptious fruit tarts, cheesecakes, tartes tatin and all manner of breakfasty pastries: croissants, *magdalenas*, brioche and huge Mallorcan *ensaimadas*. Cocoa (*xocoa*) is put to every available use from fondants to bath oil, and the 'chocolate survival kit' is the perfect gift for the family addict.

Tapas

Bar Celta

C/Mercè 16 (93 315 00 06). Metro Drassanes. **Open** *June-Sept* noon-midnight Mon-Sat. *Oct-May* noon-midnight daily. **Credit** AmEx, MC, V. **Map** p345 B4.

No-frills, noisy, brightly lit and not recommended for anyone feeling a bit rough, Bar Celta is nonetheless one of the more authentic experiences to be had. A Galician tapas bar, it specialises in food from the region, with good seafood – try the *navajas* (razor clams) or the *pulpo* (octopus) – and crisp Albariño wine served in traditional white ceramic bowls.

Bar Pinotxo

La Boqueria 466-467, La Rambla 89 (93 317 17 31). Metro Liceu. **Open** 6am-4.30pm Mon-Sat. Closed 3wks Aug. **No credit cards**. **Map** p344 A2.

Bar Pinotxo may look like an ordinary spit 'n' sawdust market-stall bar, but the number of times Jean Paul Gaultier has been spotted here is perhaps some indication of the kind of food on offer. As well as tapas, daily specials range from duck magret to *cap i pota*, a Catalan speciality involving calves' head and feet. The queue for a bar stool is subject to an invisible but watertight monitoring system.

Onofre

C/Magdalenes 19 (93 317 69 37/www.onofre.net). Metro Urquinaona. **Open** 10am-12.30am Mon-Sat. Closed Aug. **Credit** DC, MC, V. **Map** p344 B2.

Artfully crafted into a stylish tapas restaurant, this long, thin space sees a mix of ages and nationalities, drawn together by a love of good food. Generous portions of cheese, charcuterie, ham and carpaccio (and a superb warm goat's cheese salad with tomato) and anchovy are served with *pa amb tomàquet*.

El Portalón

C/Banys Nous 20 (93 302 11 87). Metro Liceu. **Open** 9am-midnight Mon-Sat. Closed Aug. **Credit** MC, V. **Map** p345 B3.

A pocket of authenticity, this trad tapas bar is located in what were once medieval stables, and doesn't seem to worry about inheriting the medieval dust. The tapas list is extensive, but the *torrades* are good too: toasted bread topped with red peppers and anchovy, cheese, ham or whatever takes your fancy, washed down with house wine from terracotta jugs.

Taller de Tapas

Plaça Sant Josep Oriol 9 (93 301 80 20/www.tallerde tapas.com). Metro Liceu. **Open** noon-11.45pm Mon-Thur, Sun; noon-12.30am Fri, Sat. **Credit** AmEx, DC, MC, V. **Map** p345 A3.

In its short life, this sleek 'tapas workshop' has spawned a rash of imitators. Perfect for tongue-tied tourists and those who aren't prepared to eat standing three-deep at a bar, both branches have multi-lingual menus and plenty of seating, inside and out. The tapas are of reliable quality and are occasionally excellent: try the succulent Palamós prawns or baby broad beans with ham.

Other locations: C/Argenteria 51, Born (93 268 85 59).

Vinissim

C/Sant Domènec del Call 12 (93 301 45 75). Metro Jaume I or Liceu. **Open** 8pm-midnight Mon; 1-5pm, 7pm-midnight Tue-Sat. **Credit** AmEx, DC, MC, V. **Map** p345 B3.

An expertly staffed wine and tapas bar, painted in warm colours and bathed in sunlight, with tables out on a quiet square. The tapas are sublime, from *cochinillo pibil* (spicy, Mexican-style shredded pork) to red peppers filled with cod brandade. Puddings are also excellent, such as delicious fig ice-cream or spiced white chocolate tart with dried fruit.

Bars

Ginger

C/Palma de Sant Just 1 (93 310 53 09). Metro Jaume I. **Open** 7pm-2.30am Tue-Thur; 7pm-3am Fri, Sat. Closed 2wks Aug, 1wk Jan. **Credit** V. **Map** p345 B3.

Dangerously comfortable buttercup-leather chairs and a soothing mix of lounge and rare groove tunes make Ginger one of the easiest places in which to while away an evening. An elegant cocktail bar on different levels, it also serves top-notch tapas – try the salmon tartare with horseradish or the wild mushroom filo pastry – and has an impressive selection of mainly Catalan wines by the glass.

La Palma

C/Palma de Sant Just 7 (93 315 06 56). Metro Jaume I. **Open** 8am-3.30pm, 7-9.30pm Mon-Thur; 8am-3.30pm, 7-11pm Fri; 7-11pm Sat. Closed Aug. **No credit cards. Map** p345 B3.

A bastion of old Catalonia, where service can seem brusque, and comes exclusively in Catalan. But this atmospheric old *bodega* has seen 'em all come and go, from the artists who used to meet here in the '50s to the mayor's cronies from the nearby city hall who frequent it nowadays. Order some *pa amb tomàquet*, some own-made sausage and some wine from the barrel, and be grateful you're not in Starbucks.

Raval

Cafés

Bar Kabara

C/Junta del Comerç 20 (93 412 7698). Metro Liceu. **Open** 8.30pm-2.30am Tue-Thur, Sun; 8.30pm-3am Fri, Sat. Closed last 2wks Aug. **No credit cards. Map** p345 A3.

The alternative-eco chic at Bar Kabara goes more than skin-deep. A truly multicultural and inclusive space, it's run by a Palestinian, a Catalan, and a Basque. Friendly staff serve up a good selection of wine and simple food to punters sitting on sofas and in a cosy conservatory. DJs (jazz, rock, blues, bossa nova) fight for airspace with earnest chat.

Bar Kaspero

Plaça Vicenç Martorell 4 (93 302 20 72). Metro Catalunya. **Open** *May-Aug* 9am-midnight daily. *Sept-Apr* 9am-10pm daily. Closed 1mth Dec-Jan. **No credit cards. Map** p344 A1/2.

A summer proposition (there's no indoor seating), with tables under shady arcades overlooking a playground for the kids. Run by two Australians,

Kasparo has good, cheap food – plenty of soups, salads and pasta, curries Thai and Indian, stews and chilli, with tapas and *bocadillos* available all day.

Bar Mendizábal

C/Junta de Comerç 2 (no phone). Metro Liceu. **Open** *June-Oct* 10am-1am daily. *Nov-May* 10am-midnight daily. **No credit cards. Map** p345 A3.

An emblematic Raval bar, its multicoloured tiles a feature in thousands of holiday snaps, Mendizábal has been around for decades but is really little more than a pavement stall. On offer are myriad fruit juices, *bocadillos* and, in winter, soup, served to tables across the road in the tiny square opposite.

Buenas Migas

Plaça Bonsuccés 6 (93 318 37 08/www.buenasmigas. com). Metro Liceu. **Open** 10am-midnight daily. **Credit** MC, V. **Map** p344 A2.

Tables outside sprawl across the square in the shade of acacia trees, while inside has a rustic *Good Life* look, with plenty of pine and Kilner jars, that tells you everything you need to know about the food. Wholesome specialities include focaccia with various toppings, leek and potato or spinach tart, the usual vegetarian-approved cakes – carrot, pear and chocolate brownies – and herbal teas.

Other locations: Baixada de Santa Clara 2, off Plaça del Rei, Barri Gòtic (93 319 13 80); Passeig de Gràcia 120, Eixample (93 238 55 49).

Granja M Viader

C/Xuclà 4-6 (93 318 34 86). Metro Liceu. **Open** 5-8.45pm Mon; 9am-1.45pm, 5-8.45pm Tue-Sat. Closed 2wks Aug. **Credit** AmEx, MC, V. **Map** p344 A2.

The chocolate milk drink Cacaolat was invented in this old *granja* in 1931, and is still on offer, along with strawberry and banana milkshakes, *orxata* (tiger nut milk) and hot chocolate. It's an evocative, charming place with century-old fittings and

Café de les Delicies. *See p179.*

enamel adverts, but the waiters refuse to be hurried. Popular with Catalan families on the way back from picking up the kids, and couples meeting after work.

Iposa

C/Floristes de la Rambla 14 (93 318 60 86). Metro Liceu. **Open** *Sept-July* 1pm-2.30am Mon-Sat. *Aug* 7pm-2.30am Mon-Sat. Closed 2wks Dec-Jan. **Credit** MC, V. **Map** p344 A2.

At lunch and dinner, Iposa functions almost exclusively as a restaurant, serving a handful of simple and low-priced dishes. The rest of the time it makes for a cosy, vaguely bohemian bar with chilled out music, decent art exhibited on its walls and coveted tables outside on a quiet, traffic-free square.

Tapas

Mam i Teca

C/Lluna 4 (93 441 33 35). Metro Sant Antoni. **Open** 1pm-midnight Mon, Wed-Fri; 8.30pm-midnight Sat. **Credit** AmEx, MC, V. **Map** p342 C5.

The name comes from an old Catalan expression meaning 'food and drink', and sums up the prevailing spirit of this little yellow and green tapas bar. All the usual tapas, from anchovies to cured meats, are rigorously sourced, and complemented by superb daily specials such as organic *botifarra*, pork confit and asparagus with shrimp.

Els Tres Tombs

Ronda Sant Antoni 2 (93 443 41 11). Metro Sant Antoni. **Open** 6am-2am daily. **No credit cards**. **Map** p342 C5.

Long the favoured meeting place for the Sunday morning book market scavengers, with great tapas and a line of tables outside in the sunshine. The *tres*

tombs in question are the 'three circuits' of the area performed by a procession of men on horseback during the Festa dels Tres Tombs in January.

Bars

Bar Pastis

C/Santa Mònica 4 (93 318 79 80). Metro Drassanes. **Open** 7.30pm-2.30am Tue-Thur, Sun; 7.30pm-3.30am Fri, Sat. **Credit** AmEx, MC, V. **Map** p345 A4.

This quintessentially Gallic bar once served pastis to the visiting sailors and the denizens of the Barrio Chino underworld. It's since moved on, but not too much: it still has a louche Marseilles feel, floor-to-ceiling indecipherable oil paintings (painted by the original owner when drunk, apparently), Edith Piaf gracing the stereo and latter-day troubadours most nights of the week.

Boadas

C/Tallers 1 (93 318 95 92). Metro Catalunya. **Open** *Jan-June, Sept-Dec* noon-2am Mon-Thur; noon-3am Fri, Sat. *July, Aug* noon-3pm, 6pm-2am Mon-Thur; noon-3pm, 6pm-3am Fri, Sat. **No credit cards**. **Map** p344 A2.

Finally the pressure of being 'so classic it's practically a stop on the tourist bus' proved too much for this tiny and well-loved cocktail bar, and in 2003 it was declared that to enter you must be appropriately dressed. If you do make the cut, this 1930s institution is elegant and relaxing, with sublimely cool barmen from another era.

Bodega Kenobi

C/Notariat 7 (no phone). Metro Catalunya or Liceu. **Open** 7-11pm Wed, Thur, Sun; 7pm-1am Fri, Sat. Closed 2wks Jan. **No credit cards**. **Map** p344 A2.

Endearingly battered but painfully cool, Kenobi offers a long list of cocktails for a song. Coolhunters queue up next to Parka'd indie kids and bespectacled mullets for €3 Daiquiris, amid wallpapered pillars, 1960s tellies, Hawaiian garlands and Alpine snowscapes. Sofas and battered armchairs are there to catch the victims of this permanent happy hour.

Cafè de les Delicies

Rambla del Raval 47 (93 441 57 14). Metro Liceu. **Open** 7pm-2am Mon-Thur, Sun; 7pm-3am Fri, Sat. **No credit cards. Map** p342 C6.
David Soul! Boney M! Olivia Newton-John! The functioning '70s jukebox is reason enough to visit this cosy little bar, even without the excellent G&Ts, the chess, the variety of teas, the terrace and the shelves of books for browsing. A coveted alcove with a sofa, low armchairs and magazines is opened at busy times, or there is a quiet dining room at the back.

Caribbean Club

C/Sitges 5 (93 302 21 82). Metro Catalunya. **Open** 7pm-2am Tue-Sat. Closed Aug. **No credit cards. Map** p344 A2.
The little sister to Boadas (*see p178*), hidden down a nearby sidestreet and known only to the cocktail cognoscenti. The prices are the same, but, as the barmen will whisper conspiratorially, the measures are a dram more generous. The apparently closed door and the tiny space filled with nautical antiques make for a delightfully intimate atmosphere.

London Bar

C/Nou de la Rambla 34 (93 318 52 61/www.london barbcn.com). Metro Liceu. **Open** 7.30pm-4.30am Tue-Thur, Sun; 7pm-5am Fri, Sat. **Credit** AmEx, MC, V. **Map** p345 A3.
The only thing familiar to Londoners will be the punters; otherwise, the swirling Modernista woodwork and smoky, yellowing charm is 100% Barcelona. A little stage at the back has seen it all over the last century, from circus to cabaret, but is now mostly used for jazz, blues and the gentler end of pub rock.

Marsella

C/Sant Pau 65 (93 442 72 63). Metro Liceu. **Open** 10pm-2.30am Mon-Thur; 10pm-3am Fri, Sat. **No credit cards. Map** p342 C6.
A well-loved bar that's been in the same family for five generations. Jean Genet, among other notorious artists and petty thieves, used to come here, attracted, no doubt, by the locally made absinthe, served to this day. Dusty, untapped 100-year-old bottles sit in tall glass cabinets alongside old mirrors and faded William Morris curtains, and chandeliers loom over the cheerful, largely foreign crowd.

Merry Ant

C/Peu de la Creu 23 (mobile 636 065 250). Metro Sant Antoni. **Open** 7pm-3am Tue-Sun. **No credit cards. Map** p342 C5.
The Merry Ant recently changed hands and is now French- and Swedish-owned, but the extraordinary jumble of wooden furniture parts that make up the bar, seating and entrance remains intact. The walls still glow womb-like red, though many of the weirder adornments have disappeared. Its licence is that of 'cultural association', meaning there is occasional cabaret, tango, acoustic sets and poetry readings.

Oddland

C/Joaquín Costa 52 (mobile 665 520 094). Metro Universitat. **Open** 7pm-2am Tue-Thur, Sun; 7pm-3am Fri, Sat. **No credit cards. Map** p342 C5.
Small and unprepossessing from without, Oddland lives up to its name inside. The loos are especially wacky, with pebbles on the floor, a profusion of plastic ivy and Astroturf, an 'inspirational' blackboard with coloured chalks for your graffiti and cartoon characters aplenty. The bar serves fine sandwiches, herbal teas and cheap cocktails, and has listening posts for you to check out the staff's favourite CDs.

The Quiet Man

C/Marqués de Barberà 11 (93 412 12 19). Metro Liceu. **Open** 6pm-3am daily. **No credit cards. Map** p342 C6.
One of the original and best of the city's many Oirish pubs, a peaceful place with wooden floors and stalls that eschews the beautiful game for occasional poetry readings and pool tournaments on its two backroom tables. There is Guinness (properly pulled) and Murphy's, but you're as likely to find Catalans here as you are to see homesick expats.

Spiritual Café

Museu Marítim, Avda Drassanes (mobile 677 634 031/reservations 93 317 52 56/www.spiritual-café. org). Metro Drassanes. **Open** *May-mid Oct* 9.30pm-3am Wed-Sun. *Mid Oct-Apr* 9.30pm-3am Thur-Sat. **Credit** MC, V. **Map** p342 C6/7.
Deliciously different, this late-night alfresco lounge bar fills the patio of the Maritime Museum with chilled sounds and zephyrs of incense. Low, round tables scrawled with Arabic script and lit with candles float on a sea of rugs and cushions, while a team of student waiters offers massages, acrobatics, juggling, Tibetan chants, and poetry.

Zelig

C/Carme 116 (no phone/www.zeligbarcelona.com). Metro Sant Antoni. **Open** 7pm-2am Tue-Thur, Sun; 7pm-3am Fri, Sat. **No credit cards. Map** p342 C5/6.
Only the stone cladding remains of the brightly lit, kebab-shop aesthetic of the working man's bar this used to be. Now, thanks to friendly barmen, artful lighting and vibrant decor, the buzz has changed from early morning Istanbul to late-night NYC.

Sant Pere & the Born

Cafés

La Báscula

C/Flassaders 30 (93 319 9866). Metro Jaume I. **Open** 1.30-11.30pm Mon-Sat. **No credit cards. Map** p345 C3.

Eat, Drink, Shop

A vegetarian cooperative-run café doesn't sound like riotous fun, but this former chocolate factory is a real gem, with excellent food and a deceptively large dining room out back. An encyclopaedic list of drinks runs from chai to glühwein, taking in cocktails, milkshakes, smoothies and iced tea, and the pasta and cakes are as good as you'll find anywhere.

Born Cooking

C/Corretger 9, Born (93 310 59 99). Metro Jaume I.
Open 1-9.30pm Mon, Thur-Sat; 4-9.30pm Wed; 1-9pm Sun. **Credit** AmEx, MC, V. **Map** p345 C3.
A tomato's toss from the leafy picnic area of the Parc de la Ciutadella is this new concept in fast food. New Yorker Christine and her Argentine partner Lucas started out making scrumptious cookies (try oat, walnut and cinnamon) and cakes for local restaurants, until the business blossomed into this small and friendly takeaway-cum-café. There are also salads, couscous, savoury tarts and meat dishes.

L'Hivernacle

Parc de la Ciutadella (93 295 40 17). Metro Arc de Triomf. **Open** 9am-midnight Mon-Sat; 9am-5pm Sun. **Credit** AmEx, MC, V. **Map** p343 E6.
Sipping coffee amid the exotic plant life of the iron and glass 'winter house' of the Ciutadella park is a thoroughly good start to the morning; sipping cava and listening to a jazz band here at night is sheer indulgence. If you *really* like it, you can have lunch here too, though the food isn't up to the setting.

Tèxtil Cafè

C/Montcada 12 (93 268 25 98/www.textilcafe.com). Metro Jaume I. **Open** 10am-midnight Tue-Sun. **Credit** MC, V. **Map** p345 C3.
Perfectly placed for C/Montcada museum-goers, and with a graceful 14th-century courtyard, this is an elegant place for a coffee in the shade, or under gas heaters in winter, with decent breakfast and lunch menus. On Sunday evenings there's a DJ followed by live jazz, though this attracts a €4 supplement.

Tapas

Euskal Etxea

Placeta Montcada 1-3 (93 310 21 85). Metro Jaume I. **Open** *Bar* 6.30-11.30pm Mon; 11.30am-4pm, 6.30-11.30pm Tue-Sat. *Restaurant* 8.30-11.30pm Mon; 1.30-4pm, 8.30-11.30pm Tue-Sat. Closed 2wks Aug, 1wk Dec-Jan. **Credit** AmEx, MC, V. **Map** p345 C3.
A Basque cultural centre and *pintxo* bar. Help yourself to dainty little croissants filled with *jamón serrano*, chicken tempura with saffron mayonnaise, melted provolone with mango and crispy ham, or a mini brochette of pork and peppers, but hang on to the toothpicks spearing each one: they'll be counted up and charged for at the end.

Mosquito

C/Carders 46 (93 268 75 69/www.mosquitotapas.com). Metro Arc de Triomf or Jaume I. **Open** 5pm-1am Tue-Thur, Sun; 5pm-2.30am Fri, Sat. **Credit** MC, V. **Map** p345 C3.

Don't be put off. The announced 'exotic tapas' are not another lame attempt to sex up fried calamares by way of tower presentation and yucca chips, but tiny versions of what owners Shilpa and Jazz do best: good to excellent dishes from the subcontinent and elsewhere in Asia. Food ranges from chicken tikka to Japanese street omelettes and masala dosas.

Bars

L'Antic Teatre

C/Verdaguer i Callis 12 (93 315 23 54/www.lantic teatre.com). Metro Urquinaona. **Open** noon-11pm daily. **No credit cards**. **Map** p344 B2.
A slightly madcap theatre run by a slightly madcap crew has as its most fabulous feature (unless you count a bloke who uses his own blood to make black pudding on stage) a hidden garden, dotted with tables cloaked in fruity vinyl and reverberating to the sound of young-enough-to-know-better hippies.

Bar Bodega Teo

C/Verdaguer i Callis 4 (93 319 10 26). Metro Jaume I or Urquinaona. **Open** 9am-6pm, 7.30pm-midnight Tue, Wed; 9am-6pm, 7.30pm-1am Thur, Fri. **No credit cards**. **Map** p344 B2.
Squeeze through the tiny front bar hanging with hundreds of key fobs, go round the counter and head to a smoky and buzzing back-room. There's a tango singer on Friday nights and flamenco on Thursdays (€6 including a drink), although you'll need to arrive early or book ahead to get in.

Casa Paco

C/Allada Vermell 10 (93 507 37 19). Metro Arc de Triomf or Jaume I. **Open** 10am-3pm Mon; 10am-2am Tue-Thur; 10am-3am Fri; 1pm-3am Sat; 1pm-2am Sun. **No credit cards**. **Map** p345 C3.
Sounds like an old man's bar, looks like an old man's bar, but this scruffy, amiable hole-in-the-wall was *the* underground hit of 2004, thanks largely to frequent visits from Barcelona's DJ-in-chief, Christian Vogel (catch him on Fridays and Saturdays). Other contributing and crucial factors include a sprawling terrace and the biggest V&Ts in the known world.

Espai Barroc

C/Montcada 20 (93 310 06 73). Metro Jaume I. **Open** 8pm-2am Tue-Sat; 6-10pm Sun. **Admission** (incl 1 drink) €20 Thur; otherwise free. **Credit** MC, V. **Map** p345 C3.
A sombre-hued riot of baroque excess, with hundreds of candles lighting oil paintings, tapestries, sculptures, flowers and bowls of fruit, to the accompaniment of Handel, Brahms and live opera on Thursdays. The location is also spectacular: deep within the 17th-century Palau Dalmases, with tables outside in the courtyard in summer. Expensive and elitist but utterly unique.

La Fianna

C/Banys Vells 15 (93 315 18 10). Metro Jaume I. **Open** 7pm-1.30am Mon-Thur; 7pm-2.30am Fri, Sat; noon-2am Sun. **Credit** DC, MC, V. **Map** p345 C3.

Strange brews

Not for nothing is Catalonia shaped like a liver. If you have a crazy idea for a drinking hole, chances are this is the town, with its couple of large local breweries and licensing laws as loose as Pavarotti's trousers on a koala bear, in which to make it happen. Just as long as no one's beaten you to it.

La Fira (C/Provença 171, no phone) is a den of freaky weirddom. Unfortunately, it's also a den of locals who enjoy really terrible music. Regardless, it's worth popping in to witness the creepy contents of the former funfair on Montjuïc rearranged in an Eixample bar, particularly the hall of mirrors in the entrance, the scary grandma in her booth and the enormous gorilla with its gaping mouth hanging over the dancefloor.

If you prefer to mix your drinks with potentially lethal steel-tipped weapons, the archery bar **L'Arquer** (Gran Via 454, 93 358 25 19) should be exactly to your disturbed fancy. Yes, it's a bar. Yes, it's a proper archery range. No, it wouldn't get past health and safety officers in any other country. Pursuits of a different sort can be found way across town at **La Primitiva** (C/Meridiana 157, no phone), the private bar of Societat Ocellaire, aka the society for the owners of small caged birds. There's nothing remarkable about the decor or the service, but there's no other bar in which the ubiquitous television in the corner has to battle with more than 60 cages of small birds. At weekends, there are even (non-contact) competitions held between prized chirrupers. The aged, male clientele usually prefer visitors to keep a low profile, as they also do at the bar in **El Canódromo** (C/Concepció Arenal 165, 93 352 20 61). This is the greyhound racing track and the bar overlooks the track itself. The carpet is an unsurprising weave of fag ends mixed with torn-up betting slips.

Bar Manolo (C/Lancaster 3, no phone) is the spiritual centre of the local skater scene. If you don't know your ollie from your nollie or your tailslide from your nosegrind, this isn't the place for you. If, on the other hand, you want to exchange tips on how to fit your enormous dreadlocks under the hood of your top, welcome home. The aesthetic, like the people, is 'unwashed', light years away from the vibe at **Kahiki** (Gran Via 581, 93 323 18 83). Here, a surprisingly yuppie crowd chooses to drink vat-sized cocktails from the scooped-out, smoke-spewing ceramic heads of Polynesian gods. Via metre-long straws.

● *Andrew Losowsky is editor of* A Weird and Wonderful Guide to Barcelona.

La Fira.

Bedouin chic has swept across town like a sirocco wind, but La Fianna has made the most dramatic use of it. Enter through heavy wooden doors into a high-arched medieval space, ablaze with diaphanous curtains, chandeliers and cushions, cushions everywhere. This Gothic seraglio also offers a reasonable selection of Mediterranean food in the evenings, and brunch from noon on Sundays.

Gimlet

C/Rec 24 (93 310 10 27). Metro Jaume I. **Open** 10pm-3am Mon, Sun; 8pm-3am Tue-Sat. **No credit cards. Map** p345 C3.

This subdued little wood-panelled cocktail bar has an Edward Hopper feel on quiet nights. The long mahogany counter has been burnished by the same well-clad elbows and patrolled by the same laconic barman for many years, and Gimlet is considered something of a classic, though the measures can be a little too ladylike for modern tastes.

Mudanzas

C/Vidrieria 15 (93 319 11 37). Metro Barceloneta or Jaume I. **Open** 10am-2.30am Mon-Thur, Sun; 10am-3am Fri, Sat. **Credit** MC, V. **Map** p345 C4.

An unpretentious and welcoming bar, with marble-topped tables and chequered tiled floor. There's a rack of newspapers and magazines, many in English, and some tables outside. In winter, it's best to sit up on the mezzanine in order to avoid the smoky fug that pervades downstairs.

La Fianna. *See p180.*

Planeta RAI

C/Carders 12, pral (93 268 13 21/www.pangea.org/ rai). Metro Arc de Triomf or Jaume I. **Open** 10am-11pm Mon-Sat. **Map** p345 C3.

Run by an earnest young collective that has 'inter-cultural awakening' at the top of the agenda, Planeta RAI exists with a number of good causes in mind, but also functions as a de facto social centre for the neighbourhood's neo-hippie element. There are workshops from acrobatics to pottery; jam sessions on Fridays, and on Tuesdays and Thursdays, world cinema is shown in the surprisingly large auditorium.

Va de Vi

C/Banys Vells 16 (93 319 29 00). Metro Jaume I. **Open** 7pm-1am Mon-Wed, Sun; 7pm-2am Thur; 7pm-3am Fri, Sat. **Credit** MC, V. **Map** p345 C3.

Opened a few years ago by a former sommelier, artist and sculptor, this Gothic-style wine bar looks like it's been around forever. There are over 1,000 wines on the list, many available in a *cata* (tasting measure). The usual Spanish selections are accompanied by wines from the New World and elsewhere.

La Vinya del Senyor

Plaça Santa Maria 5 (93 310 33 79). Metro Barceloneta or Jaume I. **Open** noon-1am Tue-Thur; noon-2am Fri, Sat; noon-midnight Sun. **Credit** AmEx, DC, MC, V. **Map** p345 C3/4.

Another classic wine bar, this one with an unmatchable position right in front of Santa Maria del Mar. With high-quality tapas and so many excellent

La Cova Fumada.

language exchange, Murphy's, Guinness and a stack of newspapers from around the world feature among them. Throughout the day, there's cheesy garlic bread, delectable filled ciabatta, tapas, dolmades and dips, and home-made chocolate or carrot cake.

Filferro
C/Sant Carles 29 (93 221 98 36). Metro Barceloneta. **Open** 9am-11pm Tue-Thur, Sun; 9am-12.30am Fri, Sat. **No credit cards. Map** p343 E7.
Simply but edgily decorated with cascades of red '50s lampshades and rusted iron balustrades, this is a peaceful, sunny spot for breakfast, lunch or tapas. As well as a decent range of fresh fruit juices (try the 'Trifàsic', with carrot, pear and lemon), there are pastries, toasted sandwiches, pasta and salads.

La Miranda del Museu
Museu d'Història de Catalunya, Plaça Pau Vila 3 (93 225 50 07). Metro Barceloneta. **Open** 10am-7pm Tue-Thur; 10am-7pm, 9-11pm Fri, Sat; 10am-2.30pm Sun. **Credit** MC, V. **Map** p345 C4.
Don't go spreading this about, but there's a secret café with terrific views, cheap and reasonable food and a vast terrace, sitting right at the edge of the marina, perched high above the humdrum tourist traps. Walk into the Catalan History Museum and take the lift to the top floor. You don't need a ticket.

Tapas

Bar Colombo
C/Escar 4 (93 225 02 00). Metro Barceloneta. **Open** noon-3am daily. Closed 2wks Jan-Feb. **No credit cards. Map** p342 D7.
Deckshod yachties and moneyed locals stroll by all day, oblivious to this unassuming little bar and its sunny terrace overlooking the port. In fact, nobody seems to notice it, odd given its fantastic location and generous portions of *patatas bravas*. The only drawback is the nerve-jangling techno that occasionally fetches up on the stereo.

Can Paixano
C/Reina Cristina 7 (93 310 08 39). Metro Barceloneta. **Open** 9am-10.30pm Mon-Sat. Closed 3wks Aug-Sept. **No credit cards. Map** p345 C4.
It's impossible to talk, get your order heard or move your elbows, yet the 'Champagne Bar', as it's invariably known, has a global following. Its narrow, smoky confines are always mobbed with Catalans and adventurous tourists making the most of dirt-cheap house cava and sausage *bocadillos* (you can't buy a bottle without a couple). A must.

La Cova Fumada
C/Baluard 56 (93 221 40 61). Metro Barceloneta. **Open** 8.30am-3.30pm Mon-Wed, Sat; 8.30am-3.30pm, 6-8.30pm Thur, Fri. Closed Aug. **No credit cards. Map** p343 E7.
This cramped, chaotic little *bodega* is the birthplace of the potato *bomba*, served with a chilli sauce. Here, when they say spicy, they mean spicy. Especially

wines on its list (the selection changes every two weeks), however, it's a crime to do as most tourists do and take up its terrace tables just for the view.

El Xampanyet
C/Montcada 22 (93 319 70 03). Metro Jaume I. **Open** noon-3.30pm, 7-11.30pm Tue-Sat; noon-3.30pm Sun. Closed Aug. **Credit** MC, V. **Map** p345 C3.
The eponymous poor man's champagne is actually a fruity and drinkable sparkling white, served in old-fashioned saucer glasses and best accompanied by the house *tapa*, superb fresh anchovies from Cantábria. Run by the same family since the 1930s, El Xampanyet is lined with coloured tiles, barrels and antique curios, and with a handful of marble tables.

Barceloneta & the Ports

Cafés

Daguiri
C/Grau i Torras 59, corner of C/Almirall Aixada (93 221 51 09). Metro Barceloneta. **Open** *June-Sept* 11am-2am daily. *Oct-May* 10.30am-1am daily. **Credit** (minimum €10) DC, MC, V. **Map** p343 E7.
Daguiri works hard not to become a one-trick, seaside summer terrace, with a raft of measures aimed squarely at foreign residents. Wi-fi connections, a

tasty are the chickpeas with morcilla sausage, roast artichokes and marinated sardines. It needs no sign, and its huge following of lunching workers means it's hard to get a table much after 1pm.

El Vaso de Oro

C/Balboa 6 (93 319 30 98). Metro Barceloneta. **Open** 9am-midnight daily. Closed Sept. **No credit cards. Map** p343 E7.
The enormous popularity of this long, narrow, cruise-ship style bar tells you everything you need to know about the tapas, but also means that he who hesitates is lost when it comes to ordering. Elbow out a space and demand, loudly, *chorizitos, patatas bravas*, cubed steak (*solomillo*) or spicy tuna (*atún*).

Bars

The loud, tacky bars lining the Port Olímpic draw a mix of stag parties staring at the go-go girls and curious locals staring at the stag parties.

Luz de Gas – Port Vell

Opposite the Palau de Mar, Moll del Diposit (93 209 77 11). Metro Barceloneta or Jaume I. **Open** *Mar-Oct* noon-3am Mon-Sat; 11am-3am Sun. Closed Nov-Feb. **Credit** AmEx, MC, V. **Map** p342 D7.
No one's saying it's not cheesy, but this boat-cum-bar also has its romantic moments. By day, bask in the sun with a beer on the upper deck, or rest in the shade below. With nightfall, candles are brought out, wine is uncorked and, if you can blot out the Lionel Richie, it's everything a holiday bar should be.

Poble Sec

Cafés

Fundació Joan Miró

Parc de Montjuïc (93 329 07 68). Metro Paral·lel, then Funicular de Montjuïc. **Open** 10am-7pm Tue-Sat; 10am-2.30pm Sun. **Credit** MC, V. **Map** p341 B6.
Inside the Miró museum is this pleasant restaurant and café; the former overlooks the sculpture garden, while the latter has tables outside in a grassy courtyard dotted with Miró's pieces. The sandwiches made with 'Arab bread' are expensive but huge; there are also pasta dishes and daily specials.

Tapas

Quimet i Quimet

C/Poeta Cabanyes 25 (93 442 31 42). Metro Paral·lel. **Open** noon-4pm, 7-10.30pm Mon-Fri; noon-4pm Sat. Closed Aug. **Credit** MC, V. **Map** p341 B6.
Packed to the rafters with dusty bottles of wine, this minuscule bar makes up for in tapas what it lacks in space. The speciality is preserved clams, cockles, mussels and so on, which are not to all tastes, but the *montaditos*, sculpted tapas served on bread, are spectacular. Try salmon sashimi with cream cheese, honey and soy, or cod, passata and black olive pâté.

Bars

Bar Primavera

C/Nou de la Rambla 192 (93 329 30 62). Metro Paral·lel. **Open** *Apr-Oct* 8am-10pm Tue-Sun. *Nov-Mar* 8am-7pm Tue-Sun. Closed 1wk Dec-Jan. **No credit cards. Map** p341 B6.
While this emphatically isn't a destination bar, it does have its charm, and makes for a perfect pit stop on the climb up Montjuïc. Positioned on the edge of Poble Sec, it has a quiet, vine-covered terrace from which to look back over the city while munching on rather basic *bocadillos*. Winter is a different proposition, however: there's no indoor seating.

La Caseta del Migdia

Mirador de Migdia, Passeig del Migdia s/n, Montjuïc (mobile 617 956 572/www.lacaseta.org). Bus 55 or bus Parc de Montjuïc/funicular de Montjuïc, then 10min walk. Follow signs to Mirador de Montjuïc. **Open** *June-Sept* 6pm-2.30am Thur, Fri; 10am-3am Sat; 10am-2am Sun. *Oct-May* 10am-6pm Sat, Sun. **No credit cards.**
Follow the Camí del Mar footpath around Montjuïc castle to find one of the few vantage points from which to watch the sun set. Completely alfresco, high up in a clearing among the pines, this is a magical space, scattered with deckchairs, hammocks and candlelit tables. DJs spinning funk, rare groove and lounge alternate surreally with a faltering string quartet; food is pizza and other munchies.

Eixample

Cafés

Bauma

C/Roger de Llúria 124 (93 459 05 66). Metro Diagonal. **Open** 8am-midnight Mon-Fri, Sun. Closed 3wks Aug. **Credit** AmEx, DC, MC, V. **Map** p338 D4.
An old-style café-bar made for lazy Sunday mornings, with battered leather seats, ceiling fans and an incongruous soundtrack of acid jazz. Along with well-priced, substantial dishes such as baked cod, and wild boar stew, there's an impressive list of tapas and sandwiches.

Café Berlin

C/Muntaner 240-242 (93 200 65 42). Metro Diagonal. **Open** 10am-2am Mon-Wed; 10am-3am Thur, Fri; 11am-3am Sat. **Credit** V. **Map** p338 C3.
Downstairs, low sofas fill with amorous couples while upstairs all is sleek and light, with brushed steel, dark leather and a Klimtesque red and gold mural. A rack of newspapers and plenty of sunlight make it popular for coffee or snacks all day long; as well as tapas there are salads, pasta dishes, *bocadillos*, cheesecake and brownies, but beware the 20% surcharge for pavement tables.

Premier

C/Provença 236 (93 532 16 50). FGC Provença. **Open** 11am-3am Tue-Sat. **Credit** MC, V. **Map** p338 C-D4.

A starkly monochrome cocktail bar for the 21st century, where perspex is the new mahogany and vodka-Red Bull is the new Martini. French owners add a little Gallic class to a short list of tapas and lunchtime dishes (expect oysters and duck magret, with champagne getting equal billing with cava) for a well-heeled thirtysomething crowd.

Tapas

La Bodegueta

Rambla Catalunya 100 (93 215 48 94). Metro Diagonal. **Open** 8am-2am Mon-Sat; 6.30pm-1am Sun. Closed 2wks Aug. **No credit cards. Map** p338 D4.
Resisting the rise and rise of the surrounding area, this former wine *bodega* is unreconstructed, dusty and welcoming, supplying students, businessmen and everyone in between with reasonably priced wine, vermouth on tap and prime-quality tapas amid the delicate patterns of century-old tiling. In summer, there are tables outside on the almost pedestrianised Rambla Catalunya.

Casa Alfonso

C/Roger de Llúria 6 (93 301 97 83). Metro Urquinaona. **Open** 9am-1am Mon-Sat. **Credit** MC, V. **Map** p344 C1.
Said to be a favourite of Madrid actors Javier Bardem and Carmen Maura, Casa Alfonso is more often patronised by Catalans of a certain age and income, and by night is a sea of beige. It has a refined, old-fashioned air: monochrome murals of early 20th-century Barcelona decorate the walls, and glass-fronted cupboards display bottles of oil and wine. Try the cheese and charcuterie served on wooden slabs.

Cervesería Catalana

C/Mallorca 236 (93 216 0368). Metro Passeig de Gràcia. **Open** 8am-1.30am Mon-Fri; 9am-1.30am Sat, Sun. **Credit** AmEx, DC, MC, V. **Map** p338 D4.
The Catalan beerhouse lives up to its name with a winning selection of brews from around the world, but the real reason to come is the tapas. A vast array is yours for the pointing: only hot *montaditos*, such as bacon, cheese and dates, have to be ordered from the kitchen. Arrive early for a seat at the bar, and even earlier to sit at one of the pavement tables.

Bars

La Barcelonina de Vins i Esperits

C/València 304 (93 215 70 83). Metro Passeig de Gràcia. **Open** *Sept-June* 6pm-2am Mon-Fri; 7.30pm-2am Sat; 8pm-1am Sun. *July, Aug* 6pm-2am Mon-Fri; 7.30pm-2am Sat. **Credit** AmEx, V. **Map** p338 D4.
With its hundreds of bottles behind chicken wire and its lighting a dentist's delight, La Barcelonina is that rare thing: an unpretentious wine bar. Oenophiles and local workers rub shoulders at the bar, poring over a long wine list that includes some excellent cavas, and preparing for the night ahead with a handful of tapas or a salad.

Dry Martini

C/Aribau 162-166 (93 217 50 72). FGC Provença. **Open** 1pm-2.30am Mon-Thur; 1pm-3am Fri; 6.30pm-3am Sat; 6pm-2.30am Sun. **Credit** V. **Map** p338 C4.
A shrine to the eponymous cocktail, honoured in Martini-related artwork and served in a hundred forms. All the trappings of a trad cocktail bar are here – bow-tied staff, leather banquettes, drinking antiques and wooden cabinets displaying a century's worth of bottles – but the stuffiness is absent: music owes more to trip hop than middle-aged crowd-pleasers, and the barmen welcome all comers.

Gràcia

Cafés

Flash Flash

C/Granada del Penedès 25 (93 237 09 90). FGC Gràcia. **Open** 1pm-1.30am daily. **Credit** AmEx, DC, MC, V. **Map** p338 D3.
Opened in 1970, this bar was a design sensation in its day, with its white leatherette banquettes and walls imprinted with silhouettes of a life-size frolicking, Twiggy-like model. They call it a *tortilleria*, with 50 or so tortilla variations, alongside a list of kid-friendly dishes and adult-friendly cocktails.

Salambó

C/Torrijos 51 (93 218 69 66). Metro Fontana or Joanic. **Open** noon-2.30am Mon-Thur, Sun; noon-3am Fri, Sat. **Credit** MC, V. **Map** p339 E3.
The time-honoured meeting place for Verdi cinemagoers, Salambó is a large and ever so slightly staid split-level café serving coffee, teas and filled ciabatta to the *barrio*'s more conservative element. At night, those planning to eat are given preference when it comes to bagging a table.

Tapas

Bodega Manolo

C/Torrent de les Flors 101 (93 284 43 77). Metro Joanic. **Open** 9.30am-7pm Tue, Wed; 9.30am-1am Thur, Fri; 12.30-4.30pm, 8.30pm-1am Sat; 10.30am-3pm Sun. Closed Aug. **No credit cards. Map** p339 E3.
Another old family *bodega* with a faded, peeling charm, barrels on the wall and rows of dusty bottles, Manolo specialises not only in wine, but in classy food: try the foie gras with port and apple. At the other end of the scale, and also with its place, comes the 'Destroyer': egg, bacon, sausage and chips.

Sureny

Plaça de la Revolució 17 (93 213 75 56). Metro Fontana or Joanic. **Open** 8.30pm-midnight Tue-Thur; 8.30pm-1am Fri, Sat; 1-3.30pm, 8.30pm-midnight Sun. Closed last wk Sept, 1st wk Oct, 2wks Dec-Jan. **Credit** MC, V. **Map** p338 D3.
A well-kept gastronomic secret, Sureny boasts superb gourmet tapas and waiters who know what they're talking about. As well as a run-of-the-mill

No shrinking Violeta

You know right away when Violeta La Burra enters the room. With a rattle of her maracas and a throaty warble, she sells her roses with the style and confidence of one who knows that she is the highlight of your evening. She knows this because she is a pro, and one of the last remaining relics of a decadent Barcelona that disappeared long ago.

Violeta is a transvestite dressed in the finest classic threads, and underneath the make-up is the aged face of Pedro Moreno. He first arrived in Barcelona from his native Seville more than 50 years ago looking for work. He found it in a bar in front of the Boqueria market, working as a flamenco dancer and rent boy. Back in those days, homosexuality was illegal, so a girl would always accompany him and his clients to the private rooms in case of a police raid.

'Dalí used to come into the bar two or three times a month,' Violeta recalled recently, 'with his wife or with a troupe of French or Italian models. They were always half-nude. Sometimes they'd just wear fur coats with nothing underneath. They loved me sitting with them: I was a very amusing innocent.'

After a brief spell performing in Belgium, where she married and then divorced a lesbian striptease artist, Moreno returned to Barcelona, and Violeta was born in a late-night cabaret in C/Escudellers. She was an instant hit, attracting the attention of Jean Marie Riviere, a famous showman who ran the Paradis Latin in Paris. He took her back with him to the French capital and she soon became a fixture of the scene, hanging out with famous artists and actors. Society columnists chatted about her relationships.

But just as people began to take notice of her exploits, Moreno got a call from Barcelona telling him that his mother had fallen ill. He returned to nurse her. But, as the old-style shows disappeared, it became near impossible to make a successful return to the cabaret stage. Money was hard to come by, and Violeta starred in low-budget pornography. The days of glamour were long gone.

These days, Moreno lives in his mother's old apartment in the Eixample with a suitcase of cuttings and a lifetime of memories as his only souvenirs of the old days. 'I was a big star,' he says wistfully. And still, on occasional weekends, he slowly becomes Violeta again, to sell red roses and to witness once more the city's affection for its favourite, now aged, night-time lover.

● *You can catch Violeta in* **Dry Martini** (see p186) *at the beginning of the night.*

tortilla 'n' calamares, look out for tuna marinated in ginger and soy, partridge and venison in season, and a sublime duck foie with redcurrant sauce.

Bars

La Baignoire

C/Verdi 6 (mobile 606 330 460). Metro Fontana or Joanic. **Open** 7pm-2am Mon-Thur, Sun; 7pm-3am Fri, Sat. **No credit cards. Map** p338 D3.

It means 'bathtub', which goes some way towards giving you an idea of the size, but the staff are unfailingly friendly and slide projections and lounge music complement the mellow vibe. Fresh fruit juices are served in summer, while cocktails and a good wine are available year round.

Casa Quimet

Rambla de Prat 9 (93 217 53 27). Metro Fontana. **Open** 6.30pm-2am Tue-Sun. Closed Feb, Aug. **No credit cards. Map** p338 D3.

Eat, Drink, Shop

Puku Café.

Yellowing jazz posters cover every inch of wall-space, dozens of ancient guitars hang from the ceiling and a succession of ticking clocks compete to be heard over the voice of Billie Holiday. This other-worldly 'Guitar Bar' (as the place is invariably known to locals) occasionally springs to life with an impromptu jam session, but most of the time, it's a perfect study in melancholy.

Noise i Art

C/Topazi 26 (93 217 50 01). Metro Fontana.
Open 6pm-1.30am Tue-Thur, Sun; 6pm-2.30am Fri, Sat. Closed 10 days end Aug. **No credit cards. Map** p338 D3.
It's known locally as the 'IKEA bar', which, though some of the plastic fittings do look strangely familiar, doesn't really do justice to the colourful, pop art interior. A chilled and convivial atmosphere is occasionally livened up with a flamenco session, and Gràcia staples such as houmus and tabbouleh are served along with various salads and pasta dishes. Mostly, though, this is a great place to sit and shoot the breeze.

Puku Café

C/Guilleries 10 (mobile 654 318 404/www.puku-cafe.com). Metro Fontana. **Open** *June-Sept* 8pm-2am Mon-Thur, 8pm-3am Fri, Sat. *Oct-May* 6.30pm-1am Mon-Wed; 6.30pm-2am Thur; 7pm-3am Fri, Sat.
No credit cards. Map p339 D3.
The Puku Café has two very different vibes. During the week it's a colourful meeting place, where the casually hip hang out over a bottle of wine and maybe some cactus and lime ice-cream. At week-ends, however, there's a transformation: the amber walls and deep orange columns instead prop up a younger, scruffier crowd, nodding along to some of the city's best DJs spinning a varied playlist based around electropop.

Samsara

C/Terol 6 (93 285 36 88). Metro Fontana or Joanic.
Open 1.30-4pm, 8.30pm-2am Mon-Thur; 1.30-4pm, 8.30pm-3am Fri; 8.30pm-3am Sat. **Credit** MC, V.
Map p338 D3.
A combination of Moroccan themed decor and intelligent cooking, Samsara has built up quite a following among Gràcia foodies. Its tapas are diminutive but don't want for flavour or imagination: try monk-fish ceviche with mango or watermelon gazpacho with basil oil. Photos line the walls, and a DJ plays lounge and the smoothest of house later in the week.

Saint-Germain

C/Torrent de l'Olla 113 (93 218 04 13). Metro Fontana. **Open** 6pm-2.30am Mon-Thur, Sun; 6pm-3am Fri, Sat. **No credit cards. Map** p338 D3.
Get here early for a leather armchair from which to survey the assembled young hip Americans sipping Caipirinhas, picking at ham and cheese crêpes and making noises of recognition at the Kruder & Dorfmeister soundtrack. Decent salads, quiches and sandwiches are served until midnight.

Other areas

Bars

Merbeyé

Plaça Doctor Andreu, Tibidabo (93 417 92 79). FGC Avda Tibidabo, then Tramvia Blau/bus 60. **Open** noon-2.30am Mon-Thur; noon-3.30am Fri, Sat; noon-2am Sun. **Credit** MC, V.
A cocktail bar straight from central casting: moodily lit, plush with red velvet and hung with prints of jazz maestros. In summer there's also a peaceful, stylish terrace. The clientele runs from shabby gentility to flashy Barça players and their bling-encrusted wives.

Shops & Services

Everything must go.

The butcher, the baker and the candlestick maker are alive and well. But in vogueish Barcelona, these traditional tradesmen are just as likely to sell cappuccino-flavoured sausages, heart-shaped brioche and candlesticks made of pink chicken wire. This mix of tradition and innovation is typical of the Barcelona shopping experience, and locals happily distribute their wealth among the small boutiques, street markets and mega malls alike.

Most shops don't open until 10am, and then close for lunch from 2pm to around 5pm. In a move that may seem like financial suicide, many small shops also close on Saturday afternoons and all day Monday. Large shops and chains, however, soldier through until 8pm,

an hour later on Saturdays. The regulations governing Sunday and holiday opening hours are fiendishly complicated. Generally speaking, however, restaurants, bakeries, flower stalls, convenience stores and shops in tourist zones such as La Rambla or the Maremàgnum can open seven days a week, and nearly all stores open on the four Sundays before Christmas.

The rate of sales tax (IVA) depends on the type of product: it's currently seven per cent on food and 16 per cent on most other items. In any of the 700 or so shops that display a Tax-Free Shopping sticker on their door, non-EU residents can request a Tax-Free Cheque on purchases of over €90.15. Before leaving the EU, these must be stamped at customs (at Barcelona airport, this is located in Terminal A by the Arrivals gate) and can immediately be reclaimed in cash at La Caixa bank.

Returning goods, even when they are faulty, can be difficult in all but the largest stores. However, all shops are required to provide a complaints book (ask for an *hoja de reclamación*). The mere act of asking for it sometimes does the trick, but, if not, take your receipt and copy of the complaint form to the local consumer information office, OMIC (Ronda Sant Pau, Raval, 43-45, 93 402 78 41, www.omic.bcn.es, open 9am-2pm Mon-Fri).

Note that if you're paying by credit card, you usually have to show photographic ID, such as a passport or driving licence. Bargain-hunters should note that sales (*rebaixes* or *rebajas*) begin after the retail orgy of Christmas and Epiphany, running from 6 January to mid February, and again during July and August.

The best Shops

For rainy day retail therapy
El Corte Inglés, L'Illa and Diagonal Mar (for all see p191).

For getting your groove back
Discos Castelló (see p212), Verdes (see p213) and FNAC (see p193).

For liquid assets
La Carte des Vins (see p209), Lavinia (see p209) and Queviures Murrià (see p208).

For Barcelona bling
Bagués (see p204), BD Ediciones de Diseño (see p195) and Loewe (see p206).

For label junkies
Jean-Pierre Bua (see p197), Loft Avignon (see p198) and Le Swing (see p203).

For style on a shoestring
Freya (see p204), Mango Outlet (see p200) and Zara (see p198).

For sensual healing
Le Boudoir (see p203), Bienestar Augusta Natural (see p210) and Enric Rovira Shop (see p208).

For dastardly disguises
Arlequí Mascares (see p213), Flora Albaicín (see p213) and Lailo (see p201).

One-stop shopping

Barcelona Glòries
Avda Diagonal 208, Eixample (93 486 04 04/www. lesglories.com). Metro Glòries. **Open** *Shops* 10am-10pm Mon-Sat. **Map** p343 F5.

Since opening in 1995, this mall, office and leisure centre has become the focus of local life. There's a seven-screen cinema (films are mostly dubbed into Spanish) and over 220 shops, including a Carrefour supermarket, an H&M, a Mango and a Disney Store, facing on to a large, café-filled square decorated with jets of coloured water. Family-oriented attractions include a free pram-lending service, play areas and entertainment such as bouncy castles and trampolines. As a leisure zone, Glòries stays open until 1am.

enjoy CHIC OUTLET SHOPPING

La Roca Village, home to over 80 stores belonging to famous national and international brands, is located on the Costa Brava just 30 minutes from both Barcelona and Girona. Discover your favourite designer brands in fashion, accessories, sportswear and homeware, offering previous season's collections at prices reduced by up to 60% all year round.

www.ChicOutletShopping.com   www.LaRocaVillage.com

Visit La Roca Village and enjoy a unique shopping experience in a purpose built open-air XIX Century Catalan Village. In addition, combine your visit to one of the famous tourist attractions in the region including the Dalí Museum in Figueres, Monsterrat or the city of Girona.

OUTLET SHOPPING TOUR:
For information please ask at your hotel reception.

A regular bus service runs:
Monday to Friday from Fabra i Puig bus station in Barcelona.

Located off the AP-7 motorway, exit 12 (Cardedeu).

Open from Monday to Friday from 11.00 a.m. to 8.30 p.m. Saturdays and Special Openings 2005 (3 July, 6 November, 6, 8, 11 and 18 December) from 10.00 a.m. to 10.00 p.m.

LA ROCA VILLAGE
OUTLET SHOPPING
T. + 34 93 842 39 00

El Corte Inglés

Plaça Catalunya 14, Eixample (93 306 38 00/www. elcorteingles.es). Metro Catalunya. **Open** 10am-10pm Mon-Sat. **Credit** AmEx, DC, MC, V. **Map** p344 B1.

With its cult-like grip on Spanish consumer consciousness, El Corte Inglés has become synonymous with the phrase 'department store' since gobbling the last of the competition in the early 1990s. The monolithic Plaça Catalunya branch has nine floors of fashion, beauty and home decor, a seventh-floor café and a decent supermarket in the basement with services from currency exchange to key-cutting. The branch on Portal de l'Àngel has six floors of music, electronics, mobile phone services, books and sporting goods; the red-jacketed stewards by the doors will point you in the right direction.

Other locations: Portal de l'Àngel 19 (93 306 38 00); Avda Diagonal 471-473, Eixample (93 493 48 00); Avda Diagonal 617, Eixample (93 366 71 00); L'Illa, Avda Diagonal 545, Eixample (93 363 80 90).

Diagonal Mar

Avda Diagonal 3, Poblenou (902 53 03 00/www. diagonalmar.com). Metro El Maresme-Forum. **Open** *Shops* 10am-10pm Mon-Sat. *Food court & entertainment* 10am-midnight Mon-Thur; 10am-2am Fri, Sat; 11am-midnight Sun.

This new three-level mall has an airy marine theme and a sea-facing roof terrace filled with cafés and restaurants of the fast-food variety. As business is still a little slow (except at the giant Alcampo supermarket), it's a good queue-free option. Other anchors include El Corte Inglés and FNAC. There's also a bowling alley, regular exhibitions, concerts and children's entertainment every Sunday at 12.30pm.

L'Illa

Avda Diagonal 545-557, Eixample (93 444 00 00/ www.lilla.com). Metro Maria Cristina. **Open** 10am-9.30pm Mon-Sat. *Supermarket* 9.30am-9.30pm Mon-Sat. **Map** p337 B4.

It looks more like an iceberg than an island (*illa*), but this hugely popular commercial and business centre caters to a high-end, fashionable clientele with

over 130 shops, among them Camper, FNAC, Diesel, Decathlon and Mango. There are all manner of fast-food restaurants, a food market on the ground floor and a Caprabo hypermarket.

Maremàgnum

Moll d'Espanya, Port Vell (93 225 81 00/www.mare magnum.es). Metro Drassanes. **Open** 10am-10pm daily. **Map** p342 D7.

When Viaplana and Piñon's black-mirrored leisure centre and mall opened in 1995, the shops, discos, bars and restaurants were *the* places to hang out. After years of declining popularity, Maremàgnum has been brightly refurbished and now focuses on the family market with funfair rides, cinemas and all the shops the kids love, from Imaginarium to a Barça shop. Ice-cream stalls keep energy levels high.

Antiques

An long-standing antiques market is held outside the cathedral every Thursday (*see p212*) and dealers set up stands at the **Port Vell** at weekends. **C/Palla** is the main focus for antiques in the Barri Gòtic; although they're of variable quality, it's fun to trawl through their dusty back rooms in search of that hidden Picasso. Dazzlingly expensive antiques live on **C/Consell de Cent** in the Eixample, but there are more affordable shops around **C/Dos de Maig**, near Els Encants flea market (*see p212*).

L'Arca de l'Àvia

C/Banys Nous 20, Barri Gòtic (93 302 15 98/www. larcadelavia.com). Metro Liceu. **Open** 10am-2pm, 5-8pm Mon-Fri; 11am-2pm Sat. Closed Aug. **Credit** AmEx, DC, MC, V. **Map** p345 B3.

This high-quality antique clothes shop has more whalebone corsets and shirred muslin nighties than a Merchant Ivory movie. Look out for exquisite beaded flapper dresses, silk bags and other specialities of the 'Grandmother's Ark', such as lace, tapestries, infant layettes and antique dolls and fans.

Eat, Drink, Shop

Gothsland Galeria d'Art. *See p192.*

El Ingenio. *See p195.*

Bulevard dels Antiquaris

Passeig de Gràcia 55, Eixample (93 215 44 99/www.
bulevarddelsantiquaris.com). Metro Passeig de Gràcia.
Open *Jan-June, Oct-Dec* 10.30am-1.30pm, 4.30-8.30pm
Mon-Sat. *July-Sept* 10am-1.30pm, 4.30-8.30pm Mon-
Fri. **Credit** AmEx, MC, V. **Map** p338 D4.
This vast first-floor arcade houses 73 shops selling
all manner of antiques at all manner of prices. The
range covers everything from African art to stained
glass, marble fireplaces and amber jewellery;
experts inspect every object for authenticity.

Gothsland Galeria d'Art

C/Consell de Cent 331, Eixample (93 488 19 22/
www.gothsland.com). Metro Passeig de Gràcia.
Open 10am-2pm, 4-8.30pm Mon-Sat. Closed Aug.
No credit cards. Map p342 D5.
Only for the wealthy, Gothsland has an unbeatable
collection of 19th- and 20th-century Catalan art,
along with a huge variety of furniture, mirrors and
vases from the Modernista period. Portraits and
landscapes by local luminaries Santiago Rusiñol,
Ramon Casas and Joaquim Mir flank polychrome
terracotta sculptures by Casanovas and Marès and
alabaster by Cipriani. Another highlight is the spectacular furniture by Gaspar Homar.

Bookshops

Museum shops are often the best bet for books
on art, photography, film, architecture and
design. A glut of shops specialising in comics,
film and other visual art forms can be found in
the Arc de Triomf area; **Kowasa** (C/Mallorca
235, Eixample, 93 215 80 58, www.kowasa.com)
is worth a look for photography enthusiasts.
For books on Catalonia, head to the **Palau**
Robert shop (*see p321*); the old-fashioned
Llibreria Quera (C/Petritxol 2, Barri Gòtic,
93 318 07 43) has plenty of maps and literature
on outdoor pursuits in the region.

Casa del Llibre

C/Passeig de Gràcia 62, Eixample (93 272 34 80/
www.casadellibro.com). Metro Passeig de Gràcia.
Open 9.30am-9.30pm Mon-Sat. **Credit** AmEx, DC,
MC, V. **Map** p338 D4.
Part of a well-established Spanish chain, this general bookshop offers a diverse assortment of titles
that includes some English-language fiction. Glossy
Barcelona-themed coffee-table tomes with good gift
potential sit by the front right-hand entrance.

A visit to Altaïr is a must for inveterate globetrotters. For lovers of the outdoors, this spacious travel bookshop also covers nature, as well as anthropology. The outstanding selection includes guidebooks, maps, travel literature, comics, children's books and its own superb glossy magazine. What's more, you can also buy world music CDs and DVDs. A relaxed vibe, helpful staff and comfy armchairs for sampling books before you buy make it hard to leave.

BCN Books

C/Roger de Llúria 118, Eixample (93 457 76 92/ www.bcnbooks.com). Metro Passeig de Gràcia. **Open** *Sept-July* 10am-8pm Mon-Fri; 10am-2pm Sat. *Aug* 10am-8pm Mon-Fri. **Credit** MC, V. **Map** p338 D4.
This well-stocked English-language bookstore has a wide range of learning and teaching materials for all ages. There's also a decent selection of contemporary and classic fiction, a good kids' section, some travel guides and plenty of dictionaries.
Other locations: C/Rosselló 24, Eixample (93 476 33 43).

Freaks

C/Ali Bei 10, Eixample (93 265 80 05/www.libfreaks. com). Metro Arc de Triomf. **Open** 10am-2pm, 5-9pm Mon-Sat. **Credit** MC, V. **Map** p343 E5.
Books, comics and films, with an unparalleled range of off-the-wall reading matter. DVDs and videos run from art-house to martial arts, via oddball animation, gore and porn. There are also film books, a clued-up selection of comics and graphic novels, and a supremely eclectic assortment of art, design, illustration and photography books: this is just the place to get that exhaustive Barbie doll catalogue you never knew you wanted.

Hibernian Books

C/Pere Serafí 33-35, Gràcia (93 217 47 96/www. hibernian-books.com). Metro Fontana. **Open** 10.30am-8.30pm Mon-Sat. **No credit cards.** **Map** p338 D3.
Hibernian Books opened its doors in 2004 with over 30,000 titles on sale, displaying everything from popular fiction by Danielle Steele and Jane Green to more cultured works. A penned-in kiddies' corner, beckoning armchairs, shelves piled high and tea and coffee furnish this bookworm's lair, which operates a part-exchange system for those keen on offloading some suitcase ballast.

Norma Comics

Passeig de Sant Joan 9, Eixample (93 244 84 20/ www.normacomics.com). Metro Arc de Triomf. **Open** 10.30am-2pm, 5-8.30pm Mon-Thur; 10.30am-8.30pm Fri, Sat. **Credit** MC, V. **Map** p343 E5.
The city's largest comic book store comes up with all the staples, whether you're after Marvel, Tintin, manga or perennial Spanish favourites along with recherché European masters. Alternatively, head downstairs for the film section, complete with books, DVDs and collectibles. Some works are in English; there are Buffy dolls, *Star Wars* masks and other toys to keep children of all ages amused.

FNAC

El Triangle, Plaça Catalunya 4, Eixample (93 344 18 00/www.fnac.es). Metro Catalunya. **Open** 10am-10pm Mon-Sat. *Newsstand* 10am-10pm daily. **Credit** AmEx, MC, V. **Map** p344 A1.
At FNAC you'll find a sweeping book selection in several languages, and at low prices. On other floors of this French multimedia megastore, there are CDs, DVDs, hi-fis, TVs, computers, mobile phones, film processing and so on. In contrast with the rather hectic book department, the first-rate international newsstand and café on the ground floor is a pleasant place in which to have a coffee with friends or leaf through magazines on a Sunday afternoon.
Other locations: Diagonal Mar, Avda Diagonal 3, Poblenou (93 502 99 00); L'Illa, Avda Diagonal 545-557, Eixample (93 444 59 00).

Specialist

Altaïr

Gran Via de les Corts Catalanes 616, Eixample (93 342 71 71/www.altair.es). Metro Universitat. **Open** 10am-2pm, 4.30-8.30pm Mon-Sat. **Credit** AmEx, DC, MC, V. **Map** p342 D5.

Eat, Drink, Shop

Urban tribes Pijos

Description Daddy's rich, Mama's good-looking and the living is way too easy for Barcelona's Sarrià Rangers, Hooray Enrics and nice-but-dim Quims.

Essential accessories Winter tan, Daddy's platinum credit card, latest Nokia, all-weather sunglasses.

For her Pearls and pashmina, upturned collars, swingy bob (good for flicking; *see below*).

For him Pastel Lacoste shirt freshly ironed by Mummy (or rather, Mummy's Filipina maid).

How to spot them That expensively conservative look is achieved by shopping at Burberry (Passeig de Gràcia 56, 93 215 81 04), Gucci (Avda Diagonal 415, 93 416 06 20) and the like. *Pijos* are well marinated in Chanel No.5 and Hugo Boss at all times.

Natural habitat Danzatoria (*see p261*), the gym, CDLC (*see p256*) or any bar where a mineral water costs €8 or more.

Distinctive behaviour The *pijo*-patented hair flick is performed approximately every 30 seconds. There's also a tendency to knot sweaters over shoulders Kennedy Clan style, and double-park.

Speech patterns The jury is out on whether it's posher to speak Spanish or Catalan, but either way, cosmopolitan *pijos* scatter English words liberally. Unfortunately, despite a gap year in Florida and a lifetime of private classes, they're still unable to form a complete sentence in the language.

Can I join in? You can buy as many Prada handbags as you like, but if Gaudí never designed a building for one of your ancestors, you're not coming in.

Take me to your leader Julio Iglesias and ex-wife Isabel Preysler, permanently grinning in the society pages of ¡Hola! magazine.

Migratory habits Summer home in Marbella and winter home in Baqueira, the Catalan skiing resort favoured by Spanish royalty.

Do say? '*Love* your shoes.'

Don't say? 'Going to the anti-globalisation demo at the weekend?'

Children

Clothes

One floor of the Plaça Catalunya branch of **El Corte Inglés** is devoted to kids, while **Galeries Maldà** (no phone, C/Portaferrissa 22, Barri Gòtic) is a small shopping centre with plenty of kids' shops. Larger branches of **Zara** (see p198) have decent kids' sections.

Chicco
Ronda Sant Pere 5, Eixample (93 301 49 76/www. chicco.es). Metro Catalunya. **Open** 10am-8.30pm Mon-Sat. **Credit** AmEx, MC, V. **Map** p342 D5.
The market leader in Spain, this colourful store has every conceivable baby-care item, from dummies and high chairs to bottle-warmers and travel cots. Its clothes and shoes are practical and well designed, and made for kids up to eight. There's also lingerie for the pre- and post-natal mother.

Menuts
C/Santa Anna 37, Barri Gòtic (93 301 90 83). Metro Catalunya. **Open** 5-8pm Mon; 11am-1.30pm, 5-8pm Tue-Fri; 11am-8.30pm Sat. Closed 2wks Aug. **Credit** AmEx, MC, V. **Map** p344 B2.
Menuts sells handmade baby and toddler outfits in traditional styles: smocked tops, matinée jackets, crocheted hats and dangerously cute booties. The very tiniest sizes are for dolls.

Prénatal
Gran Via de les Corts Catalanes 611, Eixample (93 302 05 25/www.prenatal.es). Metro Passeig de Gràcia. **Open** 10am-8.30pm Mon-Sat. **Credit** AmEx, DC, MC, V. **Map** p342 D4.
This ubiquitous but pricey French-owned chain has unfrumpy maternity wear, clothes under-eights, buggies, car seats, cots, feeding bottles and toys. **Other locations**: Diagonal Mar, Avda Diagonal 3, Poblenou (93 356 04 03); and throughout the city.

Toys

Drap
C/Pi 14, Barri Gòtic (93 318 14 87). Metro Liceu. **Open** 9.30am-1.30pm, 4.30-8.30pm Mon-Fri; 10am-1.30pm, 5-8.30pm Sat. **Credit** AmEx, DC, MC, V. **Map** p344 B2.
A selection of painstakingly crafted dolls' mansions, perfect in every detail down to the doorbells and tiny padded hangers for the hand-carved wardrobes.

El Ingenio
C/Rauric 6, Barri Gòtic (93 317 71 38/www.el-ingenio. com). Metro Liceu. **Open** 10am-1.30pm, 4.15-8pm Mon-Fri; 10am-2pm, 5-8pm Sat. **Credit** MC, V. **Map** p345 A3.
A kaleidoscope of magic tricks, puppets, party decorations and wigs. A speciality is carnival outfits and masks, ranging from warty noses to pumpkin-like *capgrosses* (oversized papier-mâché heads).

Joguines Monforte
Plaça Sant Josep Oriol 3, Barri Gòtic (93 318 22 85). Metro Liceu. **Open** 9.30am-1.30pm, 4-8pm Mon-Fri; 10am-2pm, 4.30-8.30pm Sat. **Credit** AmEx, MC, V. **Map** p345 A3.
Make sure to try the Spanish version of snakes and ladders (*el juego de la oca*, or the 'goose game') and ludo (*parchís*) at this old-school toy shop dedicated to board games. Other quiet pursuits sold here include chess boards, jigsaw puzzles, wooden solitaire, croquet sets and kites.

Cleaning & repair

Any shop marked '*rapid*' or '*rápido*' does shoe repairs and key-cutting; El Corte Inglés (see p191) has both in the basement.

La Hermosa
C/Formatgeria 3, Born (93 319 97 26). Metro Jaume I **Open** 10am-10pm Mon-Sat; 5-9pm Sun. **No credit cards**. **Map** p345 C3.
A funky neighbourhood washing and dry-cleaning facility complete with sofas, magazines and free internet access. Opt for self-service washing and drying (€3.50 for a standard load) or go for the drop-off service (€10 for 7kg, €16 for 14kg). Dry-cleaning service takes two to three days.

LavaXpres
C/Ferlandina 34, Raval (no phone). Metro Sant Antoni or Universitat. **Open** 8am-11pm daily. **No credit cards**. **Map** p342 C5.
This completely self-service, American-owned launderette is open 365 days a year. There are special machines big enough to wash a rucksack and still have room for more. Smaller 9kg loads cost €3.50.

Tintorería Ferran
C/Ferran 11, Barri Gòtic (93 301 87 30). Metro Liceu. **Open** 9am-2pm, 4.30-8pm Mon-Fri. **Credit** V. **Map** p345 A3.
Dry-cleaning here is reasonably priced, and staff can clean larger items such as duvets and rugs, which can even be stored for you over the summer. The laundry service is pricey, but look out for seasonal special offers and bulk rates: five shirts washed and ironed costs €9. There's a delivery service too.

Design & homeware

BD Ediciones de Diseño
Casa Tomas, C/Mallorca 291, Eixample (93 458 69 09/www.bdbarcelona.com). Metro Passeig de Gràcia. **Open** 10am-2pm, 4-8pm Mon-Fri; 10am-2pm, 4.30-8pm Sat. Closed 3-4wks Aug. **Credit** AmEx, DC, MC, V. **Map** p338 D4.
A Modernista masterpiece by architect Domènech i Muntaner is an appropriately lavish setting for this prominent design centre. Best known for its reproductions of classic pieces by design deities, this is the place where anyone with a few thousand euros to spare can buy Gaudí's curving Calvet armchair

NOTÉNOM PAU CLARIS 159 08037 BARCELONA TEL 934 876 084

MUJER HELMUT LANG R.E.D. VALENTINO LEBOR GABALA P.A.R.O.S.H D-SQUARED2 LEVI'S RED COMME DES GARÇONS COMME DES GARÇONS SONIA RYKIEL MIRIAM OCARIZ DAVID DELFIN LLUIS GENERÓ MAURIZIO PECORARO **HOMBRE** R.E.D VALENTINO D-SQUARED2 LEVI'S RED P.A.R.O.S.H. HELMUT LANG DUFFER OF ST GEORGE COMME DES GARÇONS SHIRT **COMPLEMENTOS** SUSAN SUELL JUAN ANTONIO LÓPEZ ADIDAS PIRELLI **PERFUMES** BOELLIS-PANAMA 1924 COMME DES GARÇONS

or Dalí's magenta-coloured Gala love seat. The stunning space also showcases new designers alongside contemporary big guns such as Javier Mariscal and Oscar Tusquets, the shop's co-founder.

Dom

C/Provença 249-251, Eixample (93 487 11 81/www. id-dom.com). Metro Diagonal. **Open** 10.30am-8.30pm Mon-Fri; 10.30am-9pm Sat. **Credit** DC, MC, V. **Map** p338 D4.

If you want your home to look like a designer bar, this place has everything, from gleaming chrome cocktail shakers and fans to PVC sofas and beanbags. A certain '70s influence also prevails in the shape of lava lamps and discoballs; to scatter on your retro coffee table, there's a selection of books and magazines devoted to style and culture. **Other locations**: C/Avinyó 7, Barri Gòtic (93 342 55 91).

Gotham

C/Cervantes 7, Barri Gòtic (93 412 46 47/www. gotham-bcn.com). Metro Jaume I. **Open** Sept-July 10.30am-2pm, 5-8.30pm Mon-Sat. Aug 10.30am-2pm, 5-8.30pm Mon-Fri. **Credit** V. **Map** p345 B3.

Fab '50s ashtrays in avocado green, bubble TV sets, teak sideboards, coat stands that look like molecular models… Take a trip down nostalgia lane with Gotham's classic retro furniture from the '30s, '50s, '60s and '70s in warm cartoon colours.

Ici et Là

Plaça Santa Maria del Mar 2, Born (93 268 11 67/ www.icietla.com). Metro Jaume I. **Open** 4.30-8.30pm Mon; 10.30am-8.30pm Tue-Sat. Closed 2wks Aug. **Credit** AmEx, MC, V. **Map** p345 C3/4.

An eccentric collection of one-off and/or limited-series handmade furniture and accessories by over 40 artists, all sourced by a French and Spanish female collective. Pieces range from a tribal chair of ostrich leather and antelope horns by Haillard to spiky South African lightbulbs or a table lamp made of chicken wire and beach pebbles.

Maison Parfum

C/Provença 266, Eixample (93 487 49 04). Metro Diagonal. **Open** 10.30am-8.30pm Mon-Sat. Closed 2wks Aug. **Credit** AmEx, V. **Map** p338 D4.

The latest must-have for the Barcelona home is the right smell, and this lavishly feng-shuied store has over 50 artisan home fragrances, divided into the seven areas of a home, ranging in price from €5 to €150. Designed by Ramón 'the Nose' Monegal.

Nipiu

C/Urgell 32, Eixample (93 426 42 29/www.nipiu. com). Metro Urgell. **Open** 5-8.30pm Mon; 11am-2pm, 5-8.30pm Tue-Sat. **Credit** AmEx, MC, V. **Map** p342 C5.

Mario Sánchez Olivera started out as a jewellery designer, and it shows in the gem-coloured velvets, glass and bright plastics he combines with curving metal to create fantastical thrones, rainbow-shaped sofas, mirrors, coffee tables and other pieces.

Ici et Là.

Vinçon

Passeig de Gràcia 96, Eixample (93 215 60 50/www. vincon.com). Metro Diagonal. **Open** 10am-8.30pm Mon-Sat. **Credit** AmEx, DC, MC, V. **Map** p338 D4.

The first stop for Catalan interior design. The ground floor is dedicated to lighting, kitchen and bathroom goods; everything related to the bedroom is in a nearby branch. Furniture is on the lovely Modernista upper floor, where pieces of interest, such as Emili Padrós's stools made from motorbike seats, are accompanied by a blurb on the designer. **Other locations**: TincÇon, C/Rosselló 246, Eixample (93 215 60 50).

Fashion

Boutiques

Jean-Pierre Bua

Avda Diagonal 469, Eixample (93 439 71 00/www. jeanpierrebua.com). Bus 6, 7, 15, 33, 34, 67, 68. **Open** Sept-July 10am-2pm, 4.30-8.30pm Mon-Sat. Aug 4.30-8.30pm Mon; 4.30-8.30pm Tue-Sat. **Credit** AmEx, DC, MC, V. **Map** p338 C3.

One of the city's original spearheads of upmarket avant-garde fashion goes from strength to strength, with a new accessories department featuring exclusive shrines to Marni, Dries Van Noten and D&G. Clothes for male and female devotees by the likes of Jean-Paul Gaultier, Miu Miu, Ann Demeulemeester, Matthew Williamson, John Galliano and Alexander McQueen grace two immaculately appointed floors.

Loft Avignon

C/Avinyó 22, Barri Gòtic (93 301 24 20). Metro Jaume I or Liceu. **Open** 10.30am-8.30pm Mon-Sat. **Credit** DC, MC, V. **Map** p345 B3.

A smörgåsbord of international designers is on the menu at this purveyor of high-end informal fashion for men and women. Think Diesel Style Lab, Indian Rose, Vivienne Westwood and Ungaro, with a sprinkling of Bikkemberg. Add a dash of Andrew Mackenzie and JPG, and you've got the full picture. **Other locations**: C/Boters 8, Barri Gòtic (93 301 37 95); C/Boters 15, Barri Gòtic (93 412 59 10).

On Land

C/Princesa 25, Born (93 310 02 11/www.on-land. com). Metro Jaume I. **Open** *Sept-July* 5-8.30pm Mon; 11am-2pm, 5-8.30pm Tue-Fri; 11.30am-8.30pm Sat. *Aug* 11am-2pm, 5-8.30pm Tue-Fri; 11.30am-8.30pm Sat. Closed 1wk Aug. **Credit** AmEx, DC, MC, V. **Map** p345 C3.

Apart from local wonderboy Josep Abril's hip, smart and slouchy menswear, there's recycled urban fashion for men and women by the likes of Cecilia Sörensen, Montse Ibañez and Petit Bateau. T-shirts with mottos are by local outfit Divinas Palabras. **Other locations**: C/València 273, Eixample (93 215 56 25).

Suite

C/Verdi 3-5, Gràcia (93 210 02 47/www.martar gustems.com). Metro Fontana. **Open** 5-8.30pm Mon; 10.30am-2pm, 5-8.30pm Tue-Sat. **Credit** V. **Map** p339 D3.

A showcase for up and coming Spanish designers. Apart from Marta R Gustems's unfussy, flattering designs in blissfully comfy fabrics, look out for Espera Drap's imaginative use of textures, La Casita de Wendy's playful take on womenswear, quirky bags by El Bosque Animado and funky, practical shoes by Suloe. Other creators of contemporary cool include Ion Fizz, Montse Ibañez and Mónica Sarabia.

Budget

Mango

Passeig de Gràcia 65, Eixample (93 215 75 30/ www.mango.es). Metro Passeig de Gràcia. **Open** 10am-9pm Mon-Sat. **Credit** AmEx, DC, MC, V. **Map** p338 D4.

A small step up from Zara in quality and price, Mango's womenswear is less chameleonic but still victim to the catwalks. Strong points include tailored trouser suits and skirts, knitwear and stretchy tops. Unsold items end up at the Mango Outlets (*see p200*), which are packed with frenzied girls on a mission. **Other locations**: Passeig de Gràcia 8-10, Eixample (93 412 15 99); Avda Portal de l'Àngel, Barri Gòtic (93 317 69 85); and throughout the city.

Zara

Avda Portal de l'Àngel 32-34, Barri Gòtic (93 317 44 52/www.zara.com). Metro Catalunya. **Open** 10am-9pm Mon-Sat. **Credit** AmEx, DC, MC, V. **Map** p344 A1.

Zara's recipe for success has won over the world, but items are cheaper on its home turf. Well-executed, affordable copies of catwalk fashions appear on the rails in a fashion heartbeat; while the women's section is the front runner, the men's and kids' sections cover good ground. Last year saw the introduction of the 'Zara Home' department. The price you pay (for the price you pay) becomes apparent in the despair-inducing queues at peak times. **Other locations**: C/Pelai 58, Eixample (93 301 09 78); Passeig de Gràcia 16, Eixample; and throughout the city.

Designer

Antonio Miró

C/Consell de Cent 349, Eixample (93 487 06 70/ www.antoniomiro.es). Metro Passeig de Gràcia. **Open** *Sept-July* 10am-2pm, 4.30-8.30pm Mon-Sat. *Aug* 11am-2pm, 5-8pm Tue-Sat. **Credit** AmEx, DC, MC, V. **Map** p338 D5.

Sobriety and simplicity are the driving forces behind the minimalist attire designed by Antonio Miró, one of the masters of contemporary Spanish fashion. Men's smart, low-key pieces are offset by the odd hip touch; womenswear consists largely of androgynous tailored suits in a discreet palette of blacks, greys and browns, and the odd flirty dress. The more casual and accessible Miró Jeans line brings minimalism to the masses. There's also a plethora of Miró-branded merchandise: accessories, fragrances, ties and even bathroom fittings. **Other locations** (Miró Jeans): C/València 272, Eixample (93 272 24 91); C/Pi 11, Barri Gòtic (93 342 58 75); C/Vidrieria 5, Born (93 268 82 03).

Daniela Yavich

C/Escudellers 56, Barri Gòtic (93 317 49 57/ www.danielayavich.com). Metro Liceu. **Open** 11am-8.30pm Mon-Sat. Closed Feb. **Credit** DC, MC, V. **Map** p345 B3.

Each season, this young Argentine designer produces a range of atemporal garments that she repeats in a wide spectrum of colours and natural fabrics. Far from the über-trendy flash-in-the-pan sartorial acquisitions that are worn once, these refreshingly wearable skirts, tops and jackets are destined for a long, useful life. Prices are also in line with mere mortal women's wallets.

Giménez y Zuazo

C/Elisabets 20, Raval (93 412 33 81/www.gimenez zuazo.com). Metro Catalunya. **Open** 10.30am-3pm, 5-8.30pm Mon-Sat. **Credit** AmEx, MC, V. **Map** p344 A2.

This designer duo produces women's clothing that brings together vivid colours and patterns in T-shirts and tops with the more elaborate cuts and styles of their urbanwear. Perennially quirky designs centre on intricate prints, seemingly casual scribbled drawings and an almost obsessive attention to detail, including buttons, lapels and cuffs. **Other locations**: C/Rec 42, Born (93 310 67 43).

Buying the flag

with backgrounds in architecture and fine art, Demano reuses defunct banners to create environmentally friendly urban luggage. Three years after convincing a maintenance man to let them keep a flag, the girls have secured deals with City Hall and other institutions, such as the MACBA or Fundació Antoni Tàpies, to use their old banners and turn them into bags. The 20 models are instantly recognisable for their funky, practical designs, bright colours, tough waterproof material and dissected words, pictures or shapes. They're also inherently exclusive: finite stocks of banners mean that there are only ever ten bags (or fewer) that look the same.

Although Demano occasionally collaborates with banner-makers in other cities, Barcelona is the home and essence of the concept. Each bag is named after a local neighbourhood, street or place. The roomy Boqueria

Ever doubted that this is a stylish city? Doubt no more: hell, even the lamp-posts here get dressed up. On Barcelona's main thoroughfares, the lamp-posts are decked out in a variety of hanging PVC banners advertising events such as plays, concerts and exhibitions. With a lively cultural agenda in place, this makes for a blizzard of bunting. With an average of 300 banners per exhibition, the side effect of a dynamic annual cultural scene is 19,800 square metres (213,000 square feet) of non-recyclable polyester waste. Luckily for the environment, the city's politically correct credentials, souvenir shoppers and fashion buffs, **Demano** (93 300 48 07, www.demano.net) has made recycling Barcelona's cultural by-products its business.

The brainchild of Liliana, Marcela and Eleonora, three Barcelona-based Colombians

model is for fashion-conscious shoppers to cart groceries home; the Mar Bella and Barceloneta are for stylish beach bums; the Borne is for aspiring DJs and their vinyl; and the Estación de Francia is for weekends away.

Handmade in specialised workshops, each bag comes with a pedigree detailing the banner from which it's been made. You can order online: check the stock, pick a model, and in a few clicks you've got a personalised creation. Alternatively, a selection of Demano products – which will soon also include belts, wallets and other accessories – is on sale in many museum gift shops around town, as well as at the likes of Red Market (*see p201*), Anna Povo (C/Vidrieria 11, 93 319 35 61) and Vinçon (*see p197*). It gives the idea of Barcelona streetwear a whole new meaning.

Le Boudoir. See p203.

Lydia Delgado

C/Minerva 21, Gràcia (93 415 99 98/www.lydia delgado.es). Metro Diagonal. **Open** 10am-2pm, 4.30-8.30pm Mon-Sat. **Credit** AmEx, MC, V. **Map** p338 D3.

Lydia's womenswear and accessories pull off purposeful femininity without descending into chi-chi frothiness. A medley of modern, retro and antique influences is fused in these covetable designs, which have recently toyed with flamenco chic and '40s-inspired cuts; expect luxuriant brocades and satins, appliqué motifs, diaphanous layers, flowing cuts and tailored wools and tweeds.

Purificación García

Passeig de Gràcia 21, Eixample (93 487 72 92/www. purificaciongarcia.es). Metro Passeig de Gràcia. **Open** 10am-8.30pm Mon-Sat. **Credit** AmEx, DC, MC, V. **Map** p342 D5.

Purificación's sleek, sophisticated creations occasionally take off on brief flights of fancy. The conservatively cut men's garments are jazzed up with a wide palette of colours and an inventive use of fabrics; the slightly more whimsical women's styles flirt maturely with informality and bohemian chic. Yet, on the whole, Purificación's collections remain anchored in pure, understated designs.

Designer bargains

One of Barcelona's hotspots for bargain clothes shopping is C/Girona. The two blocks between C/Ausiàs Marc and Gran Via de les Corts Catalanes are lined with remainder stores and factory outlets of fluctuating quality. **Mango Outlet**, crammed with last season's unsold stock, far outshines the rest: the C/Girona branch (No.37, 93 412 29 35) is larger and more frantic, while the uptown branch (C/Pau Casals 12, 93 209 07 73) offers a more select choice.

If you're a dedicated designer bargain-hunter, make the 30-minute pilgrimage outside the city to **La Roca Village** (93 842 39 39, www.laroca village.com); more than 50 discount outlets tempt you with designer apparel from Antonio Miró, Versace, Diesel, Camper and others.

Contribuciones y Moda

C/Riera Sant Miquel 30, Gràcia (93 218 71 40). Metro Diagonal. **Open** 11am-2pm, 5-9pm Mon-Fri; 11am-2pm Sat. Closed 1-2wks Aug. **Credit** AmEx, DC, MC, V. **Map** p338 D3/4.

Discount designerwear for men and women in an airy store on the fringes of the uptown shopping district. An impressive array of international designers is represented: on a good day, you could walk off with *gangues* (bargains) from the likes of Cacharel, Comme des Garçons, Moschino or Versace.

Stockland

C/Comtal 22, Barri Gòtic (93 318 03 31). Metro Urquinaona. **Open** *Sept-July* 10am-8.30pm Mon-Sat. *Aug* 10am-2pm, 4.30-8.30pm Mon-Sat. **Credit** AmEx, MC, V. **Map** p344 B2.

A far cry from the elbow-deep frenzy found at many remainder stores, this neat and elegant boutique specialises in end-of-line clothing for women designed by respected Spanish names such as Josep Font, Jesus del Pozo and Purificación García at discount prices. Smart, grown-up styles predominate; there's a selection of eveningwear upstairs.

Mid-range

Adolfo Domínguez

C/Ribera 16, Born (93 319 21 59/www.adolfo-dominguez.es). Metro Barceloneta. **Open** 11am-9pm Mon-Sat. **Credit** AmEx, DC, V. **Map** p345 C4.

Men's tailoring remains Domínguez's forte, with his elegantly cut suits and shirts. The women's line reciprocates with tame, immaculately refined outfits,

also squarely aimed at the 30- to 45-year-old market. The more casual U de Adolfo Domínguez line courts younger traditionalists, but doesn't quite attain the effortless panache of its grown-up precursor. This new two-storey flagship store is supplemented by several others around the city.
Other locations: Avda Diagonal 490, Gràcia (93 416 17 16); Passeig de Gràcia 32, Eixample (93 487 41 70); Passeig de Gràcia 89, Eixample (93 215 13 39).

Cortefiel
Avda Portal de l'Àngel 38, Barri Gòtic (93 301 07 00/www.cortefiel.com). Metro Catalunya. **Open** 10am-8.30pm Mon-Sat. **Credit** AmEx, DC, MC, V. **Map** p344 B2.
This popular chain casts a wider net than Mango or Zara, its fine tailored jackets and elegant, mature renditions of current trends appealing to a variety of women, from conservative students to fashion-conscious fiftysomethings. If you like a bit of glitz in your wardrobe, take a peek at the swankier Pedro del Hierro collection downstairs. Both labels have less prominent but successful menswear lines.
Other locations: Passeig de Gràcia 27, Eixample (93 215 19 07); and throughout the city.

Custo Barcelona
Plaça de les Olles 7, Born (93 268 78 93/www.custo-barcelona.com). Metro Jaume I. **Open** 10am-10pm Mon-Sat; noon-8pm Sun. **Credit** AmEx, DC, MC, V. **Map** p345 C4.
A local predilection for amalgamating loud patterns and prints with an assortment of fabrics culminates in Custo's kaleidoscopic candy-coloured creations. Motifs have recently included 19th-century prints, psychedelic art, botanical illustrations and wallpaper. The collections now comprise a full range of casualwear, but the T-shirts remain number one on everybody's wishlists, despite the high prices.
Other locations: C/Ferran 36, Barri Gòtic (93 342 66 98).

Street

Black Jazz
C/Rec 28, Born (93 310 42 36). Metro Jaume I. **Open** 5-9pm Mon; 11am-2.30pm, 5-9pm Tue-Sat. **Credit** AmEx, DC, MC, V. **Map** p345 C4.
Exceedingly cool men's designer fashion. If you can hack the snooty gaze of the shop attendants are willing to splurge, take your pick from an ample selection of under- and outerwear by names such as D&G, Diesel Style Lab, Antonio Miró, Indian Rags and Bikkemberg. Carlo Pignatelli is one of the latest additions to this panoply of luminaries.

Free
C/Ramelleres 5, Raval (93 301 61 15). Metro Catalunya. **Open** 10am-2pm, 4.30-8.30pm Mon-Sat. **Credit** V. **Map** p344 A1.
This skate emporium has grown exponentially to cater for Barcelona's expanding population of skate enthusiasts. For boys, there are T-shirts, sweatshirts

and baggy trousers from Stüssy, Carhartt, Fresh Jive et al; the girls get plenty of Compobella and Loreak Mendian. The requisite chunky or retro footwear comes courtesy of Vans, Vision and Etnies.
Other locations: C/Bonsuccès 2, Raval (93 412 56 45); C/Viladomat 319, Eixample (93 321 72 90).

Kwatra
C/Antic de Sant Joan 1, Born (93 268 08 04/ www.kwatra.com). Metro Barceloneta or Jaume I. **Open** 11am-2pm, 4-8pm Mon-Sat. **Credit** MC, V. **Map** p345 C3.
Ex-Nike employee Robbie still has the connections to get hold of limited edition swoosh-adorned items. Diesel, Adidas and Puma shoes, bags and clothes make up the rest of the urban sportswear stock, with accessories by City Knife, Waffle and Speedsweep.
Other locations: Bulevard Rosa, Passeig de Gràcia 55, Eixample (93 488 04 27).

Red Market
C/Verdi 20, Gràcia (93 218 63 33). Metro Fontana. **Open** *Sept-July* 5-9.30pm Mon; 11.30am-2pm, 5-9.30pm Tue-Sat. *Aug* 5-9.30pm Mon-Sat. **Credit** AmEx, MC, V. **Map** p339 D3.
A choice selection of streetwear includes the latest in girls' and boys' urban outfitting by Aem Kei, Zoo York, Lambretta, Punk Royal, Diesel 55, Franklin & Marshall and others, as well as a rare crop of good-looking trainers by Gola, Puma, Nike and Adidas.

Tribu
C/Avinyó 12, Barri Gòtic (93 318 65 10). Metro Jaume I or Liceu. **Open** *June-Sept* 11am-8.30pm Mon-Sat. *Oct-May* 11am-2.30pm, 4.30-8.30pm. **Credit** MC, V. **Map** p345 B3.
One of the countless clued-up fashion platforms in town for international and homegrown casual labels such as Jocomomola, Nolita, Diesel and Freesoul. Don't miss the designer trainers at the back.

Trip Shop
C/Duc de la Victòria 13, Barri Gòtic (no phone). Metro Catalunya. **Open** 10am-2.30pm, 4.30-8.30pm Mon-Sat. **Credit** AmEx, DC, V. **Map** p344 B2.
The hip hop garb for guys and girls at this store focuses mainly on US labels: plenty of Ecko, South Pole and especially Sir Benni Miles. Seriously chilled staff hang among the hoodies.

Vintage & second-hand

The narrow C/Riera Baixa in the Raval is where most of Barcelona's second-hand clothes retailers cluster. At No.20, **Lailo** (93 441 37 49) harbours an extensive selection with which to kit out '80s comeback chicks, flapper wannabes, fancy-dress freaks, cocktail-party guests and latter-day hippies. **Holala! Ibiza** at No.11 (93 441 99 94) has affordable thrift-store staples, while at No.7, **Smart & Clean**'s '60s and '70s second-hand gear is largely made up of mod essentials, with a decent range of leather jackets and vintage trainers (93 441 87 64).

Eat, Drink, Shop

MonkeyBiz

Discover MonkeyBiz, a new concept children's store right in the centre of Barcelona's shopping zone. You will find original clothing, toys and decorational items from diffrent corners of the globe. Handpainted T-shirts, beaded animals and dolls, recycled plastic animals and bags, motorbikes from South Africa, wooden construction toys from Austria, plush animals from Germany, wooden toys from Poland, IQ Puzzles from America, clothes from Japan and more. They also organise storytelling, puppet shows and fashion shows. Come and find out when at MonkeyBiz.

C/ Balmes 114, bajos Tel. 93 272 2708
www.mon-key-biz.com
Mon-Sat 10.30am-8.30pm

Diagonal **EIXAMPLE I**

Produit National Brut

C/Avinyó 29, Barri Gòtic (93 268 27 55). Metro Jaume I or Liceu. **Open** 11am-9pm Mon-Sat. **Credit** AmEx, MC, V. **Map** p345 B3.

A dependable assortment of stock includes the usual mélange of tea-lady smocks, faded T-shirts, cords and token vintage trainers. All this lives alongside PNB's own line of equally old-school urban sportswear. Musical references and '60s, '70s and '80s retro influences are the theme for men's T-shirts and girls' stretchy cotton tank tops, dresses and skirts.

Le Swing

C/Riera Baixa 13 (no phone). Metro Liceu. **Open** 11am-2.30pm, 5-9pm Mon-Sat. **No credit cards.** **Map** p342 C6.

Today's second-hand is known as 'vintage', and thrift is not on the agenda. Fervent worshippers of Pierre Cardin, YSL, Dior, Kenzo and other fashion deities scour all corners of the sartorial stratosphere and deliver their booty back to this little powder puff of a boutique. The odd Zara number and other mere mortal brands creep in as well.

Lingerie & underwear

Rambla de Catalunya is a mecca for underwear shoppers: boutiques brimming with frivolous lingerie, such as **La Perla** (No.88, 93 467 71 49), sit alongside traditional retailers, among them **La Perla Gris** (No.118, 93 215 29 91). At the less luxurious end of the scale, you'll find inexpensive swimwear and underwear at high street chains such as **Oysho** (No.77, 93 488 36 01), from the same stable as Zara. **Saint Honoré** (No.11, 93 317 65 45) strikes a happy medium with reasonably priced Spanish labels as well as its own range. **El Corte Inglés** (*see p191*) stocks a large range of men's and women's undergarments for all ages.

Janina

Rambla Catalunya 94, Eixample (93 215 04 84). Metro Diagonal/FGC Provença. **Open** Sept-July 10am-8.30pm Mon-Sat. **Credit** AmEx, MC, V. **Map** p338 D4.

Good quality women's underwear and nightwear by Calvin Klein, Christian Dior, La Perla and others. Some larger sizes are stocked; alternatively, bras can be sent to a seamstresses to be altered overnight. Swimwear, stockings and camisoles are also on sale. **Other locations:** C/Caputxes 10, Born (93 268 72 24); Avda Pau Casals 8, Eixample (93 202 06 93).

Le Boudoir

C/Canuda 21, Barri Gòtic (93 302 52 81/www.leboudoir.net). Metro Catalunya. **Open** Sept-July 10am-8.30pm Mon-Thur; 10am-9pm Fri, Sat. *Aug* 11am-8.30pm Mon-Thur; 11am-9pm Fri, Sat. **Credit** AmEx, MC, V. **Map** p342 D5.

Sensuality abounds in Barcelona's classy answer to Agent Provocateur and Ann Summers. Sexy lingerie comes with designer labels (and prices), swimwear

is not for shrinking violets and fluffy kitten-heeled mules have not been made with practicality in mind. Erotic books, sex toys, essential oils and other seductive stuff nestle discreetly on satin chaises longues and velvet cushions at the back.

Women's Secret

C/Portaferrissa 7-9, Barri Gòtic (93 318 92 42/www.womensecret.com). Metro Liceu. **Open** 10am-9pm Mon-Sat. **Credit** AmEx, DC, MC, V. **Map** p344 B2.

Mix-and-match bras and knickers run the gamut from sexy to sensible. Whether you want strapless, halterneck, padded, racer back or several things at once, the 'basics' line has it covered. The real winners, however, are the colourful, cheap and cheerful nightwear and bikinis. Quality and durability are not guaranteed, but who cares when you can buy a whole new batch next season?

Other locations: Avda Portal de l'Àngel, Barri Gòtic (93 301 07 00); and throughout the city.

Shoes

In summer, people of all ages wear *abarcas*, sloppy peep-toe sandals from Menorca, or the traditional Catalan *espardenyes*, espadrilles of hemp and canvas. Footwear lines the main shopping strips, such as Portal de l'Àngel or C/Pelai; chains include **Casas**, **Mar Bessas**, **Royalty**, **Querol**, **Tascón** and **Vogue**, which have huge but almost identical collections.

Camper

C/Pelai 13-37, Eixample (93 302 41 24/www.camper.com). Metro Catalunya. **Open** 10am-10pm Mon-Sat. **Credit** AmEx, DC, MC, V. **Map** p344 A1.

Now internationally coveted, these bright, round-toed durable shoes in quasi-childish styles started out as Mallorcan peasant (*camper*) shoes. Some of the more extraordinary new lines include bright, plastic wellies, boots inspired by boxing gloves, and wobbly rubber high heels for the girls.

Other locations: Rambla de Catalunya 122, Eixample (93 217 23 84); C/València 249, Eixample (93 215 63 90); and throughout the city.

Czar

Passeig del Born 20, Born (93 310 7222). Metro Jaume I. **Open** *Mid Sept-June* 5-9pm Mon; 11.15am-2.30pm, 5-9pm Tue-Sat. *July-mid Sept* 5-10pm Mon; noon-2pm, 5-10pm Tue-Sat. **Credit** MC, V. **Map** p345 C3.

Spain is generally weak on sneakers but Czar represents a small shard of light in the gloom. Its small, ferociously hip selection of trainers includes Puma, Diesel and Paul Smith, but also harder-to-find labels such as Rizzo, Fluxa and Le Coq Sportif.

La Manual Alpargatera

C/Avinyó 7, Barri Gòtic (93 301 01 72/www.lamanual.net). Metro Liceu. **Open** *Jan-Sept, Dec* 9.30am-1.30pm, 4.30-8pm Mon-Sat. *Oct, Nov* 9.30am-1.30pm, 4.30-8pm Mon-Fri; 10am-1.30pm Sat. **Credit** AmEx, DC, MC, V. **Map** p345 B3.

Eat, Drink, Shop

It has famously shod the Pope and Jack Nicholson, but La Manual Alpargatera still offers its comfy, traditional peasant espadrilles at rock-bottom prices. The impressive stack of shoes behind the counter includes the ribboned Tabarner model, which Catalans wear to dance the *sardana*, but staff can also make whatever you want, to order.

Muxart

C/Rosselló 230, Eixample (93 488 10 64/www.muxart. com). Metro Diagonal. **Open** 10am-2pm, 4.30-8.30pm Mon-Fri; 10am-2pm, 5-8.30pm Sat. **Credit** AmEx, MC, V. **Map** p338 D4.

Shoes around which to build an outfit. Materials are refined, styles are sharp, avant-garde and blatantly not intended to hide under a pair of beige slacks. Lines for men and women are complemented by equally creative bags and accessories.
Other locations: Rambla Catalunya 47, Eixample (93 467 74 23); Diagonal Mar, Avda Diagonal 3, Poblenou (93 356 23 13).

Rouge Poison

C/Flassaders 34, Born (93 310 55 46). Metro Jaume I. **Open** *Sept-June* 5-9pm Mon; noon-2.30pm, 5-9pm Tue-Sat; noon-3pm Sun. *July-Aug* 5-9pm Mon; Sun; noon-2.30pm, 5-9pm Tue-Sat. **Credit** AmEx, MC, V. **Map** p345 C3.

These kittenish designs are guaranteed to make even the clumsiest plates of meat look elegant. Rouge Poison shoes are presented in Barbarella-style plastic capsules, swings and flip-top boxes, but prices preclude all but true shoe fetishists.

U-Casas

C/Espaseria 4, Born (93 310 00 46/www.casasclub. com). Metro Jaume I. **Open** 10.30am-9pm Mon-Thur; 10.30am-10pm Fri, Sat. **Credit** AmEx, MC, V. **Map** p345 C4.

The pared-down, post-industrial decor so beloved of this neighbourhood provides the perfect backdrop for bright and quirky shoes. Strange heels and toes are out in force this season, and after all those snub-nosed winklepickers and rubber wedgies from the likes of Helmut Lang, Fly, Fornarina and Irregular Choice, you can rest your weary pins on the giant, shoe-shaped chaise longue.
Other locations: C/Tallers 2, Raval (93 318 3405); L'Illa, Avda Diagonal 345-557 (93 419 14 85); Barcelona Glòries, Avda Diagonal 208 (93 486 0145).

Fashion accessories

Jewellery

The Born's C/Argenteria takes its name from the numerous silversmiths who established themselves there in the 15th century. Even today, this street and the surrounding area are home to a number of shops selling silver jewellery, such as **Platamundi** (Plaça Santa Maria 7, 93 310 10 87), part of a successful chain that has pretty, affordable pieces in its shops

throughout Barcelona. Nearby, boutiques such as **Ad Láter** (C/Ases 1, 93 310 66 00, www.prudencisanchez.com) exhibit pieces by innovative local jewellery designers. Upmarket jewellers naturally gravitate towards the glamorous shopping districts, such as Passeig de Gràcia and Avda Diagonal.

Alea Majoral Galería de Joyas

C/Argenteria 66, Born (93 310 13 73/www.majoral. com). Metro Jaume I. **Open** *Sept-mid Aug* 10.30am-8.30pm Mon-Sat. *Last 2wks Aug* 10.30am-2pm, 4-8.30pm Mon-Sat. **Credit** AmEx, DC, MC, V. **Map** p345 C3.

Located in a small showroom at the back of one of Enric Majoral's outposts, you will find rotating displays of jewellery that are usually worth checking out as they are designed by some of the city's hippest up-and-coming jewellers. En route, take time to stop and admire Balearic-born Majoral's own collection of imaginative silver and gold jewellery, which takes its inspiration from the marine world and its natural shapes and textures.
Other locations: Majoral, C/Consell de Cent 308, Eixample (93 467 72 09); Majoral Pedralbes Centre, Avda Diagonal 609, Zona Alta (93 363 12 91).

Bagués

Passeig de Gràcia 41, Eixample (93 216 01 73/ www.bagues.es). Metro Passeig de Gràcia. **Open** *Sept-July* 10am-8.30pm Mon-Fri; 10am-1.30pm, 5-8.30pm Sat. *Aug* 10am-1.30pm, 4.30-8.30pm Mon-Fri; 10am-1.30pm Sat. **Credit** AmEx, DC, MC, V. **Map** p338 D4.

This prestigious jeweller and watchmaker is fittingly located in a Modernista landmark, the Casa Amatller. The most exclusive and astronomically priced collection dates back to the master jeweller Lluís Masriera, who is said to have revolutionised the Spanish jewellery scene of the time with the 'translucid enamel' technique, which lends the colours in a piece a vibrant luminosity. Typical motifs to be found in jewellery of the era, such as nymphs, flowers and birds, are the essence of these ornate, delicate art nouveau designs. A visit here is essential for any jewellery collector.
Other locations: Rambla de les Flors 105, Raval (93 481 70 50).

Freya

C/Verdi 17, Gràcia (93 237 36 89). Metro Fontana. **Open** 5-9pm Mon; 11am-2pm, 5-9pm Tue-Sat; 5-9pm Sun. Closed 1wk Aug. **Credit** AmEx, MC, V. **Map** p339 D3.

Unwitting passers-by are lured into this Smartie-coloured treasure trove for true accessory addicts by the kooky, colourful window displays. Owner Teresa brings together some of the city's most creative jewellery designers, and is always on the lookout for quirky designs that won't break the bank. There's something here for everyone, as any material and any budget goes, with felt hair slides, wooden bangles, plastic rings, papier-mâché earrings and a selection of more elaborate silver numbers.

Retail road map

A guide to navigating the geography of fashion hotspots.

The **Born** is dynamic fashion terrain, but its yuppification in the last few years is reflected in mercilessly hip boutiques and escalating prices. On C/Rec, its nerve centre, established alternative designers such as Giménez y Zuazo (*see p198*) sit alongside shops like Puravida (No.77) and Black Jazz (*see p201*), offering up-to-the-minute elegant designer wear. With the gentrified territory has come the invasion of brands: for a clued-up selection of sporty labels, check out Kwatra (*see p201*). Footwear fiends are well looked after by the Czar (*see p203*) trainer oasis and Rouge Poison (*see p204*) among others. Also rich in sartorial plunder are C/Esparteria, C/Vidrieria and C/Banys Vells.

The **Barri Gòtic** features local legends like Custo (*see p201*), young designers such as Daniela Yavich (*see p198*), funky boutiques and high-street players. C/Avinyó makes a good starting point whatever your wallet's attributes, with inexpensive street fashion by Produit National Brut (*see p203*), So_da (No.24, *pictured*) and Sugarhill (No.42), kooky mid-range designs by the likes of Zebra (No.46), and pricier offerings from boutiques such as Loft Avignon (*see p198*) and Tribu (*see p201*). For maximum retail therapy per square metre, go to Avda Portal de l'Àngel or C/Pelai, where all the high-street biggies roost: city-break shopping is not complete without a pilgrimage to Zara (*see p198*) and Mango (*see p198*). C/Portaferrissa also houses popular stores.

Across the fashion vacuum of the Rambla lies the **Raval**, where gritty meets trendy and bohemian chic rules. It's home to a glut of second-hand outlets on C/Riera Baixa (*see p201*), but is also a hotbed for innovative fashion. Head to the streets between C/Carme and the MACBA, where Naifa (C/Doctor Dou 11, 93 302 40 05) and others have offbeat garb by independent designers; Free (*see p201*) kits out resident skaters. The area's *pijo* pretensions emerge on C/Elisabets (*see p194*), where Born-ite style gurus like Huno (No.18, 93 412 63 05) have outposts.

Serious Catalan money doesn't muddy its designer pumps in the downtown waters. The **Eixample** shopping map has two well-traipsed arteries: Rambla de Catalunya boasts lingerie shops (*see p203*), chains and upmarket stores but Passeig de Gràcia is where Spanish big guns such as Antonio Miró (*see p198*), Adolfo Domínguez (*see p200*) and Purificación García (*see p200*) settle, along with countless international luminaries.

Gràcia's leafy streets, café terraces and alternative boutiques make for a relaxed retail outing; C/Verdi is where you'll find the action. Among a succession of arty clothes shops, Red Market (*see p201*) keeps streetwear fanatics happy and Suite (*see p198*) showcases young designers. Plaça Rius i Taulet is a focal point, as are the streets radiating out from it: on C/Penedès, you'll find well-priced goodies at Rebeca Damasco's (No. 12, 93 217 46 56).

MN

C/Sant Honorat 11, Barri Gòtic (93 325 15 36). Metro Jaume I or Liceu. **Open** 10am-1.30pm, 5-8pm Mon-Sat. Closed last 2wks Aug. **Credit** DC MC, V. **Map** p345 B3.

Montse Nuñez's hand made fired enamel silver, gold and copper jewellery is the product of a highly specialised and laborious technique that's not changed for decades. Modern, minimalist pieces – brightly coloured chunky rings, pendants and brooches – have bags of funky style. For those with a more classical penchant, there are intricate Modernista designs and Da Vinci-inspired cameos.

Leather & luggage

Casa Antich SCP

C/Consolat del Mar 27-31, Born (93 310 43 91/ www.casaantich.com). Metro Jaume I. **Open** 9am-8.30pm Mon-Fri; 9.30am-8.30pm Sat. **Credit** AmEx, DC, MC, V. **Map** p345 B4.

Stacks of hold-alls, briefcases, suitcases and metal steamer trunks big enough to sleep in. Also stocked are travel accessories, backpacks for kids and adults, briefcases, duffles, totes and handbags of all varieties from brands such as Eastpak, Dockers, Samsonite and Superga, along with bags made to your personal specifications.

Loewe

Passeig de Gràcia 35, Eixample (93 216 04 00/ www.loewe.com). Metro Passeig de Gràcia. **Open** 10am-8.30pm Mon-Sat. **Credit** AmEx, DC, MC, V. **Map** p342 D5.

The price tags are bigger than the handbags at this couturier, where the Daddy Warbucks prices go well into the thousands. With a decadent setting on two floors of Domènech i Montaner's Casa Morera, the store's products, from crocodile-skin demi bags to men's sheepskin coats, are of superb quality. **Other locations**: (for women) Avda Diagonal 570, Eixample (93 200 09 20); (for men) Avda Diagonal 606, Eixample (93 240 51 04).

Barcelona sucks

Sweet of tooth? Fan of kitschy novelties? Dubious Freudian oral fixation? You're in the right town. Whether your tastes are for old-fashioned varieties or eye-catching innovations, you'll find your dream lollipop in Barcelona.

At **Papabubble** (*see p209*), Tommy Tang and Chris King keep it sweet with artisan goodies that are cooked and shaped on view in the shop itself. As well as old-fashioned humbugs and sticks of rock, there's a kaleidoscope of swirly lollies, ranging from saucer size to bigger-than-your-face. Seasonal pops include snow-capped pine trees; the stag and hen market is blessed with a candified 'meat 'n' two veg' on a stick. One romantic even requested a personal mould as a present to his girlfriend. More popular requests range from simply writing a name across a lollipop in candy letters to playful ways of presenting cash gifts, a tradition at Catalan weddings; one request was for a transparent red candy heart inlaid with 900 1 coins. The firm has just won a contract with

Selfridges and is in talks over a candy version of Jeff Koons's emblematic *Puppy* sculpture for the Guggenheim.

'Basically, we can do anything with candy that you can do with glass,' says Tang. 'Except that it tastes better.'

Attracting more flashbulbs than buyers are the insect lollies at **Fruits del Bosc** (Stalls 866-870, Mercat de la Boqueria, 93 302 52 73, www.boletspetras.com). Gnomish owner Llorenç Petràs is known as the *duende* (spirit) of the market, his iconic stall famous for its wild mushrooms, snails and truffles and other fruits of the forest. As such, the old guard were not impressed when his son, Isaac, started selling freakshow lollies in spring 2004. Choose from tequila-marinated earthworm or crunchy vodka-soaked scorpion (sans sting) suspended inside lemon lollies, alongside other treats such

Scarves & textiles

Textiles were once one of Barcelona's main industries. It's a legacy visible in many of the street names of the Born, where the highest concentration of textile shops and workshops are to be found. Contact tourist offices (*see p321*) for information about taking a tour of the official 'Textile Itinerary'.

Almacenes del Pilar

C/Boqueria 43, Barri Gòtic (93 317 79 84). Metro Liceu. **Open** 9.30am-2pm, 4-8pm Mon-Sat. Closed 2wks Aug. **Credit** AmEx, MC, V. **Map** p345 A3.
At Almacenes del Pilar there's an array of fabrics and accessories for traditional Spanish costumes, on display in a shambolic interior dating back to 1886. Making your way through bolts of material, you'll find richly hued brocades used for Valencian *fallera* outfits and other rudiments of folkloric dress from throughout the country. Lace *mantillas* and the high combs over which they are worn are stocked along with fringed, hand-embroidered pure silk *mantones de manila* (shawls) and colourful wooden fans.

Rafa Teja Atelier

C/Santa Maria 18, Born (93 310 27 85). Metro Jaume I. **Open** 11am-9pm Mon-Sat; noon-3pm Sun. Closed 1wk Aug. **Credit** AmEx, MC, V. **Map** p345 C3.
Few Spanish women would dream of attending a wedding without a shawl, and this is something of a mecca for them. Apart from elegant pashminas, fringed silk numbers, practical classic or quirky woollen scarves and sheer evening wraps, stock also includes some pretty silk jackets.
Other locations: Conde de Salvatierra 10, Eixample (93 237 70 59).

Flowers

The 18 flower stalls along the Rambla de les Flors originated with the old custom of Boqueria market traders giving a free flower to their

makers of children's clothing, stationery, activity books, cola-flavoured toothpaste and even a suitably saccharine fragrance for little girls. It also provides the growing adult market with Margarita, piña colada and cappuccino flavours, along with sexed-up marketing tactics, such as 'Chupa Chicks' in lollipop-studded bras.

as chocolate-dipped crickets and strawberry or melon candy bars sprinkled with 'fresh farm ants'. Future plans include a takeaway service of fried ant eggs and the like.

However, it's the cheap and cheerful **Chupa Chups** (www.chupachups.com) that are making the biggest bang. The Bernat family's pops stormed the market in the '60s, and soon the flower power Dalí-designed logo was everywhere; the Catalan company now sells four billion lollies a year in over 170 countries. Inviting you to 'Chupafy your world', Chupa Chups has now licensed its brand name to

Things aren't so sweet in the accounts department, however: Chupa Chups, which also owns the Smint brand and Gaudí's Casa Batlló, is reportedly under investigation for tax evasion, and is in debt to various creditors after overexpansion abroad in the '90s. Its image was further tarnished in late 2004, when demonstrations in Plaça Sant Jaume called for a boycott of Chupa Chups over its alleged refusal to pay money owed to Danish company Spacerocket. This might be one lolly that's about to go pop.

customers, and have just celebrated their 150th anniversary. There are also stands at the **Mercat de la Concepció** (C/Aragó 311, Eixample, 93 457 53 29, www.laconcepcio.com), on the corner of C/València and C/Bruc (map p339 E4), which are open all night. Many florists offer the Interflora delivery service.

Flors Navarro
C/València 320, Eixample (93 457 40 99/www.flores navarro.com). Metro Verdaguer. **Open** 24hrs daily. **Credit** AmEx, MC, V. **Map** p338 D4.
At Flors Navarro, fresh-cut blooms, pretty house-plants and stunning bouquets explode in all directions and are available to buy 24 hours a day. A dozen red roses cost €24 or €27 and can be delivered anywhere in the city, day or night.

Food & drink

Pâtisseries & chocolate

Caelum
C/Palla 8, Barri Gòtic (93 302 69 93). Metro Liceu. **Open** 5-8.30pm Mon; 10am-9pm Tue-Thur; 10.30am-midnight Fri, Sat. Closed Aug. **Credit** AmEx, DC, MC, V. **Map** p344 B2.
Spain's nuns and monks have a naughty sideline in traditional sweets including candied saints' bones, sugared egg yolks and drinkable goodies such as eucalyptus and orange liqueur, all of which are beautifully packaged. If you'd like to sample before committing to a whole box of holy honey cake, there's a taster café downstairs on the site of some medieval Jewish thermal baths.

Enric Rovira Shop
Avda Josep Tarradellas 113, Les Corts (93 419 25 47/www.enricrovira.com). Metro Entença. **Open** 10am-2.30pm, 5-8pm Tue-Fri; 10am-2.30pm Sat. Closed Aug. **Credit** MC, V. **Map** p337 B3.
The most deluxe of Barcelona's growing tribe of chocolate boutiques, Rovira produces velvety smooth, hazelnut-studded versions of Gaudí's hexagonal pavement slabs, pink peppercorn truffles, Cabernet Sauvignon bonbons and twisty blocks of Christmas *turrón* in unusual flavours.

Escribà
Gran Via de les Corts Catalanes 546, Eixample (93 454 75 35/www.escriba.es). Metro Urgell. **Open** *July-Sept* 8am-3pm, 5-9pm Mon-Fri; 8am-9pm Sat, Sun. *Aug* 9am-3pm daily. **Credit** MC, V. **Map** p342 C5.
Antoni Escribà, the 'Mozart of Chocolate', died in 2004, but his legacy lives on. His team produces jawdropping creations for the Easter displays, from a hulking chocolate Grand Canyon to a life-size model of Michelangelo's *David*. Smaller miracles include cherry liqueur encased in red chocolate lips. The Rambla branch is worth visiting as it's situated in a pretty Modernista building.
Other locations: La Rambla 83, Raval (93 301 60 27).

General food stores

The supermarket in the basement of El Corte Inglés in Plaça Catalunya (*see p191*) has a 'gourmet' food section of local and foreign specialities. The corner shops along C/Ample, C/Escudellers and C/Sant Pau are open until at least 10pm; some serve until midnight.

Champion
La Rambla 113 (93 302 48 24). Metro Catalunya. **Open** 9am-10pm Mon-Sat. **Credit** MC, V. **Map** p344 A2.
Not the best of the supermarket sweep, but the opening hours and unbeatable location more than make up for its slight shabbiness, confusing layout and agonisingly slow checkout lines.

Colmado Quílez
Rambla Catalunya 63, Eixample (93 215 23 56). Metro Passeig de Gràcia. **Open** *Jan-mid Oct* 9am-2pm, 4.30-8.30pm Mon-Fri; 9am-2pm Sat. *Mid Oct-Dec* 9am-2pm, 4.30-8.30pm Mon-Sat. **Credit** MC, V. **Map** p338 D4.
This wonderful old corner shop is one of the monuments of the Eixample. The mirrored windows and walls are stacked rafter-high with a dazzling variety of olive oils, sweets, preserves, cheeses and Jabugo hams, plus every type of alcohol from saké, whiskies and cava to Trappist beers. The store's own gourmet label, Quílez, includes Iranian Beluga caviar, cava, Kenyan coffee, saffron and anchovies.

Queviures Murrià
C/Roger de Llúria 85, Eixample (93 215 57 89). Metro Passeig de Gràcia. **Open** 9am-2pm, 5-9pm Tue-Thur, Sat; 9am-2pm, 5-9.30pm Fri. Closed Aug. **Credit** AmEx, DC, MC, V. **Map** p338 D4.
The ultimate place to shop for a picnic, Murrià has everything from tins of tuna to €275 jars of porcini mushrooms, all beautifully displayed against original 1900s decoration by Ramon Casas. Delicacies include a superb range of individually sourced farm-house cheeses, international treats such as prime Scottish smoked salmon, and more than 300 wines, including the family's own-label brut Cava Murrià.

Food specialities

Casa Gispert
C/Sombrerers 23, Born (93 319 75 35/www.casa gispert.com). Metro Jaume I. **Open** *Jan-July, Sept* 9.30am-2pm, 4-7.30pm Tue-Fri; 10am-2pm, 5-8pm Sat. *Aug* 10am-2pm, 5-8pm Tue-Sat. *Oct-Dec* 9.30am-2pm, 4-7.30pm Mon-Fri; 10am-2pm, 5-8pm Sat. **Credit** MC, V. **Map** p345 C3.
It's almost impossible to resist the fragrance of roasting coffee beans, freshly toasted hazelnuts, pistachios and almonds, and wooden shelves full of spices and teas. The gourmet food baskets make perfect gifts and there are also special DIY packs for local specialities, such as *calçot* sauce, summer *orxata*, Hallowe'en *panellets,* and *crema catalana.*

Formatgeria La Seu

C/Dagueria 16, Barri Gòtic (93 412 65 48/www. formatgerialaseu.com). Metro Jaume I. **Open** 10am-2pm, 5-8pm Tue-Fri; 10am-3pm, 5-8pm Sat. Closed Aug. **No credit cards. Map** p345 B3.

Katherine McLaughlin sells a delectable range of Spanish farmhouse olive oils and cheeses, among them a fierce *tou dels til·lers* and a blackcurranty *picón* from Cantabria. On Saturdays from noon to 3pm, McLaughlin holds a sit-down cheese and oil tasting for €5.50, but you can wash down three cheeses and a glass of wine anytime for €2.20.

Papabubble

C/Ample 28, Barri Gòtic (93 268 86 25/www.papa bubble.com). Metro Barceloneta or Drassanes. **Open** 10am-2pm, 4-8.30pm Tue-Fri; 10am-8.30pm Sat; 11am-7.30pm Sun. Closed Aug. **Credit** MC, V. **Map** p345 B4.

Tommy and Chris flip, stretch and roll traditionally made hot candy fresh from the kitchen into lollipops, humbugs, sculptures and even edible jewellery in all flavours, from strawberry and lavender to passion fruit and Mojito. The personalised lollies are in constant demand. *See p206* **Barcelona sucks**.

Wine

Craft shop **Art Escudellers** (*see p210*) has a good selection of wines in its cellar.

La Carte des Vins

C/Sombrerers 1, Born (93 268 70 43/www.lacarte desvins.com). Metro Jaume I. **Open** 10.30am-9.30pm Tue-Fri; 10.30am-2.30pm, 3.30-9.30pm Sat, Sun. **Credit** AmEx, DC, MC, V. **Map** p345 C3.

A small but user-friendly selection of wines, champagnes and cavas, clearly laid out and labelled by region and vintage (although the prices are somewhat elevated). About 80% of the bottles are from Spain, and cover all the important names from a L'Ermita '99 to organic wines by Catalan producers Albet i Noya. Staff speak English and there's a small collection of wine accessories and books on viticulture, including titles in English.

Other locations: La Boqueria, La Rambla 89, Raval (93 342 73 85); C/Mandri 64, Sant Gervasi (93 254 00 81).

Lavinia

Avda Diagonal 605, Eixample (93 363 44 45/www. lavinia.es). Metro Maria Cristina. **Open** 10am-9pm Mon-Sat. **Credit** AmEx, DC, MC, V. **Map** p337 A2.

This ultra-slick store houses the largest selection of wines in Europe. Knowledgeable, polyglot staff happily talk customers through the thousands of horizontally displayed Spanish and international wines, including exceptional vintages and special editions at good prices. They'll also help you put together cases to send home and let you try before you buy.

Vila Viniteca

C/Agullers 7-9, Born (93 268 32 27/www.vila viniteca.es). Metro Jaume I. **Open** Sept-June 8.30am-2.30pm, 4.30-8.30pm Mon-Sat. July-Aug 8.30am-2.30pm, 4.30-8.30pm Mon-Fri; 8.30am-2.30pm Sat. **Credit** DC, MC, V. **Map** p345 B4.

Newly renovated and expanded, this family-run business has built up a stock of over 6,000 wines and spirits since 1932. With everything from a 1953 Damoiseau rum costing as much as €500, through

Faced with **Arlequí Mascares**, you may leave a completely different person. *See p213.*

to €6 bottles of table wine, the selection here is mostly Spanish and Catalan, but also takes in international favourites along with fine cheeses, cured meats and oils. Perfect for foodie gifts.

Gifts

The city's museums have some good gift shops. The Espai Gaudí at **La Pedrera** (*see p129*) is the mother of all Gaudiana purveyors, while the **MACBA** (*see p101*) and **CaixaForum** (*see p117*) shops are excellent sources of games, gifts, designer gizmos and kooky postcards. The **Fundació Joan Miró** (*see p118*) has plenty of boldly designed espresso cups, coasters and so on, while the **Museu Tèxtil** (*see p107*) has a good supply of creative scarves, ties, shirts, bags and quirky jewellery.

Art Escudellers

C/Escudellers 23-25, Barri Gòtic (93 412 68 01/ www.escudellers-art.com). Metro Drassanes. **Open** 11am-11pm daily. **Credit** AmEx, DC, MC, V. **Map** p345 A-B3.
Art Escudellers sells an extravaganza of clay and glassware that's mostly handmade by Spanish artists and labelled by region. Decorative and practical items include sturdy kitchenware, traditional *azulejos* (tiles) and Gaudi-themed coffee cups. Downstairs is a wine cellar and diminutive café, while the nearby branch (No.12) specialises in glassware: a kitsch-fest of lurid Swarovski crystal bonsais to be precise.

Baraka

C/Canvis Vells 2, Born (93 268 42 20). Metro Jaume I. **Open** 10am-2pm, 5-8.30pm Mon-Fri; 11am-2pm, 5-8.30pm Sat. **Credit** AmEx, DC, MC, V. **Map** p345 C4.

Straight from the souks of the Atlas mountains, Moroccan artefacts sit alongside books and music from throughout the Muslim world. Hennaed goatskin lamps, bejewelled slippers, clay tajines and pretty filigreed tea glasses are displayed on handmade mosaic tables; you can hardly move for the rugs, baskets, chests and lanterns.

Xilografies

C/Freneria 1, Barri Gòtic (93 315 07 58). Metro Jaume I. **Open** 10am-2pm Mon-Sat. **No credit cards. Map** p345 B3.
Using painstakingly detailed 18th-century carved boxwood blocks that have been passed down in her family for generations (some of which are displayed in a glass cabinet in the tiny shop), Maria creates *ex libris* stickers for books, bookmarks, notepaper, address books and prints. There are also prints of 18th-century maps and reproduction pocket sundials.

Hair & beauty

Beauty treatments

Bienestar Augusta Natural

Via Augusta 217, Zona Alta (93 241 69 00/ www.augustanatural.com). FGC Bonanova. **Open** 8am-9pm Mon-Sat. **Credit** AmEx, DC, MC, V. **Map** p338 C2.
This flash new health and beauty complex for both sexes is complete with minimalist decor, Japanese garden, restaurant and vitamin shop. As well as manicures and facials, there's hairdressing (with private booths), saunas, jacuzzis, new techniques such as colour therapy, and an impressive array of massages including shiatsu, Thai and ayurvedic.

Instituto Francis

Ronda de Sant Pere 18, Eixample (93 317 78 08).
Metro Catalunya. **Open** 9.30am-8pm Mon-Fri; 9am-
4pm Sat. **Credit** DC, MC, V. **Map** p344 B1.
Europe's largest women's beauty centre has seven
floors and over 50 staff dedicated to making you
beautiful inside and out. As well as all the usual
facials, massages, anti-cellulite treatments and manicures, they specialise in depilation, homeopathic
therapies and non-surgical procedures such as teeth
whitening and micropigmentation.

Masajes a 1000

C/Mallorca 233, Eixample (93 215 85 85/www.
masajesa1000.com). Metro Diagonal/FGC Provença.
Open 8am-midnight daily. **Credit** MC, V. **Map**
p338 D4.
An efficient and economic beauty centre. You can
try a half-hour massage and siesta in an ergonomic
chair, or a luxurious 90-minute 'four-hand' massage.
There are also pedicures, manicures, hair and skin
care and tanning, with no need to book ahead.
Other locations: Travessera de les Corts 178, Les
Corts (93 490 92 90); C/Numancia 76, Les Corts (93 410
87 82); C/Dante Alighieri 5-7, Horta (93 429 29 78).

Cosmetics & perfumes

The ground floor of **El Corte Inglés** (*see*
p191) also has a good range.

Regia

Passeig de Gràcia 39, Eixample (93 216 01 21/
www.regia.es). Metro Passeig de Gràcia. **Open**
10am-8.30pm Mon-Sat. **Credit** AmEx, DC, MC, V.
Map p338 D4.
Regia was founded in 1928, and all six of its
Barcelona branches have a good selection of upmarket perfumes and cosmetics on sale, as well as their
own house line of skin and hair products. What
makes this particular outlet special is the outstanding perfume museum that's hidden at the back of the
shop, past the offices (*see p127*).
Other locations: Bulevard Rosa, Passeig de Gràcia
55, Eixample (93 215 73 48); C/Muntaner 242, Sant
Gervasi (93 200 63 48); and throughout the city.

Sephora

El Triangle, C/Pelai 13-39, Eixample (93 306 39 00/
www.sephora.es). Metro Catalunya. **Open** 10am-
10pm Mon-Sat. **Credit** AmEx, DC, MC, V. **Map**
p344 A1.
Sephora is a supermarket of scents and make-up. A
gargantuan Gallic enterprise that keeps competi-
tively priced perfumes and beauty products alpha-
betically arranged to help customers navigate from
Armani to Vera Wang via Clarins. Gloved assistants
prowl around offering samples or makeovers and
everyone is fully encouraged to play with the testers:
whatever the result, there are tissues and cleansing
lotion aplenty to clean up afterwards.
Other locations: La Maquinista, C/Potosi s/n, Sant
Andreu (93 360 87 21); Diagonal Mar, Avda Diagonal
3, Poblenou (93 356 23 19).

Hairdressers

Llongueras

Passeig de Gràcia 78, Eixample (93 215 41 75/
www.llongueras.com). Metro Passeig de Gràcia.
Open *Sept-July* 9am-7pm Mon-Sat. *Aug* 9am-6pm
Mon-Fri; 9am-2pm Sat. **Credit** AmEx, DC, MC, V.
Map p338 D4.
A safe bet for all ages, this reassuringly pricey
Catalan chain of hairdressers also has well-trained
stylists, who take the time to give a proper consul-
tation, wash and massage. The cuts themselves are
up-to-the-minute but generally as natural as possible and free of the excesses of the trendier salons.
Other locations: Rambla Catalunya 16, Eixample
(93 318 81 42); and throughout the city.

Rock & Roll

C/Palma de Sant Just 12, Barri Gòtic (93 268 74
75). Metro Jaume I. **Open** 10.30am-8pm Tue-Fri;
10am-4pm Sat. **Credit** AmEx, MC, V. **Map** p345 B3.
Blinding white decor and bleeping electronica usually indicate a traumatic regime of enforced mullets
and badger streaks, but the friendly and very experienced stylists, Laura and Christian, don't insist on
the latest fashion foibles: if you demand a tiny trim,
that's what you'll get. A basic cut and blow-dry is
€33 for women and €21 for men.

La Tijereta

C/Vidrieria 13, Born (93 319 70 01). Metro
Barceloneta or Jaume I. **Open** 10am-7pm Mon-
Fri; 9am-2pm Sat. **Credit** MC, V. **Map** p345 C4.
As long as you don't mind passers-by gawking at
you through the goldfish bowl windows, tiny La
Tijereta is a little over half the price of the rest of the
Born crop of hi-design hairdressers with no dis-
cernible drop in quality. A wash, cut and blow-dry
is €17.85 for women and €11.75 for men; products
used are from Tigi's Bedhead range.

Opticians

Grand Optical

El Triangle, Plaça Catalunya 4, Eixample (93 304
16 40/www.grandoptical.com). Metro Catalunya.
Open 10am-10pm Mon-Sat. **Credit** AmEx, DC, MC,
V. **Map** p344 A1.
Some staff speak English at this sparkling optical
superstore in the town centre. Efficient service
ensures that you can have your prescription sun-
glasses or standard specs in as little as an hour.
There are over 3,500 designer frames in stock.
Products have a year guarantee, redeemable in any
Grand Optical outlet in the world.

Markets

For details of the 40 permanent neighbourhood
food markets in Barcelona, check www.bcn.es/
mercatsmunicipals. The return of the **Mercat
de Santa Caterina** (Passeig Lluís Companys,

Eat, Drink, Shop

93 319 57 40, www.mercatsantacaterina.net) to its original site on Avda Francesc Cambó has been on the cards for years, but may not take place until summer 2005 or later. When it does move, it'll be to a spectacular new building designed by the late Enric Miralles.

Other markets to look out for include the **stamp and coin market** on Plaça Reial (9am-2.30pm Sun, 93 318 93 12), and the **Fira de Santa Llúcia** on Plaça Nova (see p224). Of the city's various **artisan food fairs**, the most central is usually held on picturesque Plaça del Pi on the first and third Friday, Saturday and Sunday of every month, as well as during local fiestas.

Antiques Market

Plaça Nova, Barri Gòtic (93 302 70 45). Metro Jaume I. **Open** 10am-9pm Thur. Closed Aug. **No credit cards. Map** p344 B2.
The location of this market in front of the cathedral means that prices are targeted at tourists, so come prepared to haggle. The market itself dates from the Middle Ages but the antiques certainly don't, and generally consist of smaller items such as sepia postcards, *manila* shawls, pocket watches, typewriters, feather quills, lace, cameras and jewellery among the inevitable bibelots and bric-a-brac. In December, the market transfers to Portal de l'Àngel.

Book & Coin Market

Mercat de Sant Antoni, C/Comte d'Urgell 1, Eixample (93 423 42 87). Metro Sant Antoni. **Open** 9am-2pm (approx) Sun. **No credit cards. Map** p342 C5.
Trestle tables around the outside of the Mercat Sant Antoni's metal structure are packed with every manner of reading material from arcane old tomes to well-pawed bodice-rippers and yellowing comics. There are also stacks of coins and more contemporary wares such as music, software and posters. Arrive early to beat the crowds.

La Boqueria

La Rambla 89, Raval (93 318 25 84). Metro Liceu. **Open** 8am-8.30pm Mon-Sat. **Map** p344 A2.
Barcelona's most central food market outstrips all the rest. However, steer clear of conspicuous stalls near the front, as their neatly stacked picture-perfect fruit, mounds of sweets, candied fruit and nuts and ready-to-eat fruit salads are designed to ensnare tourists and have prices to match. The authorities appear to have cottoned on to the market's potential as a tourist attraction and are now capitalising on it with a range of Boqueria merchandise, available from a stall at the entrance.

Packed under the impressive vaulted glass and iron structure, amid a cacophony of buying and selling, is a succession of stalls trading in fresh fruit and vegetables, meat, fish, seafood, nuts and more. And if all this makes you hungry, there are great places to eat incomparably fresh food, if you can hack the noise and are prepared to pull up a stool at a frenzied bar. Visitors and residents never tire of wandering the hectic, colourful aisles and ogling the gory spectacle of tripe and sheep heads, the flailing pincers of live crabs and crayfish, bins of nuts, tubs of aromatic olives and sacks of herbs and spices. Don't miss Llorenç Petràs's woodland stall of myriad mushrooms and insect goodies, at the back.

Els Encants

C/Dos de Maig 186, Plaça de la Glòries, Eixample (93 246 30 30). Metro Glòries. **Open** 9am-5pm Mon, Wed, Fri, Sat. *Auctions* 7-9am Mon, Wed, Fri. **No credit cards. Map** p343 F5.
This sprawling flea market sells anything under the sun and more, with over 1,000 official stalls. Among the heaps of junk are second-hand clothes, toys and geriatric furniture. Although the market is officially open in the afternoons, many stalls pack up at midday; for the best stuff, get there with the larks and prepare to haggle. The auctions are best either at 7am, when the commercial dealers buy, or near midday, when unsold goods drop dramatically in price. Avoid Saturdays, when prices shoot up and the crowds move in, and be on your guard for pickpockets and short-changing.

Music

C/Tallers, C/Bonsuccès and C/Riera Baixa in the Raval are dotted with speciality music shops catering to all tastes and formats, with plenty of instruments and sheet music. Mainstream music selections are found in the huge Portal de l'Àngel branch of **El Corte Inglés** (see p191) and, more cheaply, at **FNAC** (see p193), which also has world music and acres of classical.

Casa Beethoven

La Rambla 97, Raval (93 301 48 26/www.casa beethoven.com). Metro Liceu. **Open** 9am-1.30pm, 4-8pm Mon-Fri; 9am-1.30pm, 5-8pm Sat. Closed 3wks Aug. **Credit** MC, V. **Map** p344 A2.
The sheet music and songbooks on sale in this beautiful old shop cover the gamut from Wagner to the White Stripes, but with a special concentration on opera. Books cover music history and theory, while the CD collection is particularly strong on both modern and classical Spanish music.

Discos Castelló

C/Tallers 3, 7, 9 & 79, Raval (93 302 59 46/ www.discoscastello.es). Metro Catalunya. **Open** 10am-8.30pm Mon-Sat. **Credit** AmEx, DC, MC, V. **Map** p344 A2.
Discos Castelló is a homegrown cluster of small shops, each with a different speciality: No.3 is devoted to classical; the largest, No.7, covers pretty much everything; No.9 does hip hop, rock and alternative pop plus T-shirts and accessories; and No.79 is best for jazz and '70s pop. The branch in Nou de la Rambla is good for ethnic music and electronica. **Other locations**: throughout the city.

New Phono

C/Ample 35-37, Barri Gòtic (93 315 13 61/www.
newphono.com). Metro Jaume I. **Open** 10am-2pm,
4.30-8pm Mon-Fri; 10am-2pm Sat. **Credit** AmEx,
DC, MC, V. **Map** p345 B4.

Budding Segovias will splurge on a fine Ramírez
classical guitar; others will just want a dirt-cheap
Admira to strum on the beach. New Phono's cluster
of display rooms holds a range of wind, string and
percussion instruments, and accessories, while keyboards and recording equipment reside over the
road. Check the noticeboard for musical contacts.

Verdes

C/Duc de la Victòria 5, Barri Gòtic (93 301 91 77/
www.verdesrecords.com). **Open** 11am-8pm Mon-Fri.
Credit MC, V. **Map** p344 B2.

The best vinyl shop in town for all breeds of urban
house music also comes with its own label, Verdes
Records. It's a subterranean hangout complete with
private listening booths that's great for imports, flyers, club chat and DJ spotting. Check the excellent
website for details of new releases.

Photography

If Casanova Foto doesn't have what you need,
try **ARPI** (La Rambla 38-40, Barri Gòtic, 93 301
74 04), which has a wide range but scores more
poorly on service and digital equipment.

Casanova Foto

C/Pelai 18, Raval (93 302 73 63/www.casanovafoto.
com). Metro Universitat. **Open** 10am-2pm, 4.30-
8.30pm Mon-Fri; 10am-2pm, 5-8.30pm Sat. **Credit**
AmEx, MC, V. **Map** p344 A1.

Petràs's stall in
La Boqueria.
See p212.

This well-established company provides a reliable
and comprehensive photography service along with
photographic equipment for both aficionados and
professionals. As well as new and second-hand
traditional and digital photography equipment,
there's a repair service and a reasonably extensive
lab. Tourist snaps are not the main line of business;
it takes two days to get your film processed.

Other locations: Casanova Professional, C/Tallers
68, Raval (93 301 61 12); Casanova Col·lecció, C/Pelai
9, Raval (93 317 28 69).

Fotoprix

C/Pelai 6, Raval (93 318 20 36/www.fotoprix.es).
Metro Universitat. **Open** 9.30am-8.30pm Mon-Fri;
10am-8.30pm Sat. **Credit** MC, V. **Map** p344 A1.

It's hard to miss this store, as there are over 45 bright
yellow branches throughout the city. All branches
offer 1-hour APS and standard film development
and copies from negatives. Other services are also
on offer such as passport photos, slide processing,
printing from CDs and memory cards, and converting Super 8 film to video or DVD.

Other locations: C/Ferran 33, Barri Gòtic (93 317
01 10); and throughout the city.

Speciality shops

Arlequí Mascares

C/Princesa 7, Born (93 268 27 52/www.arlequimask.
com). **Open** 10.30am-8.30pm Mon-Sat;
10.30am-4.30pm Sun. **Credit** MC, V. **Map** p345 B3.

The walls here are dripping with masks, crafted
from papier mâché and leather. Whether gilt-laden
or in feathered *Commedia Dell'arte* style, simple
Greek tragicomedy styles or traditional Japanese or
Catalan varieties, they make striking fancy dress or
decorative staples. Other trinkets and toys include
finger puppets, mirrors and ornamental boxes.

Other locations: C/Caballeros 10, Poble Espanyol
(93 426 21 69).

Cereria Subirá

Baixada de Llibreteria 7, Barri Gòtic (93 315 26
06). Metro Jaume I. **Open** *Jan-July, Sept-Nov* 9am-
1.30pm, 4-7.30pm Mon-Fri; 9am-1.30pm Sat. *Aug* 9am-
1.30pm, 4-7.30pm Mon-Fri. *Dec* 9am-1.30pm, 4-7.30pm
Mon-Sat. **Credit** AmEx, MC, V. **Map** p345 B3.

The interior, dating back to 1761, is stunning, with
grand swirling mint-green and gilt-adorned
balustrades and torch-wielding maidens, but the
range of candles is also impressive. The varieties
include simple votive candles, scented and novelty
wax creations and tapered classics. Related stock
includes large garden torches and oil burners.

Flora Albaicín

C/Canuda 3, Barri Gòtic (93 302 10 35). Metro
Catalunya. **Open** 10.30am-1pm, 5-8pm Mon-Sat.
Closed 2wks Aug. **Credit** AmEx, MC, V.
Map p344 A-B2.

If you're even mildly tempted by the frilly flamenco
dresses hanging forlornly in the tourist traps lining
the Rambla, make a beeline for this haven of ruffles

and polka dots. The tiny store is bursting to the seams with its brightly coloured flamenco frocks, shoes, head combs, bangles, shawls and so on.

Herboristeria del Rei

C/Vidre 1, Barri Gòtic (93 318 05 12/www.herbor isteriadelrei.com). Metro Liceu. **Open** 5-8pm Mon; 10am-2pm, 5-8pm Tue-Sat. Closed 1-2wks Aug. **Credit** MC, V. **Map** p345 A3.

In 1860 Queen Isabel II named this venerable herbalist official purveyor to the Royal Court. She called in Soler i Rovirosa, a famous theatre set designer of the time, to decorate it, since when it's been a local fixture. The shop continues to stock over 200 medicinal herbs and spices in gorgeous glass jars. You'll also find teas, essential oils, natural toiletries, soaps and a selection of health food.

El Rei de la Màgia

C/Princesa 11, Born (93 319 39 20/www.elreidela magia.com). Metro Jaume I. **Open** *Sept-July* 10am-2pm, 5-8pm Mon-Fri; 11am-2pm Sat. *Aug* 11am-2pm, 5-8pm Mon-Fri. **Credit** AmEx, MC, V. **Map** p345 B3.

This enclave of illusionism has been enticing wannabe Houdinis into its tiny interior since 1881. In-house professionals produce the tricks of the trade from endless shelves and drawers. Practical jokers are well served, with whoopee cushions, fake turds and more imaginative buffoon material.

Sport

The tourist shops on La Rambla stock a huge range of football strips.

La Botiga del Barça

Maremàgnum, Moll d'Espanya, Port Vell (93 225 80 45). Metro Drassanes. **Open** 10am-10pm daily. **Credit** AmEx, DC, MC, V. **Map** p342 D7.

Everything for the well-dressed Barça fan, from the standard blue and burgundy strips to scarves, hats, crested ties, aftershave and even underpants. The myriad souvenirs and gifts also include calendars, shirts printed with your name, shield-embossed ashtrays, beach towels and so on.

Other locations: Gran Via de les Corts Catalanes 418, Eixample (93 423 59 41); Museu del FC Barcelona, Nou Camp (93 409 02 71).

Decathlon

C/Canuda 20, Barri Gòtic (93 342 61 61/www. decathlon.es). Metro Catalunya. **Open** 10am-9.30pm Mon-Sat. **Credit** AmEx, DC, MC, V. **Map** p344 B2.

The city's first stop for sports gear has attire and equipment for everything from scuba diving and camping to golf, windsurfing, yachting and racket sports. In the basement, there are trustworthy repair departments for bicycles, skis (winter only) and custom stamping for team shirts. In July and August, bike rentals are available by the hour, day or week. **Other locations**: L'Illa, Avda Diagonal 545-557, Eixample (93 444 01 65); Gran Via 2, Gran Via de les Corts Catalanes 75-97, Hospitalet de Llobregat (93 259 15 92).

Ticket agents

FNAC (*see p193*) has an efficient ticket desk on its ground floor: it sells tickets to theme parks and sights, but it's especially good for contemporary music concerts and events (it's also one of the main outlets for tickets to Sónar; *see p219*). Concert tickets for smaller venues are often sold in record shops and at the venues themselves; check posters for further details. For Barça tickets, *see p271*.

Servi-Caixa – La Caixa

902 33 22 11/www.servicaixa.com. **Credit** AmEx, DC, MC, V.

Use the special Servi-Caixa ATMs (most larger branches of La Caixa have them), dial 902 33 22 11 or check the website to purchase tickets for cinemas, concerts, plays, museums, amusement parks and Barça games. You'll need the card with which you made the payment when you collect the tickets; be sure to check the pick-up deadline.

Tel-entrada – Caixa Catalunya

902 10 12 12/www.telentrada.com. **Credit** MC, V.

Through Tel-entrada you can purchase tickets for theatre performances, cinemas (including the IMAX), concerts, museums and sights over the phone, online or over the counter at any branch of the Caixa Catalunya savings bank. Tickets can be collected from Caixa Catalunya ATMs or the tourist office at Plaça Catalunya (*see p321*).

Travel services

FNAC (*see p193*) and **El Corte Inglés** (*see p191*) also have travel agencies. One worthwhile Spanish travel website is **www.rumbo.es**.

Halcón Viajes

C/Aribau 34, Eixample (93 454 59 95/902 30 06 00/www.halconviajes.com). Metro Universitat. **Open** 9.30am-1.30pm, 4.30-8pm Mon-Fri; 10am-1pm Sat. **Credit** AmEx, DC, MC, V. **Map** p342 C5.

This mammoth chain has exclusive deals with Air Europa and Globalia, among others, and can offer highly competitive rates in most areas. Service tends to be quite brisk but efficient.

Other locations: throughout the city.

Viajes Zeppelin

C/Villarroel 49, Eixample (93 412 00 13/www. viajeszeppelin.com). Metro Urgell. **Open** 9am-8pm Mon-Fri; 10am-1pm Sat. **Credit** AmEx, DC, MC, V. **Map** p342 C5.

The friendly staff at this agency speak some English and offer all the usual services, from flight, bus, train and hotel bookings to car rental and travel insurance (which is available even if you haven't booked the travel itself with this company). Viajes Zeppelin also provides international student identity cards (ISIC) and youth discount cards for under-25s. Be sure to check online for any special offers.

Arts & Entertainment

Festivals & Events   216
Children   225
Film   230
Galleries   234
Gay & Lesbian   238
Music & Nightlife   246
Performing Arts   262
Sport & Fitness   271

Features

Urban tribes Castellers   221
Urban tribes Gegants   223
Tales from the crib   229
Stars above the silver screen   232
The art of drinking   236
Urban tribes Bears   240
Don't miss Nights to…   249
Chips with everything   250
Get out   254
Quiet, please!   259
Let's do the show right here!   264
Rocking the boat   269
Urban tribes Culés   273

Festivals & Events

Shake your tail feathers.

Festa Major de
Gràcia.
See p220.

Whether they involve running through fireworks, gobbling grapes or raffling pigs, parties are the life and soul of Barcelona, and an enthusiastic crowd always materialises to make things go with a bang. Even with 15 public holidays a year, the notoriously hard-working *barcelonins* somehow find the energy to celebrate even the smallest events before an early start at the office the next day.

The annual round of some 30 or so neighbourhood *festes* share many traditional ingredients; among them are *castellers* (*see p221* **Urban tribes**) and *gegants* (*see p223* **Urban tribes**), both spectacular for rather different reasons, and the *correfoc* and the *sardana*. The *correfoc* ('fire run') is a nocturnal frenzy of pyromania, when groups of horned devils dance through the streets, brandishing tridents that spout fireworks, and generally flout just about every safety rule in the book. The more daring onlookers, protected by cotton caps and long sleeves, try to stop the devils and touch the giant, fire-breathing dragons being dragged along in their wake.

The orderly antidote to this pandemonium is the *sardana*, Catalonia's folk dance. Watching the dancers executing their fussy little hops and steps in a large circle, it's hard to believe that *sardanes* were once banned as a vestige of pagan witchcraft. The music is similarly restrained, a reedy noise played by an 11-piece *cobla* band. The *sardana* is much harder than it looks, and the joy lies in taking part rather than watching. To try your luck, check out the *sardanes populars* held in front of the cathedral (noon-2pm Sun, plus 6.30-8.30pm Sat from March to November) or www.fed.sardanista.com for monthly programmes round the city.

INFORMATION

Organisers are prone to change event dates. For more information, try tourist offices or the city's information line on 010, or the cultural agenda section at www.bcn.es. Newspapers also carry details, especially in their Friday or Saturday supplements. Events listed below that include public holidays (when many shops will be closed for the day) are marked *.

Spring

Festes de Sant Medir de Gràcia

Information www.santmedir.org. Gràcia to Sant Cugat & back, usually via Plaça Lesseps, Avda República Argentina & Carretera de l'Arrabassada. **Starting point** Metro Fontana. **Date** early Mar. **Map** p338 D2/3.

Since 1830, decorated horses and carts have gathered bright and early around the Plaça Rius i Taulet to ride up to the hermitage of Sant Medir in the Collserola hills. Mass is celebrated, *sardanes* are danced and barbecued *botifarres* are eaten with beans. At mid-morning and again in the evening, neighbourhood societies drive horse-drawn carts around the main streets of Gràcia and shower the crowd with over 100 tons of blessed boiled sweets.

Setmana Santa* (Holy Week)

Date 10-17 Apr 2006.

The main Easter event in Barcelona is the blessing of the palms on *diumenge de rams* (Palm Sunday). Crowds surge into the cathedral clutching bleached palm fronds bought from the stalls along Rambla de Catalunya and outside the Sagrada Família. Boys carry long wafting *palmons*, while girls have graceful *palmes* woven into intricate designs. Once home, the palms are hung on balconies to ward off evil.

On Good Friday a series of small processions and blessings takes place in front of the cathedral; a procession sets out from the church of Sant Agustí on C/Hospital at around 5pm and arrives at the cathedral a couple of hours later. On Easter Sunday, godparents dole out the *mones*: originally, marzipan cakes decorated with boiled eggs, but these days more likely to be a chocolate cartoon character.

Sant Jordi

La Rambla & all over Barcelona. **Date** 23 Apr.

On the feast day of Sant Jordi (St George), the patron saint of Catalonia, nearly every building bears the red and gold Catalan flag, while bakeries sell Sant Jordi bread streaked with red *sobrassada* pâté and yellow walnuts. Red roses decorate the Palau de la Generalitat and the city's many statues and paintings of Georgie in all his dragon-slaying glory. It's said that as the drops of the dragon's blood fell, they turned into red flowers; for over five centuries, this has been the Catalan version of St Valentine's Day.

Men traditionally give women a rose tied to an ear of wheat and women reciprocate with a book, although in these enlightened times many now give both. This is also the 'Day of the Book', thanks to the odd fact that both Cervantes and Shakespeare died on 23 April 1616. The day accounts for an amazing 10% of Catalonia's annual book sales; street stalls and bookshops give good discounts.

Festival de Música Antiga

CaixaForum, Avda Marquès de Comillas 6-8, Montjuïc (902 22 30 40/www.fundacio.lacaixa.es). Metro Espanya. **Date** 27 Apr-15 May 2005. **Concerts** €4-€10. **Map** p341 A5.

Go for baroque at the Festival of Early Music, which features performers from all over the globe. The 2004 line-up included tenor David Munderloh and Driss el Matoumi playing ancient Berber music. Special family concerts are staged at 12.30pm. The accompanying El Fringe festival is held over three days around the Barri Gòtic and offers young performers an opportunity to perform alongside more established musicians.

Feria de Abril de Catalunya

Nova Mar Bella beach (information Federación de Entidades Culturales Andaluces en Cataluña www.fecac.com). Metro Besòs-Mar, then special shuttle buses. **Date** end Apr/May.

Dressed to frill and entering on horseback, the city's Andalucían population parties at this joyously tacky car-park-turned-fantasy-fairground. Unlike elitist Seville's equivalent, the Barcelona version is a free-for-all with over 60 open *casetas* (decorated marquees) offering *manzanilla* sherry, free flamenco shows, throbbing speakers and heaving dancefloors. Be warned, however, that the Portaloos are mobbed and filthy, and the food tents are overpriced.

Dia del Treball* (May Day)

Various venues. **Date** 1 May.

A day of mass demonstrations led by trade unionists representing an alphabet soup of organisations including the communist CCOO, the socialist UGT and anarcho-syndicalist CGT. Main routes cover Plaça da la Universitat, Via Laietana, Passeig de Gràcia, Passeig Sant Joan and Plaça Sant Jaume and the Sants neighbourhood.

Barcelona Poesia & Festival Internacional de Poesia

All over Barcelona (information Institut de Cultura 93 316 10 00/www.bcn.es/cultura). **Date** 11 May 2005.

This poetry festival started as the courtly Jocs Florals (Floral Games) in 1393, which were named after the prizes: a silver violet for third; a golden rose as second prize; and, naturally, a real flower for the winner. The games died out in the 15th century, but they were resuscitated in 1859 as a vehicle for the promotion of the Catalan language. Prizes went to the most suitably florid paeans to the motherland; these days, however, Spanish is also permitted, and many foreign languages can be heard at the International Poetry Festival. Held in the Palau de la Música on the festival's final evening, in 2004 it staged readings by Anne Waldman and Eva Runefeld.

Festival de Flamenco de Ciutat Vella

Information 93 443 43 46/www.tallerdemusics.com. **Date** 1wk late May.

Not for old-school purists, the Old City flamenco festival stages five days and nights of vanguard performers and DJs fusing flamenco with anything from electronica to jazz and rock. There are also films, exhibitions, conferences and children's activities, all centred around the CCCB (*see p99*).

Arts & Entertainment

Festa dels Cors de la Barceloneta

Barceloneta. **Date** 14-16 May 2005.
In a tradition dating back 150 years, some 24 choirs of workers and regulars from Barceloneta's restaurants and bars sing traditional *caramelles* and march in carnival parades around the district. Singers wear costumes garlanded with objects typical of their profession – nets and oars for a fisherman, paintbrushes and hammers for a decorator – and carry long, decorated hatchets, oars or pitchforks bearing their choir's symbol. The first parade is on Saturday morning; at midday, the choirs take off for an overnight jolly on the coast, returning on Monday afternoon for song, dance, drink and fireworks.

Primavera Sound

Various venues (information www.primaverasound. com). **Tickets** €62 until Mar; €75 Apr; €100 May.
Date 26-28 May 2005.
Fast stealing Sónar's thunder, this three-day, six-stage music festival is one of the best in Spain. Credit its success to its raid of genres: Wilco played in 2004, alongside Franz Ferdinand, Miss Kittin, Pixies and Scissor Sisters, plus rafts of electronica acts, DJs and local bands. There's also a record fair and the Soundtrack Film Festival, which in 2004 focused on rockumentaries and pop cinema. The 2005 edition is to move from Montjuïc to the Fòrum space on the waterfront at the end of Avda Diagonal.

L'Ou Com Balla

Ateneu Barcelonès, C/Canuda 6; Casa de l'Ardiaca, C/Santa Llúcia 1; Cathedral cloisters; Museu Frederic Marès; all in Barri Gòtic (information Institut de Cultura 93 301 77 75/www.bcn.es/icub). **Date** wk of 26 May 2005.
L'Ou Com Balla (the 'dancing egg') is a local Corpus Christi tradition dating from 1637: a hollowed-out eggshell in spinning and bobbing *perpetuum mobile* on the spout of a fountain garlanded with flowers and cherry blossom. The white egg symbolises the body of Christ: along with the flowing water, it's a potent symbol of renewal, and if it doesn't break, it's said to be a good omen for the year ahead. The Sunday Corpus procession leaves from the cathedral in the early evening; on Saturday 28 May there's free entrance to the Ajuntament, the Palau Centelles behind it and the Museu d'Història de la Ciutat (*see p92*) along with *sardanes* at 7pm outside the cathedral.

Get loved up at **Sónar**.

or a transvestite striptease. In principle, anything is welcome; the programme has recently broadened to include music, video and animation.

Sónar

Information www.sonar.es. **Date** 16-18 June 2005.
Tickets (approx) €15-€93.
The three-day International Festival of Advanced Music and Multimedia Art is still a must for anybody into electronic music, contemporary urban art and media technologies. The event is divided into two parts: SónarDay comprises record fairs, conferences, exhibitions and soundlabs around the CCCB, while DJs play. SónarNight means a scramble for the desperately overcrowded shuttle bus from the bottom of La Rambla out to the Polígon Pedrosa in the industrial hinterland of L'Hospitalet de Llobregat, where concerts and DJs spread out over SónarClub, SónarPark and SónarPub. Advance tickets are available from the Palau de la Virreina (*see p321*).

Summer

Marató de l'Espectacle

Mercat de les Flors, C/Lleida 59, Poble Sec (information Associació Marató de l'Espectacle 93 268 18 68/www.marato.com). Metro Poble Sec or Espanya. **Date** 3-4 June 2005. **Map** p341 B6.
An anarchic performance marathon in which over 200 artists get between three seconds and ten minutes to grab the crowd's attention. As you wander about the Ciutat de Teatre, expect to see anything from dance and circus acts to singing bellybuttons

Festa de la Música

All over Barcelona (information Institut de Cultura 93 316 10 00/www.bcn.es/icub). **Date** 1 Sat, mid-late June.
Started in France in 1982 and now celebrated in over 100 countries, the Festival of Music sees amateur musicians from 100 countries take to the streets. All events are free, and you're as likely to see a kid slapping a bongo as a first-rate blues band, symphonic orchestra or choir.

Setmana Santa. *See p217.*

Sant Joan*

All over Barcelona. **Date** night of 23 June.

The beach is the place to be for an orgy of all-night pyromania on the eve of Sant Joan (St John the Baptist). Being summer solstice, it's traditional to stay up 'til dawn, munching *coca de Sant Joan* – flat, crispy bread topped with candied fruit – with endless bottles of cava while partying by the light of huge bonfires. The biggest fireworks displays are at Montjuïc, Tibidabo and L'Estació del Nord. Don't miss Barceloneta's Nit del Foc (Night of Fire), where devils incite the crowds to dance around the bonfires before everyone drunkenly heads down to the beach at dawn for skinny-dipping. Special metro and FGC trains run all night; 24 June is the quietest day of the whole year as the city sleeps off its collective hangover.

Clàssics als Parcs

Information Parcs i Jardins 93 413 24 00/www.bcn. es/parcsijardins). **Date** 1-24 July 2005.

What nicer way can there be to spend a balmy summer evening than listening to some classical music in one of Barcelona's most beautiful parks? Throughout July, young musicians perform a varied concert programme, alfresco and for free. On Thursdays, concerts are held at the secluded Jardins de la Tamarita and the pretty Turó Park, on Fridays at the futuristic Diagonal Mar and the Jardins de Ca n'Altimira, and on Saturdays at the Parc de la Ciutadella.

Festival del Grec

Information Institut de Cultura 93 316 10 00/ www.bcn.es/grec). **Date** June-Aug 2005.

An integral part of summer in the city, El Grec began in 1976 as a series of plays in the eponymous Greek-style amphitheatre on Montjuïc and has grown into a two-month spree of dance, music and theatre all over the city. There's no shortage of avant-garde acts, but some of the better-known acts in 2004 included Cape Verdean Cesária Evora and the excellent Compañía Nacional de Danza.

Gran Trobada d'Havaneres

Passeig Joan de Borbó, Barceloneta (information Institut de Cultura 93 316 10 00/www.bcn.es/icub). **Date** last Sat in June.

The barnacled legacy of Catalonia's old trade links with Cuba, *havaneres* are melancholy 19th-century sea shanties accompanied by accordions and guitars. The main event is at the port town of Calella de Palafrugells, but the Barcelona satellite is no less fun. Performances by groups dressed in stripy shirts, with salty sea dog names such as Peix Fregit (fried fish) and Xarxa (fishing net), are followed by *cremat* (flaming spiced rum) and fireworks.

Dies de Dansa

Information Associació Marató de l'Espectacle (93 268 18 68/www.marato.com). **Date** 8-10 July 2005.

This three-day Festival of Dance aims to create what insiders like to call a 'dialogue' between public spaces and individual expression. All shows are free and most centre around the terraces of the CCCB, MACBA, CaixaForum and Fundació Miró, including popular events such as dance-offs and the Spanish-Portuguese breakdancing championships. Local dancers are supplemented by international troupes such as Alias Compagnie from Switzerland.

Festa Major de Gràcia

All over Gràcia (information 93 459 30 80/www. festamajordegracia.org). Metro Fontana. **Date** 3rd wk in Aug. **Map** p338 D/E2/3.

Gràcia's extravagant *festa major* is most distinctive for its best-dressed street competition, where residents transform some 25 streets into pirate ships, rainforests and even a giant strawberry gâteau; C/Verdi del Mig carried off the prize in 2004 with a journey through the Jurassic period. The festival opens with giants and castles in Plaça Rius i Taulet, and climaxes with a *correfoc* and a *castell de focs* (castle of fireworks). In between, 600 activities, from concerts to *sardanes* and kids' bouncy castles, are centred around Plaça Rius i Taulet, Plaça de la Revolució, Plaça del Sol and Plaça de la Virreina.

Festa Major de Sants

All over Sants (information Federació Festa Major de Sants 93 490 62 14/www.festamajordesants.org). Metro Plaça de Sants or Sants Estació. **Date** last wk Aug.

One of the less well-known *festes majors*, Sants has a traditional flavour, with floral offerings to images of St Bartholomew at the church and the market.

Arts & Entertainment

Major events, such as the *correfoc* on the night of the 24th, are held in the Parc de l'Espanya Industrial; others are at Plaça del Centre, C/Sant Antoni, Plaça de la Farga and Plaça Joan Peiro, behind Sants station.

Festival L'Hora del Jazz, Memorial Tete Montoliu
Various venues (information L'Associació de Músics de Jazz i Música Moderna 93 268 47 36/www.amjm. com). **Date** Sept.
The 'Jazz Time' festival honours the memory of Barcelona's most famous jazzman, blind pianist Tete Montoliu (1933-97), with performances from local acts. Free daytime concerts are held in Plaça Rius i Taulet in Gràcia, and the night-time programme is spread over the Barcelona Pipa Club (*see p247*), Corto Club (C/Tallers 68, 93 302 27 95) and Can Deu Civic Centre (Plaça Concòrdia 13, Les Corts, 93 410 10 07), with styles ranging from Latin jazz to gypsy swing.

Diada Nacional de Catalunya*
All over Barcelona. **Date** 11 Sept.
Catalan National Day commemorates Barcelona's capitulation to the Bourbon army in the 1714 War of the Spanish Succession, a bitter defeat that led to the repression of many Catalan institutions. It's lost some of its vigour but is still a day for national re-affirmation, with the Catalan flag flying on buses

Urban tribes Castellers

Description Groups of up to 400 people who make human castles up to ten storeys high.
Natural habitat Usually to be found in the main square of a district on its fiesta day.
Appearance Bright shirts, white trousers and a *faixa*, a long red woollen cummerbund wrapped tightly to protect the back.
Distinctive behaviour Often seen biting the tips of their collars. Good at landing.
Group composition Of all ages, from six to 80, and of both sexes, with a preponderance of young males. A small child is chosen to be the *anxaneta*, who climbs to the very top.
First sighted The first records of *castells*, as we know them, date from the middle of the 19th century.
Evolution Having enjoyed their golden years in the romantic *fin-de-siècle* flowering of Catalan culture, they were banned by Franco and became virtually extinct. Recent years have seen quite a revival.
Philosophy Equality, team effort and national fervour. The unsung heroes are the *castellers* taking the most strain in the middle of the *pinya*, the bottom level.
Jargon *Castells* are referred to, in Catalan, by the number of *castellers* in the core of the structure, and the number of storeys high they reach. Thus a *quatre de nou* (four of nine) is nine storeys of four castellers.
Take me to your leader The *Cap de colla* is the head, and shouts instructions to the others. Everybody else is considered equal, though the *anxaneta* is the star of the show.
Endangered species? There are 60 official *colles de castellers*, containing a sum total of approximately 8,000 participants, from all over Catalonia.

Can I join in? You can find out your local *colla* by ringing the group Coordinadora de Colles Castelleres de Catalunya on 977 605 206.
Are they dangerous? Only to themselves. *Castells* always wobble and occasionally fall. Fifteen metres (almost 50 feet) is a long way to go.
Do say 'I think the collective effort shown by you fellows is much more impressive than the individual flair demonstrated by Spanish bullfighters.'
Don't say 'Isn't it immoral to put a six-year-old child in such mortal danger?'

and balconies. There are several marches throughout the city, the epicentre being the statue of Rafael Casanova (who directed the resistance) on the Ronda Sant Pere. Many make a pilgrimage to the monastery at Montserrat, the spiritual heart of the region and an important guardian of Catalan language and culture during the dictatorship.

Festes de la Mercè*

All over Barcelona (information tourist offices or www.bcn.es. **Date** 19-25 Sept 2005.

What was once a small religious parade in honour of the patron saint of the city, Our Lady of Mercy, has gradually swollen to a week-long party with all things bright and Catalan hitched to its wagon. The event opens with *castellers* in the Plaça de la Mercè followed by over 400 events including *gegants, capgrosses, sardanes* and the biggest and boldest *correfoc* of them all on the Saturday night.

The highlights of this immense event include dazzling firework displays along the city beaches, a seafront air show and the solidarity festival, now returned to its original location on the Passeig de Gràcia. Free concerts fill the squares (everything from sea shanties to hip hop), while sporting events include a fun run through the city centre, a swim across the port and a regatta. Add to that exhibitions, children's activities, street entertainers and free entrance to many museums on 24 September, and it's a full, full week.

Mostra de Vins i Caves de Catalunya

Maremàgnum, Moll d'Espanya, Port Vell. Metro Drassanes. **Date** 6-8pm 21, 22 Sept; noon-10pm 23-25 Sept 2005.

This wine and cava fair has been running since 1980 and now showcases over 400 labels from around 50 Catalan *bodegas*. Big names include Torres, Freixenet, Codorníu, Pinord and Mont Marçal; also on show are fine cheeses, charcuterie and related oenophilia. Five wine or cava tastings with a commemorative glass cost €6; two food tastings cost €2.

Barcelona Acció Musical (BAM)

Various venues (information www.bam.es). **Date** 20-25 Sept 2005.

Held during the Mercè, BAM stages a good number of free concerts on Plaça del Rei, La Rambla del Raval and outside the cathedral. The prime mover of what has become known as 'So Barcelona' (Barcelona Sound), BAM largely promotes leftfield *mestissa* (vaguely, ethnic fusion) in its mission to provide 'music without frontiers'. The line-up of around 40 bands usually includes several international headliners, although 2004 offered mostly local fare. Large concerts are in the Sala Apolo (*see p257*) and the echoing Estació de França train station.

Festa Major de la Barceloneta

All over Barceloneta (information 93 221 72 44). **Date** last wk Sept.

This tight-knit maritime community throws itself into the local *festes* with incredible gusto. The fun kicks off with fireworks on the beach, a 24-hour football tournament, *sardana* dancing, falcons (acrobatic groups) and a free tasting of traditional crispy *coca* bread washed down with *muscatel*, and finishes with more of the same ten days later. In between, expect parades, music, fire-breathing dragons, open-air cinema and bouncy castles. Look out, too, for a character called General Bum Bum, who parades with a wooden cannon but stops periodically to fire sweets into crowds of scrabbling children.

LEM Festival

Various venues, Gràcia (information 93 241 6819/ www.gracia-territori.com). Metro Joanic or Fontana. **Date** end Sept-mid Oct.

LEM stands for something different with every edition of this experimental music festival (Lateralities, Effervescences and Magnetisms in 2004), where the saucepan is as likely to be employed as the guitar. Over 60 concerts and happenings of electronic music, improvisation and multimedia art take place all over Gràcia.

Festival de Tardor Ribermúsica

Various venues, Born (information www.riber musica.org). Metro Barceloneta or Jaume I. **Date** 3 days in late Oct.

This lively autumn music festival boasts more than 100 free performances around the Born, and fills the squares, bars, galleries, shops, churches and clubs with concerts of all stripes. Wander down the tributaries of the Passeig del Born to see baroque quartets, Celtic rockers or flamenco flautists playing at the Santa Maria del Mar church, the Picasso Museum, open squares and in among the clothes hangers of a number of boutiques.

Festival International de Jazz de Barcelona

Information The Project 93 481 70 40/ www.the-project.net). **Date** Nov.

One of Europe's most well-respected jazz festivals has grown to embrace everything from bebop to gospel around a core of mainstream performers. Highlights in 2004 included Caetano Veloso, Keith Jarrett and Bebo Valdés, performing at the Palau de la Música, Luz de Gas, Razzmatazz and L'Auditori. There are big band concerts in the Ciutadella park.

La Castanyada*

All over Barcelona. **Date** 31 Oct-1 Nov.

All Saints' Day and the evening before are known as the Castanyada after the traditional treats of *castanyes* (roast chestnuts) along with *moniatos* (roast sweet potatoes) and *panellets* (small almond balls covered in pine nuts). The imported tradition of Hallowe'en has rocketed in popularity of late, and there are now several celebrations around town. The largest is in Poble Espanyol, with music and a monsters' ball late into the witching hours. Tots Sants (All Saints') is also known as the Dia dels Difunts

(Day of the Dead); the snacks switch to white, bone-shaped *ossos de sant* cakes. Thousands visit local cemeteries over the weekend to sprinkle the graves with holy water, leave flowers and hold vigils.

Festival de Músiques del Món

CaixaForum, Avda Marquès de Comillas 6-8, Montjuïc (902 22 30 40/www.fundacio.lacaixa.es). Metro Espanya. **Date** Oct 2005. **Tickets** €10; €8 concessions. **Map** p341 A5.

CaixaForum's annual World Music Festival hosts about 20 concerts, along with related exhibitions, films and workshops. Highlights last year included queen of rai Cheikha Remitti, and Syrian stars Al-Kindi and Sheik Hamza Chakour, but expect anything from Mongolian throat-singing to Turkish whirling dervishes alongside homegrown talent such as flamenco singer Miguel Poveda. Family concerts (tickets €3) are at 12.30pm on weekends.

Wintercase Barcelona

Sala Razzmatazz 1, C/Almogàvers 122, Poblenou. (information www.wintercase.com). Metro Marina. **Date** late Nov. **Map** p343 F6.

Urban tribes Gegants

Description The immense, regal giants heading up any festival procession. Usually in couples, they're dressed as princesses, knights-at-arms, fishwives, swarthy sultans or buxom milkmaids.

Natural habitat Some are on display at the Palau de la Virreina throughout the year, but all are wheeled out on the slightest pretext.

Appearance Fibreglass heads with impassive Botox features and a barnet of real human hair. Trainer-clad feet stick out from under their dresses. Oh, and they're about five metres (16 feet) tall.

Distinctive behaviour Twirl around excitably when they hear the music of the *gralles*, traditional reedy recorders.

First sighted Originated in medieval travelling theatre, starring in religious tableaux and plays designed to explain the Bible to illiterate pagan peasants.

Evolution The *gegants* del Pi, Laia and Oriol were built in 1772. Superstars in their own right, they've partied across the globe.

Take me to your leader The city's official *gegants* represent King Jaume I, Queen Violant and the apple-cheeked Santa Eulàlia, but each neighbourhood has its own figures.

Seen in the company of Dwarfish mischief-makers known as *capgrossos* (fatheads) on account of their grotesquely swollen bonces. Also seen with their menagerie of giant lions, mules, eagles and dragons.

Endangered species? Quite the contrary. After something of a renaissance there are now over 200 *gegants* in the city.

Can I join in? Only if you're prepared to stick your head up their skirts and shuffle along with 60 kilos (19 stone) or so on your shoulders, squinting out of a burkah-style mesh window.

Do say Actually, it's better to sing: each pair of giants has their own special ditty.

Don't say 'Your shoelaces are undone.'

Arts & Entertainment

This music festival showcases some of the finest indie bands over four nights in Barcelona, Bilbao, Madrid and Valencia. The Barcelona leg takes place in Razzmatazz with shows from the likes of Tindersticks, the Dears and the Detroit Cobras.

Winter

Fira de Santa Llúcia

Pla de la Seu & Avda de la Catedral (93 402 70 00/ www.bcn.es/nadal). Metro Jaume I. **Dates** end Nov-23 Dec. **Map** p344-345 B2-3.

Dating from 1786, this traditional Christmas fair has expanded to over 300 stalls selling all manner of handcrafted Christmas decorations and gifts, along with mistletoe, poinsettias and Christmas trees. Kids line up for a go on the giant *caga tió*, a huge, smiley-faced 'shit log' that poops out pressies upon being beaten viciously by a stick; smaller versions are on sale in the stalls. There's also a nativity scene contest, musical parades and exhibitions, including the popular life-size nativity scene in Plaça Sant Jaume.

Nadal* & Sant Esteve* (Christmas Day & Boxing Day)

Dates 25 & 26 Dec.

The Catalan equivalent of the Christmas midnight mass is the *missa del gall* (cockerel's mass), held at dawn. Later, the whole family enjoys a traditional Christmas feast of *escudella i carn d'olla* (a meaty stew), seafood and roast truffled turkey, finishing off with great ingots of *turrón*. The *caga tió* (*see above*) gives small gifts but the real booty doesn't arrive until the night of 5 January.

Cap d'Any (New Year's Eve)*

Date 31 Dec & 1 Jan.

During the day, look out for L'Home dels Nassos, the man who has as many noses as days of the year – it being the last day, the sly old fox has only one – who parades and throws sweets to the children. At night, bars and discos charge hoiked-up prices, but free public celebrations are held around the city, mainly on La Rambla and Plaça Catalunya. At midnight everyone stops swilling cava and starts stuffing 12 grapes into their mouths, one for every chime of the bell. Wear red underwear for good luck.

Cavalcada dels Reis

Kings usually arrive at Parc Ciutadella, then parade along C/Marquès de l'Argentera up Via Laietana to Plaça Catalunya & continue to Montjuïc. The detailed route changes each year (information Centre d'Informació de la Virreina 010). **Date** 5 Jan, 5-9pm. **Map** p344-5 B/C1/4.

Melchior, Gaspar and Balthasar arrive aboard the *Santa Eulàlia* boat at the bottom of La Rambla before beginning a grand parade around town with a retinue of acrobats, circus clowns and pages. The televised route is published in the newspapers but the biggest crowds are on C/Marquès de l'Argentera. Later that night, children leave their shoes out on

the balcony stuffed with hay for the kings' camels; in the morning, they're either full of presents or edible coal, depending on their behaviour.

Festa dels Tres Tombs

Sant Antoni. Metro Sant Antoni. **Date** 17 Jan. **Map** p341-2 B/C5.

St Anthony's day also marks the *festa major* of the district; all the usual ingredients of music and *gegants* here include a monstrous, symbolic fire-breathing pig. The devil is meant to have tempted the saint by taking the form of a pig; indeed, Sant Antoni is often depicted with a porker by his side. However, he is in fact the patron saint of all domestic animals, and on his feast day it's still the custom to bring animals to the church of St Anthony to be blessed. Afterwards, horsemen ride three circuits (*tres tombs*) in a formal procession from Ronda Sant Antoni, through Plaça Catalunya, down La Rambla and along C/Nou de la Rambla.

Santa Eulàlia

All over Barcelona. **Date** wk of 12 Feb.

The city's blowout winter festival is in honour of Santa Eulàlia (Laia), Barcelona's co-patron saint and a special favourite of the children. In the fourth century, 13-year-old Laia spoke out against the Romans' persecution of the Christians and was promptly arrested, locked in a box of fleas and whipped with flaming scourges before being crucified naked (a miraculous snow fell to save her modesty). Her feast day on 12 February kicks off with a ceremony in Plaça Sant Jaume followed by music, *sardanes* and parades, with masses and children's choral concerts held in the churches and cathedral. In the evening, the female giants gather in Plaça Sant Josep Oriol, then go to throw flowers on the Baixada de Santa Eulàlia (where the Romans rolled Laia down the hill in a barrel of broken glass) before a final boogie in the Plaça Sant Jaume. The Ajuntament and the cathedral crypt (where she's buried) are free and open to the public, as are over 30 museums. The festival closes on Sunday evening with *correfocs* (for adults and children) centred around the cathedral.

Carnestoltes (Carnival)

All over Barcelona. **Date** Shrove Tuesday/Ash Wednesday.

The city drops everything for a last hurrah of overeating, overdrinking and underdressing prior to Lent. You'll have to hop on a Tuesday-night train to Sitges for the best carnival, but there's still plenty going on in Barcelona. The celebrations begin on Dijous Gras (Mardi Gras) with the appearance of potbellied King Carnestoltes – the masked personification of the carnival spirit – followed by the grand weekend parade, masked balls, *fartaneres* (neighbourhood feasts, typically with lots of pork), food fights and a giant *botifarrada* (sausage barbecue) on La Rambla, with most of the kids and market traders in fancy dress. It's over on Ash Wednesday when the effigy of Carnestoltes goes up in flames and revellers celebrate the mock Burial of the Sardine on the beach.

Children

Playing away.

Compact and colourful Barcelona has plenty of distractions for pint-sized concentration spans. Pester power will ensure endless stops along **La Rambla** for the entertainers and animals, not to mention visits to the **zoo** (*see p226*) and the **Magic Fountain** (*see p118*) or trips on the **cable car** (*see p113*). Even the local museums are feeling the pull of small, sticky hands on the purse strings and provide an ever-growing choice of extra kids' activities, from making chocolate figurines at the **Museu de la Xocolata** (*see p226*) to blowing giant paint bubbles at **CosmoCaixa** (*see p226*). The city's beaches, meanwhile, are fairly clean and have plenty of lifeguards, play areas, showers and ice-cream kiosks, but the beaches further out of town towards the south, such as Castelldefels or Sitges (*see p279*), have shallower waters. (Unfortunately, none has many public toilets.)

In stereotypical Mediterranean manner, Catalans find it very natural to touch and coo over other people's children; don't be surprised if your waiter whips away your wee one for a quick cuddle between courses, or an old lady comes over to pull up your child's droopy socks. However, the nuts and bolts of childcare, such as changing nappies and breastfeeding, rarely take place in public. As mother and baby facilities are almost non-existent – the newer parts of the airport, the larger shopping malls and Poble Espanyol are among the few exceptions – most operations occur in the car and any emergency changes will have to happen in the pram.

Public transport is only free for children under four, and only stations on line 2 and some on line 4 have lifts. Officially, pushchairs are supposed to be folded up on the metro (indeed, the turnstiles are too narrow for many prams) but in practice, most people just grapple gamely with the obstacle course and the guards don't interfere. The newer buses are low enough to allow parents to wheel prams on board, and even have special safety belts to secure them.

Entertainment

Attractions

From a child's-eye view, **La Rambla** is half theatre and half petting zoo; the animal stalls, Boqueria market, entertainers and caricature

Giant mammoth at Parc de la Ciutadella.

artists can easily fill an afternoon. At the bottom end, the Maremàgnum centre attracts families with ice-creams, a summer funfair and sea views. The pedestrianised streets and squares of the Barri Gòtic and the Born are especially kid-friendly areas, as is the **Poble Espanyol** (*see p121*), in the green hills of Montjuïc. The nearby music and light show of the **Magic Fountain** makes for a good evening activity.

Many museums run children's activities for the Estiu als Museus summer programme from June to September, but there's also an ever-increasing spectrum of year-round children's options. Those aimed at younger kids will be more accessible to non-Catalan-speakers. The **CaixaForum** (*see p117*) runs 'Playing With Art', for children aged three and over, every Saturday and Sunday (11am-2pm, 4-8pm). **MACBA** (*see p101*) has various free Sunday morning workshops for children up to 14, and the **Museu d'Història de Catalunya** (*see p113*) runs tours for three- to eight-year-olds at noon on Saturdays. A must-see for junior footie fiends is the **Museu del FC Barcelona** (*see* *p134*), where the guided tour includes a walk from the dressing rooms through the tunnel, a few steps on the pitch and a spell on the bench.

L'Aquàrium

Moll d'Espanya, Port Vell (93 221 74 74/www. aquariumbcn.com). Metro Barceloneta or Drassanes. **Open** *Oct-May* 9.30am-9pm Mon-Fri; 9.30am-9.30pm Sat, Sun. *June, Sept* 9.30am-9.30pm daily. *July, Aug* 9.30am-11pm daily. **Admission** €13.50; €9.25 concessions; free under-4s. **Credit** AmEx, DC, MC, V. **Map** p342 D7.

The main draw here is the Oceanari, a giant shark-infested tank traversed via a glass tunnel. Many of the larger tanks are surrounded by benches for lingering observation; smaller animals, such as starfish and the newly expanded collection of sea horses, are at kids'-eye level. Upstairs is devoted to children: for pre-schoolers, Explora! has 50 knobs-and-whistles style activities such as turning a crank to see how ducks' feet move underwater, climbing inside a deep-sea diver's suit or crawling through a tube wave. Older children prefer Planet Aqua, a stunning, split-level circular space with Humboldt penguins, a walk inside a model sperm whale or a petting tank of skates and eagle rays.

CosmoCaixa

C/Teodor Roviralta 47-51 (93 212 60 50/www. fundacio.lacaixa.es). Bus 60/FGC Avda Tibidabo, then Tramvia Blau (see p140*).* **Open** 10am-8pm Tue-Sun. **Admission** €3; €2 concessions; free under-3s. *Planetarium* €2; €1.50 concessions; free under-3s. **Credit** AmEx, DC, MC, V.

It's a bit of a schlep from the centre of town, but you could easily spend a day at the lavishly revamped Science Museum. Two highlights: the gargantuan geological wall of Iberian rocks, and the Flooded Forest, the world's first living, breathing Amazonian rainforest inside a museum. Attractions designed specifically for kids include the Bubble Planetarium, the touchy-feely Toca Toca! space for exploring natural phenomena such as giant snails or scorpions, and the candy-bright, Javier Mariscal-designed spaces of Clik (for three- to six-year-olds) and Flash (for seven- to nine-year-olds), where supervisors guide hands-on exploration of how boats float, how to mix colours or how to walk on the moon.

Museu de Cera

Ptge de la Banca 7, Barri Gòtic (93 317 26 49/www. museocerabcn.com). Metro Drassanes. **Open** *July-Sept* 10am-10pm daily. *Oct-May* 10am-1.30pm, 4-7.30pm Mon-Fri; 11am-2pm, 4.30-8.30pm Sat, Sun. **Admission** €6.65; €3.75 children; free under-5s. **No credit cards. Map** p345 A4.

More a giggle than an educational visit, this wax museum belongs to the so-bad-it's-good school of entertainment. Expect the Playstation generation to be underwhelmed by clumsy renderings of Gaudí and Princess Diana jumbled in with Frankenstein, squatting Neanderthals and ET (mysteriously perched on top of the Millennium Falcon). Recover with a drink at the museum's enchanted-forest-cum-café.

Museu de la Màgia

C/Oli 6, Born (93 319 73 93/www.elreidelamagia. com). Metro Jaume I. **Open** 6-8pm Thur. *Show* 6pm Sat; noon Sun. Closed Aug. **Admission** €7; free Thur. **No credit cards. Map** p345 B3.

This small collector's gallery of 19th- and 20th-century tricks and posters from the magic shop El Rei de la Màgia will enchant any budding Paul Daniels out there. To see some live sleight of hand, book for the shows on Saturday or Sunday; places are limited. The show's not in English, but it's fairly accessible regardless.

Museu de la Xocolata

C/Comerç 36, Born (93 268 78 78/www.museudela xocolata.com). Metro Arc de Triomf or Jaume I. **Open** 10am-7pm Mon, Wed-Sat; 10am-3pm Sun. **Admission** €3.80; €3.20 concessions; free under-7s. **Credit** MC, V. **Map** p345 C3.

This delicious collection of chocolate sculptures includes characters from *Finding Nemo, Chicken Run* and *Ben-Hur,* along with painstaking models of Gaudí's buildings that take all the work out of tourism. Audio-visual shows and touch-screen computers help kids through the otherwise rather dry history of the cocoa bean; several children's weekend workshops are available if you reserve in advance and include making a chocolate figurine, cooking desserts, or printing T-shirts.

Tibidabo funfair

Plaça del Tibidabo, Tibidabo (93 211 79 42). FGC Avda Tibidabo. **Open** *Nov-mid Dec, mid Jan-Feb* noon-6pm Sat, Sun. *Mar, Apr* noon-7pm Sat, Sun. *May, June* noon-8pm Sat, Sun. *July* noon-8pm Wed-Fri; noon-11pm Sat; noon-10pm Sun. *Aug* noon-10pm Mon-Thur; noon-11pm Fri-Sun. *1st 2wks Sept* noon-8pm Wed-Fri; noon-9pm Sat, Sun. *2nd 2wks Sept* noon-9pm Sat, Sun. *Oct* noon-7pm Sat, Sun. Closed mid Dec-mid Jan. **Admission** *Seven rides* €11. *Unlimited rides* €22; €16 concessions; €9 children under 1m20cm tall; free children under 90cm tall. **Credit** MC, V.

Dating from 1889, this charming, mountain-top fairground has more than 30 rides, from bumper cars and rollercoasters to the wonderful Aeromàgic – a stunning mountain ride on a train suspended from a rail – and the 1928 Avió, the world's first popular flight simulator. Few are very hair-raising by today's standards, but more state-of-the-art attractions are being added, such as a multimedia 'experience' that lets children become part of a cartoon. Don't miss the collection of antique mechanical puppets and contraptions at the Museu d'Autòmates or the hourly puppet shows at the Marionetàrium (from 1pm).

Zoo de Barcelona

Parc de la Ciutadella, Born (93 225 67 80/www.zoo barcelona.com). Metro Barceloneta or Ciutadella-Vila Olímpica. **Open** *Nov-Feb* 10am-5pm daily. *Mar, Oct* 10am-6pm daily. *Apr, Sept* 10am-7pm daily. *May-Aug* 9.30am-7.30pm daily. **Admission** €12.50; €8.20 3-12s. **Credit** MC, V. **Map** p343 E6.

Tibidabo funfair. *See p226.*

Now that Snowflake the albino gorilla has gone to the swinging tyre in the sky, the zoo is a notably emptier place despite the new multimedia gorilla museum. Fortunately, kids still love old favourites like the dolphins, sea lions, elephants, monkeys and hippos, although there's barely enough room to swing a bobcat in some of the enclosures. Child-friendly features include a farmyard petting zoo, pony rides, mini-train and plenty of restaurants, picnic areas and playgrounds. If all that walking is too much for tiny legs, you can rent electric cars from the C/Wellington entrance.

Festivals

Barcelona specialises in noisy, charming festivals that take all the work out of child entertainment. Look out for the local *festes majors* of each district, especially **La Mercè** (*see p222*), the biggest and baddest of them all. Older kids will enjoy the late-night pyromania of the **Sant Joan** summer solstice festival (*see p220*) and music festivals such as **Primavera Sound** (*see p219*), while younger ones will go for the carnival parades of **Carnestoltes** (*see p224*) or gathering sweeties from the streets at the **Festes de Sant Medir de Gràcia** (*see p217*). Christmas traditions are particularly child-centred, with racks of pooping *caganers* and shitting logs at the **Santa Llúcia market** (*see p224*). The Three Kings' procession (*see p224*) on 5 January is also a guaranteed hit.

Film & theatre

English-language children's theatre is rare in Barcelona, with the exception of the Christmas pantomime; check *Metropolitan* magazine for details. To catch a film in English, the best bet for undubbed films is the huge **Yelmo Icària Cineplex** (*see p231*) for mainstream blockbusters and jumbo buckets of popcorn, while the **Filmoteca** (*see p232*) shows original-language children's films on Sundays at 5pm. On a rainy day, a good but pricey standby can be the **IMAX Port Vell** (*see p232*), although films are only shown in Spanish and Catalan, and tend to be rather dreary nature or sport documentaries and such like.

Parks & playgrounds

The star spot is the leafy **Parc de la Ciutadella**, where the shady gardens, giant mammoth, playgrounds, picnic area, rowing boats and zoo make for a relaxing day out. Gaudí's wonderfully quirky **Park Güell** makes up for its lack of grass with bright gingerbread houses, winding coloured benches and stalactite caves. Even higher above the city, the **Parc de la Creueta del Coll** has a large playground, ping pong tables, a picnic area and great views, and the large artificial lake is filled up in the summertime to act as an outdoor public swimming pool. The delightful **Parc del Laberint** has hidden benches and elfin tables, picnic areas and a deceptively difficult maze, while the **Jardins de la Tamarita** form a tranquil dog-free enclave of swings and slides hidden away next to the stop for the Tramvia Blau. On the **Plaça Vicenç Martorell** in the Raval and the **Plaça de la Revolució** in Gràcia, you'll find pint-sized playgrounds situated on (almost) traffic-free squares close to adult-friendly café terraces.

Parc del Castell de l'Oreneta.

Parc del Castell de l'Oreneta

Camí de Can Caralleu & Ptge Blada, Zona Alta (93 413 24 80/www.bcn.es/parcsijardins). By car Ronda de Dalt exit 9/by bus 22, 34, 64, 66, 75. **Open** (daily) *May-Aug* 10am-9pm. *Apr, Sept* 10am-8pm. *Mar, Oct* 10am-7pm. *Nov-Feb* 10am-6pm.

The castle (*castell*) may be long gone, but the old grounds remain a wonderful place to roam through forest glades and flowery meadows. There are two signposted walks with wonderful views, plus picnic areas, supervised pony rides for 3- to 12-year-olds on Saturdays and Sundays (10.30am-2pm, €5), ping pong tables and various adventure playgrounds. On Sundays, hop aboard one of 20 miniature trains (11am-2pm, €1.20).

Out of town

As well as the water parks mentioned below, Catalonia has four others: **Aqua Brava** (in Roses), **Aquadiver** (Platja d'Aro), **Water World** (Lloret de Mar) along the Costa Brava and **Marineland**, in Palafolls. For the endlessly popular **Port Aventura** theme park, *see p291.*

Catalunya en Miniatura

Can Balasch de Baix, Torrelles de Llobregat, Outer Limits (93 689 09 60/www.catalunyaenminiatura. com). By car A2 south to Sant Vicens dels Horts, then left to Torrelles de Llobregat (5km/3 miles)/by bus Soler i Sauret (information 93 632 51 33) from Travessera de les Corts. **Open** *Mar-Sept* 10am-7pm daily. *Oct-Feb* 10am-6pm Tue-Sun. **Admission** €9.50; €6.50 4-12s; free under-4s. **Credit** MC, V.

Make like Gulliver as you stroll around tiny renderings of 170 of Catalonia's most emblematic buildings and sights. Highlights include a miniature Montserrat, Girona cathedral and everything Gaudi

ever laid a finger on, although it's hard to figure out what the not-especially-exciting train station at Girona is doing here. For the kiddies, an appropriately munchkin-sized train circles part of the complex, and clowns perform at 1pm on Sundays in the amphitheatre.

Illa de Fantasia

Finca Mas Brassó, Vilassar de Dalt (93 751 45 53/ www.illafantasia.com). By car NII north to Premià de Mar, then left (24km/15 miles). **Open** *Mid June-Aug* 10am-7pm daily. Closed Sept-mid June. **Admission** €12; €9 2-10s; free under-2s. **Credit** AmEx, DC, MC, V.

Port Aventura on a budget, this water park has 22 attractions such as foam slides, kamikaze rides and rubber dinghy chutes, along with different pools, a restaurant, a disco, a supermarket and a range of activities that include salsa and aerobics classes. There's a picnic/barbecue area in a pine grove; bring your own food. The atmosphere is Spanish rather than touristy.

Parc de les Aus

Ctra de Cabrils, Vilassar de Mar, Outer Limits (93 750 17 65/www.elparcdelesaus.com). By car (24km/ 15 miles) A2 north to Vilassar de Mar, then left to park (1km)/by train RENFE from Sants or Plaça Catalunya to Vilassar de Mar, then taxi. **Open** 10am-sunset Tue-Sun. **Admission** €10.50; €7.50 3-12s; free under-3s. **Credit** AmEx, DC, MC, V.

Over 300 species of local and exotic birds live in this colourful park and nature reserve. For the younger children, there is a miniature train and trampolines, as well as a petting zoo, pony rides and maybe even a cuddle with the park chimps, Tico and Julio.

Eating & drinking

It's rare to find a children's menu in Barcelona, but many restaurants will provide smaller portions on request. That said, there's little need to do so when children and tapas were so clearly made for each other. Remember that most restaurants don't serve lunch before 1.30pm or dinner before 9pm. If you're desperate for a snack, there are plenty of options: **Bar Mendizábal** is good for fresh milkshakes and fruit juices, and there's all-day pizza at **Al Passatore** in the Born (Pla del Palau 8, 93 319 78 51). For kicking back and relaxing in the sun (near a playground), try the outdoor terraces at **Bar Kasparo** or **Iposa** in the Raval, **L'Hivernacle** in the Ciutadella park or **Bar Colombo** at the port.

Museum cafés are often child-friendly spots, and you don't always have to buy a ticket for the museum itself to enjoy them. **La Miranda del Museu**, at the Catalan history museum, has fantastic views and plenty of terrace space in which to play. The café of the **Fundació Joan Miró** is an oasis of sustenance on

Montjuïc; the adjacent **El Bosc de les Fades** is a must after a visit to the waxworks museum. For all, *see* **pp172-188**.

Babysitting & childcare

Canguro Gigante

Passeig de Sant Gervasi 20, Sant Gervasi (93 211 69 61). FGC Avda Tibidabo. **Open** 9am-9pm Mon-Fri. **No credit cards.**

A daycare centre for kids aged from one to ten. The starting rate is €4 per hour; meals are available if required. Some English is spoken.

Cinc Serveis

C/Pelai 50, 3° 1ª, Eixample (93 412 56 76/24hr mobile 639 361 111/www.5serveis.com). Metro Catalunya. **Open** 9.30am-1.30pm, 4.30-8.30pm Mon-Fri. **No credit cards.** **Map** p344 A1.

The basic rate after 8pm is €8.40 per hour, plus the cost of the sitter's taxi home. Long-term rates are cheaper and vary according to the age of the child.

Happy Parc

C/Pau Claris 97, Eixample (93 317 86 60/www. happyparc.com). Metro Passeig de Gràcia. **Open** 5-9pm Mon-Fri; 11am-9pm Sat, Sun. **Rates** €3.60/hr; 90¢ each subsequent 15mins. **No credit cards.** **Map** p342 D5.

Ball pools, twister slides and more at this giant indoor fun park and drop-in daycare centre for kids up to 11 (the maximum height is 1m 45cm/4ft 7in.) Birthday parties for groups of ten or more can also be organised here.

Tender Loving Canguros

Information *mobile 647 605 989/www.tlcanguros. com.* **Open** 9am-9pm Mon-Sat. **No credit cards.**

English residents Julie Stephenson and Julia Fossi provide short- and long-term nannies and babysitters for Barcelona and surrounds. All babysitters and nannies speak fluent English and can come to your hotel, apartment or home at short notice to sit one or several children of any age. Prices start at €7 an hour; the agency fee is €15 per session.

Tales from the crib

What to do if little Johnny won't go to sleep at bedtime? A glass of warm milk? A gentle lullaby? Or a blood-curdling horror story of child abduction and flesh-eating monsters? Catalan folklore is full of decidedly non-PC *espantanens* ('child frighteners'), designed to make kids behave and – as a side effect – turn them into gibbering emotional wrecks.

El Coco is one of the best known. With shaggy black hair and fluorescent eyes, El Coco preys on children who don't go to bed when they're told to. Only leaving his hidey-hole in the dead of night, he lingers in the shadowy corners of children's bedrooms and taunts them with a scary grunting noise, before grabbing them and carrying them home to eat raw. Sadly, it can be just as dangerous to go to sleep, at least when **La Pesanta** is around. In the form of a huge black dog with human hands, she jumps on to the chest of those who sleep on their backs; her great weight gives them terrible nightmares before suffocating them to death.

Warning of 'stranger danger' is **L'Home del Sac** (the 'bag man'), a sinister old man dressed in old brown rags with shaggy hair and a giant sack on his back. Wandering the streets of Barcelona, he lures over any children he sees out alone with sweets and toys and then tosses them in his sack. Back in his castle, he boils down the children's juicy flesh to produce a fine oil, which he uses to grease the train tracks.

Then there's the **Caçamentides** ('liar hunter'), a man as tall and wide as the towers of the cathedral and with fingers as sharp as claws, which he uses to snatch up children who tell lies. He knows who they are because when a lie comes out of a child's mouth, it turns into an invisible bird that flies away after leaving a dark stain on their teeth. The birds fly to the Caçamentides and tell him where the child is to be found. Then he goes to the beach to barbecue his hostages and eat them seven by seven.

Much feared by little girls who live in Bruc, Esparreguera and Piera is the **Cardapeçols**, a strange and foul-tempered old woman who's obsessed with well-combed hair. She visits little girls with long, tangled locks and goes at them with thistle heads and, in especially bad cases, the sharp iron spikes used to card sheep wool. She combs until she's pulled all the hair out, and the offender is left bleeding and bald.

Putting on the frighteners out in La Vall de Ribes de Freser is **Jan del Gel**, a boy made of solid ice, and so cold-hearted that children freeze just by looking at him. He throws the human popsicle on his back and carries it to his ice cave where he makes it into a hearty soup. Another winter sprite is **La Tinyosa**, who appears as a mass of foggy cloud, descending over any lost children wandering her territory of the Montserrat mountains and the plains of Vic, and carrying them away.

Film

Classic movies, Hollywood blockbusters and cinema under the stars.

The **Renoir-Floridablanca** majors in off-beat independent cinema. *See p231.*

Pedro Almodóvar is a fan. Peter Greenaway is a fan. Alan Parker is a fan. Half the commercials directors in Europe are fans. As a film location, Barcelona has it all: sun, sea, seedy streets, skyscrapers and administrative acquiescence.

It also has the advantage of being able to double up as all sorts of other locations. As Almodóvar said after shooting *All About My Mother*, 'I have now discovered that Barcelona is also Marseille, Havana and Naples.' But as well as standing in for specific locations, it can look like none at all: Catalan production company Filmax has discovered that locations in Catalonia can play unnamed Everytowns; the company produces a constant stream of low- and mid-budget, English-language horror flicks here. Most make only brief appearances at the box office here, but have an extended afterlife at video stores around the world.

As Spain's most hallowed living film-maker, both at home and abroad, Almodóvar's position remains – for the moment – unassailable. There are signs, though, that he may soon have to hand over his crown to a younger generation of film-makers currently biting at his heels. Notable among them are Fernando León de Aranoa, whose *Mondays in the Sun* was chosen as Spain's 2003 Oscar candidate for Best Foreign Film ahead of Almodóvar's *Talk to Her*; a year later Alejandro Amenábar's *The Sea Inside* was picked over *Bad Education*. Both León de Aranoa and Amenábar cast as their lead actor Javier Bardem; currently Spain's most compelling leading man, he's also a far better actor, either in Spanish or in English, than any of the recent exports to Hollywood, Antonio Banderas included.

Other Spanish film-makers producing distinctive films include Alex de la Iglesia: the leering love-child of Terry Gilliam and the Coen brothers, he manically subverts genre after genre with irreverent glee. Julio Medem broke his chain of ethereal, magical-realist movies like *Cows*, *Earth* and *Sex and Lucía* to make *Basque Ball*, a polemical documentary featuring interviews with people on all sides of the Basque nationalist dispute. The movies of Isabel Coixet owe more to American independents than to Spanish cinema. Marc Recha, meanwhile, makes painfully slow, hyper-realist films; his second feature, *Pau and his Brother*, was shown in competition in Cannes in 2001, but bombed at the box office.

Apart from Hollywood blockbusters, the big box office favourite here is screwball comedy, which accounts for a high proportion of Spanish film-making. Social and historical drama also figure strongly, as Spanish film-makers continue to exorcise the ghost of Franco and the Civil War. In 2003 box office records were broken by a cinematic version of a cartoon strip, *La Gran Aventura de Mortadelo y Filemón*, which beat *Lord of the Rings* and *Finding Nemo* to top the overall film charts. In 2004, though, things got back to normal, and *The Sea Inside* was the only non-American film to scrape into the top ten.

SEEING FILMS

There's a reasonably wide choice of subtitled cinema in Barcelona, with the inevitable preponderance of Hollywood pap. Release dates vary widely: blockbusters are usually released more or less simultaneously across Europe, while smaller, independent productions can sometimes take up to three years to hit cinemas, long after they are available on DVD. Several of the charming, idiosyncratic local cinemas that used to screen subtitled films have either closed or switched to dubbed films during the last few years, as the multiscreens have grabbed audience share.

Newspapers carry full details of all cinema screenings, as does the weekly *Guía del Ocio*. Subtitled films are marked VO or VOSE (for '*versió original subtitulado en espanyol*'). Some of the larger cinemas open at 11am, though most have their first screenings around 4pm. Early evening showings start between 7.30pm and 8.30pm; later screenings begin between 10.15pm and 10.45pm. Weekend evenings can be very crowded, especially for recent releases, so turn up early. On Fridays and Saturdays, many cinemas have a late-night session starting around 1am. All cinemas have a cheap night: usually Monday, occasionally Wednesday. You can buy tickets for an increasing number of cinemas online at www.cinentradas.com or via **Servi-Caixa** (*see p214*).

Original-language cinemas

Maldà
C/Pi 5, Barri Gòtic (93 317 85 29). Metro Liceu. **Tickets** call for details. **Credit** call for details. **Map** p344 B2.
Barcelona lost a well-loved institution when the Maldà was closed down by safety officials. The cinema, which had screened a weekly double-bill of recent, thematically linked independent films, was scheduled to reopen in early 2005, complete with spanking new fire exits and scrubbed-up seating.

Méliès Cinemes
C/Villarroel 102, Eixample (93 451 00 51). Metro Urgell. **Tickets** *Mon* €2.70. *Tue-Sun* €4. **No credit cards. Map** p342 C5.
More accessible than art-house but more eclectic than a commercial cinema, the Méliès is run by and for film lovers. Programming is an eccentric combination that takes in classic movies, fairly recent contemporary works and whatever else the owner feels like screening. There are up to eight films per week, with regular seasons organised by director, star or theme.

Renoir-Floridablanca
C/Floridablanca 135, Eixample (info 93 228 93 93/ tickets 902 88 89 02/www.cinesrenoir.es). Metro Sant Antoni. **Tickets** *Mon* €4. *Tue-Sun* €5.80; €4 concessions, & late show Fri & Sat. **Credit** MC, V. **Map** p342 C5.
The closest first-run original-version cinema to the centre of town, this four-screen branch of the Renoir chain screens up to eight independent, off-beat American, British and Spanish films per day, though note that programming tends towards the worthy rather than the exciting.
Other locations: Renoir-Les Corts *C/Eugeni d'Ors 12, Les Corts (info 93 490 55 10/tickets 902 88 89 02).*

Verdi
C/Verdi 32, Gràcia (93 238 79 90/www.cines-verdi. com). **Tickets** *Mon* €4. *Tue-Fri* €5.80; €4 1st screening daily. *Sat, Sun* €6. **No credit cards. Map** p338 D3.
A long-standing champion of foreign cinema, the original five-screen Verdi, plus its four-screen annexe Verdi Park on the next street over, offer a diverse programme of interesting, accessible cinema from around the world, concentrating on Asia and Europe, as well as some Spanish repertoire. At peak times, chaos reigns; arrive early and make sure you don't mistake the line to enter for the ticket queue.
Other locations: Verdi Park *C/Torrijos 49, Gràcia (93 238 79 90).*

Yelmo Icària Cineplex
C/Salvador Espriu 61, Vila Olímpica (info 93 221 75 85/tickets 902 22 09 22/www.yelmocineplex.es). Metro Ciutadella-Vila Olímpica. **Tickets** *Mon* €4.50. *Tue-Sun* €6; €4.50 before 3pm & concessions. **No credit cards. Map** p343 F7.

Arts & Entertainment

Stars above the silver screen

The schlock horror of holiday blockbusters; the cruelly glacial air-conditioning; the sense that balmy evenings are passing you by... The lot of the cinema-goer in summer is not a happy one. Thank goodness, then, for Barcelona's crop of annual outdoor film screenings, a crop that increases in size every year.

Every Thursday over the summer, **Cine Sin Techo** (93 207 53 69, www.cinesintecho.org) lights up the ancient walls of the Plaza Isidre Nonell with classics of independent and mainstream cinema, shown in their original language with Spanish subtitles. A makeshift bar and seating for 400 are arranged; admission is free. On Wednesdays and Fridays, meanwhile, the action moves up the hill to the **Sala Montjuïc** (www.sala montjuic.com), for which the sombre Montjuïc castle becomes the backdrop (and indeed, screen) for picnicking film-goers and jazz fans. Bring your own beer and a blanket and enjoy a smattering of live music and a smörgåsbord of world cinema, with a couple of classics thrown in for good measure. A special free bus service runs before and after the film from metro Espanya.

Also on Montjuïc, the description-defying fake Spanish village of **Poble Espanyol** (93 508 63 00, www.poble-espanyol.com; see p121) has also run decent open-air cinema seasons, though 2005 still hangs in the balance: check the website. Nearby, a more stable and utterly unique run of movies takes place at the former Olympic pools of **Piscina Bernat Picornell** (see p276). Throughout July and August, there are late-night sessions where you can work on your breaststroke while genning up on your Bergman. Filmic hipsters, meanwhile, can head to supercool bar-restaurant **Oven** (C/Ramon Turró 126, Poblenou, 93 221 06 02) of a Wednesday, to catch one of its themed movie series. In 2004 this meant Peter Greenaway during July and Peter Sellers in August.

Keep an eye out, too, for occasional one-off festivals throughout the summer. One that looks set to become a regular August fixture is **Gandules** at the CCCB (C/Montalegre 5, Raval, 93 306 41 00, www.cccb.org). Gandules means 'idlers', which tells you all you need to know about the atmosphere at this season of animated shorts. The films are shown outdoors on the deckchair-strewn patio of the city's most innovative cultural space, and topped and tailed with DJ sessions.

In a sterile mall by the Olympic port, this 15-screen multiplex is low on atmosphere but high on choice. Films are mostly mainstream Americana, with the odd Spanish or European movie. Weekends are seat-specific, so queues tend to be slow-moving; it's worth booking your seat on the internet before you go.

Specialist cinemas

An increasing number of bars are showing films. **Planeta Rai** (C/Carders 12, pral, 93 268 13 21, www.pangea.org/rai) runs mainly classic movies twice a week.

Cine Ambigú

Sala Apolo, C/Nou de la Rambla 113 (93 441 40 01/www.retinas.org). Metro Paral·lel. **Shows** 8.30pm, 10.30pm Tue. Closed June-Sept. **Tickets** €4-€6 (incl 1 drink). **No credit cards. Map** p342 C6.

This charming '30s music hall, reminiscent of a louche, candlelit cabaret, hosts weekly screenings of accessible but alternative art-house cinema from around Europe, usually on Tuesdays. Seating is somewhat monastic, but you can dull the discomfort with alcohol, and smoking of all types is permitted. The website provides details of forthcoming shows.

Filmoteca de la Generalitat de Catalunya

Cinema Aquitania, Avda Sarrià 31-33, Eixample (93 410 75 90/www.cultura.gencat.net/filmo). Metro Hospital Clínic. Closed Aug. **Tickets** €2.70; €2 concessions; €33 20 films; €66 50 films. **Credit** (block tickets only) AmEx, MC, V. **Map** p338 C3.

Funded by the Catalan government, the Filmoteca is a little dry for some tastes, offering comprehensive seasons of cinema's more recondite auteurs, alongside better-known classics, plus screenings each spring of all films nominated in the Goya awards. Overlapping cycles last two or three weeks, with each film screened at least twice at different times. Books of 20 and 100 tickets bring down the price per film to a negligible amount. The 'Filmo' also runs a library of film-related books, videos and magazines at Portal Santa Madrona 6-8, just off La Rambla.

IMAX Port Vell

Moll d'Espanya, Port Vell (93 225 11 11/www.imax portvell.com). Metro Barceloneta or Drassanes. **Tickets** €7-€10. **Credit** MC, V. **Map** p342 D7.

A squat white hulk in the middle of the marina, the IMAX has yet to persuade many that it's anything more than a gimmick. Its predictable programming,

Sala Montjuïc.

recognisable from similar enterprises the world over, covers fish, birds, ghosts and adventure sports, possibly in 3D. (If it's fish in 3D you want, the Aquarium next door is excellent; *see p226*.)

VOID/Sala Zelig

C/Ferlandina 51, Raval (93 443 42 03/www.void-bcn. com). Metro Sant Antoni or Universitat. **Shows** 9pm Wed-Sun. **Tickets** (incl 1 drink) €3. **Credit** AmEx, MC, V. **Map** p342 C5.

VOID offers an excellent art-house video and DVD rental service, and also has a small screening room on the premises. From Wednesday to Saturday, the programme consists of vaguely avant-garde classics; on Sunday, democracy rules, and the audience votes on what to watch.

Festivals

There are an increasing number of film festivals in Barcelona. Though none is as big or brash as **Sitges** (*see below*), they all show interesting work unlikely to feature elsewhere. New events pop up every year, but regular festivals include the following: **Asian** (April/May), **Jewish** (May), **Women's** (June),

Animation (June), **Gay and Lesbian** (July and October), **Open-Air Shorts** (September), **Documentaries** (October), **Human Rights** (October), **African** (November) and **Alternative Film** (November). OVNI, a well-established alternative video festival, takes place every 18 months, in early spring and late autumn; the next is scheduled for spring 2006.

Festival Internacional de Cinema de Catalunya, Sitges

93 894 99 90/www.cinemasitges.com. **Advance tickets** available from Tel-entrada. **Date** Dec.

After a decade or so flirting with the mainstream, Sitges has realised it just can't compete with Venice or even San Sebastián, and has returned to what it does best: chills 'n' thrills beside the seaside. The festival dropped its token mainstream section in 2004, and now exclusively screens gore, horror and sci-fi. It attracts strong contributions from Japan and Korea, current world leaders of ground-breaking genre movies, and there are various retrospectives and thematic cycles to add to the fun. A special late-night train service returns to Barcelona after the final screening of the evening.

Galleries

Where art is a serious, if not altogether lucrative, business.

Coldcreation. *See p236.*

For all its past limitations and insecurities, the Barcelona art world proves an irresistible attraction for the creative at heart. Drawn by the spirit of artistic liberalism championed by the city's freethinking figureheads, among them Dalí, Miró and Picasso, many artists have chosen Barcelona as their base.

For years institutions were reluctant to tap into the creative source on their doorsteps. The early 20th-century avant-garde, which enjoyed a short-lived but vital spell here, persisted as the artistic trademark while local innovators remained low-key. The '50s saw the emergence of abstract painting, and conceptualism made a mark in the '70s, but it wasn't until the '80s and '90s that the spiritual and economic revival of the city forced a redefinition of its cultural identity. Encouraged by governmental and public interest, the art world blossomed, confidence bolstered by Catalan artists such as Antoni Tàpies and Susana Solano already moving freely on the international scene.

Commercial galleries struggle with a lazy local collecting tradition. But creativity is born of trauma, and the various cultural and economic opportunities and frictions brought by globalised culture have had a beneficial impact on the arts. Institutions such as the CaixaForum's Mediateca (*see p117*) now offer encouragement; and in collaboration with the work of **Metrònom** (*see p105*) and artist associations such as **Hangar** (*see p237*) on the fringe scene, the art world is creating an arena in which artists can act and interact.

Loop, a video art fair organised by the gallery association Art Barcelona (Rambla de Catalunya 50, pral 1ª, www.loop.artbarcelona. es), and its wider circuit **Off Loop**, was founded to international applause in November 2003 and takes place in galleries around the city. Aiming at raising awareness of video both as an art form and as a commercial product, the fair proposes to be an annual event.

Gallery listings appear in the weekly *Guía del Ocio*, sold in most kiosks; *Curator*, which comes out every three months, has a glossier version. For younger galleries, particularly in the Raval area, **FAD** (Convent dels Àngels, Plaça dels Àngels 5-6, www.fad.es) has an information point with a plethora of publicity materials.

Arts & Entertainment

Commercial galleries

Barri Gòtic

In addition to the galleries listed below, **Artur Ramon** deals in historic art and objects from several different spaces on the same street (C/Palla 10, 23 & 25, 93 302 59 70).

Antonio de Barnola

C/Palau 4 (93 412 22 14). Metro Jaume I or Liceu. **Open** 5-9pm Tue-Fri; noon-2pm, 5-9pm Sat. Closed Aug. **No credit cards. Map** p345 A4.
Works by Spanish contemporary artists are shown in this handsome space, with a particular emphasis on architectural themes. Catalan installation artist Margarita Andreu and the acclaimed Argentine photographer Humberto Rivas are regulars. The photographer Pablo Genovés shows in 2005.

Galeria Loft

C/Ample 5 (93 301 11 12). Metro Jaume I. **Open** 11am-2pm, 5-8.30pm Tue-Sat. Closed Aug. **Credit** AmEx, MC, V. **Map** p345 B3.
Bertrand Cheuvreux recently opened this delightful branch of the Parisian gallery, dedicated to the Chinese avant-garde. Shows by talented contemporaries such as Yan Ley and Guo Wei make their impact, their dark compositions contrasting with the gentle humour of the kitsch decor. The basement (Galeria DART) shows French contemporary works. **Other locations: Galeria OFF Ample** Ptge de la Pau 10, Almacén 2 (no phone).

Sala Parés

C/Petritxol 5 (93 318 70 08/www.salapares.com). Metro Liceu. **Open** *Oct-May* 10.30am-2pm, 4.30-8.30pm Mon-Sat; 11.30am-2pm Sun. *June-Sept* 10.30am-2pm, 4.30-8.30pm Mon-Sat. Closed 3wks Aug. **Credit** AmEx, MC, V. **Map** p344 A2.
The delicious scent of wood polish and oil paint wafts through the elegant Sala Parés, which, since 1840, has specialised in figurative and historical painting. It was here that Picasso had his first one-man show a century ago; nowadays the gallery plays host to the Fundació Banco Sabadell's annual young painter award, displayed in September. The nearby Galeria Trama (C/Petritxol 8, 93 317 48 77, www.galeriatrama.com) offers contemporary work; Barcelona-based Toni Catany and the digital imagery of internationals Aziz + Cucher are keyed in for spring 2005.

Raval

Additionally, the **Nogueras Blanchard Gallery** (Xuclà 7, 93 224 71 60, www.noguerasblanchard.com) plays host to a promising line-up of dynamic young locals and internationals.

Ego Gallery

C/Doctor Dou 11 (93 302 36 98/www.egogallery.com). Metro Catalunya. **Open** 11am-1.30pm, 5-8.30pm Tue-Sat. **Credit** MC, V. **Map** p344 A2.

This small, simple space is put to its best use with unpretentious shows by young talents such as pop photographer Victòria Campillo. The landscapes of Dik Bouwhuis and crochet sculpture of Patricia Waller sew up 2005.

Galeria dels Àngels

C/Àngels 16 (93 412 54 54/www.galeriadelsangels.com). Metro Catalunya. **Open** noon-2pm, 5-8.30pm Tue-Sat. Closed Aug. **No credit cards. Map** p344 A2.
Collector Emilio Álvarez has widened his tastes beyond painting to include innovative shows in sculpture, contemporary photography and video art. His exhibitions feature the witty object-installations of Jaume Pitarch, the abstract painting of Miquel Mont and the landscape photography of Mayte Vieta.

Ras Gallery

C/Doctor Dou 10 (93 412 71 99/www.actar.es). Metro Catalunya. **Open** 11am-9pm Tue-Sat. **Credit** AmEx, MC, V. **Map** p344 A2.
Run by a respected publishing house, Ras has a small but savvy arts bookshop fronting a gallery with fine shows often related to the contents of new publications. Hi-tech exhibitions of original architectural drawings, photos and maquettes by contemporary masters pay compliment to Actar's thematic and historical volumes.

Born

Galeria Maeght

C/Montcada 25 (93 310 42 45/www.maeght.com). Metro Jaume I. **Open** 10am-2pm, 4-7pm Tue-Sat. **Credit** AmEx, DC, MC, V. **Map** p345 C3.
Paris-based Maeght opened this handsome space in the 1970s, occupying a Renaissance palace with a lovely courtyard and staircase. Spanish figureheads – Tàpies, Arroyo, Palazuelo – are presented alongside other European painters and sculptors. Prestige and quality combine, though the Maeght still struggles for relevance on the crowded Barcelona scene.

Iguapop Gallery

C/Comerç 15 (93 310 07 35/www.iguapop.net). Metro Jaume I. **Open** 11am-2.30pm Tue-Sat; 5-9pm Mon-Sat. **Credit** AmEx, DC, MC, V. **Map** p345 C3.
After ten years in concert promotion, Iguapop has nowadays branched out into art and streetwear, and given each equal space in this showroom. The gallery shows the latest trends in photography, graffiti and graphic design by hip young locals and international names.

Eixample

In addition to those below, the rough and ready **ADN Galeria** (Enric Granados 49, 93 451 00 64, www.adngaleria.com) and the Barcelona branch of the prestigious Portuguese gallery **Inter-Atrium** (C/Consell de Cent 295, 93 511 48 77, www.interatrium.com) are worth a look.

Coldcreation

C/Aragó 379 (93 457 97 53/www.coldcreation.com).
Metro Girona. **Open** 4-9pm Tue-Sat. Closed 2wks
Aug. **No credit cards. Map** p339 E4.
This sophisticated space promotes the fusion of art
and science, mathematics and psychology in sharp
shows incorporating installation, video/data art, performance and sound art. Josep Bofill, Luis López,
Thomas Charveriat and actor Jordi Mollà feature
among the extensive list of contributors.

Galeria Carles Taché

*C/Consell de Cent 290 (93 487 88 36/www.carles
tache.com). Metro Passeig de Gràcia.* **Open** *Mid
Sept-June* 10am-2pm, 4-8.30pm Tue-Sat. Closed
Aug. **No credit cards. Map** p342 D5.
Established Spanish names (Arroyo, Broto,
Campano) are represented, along with internation-
als such as Sean Scully, Lawrence Durrell and Tony
Cragg. Look out for the juicy scrawlings of Frederic
Amat and the deconstructed Disney of Carlos Pazos.

The art of drinking

A Barcelona artist thoughtfully fingers his
empty glass, as a price tag dangles above
his head and a gaunt, acrylic face in a
crooked wooden frame peers apologetically
down at him. Eight or so of these sketchy
characters are for sale, exhibited haphazardly
on opposite walls of bar **El 24** in the Barri
Gòtic (C/Ferran 24, 93 317 08 07). 'People
don't buy art,' laments the painter, 'They
buy bigger, flatter televisions.'

A century ago, and Picasso would have
agreed, at least with the former part: his first
exhibition at Modernista tavern **Els Quatre
Gats** (C/Montsió 3, 93 302 41 40) was a
financial flop, yet no one was prompted to
remove the mosaic of paintings and drawings
that have animated its walls, its menus, and
its constant flow of visitors ever since.

In Barcelona, there's no scarcity of artists –
as the local saying goes, 'Kick the dirt and
ten scuttle out' – and with most commercial
galleries closed to newcomers, it's not easy
to get noticed. Yet while there are bars ready
to follow the Quatre Gats example, there is
a profitable alternative for both artist and
proprietor, and one that upholds the
centuries-old pairing of booze and bohemia.
The city has any number of restaurants
and bars open to artistic proposal, with few
limitations other than practicalities of space
and the proximity of alcohol. They offer
decent facilities (space, light, toilets), a
more relaxed, free-spending environment, and
greater punter turnover than most commercial
galleries. The establishments, meanwhile, get
their walls redecorated for free and (assuming
the artist has a few friends) make some
money on opening night.

Al Limón Negro (C/Escudellers Blancs 3,
Barri Gòtic, mobile 656 376 927) has been
host to regular exhibitions for years, from
audiovisual projections to displays of graffiti.
In the same area, **Leticia** (C/Còdols 21, 93
302 00 74) opts for stills, large prints and

digital photography. Up in Gràcia, **i Què?**
(C/Topazi 8, 93 416 07 33) favours colourful
abstracts that complement the cheerful
bar-room atmosphere; nearby restaurant
Big Sur (C/Verdi 64, 93 415 92 17,
www.bigsurlife.com) proves its cool with large,
confident works. Downtown, the playful **Iposa**
(*pictured*, and *see p178*) adorns its limited
space with small, intriguing collages,
brimming with Ravalian cheek and charm.

For more ambitious visual arts projects,
'cultural associations' – not licensed bars,
but small arts collectives that may sell
alcohol in support of organised cultural
events – offer greater freedom to the artist.
The wonderfully thrown together **Merry Ant**
(*see p179*) and the bohemian den **L'Atelier**
(Rambla del Raval 49, mobile 600 386 049)
are among the most reliable, the latter in
particular offering regular activities and a
wild array of performances.

Galeria Estrany-de la Mota

Ptge Mercader 18 (93 215 70 51/www.estrany delamota.com). FGC Provença. **Open** *Sept-June* 10.30am-1.30pm, 4.30-8.30pm Tue-Sat. *July* 10.30am-1.30pm, 4.30-8.30pm Mon-Fri. Closed Aug. **No credit cards. Map** p338 D4.

This basement space works well for Antoni Estrany's selection of neo-conceptualists, including the photo-montages of Montserrat Soto and the disarmingly simple drawings of Francesc Ruiz. International artists include Douglas Gordon, Jean-Marc Bustamante and Thomas Locher.

Galeria Joan Prats

Rambla Catalunya 54 (93 216 02 84/www.galeria joanprats.com). Metro Passeig de Gràcia. **Open** *Sept-June* 10.30am-1.30pm, 5-8.30pm Tue-Sat. *July* 10.30am-1.30pm, 5-8.30pm Tue-Fri. Closed Aug. **Credit** AmEx, MC, V. **Map** p342 D4.

This elegant gallery was born of the '20s friendship between Joan Prats, son of a fashionable milliner, and Joan Miró. It's still hats off to the shows, with high-profile Eulàlia Valldosera and the quirky Catalan Perejaume regulars, and the lush abstractions of José Maria Sicilia promised for 2005.

Galeria Toni Tàpies

C/Consell de Cent 282 (93 487 64 02/www.toni tapies.com). Metro Passeig de Gràcia. **Open** 10am-2pm, 4-8pm Tue-Fri; 11am-2pm, 5-8.30pm Sat. Closed Aug. **Credit** MC, V. **Map** p339 F4.

Run with verve by the son of the prestigious Catalan painter, this gallery shows Catalan innovators Tere Recarens and Martí Anson, along with established creators Jaume Plensa and Tàpies himself.

ProjecteSD

Ptge Mercader 8 (93 488 13 60). FGC Provença. **Open** 11.30am-8.30pm Tue-Sat. Closed 2wks Aug. **No credit cards. Map** p338 D4.

Silvia Dauder has founded a handsome space on either side of this tranquil Eixample courtyard. Her shows exemplify her passions for new drawing, stylish photography and film; limited-edition artists' texts complement the exhibits. Patricia Dauder's provocative drawings will be here in 2005.

Gràcia & Zona Alta

In addition to those below, **Galeria L'Espai [B]** (C/Torrent de l'Olla 158, 93 217 10 90, www.espaib.com) has an interesting collection of contemporary newcomers.

Galeria Alejandro Sales

C/Julián Romea 16 (93 415 20 54/www.alejandro sales.com). FGC Gràcia. **Open** *Oct-June* 11am-2pm, 5-8.30pm Tue-Sat. *July, Sept* 11am-2pm, 5-8.30pm Tue-Fri. Closed Aug. **No credit cards. Map** p338 D3.

Impeccable shows by blue-chip artists, with a solid Spanish stable. High-profile artists Eduardo Chillida and Eugenio Estrada feature alongside young creators Carla Tarruella and local light Lluís Hortalà, seen in a smaller room called Blackspace.

Galeria H²O

C/Verdi 152 (93 415 18 01/www.h2o.es). Metro Lesseps. **Open** 4-8pm Tue-Fri; 11am-1pm Sat. Closed Aug. **Credit** V. **Map** p339 E2.

This dynamic gallery boasts diverse shows on photographic, design and contemporary art themes. The provocative photography of Christian Maury and the visual poetry of JM Calleja will feature in 2005.

The fringe

Lamentably, a lack of funding has forced some of Barcelona's more active and original artists' groups to disband, while others hang in the balance. The fringe has an inherently organic nature, however, that has ensured its survival in the past. In Poblenou, the spacious **Centre Civic Can Felipa** (C/Pallars 277, 93 266 44 41) hosts regular shows. **Theredoom Galeria** (C/Marina 65-67, 93 221 13 69, www.theredoom. com) and the neighbouring **La Santa Proyectos Culturales**, organiser of the free-flowing art festival BAC! in autumn (address/phone as above, www.lasanta.org), also act as information points for extemporary events.

In the Raval, **Kültur Büro Barcelona** (C/Joaquim Costa 24, 4°, 93 442 06 95, www.kbb.org.es) shows video art, and, in summer, experimental cinema with views from its roof terrace. In late spring **Tallers Oberts** sees artists open their studios in Poblenou and the Old City; for details, try the **FAD** (Convent dels Àngels, Plaça dels Àngels 5-6, www.digi teca.com/tallersoberts). Some studios remain open to visitors all year, though usually only in the afternoons. **Vesartesiempre** (Passeig Bernardí Martorell 22, no phone) is an eyebrow-raising option, while the intriguingly named **___ión** (Ptge Bofarull 7, Sagrera, mobile 659 205 943) incorporates an exhibition area, studios and dance and theatre workshops.

Hangar

Passatge del Marqués de Santa Isabel 40, Poblenou (tel/fax 93 308 40 41/www.hangar.org). Metro Poblenou. **Open** *Information* 9am-2pm Mon-Fri. Closed Aug. **No credit cards**.

Not a commercial gallery but a multi-disciplinary centre, with a number of artists' studios and a showroom exhibiting residents' work (generally not for sale). Run by the Catalan Visual Artists Association, it spearheads an open studio project for Poblenou artists in late November and June.

La Xina A.R.T.

C/Doctor Dou 4 (93 301 67 03/www.laxinaart.org). Metro Catalunya. **Open** 5.30-8.30pm Mon-Fri; 11am-2pm, 5.30-8.30pm Sat. Closed Aug. **Map** p342 A2.

A collective of 14 artists runs this small but essential space near the MACBA as a base for lively exchanges and fresh, inventive exhibitions. Artists include Benxamín Álvarez and Tito Inchaurralde.

Arts & Entertainment

Gay & Lesbian

Out and about.

Only a couple of decades ago, the moral legacy of the Spanish dictatorship confined homosexual behaviour to a handful of underground bars, and the city's gay population lived in fear of abuse on the streets. Nowadays, men with shaved heads and combat fatigues are more likely to be on their way to a leather bar than anything more sinister, and recent legislation introducing same-sex marriages caused hardly a ripple of dissent.

The gay scene is referred to in Spanish as the *ambiente*, but the label is not as useful as it might seem. In Barcelona, anything goes; most gay bars welcome straight drinkers, and vice versa. The lack of segregation means that there isn't a gay ghetto as such. The area bordered by the streets of Diputació and Aragó, Balmes and Villarroel in the Eixample is known as the 'Gaixample', and is where most gay venues are concentrated. Yet even this isn't really a gaybourhood: although it has a buzz at night, the wide streets make it anything but villagey. Most outdoor cruising is done elsewhere: especially on Montjuïc, up from the Plaça Espanya. While this area has undergone major changes of late, with much of the vegetation cut away and oh-so-unflattering floodlights installed, there are still a couple of shadowy corners where it's business as usual.

Pick up a copy of the free gay map or magazines such as *Nois* or *Shanguide* from bars and gay shops. Good websites include www.mensual.com, www.naciongay.com, www.barcelonagay.com and www.guiagay.com.

Cafés & bars

Gaixample

In addition, bars worth checking out include **Dietrich** (C/Consell de Cent 255, 93 451 77 07), **Oui Café** (C/Consell de Cent 247, no phone) and **Escandalus** (C/Villarroel 86, 93 454 44 57). Unless stated, women are mostly welcomed in the bars listed here.

Átame

C/Consell de Cent 257 (93 454 92 73). Metro Universitat. **Open** 6.30pm-2.30am daily. **No credit cards. Map** p342 C5.
This long space is a wee bit tacky, but still a classic. La Moderna is a kitsch drag show on Thursdays; not so *moderna*, but certainly surreal. Four TV screens show an endless cycle of music videos.

Col·lectiu Gai de Barcelona

Ptge Valeri Serra 23 (93 453 41 25/www.colectiugai. org). Metro Urgell. **Open** 7-9pm Mon-Thur; 7pm-1am Fri, Sat. **No credit cards. Map** p342 C5.
The headquarters of this gay association has an easygoing and unpretentious bar, with cheap drinks and few tourists. It's a long, narrow space, where strangers have little choice but to talk to each other.

Crazy's

C/Consell de Cent 245 (no phone). Metro Universitat. **Open** 5pm-3am daily. **No credit cards. Map** p342 C5.
This long bar with silver painted walls and coloured light panels opens (unofficially) at 6am at weekends to serve breakfast for exhausted clubbers, while Carla the drag queen works to boost their spirits.

Fénix

C/Casanova 64 (93 323 66 07). Metro Urgell. **Open** midnight-3am daily. **No credit cards. Map** p342 C5.
With its curlicued mirrors, low lighting and pool table, this is a good place for a quiet early drink. Push past the red curtains to a friendly, unpretentious space with Christmas lights on the walls blinking in time with the fruit machine.

Mi Madre!

C/Consell de Cent 223 (93 454 86 74). Metro Urgell. **Open** 10.30pm-2.30am Thur, Sun; 10.30pm-3am Fri-Sat. **No credit cards. Map** p342 C5.
A new stone-clad bar with snakeskin stools and handbag house, Mi Madre! wouldn't win any design prizes, but is still a good option when the other bars are rammed. Happy hour runs 10.30pm-12.30am.

Punto BCN

C/Muntaner 63-65, Eixample (93 453 61 23/www.arenadisco.com). Metro Universitat. **Open** 6pm-3am daily. **No credit cards. Map** p342 C5.
One of Barcelona's oldest gay bars, this unpretentious, friendly spot is one of the few places that gets busy early in the evening. It draws birds of many feathers, from besuited fiftysomethings to teenagers having their first drink out of the closet. Screens at the back show images from the various Arena clubs.

Sal i Pebre

C/Diputació 214 (no phone). Metro Universitat. **Open** 11pm-3am Thur-Sat. **No credit cards. Map** p342 C5.
Sal i Pebre's cheap drinks and cheesy music attract a young, studenty crowd, including a number of women. Drinks are two for the price of one all night on Thursdays and until midnight on Fridays and Saturdays. Packed at weekends.

Marlene presides over a classy kind of kitsch at **Burdel 74**.

Sweet

C/Casanova 75 (no phone). Metro Universitat.
Open 8pm-2.30am Tue-Thur, Sun; 8pm-3am Fri,
Sat. **No credit cards. Map** p345 C5.
Sweet has managed to attract an impressive number of regulars during its short life, despite having plenty of fierce local competition. It's a large, slick bar with red lighting, low seating and chill-out music in a relaxed atmosphere with friendly staff. Prices rise after midnight.

Z:eltas Club

C/Casanova 75 (93 454 19 02/www.zeltas.net).
Metro Universitat. **Open** 11pm-3am Wed-Sun.
No credit cards. Map p342 C5.
Z:eltas has the feel of a large cocktail bar, its stylish design accentuated by spectacular orange and green spotlighting. The DJ spins funky house for those warming up on the tiny dancefloor.

The rest of the city

Schilling (*see p175*) and **La Concha** (*see p250*), though not gay per se, are worth a look.

Burdel 74

C/Carme 74, Raval (93 442 69 86). Metro Liceu.
Open 5.30pm-3am Tue-Sun. **No credit cards.**
Map p342 C6.
Presided over by a huge picture of Marlene Dietrich, Burdel is mixed and friendly. Tables are papered with pictures of actresses and male models, and the decor is classily kitsch, with fuchsia walls and polka-dot lampshades. There's also bingo.

Nightclubs

Gaixample

Arena Classic

C/Diputació 233 (93 487 83 42/www.arenadisco. com). Metro Passeig de Gràcia or Universitat. **Open** 12.30am-5am Fri, Sat. **Admission** (incl 1 drink) €5 Fri; €10 Sat. **No credit cards**. **Map** p342 D5.

There are three discos called Arena in the city, and they all offer variations on a well-worn theme; you can switch between one and another freely after getting your hand stamped at your first port of call. Of the trio, Classic is the most light-hearted, with plenty of dancefloor-filler anthems of the 'Dancing Queen' ilk, a campy-kitsch atmosphere and a healthy mix of the sexes.

Arena Madre

C/Balmes 32 (93 487 83 42). Metro Passeig de Gràcia or Universitat. **Open** 12.30am-5am Tue-Sat; 7pm-5am Sun. **Admission** (incl 1 drink) €5 Tue-Fri, Sun; €10 Sat. **No credit cards**. **Map** p342 D5.

The cavernous Arena Madre has a spacious dancefloor, a darkroom and a soundtrack that mixes pounding house and current chart hits. It attracts a younger crowd than Arena Classic, and is more of a cattle market too. In the early part of the week there are shows and strippers; on Sundays, there's a party where badge-wearing punters can send messages to one another.

Arena VIP

Gran Via de les Corts Catalanes 593 (93 487 83 42). Metro Universitat. **Open** 12.30am-5am Fri, Sat. **Admission** (incl 1 drink) €5 Fri; €10 Sat. **No credit cards**. **Map** p342 D5.

Urban tribes Bears

Description Bears (*osos* in Spanish/*óssos* in Catalan) are gay men who don't fit most current stereotypes of male beauty and are proud of it. Being over 30, fat and hairy is where it's at.

Natural habitat In Barcelona, the Bear Factory (Ptge Domingo 3, Eixample, www.bearfactory. tk) and Ursus Cave, located in La Luna (*see p241*). In Sitges, the Bears Bar (C/Bonaire 17, 93 894 62 96). They can also be spotted in leather bars and cruisey parks.

Grooming Normally seen in jeans, leather, white tank tops, lumberjack shirts or no shirt

at all. Accessories include bondage collars, cuffs, blindfolds and picnic baskets.

Distinctive behaviour Bears are extremely affectionate beasts and into hugging. A pat on the belly is usually a good sign. At the back of many bars there are dark cave-like rooms that are often used for more than just hibernation.

Types A cub (*cachorro/cadell*) is a young bear. Those of Asian origin are called panda bears (*oso panda/ós panda*). If they're hairy but not fat, they're otters (*nutrias/llúdries*). A wolf (*lobo/llop*) is a bear with an above-average sexual appetite, while a 'Santa' (Papá Noel/ Pare Noel) is a white-haired bear and a 'daddy' (*papi/papi*) is a paternal bear. Bear admirers are called hunters (*cazadores/caçadors*).

First sighted In San Francisco in the '80s. A bunch of guys, tired of body and age fascism, launched *Bear* magazine and a breed was born.

Evolution Coming on nicely: the Ursus Planet group (www.ursusplanet.com) organises bear gatherings with picnics, meals, walks and other typically ursine activities in Sitges. The ursophile group Bearcelona (C/Verdaguer i Callís 9, 93 268 47 00/www.bearcelona.org) hosts similar events in Barcelona.

Philosophy Bearness is more an attitude than a physical type. Bears are men at ease with their bodies and their masculinity. Being a bear is about not excluding anyone.

Take me to your leader Every July, the Mr Bearcelona beauty pageant crowns one furry aspirant King of the Catalan bears.

Do say 'Who's been eating my porridge?'
Don't say 'That Brad Pitt's a bit of all right.'

The last and tackiest of the Arena troika is the most mixed; again, it's a youthful venue with lots of space, but it's nonetheless heaving at weekends. Like the other Arenas, the VIP does its bit for the Spanish retro pop industry, along with the usual divas.

Martins

Passeig de Gràcia 130 (93 218 71 67). Metro Diagonal. **Open** midnight-5am Thur-Sun. **Admission** (incl 1 drink) €10. **No credit cards.** **Map** p338 D3/4.
Martins has three bars, a porno lounge, a shop selling accessories (cockrings, not handbags) but is desperately low on punters. It does liven up a bit once the crowds from the Eagle and New Chaps turn out, when the action moves to a darkroom with so much history it should be listed.

Metro

C/Sepúlveda 185 (93 323 52 27/www.metro disco.bcn). Metro Universitat. **Open** midnight-5am Mon-Thur, Sun; midnight-6am Fri, Sat. **Admission** (incl 1 drink) €10. **Credit** MC, V. **Map** p342 C5.
Walk down past a silver-painted, caged Venus di Milo and enter a real party. The smaller dancefloor plays Latin tunes and pop classics, while the packed main area focuses on disco greats. The darkroom gets rammed: watch your pockets. On Mondays there are drag shows, and on Tuesdays strippers; other events include foam parties and bingo.

New Chaps

Avda Diagonal 365 (93 215 53 65/www.newchaps. com). Metro Diagonal. **Open** 9pm-3am Mon-Sat; 7pm-3am Sun. **No credit cards.** **Map** p338 D4.
A well-used bar for stockmen *d'un certain âge*, and true to its butch name: steer horns on the wall, porn on the video, all sorts of goings-on in the darkroom downstairs and nary a dame to be seen.

Gay Day

Space Barcelona, C/Tarragona 141-147 (93 426 84 44/www.gaydaybcn.com). Metro Tarragona. **Open** 7.30pm-3am Sun. **Admission** (incl 1 drink) €10. **No credit cards.** **Map** p341 A/B4.
The new outpost of globally renowned Ibiza club Space has taken the city by storm, mostly for its gay house night on Sundays. A superslick and shiny venue, with a clientele to match. Dress minimally and intriguingly to get past the velvet rope: this is no place for wallflowers. Boys only.

XT

C/Comte Borrell 143 (mobile 646 622 307). Metro Urgell. **Open** 6pm-1am Tue-Fri; 6am-noon Sat-Mon. **Admission** €6. **No credit cards.** **Map** p342 C5.
An upfront sex club for men, with darkroom, glory holes, slings, private cabins and screens with porn. There's also a small range of sex-shop products.

The rest of the city

Other clubs with gay followings include **La Terrrazza** and **Discothèque** (*see p256*), which draw a hip bridge-and-tunnel crowd.

Eagle

Passeig de Sant Joan 152, Eixample (93 207 58 56/www.eaglespain.com). Metro Verdaguer. **Open** 10pm-2.30am Mon-Thur, Sun; 10pm-3am Fri, Sat. **No credit cards.** **Map** p339 E4.
The clientele at the Eagle is over 30 and hirsute, and may well drop the obligatory leather once inside. A small bar gives off to a backroom with all manner of contraptions, including a bathtub for watersports. The videos and theme nights are pretty hardcore.

Gay T Dance

Sala Apolo, C/Nou de la Rambla 113, Poble Sec (93 441 40 01/www.gaytdance.com). Metro Paral·lel. **Open** 11pm-3am Sun. **Admission** (incl 1 drink) €10. **No credit cards.** **Map** p342 C6.
A hugely popular gay party held on Sundays in the impressive Sala Apolo (*see p256*). Each night has a different theme, from pirates to Arabian Nights, with performances and projections to match. Many gay after-hours clubs hand out free tickets at the exit. The crowd is mixed but more muscled than not.

La Luna

Avda Diagonal 323, Eixample (no phone). Metro Verdaguer. **Open** 11pm-3am Mon-Thur; 11pm-10.30am Fri, Sat. **Admission** €15; free before 5am. **No credit cards.** **Map** p339 E4.
The place to be between 6am and 8am on weekend mornings. It's surprisingly friendly, and its dancefloor is packed with a mixed bunch of survivors dancing to club hits and, later in the morning, older tunes. There's a quiet bar and a busy darkroom. Also hosts Ursus Cave (*see p240* **Urban tribes**).

Salvation

Ronda Sant Pere 19-21, Eixample (93 318 06 86/ www.matineegroup.com). Metro Urquinaona. **Open** midnight-5am Fri, Sat; 6pm-5am Sun. **Admission** (incl 1 drink) €12. **No credit cards.** **Map** p342 D5.
One of Salvation's two large dancefloors sees disdainful barebacked Muscle Marys pumping to house among swirls of dry ice, while the other reverberates to cheesy disco. On Sundays, the club becomes La Madame, with a fun-loving gay/straight mix. Again, watch your wallet in the claustrophobic darkroom.

SM55

C/Riera Sant Miquel 55, Gràcia (no phone/www. sm55.com). Metro Diagonal. **Open** 10pm-3am daily. **Admission** €2 Mon-Thur; €10 Fri-Sun. **Credit** AmEx, DC, MC, V. **Map** p338 D3.
This recently opened leather bar offers nights for older guys who like a bit of rough in an otherwise gay-deserted area. The walls are decorated with fetish items from military boots to nipple pins. There are naked, underwear and sports clothes nights; check online for details.

Topxi

C/València 358, Eixample (93 207 01 20/www.topxi. com). Metro Diagonal or Verdaguer. **Open** 11pm-5am Wed-Thur; 11pm-6am Fri, Sat; 7pm-5am Sun. **Admission** €5. **No credit cards.** **Map** p339 E4.

Arts & Entertainment

A small bar for men over 40, with a busy darkroom showing porn films. Viper-tongued septuagenarian drag queens dressed in flamboyant national costume perform on Friday and Saturday around 1am.

Lesbian bars & nightclubs

The traditional lesbian bars tend to be uptown, while the new ones tend to be in the Eixample. You'll also find lesbians in some spots favoured by gay men, such as **Arena** (*see p240*) or La Madame at **Salvation** (*see p241*). Regular events are organised by a variety of groups: **Ca La Dona** (*see p324*) and **Casal Lambda** (*see p312*) are good places to get information, as is **Complices** (*see p244*). Admission to bars listed below is free unless stated.

Aire

C/València 236, Eixample (93 454 63 94/www.arena disco.com). Metro Passeig de Gràcia. **Open** *Sept-June* 11pm-3am Thur-Sat. *July, Aug* 11pm-3am Tue-Sat. **Admission** (incl 1 drink) €5 Tue-Fri; €6 Sat. **No credit cards. Map** p338 C4.
The lesbian outpost of the Arena group is an airy bar with a pool table, a dancefloor and Egyptian columns to lend support to kissing couples. Customers range from younger lesbians to thirtysomethings and a handful of their gayboy friends. Busy at weekends.

La Bata de Boatiné

C/Robadors 23, Raval (no phone). Metro Liceu. **Open** 10pm-3am Tue-Sun. **No credit cards. Map** p342 C6.
This battered and slightly grungy bar has recently become popular among a young lesbian crowd, but is very mixed, with gay and straight regulars. It's a good place to meet after midnight and to find out what's going on in other alternative late-night bars.

Divina's

Avda Diagonal 337, Eixample (93 458 21 60). Metro Verdaguer. **Open** 7pm-3am Thur-Sun. **No credit cards. Map** p339 E4.
The admission-free policy of this lesbian bar has made it popular with a mixed clientele: it's always crowded. The decor is low-key but for an unforgettable blown-up photo of the owner as femme fatale, and there's pool and table football at the back.

D-Mer

C/Plató 13, Sant Gervasi (93 201 62 07/www.d-mer. com). Metro Lesseps/FGC Muntaner. **Open** midnight-3am Fri, Sat. **No credit cards. Map** p338 C2.
Hip dance music, comfortable seating, red and green neon lighting and pretty people on both sides of the long bar. The clientele ranges from trendy young things to women in their forties, but while it's relaxed and light-hearted, this is not a place for boys.

¿Entiendes?

Ptge Domingo 3, Eixample (no phone). Metro Passeig de Gràcia. **Open** 11.30pm-3am Thur-Sat. **Admission** *Thur* free. *Fri, Sat* (women, incl drink) €4; (men) €10. **No credit cards. Map** p338 D4.

Foam party at **Arena Madre**. *See p240.*

Run by Raquel and Noemí, who met as contestants on Spanish *Big Brother*, this is a small and friendly space where you can dance to salsa, pop and decaffeinated house. Always packed with a mixed crowd.

LesFatales

C/Balmes 90, Eixample (www.lesfatales.com). Metro Universitat. **Open** 11pm-3am Thur-Sat. **No credit cards. Map** p342 D5.
The most interesting and alternative addition to the lesbian scene this year, run by a dynamic group of women, many of them DJs. The music runs from pop to electronica and techno, and there are occasional performances, including a politically aware cabaret.

Restaurants

In addition to those listed here, plenty of mixed restaurants in Barcelona have thriving gay followings. Among the most popular are **La Verònica** (*see p149*) and Barri Gòtic's **Venus Delicatessen** (C/Avinyó, 93 301 15 85).

Café Miranda

C/Casanova 30, Eixample (93 453 52 49). Metro Universitat. **Open** 9pm-midnight Tue-Thur, Sun; 9pm-1am Fri, Sat. **Set dinner** €25.70. **Credit** MC, V. **Map** p342 C5.
Elaborate decor, spectacular waiters, drag queens, singers and acrobats; when they pause for breath the music is loud and uptempo. The food is generally nothing special but the atmosphere is; booking is essential, particularly at weekends.

Castro

C/Casanova 85, Eixample (93 323 67 84/www.castro restaurant.com). Metro Universitat. **Open** 1-4pm, 9pm-midnight Mon-Fri; 9pm-midnight Sat. **Main courses** €10-€18. **Set lunch** €8.30 Mon-Fri. **Credit** MC, V. **Map** p342 C5.

Arts & Entertainment

A heavy chain curtain welcomes you into the black leather and grey metal interior. Starters comprise salads and carpaccios, while mains include chargrilled steak, kangaroo and duck magret, or cod with honey and peppers stuffed with crab.

Cubaneo

C/Casanova 70, Eixample (93 454 31 88). Metro Universitat. **Open** 1-4.30pm, 8.30pm-midnight Tue-Thur; 8.30pm-1am Fri-Sun. Closed lunch in Aug. **Main courses** €8.50-€11.80. **Set lunch** €7. **Set dinner** €20. **Credit** MC, V. **Map** p342 C5.

Cuban soul food, invigorating Mojitos and handsome muscled waiters, not to mention an unholy mix of Cuban personalities and gay icons on the walls. The set meals start with salads, followed by a choice of mains and include a bottle of wine or cava.

Iurantia

C/Casanova 42, Eixample (93 454 78 87). Metro Universitat. **Open** 1.30-4pm Mon-Fri; 9pm -12.30am Mon-Sat. **Main courses** €8.50-€13.40. **Credit** MC, V. **Map** p342 C5.

A very sleekly designed restaurant, serving imaginative fusion alongside the pizza and pasta. Try cheesecake with chocolate-coated peanuts and rose petal marmalade, among other things.

Shops & services

General shops

Antinous Libreria Café

C/Josep Anselm Clavé 6, Barri Gòtic (93 301 90 70/ www.antinouslibros.com). Metro Drassanes. **Open** 10.30am-2pm, 5-8.30pm Mon-Fri; noon-2pm, 5-8.30pm Sat. **Credit** AmEx, DC, MC, V. **Map** p345 A4.

An elegant store with gay and lesbian literature, some in English, plus plenty of other handy items and a noticeboard with information on events and places to stay outside town. When you're done, have a coffee and cake in the tea shop at the back.

Complices

C/Cervantes 2, Barri Gòtic (93 412 72 83/www. libreriacomplices.com). Metro Jaume I. **Open** 10.30am-8.30pm Mon-Fri; noon-8.30pm Sat. **Credit** AmEx, MC, V. **Map** p345 B3.

Two women run Barcelona's oldest gay bookshop, stocking women's books, magazines and videos on one side and men's on the other. Go downstairs for spicier material and a selection of books in English.

Ovlas

Via Laietana 33, Barri Gòtic (93 268 76 91). Metro Jaume I. **Open** 10.15am-8.30pm Mon-Sat. **Credit** AmEx, MC, V. **Map** p345 B3.

Ovlas has a variety of attention-grabbing outer- and underwear and a good selection of footwear. Leather accessories, partying outfits, military boots, Billy Boys dolls and all kinds of gay clothing can be found here, from see-through shirts to sequined tank tops. There's also a bar on the premises.

Spike Urban

C/Hospital 46, Raval (93 412 64 67). Metro Liceu. **Open** 11am-9pm Mon-Sat. **Credit** AmEx, MC, V. **Map** p342 C6.

Handsome and helpful shop assistants, modern clothing, sexy underwear and high-fashion trainers. Not a shop for the thrifty, but during the sales it offers pretty good deals on G Star, Levi's engineered jeans, Diesel, Energie and Puma gear.

La Tienda de Ken

C/Casanova 56, Eixample (93 534 67 70/www. latiendadeken.com). Metro Universitat. **Open** 5.30-9pm Mon; 11am-2pm, 5.30-9pm Tue-Sat. Closed 2wks Aug. **Credit** MC, V. **Map** p342 C5.

This tiny shop sells a variety of gay clothing and accessories. Male Barbie fans can buy anything from Tarzan-like swimming wear in rags to chains and kinky leather bracelets. But the best are some original badges, portraying popular soap opera divas from the '80s and *Sesame Street* characters.

Hairdressers

Fashion Chaning

C/Diputació 159, Eixample (93 454 24 10). Metro Urgell. **Open** 11am-7.30pm Tue-Sat; 3-7.30pm Mon. **Credit** AmEx, DC, MC, V. **Map** p342 C5.

A gay hairdressing salon for boys and girls, and one place where men ask for manicures, pedicures and facials without getting odd looks. You can get your eyebrows, eyelashes and even your body hair dyed, along with getting party makeovers.

Saunas

At all of the establishments listed below, you'll find enough showers, steam rooms and dry saunas to justify the name, along with bars and colourful porn lounges. On arrival, you'll be supplied with locker key, towel and flip-flops.

Corinto

C/Pelai 62, Eixample (93 318 64 22). Metro Catalunya. **Open** noon-5am Mon-Thur; 24hrs Fri-Sun. **Admission** €13 Mon, Wed, Thur, Sat, Sun; €10.50 Tue, Fri. **Credit** V. **Map** p342 D5.

This well-equipped sauna in the heart of the city is attended by a wide cross-section of men. It has big glass windows from where, half-naked, you can overlook the living statues on La Rambla.

Sauna Casanova

C/Casanova 57, Eixample (93 323 78 60). Metro Urgell. **Open** 24hrs daily. **Admission** €13 Mon, Wed, Fri-Sun; €10.50 Tue, Thur. **Credit** MC, V. **Map** p342 C5.

Recently refurbished, Casanova is the city's most popular sauna, attracting plenty of well-muscled eye-candy. It's at its busiest on Tuesday and Thursday evenings, every night after the clubs close and all day Sunday.

Sex shops

All the following gay-oriented sex shops have viewing cabins for videos.

Nostromo

C/Diputació 208, Eixample (93 323 31 94). Metro Universitat. **Open** 11am-10pm Mon-Fri; noon-10pm Sat, Sun. **No credit cards. Map** p342 C5.

Skorpius

Gran Via de les Corts Catalanes 384-390, Eixample (93 423 40 409/www.sexshop-skorpius.com). Metro Plaça Espanya. **Open** 10am-midnight daily. **Credit** MC, V. **Map** p341 B6.

Zeus

C/Riera Alta 20, Raval (93 442 97 95). Metro Sant Antoni. **Open** 10am-9pm Mon-Sat. **Credit** MC, V. **Map** p342 C5.

Sitges

Half an hour down the coast from Barcelona is the little fishing village of Sitges. A gay resort since the '60s, it's full of friendly bars and nightclubs and host to riotous street parties at weekends, in summer and during its carnival celebrations. About an hour's walk south of town is a gay nudist beach, with a bar that serves food and a cruising area in the bushes behind. It's quite a hike, though: wear trainers, at least until you get there.

Accommodation

Built in a Modernista palace and furnished throughout with period furniture, **El Xalet** (C/Illa de Cuba 35, 938 94 55 79, www. elxalet.com, rates €64.20-€99.50 incl breakfast) offers extraordinarily good value rooms. Book weeks in advance in the summer and ask for room 104, with its fits-two marble bath, outrageous crystal chandelier and marry-me wardrobe. The same family runs the **Hotel Noucentista** (C/Illa de Cuba 21, 938 94 85 53, rates €64.20-€99.50 incl breakfast, closed Nov-Feb) up the road. More or less opposite, the **Hotel Liberty** (C/Illa de Cuba 45, 938 11 08 72, www.hotel-liberty-sitges.com, rates €70-€120 incl breakfast) is a reasonably priced option with spacious rooms and a lush garden. Be sure to book three months ahead in summer, but the owners also have 32 apartments for rent; for these, see www.staysitges.com. The follow-the-herd choice is the **Hotel Romàntic**, a beautifully restored 19th-century house with a secluded palm-filled garden (C/Sant Isidre 33, 938 94 83 75, www.hotelromantic.com, rates €84-€99 incl breakfast, closed Nov-Mar). Peter and Rico at **RAS** (607 14 94 51, www.raservice. com) can help you out if you're stuck.

Bars & nightclubs

Most begin a night on 'Sin Street', aka C/Primer de Maig, a brightly lit strip of gawdy bars such as famous drink-and-dance joint **Parrots Pub** (Plaça Indústria 2, no phone), and its sidekick **Parrots Pub 2**. A cheerful stopping-off point is **Orek's Bar Musical** (C/Bonaire 13, no phone), which pumps out Gloria Gaynor et al and is run by friendly French couple Noel and Gilles. Next door is the sweaty disco **Organic** (C/Bonaire 15, no phone). You'll invariably end up in **Trailer** (C/Angel Vidal 36, 93 894 04 01), with music until 5am. For a quieter and older experience, try **El Horno** (C/Joan Tarrida Ferratges 6, no phone), opposite Sitges' main lesbian haunt, **Maripili** (C/Joan Tarrida Ferratges 14, no phone).

Restaurants

A cardboard cut-out Marilyn Monroe and '80s disco soundtrack invite you to **Ma Maison** (C/Bonaire 28, 93 894 60 54, mains €11, closed Nov), where the waiters are friendly, ceilings are Wedgwood blue and food (speciality couscous) is reasonably priced. At the bottom of a little passageway off C/Mayor is the charming **Flamboyant** (C/Pau Barrabeitg s/n, 16 93 894 58 11, mains €10, closed Oct-Feb). The food is fairly average, but served in a magical leafy courtyard. The Australian-run **Beach House** (C/Sant Pau 34, 93 894 90 29, mains €6.50, closed Mon-Wed from Oct-Apr) has a lavish set menu in summer, and theme nights in winter: Thursday is pie night, Friday fish 'n' chips, bingo and drag acts, and Saturday's curry night.

Metro. *See p241.*

Music & Nightlife

Twist and pout.

No one's pretending it's Ibiza, or even Madrid, but it's all too easy to find yourself still on a Barcelona night out as the first fingers of sunlight are creeping up the cathedral spires. It's all here, from superclubs hosting famed international celebrity DJs to tiny little clubs specialising in the latest experimental electro, ear-bleeding drum 'n' bass and boom-busting techno. There are lounge clubs and gilded ballrooms, *salsatecas* and Brazilian samba bars, seductive tango emporiums and alternative club nights offering anything from northern soul to Bollywood bhangra and crooning drag queens. There are even bars with beds (**Sugar Club** and **CDLC**, for both, *see p256*), so why would you ever go home?

Going out in Barcelona happens late. People rarely meet for a drink much before 11pm. Bars don't shut until 3am, and it's not until they kick people out that the clubs (cutesily still known as *discotecas*) really get going. If you're still raring to go at 6am, there's a good chance you'll find an after-party party for even more hedonism if you keep your ear to the ground. Like most other places, the biggest nights are Thursday, Friday and Saturday, with Sunday teatime chill-out sessions fast catching on.

Traditionally, you had to head uptown to hit the posh clubs, but the Port Olímpic is putting out some serious competition with places like **Club Catwalk** (*see p256*) and CDLC luring the *pijos* downtown. There are also nightly beach parties running up and down the coast from Bogatell (**El Chiringuito**, *see p254* **Get out**) to Mataró through the summer. Meanwhile, you'll find smaller venues pulsating with life in the Barri Gòtic, particularly around the Plaza Reial and C/Escudellers. Across La Rambla, in the Raval, you can skulk the grittier, grungier places. If hippie chic, joints and chillums are your thing, Gràcia is good for hanging with the artsy crowd, though in truth it's a far better place for drinking than it is for dancing.

LIVE MUSIC

The term 'live music' has been threatening to become a bit of a misnomer in Barcelona over the last year. The closure of grown-up venues La Boîte and Jazzroom and the threatened closure of **Harlem Jazz Club** (*see p248*) was seen by some as a worrying symptom of the music scene's sickly state, particularly as these venues were run by long-time champions of live

music in Barcelona. But perhaps the rumours of the death of music in the city are exaggerated. There is still plenty of variety, though most enthusiasm does seem to be reserved for genres and bands from the supposedly 'cooler' countries of northern Europe and America – good news for visitors, who often get to see their favourite bands in venues half the size they'd normally play at home. But rocketing ticket prices (perhaps to support seemingly ever-growing guest lists – blaggers, take note!) mean you pay for such privilege.

Barcelona does have some homegrown talent, it's just rare to see it at the main venues. Some

of the leading bands were given a showcase at the 2004 BAM festival (*see p222*), from post-rockers 12Twelve, to the wistful vocal house of trio Pastora, indie-pop-rockers Mishima and hardcore band Standstill. Where Catalans have had most success internationally, however, is with *mestizaje* – a word that basically means mix, and whose performers generally draw from a blend of influences including rock, flamenco, rai, hip hop, and various South American, Asian and African styles. The *mestizaje* top draws at the moment are Ojos de Brujo and the Raval's 08001.

As well as the venues listed below you can catch the occasional visits of pop-rock superstars in one of Montjuïc's sports stadiums (if you hang out in the area on the afternoon of the concert, you could catch the soundcheck) and Vall d'Hebron, or even way out in Badalona's Palau Olímpic. The other main music venues for seeing international names (as well as hotly tipped unknowns and local

musicians) are the multi-faceted industrial space **Razzmatazz** (*see p261*), the old dancehall **Sala Apolo** (*see p257*), which, with a smaller space, mainly hosts weirder, less known or slightly on-the-descendent acts, and the mall-like **Bikini** (*see p260*), which has revived the quality of its programming with an impressively eclectic roster of recent acts including Radio 4, Terry Callier, Marianne Faithfull and Everlast.

INFORMATION AND TICKETS

For concert information buy the weekly (out on Thursday) listings guide *Guía del Ocio* or the Friday papers, which usually include listings supplements. Look in bars and music shops for free mags such as *Metropolitan, Go, AB, Mondo Sonoro* (all mostly independent pop/rock/electronica) and *Batonga!* (world music). *Punto H* and *Suite* are good for keeping up to date on the club scene, or there is *Movin' BCN,* a monthly, bilingual publication available from news kiosks.

On the web, try listings sites www.lecool. com, www.barcelonarocks.com, www.atiza.com, www.salirenbarcelona.com and www.clubbing spain.com. For festivals try www.festivales.com and www.whatsonwhen.com. You can also get information and tickets from Tel-entrada and Servi-Caixa (*see p214*). Specialist record shops, such as those on C/Tallers in the Raval, are good for info and club flyers.

Barri Gòtic

Barcelona Pipa Club
Plaça Reial 3, pral (93 302 47 32/www.bpipaclub.com). Metro Liceu. **Open** 6pm-1am daily. **Admission** free. **No credit cards**. **Map** p345 A3.
One of Barcelona's best-loved bars, where Catalan celebrities mingle with the bourgeoisie and American year-abroad students, and courses in the art of pipe smoking are offered along with live jazz and gastronomic evenings. Licensing problems have put the bar under threat of closure and the opening hours have been drastically abridged, though it's still worth a shot after-hours. To try, ring the buzzer next to the sign of the pipe.

Café Royale
C/Nou de Zurbano 3 (93 412 14 33). Metro Liceu. **Open** 6pm-2.30am Mon-Thur, Sun; 6pm-3am Fri, Sat. **Admission** free (1 drink minimum). **Credit** AmEx, MC, V. **Map** p345 A3.
Just off Plaça Reial, Café Royale offers a little more conversation, a little less action. Early in the evening it's a chilled place to slump on sofas, but even later, when Fred Guzzo's funk, soul and jazz-driven beats and the doorman's snotty attitude are cranked up a notch, the youngish mixed tourist/local crowd seems happier rubbing up against each other in the narrow bar than on the dancefloor.

Jamboree. *See p249.*

New York.
See p250.

Dot

*C/Nou de Sant Francesc 7 (93 302 70 26/
www.dotlightclub.com). Metro Drassanes.* **Open**
11pm-2.30am Tue-Thur, Sun; 11pm-3am Fri, Sat.
Admission free. **No credit cards. Map** p345 A4.
Don't miss this vital Dot on Barcelona's electronica
landscape: turn down a seedy street at the sign of
the roasting chickens. It may be small but it scores
large for a combination of great playlist (hip hop,
breaks, funk, house… plus a sprinkling of punk and
indie) in the hands of resident DJ Kosmos, non-stuffy
staff and a crowd that's like a baked alaska – cool,
yet somehow still warm and welcoming.

Downstairs@Club13

Plaça Reial 13 (93 412 43 27). Metro Liceu. **Open**
Apr-Oct 2pm-2.30am Mon-Thur, Sun; 2pm-3am Fri, Sat.
Nov-Mar 6pm-2.30am Mon-Thur, Sun; 6pm-3am Fri,
Sat. **Admission** free. **Credit** MC, V. **Map** p345 A3.
Sounds glam, is glam. A relative newcomer to the
scene, this little nightspot adds a touch of class to
the grungy Plaça Reial, what with its glittering chandeliers and posh-nosh restaurant. The red flock wallpaper, exposed brick cellar and black leather sofas
downstairs make an ideal backdrop for smooth
grooves from deep house to nu breaks via hip hop.
Each night has a different musical flavour, though
Thursday is the most 'exclusive', with a stricter door
policy. Good for posing and pulling – the look is
designer denim and razor-cut Hoxton hairstyles.

Fantastico

*Ptge dels Escudellers 3 (93 317 54 11/www.
fantasticoclub.com). Metro Drassanes or Liceu.*
Open 10.30pm-3.30am Wed-Sat. **Admission** free.
No credit cards. Map p345 A4.
If you're tired of the prevailing electronic beats and
hip hop and need a dose of Brit pop to pull you
through, this is your place. Hip indie pop kids flock
here to dance to the latest UK invasion mixed in with
the occasional German electro pop or New York no
wave punk funk and the Spanish versions they've
spawned. Classified ads projected on to its candy-
coloured walls give this place its pop charm.

Fonfone

*C/Escudellers 24 (93 317 14 24/www.fonfone.com).
Metro Drassanes or Liceu.* **Open** 9.30pm-2.30am
Mon-Thur, Sun; 9.30pm-3am Fri, Sat. **Admission**
free. **Credit** MC, V. **Map** p345 A3.
A refreshingly spacious bar on one of the Gòtic's
seedier backstreets, Fonfone stands out by virtue of
its green and orange glowing decor. It pulls a mixed
crowd of locals and lost tourists of a studenty bent.
Pop, electronica, house and breakbeats attempt to
distract the punters from their conversation.

Harlem Jazz Club

*C/Comtessa de Sobradiel 8 (93 310 07 55). Metro
Jaume I.* **Open** 8pm-4am Tue-Thur, Sun; 8pm-5am
Fri, Sat. *Gigs* 10.30pm, midnight Tue-Thur, Sun;
11.30pm, 1am Fri, Sat. Closed 2wks Aug. **Admission**
free Mon-Thur; €5 (incl 1 drink) Fri-Sun. **No credit
cards. Map** p345 B3.

It doesn't look like much from the outside, but you can't judge this club by its cover or, in fact, its rather sterile decor. An international studenty crowd braves the oxygen-free atmosphere and crushed space to enjoy what is perhaps the most eclectic music programming in town. Despite the name, the genres heard here encompass everything from klezmer to flamenco fusion via Moroccan music. Unless Harlem succeeds in its bid for public funding, it may have to close in June 2005.

Jamboree/Los Tarantos

Plaça Reial 17 (93 301 75 64/www.masimas.com). Metro Liceu. **Open** 12.30pm-5.30am daily. *Gigs* 10pm Mon; 11pm Tue-Sun. **Admission** (incl 1 drink) €8. *Gigs* €8-€10. **Credit** V. **Map** p345 A3.

Every night Jamboree hosts jazz, Latin or blues gigs by mainly Spanish groups; when they're over the beards wander off and the beatbox comes out. On Mondays, particularly, the outrageously popular What the Fuck (WTF) jazz jam session is crammed with a young local crowd waiting for the funk/hip hop night that follows. Upstairs, sister venue Los Tarantos stages flamenco performances, then joins forces with Jamboree as a smooth-grooves chill-out space.

Karma

Plaça Reial 10 (93 302 56 80). Metro Liceu. **Open** midnight-5am Tue-Sun. **Admission** free Tue-Thur, Sun; €8 or 2-3 drinks minimum Fri, Sat. **No credit cards. Map** p345 A3.

Tunnel-shaped cellar club Karma has long been the embarrassing elderly uncle of the Barcelona nightlife scene, steadfastly unhip, but still knowing how to have a good time with its failsafe cocktail of booze and cheesy rock for backpackers and those who want to meet them.

La Macarena

C/Nou de Sant Francesc 5 (no phone). Metro Drassanes. **Open** 11.30pm-4.30am Mon-Thur, Sun; 11.30pm-5.30am Fri, Sat. **Admission** free before 2.30am; €5 afterwards. **No credit cards. Map** p345 A4.

Not a centre for embarrassing synchronised arm movements performed to cheesy pop toons, but a completely soundproofed cosy little dance space/bar with a kicking sound system that will pound away electro, minimal and house beats until very late. Guest house DJs Brett Johnson and Vincenzo have shared the decks with locals at this coveted little place, usually a day before or after a bigger gig elsewhere in town.

Don't miss   Nights to...

Make jazz cool again

The What the Fuck night at jazz cave **Jamboree** (*see above*) offers the bizarre vision of baggy-panted b-boys won over to the jazz thang by the hot, hard, funk-tinged playing on stage and a young, up-for-it crowd on the floor.

Come dancing

La Gardenia Blanca orchestra at **La Paloma** (*see p253*) is a classic, with moustachioed, fedora-ed guys crooning cruise-ship favourites, and well-endowed ladies squeezed into sequin-laden, thigh-split gowns. Watch them rumba and cha cha cha 6-9.30pm Thursday to Saturday.

Get up close and personal

The tiny performance space at the Mercat de les Flors hosts indie performers of varying flavours for the **Pocket Club** (*see p257*). It doesn't get any more intimate than this.

Hang with big ballers

Claim to be on the Australian water polo team and hang out with affluent and glamorous athletes, and their entourage of fabulous friends and bewitching beauties dripping in bling. The best places to get

away with it include **CDLC** and nearby **Club Catwalk** (for both, *see p256*).

Show off your snorkel

Board shorts, wet T-shirts, bikinis and that Barcelona glow are choice for strutting your stuff at **El Chiringuito** and **Liquid** (for both, *see p254* **Get out**).

Strike a pose

Youthful beauties are lured to Disney-like Poble Espanyol to battle it out for their 15 seconds of fame on the starlit dance platforms, at open-air **La Terrrazza** (*see p257*) in the summer and megaclub **Discothèque** (*see p256*) in the winter.

Blag it

Don't miss the monthly residencies of Barcelona's favourite international superstars: Miss Kittin at **Razzmatazz** (*see p261*) attracts electro-cuties by way of her hard-hitting Berlinesque sound; Powder Room at **Sala Apolo** (*see p257*) sets the stage for Keb Darge's impossible-to-find soul tunes, and sexy Swedes come out in droves when Scandinavian chart topper Jay Jay Johanson mixes up his blend of discopop at **Mond Club** (*see p260*).

Arts & Entertainment

New York

C/Escudellers 5 (93 318 87 30). Metro Drassanes or Liceu. **Open** midnight-5am Thur-Sat. **Admission** (incl 1 drink) €8 with flyer, €10 without. **No credit cards**. **Map** p345 A3.

Recently reopened with a facelift, this ancient former brothel turned rock club now hosts some of the best nights in *musica negra* (black music), a term used by soul-deprived Spaniards to describe anything from funk to northern soul. A long hallway bar leads to the main dancefloor, where fairground figures leer from the stage and wallflowers gaze from the mezzanine. Every Friday, Black Magic Sounds covers the ground between ska, rocksteady, reggae, funk, soul and '70s disco to a crowd of diehard followers and late-night wanderers. Gilles Peterson, King Britt and Norman Jay have all played here.

Sidecar Factory Club

Plaça Reial 7 (93 302 15 86/www.sidecarfactoryclub.com). Metro Liceu. **Open** 8pm-4.30am Tue-Thur, Sun; 8pm-5am Fri, Sat. *Gigs* (Oct-July) 10.30pm Tue-Sat. **Admission** (incl 1 drink) €6. *Gigs* €5-€10. **No credit cards**. **Map** p345 A3.

Don't be fooled by the flashy entrance, this is a pure basement rock club hosting fledgling Barcelona indie acts, as well as intimate concerts by guests ranging from Superchunk-fronted Portastatic to Detroit trash rockers Demolition Doll Rods. Between times, the club holds DJ sessions – with house, techno and electro on Wednesdays, electropop and glam on Thursdays, and the latest pop and rock at weekends – to the fashionably punk and Plaça Reial stragglers who absolutely must have another beer after 3am.

Raval

Aurora

C/Aurora 7 (93 442 30 44). Metro Paral·lel. **Open** 8pm-3am daily. **Admission** free. **No credit cards**. **Map** p342 C6.

Aurora used to be an unkempt ramshackle place inhabited by unkempt ramshackle arty types in the wee hours. It was renovated a couple of years ago and given a smarter, shinier, pop-arty look, and some of the clientele (party-hungry tourists and a mixed bag of locals) look as if they've scrubbed up a bit too. Aurora now offers infusions and flamenco fusion along with the harder stuff.

Chips with everything

While scratching around for gimmicks to launch a new VIP section, the American owner of tourist favourite the Baja Beach Club came up with an idea. Instead of just giving out VIP cards to members, why not implant each of them with a microchip?

There are several reasons why not, you might think, but there is no legal reason among them. At the time of writing, more than 50 people in Barcelona, and subsequently 40 in Baja's sister club in Rotterdam, had signed up. And so, once a month, a nurse turns up to apply a local anaesthetic and then inject a small chip the size of a grain of rice into the next set of wannabe VIPs' forearms. There are currently more than a hundred people on the waiting list. Although the removal process is supposed to be very straightforward, no one has yet asked for it.

Civil libertarians don't seem very impressed by the idea of scanning and tracking people's movements; the club has also found fame with religious extremists and features prominently on hundreds of loony apocalyptic websites describing the chip as the mark of the beast, pointing at the bar tab system and quoting Revelations: '...and that no man might buy or sell, save he that had the mark.'

Benidorm

C/Joaquín Costa 39 (no phone). Metro Universitat.
Open *Apr-mid Oct* 8pm-2.30am Mon-Thur, Sun; 8pm-
3am Fri, Sat. *Mid Oct-Mar* 7pm-2.30am Mon-Thur,
Sun; 7pm-3am Fri, Sat. Closed Aug. **Admission** free.
No credit cards. Map p342 C5.
This lively, smoky little place is a kitsch paradise of
brothel-red walls, crystal lanterns and '80s disco
paraphernalia, boasting the world's smallest toilet,
dancefloor and chill-out room. The sounds being
absorbed by the mass of humanity packed in here
on weekends (watch your wallet) range from hip hop
to '70s stuff, although mostly they are variations on
the same electronica theme.

Big Bang

*C/Botella 7 (93 443 28 13/www.bigbangbcn.net).
Metro Liceu or Sant Antoni.* **Open** *Bar* 10.30pm-
2.30am Wed, Thur, Sun; 10.15pm-3am Fri, Sat. *Gigs*
around 10.30pm-1am Fri, Sat. *Jam sessions* 11pm-
1am Wed, Thur, Sun. **Admission** *Bar & jam
sessions* free. *Gigs* varies. **No credit cards.**
Map p342 C5.
An oddity this – one of the few ungentrified bars
in the Raval, the shabby but somehow characterful
Big Bang attracts a queer bunch, from crusty types
to ageing rockers via boyz from the 'hood and some
slightly confused-looking backpackers. Just what
attracts them? Is it the erratic behaviour of the bar
staff, the comically limb-deprived table football, or
the gigs of an industrial/punk rock bent held in the
stark backroom? Or is it being able to get a drink
here when everything else is closed? Bang on the
shutters to try your luck.

El Cangrejo

C/Montserrat 9 (93 301 29 78). Metro Drassanes.
Open 10pm-3.30am Thur-Sun. **Admission** free.
Credit MC, V. **Map** p345 A4.
The original Barcelona drag cabaret, El Cangrejo
attracts a mixed bag of old-timers, honeymooners,
gay couples and revellers. Tuesday and Wednesday
evenings feature DJ sessions, but otherwise the acts
consist largely of performers lip-synching golden-
oldie Spanish ballads interspersed with raconteurs
whose outrageous get-ups combine early Divine,
Prince and the Jolly Green Giant. You'd have to go
a long way to find a more sequin-spangled line-up.
As for the decor, if you can imagine being sandwiched between a lemon meringue pie and a paella,
you'll get the general idea.

Cynics might point out that many of the
scantily clad visitors to Baja won't be
strangers to implants. The club, where the
DJ sits in a fake speedboat, is the liquid
camembert end of cheesy. Topless barmen
and bikini-clad waitresses serve stag and hen
parties as much drink as they can bathe in,
from differently themed bars. Accompanying
the ensuing mayhem is a soundtrack of so-
bad-it's-good pop, movie theme tunes and
even the occasional sports anthem.

For those who can't get enough of this kind
of thing, here's how it works. When scanned,
your Baja-chipped arm gives off a unique ID
number that is then linked both to entry and
to a bar tab, topped up straight from your
bank. Payment is just a case of waving your
arm in front of the bar staff. The idea is that
you can go for a night out unencumbered by
a wallet. How you pay for your taxi, however,
hasn't been explained.

Baja Beach Club

*Passeig Marítim 34 (93 225 91 00/www.
bajabeach.es). Metro Ciutadella-Vila Olímpica.*
Open *June-Oct* 1pm-3am Mon-Wed; 1pm-5am
Thur, Sun; 1pm-6am Fri, Sat. *Nov-May* 1pm-
5am Thur, Sun; 1pm-6am Fri, Sat. **Admission**
(incl 1 drink) €12 Thur, Sun; €14 Fri; €15
Sat. **Credit** AmEx, MC, V. **Map** p343 E7.

La Concha

C/Guàrdia 14 (93 302 41 18). Metro Drassanes.
Open 5pm-2.30am Mon-Thur, Sun; 5pm-3am Fri, Sat.
Admission free. **No credit cards**. **Map** p345 A3.
Manager Rashid has made such an impressive turnaround of this classic bar that these days it's talked about from Ronda to Rio, with as many in-the-know tourists as locals and doe-eyed drag queens taking up space along the bar. Spanish screen siren Sara Montiel remains immortalised in a hundred faded photographs, while the exotic Arabic music mixes with flamenco.

Corto Club

C/Tallers 68 (93 302 27 95). **Open** 9pm-3am Mon-Sat. **Admission** varies. **Credit** V. **Map** p344 A1.
The people who brought us late-night drinking at the Pipa Club give us another place to whet our palate, this time with music. Live jazz, blues, funk, and bossa nova fill the spaces amid the thought balloons and original drawings of Hugo Pratt's comic-book sailor Corto Maltese. Starry-eyed Argentines wax nostalgic with locals and tourists for the *milonga* on Tuesdays, where professionals encourage amateurs to choose a partner and dance to the tango band. Wearing the right shoes is optional, but a rose between the teeth is a must.

DAF

Plaça dels Àngels 5-6 (93 329 00 21). Metro Catalunya or Universitat. **Open** 9pm-3am Thur-Sat. **Admission** free. **Credit** AmEx, MC, V. **Map** p344 A1.
A restaurant and lounge bar housed in an ancient convent, where beeps and bloops echo through cavernous vaulted stone ceilings as DJs serve up electronica long after the kitchen closes. A hip, artsy university crowd drinks Mojitos while practically supine, discussing the merits of the art installation next door, the latest free lecture at nearby CCCB, or why electronic music is not for dancing.

Jazz Sí Club

C/Requesens 2 (93 329 00 20/www.tallerdemusics. com). Metro Sant Antoni. **Open** Sept-July 9am-11pm Mon-Fri; 6-11pm Sat, Sun. *Aug* 6-11pm Thur, Fri, Sun. **Admission** (incl 1 drink) €4 Mon; 1 drink minimum Tue, Wed, Sun; (incl 1 drink) €5 Thur-Sat. **No credit cards**. **Map** p342 C5.
This tiny music school auditorium-cum-bar is a space where students, teachers and music lovers can meet, perform and listen. Each night is dedicated to a different musical genre: trad jazz on Mondays, pop/rock/blues jams on Tuesdays, jazz jams on Wednesdays, Cuban music on Thursdays, flamenco on Fridays, rock on Saturdays and Sundays.

Kentucky

C/Arc del Teatre 11 (93 318 28 78). Metro Drassanes. **Open** 10pm-3am Tue-Sat. Closed Aug. **Admission** free. **No credit cards**. **Map** p345 A4.
One-time pick-up bar and haunt of wayward US sailors and lowlifes of the old Barrio Chino, haven of lost souls and chancers steering by the wrong star, what epic lock-ins have unrolled behind that rattling shutter? What tales could be told of Kentucky? There must be a million, if only anyone could remember any of them…

Moog

C/Arc del Teatre 3 (93 301 72 82/www.masimas. com). Metro Drassanes. **Open** 11.30pm-5am daily. **Admission** €8. **Credit** V. **Map** p345 A4.
Moog has been programming electronic music for years with admirable consistency. Residents Omar, Robert X and Juan B share deck space with guest DJs on Wednesdays. Sunday's Affair guarantees eclecticism: entry is free, so what have you got to lose? A bar in the entryway, a few tables, a small downstairs dancefloor for house and techno and a chill-out room (of sorts) upstairs combine to form a compact and scaled-down club.

La Paloma

C/Tigre 27 (93 301 68 97/www.lapaloma-bcn.com). Metro Universitat. **Open** 6-9.30pm, 11.30pm-5am Thur; 6-9.30pm, 11.30pm-2am; 2.30am-5am Fri, Sat; 6-9.30pm Sun. **Admission** (incl 1 drink) €3-€8. **Credit** (bar only) MC, V. **Map** p342 C5.
La Paloma recently celebrated its 100th birthday, despite the neighbourhood's efforts to silence it. A walk through the surrealist red velvet-lined foyer reveals a lavishly restored belle époque theatre and dancehall complete with shimmering chandeliers and plush balconies. It's a strange spectacle for those who arrive early – Grandma and Grandpa in full evening wear still foxtrotting after the ballroom sessions finish and the house and broken beats begin. On Thursday nights the Bongo Lounge DJs

Less is more: minimal **Zentraus**. *See p254.*

Get out

Summer's here and the time is right for dancing in the... er... where? The street? What, and fall foul of the Ajuntament's *civisme* project? Spoil the 'everyone can still have fun and respect each other' fantasy? OK, the streets are out. Dancing in the... clubs? Oh yes, that's why you left your northern European climes, so you can be stuck inside a sweaty airless smokebox. If you really want to appreciate summer in (and out of) the city, you should seek out the spots that are made for it. Just as the best food is eaten in its season, so the best summer clubbing happens in the seasonal clubs that sprout in the sunny months.

One venue particularly suited to this convoluted organic metaphor is **La Caseta de Migdia** (*see p185*), a laid-back space on the edge of Montjuïc, with a peaceful isolated location and a great view. A more accessible alternative is the **Chiringuito de Barceloneta** (no phone, www.chiringuito-barceloneta.com, Apr-Oct only) on Platja Sant Sebastià, near Rebecca Horn's stack of rusty cubes. Not to be confused with any of the other lookalike beach bars along the front, this one has the friendliest staff, the stiffest drinks, and the drunkest DJs. A mostly young, hip crowd, an even blend of locals and tourists, swarms around the sun-loungers or sways to soulful house from DJs Supa Stevie and Guillermo, or the Sunday reggae sessions. It comes into its own at nightfall when flares flicker and the sound of the surf adds a backbeat.

A little more effort is needed to reach the iconic beach bar **Lasal** (93 755 40 49, www.lasal.com, May-Sept only) on Sant Simó beach in Mataró, north of Barcelona. DJs such as Mad Professor, the Herbaliser and Mixmaster Morris have done duty behind the decks here at the Café del Mar of the Catalan coast. Resident DJs include Barcelona stars Kosmos and DJ2D2, setting the funky, breakbeat-friendly tone of the music policy. Wicker chairs and palm-leaf umbrellas create a kick-back tropical feel, and when the sun goes down, the candles and flares come out.

Going up the scale in terms of both altitude and attitude, **Liquid** (Complex Esportiu Hospitalet Nord, C/Manuel Azaña, mobile 670 221 209, www.liquidbcn.com) is a select uptown club with a difference – rather than a feng-shui-ed converted mansion, its USP is an enormous swimming pool, though the mix funk and Latin rhythms with psychedelic lights and live jazz, while Vegas-style go-go dancers compete for attention.

Salsitas

C/Nou de la Rambla 22 (93 342 52 70/www.grupo salsitas.com). Metro Liceu. **Open** 9pm-2.30am Tue-Sun. **Admission** free. **Credit** AmEx, DC, MC, V. **Map** p345 A3.

'Babes, babes, babes...' declares one happy visitor to this resto-club, which fills the gap at the more sophisticated end of the meat market. Dress code is fashion-conscious and dressed up, but don't try too hard – you'll never compete with the exotic decor of enormous white palm-tree pillars anyway. The house music from resident DJs Toni Bass and Flavio Zarza almost seems secondary – this place is about looking, not listening.

Zentraus

Rambla del Raval 41 (93 442 13 23/www.zentraus. com). Metro Liceu. **Open** 9pm-2.30am Tue-Thur; 9pm-3am Fri, Sat. Closed 2wks Aug. **Admission** free. **No credit cards**. **Map** p342 C6.

Stepping into this minimalist black, grey and red setting you'd forget that you're smack in the middle of the Raval and not some uptown dig. The uplit bar, black-clad bartenders, and completely soundproofed dancefloor make this a prime hotspot for beatseekers in the area, bringing in a diverse and unpredictable crowd. The harder side of techno, electro, drum 'n' bass, breakbeats and minimal house, normally take control of the dancefloor.

Sant Pere & the Born

Bass Bar

C/Assaonadors 25 (mobile 699 326 594). Metro Jaume I. **Open** 7pm-2.30am Mon-Thur, Sun; 7pm-3am Fri-Sat. *Gigs* around 10-11pm Fri, Sat. **Admission** free. **No credit cards**. **Map** p345 C3.

10-watt coloured light bulb? Check. Rich-coloured walls? Check. Battered sofa? Check. Badly photo-copied flyers? Oh yes. Dreadlocks on staff and clients? Of course! This tiny classic on the local protest-chic scene has a dedicated cliquey following, attracted by late beers and, on Fridays and Saturdays, music from very, very small bands playing 'global' sounds, mainly flamenco fusion.

Dr Astin

C/Abaixadors 9 (93 310 10 58). Metro Jaume I. **Open** 10pm-3am Wed-Sat. **Admission** free. **No credit cards**. **Map** p345 B-C3.

Arts & Entertainment

La Terrrazza.

majority of young and stylish punters are happy to hang poolside and keep their gel intact.

The most classic summer-only offering, however, is the open-air club **La Terrrazza** (*see p257*). The young, scantily dressed, mixed-sexuality crowd goes wild to invited DJs such as Dimitri from Paris and Sven Vath, as well as slightly lesser-known deck hounds from top house and techno clubs throughout Europe. The dress code ranges from sexy to glam to outrageous – and you'll be competing for attention with the outlandish decor; 2004's was based on surrealist art in honour of the year of Dalí.

Thankfully, the club is only open May to October – you'll need to spend the winter getting buff and preparing your wardrobe to pass muster at the door or to jump the excruciating queues.

Minute and slightly grungy, this spot has been hammering out house and techno beats for years, in spite of a recent change of management. The Born's cool army of hipsters come here to get their groove on before heading out to the bigger venues. Free and completely soundproofed, it's a perfect choice to start the night.

Drop Bar

Via Laietana 20 (93 310 75 04). Metro Jaume I.
Open 8am-2.30am Thur; 8am-3am Fri; 11pm-3am Sat.
Admission free. **No credit cards. Map** p345 B3.
Long ignored on its corner of Via Laietana with C/Argenteria, Drop Bar sports unpromising '80s-style curved windows overlooking the street and has three different spaces inside, including an open-air area, and a daytime café. Cool, cutting-edge programming includes EBM, IDM and ICBM nights (whatever the vogue of the week happens to be). Dance music for the head bobbers.

Magic

Passeig Picasso 40 (93 310 72 67/www.magic-club.net). Metro Barceloneta. **Open** 11pm-5.30am Thur; 11pm-6.30am Fri, Sat. **Admission** (incl 1 drink) €10. *Gigs* €3-€15. **No credit cards. Map** p343 E6.
An awkward, L-shaped and airless basement club that could never be called comfortable. Still, the pull

for the quirky and cliquey locals who crowd in here is the music: a strange odds and sods mix of tribute bands and tongue-in-cheek pop-rock.

Over the Club

C/Fusina 7 (93 268 10 80/www.overtheclub.com). Metro Barceloneta or Jaume I. **Open** 11pm-3am Thur-Sat. **Admission** free. **No credit cards. Map** p345 C3.
First restaurants were at it, then clothes shops and hairdressers, now internet cafés are doing a Cinderella and turning into a club when midnight strikes. Thursdays are chilled, with just the front futuristic neon-lit bar and small leather-pouffe-littered back room open. On Fridays and Saturdays the dancefloor opens up to a soundtrack of pounding commercial house.

Port Vell & Port Olímpic

Around the right-angled quayside of the Port Olímpic, you'll find dance bars interspersed with seafood restaurants, fast-food outlets, ice-cream parlours, coffee shops and mock-Irish pubs; with video screens, glittery lights and go-go girls and boys in abundance, it makes little difference which one you choose.

Arts & Entertainment

CDLC

Passeig Marítim 32 (93 224 04 70/www.cdlc barcelona.com). Metro Ciutadella-Vila Olímpica. **Open** noon-3am daily. **Admission** free. **Credit** AmEx, MC, V. **Map** p343 E7.

Carpe Diem Lounge Club is the darling of the Barça football team (it's owned by the wife of ex-Barça man Patrick Kluivert) and other celebs staying at the Hotel Arts. It works hard to be the most exclusive club on the circuit, sometimes even going so far as to refuse entry to its own invited VIPs. But, hey, if Rod Stewart got in, you should be able to. There's a space to suit any kind of lounge lizard or livewire – from the swanky bed-size sofas to the fast-moving dancefloor and beachfront terrace (even the toilets are luxurious enough to linger in). Resident DJ Anne-Miek and guests play soulful, vocal house.

Club Catwalk

C/Ramon Trias Fargas s/n (93 221 61 61/www. clubcatwalk.net). Metro Ciutadella-Vila Olímpica. **Open** midnight-5am Thur; midnight-5.30am Fri-Sun. **Admission** (incl 1 drink) €15. **Credit** V. **Map** p343 F7.

As the bitter nightclub wars rage on, so then Club Danzatoria must become Club Catwalk. The same vibe as before, as the fashionable sashay over from neighbouring CDLC and Shôko to strut their stuff in this A-list hedonist paradise. Get past the impassive doormen to enter two separate dancefloors, one house and the other hip hop and R&B. White canopied sofas where anything goes set the tone for its South Beach-inspired glam. Once a month Subliminal Sessions host DJs Erick Morillo and others from the New York house label.

Le Kasbah

Plaça Pau Vilà (Palau del Mar) (93 238 07 22/ www.ottozutz.com). Metro Drassanes. **Open** 10.30pm-3am daily. **Admission** free. **Credit** AmEx, MC, V. **Map** p345 C4.

A white awning over terrace tables heralds the entrance to this louche bar beind the Palau de Mar. Inside, a North African harem look seduces a young and up-for-it mix of tourists and students on to its plush cushions for a cocktail or two before going out. As the night progresses so does the music, from chill-out early on to full-on boogie after midnight.

Shôko

Passeig Marítim 36 (93 225 92 03/www.shoko.biz). Metro Ciutadella-Vila Olímpica. **Open** midnight-3am Wed-Sun. **Admission** free. **Credit** AmEx, MC, V. **Map** p343 E7.

Another Jekyll and Hyde restaurant-club, where the staff look miserable in their role as waiters, but once it's party time their joie de vivre knows no bounds. The restaurant has had horrendous reports, but thanks largely to its attempt at a harmonious oriental atmosphere (the decor has been feng shui-ed) the club is an oasis of good vibes and relative friendliness in the notoriously snooty-or-seedy Port Olimpic.

Sugar Club

World Trade Center, Moll de Barcelona (93 508 83 25/www.sugarclub-barcelona.com). Metro Drassanes. **Open** *Bar* 8-11.30pm Wed-Sat. *Club* 11pm-3am Wed-Sat. **Admission** free. **Credit** MC, V. **Map** p342 C7.

Grupo Salsitas continues its quest to rule all that's cool with this latest addition to the stable of Salsitas, Danzatoria, Danzarama et al. Beautiful people and a twinkling view across the marina provide the decoration in this otherwise minimal couple of spaces, one small and intimate with a splash of smooth and soulful vocal house, the other a large dancefloor with sofas. DJs blend tribal, electro and tech house beats with the odd remixed '80s classic thrown in to keep the well-dressed 25- to 35-year-old Sugar babes sweet.

Montjuïc & Poble Sec

Barcelona Rouge

C/Poeta Cabanyes 21 (93 442 49 85). Metro Paral·lel. **Open** 11pm-4am Tue-Sat. **Admission** free. **No credit cards. Map** p341 B6.

A hidey hole of a place in one of Barcelona's unsung *barrios*. It's small enough to get packed even though it's little known, hard to get into and hard on the wallet. Once inside there's ambient music, good cocktails and battered sofas draped with foreign and local thirtysomethings – those with a bit of money and a bit of class who want to avoid the more obvious nightspots. Ring the buzzer to get in.

Discothèque

Poble Espanyol, Avda Marquès de Comillas (93 289 21 97/93 424 24 98). Metro Espanya. **Open** midnight-6am Fri, Sat. **Admission** (incl 1 drink) €18 with flyer, €12 without. **Credit** MC, V. **Map** p341 A5.

New promoters have taken on the arduous task of keeping Discothèque at the forefront of the A-list clubs. As at neighbouring Terrrazza, a snaking queue of the young and the beautiful use looks and attitude to blag their way in. Nights with names like 'Ken loves you' or 'Fuck me, I'm famous' mix up house and techno in the main room, while hip hop and R&B sounds fill the smaller room. Projections, drag queens, podium dancers and an aspirational VIP bar all recreate the Ibiza-when-it-was-still-hot vibe.

Maumau

C/Fontrodona 33 (93 441 80 15/www.mauma underground.com). Metro Paral·lel. **Open** 11pm-2.30am Thur; 11pm-3am Fri, Sat; 7pm-midnight Sun. **Admission** (membership) €5. **No credit cards. Map** p342 C6.

Recently renovated to include, among other things, a wheelchair ramp and better lavatories, Mauma is the long-time favourite of the Poble Sec haunts. Behind the anonymous grey door (ring the bell), first-timers to this likeable little chill-out club pay €5 to become members. In practice it rarely charges out-of-towners. Inside, a large warehouse space is humanised with colourful projections, IKEA sofas and scatter cushions, and a friendly, laid-back crowd. DJ Wakanda schools us in the finer points of deep house, jazz, funk or whatever takes his fancy.

Mercat de les Flors/Pocket Club

Ciutat del Teatre, C/Lleida 59 (93 426 18 75/ 21 02/www.pocketbcn.com). Metro Espanya or Poble Sec. **Open** 9.30pm-2am every other Thur. **Admission** €9. *Gigs* varies. **No credit cards.** **Map** p341 B6.

Mercat de les Flors is normally the host for performances programmed for one festival or another – anything from film to digital art happenings to experimental drama. But it has appeared on the urban hipster's radar recently as one of the venues for Pocket Club (*see also* Distrito Diagonal, *p258*). This bi-monthly night features the most independent of musical performers, from beardy folk twiddler Iron and Wine to laptop-wielding, mash-up audio guerrilla Jason Forrest.

Sala Apolo

C/Nou de la Rambla 113 (93 441 40 01/www.sala-apolo.com). Metro Paral·lel. **Open** midnight-5.30am Wed; 12.30-5.30am Thur; 12.30-6.30am Fri, Sat. **Admission** (incl 1 drink) €4 Wed; €6-€12 Thur; €12 Fri, Sat. **No credit cards.** **Map** p342 C6.

This 1940s dancehall is a curious and rather musty backdrop for some of the most eclectic alternative music programming in Barcelona. Local bands and international groups from Lee Scratch Perry to Gotan Project play from Thursday to Saturday before the club sessions kick off the night proper. Wednesday's Canibal Sound System night stretches the term Latin music to include hip hop and funk. Thursday is funk night in the Powder Room. Pick up a flyer for free entry to Maumau on Sunday. Friday and Saturday's Nitsa Club is an elder statesman of the techno scene.

La Terrrazza

Poble Espanyol, Avda Marquès de Comillas (93 272 49 80/www.nightsungroup.com). Metro Espanya. **Open** *Mid Oct-mid May* midnight-6am Thur-Sat. **Admission** (incl 1 drink) €15 with flyer, €18 without. **Credit** MC, V. **Map** p341 A5.

What used to be the summer face of the city's best-known club combo in the bizarre environs of the Poble Espanyol is now its own separate entity. Beautiful (or at least young, or at least gay) people queue out front from May to October to dance under the stars. You don't have to dress up but you may skip the queue or the ticket price if you do. Guests like house DJs Dimitri from Paris and Miguel Migs share the decks with resident DJs.

Tinta Roja

C/Creu dels Molers 17 (93 443 32 43/ www.tintaroja.net). Metro Poble Sec. **Open** *Bar* 8pm-1am Wed, Thur, Sun; 8pm-3am Fri, Sat. *Shows* 10pm-midnight Wed-Sun. Closed 2wks Aug. **Admission** *Bar* free. *Shows* (incl 1 drink) €8. **No credit cards.** **Map** p341 B6.

Push through the depths of the bar to be transported to a Buenos Aires bordello/theatre/circus/cabaret by plush red velvet sofas, smoochy niches and ancient ticket booth. It's an atmospheric place for a late-ish drink, and a distinctly different entertainment experience from Friday to Sunday when there are live performances of tango, jazz and flamenco, in a small theatre at the back. Tango classes are also offered.

Eixample

242

C/Entença 37 (www.dosquatredos.com). Metro Espanya or Rocafort. **Open** varies. **Admission** varies. **No credit cards.** **Map** p341 B5.

DosQuatreDos (242 in Catalan) had its inception in 1999 as a goth-friendly joint playing dark European electronica by the likes of Depeche Mode. Things have lightened up a bit since then, with the studded dog collars now sharing dancefloor space with the glitter of electroclash. Brit-music-loving locals old enough to remember Blue Monday's original release come here to shug to anything electronic, from Peaches to the Postal Service via the Pet Shop Boys. Check out the website for your free entry password and the wildly varying opening hours.

Antilla BCN Latin Club

C/Aragó 141 (93 451 45 64/www.antillasalsa. com). Metro Urgell. **Open** 11pm-4am Mon-Thur, Sun; 11pm-5.30am Fri, Sat. *Gigs* around 11.30pm. **Admission** (incl 1 drink minimum) €10. **No credit cards.** **Map** p341 B5.

The Antilla prides itself on being a 'Caribbean cultural centre', hosting exhibitions and publishing its magazine *Antilla News*. But its true calling lies in being the self-claimed best *salsateca* in town, with dance classes (including acrobatic salsa and Afro-Cuban styles) and a solid programme of live music covering all Latin flavours from *son* to merengue and Latin jazz.

Astoria

C/París 193 (93 200 98 25/www.grupocostaeste. com). Metro Diagonal. **Open** 9pm-3.30am Mon-Sat. Closed Aug. **Admission** free. **Credit** AmEx, MC, V. **Map** p338 C3.

From the same people who brought you Bucaro and the Sutton Club, Astoria offers a break from the norm. For a start, the club is housed in a converted 1950s cinema, which means the projections are big and actually watchable. There are three bars, so you're spared endless queues, there's plenty of comfortable seating along with a small dancefloor, and if you're very wonderful you may get to sit on a heart-shaped cushion in the tiny VIP area. With all this going for it, it has inevitably become the domain of Barcelona's moneyed classes.

Bucaro

C/Aribau 195 (93 209 65 62/www.grupocostaeste. com). FGC Provença. **Open** 10.30pm-3.30am Mon-Wed; 10pm-4am Thur; 10pm-5am Fri, Sat. **Admission** free. **Credit** AmEx, MC, V. **Map** p338 C3.

Looking a tad jaded these days, Bucaro's worn leather sofas and grubby pouffes still manage to pull a crowd of glamourpusses – those floor-to-ceiling mirrors allow plenty of preening space for Barcelona's peacocks. With the giant skylight looming above the dancefloor like a portal to another world, and a mezzanine where you can stalk your prey before swooping on to the dancefloor, this is a place that knows class when it sees it. Drinks are a couple of euros more expensive if you're sitting at a table. A list of dress code dos and don'ts and a friendly but firm bouncer to enforce them greet you at the entrance.

Buda Restaurante

C/Pau Claris 92 (93 318 42 52/www.buda restaurante.com). Metro Catalunya. **Open** 9pm-3am daily. **Admission** free. **Credit** MC, V. **Map** p344 B1.

The centre of Barcelona is strangely devoid of glamorous nightspots, or at least it was until Buda came along and put some sparkle back into the mix. The place has lots of throne-style furniture and gilded wallpaper, topped off with a colossal chandelier. The laid-back nature of the staff (dancing on the bar seems completely acceptable) and upbeat house music make it excellent for drinks and an ogle. Tuesday is 'Model's night' (which model isn't clear), Wednesday is ballroom dancing night, and every second Thursday is Asian night, complete with geishas.

City Hall

Rambla Catalunya 2-4 (93 317 21 77/www.grupo ottozutz.com). Metro Catalunya. **Open** midnight-6am Tue-Sun. **Admission** (incl 1 drink) €12. **Credit** (door only) MC, V. **Map** p344 A1.

Packs in a sweaty stream of clubbers thanks to its cutting-edge musical selection on any given day of the week. Trendspotting City Hall has Old is Cool night on Mondays, acid and electro house on Wednesdays, Soul City providing hip hop and R&B on Thursdays, and Underground Sessions on Fridays and Saturdays, with such ambassadors of house as Derrick L Carterh.

Danzarama

Gran Via de les Corts Catalans 604 (93 301 97 43/ reservations 93 342 5070/www.gruposalsitas.com). Metro Universitat. **Open** 7am-3am daily. **Admission** free. **Credit** AmEx, DC, MC, V. **Map** p342 D5.

A new opening from the ever-expanding Salsitas group, takes the restaurant-club concept to the extreme, opening from 7am for breakfast and serving snacks, lunches and dinner throughout the day into the night. From 6pm Café Chillout eases you into the evening with lounge music and infusions. Each evening sees a different event, such as special singles nights or comedy performances. Resident DJs, including local muso legend David Mas, play grown-up house for clubbers who've grown out of glowsticks.

Distrito Diagonal

Avda Diagonal 442 (mobile 607 113 602/ www.distritodiagonal.com). Metro Diagonal. **Open** 10pm-3.30am Wed, Thur, Sun; 10pm-4.30am Fri, Sat. **Admission** free, Fri-Sun; €5 Thur. **No credit cards. Map** p338 D4.

Housed in the stunning Casa Comalat, Distrito Diagonal attracts a slightly older crowd with an easygoing atmosphere bathed in red light, sounds from nu jazz to deep house and plenty of chairs to sink into. It's become a sought-after venue for small promoters and one-off parties, which means the music can veer from Bollywood to hip hop. Thursday nights Cabaret Club educates listeners with the latest indietronica.

Domèstic

C/Diputació 215 (93 453 16 61). Metro Universitat. **Open** 7.30pm-2.30am Mon-Thur; 7.30pm-3am Fri, Sat. **Admission** free. **Credit** AmEx, MC, V. **Map** 342 C5.

Domèstic is another multi-tasking venue, combining a rather half-hearted restaurant, a bar/club and an occasional live venue. The colours are bold, the crowd is studenty and the music is laid-back, ranging from electropop to tribal house, with a new roster of DJs every month. It tends to be more of a meeting place rather than a destination, though the cosy, battered leather chairs can be hard to leave.

La Fira

C/Provença 171 (mobile 650 855 384). Metro Hospital Clínic. **Open** 10pm-3am Tue-Thur; 10pm-4.30am Fri, Sat. **Admission** free before 1am; (incl 1 drink) €10 after 1am. **No credit cards. Map** p338 C4.

It's called a 'bar-museum', but don't worry, you don't get a history lesson with your pint of lager. The exhibits are old fairground rides: bumper cars, merry-go-rounds, crazy mirrors... which all seem a little spooky when in a dark, warehouse-sized space and surrounded by beered-up students flirting to a soundtrack of tacky pop.

Luz de Gas

C/Muntaner 246 (93 209 77 11/www.luzdegas.com). FGC Muntaner. **Open** 11.30pm-5am daily. *Gigs* around 12.30am Mon-Sat; midnight Sun. **Admission** (incl 1 drink) €15. **Credit** AmEx, DC, MC, V. **Map** p338 C3.

This lovingly converted old music hall, garnished with chandeliers and classical friezes, occasionally hosts classic MOR acts: Kool and the Gang or Bill Wyman's Rhythm Kings. In between the visits from international 'names', you'll find nightly residencies: blues on Mondays, Dixieland jazz on Tuesdays, cover bands on Wednesdays, Saturdays and Sundays, soul on Thursdays and rock on Fridays.

The Pop Bar

C/Aribau 103 (93 451 29 58). Metro Hospital Clínic. **Open** 9pm-3.30am Wed-Sun. **Admission** free. **Credit** AmEx, DC, MC, V. **Map** p338 C4.

Balls to house, hip hop and the rest of it, when you can have pure, unadulterated pop and one-hit

Quiet, please!

A night-time cruise through the Barri Gòtic in search of that next drink can seem like an enchanting ride in some surreal theme park of decadence and depravity, complete with costumed characters acting out wild fantasies and street vendors catering to your every need. Some people, however, have to live here, and Barcelona's residents have had enough, mobilising entire neighbourhoods to combat public enemy number one: noise.

From the Marcel Marceau lookalikes outside La Paloma trading lollipops for your silence, to the bed sheets hanging from Born balconies begging '*Sense soroll*' ('No noise'), the city has taken a hands-on approach to the issue. In Gràcia, an entire movement of neighbours has banded together with the city council to enforce strict ordinances in the squares and bars. Cops armed with decibel counters place tamper-proof sound limiters to baffle DJs and drinkers; on the squares, the erstwhile anarchy of terraces and crusties has been replaced with strict grids and schedules for placing tables, and absolutely no congregation of noisy youths is allowed. Loitering past 11pm is prohibited, and government-sponsored posters of sleeping babies loom overhead.

While draconian club laws such as the ones imposed in Britain and New York seem unlikely to land in Barcelona anytime soon, the fact remains that the authorities will always side with the residents before the establishments. Many places have been forced to cancel all music-related events and others have been forced to schedule DJs only at weekends. The relatively recent law bringing a 3am closing time has been a mixed blessing, meaning the only place for inebriated punters to carry on is the street. Most bars have strict guidelines asking that as you leave you are quiet, keep moving, don't loiter, and so on, the obvious flaw in the plan being that even the best-intentioned drunk is still, well, drunk.

wonders that you never thought you'd hear again – we're talking early Kylie, Rick Astley and Donna Summer. The retro decor is appropriate to the sounds, with funky brown, orange and white, augmented by things like polka dot toilets, and deep orange sofa booths. This place also gets two thumbs up for its big screens showing FashionTV, a welcome change from all those darned projections that you find absolutely everywhere else these days.

Santa Locura

C/Consell de Cent 294 (93 487 77 22). Metro Passeig de Gràcia. **Open** midnight-5.30am Thur-Sat. **Admission** (incl 1 drink) €10. **No credit cards**. **Map** p342 D5.

Perhaps the most extraordinary clubbing experience in Barcelona, Santa Locura has three floors filled with weird and wonderful, pseudo-religious, nocturnal pleasures: marry your honey at the bar; watch a Chippendale-style show; plead guilty at the confessional box, and hit the dancefloor to the music of Kylie and Sophie Ellis-Bextor.

Gràcia

L'Espai

Travessera de Gràcia 63 (93 241 68 10). Metro Diagonal. **Open** *Gigs* 10pm Tue-Sat, 7pm Sun. Closed July-Sept. **Admission** €7-€22. **Credit** MC, V. **Map** p338 C3.

The Catalan local authority runs this music and dance performance space, and there's a certain air of worthiness about the programming here, with a strong local bias. Still, it has a serious offering of world, jazz and experimental rock music, and many performances are recorded for national radio.

Gusto

C/Francisco Giner 24 (no phone/www.fatproducts. com). Metro Diagonal. **Open** 10pm-2.30am Wed, Thur, Sun; 10pm-3am Fri, Sat. **Admission** free. **No credit cards. Map** p338 D3.

Gusto gets full to bursting on weekend nights, seemingly due to one rather bizarre feature – past the normal but attractive red-painted front bar, where a DJ plays chilled electronica, a quirky backroom lures a young crowd with a floor covered in sand and with sands as seats.

KGB

C/Alegre de Dalt 55 (93 210 59 06). Metro Joanic. **Open** 3-7am Thur; 1-7am Fri, Sat. **Admission** (incl 1 drink) €9. **No credit cards. Map** p339 E3.

This aptly named spot looks like it sounds – hardcore. A dark, intimidating space, it's been Barcelona's top choice for ear-bleed techno for over two decades. These days it's also experimenting with a wider music policy, including ska and reggae nights. Mostly, though, the promoters stick to the tried-and-tested recipe of any music that makes kids think they're hard: hip hop, punk, hardcore and nu-metal.

Mond Bar

Plaça del Sol 21 (93 272 09 10/www.mondclub.com). Metro Fontana. **Open** 8.30pm-3am daily. **Admission** free. **No credit cards. Map** p338 D3.

The pop child of the Mond Club and Sinnamon Promotions, the juggernaut music promoter behind all things Mond and most things Razzmatazz. This tiny two-level bar gets sweaty and smoky as the coolest cats in Gràcia pack in for an early drink. Recent problems with the neighbours have meant the music is quieter now, but that doesn't stop the guest DJs from churning out pop, soul and electro funk.

Mond Club

Sala Cibeles, C/Còrsega 363 (93 272 09 10/ www.mondclub.com). Metro Diagonal. **Open** 12.30-6am Fri. Closed 2wks Aug. **Admission** (incl 1 drink) €12. **No credit cards. Map** p338 D4.

Friday nights this vintage dancehall, upgraded with nasty floor tiles, turns into the Mond Club, with DJs playing old-school tunes from northern soul to '80s pop via new wave. It attracts pop or die youngsters and downtown music enthusiasts who're willing to travel up here for their night of nostalgia. Look out for occasional DJs turns from the likes of Jarvis Cocker, Arthur Baker and Swedish sensation Jay Jay Johanson.

Otto Zutz

C/Lincoln 15 (93 238 07 22/www.grupo-ottozutz. com). FGC Gràcia. **Open** midnight-5am Wed; midnight-5.30am Thur-Sat. **Admission** (incl 1 drink) €15. **Credit** AmEx, DC, MC, V. **Map** p338 D3.

Nightclubs and supermodels go hand in hand, so its no wonder that a club would give its name to a modelling agency. Its young superbabes come here to spend their hard-earned cash posing and strutting on the distinct dancefloors. Hip hop and R&B are the choice rhythms in one, there's deep house in the Velvet Room, while electro and tech house prevail on the main floor, where every month the Poker Flat boys lend their technical wizardry.

Sutton Club

C/Tuset 13 (93 414 42 17/www.thesuttonclub.com). Metro Diagonal. **Open** 11.30pm-4am Tue-Thur; 11.30pm-5am Fri, Sat; 6.30pm-midnight Sun. Closed 2wks Aug. **Admission** varies. **Credit** MC, V. **Map** p338 C3.

Glam, groovy and disco, in the truest sense of the word – with plenty of mirrors and chrome, and liveried waiters to bring your drinks to the table while sequinned podium dancers strut their stuff with feathers in their hair. View the grown-up, dressed-up crowd from your own balcony table – call to reserve.

Other areas

Bikini

C/Déu i Mata 105, Les Corts (93 322 08 00/www.bikinibcn.com). Metro Les Corts or Maria Cristina. **Open** midnight-5am Tue-Sun. **Admission** (incl 2 drinks before 1am, 1 after) €12 Tue-Sat; €14 Sun. **Credit** MC, V. **Map** p337 B3.

Bikini is hard to find in the soulless commercial streets behind the L'Illa shopping centre, but it's worth seeking out for top-flight gigs by serious musicians of any stripe, from Femi Kuti to the Thievery Corporation, Marianne Faithfull to Amp Fiddler. After the gigs, the slick spaces host club nights with house, funk and hip hop on the turntables. On Sunday watch Barça football matches on the big screen from 8.30pm, then party on to the latest dance sounds from 10.30pm.

Danzatoria

Avda Tibidabo 61 (93 272 00 40/www.grupo salsitas.com). FGC Avda Tibidabo, then 10min walk. **Open** 9pm-2.30am Tue-Sun. **Admission** free. **Credit** AmEx, DC, MC, V.

The uptown location attracts an upscale crowd to this spectacular converted manor house on a hill overlooking Barcelona. The top floor was recently converted to a restaurant, serving until midnight. The hipness factor goes up as you climb the club's glamour-glutted storeys. Preened *pija* flesh is shaken on hot-house dancefloors, or laid across sofas hanging from the ceiling in the chill-out lounges. We've had reports of snotty staff, but who cares when you're lounging in one of the layers of palm-filled gardens, accompanied by some gorgeous creature and some (very expensive) champagne, gazing at the city lights below.

Elephant
Passeig dels Til·lers 1 (93 334 02 58/www.elephant bcn.com). Metro Palau Reial. **Open** 11pm-3am Wed; 11pm-5am Thur-Sun. **Admission** free Wed, Thur, Sun; €15 Fri, Sat. **Credit** MC, V. **Map** 337 A2.
If you have a Porsche and a model girlfriend, this is where you meet your peers. A converted mansion, Elephant is as elegant and hi-design as its customers. The big attraction (apart from the aforementioned models) is the outdoor bar and terrace dancefloor – though the low-key, low-volume (due to neighbours' complaints) house music doesn't inspire much hands-in-the-air action.

Mirablau
Plaça Doctor Andreu 1, Tibidabo (93 418 58 79). FGC Avda Tibidabo, then Tramvia Blau. **Open** 11am-4.30am Mon-Thur, Sun; 11am-5.30am Fri, Sat. **Credit** DC, MC, V.
It doesn't get any more uptown than this, geographically and socially. Located at the top of Tibidabo and at the end of the road, this small bar is packed with the perfumed high rollers of Barcelona, from local footballers living on the hill to international businessmen on the company card, as well as young *pijos* stopping by for a drink before heading off to nearby Danzatoria on daddy's ride. Apart from the blaring cheesy Spanish pop, its only attraction is the breathtaking view.

Universal
C/Marià Cubí 182 bis-184 (93 201 35 96/www. grupocostaeste.com). FGC Muntaner. **Open** 11pm-5.30am Mon-Sat. **Credit** AmEx, MC, V. **Admission** free. **Map** p338 C3.
One of a very few clubs in the city that cater to an older, well-dressed crowd, Universal doesn't charge to get in, but the drink prices are steep. Recent renovations by the designer of the Salsitas chain have brought about aquatic slide projections in the upstairs chill-out area, along with a sharper look downstairs. As it gets later, the music moves from downtempo to soft house, which works the crowd up to a gentle shimmy.

Poblenou

Oven
C/Ramon Turró 126 (93 221 06 02). Metro Poblenou. **Open** 1.30pm-4am Mon; 1.30pm-3am Tue-Fri; 9pm-3am Sat. **Credit** AmEx, MC, V. **Map** p343 F6.

The slickest outfit in the newly hip Poblenou, Oven is a bit tiresome to get to but well worth the effort, especially if you make a night of it by having cocktails and dinner here first. The industrial interior segues into grown-up clubland come midnight, when the tables are cleared to make way for dancing, and Barcelona's best-known DJ, Professor Angel Dust, hits the decks with his own mix of house and Afro-Latin tunes.

Razzmatazz
C/Almogàvers 122 (93 320 82 00). Metro Bogatell or Marina. **Open** 1-5am Fri, Sat. **Admission** (incl 1 drink) €12. **Credit** V. **Map** p343 F6.
Five thousand clubbers just can't be wrong. The mother of all warehouse superclubs and the best live venue in town, Razzmatazz recently opened up to its backdoor buddy the Loft, and now offers neophyte clubbers the chance to take in five rooms for just one admission price. Whether they're goths, punks, mods, technophiles or electrotrash, young Catalans from Badalona and beyond trek here to dance until they drop – or until the trains start running again. This is a place Jarvis Cocker, Miss Kittin and Dave Clark, as well as bands from Air to Blur, call home when they visit.

Outer limits

Pacha
Avda Doctor Marañon 17 (93 334 32 33/www. clubpachabcn.com). Metro Zona Universitaria. **Open** 11.30pm-4.30am Wed; midnight-7am Thur-Sat; 8pm-2am Sun. **Admission** (incl 1 drink) €15. **Credit** MC, V.
The international *über*club lands in Barcelona and loses none of its charm in doing so. This Pacha is huge and brightly lit, and has one of the best sound systems in town – not a penny has been spared in creating the club's six bars, two VIP areas, chill-out room and terrace. The crowd is young, comprising a mix of students and fresh-faced foreign tourists. Sunday is Sundown 'Teadance' sessions day, with big-in-Ibiza guest DJs playing uplifting house from 8pm.

Space Barcelona
C/Tarragona 141-147 (93 426 84 44/ www.spacebarcelona.com). Metro Tarragona. **Open** midnight-6am Fri, Sat. **Admission** (incl 1 drink) €15; €12 with flyer. **No credit cards**. **Map** p341 A-B4.
Space? Well, there's actually not much of it in this mainland version of the Balearic superclub, but that doesn't stop Barcelona's youngest citizens, who parade the latest H&M designer imposter threads and head to this meat market of raging hormones to relive memories of last summer in Ibiza. The decor is very Bauhaus, and its four ample bars make for a short wait. The DJ sets orbit around house, with occasional guests like the Basement Boys bringing in an older mixed crowd.

Performing Arts

Let them entertain you.

Gran Teatre del Liceu. *See p263.*

Classical Music & Opera

A decade ago, with its opera house still smouldering, Barcelona only had one decent venue. How times change. The architecturally exuberant Palau de la Música remains, but the last few years have seen the phoenix-like Liceu spread its wings, the stark Auditori provide the city with a bleeding-edge concert hall, the Auditori Winterthur become a small, charming outpost in the otherwise soulless business and university district, and the Palau de la Música demolish the church next door to make space for a subterranean 500-seat auditorium. These venue changes have been supplemented by a subtle switch in repertoire. The canon still reigns, of course. But as a younger generation of cultural programmers takes charge, newer work has found an audience. You no longer have to be dead to get your music heard.

The last few years have seen the deaths of two leading Catalan composers – Joaquim

Homs and Xavier Montsalvatge – leaving Joan Guinjoan as Catalonia's most important living composer. Another local, manic genius Carles Santos, composes, directs and performs in surreal operatic-theatrical performances that combine sex, psychology and sopranos. Now in his sixties, he still manages to average a new show a year.

The main musical season runs September to June. During this time the city orchestra, the **OBC**, plays weekly at the **Auditori**, while the **Liceu** hosts a different opera every three or four weeks. Both the Auditori and the **Palau de la Música** hold several concert cycles of various genres, either programmed by the venues or by independent promoters (Ibercamera and Euroconcert are the most important). Several festivals are also staged, the foremost of which are the **Festival de Música Antiga** (*see p217*) and the **Nous Sons** festival of contemporary music (*see p266*).

In summer, the focus moves. Various museums, among them the **Museu Marítim** (*see p112* **Making waves**), the **Fundació Miró** (*see p118*), the **Museu Barbier-Mueller** (*see p105*) and **La Pedrera** (*see p129*), hold small outdoor concerts, and there are weekly events in several of the city's parks (*see p220* **Clàssics als Parcs**). More serious musical activity, though, follows its audience and heads up the coast, to major festivals in the towns of Perelada, Cadaqués, Toroella de Montgrí and Vilabertrán.

INFORMATION AND TICKETS

The most thorough source of information is the monthly *Informatiu Musical*, published by Amics de la Música (93 268 01 22, www.amics musica.org), which lists concerts in all genres. You can pick up a copy at tourist offices (*see p321*) and record shops. Weekly entertainment guide *Guía del Ocio* has a music section; both *El País* and *La Vanguardia* list forthcoming concerts, and usually publish details for that day's more important events. The council website, www.bcn.es, also has details. Tickets for most major venues can be bought by phone or online from the venue itself, or from **Tel-entrada** or **Servi-Caixa** (for both, *see p214*).

Venues

In addition to the venues below, a number of churches hold concerts. The most spectacular is **Santa Maria del Mar** (*see p109*) in the Born, whose tall, ghostly interior exemplifies the Gothic intertwining of music, light and spirituality. Concerts include everything from Renaissance music to gospel. There's a monthly free organ concert at the cathedral, usually (but not always) held on the second Wednesday of the month. Other churches with regular concerts include **Santa Maria del Pi**, **Sant Felip Neri**, **Santa Anna** and the monastery in **Pedralbes**. In May, keep an eye out for the **Festival de Música Antiga** (*see p217*), when concerts of early music are held in different locations in the Old City.

L'Auditori

C/Lepant 150, Eixample (93 247 93 00/www. auditori.org). Metro Marina. **Open** *Information* 8-10pm daily. *Box office* noon-9pm Mon-Sat; 1hr before performance Sun. *Performances* 8pm Mon-Thur; 9pm Fri; 7pm Sat; 11am Sun. **Tickets** varies. **Credit** MC, V. **Map** p343 F5.

Rafael Moneo's sleek design is anodyne to the point of anonymity, all pale beech and sharp lines, and the Auditori is never likely to arouse the same affection as the Palau de la Música. Nevertheless, the newish, 2,400-seat hall has provided the city with a world-class music venue and a home to its orchestra, the OBC. The Museu de la Música is expected to open here towards the end of 2005, as is a new 600-seat auditorium, which will add more variety to an already impressive programme that covers not just classical

music but jazz, contemporary and world music. A late-night bus service connects the Auditori with Plaça Catalunya after evening performances.

Auditori Winterthur

Auditori de l'Illa, Avda Diagonal 547, Les Corts (93 290 11 02/www.winterthur.es). Metro Maria Cristina. **Open** *Information* 9am-1.30pm, 3-7pm Mon-Fri. **Tickets & credit** varies. **Map** p337 B3.

A charming, intimate venue in the unlikely setting of L'Illa, a monolithic shopping centre. Though it hosts few concerts, they're generally of a high quality; the Schubert cycle and series of song recitals, both annual events, are well worth catching.

Gran Teatre del Liceu

La Rambla 51-59, Barri Gòtic (93 485 99 13/tickets 902 53 33 35/www.liceubarcelona.com). Metro Liceu. **Open** *Information* 10am-10pm Mon-Fri. *Box office* 2-8.30pm Mon-Fri; 1hr before performance Sat, Sun. Closed 2wks Aug. **Tickets** varies. **Credit** AmEx, DC, MC, V. **Map** p345 A3.

The Liceu has gone from strength to strength of late, steadily increasing the number of performances but still often selling out. The flames that swept away an outdated, rickety structure a decade ago cleared the decks for a fine new opera house. Compared with the restrained façade, the 2,340-seat auditorium is an elegant, classical affair of red plush, gold leaf and ornate carvings, but with mod cons that include seat-back subtitles in various languages that complement the Catalan surtitles above the stage.

In addition to its own operas, the Liceu hosts some of the best itinerant productions and co-productions with leading opera houses Europe-wide, as well as major international dance companies and even the (very) occasional pop concert. The large basement bar hosts pre-performance talks, recitals, children's shows and other musical events; the Espai Liceu is a 50-seat auditorium with a regular programme of screenings of past operas.

Palau de la Música Catalana

C/Sant Francesc de Paula 2, Sant Pere (93 295 72 00/ www.palaumusica.org). Metro Urquinaona. **Open** *Box office* 10am-9pm Mon-Sat; 1hr before performance Sun. **Tickets** varies. **Credit** MC, V. **Map** p344 B/C2.

The astonishing, overwrought architectural flights of fancy of the Palau de la Música's interior are only hinted at by its façade. Built in 1908 by Lluís Domènech i Montaner, it ranks alongside any Gaudi building for imagination and colour. A recent extension, adding a terrace, a restaurant and a subterranean hall, has been controversial: concert-goers approve, but architecture critics have been less sure.

The Orquestra Simfònica del Vallès is the most regular visitor, its Saturday evening concerts made up mostly of symphonic classics. Various performances by more internationally recognised names either form part of the 16-concert Palau 100 cycle, or are brought by independent promoters. If you can't make it to a concert, there are several tours of the building every day in either Spanish or English (*see p107*).

Orchestras & ensembles

La Capella Reial de Catalunya, Le Concert des Nations & Hespèrion XXI

Information 93 580 60 69.

That Catalonia has a rich heritage in early music is due in large part to the indefatigable Jordi Savall, the driving force behind these three interlinked groups that, between them, play around 300 concerts a year worldwide. La Capella Reial specialises in Catalan and Spanish Renaissance and baroque music; Le Concert des Nations is a period-instrument ensemble playing orchestral and symphonic work from 1600 to 1850; and Hespèrion XXI plays pre-1800 European music.

Orfeó Català

Information 93 295 72 00/www.palaumusica.org.

The Orfeó Català began life as one of 150 choral groups that sprang up in Catalonia as part of the patriotic and social movements at the end of the 19th century. While it's no longer as pre-eminent as it once was, the group still stages around 25 performances a year, giving a cappella concerts as well as providing a choir for the Orquestra Simfònica and other Catalan orchestras. The largely amateur group also includes a small professional nucleus, the Cor de Cambra del Palau de la Música, which gives 50 performances a year.

Orquestra Simfònica de Barcelona Nacional de Catalunya (OBC)

Information 93 247 93 00/www.obc.es.

Representing both Barcelona and Catalonia, the awkwardly named OBC is the busiest orchestra in town, performing at the Auditori almost every weekend of the season. Under the right baton the Simfònica can excel, though it's difficult to know who wields it: the 2004/5 season features no fewer than 18 different conductors for 30 concerts. The orchestra provides a fairly standard gallop through the symphonic repertoire, though new artistic director and principal conductor Ernest Martínez

Let's do the show right here!

When Laurie Lee set out one midsummer morning with his fiddle under his arm, he joined a centuries-long tradition of troubadours slacking round the Med postponing difficult career choices. This same tradition now brings us motionless men in white make-up sitting on the toilet, grim reapers reaping grimly at the cathedral doors and every crusty and his inevitable dog importuning passers-by with *Ode to Joy* on the penny whistle. With or without the joy. But before you strap on your guitar with dreams of wine and wealth, a note of warning: as befits a flourishing free-market economy, competition is intense, standards are high and off-key renditions of *Stand By Me* aren't going to impress anyone. Unless, of course, you can play it on the saw, the sousaphone or the shower attachment.

The good news is that you don't need to be musical to busk successfully in Barcelona. You don't need to be a good juggler. In fact, you don't have to be able to do anything at all except stand very, very still. From the spectacular to the surreal, with occasional forays into the shoddy, Barcelona's human statues are an impressive menagerie, encouraged by a sympathetic urban setting. At peak times human statues line up like models at a beauty parade, each attracting an expectant crowd. There's no accounting for taste: the stunning sylvan tree nymph emerging from an elaborate creation of twigs, glitter and tulle gets less attention than Bart Simpson, whose efforts extend to buying a yellow mask, and occasionally squirting kids with his water-pistol. It's the whole high art versus low art argument in microcosm: the few might want Titania, the masses want Bart and Darth and the Devil and someone sitting on the toilet.

Musically, there's a similar range, apparently distributed according to area: Spanish classical guitar in the squares and spaces around the cathedral, alternating with baroque violins and flutes; Dixieland on shopping streets; bleary crusties and over-qualified music students in quiet sidestreets, and the regulation troupes of amped-up Peruvians at the top of La Rambla, with pan pipes, playback and please-buy-our-CD smiles.

One change in the musical cosmos of late has been the influx of eastern Europeans. No restaurant terrace is now complete without an accordion and fiddle combo. So well have they adapted that rather than Romanian folk songs and Ukrainian laments, they play the same French and Spanish standards as everyone else. However, they don't do so with quite as much verve, and nerve, as the two women in front of the cathedral playing synchronised cimbalos (like a piano stripped of keys, hammers and casing) who treat passers-by to euphonious renditions of Abba.

Contemporary music gets a hearing in the **AvuiMúsica** concert series.

Izquierdo has brought in a more adventurous programme. The orchestra is also committed to new Catalan composers, commissioning two works a year and giving a handful of others their first performance. In 2004 it performed at the electronic music festival Sónar (*see p219*), in conjunction with various non-classical musicians.

Orquestra Simfònica i Cor del Gran Teatre del Liceu
Information 93 485 99 13/www.liceubarcelona.com.
Verdi and Wagner are the sine qua nons of the Liceu season. Following huge success with an excellent *Ring* cycle performed over two years, in 2005 it's the turn of *Parsifal* and *Rigoletto*, as well as a concert version of *Il Corsaro*. Italian staples by the likes of Puccini and Rossini also feature regularly, as do Britten and Janácek, with *A Midsummer Night's Dream* and *Jenufa* staged in 2005. The season ends in July with a revival of a crowd-pleaser: *Turandot* is due in 2005. There's also a programme of concerts and recitals, including sessions linked to the current opera, and a half-dozen mini-operas for children; favourites include *Peter and the Wolf* and *The Magic Flute*.

Orquestra Simfònica del Vallès
Information 93 727 03 00/www.osvalles.com.
This run-of-the-mill provincial orchestra, based in the nearby town of Sabadell, performs regularly in Barcelona, often at the Palau de la Música, where it plays a dozen symphonic concerts each season.

Contemporary music

AvuiMúsica
Associació Catalana de Compositors, Passeig Colom 6, space 4, Barri Gòtic (93 268 37 19/ www.accompositors.com). Metro Jaume I.
Open *Information* 9.30am-1.30pm Mon-Fri. **Tickets** €9; €4.50 concessions. **No credit cards. Map** p344 B4.
A season of small-scale contemporary concerts run by the Association of Catalan Composers at various venues around the city. Members of the association are well represented, and around half the works each year have not been played in public before.

Barcelona 216
Information 93 487 87 81.
A small ensemble with a strong commitment to contemporary music of all types, including written compositions and more experimental works.

CAT
Travessera de Sant Antoni 6-8, Gràcia (93 218 44 85/www.tradicionarius.com). Metro Fontana. **Open** *Gigs* about 10pm Fri. Closed Aug. **Admission** €10-€15. **No credit cards. Map** p338 D3.
The Centre Artesà Tradicionàrius promotes traditional Catalan music and culture and hosts a number of festivals, including a showcase of folk music and dance staged between January to April. The Centre's concerts, workshops and classes also cover indigenous music from the rest of Spain as well as other countries.

Diapasón

Information 93 415 51 15.

A septet specialising in Satie and more playful works of contemporary classical music led by composer/performer Domènec González de la Rubia.

Festival d'Òpera de Butxaca i Noves Creacions

Mobile 659 454 879/www.festivaloperabutxaca.org. **Date** 2nd half Nov.

A successful series of small-scale chamber operas performed in various venues, including the former anatomy theatre of the Royal Academy of Medicine.

Fundació Joan Miró

Parc de Montjuïc, Montjuïc (93 443 94 70/ www.bcn.fjmiro.es). Metro Paral·lel, then Funicular de Montjuïc/bus 50, 55. **Open** *(Mid June-July) Box office* 1hr before performance Thur. **Tickets** €6; €15 for 3 concerts. **Credit** MC, V. **Map** p341 B6.

When the rest of the city gets too hot, head up to the Fundació Miró for its annual festival of jazz, improv and other performance-based music. It's not the greatest venue in the city, but the electric performances soon dispel any discomfort. Some concerts take place on the roof terrace.

Gràcia Territori Sonor

Information 93 237 37 37/www.gracia-territori.com.

The main focus of this dynamic, tirelessly creative collective is the LEM festival: held in various venues in Gràcia, it's a rambling, eclectic series of musical happenings, much of them experimental, improvised and electronic, and most of them free. The concerts are supplemented by dance performances, sound installations and poetry readings. The larger, more formal events are held at L'Espai and CaixaForum.

Metrònom

C/Fusina 9, Born (93 268 42 98/www.metronom-bcn. org). Metro Arc de Triomf or Jaume I. **Concerts** 10pm. **Admission** free. **Map** p345 C3.

Known predominantly for its exhibitions and installations, Metrònom also hosts concerts of experimental music. The main focus is a week-long series of concerts in late January/early February, featuring key international figures from the experimental music scene. Concerts also take place at other times throughout the year; some are in collaboration with the Barcelona foundation Phonos, which specialises in experimental electro-acoustic music.

Nous Sons – Músiques Contemporànies

Information 93 247 93 00/www.auditori.org. **Date** 9 Feb-18 Mar 2005.

Previously known as the festival of contemporary music, New Sounds is an interesting burst of new music that continues to evolve year by year, and features national and international ensembles. The emphasis in 2005 is on written music, particularly the work of Arvo Pärt and Magnus Lindberg.

Trio Kandinsky

Information 93 301 98 97/www.triokandinsky.com. Formed in 1999, the Trio Kandinsky have an excellent reputation, performing contemporary repertoire across Spain and all over the Mediterranean.

Theatre & Dance

Barcelona has a long tradition of dynamic theatre, and 2004 was a particularly busy year. The five-month Fòrum 2004, a kind of non-competitive cultural Olympics, saw dozens of companies from all over the world stage shows both on the Fòrum site and around town.

Key Catalan theatre players making waves internationally include La Fura dels Baus, Els Comediants and Tricicle, while Dagoll Dagom (*see p269* **Rocking the boat**) creates huge money-spinning musicals. And don't forget ever-controversial Calixto Bieito: renowned for his wildly polemical interpretations of *Hamlet* and *Don Giovanni*, he's directed classics at the Edinburgh Festival and worked at the English National Opera.

Although Barcelona has many thriving contemporary dance companies, there are few major dance venues and most companies spend a large amount of their time touring. Performers such as Pina Bausch and the Compañía Nacional de Danza (directed by the revered Nacho Duato) have played to sell-out crowds in the **Teatre Nacional** and the **Liceu**, while the Teatre Nacional has a resident company led by Marta Carrasco and the **Teatre Lliure** hosts quite a lot of new work. However, it's generally difficult for companies to find big audiences.

Innovative companies such as Sol Picó and Mar Gómez usually run a new show every year, as do emblematic, influential companies such as Metros, Mudances and Gelabert-Azzopardi. The **Institut del Teatre** is the main official training ground for future actors and dancers. Its own dance company, IT DANSA, will be performing at the Teatre Nacional in June 2005.

SEASONS AND FESTIVALS

The **Sitges Teatre Internacional** festival (www.teatresitges.com) is held from late May to early June, mixing new Catalan work and better-known international companies. The **Grec Festival** (*see p220*) is another must – apart from having impressive shows from all over the world, its open-air venues are magical on a summer night. New companies have a chance to launch their work at the **Mostra de Teatre** (www.mostradeteatre debarcelona.com) in October and November, when they're assigned two nights apiece and are judged by a panel of directors. The

Marató de l'Espectacle at the Mercat de
les Flors (*see p219*) is in May, with a fun but
exhausting two nights of non-stop five-minute
performances. **Dies de Dansa** (*see p220*)
offers three days of national and international
dance in public sites such as the Port, the
CCCB or the MACBA.

TICKETS AND TIMES
Main shows start around 9-10.30pm, although
many theatres have earlier (and cheaper) shows
at 6-7pm on Saturdays. On Sundays there are
morning matinées aimed at family audiences;
most theatres are dark on Mondays. Advance
bookings are best made through Servi-Caixa or
Tel-entrada (*see p214*). The best places to find
information are *Guía del Ocio* and the *cartelera*
(listings) pages of the newspapers. Online,
check www.teatral.net and www.teatrebcn.com;
for dance, try www.dancespain.com.

Major venues

Large-scale commercial productions are shown
in the massive **Teatre Condal** (Avda Paral·lel
91, 93 42 31 32), home to the ever-popular
Tricicle group; the **Borràs** (Plaça Urquinaona
9, 93 412 15 82); and the **Tívoli** (C/Casp 10-12,
93 412 20 63), which hosts giant productions
such as the musical *Fame*. The **Monumental**
bullring (*see p272*) and the **Palau d'Esports**
(C/Guàrdia Urbana s/n, 93 423 64 63) are used

for mega-shows in the off-season. Ballet and
modern dance troupes occasionally appear at
the **Liceu** and the **Teatre Nacional**, while
cultural centres such as the **CCCB** (*see p99*)
and gallery **Metrònom** (*see p105*) are often
used for contemporary dance.

L'Espai
Travessera de Gràcia 63, Gràcia (93 241 68 10).
FGC Gràcia. **Box office** 6.30-10pm Tue-Sat; 5-7pm
Sun. **Tickets** €11-€20; €8.25-€15 concessions.
Credit AmEx, DC, MC, V. **Map** p338 C3.
Funded by the Catalan government, and therefore
able to programme more experimental work as well
as more popular performers, this is just about the
only venue dedicated to dance. There are fine dance
shows for kids from the very visual Nats Nus, and,
in 2005, from the Mudances company.

Mercat de les Flors
Plaça Margarida Xirgú, C/Lleida 59, Montjuïc
(93 426 18 75/www.mercatflors.com). Metro Poble
Sec. **Box office** 1hr before show. Advance tickets
also available from Palau de la Virreina. **Tickets**
varies. **No credit cards. Map** p341 B6.
A huge converted flower market housing three
performance spaces, the Mercat is one of the most
innovative venues in town. Performances here
experiment with unusual formats and mix new
technologies, pop culture and the performing arts.
Film nights and DJ sessions (as part of Pocket Club
on Thursdays; *see p257*) also feature; events include
May's Marató de l'Espectacle (*see p219*) and an
Asian festival in autumn.

Publicly funded space, large-scale theatre: **Teatre Nacional de Catalunya (TNC)**. *See p268.*

Arts & Entertainment

Teatre Lliure

Plaça Margarida Xirgú, Montjuïc (93 289 27 70/ www.teatrelliure.com). Metro Poble Sec. **Box office** 11am-3pm, 4.30-8pm Mon-Fri; 2hrs before show Sat, Sun. **Tickets** €12-€16 Tue, Wed; €16-€24 Thur-Sun; €12 concessions Tue-Sun. **Credit** MC, V. **Map** p341 B6.

Many of Barcelona's most interesting actors, designers and directors have started out at this venue, founded in 1976. Young director Alex Rigola has compiled an eclectic programme for 2005 that includes *La meva filla sóc jo*, a new Carles Santos avant-garde musical creation. Bigger shows are subtitled in English on Wednesdays.

Teatre Nacional de Catalunya (TNC)

Plaça de les Arts 1, Eixample (93 306 57 00/www. tnc.es). Metro Glòries. **Box office** 3-9pm Tue-Sun. **Tickets** €15-€25; €10-€15 concessions. **Credit** AmEx, DC, MC, V. **Map** p343 F5.

Funded by the Generalitat, designed by architect Ricard Bofill and built in 1996, the huge Parthenon-like TNC has three superb performance spaces. Its main stage promotes large-scale Catalan and Spanish classical theatre; shows include *Mar i Cel*, slated at the time of writing to run through the spring (*see p269* **Rocking the boat**), and, in summer 2005, *Fuenteovejuna* by Lope de Vega. More contemporary European theatre and works by new writers are normally staged in the more experimental Sala Tallers. The Projecte T-Dansa gives young dancers their first professional experience; the excellent Marta Carrasco is in residence until 2006.

Teatre Poliorama

La Rambla 115, Barri Gòtic (93 317 75 99/www.teatre poliorama.com). Metro Catalunya. **Box office** 5-8pm Tue; 5-9.30pm Wed-Sat; 5-7pm Sun. Closed 2wks Aug. **Tickets** varies. **Credit** MC, V. **Map** p344 A2.

Run by private producers 3xtr3s, this central theatre specialises in new work, normally by Catalan writers. On Sundays there are musicals for children.

Teatre Romea

C/Hospital 51, Raval (information 93 301 55 04/ tickets 902 10 12 12/www.fundacioromea.org). Metro Liceu. **Box office** 5-8pm Tue-Sat. **Performances** 9pm Tue-Fri; 6.30pm, 10pm Sat; 6.30pm Sun. **Tickets** €10-€24. **Credit** (phone bookings only) AmEx, DC, MC, V. **Map** p342 C6.

Calixto Bieito is the artistic director of the Teatre Romea, which starts its sixth season under huge private producer Focus. The theatre looks to contemporary European theatre for inspiration; highlights of the 2004/5 season include *Kiss of the Spider Woman*, *Festen* and *The People Next Door*, about the damage caused by the fearmongering after the 9/11 attacks.

Alternative theatres

Things are not looking good for smaller venues; a few have had to close lately, tired of fighting for funding and audiences. However, theatres such as the **Nou Tantarantana** (C/Flors 22,

93 441 70 22), the **Espai Escènic Joan Brossa** (C/Allada-Vermell 13, 93 310 13 64) and the **Versus Teatre** (C/Castillejos 179, 93 232 31 84) often produce interesting work. The **Teatre de la Riereta** (C/Reina Amalia 3, 93 442 98 44) hosts a few English works, as does the **Teatre Llantiol** (C/Riereta 7, 93 329 90 09).

Sala Beckett

C/Alegre de Dalt 55 bis, Gràcia (93 284 53 12/www. salabeckett.com). Metro Joanic. **Box office** from 8pm Wed-Sat. Closed Aug. **Tickets** €6-€16; €4-12 concessions. **No credit cards. Map** p339 E3.

This small venue was founded by the Samuel Beckett-inspired Teatro Fronterizo group, run by playwright José Sanchis Sinisterra. He's no longer based at the theatre, but his influence prevails; exciting innovative work is still the norm.

Theatre companies

As well as those reviewed below, companies to check include the satirical, camp **Chanclettes**, and the **Compañía Nacional Clásica** for versions of the Spanish masters. For English-language theatre, look out for the **Jocular** company and **Black Custard Theatre**.

Els Comediants

www.comediants.com.

Els Comediants have their roots in *commedia dell' arte* and street performance; their mix of mime, circus, music, storytelling and fireworks is as likely to appear on the street to celebrate a national holiday as at any major theatre festival. *L'Arbre de la Memòria* (*The Memory Tree*), a play starring a 12m (39ft) tree as imagined by the nature-starved occupants of a post-holocaust future, tours until July 2005.

Compañía Mar Gómez

www.danzamargomez.com

A wonderful mix of contemporary dance and theatre with a wicked sense of humour, fun images and and good music. The company's latest show, *Despues te lo cuento* (*I'll Tell You About It Later*), is touring nationally until the end of 2005.

La Cubana

www.lacubana.es.

Both satirical and spectacular, La Cubana's shows have a cartoonish quality, using multimedia effects, camp music and audience participation. Its most recent sell-out show has been *Una Nit d'Opera,* a comic look at the diva-ridden world of opera.

La Fura dels Baus

www.lafura.com.

Barcelona's bad boy company has been going for 25 years and has toured the world with polemical and stimulating shows such as the 2003 *XXX*, a porn cabaret inspired by the Marquis de Sade. It describes its new show, *Obit*, as a voyage through life to death; once premièred, the show will be staged aboard the company's boat *Naumon*, which will first be moored in the Port Vell and then taken to various countries in the second half of 2005.

Els Joglars
www.elsjoglars.com.

Darkly satirical, Els Joglars have been at the forefront of political theatre for 30 years. Albert Boadella, the company's founder and leader was imprisoned under the Franco regime for his political stance and his theatre continues with the same basic ideology today. Recent creations include touring Cervantes farce *El Retablo de las Maravillas*.

Tricicle
www.tricicle.com.

Local boys Carles Sans, Paco Mir and Joan Gràcia founded this mime trio 25 years ago. The goofy,

Rocking the boat

Specialising in deliciously kitsched-up musicals in the old-time Broadway vein, **Dagoll Dagom** kickstarted big-style Catalan musicals 30 years ago. The company began as a university theatre company radically opposed to Franco's regime: in 1977, its first show, *No hablaré en clase* (*I Will Not Speak in Class*), a blatant attack on the oppressive educational system at that time, was banned, a problem the company solved by changing the name of the show and disguising its content.

The group's next show, *Antaviana* (1978), was the piece that consolidated the its reputation. More poetic than political, it toured all over Europe with more than a thousand shows. More recently the satirical works *Cacao* (2000) and *La Perritxola* (2003) spoofed various political goings-on of the day, all in the company's initimably anarchic style. However, its shows are not all its own:

among other works given Dagoll Dagom's fantastical treatment are a couple of Gilbert and Sullivan operettas, *The Mikado* and *The Pirates of Penzance*.

To celebrate the company's 30th anniversary, its emblematic 1988 musical *Mar i Cel* (*Sea and Sky*) has been revived for an indefinite run at the TNC. The show was a real turning point for theatre here; previously, writers and directors had looked to the West End or Broadway for inspiration or to adapt existing work, but this was an all-Catalan production. Based on a classic by nationalist playwright Àngel Guimerà, it's a tragic tale of Moors and Christians, pirates and damsels-in-distress, with a tear-jerking doomed love story at its core... all set aboard a gigantic boat marooned in the middle of the stage. The music, composed by Albert Guinovart, forms part of every drama student's vocal repertoire and every Catalan's record collection.

Arts & Entertainment

clean-cut humour appeals to the Spanish taste for slapstick; they're not above the odd Benny Hill moment of crossdressing or chase sequences.

Dance companies

In addition, groups worth seeing include popular and established company **Metros**, the collective **La Caldera**, newer group **Búbulus**, and Toni Mira's company **Nats Nus**. Its highly successful offshoot **Nats Nens** produces contemporary dance shows for children.

Andrés Corchero-Rosa Muñoz
www.iespana.es/andrescorchero.
This is the dance company that dancers love, but its experimental style, based on improvisation and butoh, can make it a little difficult for the uninitiated. Look out for the company's collaborative works too.

Gelabert-Azzopardi
www.gelabertazzopardi.com.
The influential duo of Cesc Gelabert and Lydia Azzopardi are at that moment when mental maturity and physical ability exist in more or less equal measure. Their emotional range and versatility can be seen in the forthcoming *Com un rossinyol amb mal de queixal (Like a Nightingale with Toothache)* at the Teatre Lliure in spring 2005.

Mal Pelo
www.malpelo.com.
Mal Pelo has a particular Catalan sensibility, creating expressive, earthy and somewhat surreal choreographies. Their new show exploring silence, *An (el silenci)*, is a mixture of dance, text and live music; it should be seen here in 2005.

Marta Carrasco
www.martacarrasco.com.
Carrasco has choreographed many plays and musicals, but she's now resident at the TNC (*see p268*), where her latest show, *Ga-gá*, opens in June 2005. The show promises to mix dance, drama and music in an exploration of old-style circus.

Mudances
www.margarit-mudances.com.
Director Àngels Margarit has been growing in stature as a choreographer for the past decade, producing highly structured work with a creative use of video. His new piece *Sólo Por Placer (Only For Pleasure)* will be staged at the Teatre Lliure in April 2005. Mudances often programmes shows for children.

Sol Picó
www.solpico.com.
Through perserverance, charisma, hard work and lots of energy, Sol Picó and her company are probably the best known of the younger generation of dancers. The company's recent works have enjoyed no little success, thanks to Picó's energy, curiosity and willingness to explore.

Flamenco

Bar-restaurant **TiriTiTran** (C/Buenos Aires, 28, 93 363 05 91) is a favourite with flamenco aficionados; impromptu performances often happen at weekends. The flamenco shows at the restaurant **Nervion** (C/Princesa 2, 93 315 21 03) seem to be aimed at curious tourists, but it is a lot cheaper than the established *tablaos*: if you don't eat, entry is €9, which includes a drink. **Soniquete** (C/Milans 5, mobile 639 382 354) is the most reliable and central place to hear spontaneous, and free, flamenco from Thursday to Sunday. If no one shows up, you'll still hear some decent *sevillanas* on the sound system.

El Tablao de Carmen
Poble Espanyol, Avda Marquès de Comillas, Montjuïc (93 325 68 95/www.tablaodecarmen.com). Metro Espanya. **Open** 8pm-2am Tue-Sun. *Shows* 9.30pm, 11.30pm Tue-Thur, Sun; 9.30pm, midnight Fri, Sat. Closed Jan. **Admission** show & 1 drink €29; show & dinner €55. **Credit** AmEx, DC, MC, V. **Map** p341 A5.
This rather sanitised version of the traditional flamenco *tablao* sits in faux-Andalucían surroundings in the Poble Espanyol. You'll find both established stars and new young talent, displaying the various styles of flamenco singing, dancing and music. The emphasis is on panache rather than passion, so you might prefer your flamenco with a bit more spit and a little less polish. You must reserve in advance (up to a week ahead in summer), which will allow you to enter the Poble Espanyol free after 7pm.

Los Tarantos
Plaça Reial 17, Barri Gòtic (93 318 30 67/www. masimas.com). Metro Liceu. **Open** *Flamenco show* 8.30pm, 9.30pm, 10.30pm daily. **Admission** €5. **Credit** MC, V. **Map** p342 D6.
This flamenco *tablao* has presented many top stars over the years. It now caters mainly to the tourist trade, but avoids the fripperies of some coach-party venues. Now under new ownership, prices have gone down, but the performers are less experienced.

Dance schools & workshops

Many of the major companies allow you to join their own classes for short periods, but call to check first. Some, like **Mudances** and **Lanónima Imperial**, also run special workshops. The **Institut del Teatre** runs summer classes, but they're often expensive. Two good spots for contemporary dance classes are **Area Espai de Dansa i Creació** (C/Alegre de Dalt 55, 93 210 78 50) and its neighbour **Company & Company** (C/Alegre de Dalt 57, 93 210 59 72). A more complete list of dance schools in Barcelona can be found at www.dancespain.com/schools.html.

Sport & Fitness

The Olympics left a multi-sport legacy, but football remains king.

Barcelona owes much of its current global prestige to the 1992 Olympics, an important legacy of which has been an impressive range of sporting facilities that are now open to the public. The city council has been at pains to make the most of the tracks, stadia and pools bequeathed by the event, not only in providing the infrastructure to practise 138 different sports – hapkido to fencing, jai alai to five-a-side football – but also to attract a variety of top-class events to Barcelona.

Reigning supreme over all this variety is FC Barcelona: El Barça, a symbol of Catalan identity, famously claims to be 'more than just a club'. It's certainly more than just a *football* club: as well as the team, whose massive Nou Camp stadium is the biggest in Europe, Barça run basketball, handball and roller-hockey teams, all wearing the hallowed '*blaugrana*' (blue and burgundy) strip.

Spectator sports

Tickets can often be purchased by credit card with **Servi-Caixa** or **Tel-entrada** (*see p214*). Check www.agendabcn.com or newspapers such as *El Mundo Deportivo* for event details.

Basketball

'*Baloncesta*' – or, simply, '*basket*' – is easily Spain's second most popular sport; the country even hosts Europe's most competitive league, the ACB. **FC Barcelona** are the most powerful side, fielding top-drawer European players; there are two other top local clubs, **DKV Joventut**, from Badalona, and **Basquet Manresa**. The season runs September to early June: league matches are on weekend evenings, with European matches played midweek.

FC Barcelona

Palau Blaugrana, Avda Aristides Maillol, Les Corts (93 496 36 00/www.fcbarcelona.com). Metro Collblanc or Palau Reial. **Ticket office** 9am-1.30pm, 3.30-6pm Mon-Thur; 9am-2.30pm Fri; also 2hrs before a game. Advance tickets available from day before match; if match is Sun, tickets available from Fri. **Tickets** €5-€30. **No credit cards.**
Five seconds were left on the clock on the last day of the 2003/4 ACB season when Rodrigo de la Fuente scored the points for Barça to lift the ACB for the 11th time, making up for the team's failure to retain the European Cup. Coach Svetislav Pesic has since left under a cloud, but his team remains intact, including the man-mountain Slovene Gregor Fucka ('fooch-ka').

Bullfighting

Plaza de Toros Monumental

Gran Via de les Corts Catalanes 749, Eixample (93 245 58 04/93 215 95 70). Metro Monumental. **Open** *Bullfights* Apr-Sept 5.30-7pm Sun. *Museum* Apr-Sept 11am-2pm, 4-8pm Mon-Sat; 10.30am-1.30pm Sun. **Admission** *Bullfights* €18-€95. Advance tickets available from Servi-Caixa. *Museum* €4; €3 concessions. **No credit cards**. **Map** p343 F5.

In April 2004 the council voted the city to be *'anti-taurino'* (anti-bullfighting), though this was largely a symbolic gesture: 100 bulls are still killed every year at the city's one remaining bullring. *Corridas* take place on Sundays in summer, largely in front of tourists and immigrant Andalucians.

Castellers

Not for Catalans the dangerous flamboyance of the bullfight; they prefer to celebrate their feast-days by forming *castells* in the sky. These human towers, up to ten people-storeys high and consisting of up to 300 *castellers*, rely on traditional Catalan values of good organisation, teamwork and reliability, and are an amazing sight as they rise, wobble and occasionally fall. The star of the show is the *anxaneta*, a six- to nine-year-old child who climbs to the top and 'crowns' the *castell* by raising an arm into the air. For information, contact the Coordinadora de Colles Castelleres de Catalunya (977 60 52 06, www.coordinadoracollescastelleres.info).

Football

Barcelona boasts two Primera (top flight) teams, **FC Barcelona** and **Espanyol**. Barça finished 2003/4 in second place and are hoping for a return to the glory years at the majestic Nou Camp after a five-year trophy famine. Espanyol, who just avoided relegation in 2004, can be entertaining on a good day. Every weekend from September to May, one or the other will be playing, usually on Saturday or Sunday evening; check press for details, and keep checking as kick-off times can change. **Europa** (based in Gràcia) and **Júpiter** (in Poblenou) are worthwhile semi-pro teams.

FC Barcelona

Nou Camp, Avda Aristides Maillol, Les Corts (93 496 36 00/www.fcbarcelona.com). Metro Collblanc or Palau Reial. **Ticket office** 9am-1.30pm, 3.30-6pm Mon-Thur; 9am-2.30pm Fri; from 11am match days. Tickets available from 2wks before each match. **Tickets** €19-€125. Advance tickets for league games available from Servi-Caixa. **Credit** AmEx, DC, MC, V. **Map** p337 A3.

The sale of Luis Figo to arch-rivals Real Madrid in 2000 sent FC Barcelona into a spiral of decline from which they seem only now to be emerging. The canny presidency of Joan Laporta has made them a potentially exciting side to watch. Around 4,000 tickets usually go on sale on the day of the game: phone to find out when, and join the queue an hour or so beforehand at the intersection of Travessera de les Corts and Avenida Arístides Maillol. 'Rented out' seats go on sale from these offices, and can also be bought through Servi-Caixa. If there are none left, buy a *'revendita'* ticket from touts at the gates. The 'B' team, a couple of divisions down the league system, play in the mini-stadium over the road.

RCD Espanyol

Estadi Olímpic de Montjuïc, Passeig Olímpic 17-19, Montjuïc (93 423 86 44/www.rcdespanyol.com). Metro Espanya then free bus, or Paral·lel then Funicular de Montjuïc. **Ticket office** 9.30am-1.30pm, 5-8pm Mon-Fri. *Match weekends* also 8am-3pm Fri; 10am-1.30pm Sat; 10am-kick-off Sun. **Tickets** €35-€65. **Credit** V. **Map** p341 A6.

The Estadi Olímpic, on the side of Montjuïc, where Espanyol are temporarily playing their home games, is one of the most beautiful locations in Europe to watch football. The trouble is that the team rarely half-fill their 56,000-capacity stadium, many of their hard-core *'ultras'* are fascists, and the athletics track around the pitch makes for a subdued atmosphere. Free buses ferry ticket holders from Plaça Espanya, from 90 minutes before kick-off. The club is scheduled to move to a new ground in Cornellà in 2006.

Other team sports

Catalonia's best **rugby** team, UE Santboiana (93 640 07 26, www.uesantboiana.com), from the suburb of Sant Boi, will be inaugurating the newly furbished 2,000-capacity Baldiri Aleu stadium, a short walk from the Sant Boi FGC station, in March 2005. Tickets cost €5. **Handball** and **roller hockey** are also well represented in the region; FC Barcelona's teams (www.fcbarcelona.com) will both be challenging for national and European honours in 2005. Terrassa Hockey, a top-level **hockey** team based in Terrassa (93 787 03 51, www.athc.es), and Viladecans, Spain's main baseball team (93 637 25 88), both welcome spectators. A lot.

Special events

La Cursa del Corte Inglés

Information & entry forms *El Corte Inglés (93 270 17 30/www.elcorteingles.com).* **Date** May. Barcelona's biggest fun run takes place in May, challenging over 50,000 runners, joggers and, yes, walkers, to take on the 11km (7-mile) course.

Motor sports

Circuit de Catalunya, Ctra de Parets del Vallès a Granollers, Montmeló, Outer Limits (93 571 97 00/www.circuitcat.com). By car: C17 north to

Parets del Vallès exit (20km/13 miles). **Times & tickets** vary by competition; available from Servi-Caixa. **Credit** MC, V.

One of the few things that kicks football off the front page of Spain's sports papers is Formula One, thanks to the recent success of the exciting young Asturian driver Fernando Alonso. *'Los alonsistas'*, his fanatical followers, who perform a Mexican wave every time he passes, will be desperate to see a podium finish for the Renault driver in the Spanish Grand Prix, held at Montmeló (6-8 May 2005); in 2004 this event attracted a record 108,000 fans. The circuit also hosts the motorcycle racing Grand Prix in mid June.

Tennis

Reial Club de Tennis Barcelona-1899, C/Bosch i Gimpera 5, Les Corts (93 203 78 52/www.rctb1899. es). FGC Reina Elisenda/bus 63, 78. **Ticket office** *During competitions* 8.30am-1.30pm, 3.30-6.30pm Mon-Fri; 9am-1pm Sat. **Tickets** €19.80-€64; available from Servi-Caixa. **Credit** AmEx, MC, V.

Mallorquín Carlos Moyá lives in Barcelona and is considered the local hero in the annual Open Seat Comte de Godó tournament in Pedralbes, which is on the ATP circuit and attended by 40,000 enthusiastic fans. The 2005 tournament runs 18-25 April, the only time the club opens to non-members. The Catalan equivalent of 'C'mon Tim' is *'Vinga Carlos'*.

Urban tribes Culés

Description *Los culés* means 'the arses'. The nickname for FC Barcelona fans comes from the days when they would watch the match sitting along the high perimeter wall of the old stadium, offering a unique view to those below.

Natural habitat The biggest stadium in Europe, the 98,000-capacity Nou Camp, is the major *culé* haunt, but matches are watched with some passion in bars around the city, and in most Catalan homes. Every time 'Barça' score, you can hear the cheers all over the region.

Grooming The most fanatical *culés*, the Boixos Nois (the *soi-disant* 'No.1 hooligan group of Spain'), are rarely seen out of a team shirt or without a flag. Most Barça fans dress more sombrely, at most wearing a red and blue scarf. The 'Catman' look (Catalan flag worn as cape) is de rigueur for matches against arch-enemy Real Madrid.

Distinctive behaviour Prone to waving white handkerchiefs in the air, a gesture known as '*la panyolada*', to show their displeasure with what is happening on the pitch.

First sighted The team started playing in 1899, and soon started up a solid fan base. By 1910 they had 560 members.

Endangered species? Not exactly. There are currently 125,000 club members, one of whom is the Pope.

Philosophy Summed up in the words of the club hymn: 'The whole stadium is as one, we are the blue and purple people, a single flag unites us.'

Take me to your leader Joan Laporta, the suave president of the club, is head *culé*.
Are they dangerous? Over the last 12 years the Boixos Nois have been responsible for two deaths during and after matches. In 2003, when Joan Laporta stopped giving them free tickets, they painted a series of death threats on his garage door. But generally there's very little violence at the Nou Camp.
Do say 'Who needs David Beckham when you've got Ronaldinho?'
Don't say Anything polite about Real Madrid. Ever.

Arts & Entertainment

Base Nàutica de la Mar Bella. *See p276.*

Active sports & fitness

The 237 municipally run facilities include a
network of *poliesportius* (sports centres), most
of which have a gym with fitness equipment, a
sports hall and a covered pool. Charges are low
and you don't have to be a resident to use the
facilities. Still, you can just head to the beach:
there's a free outdoor gym and ping pong table
at Barceloneta, and the sea is swimmable from
May to October. All beaches have wheelchair
ramps and most of the city's pools are fully
equipped for disabled people. Check with the
Servei d'Informació Esportiva for details.

Servei d'Informació Esportiva

Avda de l'Estadi 30-40, Montjuïc (93 402 30 00).
Metro Espanya then escalators, or Paral·lel then
Funicular de Montjuïc/bus 50. **Open** *25 Sept-23*
June 8am-2pm, 3.45-6pm Mon-Thur; 8am-2.30pm Fri.
24 June-24 Sept 8am-2.30pm Mon-Fri. **Map** *p341 A6.*
The Ajuntament's sports information service is
based in the Piscina Bernat Picornell building. Call
for information on sports facilities (although not all
the staff speak English), or consult the Ajuntament's
very thorough listings on the Esports section of its
website: www.bcn.es.

Bowling

Bowling Pedralbes

Avda Dr Marañón 11, Les Corts (93 333 03 52).
Metro Collblanc or Zona Universitaria. **Open** *10am-*
2am Mon-Thur; 10am-4am Fri, Sat; 10am-midnight
Sun. Aug open only from 5pm daily. **Rates** *€1.50-*
€3.80/person. **Credit** MC, V.
Fourteen lanes to try for that perfect 300, in an alley
that hosts international tournaments. Early afternoons are quiet; otherwise, sit at the bar and wait to
be paged. Shoe hire is available (€1), as are pool,
snooker and *futbolín* (table football).

Cycling

Tourist offices (*see p321*) have maps detailing
the system of cycle routes around town. These
make cycling just about viable as a mode of
transport, though major roads in the Eixample
can get a bit hairy. The seafront is a good
bet for leisure cycling; otherwise, try the
spectacular **Carretera de les Aigües**, a
flat gravel road that skirts along the side of
Collserola mountain. To avoid a killer climb
getting up there, take your bike on the FGC
to Peu del Funicular station, then take the
Funicular de Vallvidrera to the midway
stop. For serious mountain biking, check
http://amicsbici.pangea.org, which also has
information on when you can take your bike on
public transport. A really good lock is a must ;
bicycle theft is big business in Barcelona.

Probike

C/Villarroel 184, Eixample (93 419 78 89/www.
probike.es). Metro Hospital Clínic. **Open** 4.30-8.30pm
Mon; 10.30am-2pm, 4.30-8.30pm Tue-Sat. **Credit**
AmEx, MC, V. **Map** p338 C4.
The Probike club organises regular excursions, from
day trips to a summertime cross-Pyrenees run. Its
centre, which has a broad range of equipment and
excellent service plus maps and information on all
manner of routes, is a magnet for mountain bikers.

Football

Barcelona International Football League

*Info 93 218 67 31/649 261 328/nicksimons
bcn@yahoo.co.uk.*
Matches, of Sunday League standard, are generally
played at weekends from September to June among
teams of expats and locals. New players are welcome.

Golf

Catalonia is currently *a la moda* as a golfing
holiday destination. Visitors should book in
advance; courses can be full at weekends.

Club de Golf Sant Cugat

*C/Villa, Sant Cugat del Vallès, Outer Limits (93 674
39 58/www.golfsantcugat.com). By car Túnel de
Vallvidrera (C16) to Valldoreix/by train FGC from
Plaça Catalunya to Sant Cugat.* **Open** 8am-8pm
Mon; 7.30am-8pm Tue-Fri; 7am-9pm Sat, Sun.
Rates (non-members) €65 Mon-Thur; €150 Fri-Sun.
Club hire €19. **Credit** MC, V.
Designed by Harry S Colt back in 1917 and built by
British railway workers, the oldest golf course in
Catalonia is a tight, varied 18-hole set-up, making
the most of natural obstacles, that's challenging
enough to host the Ladies' World Matchplay Tour.
There's a restaurant and swimming pool on site.

Gyms & fitness centres

Sports centres run by the city council are
cheaper and generally more user-friendly than
most of the private clubs. Phone the **Servei
d'Informació Esportiva** (*see p274*).

Centres de Fitness DiR

*C/Casp 34, Eixample (901 30 40 30/93 301 62 09/
www.dirfitness.es). Metro Urquinaona.* **Open** 7am-
10.45pm Mon-Fri; 9am-3pm Sat, Sun. **Rates** vary.
Credit MC, V. **Map** p344 B1.
This plush, well-organised private chain has ten fitness centres scattered around the city, offering a
broad range of facilities as well as classes in a range
of activities. Additional installations vary from a
huge outdoor pool (at DiR Diagonal) to a squash centre (DiR Campus). An infuriating policy means that
rates cannot be given over the phone; each is 'tailored to the individual', who must visit in person.

Branches: DiR Campus, Avda Dr Marañón 17, Les
Corts (93 448 41 41); DiR Diagonal, C/Ganduxer 25-27
Eixample (93 202 22 02); and throughout the city.

Europolis

*Travessera de les Corts 252-254, Les Corts (93 363
29 92/www.europolis.es). Metro Les Corts.* **Open**
7am-11pm Mon-Fri; 8am-8pm Sat; 9am-3pm Sun.
Rates *Non-members* €9.50/day. *Membership* approx
€42.50/mth, plus €77 joining fee. **Credit** MC, V.
Map p337 A3.
Europolis centres, as large and well equipped as any
private gym in town, are municipally owned but run
by British chain Holmes Place, and provide exercise
machines for every conceivable muscle, as well as
pool areas, classes, trainers and weight-lifting gear.
Other locations: C/Sardenya 549-553, Gràcia
(93 210 07 66).

Ice skating

FC Barcelona Pista de Gel

*Nou Camp, entrance 7 or 9, Avda Joan XXIII, Les
Corts (93 496 36 00/www.fcbarcelona.com). Metro
Collblanc or Maria Cristina.* **Open** 10am-2pm, 4-
5.45pm Mon; 10am-2pm, 4-7.15pm Tue, Thur; 10am-
2pm, 4-7.30pm Wed; 10am-2pm, 4-8pm Fri; 10.30am-
1.45pm, 4.30-8.45pm Sat, Sun. Closed Aug. **Rates**
(incl skates) €8.70. **No credit cards. Map** p337 A3.
Functional rink next to the Nou Camp complex, also
used for ice hockey matches. It's perfect for the non-
football fans in the family to kill 90 minutes or so.

Skating Roger de Flor

*C/Roger de Flor 168, Eixample (93 245 28 00/
www.skatingbcn.com). Metro Tetuan.* **Open**
10.30am-1.30pm Mon, Tue; 10.30am-1.30pm, 5-9pm
Wed, Thur; 10.30am-1.30pm, 5pm-midnight Fri, Sat;
10.30am-1.30pm, 5-10pm Sun. **Rates** (incl skates)
€10. **Credit** MC, V. **Map** p339 E4.
A family-oriented ice rink in the Eixample. Gloves
are compulsory, and are on sale for €2.60. Any non-
skaters in a group get in free and can use the café.

Jogging & running

The seafront is a good location for an enjoyable
jog. If you can handle the initial climb, or use
other transport for the ascent, there are scenic
runs on Montjuïc, especially around the castle
and Olympic stadium, the Park Güell/Carmel
hills and Collserola.

Rollerblading

Flocks of rollerbladers have become a common
sight in the city centre. The **APB** (Asociacion
de Patinadores de Barcelona, www.patinar-bcn.
com) organises skating convoys: beginners meet
at the Baja Beach Club (*see p250* **Chips with
everything**) at 10.30pm on Fridays, while better
skaters hook up at Plaça Catalunya (10.30pm,
Thursdays). Both follow routes pre-determined

by the association, which also offers classes (free for beginners, €7 for equipment) at 10pm on Tuesdays in Parc Clot. Going it alone, you're not officially allowed on roads or cycle paths, and the speed limit is 10kph. The pedestrian broadways of Rambla de Catalunya, Avda Diagonal and Passeig Maritim are popular haunts.

Sailing

Base Nàutica de la Mar Bella

Avda Litoral, between Platja Bogatell & Platja de Mar Bella (93 221 04 32/www.basenautica.org). Metro Poblenou. **Open** *Mar-Sept* 10am-8pm daily. *Oct-Dec* 10am-7pm daily. *Jan-Feb* 10am-5pm daily. **Rates** *Windsurfing* €150/10hr course; €16.50/hr hire. *Catamaran* €176/16hr course; €23.50-€38.50/hr equipment hire. *Kayak* €11.50-€19/hr equipment hire. **Credit** MC, V.

Situated next to Barcelona's official nudist beach, the Base Nàutica hires out catamarans and windsurf gear to those with experience. There's a proficiency test when you first get on the water (€12 fee if you fail); unofficial registered 'friends', who will join your catamaran team for a fee, are usually available for beginners. You can hire a kayak without a test.

Skiing

If you sicken of the urban bustle, within three hours you can be in the Pyrenees. The best bet for a skiing day trip is the resort of La Molina (972 89 20 21). A RENFE train from Plaça Catalunya at 7.05am (€7.30 single, €13.20 return) takes you to the train station (get off at La Molina) and a bus takes you up to the resort. A day's ski pass (known as the *'forfait'*) will set you back €31. Trains return at 4.41pm and 7.18pm (check the timetable in the station). There are runs to suit all comers, from green for relative beginners to black for speed freaks.

Swimming

The city has dozens of municipal pools, many of them open air, and also has more than three miles of beach, patrolled by lifeguards in summer. For a list of pools, contact the **Servei d'Informació Esportiva** (*see p274*). Flip-flops and swimming caps are generally obligatory.

Club de Natació Atlètic Barceloneta

Plaça del Mar, Barceloneta (93 221 00 10/www.cnab.org). Metro Barceloneta, then bus 17, 39, 64. **Open** *Oct-Apr* 6.30am-11pm Mon-Fri; 7am-11pm Sat; 8am-5pm Sun. *May-Sept* 7am-11pm Mon-Sat; 8am-8pm Sun. **Admission** *Non-members* €8/day. *Membership* €27.50/mth, plus €58 joining fee. **Credit** AmEx, DC, MC, V. **Map** p342 D7.

This historic beachside centre, counting down to its centenary in 2007, has an indoor pool and two outdoor pools (one heated), as well as sauna and gym

facilities. There's a *frontón* if you fancy a go at the world's fastest sport: jai alai, a fierce Basque game somewhere between squash and handball.

Piscina Bernat Picornell

Avda de l'Estadi 30-40, Montjuïc (93 423 40 41/ www.picornell.com). Metro Espanya then escalators, or Paral·lel then Funicular de Montjuïc/bus 50. **Open** *June-Sept* Outdoor pool only 9am-9pm Mon-Sat; 9am-8pm Sun. *Oct-May* Outdoor pool 10am-7pm Mon-Sat; 10am-4pm Sun. Covered pool, rest of complex 7am-midnight Mon-Fri; 7am-9pm Sat; 7.30am-4pm Sun. **Admission** *June-Sept* €4.50; €3.20 concessions; free under-6s. *Oct-May* €8.50; €4.50-€5.60 concessions; free under-6s. **Credit** MC, V. **Map** p341 A6.

The 50m (164ft) indoor pool here was the main venue for the Olympics; there's also a 50m outdoor pool, a climbing wall and a gym. During the annual Grec festival, the centre offers special late-night sessions with swimming and film projections. There are also regular sessions for nudists (9-11pm Saturday all year, 4.15-6pm Sundays from October to May).

Poliesportiu Marítim

Passeig Marítim 33-35 (93 224 04 40/www.claror. org). Metro Ciutadella-Vila Olímpica. **Open** 7am-midnight Mon-Fri; 8am-9pm Sat; 8am-5pm Sun. **Admission** *Non-members* €13 Mon-Fri; €15.50 Sat, Sun; 5-visit pass €54; 10-visit pass €96. **Credit** AmEx, DC, MC, V. **Map** p343 E7.

This spa centre specialises in thalassotherapy, a popular hydrotherapy treatment using seawater. There are eight saltwater pools of differing temperatures, including a vast jacuzzi with waterfalls to massage your shoulders. There's also an icy plunge-pool, a sauna and a steam room. Other services include a bigger freshwater pool, a gym, bike hire, and some well-priced classes. The centre has access to Barceloneta beach; in the summer, leave your belongings safe in a locker while you're on the beach.

Tennis

Barcelona Tenís Olímpic

Passeig de la Vall d'Hebron 178-196, Vall d'Hebron (93 427 65 00/www.fctennis.org). Metro Montbau. **Open** *Dec-Apr* 8am-11pm Mon-Fri; 8am-7pm Sat, Sun. *May-Nov* 9.45am-9pm Sat, Sun. **Rates** (non-members) courts €16/hr; floodlights €4.60. **No credit cards.**

Originally built for the Olympics, these tennis courts are a little way from the city centre, but there's a good metro connection. There are 24 mostly clay courts, as well as paddle courts and racket hire (€3).

Club Tennis Pompeia

C/Foixarda, Montjuïc (93 325 13 48). Bus 13, 50. **Open** 8am-11pm Mon-Fri; 8am-10pm Sat, Sun. **Rates** €131/3mths. *Non-members* €10/hr; €3.80 floodlights. **No credit cards.**

There are good rates for non-members at this pleasant club above the Poble Espanyol, with a wonderful view of Barcelona to distract your smashes. There are seven clay courts; racket hire is €3.

Trips Out of Town

Getting Started   278
Around Barcelona   279
Tarragona &
  the Costa Daurada   283
Girona & the
  Costa Brava   290
Vic to the Pyrenees   298

Features

What's the time, Mr Wolf?   280
Rolling out the barrels   285
Tales of the city   294

Maps

Tarragona   283
Girona   290

Getting Started

Welcome to Catalonia.

To most foreigners, Catalonia is part of Spain, the part containing Barcelona and the Costa Brava. Spend any time here, however, and Catalonia's otherness begins to emerge. Geographically, it boasts an embarrassment of riches, from the tiny Romanesque villages on the skirts of the Pyrenees to the sandy expanses and abundant wildlife of the Ebre delta wetlands. Over and above this, the region is culturally distinct from the rest of Spain, a fact manifested most notably in its food, architecture and festivals.

For information on roads and public transport within Catalonia, see the Generalitat's www.mobilitat.org. The Palau Robert tourist centre (*see p321*) deals specifically with Catalonia and has a useful range of leaflets, guides and maps of the region.

Catalonia has a network of *casa de pagès* – country houses or old farmhouses – where you can rent a room or a whole house. For details, see the Generalitat's widely available guide *Residències – casa de pagès*. For holiday cottages, try the Rural Tourism Association, online at www.ecoturismorural.com.

On foot

Catalonia's hills and low mountain ranges make it hugely popular for walking. In many places this is made easier by GR (*gran recorregut*) long-distance footpaths, indicated with red and white signs. Good places for walking within easy reach of the city include the **Parc de Collserola** (*see p135*), **Montserrat** (*see p282*) and **La Garrotxa** (*see p302*). Another excellent Generalitat website, **www.gencat.net** (click on 'information centre' and 'routes'), has particularly good information on walks. For detailed walking maps, try Altaïr (*see p193*) or **Llibreria Quera** (C/Petritxol 2, 93 318 07 43).

By bus

The **Estació d'Autobusos Barcelona-Nord**, C/Ali Bei 80 (map p343 E5) is the principal bus station for coach services around Catalonia. General information and timetables for all the different private companies are on 902 26 06 06. The **Costa Brava** is better served by buses than trains (with the **Sarfa** company) however, as is the high **Pyrenees** (with **Alsina-Graëlls**), though the latter region is beyond the scope of this guide.

By road

Be warned that over the last few years Spain's roads have undergone a gradual process of renaming, and many locally bought maps remain woefully out of date. The most recently renamed of major roads around Barcelona are the C17 to Ripoll (formerly the N152), the C33 (A17) and the C32 (B-20).

Roads beginning C1 run north–south; those starting C2 run east–west; and those beginning C3 run parallel to the coast. Driving in or out of Barcelona, you will come across either the **Ronda de Dalt**, running along the edge of Tibidabo, and the **Ronda Litoral** along the coast, meeting north and south of the city. They intersect with several motorways (*autopistes*): the C31 (heading up the coast from Mataró); the C33/A7 (to Girona and France) and the C58 (Sabadell, Manresa), which both run into Avda Meridiana; the A2 (Lleida, Madrid), a continuation of Avda Diagonal which connects with the A7 south (Tarragona, Valencia); and the C32 to Sitges, reached from the Gran Via.

All are toll roads, but where possible, we've given toll-free alternatives in the following pages. Avoid the automatic ticket dispensers if on a motorbike: you'll pay less in the 'Manual' lanes. The **Túnel de Vallvidrera**, the continuation of Via Augusta that leads out of Barcelona under Collserola to Sant Cugat and Terrassa, also has a high toll, as does the **Túnel de Cadí**, running through the mountains just south of Puigcerdà. For more information on tolls, call 902 20 03 20 or see www.autopistas.com.

By train

All **RENFE** (902 24 02 02/www.renfe.es) trains stop at **Sants** station, and some at **Passeig de Gràcia** (Girona, Figueres, the south coast), **Estació de França** (the south coast) or **Plaça Catalunya** (Montseny, Vic, Puigcerdà). RENFE's local and suburban trains (*rodalies/cercanias*) are integrated into the metro and bus fares system (for a map, *see p346*). Tickets for these are sold at separate windows. Catalan Government Railways (**FGC**) serve destinations from **Plaça d'Espanya** (including Montserrat) and **Plaça Catalunya** (Tibidabo, Collserola, Sant Cugat and Terrassa). FGC information is available on 93 205 15 15 and at www.fgc.net.

Around Barcelona

Take a hike, say a prayer or soak up some rays.

South along the coast

A short hop south of Barcelona lands you in the popular resort of **Castelldefels**, famous for its broad sandy beaches and its seafood restaurants. It's not a pretty place, though, and its proximity to the city means there's little towel space on the sand from July to September when wind- and kitesurfers share the choppy water with shoals of mainly local bathers. The city has a large recreational port, where kayaks and catamarans can be hired from the **Catamaran Center** (Port Ginesta, local 324, 93 665 22 11 www.catamaran-center.com).

Much more charming is the village of **Garraf**, a few kilometres south, with a small curved beach backed by wooden huts that lend a retro air. It's worth taking a stroll to the **Celler de Garraf** at the northern tip of the bay, a magical Modernista creation built by Gaudí for the Güell family in 1895, and now housing a restaurant. Behind the village stretches the **Parc del Garraf** nature reserve, with hiking and biking opportunities on trails marked out on maps available from the tourist office in Sitges.

Sitges is the *pièce de résistance* of this stretch of coastline, a beautiful low-rise white-painted Jekyll-and-Hyde of a town, a relaxing getaway in the winter that moves at a furious pace in the summer, when the beaches and clubs burst with party-goers. Sitges was 'discovered' by Modernista artist Santiago Rusiñol in the 1890s: this legendary figure threw massive parties for the great and the good of Barcelona's cultural heyday, among them a teenage Pablo Picasso. It has remained a magnet for artists, writers and assorted leisure lovers, and since the '60s has become Spain's principal gay resort, served by a hotchpotch of gay bars and discos (*see p245*). The *madre* of all Sitges' parties, in the week leading up to Shrove Tuesday, is the camp-as-they-come carnival, a riot of floats, fancy dress and men in high heels.

Much of Sitges' architecture is as flamboyant as its carnival queens. It became the fashionable retirement spot for the merchants, known as '*los americanos*', who made fortunes in the Caribbean in the 19th century and spent them on increasingly lavish mansions until beyond the turn of the 20th. There are over 100 of these palaces dotted around the centre of town: in the tourist office you can pick up an excellent

booklet that takes you round the most important. Alternatively, **Agis Sitges**, (C/Rafael Llopart 12, 2°, mobile 619 793 199) offers guided tours every third Sunday of the month (€7).

Sitges' highest building, topping a rocky promontory overlooking the sea, is the pretty 17th-century **Sant Bartomeu I Santa Tecla church**, offering wonderful views of the Mediterranean. Behind the church is the **Museu Cau Ferrat** (C/Fonollar, 93 894 03 64, admission €3, closed Mon). Rusiñol set up his home here: the building houses his collection of paintings (including works by El Greco, Picasso and Ramon Casas, as well as his own) and wrought-iron sculptures, all on view. Over the road is the **Palau Maricel** (C/Fonollar, 93 894 03 64, admission €6), an old hospital converted into a Modernista palace and now used as a concert hall on summer nights. The building contains medieval and baroque paintings and sensuous marble sculptures from the American Catalanophile Charles Deering's collection.

Also worth visiting is the **Museu Romàntic** in the Casa Llopis (C/Sant Gaudenci 1, 93 894 29 69, admission €3, closed Mon), which portrays the lifestyle of the aristocratic 19th-century family that once lived there. The original furnishings and decorations haven't been changed; you can wander from room to room among grandfather clocks, music boxes and

Garraf.

antique dolls. Those who prefer messing about in boats are served well at the Port Esportiu Aiguadolç. The **Centro Náutico Aiguadolç-Vela** (93 811 31 05, www.advela.net) rents sailing boats and organises sailing excursions; a private hour-long session costs €40 (Mar-Nov only). The Yahoo Motor Centre rents jet skis with guides (93 811 30 61, €40 for 15min ride).

But Sitges is most famous for more hedonistic pleasures. At mealtimes, tourists throng the Passeig de la Ribera, a beachside promenade lined with restaurants and bars, and at night they head up the hill into the town's narrow streets, especially C/Primer de Maig – known to locals as 'Carrer de Pecat' (Sin Street) – the epicentre of Sitges' nightlife. The partying is at its fiercest in the carnival and in the town's noisy and colourful *festa major* at the end of August. Sitges also hosts an annual international film festival in autumn (*see p233*).

Where to eat

In Sitges, paella on the seafront is something of an institution. Try the patio of the elegant **Hotel La Santa Maria** (Passeig de la Ribera 52, 93 894 09 99, www.lasantamaria.com, rates €85.60-€115.50, mains €10.50, closed Christmas-mid Feb). Locals, meanwhile, escape the tourists in the colourful **Reves** (C/Sant Francesc 35, 93 89 476 25), which offers a good fixed lunch menu with wine for €8.50. A nice seafood option is **El Greco** (Passeig de la Ribera 70, closed Tue & lunch Wed, mains €23.50). For Catalan classics such as rabbit with snails and *xató* salad with cod and *romesco* sauce, head to **La Masia** (Passeig de Vilanova 164, 93 894 10 76, mains €14). The restaurant in **El Xalet** (C/Illa de Cuba 35, 938 94 55 79, mains €16, rates €64.20-€99.50 incl breakfast) is on the pricey side, but is worth it for the Modernista decor in the dining room.

What's the time, Mr Wolf?

Playground skills will generally stand you in good stead in later life, and nowhere more so than when ingratiating yourself with the locals along the Costa Maresme. Sweating over your Catalan phrasebook is an option, but a far easier way to endear yourself is to indulge in a little inter-*pueblo* taunting, an apparently limitless form of entertainment round here.

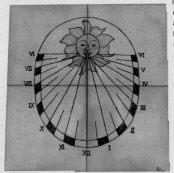

Some villagers, like those from Canet, get off with a mild local insult – in this case, 'snail-eaters' – but those from Sant Pol and Calella have reputations all over the region. Calella '*de la llopa*' is so called after an incident a couple of hundred years ago, when a wolf was terrorising the village and killing the livestock. A band of brave shepherds hunted down and killed this terrifying creature, and once they had succeeded in doing so the mighty beast was stuffed and placed on display in the village square. So far, so valiant. It was only when a woman from Sant Pol ran into the square screaming that they'd killed her dog that the trouble began...

The Sant Pol tale is no less enduring. The story goes that the *santpolencs* were so proud of their new sundial, they built a little roof over it to protect it from the elements, rendering it useless in the process. Hence the traditional cry '*Sant Pol! Quina hora és?*' ('What time is it?') whenever a train pulls into its station. Unlike the *calellencs*, however, who are at ease with their moniker (in fact, the school mascot is a wolf, and the pupils are 'wolfcubs'), the *santpolencs* have something of a sense-of-humour failure on the sundial issue, and work hard to propagate another version.

In this stirring tale, a band of Sant Pol martyrs hid in a tower to fight off Philip V's troops after they had taken control of the town in 1714. Realising that the bells of the clock-tower had been used to alert the good guys to danger, the commanding officer had them removed. Ask a *santpolenc* what time it is and you will get one of two responses. In the first, from those who buy the resistance theory, the answer generally given is: 'Time for Catalonia to have her rights returned.' In the second, from those still sensitive about the sundial, the response might just be a sock on the jaw.

Sant Pol de Mar.

Castelldefels has plenty of cheapish seafront restaurants, though the fare is better at the more upmarket **Nàutic** (Passeig Marítim 374, 93 894 06 00, mains €17). Vilanova i la Geltrú, further down the coast from Sitges, has two excellent restaurants: **Can Pagès** (C/Sant Pere 24, 93 894 11 95, closed lunch Mon-Fri & all day Nov, set menu €30) has grilled meat, while **Peixerot** (Passeig Marítim 56, 93 815 06 25, closed Sun dinner Sept-June, mains €15) offers fish.

Tourist information

Oficina de Turisme de Castelldefels

C/Pintor Serrasanta 4 (93 635 27 27/www. turismocastelldefels.com). **Open** *June-Sept* 9am-7.30pm daily. *Sept-mid June* 4-6.30pm Mon; 9am-2.30pm, 4-6.30pm Tue-Fri; 9am-2.30pm Sat.

Oficina de Turisme de Sitges

C/Sínia Morera 1 (93 894 42 51/www.sitgestur.com). **Open** *July-Sept* 9am-9pm daily. *Oct-June* 9am-2pm, 4-6.30pm Mon-Fri.

Getting there

By bus

Mon-Bus runs an hourly night service to Plaça Catalunya from Sitges between 12.11am and 3.11am.

By car

C32 toll road to Castelldefels, Garraf and Sitges (41km/25 miles), or C31 via a slow, winding drive around the Garraf mountains.

By train

Trains leave every 20mins from Passeig de Gràcia for Platja de Castelldefels (20min journey) and Sitges (30mins); not all stop at Castelldefels and Garraf. The last train back leaves Sitges at 10.26pm.

North along the coast

An excellent half-hourly train service runs up the coastline from Barcelona to **Blanes**, passing beach-fringed towns such as **El Masnou**, **Caldes D'Estrec** (popularly known as **Caldetes**), **Sant Pol de Mar** and **Calella**, and offering wonderful views of the sea. The flip side of this is that the tracks are normally between the town and the beach, which somewhat diminishes the atmosphere.

El Masnou is just a 15-minute ride away from Plaça Catalunya, and its beaches are broader and less crowded than those in the city, but Caldetes, 45 minutes up the line, is the first really attractive beach town, with a string of Modernista mansions. The town of Sant Pol, a few kilometres up the coast, is less pleasant on the eye, but its beaches are the prettiest between Barcelona and the Costa Brava. Calella is more touristy, but its lush Parc Dalmau is worth a visit and there are several interesting Gothic buildings.

Where to eat

In Caldes d'Estrac, the **Fonda Manau Can Raimón** is a small *pensión* that serves great food (C/Sant Josep 11, 93 791 04 59, mains €13, closed Tue & dinner Sun-Thur Oct-May). Another good mid-price restaurant is **Can Suñe** (C/Callao 4, 93 791 00 51, closed Mon, closed Mon-Wed Oct-June, mains €14). In Sant Pol, **La Casa** (C/Riera 13, 93 760 23 73, closed Mon-Thur, mains €7) is a colourful, stylish place; for something more upmarket, head to the wonderful, Michelin-starred **Sant Pau** (C/Nou 10, 93 760 06 62, closed all Mon, Thur lunch & Sun dinner, closed 2 wks May & all Nov, mains €35).

Trips Out of Town

Colònia Güell.

Getting there

By car
NII to El Masnou (10km/6 miles), Caldes d'Estrac (36km/22 miles), Canet de Mar (42km/26 miles), Sant Pol (48km/30 miles) and Calella (52km/32 miles).

By train
RENFE trains leave every 30mins from Sants or Plaça Catalunya for El Masnou, Caldes d'Estrac, Canet, Sant Pol and Calella. Journey approx 1hr.

Montserrat & Colònia Güell

It's unsurprising that **Montserrat** ('jagged mountain'), the vast bulbous-peaked sandstone mass that dominates the landscape to the west of Barcelona, is seen as the spiritual heart of Catalonia: its other-worldly appearance lends it a mystical aura that has for centuries made it a centre of worship and veneration. In the Middle Ages, the mountain was an important pilgrimage site; the **Benedictine monastery** that sits near the top became the jewel in the crown of a politically independent fiefdom. Surrounded by hermitages and tiny chapels, the monastery is still venerated by locals, who wait in line (8.30-10.30am, noon-6.30pm) in the 16th-century **basilica** (7.30am-7.30pm daily) to say a prayer while kissing the orb held by **La Moreneta**, or the 'Black Virgin', a small Romanesque figure discovered in a nearby mountain cave in the 12th century. The basilica is most crowded at 1pm, when the monastery's celebrated boys' choir sings mass. The monastery's **museum** (10am-7pm, admission €5.50) is stocked with fine art, including paintings by Picasso, Dali, El Greco, Monet and Caravaggio, as well as a collection of liturgical gold and silverware, archaeological finds and gifts for the virgin.

If all this piety isn't to your taste, it's still worth the trip up the mountain (there's a road, a cable car and a rack railway if you don't fancy the walk). The tourist office gives details of a number of fine walks to the various caves, among them **Santa Cova**, where the statue was discovered, a 20-minute hike from the monastery or a funicular ride (10am-1pm, 2-5.30pm daily, €2.50). The most accessible hermitage is **Sant Joan**, also 20 minutes away or a funicular ride (€6.10, 10am-6pm daily). But the most rewarding trek is the longest, to the peak of **Sant Jeroni**, at 1,235 metres (4,053 feet), which offers 360-degree views from a vertigo-inducing platform. Montserrat is something of a tourist trap and gets unbearably crowded in the summer. Its characterless, overpriced restaurants are also best avoided. But it is nonetheless a worthwhile excursion, if only for the views.

Closer to Barcelona, on the western outskirts of Santa Coloma de Cervelló, is the **Colònia Güell** (93 630 58 07, open daily, admission €4, guided tours €5-€8) commissioned by the textile baron Eusebi Güell, designed by Antoni Gaudí and, like many of the great projects started by the architect, never completed. The utopian idea was to build a garden city for the textile workers around the factory where they worked. Gaudí did complete the crypt of the church, and, with its ribbed ceiling and twisted pillars, it's an extraordinary achievement.

Tourist information

Oficina de Turisme de Montserrat
Plaça de la Creu, Montserrat (93 877 77 77/www. abadiamontserrat.net). **Open** *Apr-Aug* 9am-7pm Mon-Fri; 9am-8pm Sat, Sun. *Sept-Mar* 9am-6pm Mon-Fri; 9am-7pm Sat, Sun.

Getting there

By bus
Montserrat A Julià-Via (93 490 40 00) bus leaves at 9.15am from Sants bus station and returns at 5pm (6pm June-Sept) daily; journey time is approx 80mins.

By car
Colònia Güell A2 to Sant Boi exit, then turn towards Sant Vicenç dels Horts (3 miles/5km).
Montserrat Take the NII to exit km 59, or the A2 to the Martorell exit, then the C55 towards Monistrol (60km/37 miles).

By train
Colònia Güell FGC trains go from Plaça Espanya. Journey takes 10-25mins.
Montserrat FGC trains from Plaça Espanya hourly from 8.36am to the Aeri de Montserrat (approx 1hr) for the cable car (every 15mins); or Monistrol de Montserrat for the rack train (every hour) up to the monastery. Last cable car and rack train around 6pm.

Trips Out of Town

Tarragona & the Costa Daurada

Something for everyone, from sandcastles to amphitheatres.

Tarragona

Its hilltop location, port and grand buildings ensured Tarragona's popularity and prosperity for years. The city was known as Tarraco in Roman times, when it was capital of half of Spain; it ceded much of its importance to Barcelona in the 14th century and is now Catalonia's second city. However, its history has been preserved in many fine buildings and an impressive legacy of Roman remains.

For past glories and great views, begin along the Roman walls that once ringed the city. The path is known as the **Passeig Arqueològic** (Avda Catalunya, 977 24 57 96); the entrance is at **Portal del Roser**, one of remaining three towers, two of which were rebuilt in medieval times. Inside the walls, the superbly preserved Roman remains include the ancient **Pretori**, or

'praetorium' (977 24 19 52), used as both palace and government office and reputed to have been the birthplace of Pontius Pilate. From here, walk to the ruins of the **Circ Romans**, the first-century Roman circus where chariot races were once held. The **Museu Nacional Arqueològic**, home to an important collection of Roman artefacts and some stunning mosaics, is nearby.

To see all of the **Catedral de Santa Maria**, not to mention some wonderful religious art and archaelogical finds, you'll need a ticket for the **Museu Diocesà** (Pla de la Seu, 977 23 86 85, closed Sun). The majestic cathedral was built on the site of a Roman temple to Jupiter, and is Catalonia's largest. The cloister, built in the 12th and 13th centuries, is glorious, and the carvings alone are worth the trip.

Leading from the old town towards the sea, the **Passeig de las Palmeres** runs to the

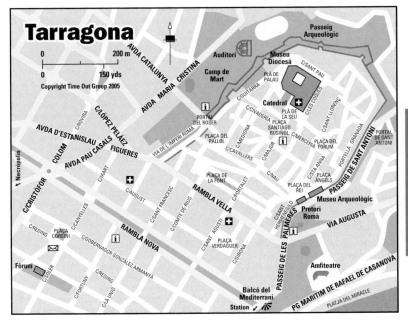

Balcó del Mediterrani overlooking the
Roman **amphitheatre** (Parc del Miracle, 977
24 25 79). The same street also leads to the
bustling, pedestrianised **Rambla Nova**, from
where you can follow C/Canyelles to the **Fòrum**
(C/Lleida, 977 24 25 01) to the remains of the
juridical basilica and Roman houses.

Tickets for the Museu Arqueològic also
allow entry to the **Museu i Necròpolis
Paleocristians** (Avda Ramón y Cajal 80, 977
21 11 75, closed Mon) on the site of an early
Christian cemetery, although it was undergoing
long-term renovation in early 2005. A couple of
miles north of the city (but an unpleasant walk
along a busy main road; take bus No.5 from
the top of the Rambla Nova) is the spectacular
Pont del Diable (Devil's Bridge), a Roman
aqueduct built in the first century.

Entry to the Passeig Arqueològic, the circus
and praetorium, the amphitheatre and the
Fòrum costs €2 (€1 concessions, free under-
16s); entry is free to holders of **Port Aventura**
tickets (*see p287*). An all-in ticket for the city's
five main museums is €8 (€4 concessions).
Hours for all are 9am-9pm Tue-Sat and 9am-
7pm Sun from Easter to mid October, and 9am-
5pm Tue-Sat and 9am-3pm Sun at all other
times of the year.

Museu Nacional Arqueològic de Tarragona

Placa del Rei 5 (977 23 62 09/www.mnat.es).
Open *June-Sept* 10am-8pm Tue-Sat; 10am-2pm
Sun. *Oct-May* 10am-1.30pm, 4-7pm Tue-Sat; 10am-
2pm Sun. **Admission** (incl entrance to Museu i
Necròpolis Paleocristians) €2.40; €1.20 concessions;
free under-18s, over-65s. **No credit cards**.

Where to eat

The fishing neighbourhood of El Serrallo is
home to the best seafood restaurants: try the
paella at **Cal Martí** (C/Sant Pere 12, 977 21 23
84, closed dinner Tue, closed Sept-June, mains
€15), the super-fresh fish at **La Puda** (Moll
Pescadors 25, 977 21 15 11, mains €22), or, a
little out of the centre to the west, **Sol-Ric** (Via
Augusta 227, 977 23 20 32, closed dinner Wed
& all day Sun, closed Jan, mains €23).

Those on a budget can fall back on the **Bufet
el Tiberi** (C/Martí d'Ardenya 5, 977 23 54 03,
closed dinner Sun & all day Mon, buffet
€12.80), while below the cathedral is **La Cuca
Fera** (Plaça Santiago Rusiñol 5, 977 24 20 07,
closed Mon & dinner Sun, set lunch €9.70),
which has great fish *suquet*. In the old town,
Palau del Baró serves huge portions of
Catalan classics in the colourful rooms of a
former baronial mansion (C/Santa Anna 3, 977
24 14 64, closed dinner Sun, closed Oct-May,
mains €13.50).

Where to stay

The smartest hotel is the towering **Imperial
Tarraco** (Passeig de les Palmeres, 977 23 30 40,
www.husa.es, rates €79-€138). The **Lauria**
(Rambla Nova 20, 977 23 67 12, rates €58-€70)
has a pool and gives big discounts at weekends
out of season. Other mid-range hotels include
the **Astari** (Via Augusta 95, 977 23 69 00, rates
€64-€85), which has a pool, and the central
Hotel Urbis (C/Reding 20 bis, 977 24 01 16,
www.urbis.com, rates €53-€97). You'll find
cheaper digs at the **Pensión Forum** (Plaça de
la Font 37, 977 23 17 18, closed Nov, rates €34-
€40) and the nearby **Pensión La Noria** (Plaça
de la Font 53, 977 23 87 17, rates €32-€42);
there's little to choose between them.

Tourist information

Oficina de Turisme de Tarragona

C/Fortuny 4 (977 23 34 15). **Open** 9am-2pm,
4-6.30pm Mon-Fri; 9am-2pm Sat.

Getting there

By car

Take the A2, then the A7 via Vilafranca (Tarragona
98km/60 miles); or the toll-free N340 (Molins de Rei
exit from A2).

By train

RENFE from Sants or Passeig de Gràcia. Trains
hourly (journey time 1hr 6mins).

The Wine Country

Just southwest of Barcelona is prime wine
terrain, where the majority of Catalan wines are
produced. Various of the region's many wine
denominaciones de origen are found here, but
the main suppliers are found in the **Penedès**.
The town of **Vilafranca**, at the centre of the
area, is worth a look for its handsome medieval
buildings and the elegant 14th-century **Basílica
de Santa Maria**. Vilafranca's wine museum,
the **Museu del Vi** (Plaça Jaume I 1-3, 93 890 05
82, closed Mon), has old wooden presses and
wine jugs, some dating to the fourth century.

While Vilafranca itself is easy to navigate on
foot, a car is almost essential to explore the
surrounding region. **Torres**, Penedès's largest
winemaker, runs tours at its cellars outside town
(not to be confused with its offices opposite the
train station), for which *see p285* **Rolling out
the barrels**. **Jean León** (Pago Jean León, 93
899 55 12, www.jeanleon.com, admission €3),
another pioneering brand but now owned by
Torres, recently inaugurated its visitors' centre
near Torrelavit, in a modern building with

Rolling out the barrels

beating the once-unassailable French offerings. Globally, the Torres mark is now a badge of quality, his empire stretching to Chile (Torres was the first foreign winemaker and responsible for introducing decent levels of pay into the industry), California and even China. As well as his famous selection of top-notch fine wines, his good value Viña Sol, Sangre de Toro and Viña Esmeralda are familiar names in more than 120 countries around the world.

Spanish empire-building is a fine art, and in the 21st century, there's nobody more adept at its execution than calm, controlled and highly ambitious wine baron Miguel Torres. It's a measure of the man that Corona, the Mexican beer, is labelled Coronita in Spain, after Torres successfully argued that the original name was too close to his red wine, Coronas. And brand is everything to Torres, who has changed the taste of Spanish wine.

Torres's family have been making wine for centuries, and this is still a family business: Torres's father, Miguel Torres Carbo, built up the firm following the bombing of the winery during the Spanish Civil War, and his sister Miramar runs the firm's California vineyards. But Torres has also been a decisive moderniser. He was among the first winegrowers to plant non-Spanish varietals (such as merlot, cabernet sauvignon and chardonnay), he pioneered the use of stainless steel tanks in the vinifying process, and he was responsible for the widespread introduction of temperature control.

The results of these changes were sensational, giving birth to fruitier, fresher Spanish wines that took on the world's best. At the prestigious 1979 Gault Millau wine olympics, the Torres' 1970 Gran Coronas Black Label, now rebranded as Mas La Plana, won the gold medal in the cabernet section,

Torres is also extremely proud of what he has done locally. The company cultivates 20 estates over 2,300 acres in Catalonia, mainly in the Penedès DO, and has helped to establish a new Catalonia DO for the whole region. Torres has also recovered several of Catalonia's near-extinct indigenous grape varieties, including samso and garro, and made a feature of them in single-grape vineyards such as Grans Muralles as well as planting them in Chile. He even cultures its own yeasts from local varieties.

Happily, this determination is coupled with a strong ecological commitment. Herbicides and insecticides are avoided at the wineries (which has sometimes meant major yield losses, notably in Chile), and the Torres Foundation focuses on conservation issues such as protecting the native Bonnelli's Eagle (Àguila Perdicera) from extinction.

You can see the empire for yourself while you're here. Free tours include the obligatory visits to the cellars, bottling area and fermentation tanks, along with a train ride through a virtual reality tunnel that shows how the weather and soil create aromas in wine.

Torres

Finca El Maset, Pacs del Penedès (93 817 74 87/www.torres.es). **Open** 9am-5pm Mon-Fri; 9am-6pm Sat; 9am-1pm Sun. **Admission** free.

Trips Out of Town

breathtaking views of a valley lined with vineyards. The price includes a video, a tour through the museum and winery, and a tasting.

Some nine kilometres (six miles) away is **Sant Sadurní d'Anoia**, the capital of the Penedès cava industry and Vilafranca's main rival. More than 90 per cent of Spain's cava, a sparkling wine traditionally made with local parellada, macabeo and xarel·lo grapes, is made in this tiny town. **Codorníu** (Avda Codorníu, 93 818 32 32, www.grupocodorniu.com, admission €2), one of the largest producers, offers a wonderful tour of its Modernista headquarters, designed at the end of the 19th century by Puig i Cadafalch. A train takes visitors through parts of the 26 kilometres (16 miles) of underground cellars, finishing with a tasting. **Freixenet** (C/Joan Sala 2, 93 891 70 00, www.freixenet.es), another mega-producer, is Sant Sadurní station and offers free tours and tastings.

South of here, the **Priorat** area has gained fame in the past decade for its full-bodied (and pricey) red wines. Monks were producing wine in the Priorat as long ago as the 11th century, but the area had been all but abandoned when young winemaker **Alvaro Palacios** set up a tiny vineyard here in the late 1980s. He battled steep hills and a sceptical wine industry, but within a few years he was winning global acclaim, and the region is now one of Spain's most popular among wine buyers. One of the more charming vineyards is the **Cellers Scala Dei** (Rambla de la Cartoixa, Scala Dei, 977 82 70 27, open by appointment only).

The small **Alella** district, east of Barcelona, is best known for whites, but more important is **Terra Alta**: near the Priorat in Tarragona, with Gandesa as its capital, it's renowned for its heavy reds. **Montsant** (capital: Falset), a newly created DO, is growing in popularity. Look out for the odd **Cooperativa Agrícola** in Gandesa, and the **Bodega Cooperativa** in Falset, designed by a disciple of Gaudí, César Martinell. Montsant's **Celler Capçanes** makes one of the world's top kosher wines.

Where to stay & eat

To try excellent and unusual local wines in Vilafranca, head to the **Inzolia** wine bar and store (C/Palma 21, 93 818 19 38). **El Purgatori** (Plaça Campanar 5, 93 892 12 63, dinner only, mains €12.50) serves *pa amb tomàquet* with charcuterie and cheese in a tiny, secluded square. **Taverna Ongi Etorriak** (C/Sant Bernat 4, 93 890 43 54, closed Mon, tapas average €1.25) is a Basque bar with a wide variety of *pintxos* and a great wine list, many available by the glass. Try **La Fabrica** (C/Hermenegild Clascar 4, 93 817 15 38, closed

Sun, mains €10) for finer dining, with an emphasis on Asian flavours. A good traditional restaurant in the region is **Sol i Vi**, in a nice hotel between Vilafranca and Sant Sadurní (Ctra Sant Sadurní a Vilafranca, 93 899 32 04, www. solivi.com, closed 2wks Jan, rates incl breakfast €82.50, mains €15). Another lodging option is the three-star **Hotel Pere III** (Plaça del Penedès 2, 93 890 31 00, www.hotelpedrotercero. com, rates €58-€72), in the centre of Vilafranca. In Torrelavit is **Masia Can Cardús** (93 899 50 18, www.agroturismealtpenedes.net, rates €40), a farm and vineyard with rooms to rent.

Tourist information

Falset

C/Sant Marcel 2 (977 83 10 23). **Open** 9am-2pm Mon-Fri; 10am-2pm Sat; 11am-2pm Sun.

Sant Sadurní d'Anoia

C/Hospital 26 (93 891 31 88). **Open** *Sept-July* 10am-2pm, 4.30-6.30pm Mon-Fri; 10am-2pm Sat, Sun. *Aug* 10am-2pm Tue-Sun.

Vilafranca del Penedès

C/Cort 14 (93 818 12 54). **Open** 4-7pm Mon; 9am-1pm, 4-7pm Tue-Fri; 9am-1pm, 5-8pm Sat.

Getting there

Alella

By bus Barcelona Bus (93 232 04 59) from Plaça Urquinaona.
By car NII north to Montgat, then left turn to Alella (15km/9 miles).

Alt Penedès

By car A2, then A7 to Sant Sadurní (44km/27 miles) and Vilafranca (55km/34 miles), or A2, then toll-free N340 from Molins de Rei, which is much slower.
By train RENFE from Sants or Plaça Catalunya; trains leave hourly 6am-10pm (journey time 45mins), then taxi for Torres, Jean León and Codorníu.

Falset, Scala Dei & Gandesa

By car A2, then A7 to Reus, and right on to N420 for Falset (143km/89 miles) and Gandesa (181km/ 112 miles). For Scala Dei, take T710 from Falset, then turn right at La Vilella Baixa.
By train RENFE from Sants or Passeig de Gràcia to Marçà-Falset. Six trains daily (journey time 2hrs). For Gandesa, continue to Mora d'Ebre (20mins) and catch a local bus.

Costa Daurada

Beyond Sitges and Vilanova, the coastline offers little relief from the towering concrete apartments erected in the 1970s. **Calafell** is worth half a day's mooch for its Iberian citadel, lively seafront and decent beaches not far away at **Sant Salvador**. Really, though, there's not much of interest until **Altafulla**, a few minutes north of Tarragona on the train.

Altafulla is split into two parts. Altafulla Playa hugs the sea with a modern but elegant esplanade of low-rise houses and the stately **Tamarit castle** overlooking a sandy bay. The castle is under private ownership; to get a better look, walk around to the far side and find the lovely hidden sandy cove. Altafulla Pueblo, meanwhile, is a jumble of cobbled streets with a medieval feel; it's a ten-minute walk inland. Local folklore has it that the old town has long been home to a coven of witches. Further south along the coast, towards the unlovely resort of **Salou**, is the **Port Aventura** theme park.

Universal Mediterránea/ Port Aventura

977 77 90 90/www.portaventura.es. By car A2, then A7 or N340 (108km/67 miles)/by train fromPasseig de Gràcia (1hr 15mins). **Open** *Mid Mar-mid June, mid Sept-Oct* 10am-7pm daily. *Mid June-mid Sept* 10am-midnight daily. *Nov, Dec* 10am-6pm Fri; 10am-7pm Sat, Sun.* **Admission** *Port Aventura* €33-€35; €26.50-€28 concessions; €23 night ticket. Free under-4s. *Costa Caribe* (mid June-mid Sept) €9-€18; €7.50-€14.50 concessions. *3-day combined ticket* €61; €49 concessions. **Credit** AmEx, DC, MC, V.

Port Aventura theme park is the main attraction of this beach resort, but there are also two hotels and the tropically landscaped Costa Caribe water park. Port Aventura has 90 rides spread over five internationally themed areas (Mexico, the Far West, China, Polynesia and the Mediterranean), while Popeye and the Pink Panther roam the time-space continuum and hug your kids. The truly stomach-curdling Dragon Khan rollercoaster is one of the highlights; for the little ones, there's the usual slew of carousels and spinning teacups. There are also 100 daily live shows and a spectacular lakeside Fiesta Aventura with lights, music and fireworks.

Where to stay & eat

Located in Calafell, the **Hotel Ra** is a spa and thalassotherapy centre on the site of an old sanatorium (Avda Sanatori 1, 977 69 42 00, www.hotelra.com, rates incl breakfast €210-€310). In the old centre of the town is an eccentric, colourful bar-restaurant, **Angelitos Negros**, with a globe-trotting range of dishes and great salads (C/Vilamar 33, 977 693 402, closed Mon-Wed in Oct, mains €10.50). Altafulla now has an upmarket hotel in the shape of the elegant **Hotel Gran Claustre** (C/Cup 2, 977 65 15 57, www.granclaustre.com, rates €138-€170), housed in an old convent that now also boasts a swimming pool. The **Hotel San Martín** (C/Mar 7, 977 65 03 07, rates €51-€76) also has a pool. The **Faristol**,

in the old town, is a hotel, bar and particularly good restaurant in an 18th-century house run by an Anglo-Catalan couple (C/Sant Martí 5, 977 65 00 77, closed lunch June-Sept, closed Mon-Thur Oct-May, rates incl breakfast €60, mains €11). For rooms in the old town, ask at the **El Corral** bar (977 65 04 86) or the Faristol. For seafood tapas and grilled meats on the seafront, try **Botigues de Mar** (C/Botigues de Mar 81, 977 65 25 60, closed Mon-Thur Sept-May, mains €10). Another good, cheap eating option is **La Chunga** (C/Mar 13, 977 65 22 81, mains €8).

Tourist information

Oficina de Turisme de Altafulla
Plaça dels Vents (977 65 07 52). **Open** *Mid June-mid Sept* 11am-1pm Mon, Tue, Thur-Sun.

Getting there

By car
Take the A2, then A7 via Vilafranca; or the toll-free N340 (Molins de Rei exit from A2).

By train
RENFE from Sants or Passeig de Gràcia to Altafulla (1hr 15mins). Trains run hourly approx 6am-9.20pm.

The Cistercian Route

The three architectural gems of the area inland from Tarragona are the Cistercian monasteries: **Poblet**, **Santes Creus** and **Vallbona de les Monges**. A signposted path, the GR175, runs between them; the trail, over 100 kilometres (62 miles) long, is known as **La Ruta del Cister** (the Cistercian Route). There are plenty of places to stay en route, though, and all three monasteries are easily accessible by car from **Montblanc**, 112 kilometres (70 miles) west of Barcelona and a beautiful town in its own right. In the Middle Ages, it was one of Catalonia's most powerful centres, with an important Jewish community. Its past is today reflected in its **C/Jueus** (Jews' Street), the magnificent 13th-century town walls (two-thirds are still intact), its churches, the **Palau Reial** (royal palace) and the **Palau del Castlà** (chamberlain's palace).

Poblet, a few kilometres west, was founded in 1151 as a royal residence and monastery. The remarkable complex includes a 14th-century **Gothic royal palace**, the 15th-century **chapel of Sant Jordi** and the main **church**, which houses the tombs of most of the Count-Kings of Barcelona. The monastery can be visited only on a guided tour. **Santes Creus**, founded in 1158 and perhaps more beautiful than Poblet, grew into a small village when

Monestir de Santes Creus.

families moved into the old monks' residences in the 1800s. Fortified walls shelter the **Palau de l'Abat** (abbot's palace), a monumental fountain, a 12th-century church and a superb Gothic cloister and chapterhouse. Visits include an audio-visual presentation.

Vallbona de les Monges, the third of these Cistercian houses, was, unlike the others, a convent of nuns. It was particularly favoured by Catalan-Aragonese queens, including Violant of Hungary (wife of Jaume I), who was buried here. It has a fine part-Romanesque cloister, but is less grand than the other two. Like them it still houses a religious community.

Monestir de Poblet

977 87 02 54. **Open** *Mar-Sept* 10am-12.40pm, 3-6pm daily. *Oct-Feb* 10am-12.40pm, 3-5.30pm daily. **Admission** €4.50; €2.50 concessions. **No credit cards**.

Monestir de Santa Maria de Vallbona

973 33 02 66. **Open** *Mar-Oct* 10.30am-1.30pm, 4.30-6.30pm Mon-Sat; noon-1.30pm, 4.30-6.30pm Sun. *Nov-Feb* 10.30am-1.30pm, 4.30-5.30pm Mon-Sat; noon-1.30pm, 4.30-5.30pm Sun. **Admission** €2.50; €2 concessions. **No credit cards**.

Monestir de Santes Creus

977 63 83 29. **Open** *Mid Mar-mid Sept* 10am-1.30pm, 3-7pm Tue-Sun. *Mid Sept-mid Jan* 10am-1.30pm, 3-5.30pm Tue-Sun. *Mid Jan-mid Mar* 10am-1.30pm, 3-6pm Tue-Sun. **Admission** €3.60; €2.40 concessions. Free Tue. **No credit cards**.

Where to stay & eat

In Montblanc, you'll need to book in advance to secure a room at the popular **Fonda dels Àngels**, which also has a great restaurant (Plaça dels Àngels 1, 977 86 01 73, closed dinner Sun and 3wks Sept, rates €37, mains €14). If it's full, try the **Hotel Ducal** (C/Francesc Macià 11, 977 86 00 25, rates €43.50). The **Fonda Colom** is a friendly old restaurant behind the Plaça Major (C/Civaderia 5, 977 86 01 53, mains €15, closed Mon).

In L'Espluga de Francolí, on the way to Poblet, the **Hostal del Senglar** (Plaça Montserrat Canals 1, 977 87 01 21, www.hostal delsenglar.com, rates €60-€67) is a great-value country hotel with gardens, a pool and an atmospheric if slightly pricey restaurant (mains €12). Santes Creus is very well served for hotels and restaurants. The **Fonda La Plana del Molí** is set in extensive gardens, with a swimming pool (Avda Plana del Molí 21, 977 63 83 09, rates €51). Try the partridge broth or wild boar stew at its restaurant (mains €8). The **Hostal Grau** (C/Pere El Gran 3, 977 63 83 11, closed mid Oct-June, rates €41-€43) is another very reasonable option. Good Catalan food can also be had at the restaurant here (closed Mon and mid Dec-mid Jan, mains €12) or at the **Restaurant Catalunya** (C/Arbreda 2, 977 63 84 32, closed Wed, mains €10) further down the hill.

Trips Out of Town

Tourist information

Oficina de Turisme de Montblanc
Antiga Esglesia de Sant Francesc (977 86 17 33/ www.montblancmedieval.org). **Open** 10am-1pm, 3-6pm Mon-Sat; 10am-2pm Sun.

Getting there

By bus
Hispano Igualadina (93 488 15 63) runs a daily service to Montblanc from Sants station. There are more buses running from Valls and Tarragona.

By car
For **Montblanc**, take the A2, then A7, then back on the A2 to exit 9; or take the toll-free N340 to El Vendrell, then the C51 for Valls, and the N240 for Montblanc (112km/70 miles). For **Poblet**, take the N240 west from Montblanc and turn left in L'Espluga de Francoli. For **Vallbona de les Monges**, take the C14 north from Montblanc towards Tàrrega and turn left on to a signposted side road. For **Santes Creus**, turn off the C51 or A2 before Valls, following signs to Vila-rodona.

By train
RENFE trains leave from Sants or Passeig de Gràcia to Montblanc. There are 5 trains a day. The journey takes about 2hrs.

Tortosa & the Ebre Delta

About an hour further down the coast from Tarragona, the railway dips inland to **Tortosa**, a little-visited town with a rich history evident in the fabric of its buildings. A magnificent Gothic **cathedral**, built on the site of a Roman temple, is surrounded by narrow medieval alleyways, and traces of the town's **Jewish** and **Arab quarters** can still be seen (and are clearly signposted). Interesting Modernista buildings around town include the colourful, Mudéjar-inspired pavilions of the former slaughterhouse (**Escorxador**), on the banks of the Ebre river.

East of here is the extraordinary **Parc Natural del Delta de l'Ebre**, an ecologically remarkable protected area. The towns of the delta are nothing special, but the immense, flat, green expanses of wetlands, channels, dunes and still-productive rice fields are eerily beautiful. The town of **Deltebre** is the base for most park services; from here, it's easy to make day trips to the bird sanctuaries, especially the remote headland of **Punta de la Banya**. The delta's flatness makes it an ideal place for walking or cycling; for bicycle hire, check at the tourist office in Deltebre). Small boats offer trips along the river from the north bank about eight kilometres (five miles) east of Deltebre.

It's also a hugely popular birdwatching destination, home to nearly half the 600 bird species found in Europe. The area is a vital breeding ground for birds who rest and feed in the delta during the winter migratory season. The flocks of flamingos make a spectacular sight, and the wetlands are inundated with herons, great crested grebes, spoonbills and marsh harriers. Even non-birdwatchers are enthused by the evocatively named whiskered tern, the moustached warbler, the lesser short-toed lark and the red-necked nightjar.

Where to stay & eat

Tortosa has a wonderful *parador*, **Castell de la Suda** (977 44 44 50, rates €102-€112), built on the site of a Moorish fortress with panoramic views. See www.paradors.es for occasional offers. On the eastern edge of the Ebre delta is a wide, sweeping beach, Platja dels Eucaliptus, where you'll find the **Camping Eucaliptus** (977 47 90 46, closed Oct-Apr, €4 per person & per tent). The **Hotel Rull** in Deltebre is large but friendly, and organises occasional 'safaris' for guests (Avda Esportiva 155, 977 48 77 28, www.hotelrull.com, rates incl breafast €54.25-€87.74, mains €12). You can also stay and eat at the ecologically friendly **Delta Hotel** (Avda del Canal, Camí de la Illeta, 977 48 00 46, www.deltahotel.net, rates €60-€81). Local specialities include dishes made with delta rice, duck, frogs' legs and the curious *chapadillo* (sun-dried eels): try them all at **Galatxo**, at the mouth of the river (Desembocadura Riu Ebre, 977 26 75 03, closed Tue, mains €14).

Tourist information

Centre d'Informació Delta de l'Ebre
C/Doctor Martí Buera 22, Deltebre (977 48 96 79/www.parcsdecatalunya.com). **Open** 10am-2pm, 3-7pm Mon-Sat; 10am-1pm Sun.

Tortosa Oficina de Turisme
Parc Municipal Teodoro González (977 44 25 67/ www.tortosa.altanet.org). **Open** *Oct-Mar* 10am-1.30pm, 3.30-6.30pm Tue-Sat. *Apr-Sept* 10am-1.30pm, 4.30-7.30pm Tue-Sat; 10.30am-1.30pm Sun.

Getting there

By car
Take the A2, then A7 via Vilafranca; or the toll-free N340 (Molins de Rei exit from A2) to the delta, then the C42 to Tortosa.

By train & bus
RENFE from Sants or Passeig de Gràcia every 2hrs to Tortosa (2hrs) or L'Aldea (2hrs 30mins), then 3 buses daily (HIFE 977 44 03 00) to Deltebre.

Girona & the Costa Brava

Sedate town, wild coastline.

Girona

It's only just over an hour north of Barcelona, but **Girona** is worlds apart: traditional, peaceful and solidly middle class. It's also a handsome city: though it boasts few of the wilder fancies of Modernisme, its medieval heart has been beautifully preserved, and its modest size means that a glimpse of green hills or parkland is possible from almost anywhere.

The **River Onyar**, lined by buildings in red and ochre, divides the old city from the new, and though it is rarely much more than a trickle these days, it's a good place to start a stroll. Note the Eiffel-designed bridge, the **Pont de les Peixateries**. A walk up the lively riverside **Rambla de la Llibertat** takes you towards the city's core and major landmark, the magnificent **cathedral**. Its 1680 baroque façade conceals a graceful Romanesque cloister and understated Gothic interior, which happens to boast the widest nave in Christendom. In the cathedral museum is the stunning 12th-century '**Tapestry of Creation**' and the **Beatus**, an illuminated tenth-century set of manuscripts.

Before their expulsion in 1492, the city's sizeable Jewish population had their own district: the **Call**, whose labyrinthine streets around the C/Força are beautifully preserved to this day. The story of this community is told in the Jewish museum in the **Centre Bonastruc ça Porta** (C/Sant Llorenç, 972 21 67 61), built on the site of a 15th-century synagogue. Nearby is the **Museu d'Història de la Ciutat**

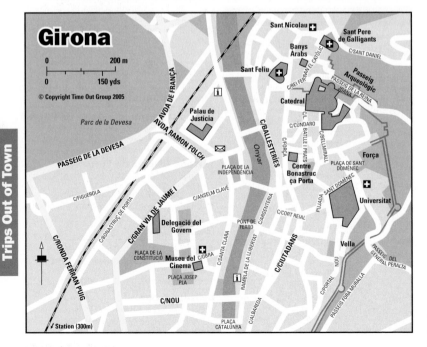

Trips Out of Town

(C/Força 27, 972 22 22 29, www.ajuntament.
gi/museu_ciutat, closed Mon), set in an 18th-
century monastery. Look out for the alcoves
with ventilated seating on the ground floor,
which is where the deceased monks were placed
to dry out for two years before their mummified
corpses were put on display.

Heading north from here, the Mudéjar **Banys
Àrabs** (C/Ferran el Catòlic, 972 21 32 62) is
actually a Christian creation, a 12th-century
bathhouse with a blend of Romanesque and
Moorish architecture. The nearby monastery
of **Sant Pere de Galligants** is one of the
finest of the countless examples of Romanesque
architecture in Catalonia, its beautiful 12th-
century cloister rich with intricate carvings. The
monastery also houses the **Museu Arqueològic**
(C/Santa Llúcia 1, 972 20 26 32, www.mac.es),
showing day-to-day objects from the Paleolithic
to the Visigothic periods. Continuing from here,
the **Passeig Arqueològic** runs along what's
left of the old city walls, intact until 1892.

Where to stay & eat

A couple of decent hotels opened in 2004 to fill
something of a gulf at the higher end of the
market: the **Hotel Ciutat de Girona** (C/Nord
2, 972 483 03, www.hotel-ciutatdegirona.com,
rates €139.10) and the **Hotel Històric**
(C/Bellmirall 6, 972 22 35 83, www.hotelhistoric.
com, rates €149.80-€160.50). The owners of
the latter also rent fully equipped apartments
(rates €90) in the adjacent building. **Pensión
Bellmirall** (C/Bellmirall 3, 972 20 40 09, closed
Jan & Feb, rates incl breakfast €60) is in a
pretty 14th-century building with a shady
breakfast courtyard. The **Hotel Peninsular**
(C/Nou 3 & Avda Sant Francesc 6, 972 20 38 00,
rates €60-€65) is good value.

The best restaurant in town, and one of the
best in Spain, is the **Celler de Can Roca**
(C/Taialà 40, 972 22 21 57, closed Mon & Sun,
mains €21.50). Located in an unprepossessing
suburb just north of the city, it's an essential
trip for food lovers, though you'll need to book
ahead. In the 19th-century area over the river
from the old town, you'll find Girona's oldest
and possibly best value restaurant, **Casa
Marieta** (Plaça de la Independència 5-6, 972 20
10 16, www.casamarieta.com, mains €8), while
the old Modernista flour factory houses **La
Farinera** (Ptge Farinera Teixidor 4, 972 22 02
20, mains €16), a good Basque restaurant with
excellent tapas. **La Crêperie Bretonne**
(C/Cort Reial 14, no phone, mains €7) transports
visitors to northern France with a menu
including crêpes and cider. Halfway up a
medieval flight of steps nearby is another
Francophile's delight, **Le Bistrot** (Pujada Sant

Domènec 4, 972 21 88 03, mains €12), with a
cheap (and good) set lunch in a gorgeous setting.
For more typically Catalan dishes, and the odd
Jewish one (plus kosher wine), try **El Pou del
Call** (C/Força 14, 972 22 37 74, mains €11).

Tourist information

Oficina de Turisme de Girona

*Rambla de la Llibertat 1 (972 22 65 75/www.
ajuntament.gi).* **Open** 8am-8pm Mon-Fri; 8am-2pm,
4-8pm Sat; 9am-2pm Sun.

Getting there

By bus

Barcelona Bus (93 232 04 59), approx 5 buses daily
from Estació del Nord.

By car

A7 or toll-free NII.

By train

RENFE from Sants or Passeig de Gràcia (1hr
15mins). Trains leave hourly approx 6am-9.15pm.

From Girona to the coast

The C66 takes you from Girona to the coast
through the Baix (Lower) Empordà, whose
strategic importance in medieval times is
demonstrated by a legacy of castles and walled
towns. The road splits in dignified **La Bisbal**,
the administrative centre of the region, where
you can buy no end of ceramic goods and visit
the **Terracotta Museum** (C/Sis d'Octubre
de 1869 99, 972 64 20 67, open May-Sept,
evenings only). Nearby **Verges** is most famous
for its grotesque 'dance of death' procession on
Maundy Thursday. Just up the road is the
12th-century **Castell de Púbol**, bought by
Salvador Dalí to house (and eventually bury)
his wife-muse Gala in her later years. Relations
were strained by then: Dalí had to book
appointments to see her, and the tomb that he
prepared for himself next to hers lies empty (he
changed his mind), guarded by a stuffed giraffe.

A few miles further east lies the walled,
moated town of **Peratallada**, dominated by
an 11th-century castle and famous for its good
food. Nearby **Ullastret** takes you further
back in time, with extensive ruins from a third-
century BC Iberian settlement, explained in the
small **Museu d'Arqueologia** (Puig de Sant
Andreu, 972 17 90 58, closed Mon). The friendly
medieval town of **Pals**, with its imposing
Torre de les Hores, has great views of the
coast, as does **Begur**, a 14th-century town built
around its castle. The latter acts as a gateway
to the Costa Brava, and is a steep three-
kilometre (two-mile) walk from the sea.

Trips Out of Town

Castell de Púbol

Information Teatre-Museu Dalí (972 67 75 00/
www.salvador-dali.org). **Open** *15 Mar-14 June, 16*
Sept-1 Nov 10.30am-5.30pm Tue-Sun. *15 June-15*
Sept 10.30am-7.30pm daily. Closed 2 Nov-14 Mar.
Admission €5.50; €4 concessions. **No credit cards**.

Where to stay & eat

In **Peratallada**, the **Hostal Miralluna** (Plaça
de l'Oli 2, 972 63 43 04, www.hostalmiralluna.
com, rates €135-€150 incl breakfast) is a tranquil
14th-century place filled with antiques. The
charming **Ca l'Aliu** (C/Roca 6, 972 63 40 61,
rates incl breakfast €56-€64) is probably the best
value in town. In **Pals**, the **Hotel Mas Salvi**
(C/Carmany 13, 972 63 64 78, www.massalvi.
com, closed Jan-mid Feb, rates €187.25-
€353) is the luxury option, with 22 suites in
an old farmhouse with gardens, a pool and a
tennis court. At the other end of the scale is
Barris (C/Enginyer Algarra 51, 972 63 67 02,
rates €36). In **Begur**, try the **Hotel Rosa** (C/Pi
i Ralló 19, 972 62 30 15, www.hotel-rosa.com,
closed Nov-Feb, rates incl breakfast €56-€84).

Locals travel from far and wide to eat in
Peratallada's restaurants; try the famous
galtes de porc a l'empordanesa (pigs' cheeks
with artichoke and carrots) at the **Restaurant
Bonay** (Plaça de les Voltes 13, 972 63 40 34,
www.bonay.com, closed Dec & Jan, mains €15).
In **Begur**, **Els Patis de Begur** (C/Pi i Rallo 9,
972 62 37 41, mains €15) specialises in paellas;
in **Pals**, **Restaurant Sa Punta** (Urbanizació
Sa Punta, 972 66 73 76, mains €21.50) serves
excellent poolside Mediterranean dishes.

Tourist information

Oficina de Turisme de Begur

Avda 11 de Setembre 5 (972 62 45 20). **Open** *Apr-*
June 9am-2.30pm, 5-9pm Mon-Fri; 10am-2pm, 5-9pm
Sat, Sun. *July-Sept* 9am-9pm daily. *Oct-Mar* 9am-2pm
Mon-Fri; 10am-2pm Sat, Sun.

Oficina de Turisme de Pals

Plaça Major 7 (972 63 73 80/www.ajuntament
depals.com). **Open** *June-Sept* 10am-2pm, 4-8pm daily.
Oct-May 10am-2pm, 4-7pm Mon-Sat; 10am-2pm Sun.

Getting there

By bus

Barcelona Bus (93 232 04 59) to Girona from Estació
del Nord. Sarfa (902 302 025) has 9 daily buses to
Palafrugell (some continue to Begur), and regular
buses to La Bisbal, which stop at Púbol.

By car

A7 or toll-free NII to Girona. For Peratallada, Pals
and Begur take exit 6 from A7 or leave NII after
Girona and take C66.

Costa Brava

Costa Brava means 'wild' or 'rugged' coast. The
name, coined by a journalist in the 1900s, refers
to its many rocky coves, whose presence has
prevented the area from being swamped by the
sort of high-rise monstrosities that plague the
seaside just north of Barcelona, in home-from-
home tourist traps like **Calella**, **Blanes** and
Lloret de Mar. North of these, **Tossa del
Mar** heralds the Costa Brava proper, and is just
about worth a look out of season. Once a haven
for artists, it has a beachside medieval castle
and pretty, narrow bar-filled streets.

The tortuous 20-kilometre (12-mile) drive
through coastal pine forests from here to
Sant Feliu de Guíxols offers brief but
unforgettable views of the sea. Sant Feliu
itself has some fine Modernista buildings along
the dignified Passeig Marítim, and the town
museum has a fine collection of local ceramics.
Sant Pol beach is three kilometres (two miles)
north of the crowded town sands, and offers
more towel room. You can explore further along
the coast on foot: the **Camí de Ronda** slaloms
its way along the undulating shoreline.

Further along the coast, **Platja d'Aro** and
Palamós are worth avoiding; the latter has
never recovered from an attack by the famous
pirate Barba Roja (Redbeard) in 1543. Instead,
continue to **Palafrugell**, which has a great
Sunday market and offers access to a number of
picturesque villages built into the rocky coves.
Calella de Palafrugell, not to be confused
with its near namesake down the coast, is a
quiet, charming town, even during its annual
Cantada d'Havaneres song festival in July. A
scenic 20-minute walk away, **Llafranc** offers
a long curved beach from where you can swim
between fishing boats at anchor in the bay.

Tamariu is known for its good seafood, and
is a base for waterskiing and fishing. Between
May and October, call Paco Heredia (972 30 1310,
www.gironautic.com) or Albert Muñoz (972 61
15 48) to hire a boat; the latter also runs two-hour
excursions by boat for €16 per person. Next up is
Aiguablava, with its modern *parador* and white
sandy beach, and **Fornells**, both accessible from
Begur, as is the small **Aiguafreda**, a cove
sheltered by pines. Nearby **Sa Riera**, the
northernmost cove, shelters two beaches, **La
Platja del Raco**, where bathing costumes must
be worn, and **Illa Roja**, where they mustn't.

Beyond the Ter estuary and the Montgri
hills, which divide the Baix and Alt Empordà,
is **L'Estartit**. This small resort town makes
much of its living catering to tourists interested
in exploring the **Illes Medes**, a group of rocky
limestone outcrops of which only two are
habitable (but uninhabited) islands. The biggest

Traditional, peaceful and handsome: **Girona** has a well-preserved heritage. *See p290.*

Tales of the city

Nearby, there's more I-Spy to be played on the façade of the cathedral, where, if you squint, you can see a little old lady among the otherwise beastly gargoyles. Once the town witch, she would spend her days cursing against religion and chucking stones at the cathedral, the priest and any religious processions, until the Almighty's patience was too sorely tested and he turned her into stone. She was condemned to stay, facing away from heaven, at the highest part of the church where the purest rainwater would be channelled through her mouth in place of blasphemous utterance.

Having ticked these two off, you also might like to play 'spot the chocolate fly' in the various *pastisseries* around town. These tasty little critters are reminders of one of the city's more extravagant miracles, during one of the many invasions which won it the soubriquet 'City of a Thousand Sieges'. During this particular attack in 1285, the troops of Philip the Bold ransacked the Sant Feliu church, smashing open the tomb of Girona's patron saint, Narcissus – had they known that Narcissus is also the patron saint of insect bites (no, really) they might have thought twice. Cloud of venomous flies issued forth, driving the soldiers and horses into such a frenzy that they turned against each other, man against beast, and Girona survived to live another day.

Splayed miserably at the top of a stone column in front of the cathedral in the Plaça Sant Feliu, looking more like royal roadkill than the King of the Jungle, is Girona's celebrated lion. It's easily missed, but worth the effort to spot, for shinning up the pole and kissing the lion's butt will bring luck to newly weds, full citizenship to *gironins*, and the promise of a return trip for outsiders. Nowadays the council has made these dreams a reality for everyone, with a nice handy set of steps.

housed a British prison in the 19th century, but Les Illes are now home only to a unique ecosystem, an underwater paradise where divers can contemplate the colourful coral and hundreds of different species of sealife. Glass-bottomed boats do tours in the summer months. For a view of the islands, it's worth the 45-minute climb up to the 12th-century **Castell de Montgrí**.

Watersports

In Calella de la Costa, catamarans, kayaks and windsurfing equipment can all be hired at **Club Nàutic Calella** (Passeig Platja, 93 766 18 52). In L'Estartit, for diving around the Illes Medes, try the **Diving Center La Sirena** (C/Camping

La Sirena, 972 75 09 54, www.la-sirena.net, closed mid Nov-Apr), **Unisub** (Passeig Marítim 10, 972 75 17 68, www.unisub.es), or **Quim's Diving Center** (Ctra Torroella de Montgrí, km 4.5, 972 75 01 63, www.quimsdivingestartit.com).

Where to eat

In **Sant Feliu de Guíxols**, try the **Nàutic** in the Club Nàutic sailing club, for great views and superb seafood (Port Esportiu, 972 32 06 63, closed Mon and 2wks Oct, set lunch €25). **Calella** has the excellent **Tragamar** (Platja de Canadell s/n, 972 61 43 36, mains €11), a branch of the restaurant Tragaluz in Barcelona. In **Tamariu**, there's more good seafood at the

Royal on the beachfront (Passeig de Mar 9, 972 62 00 41, closed Dec & Jan, mains €12), while in Aiguablava, the **Hotel Aiguablava** (Platja de Fornells, 972 62 20 58, closed Nov-Feb, mains €20) has an excellent beachfront restaurant.

Where to stay

In **Sant Feliu de Guixol**, try the **Hotel Les Noies** (Rambla de Portalet 10, 972 32 04 00, closed late Oct-early June, rates €34.30), or the small, friendly **Hotel Plaça** (Plaça Mercat 22, 972 32 51 55, rates €75-€107), close to the beach. North of Sant Feliu, in **S'Agaró**, is the nearest luxury option, the **Hostal de la Gavina** (Plaça de la Rosaleda, 972 32 11 00, closed Nov-Easter, rates €192-€288), a five-star in the European grand hotel tradition. **Llafranc** has the **Hotel Llafranc** (Passeig de Cipsela 16, 972 30 02 08, www.hllafranc.com, rates €87-€136 incl breakfast) and the friendly **Hotel Casamar** (C/Nero 3-11, 972 30 01 04, closed Jan-Mar, rates incl breakfast €72-€94).

Tamariu is home to the relaxed **Hotel Tamariu** (Passeig de Mar 2, 972 62 00 31, www.tamariu.com, closed Nov-Mar, rates incl breakfast €84-€121), while in **Aiguablava**, there's the pleasant local *parador*, **Platja d'Aiguablava** (972 62 21 62, www.parador.es, rates €120-€45) or the stately, family-run **Hotel Aiguablava** (972 62 21 62, www.parador.es, rates incl breakfast €120-€145). **Sa Tuna** has the **Hostal Sa Tuna** (Platja Sa Tuna, 972 62 21 98, closed mid Oct-mid Mar, rates incl breakfast €96.30), with five rooms in a perfect spot by the sea. In **Sa Riera** is the **Hotel Sa Riera** (Platja de Sa Riera, 972 62 30 00, closed mid Oct-Easter, rates incl breakfast €97.40-€113.60). L'Estartit has the **Santa Clara** (Passeig Marítim 18, 972 75 17 67, rates incl breakfast €45-€52).

Tourist information

Oficina de Turisme de L'Estartit

Passeig Marítim (972 75 19 10). **Open** *May* 9am-1pm, 4-7pm Mon-Fri; 10am-2pm Sat, Sun. *June-Sept* 10am-2pm, 4-9pm Mon-Sat; 10am-2pm Sun. *Oct-Apr* 9am-1pm, 3-6pm Mon-Sat; 10am-2pm Sun.

Oficina de Turisme de Palafrugell

C/Carrilet 2 (972 30 02 28/www.palafrugell.net). **Open** *May-June, Sept* 10am-1pm, 5-8pm Mon-Sat; 10am-1pm Sun. *July, Aug* 9am-9pm Mon-Sat; 10am-1pm Sun. *Oct-Apr* 10am-1pm, 4-7pm Mon-Sat; 10am-1pm Sun.

Oficina de Turisme de Sant Feliu de Guixols

Plaça del Mercat 28 (972 82 00 51/www.guixols.net). **Open** *Mid June-mid Sept* 10am-2pm, 4-8pm daily. *Mid Sept-mid June* 10am-1pm, 4-7pm Mon-Sat; 10am-2pm Sun.

Getting there

By bus

Sarfa (902 302 025) has 15 buses daily to Sant Feliu from Estació del Nord (journey time 1hr 20mins), and 9 to Palafrugell (2hrs); some continue to Begur. Change in Palafrugell or Torroella for L'Estartit.

By car

A7 north to exit 9 on to C35/C65 for Sant Feliu de Guíxols, then C31 for Palafrugell (123km/76 miles); or A7 exit 6 for Palafrugell and Begur via La Bisbal.

North to France

The seaside town of **L'Escala**, famous for its anchovies, provides a great place for refuelling with coffee and provisions before making the worthwhile 15-minute walk to **Empúries**. Here, you'll find the well-preserved remains of an ancient city that dates back to 600 BC, when it was founded by the Phoenicians, before being recolonised by the Greeks and finally by the Romans in AD 2. Today, ruins from all three periods, as well as the layout of the original Greek harbour, are clearly visible. The whole site is picturesque and atmospheric, lending a rare immediacy to history in an ancient site.

Just visible on the other side of the huge Golf de Roses is the overcrowded tourist resort of **Roses**, which has little to recommend it apart from a 16th-century citadel and the nearby legendary restaurant **El Bulli** in Cala Montjoi. From Roses, the road coils over the hills that form the **Cap de Creus** nature reserve, before dropping spectacularly down to **Cadaqués**. The town's relative isolation has made it a destination for the discerning: Picasso painted much of his early Cubist work here, but it was Salvador Dalí who really put the place on the map. The artist spent his childhood summers here, brought his surrealist circle to see it, and ended up building his home in **Port Lligat**, a short walk away.

Cadaqués later became the preferred resort among the Catalan cultural elite, and has kept its charm primarily thanks to a ban on the high-rise buildings that have blighted the rest of coastal Spain. Dalí's house, with much of its zany furniture, peculiar fittings and some impertinent stuffed animals, is now a museum, which offers great insight into the eccentric genius's strange lifestyle. Note that you should book some days before you visit, as only eight people are allowed in at a time.

On the north side of the cape, **Port de la Selva**, looking towards France, is less touristy than Cadaqués and within hiking distance of the remarkable **Sant Pere de Rodes** fortified abbey, the area's most accomplished example of Romanesque architecture. A further climb takes you up to the remarkable **Castell de Sant Salvador**, an imposing tenth-century castle that seems to grow out of the rock with unparalleled views out over the Pyrenees to France, and back over the Gulf of Roses into Catalonia.

The capital of the Alt Empordà region is **Figueres**, where Dalí was born and is buried in his own museum in the city's old theatre, the **Teatre-Museu Dalí**. The artist donated many of his works to the museum and also redesigned the place, putting thousands of yellow loaves on the external walls and huge eggs on its towers. The highlight inside is the three-dimensional room-sized Mae West face, a collection of furniture arranged to look like the star when viewed from a certain angle. All of this rather overshadows the city's other two (rather good) museums: the **Museu de l'Empordà** (Rambla 2, 972 50 23 05), which gives an overview of the history of the area, and the **Museu del Joguet** (C/Sant Pere 1, 972 50 45 85), full of 19th-century toys, some of which belonged to Dalí and Miró.

Dalí's **Castell de Púbol**. *See p291*.

Between Figueres and the sea sits the nature reserve of **Aiguamolls de l'Empordà**, a haven for rare species of birds that flock to the marshy lowlands at the mouth of the Fluvia river in spring and autumn. As well as flamingos, bee-eaters and moustached warblers, it is home to turtles, salamanders and otters.

Casa-Museu de Port Lligat

972 25 10 15/www.salvador-dali.org. **Open** *Mid Mar-mid June, mid Sept-Dec* 10.30am-5.10pm Tue-Sun. *Mid June-mid Sept* 10.30am-8.10pm Tue-Sun. Closed Jan-Mar. **Admission** €8; €6 concessions. **No credit cards.**

Sant Pere de Rodes

972 38 75 59. **Open** *June-Sept* 10am-7.30pm Tue-Sun. *Oct-May* 10am-5pm Tue-Sun. **Admission** €3.60; €2.40 concessions; free Tue. **No credit cards.**

Teatre-Museu Dalí

Plaça Gala-Salvador Dalí 5, Figueres (972 67 75 00/www.salvador-dali.org). **Open** *July-Sept* 9am-7.45pm Tue-Sun. *Oct-May* 10.30am-5.45pm Tue-Sun. *June* 10.30am-5.45pm daily. **Admission** €9; €6.50 concessions. **No credit cards.**

Where to stay & eat

Right next to the Greek ruins in **Empúries**, the **Hostal Ampurias** (Platja Portitxol, 972 77 02 07, rates €85-€107 incl breakfast, set menu €21) offers sparse but clean rooms in a fantastic setting in front of the rocky beach, and does good Mediterranean food all year round. Fifteen minutes' walk away in the pretty little village of Sant Martí d'Empúries, is the comfortable **Riomar** (Platja del Riuet, closed mid Oct-Easter, 972 77 03 62, rates incl breakfast €62-€94). Over the bay, a twisting seven-kilometre (four-and-a-half-mile) drive from Roses is the extraordinary and world-famous **El Bulli** (*see p171*), the best restaurant in Spain (for those who can afford it).

Cadaqués has few hotels, and most are closed in winter, so always call first. Try the friendly *pensión*/restaurant **Fonda Cala d'Or** (C/Sa Fitora 1, 972 25 81 49, rates €25, mains €9) or the **Hostal Marina** (C/Riera 3, 972 25 81 99, closed Jan-Easter, rates €35-€65). **Playa Sol** (Platja Pianc 3, 972 25 81 00, www.playasol. com, closed Dec & Jan, rates €88.60-€156 incl breakfast) has lovely sea views. The **Misty** (C/Nova Port Lligat, 972 25 89 62, closed Jan-mid Mar, rates €52-€83) has a pool; otherwise, try the **Llane Petit** (C/Doctor Bartomeus 37, 972 25 10 20, www.llanepetit.com, closed Jan & Feb, rates €92-€140 incl breakfast).

Restaurants, too, have a habit of closing in winter, so it pays to call ahead. **Restaurant Can Rafa** (C/Passeig Marítim 7, 972 15 94 01, closed Wed & Sun dinner mid Jan-June & Oct-mid Nov, closed mid Nov-mid Jan, mains €21) has local lobster as its speciality, while the pretty **Es Balconet**, up a winding street back from the bay (C/Sant Antoni 2, 972 25 88 14, mains €15, closed Tue, Wed & Nov) is good for paella. **Casa Anita** (C/Miguel Roset, 972 25 84 71, www.casa-anita.com, closed Nov & Mon, mains €15) is a popular, friendly and family-owned place with excellent fresh seafood and long queues. Dalí used to eat here. At Cap de Creus, the **Restaurant Cap de Creus** (972 19 90 05, mains €16.50) serves an eclectic range of dishes from seafood to curry, all in a spectacular setting on a headland jutting out to sea.

In Figueres, the **Hotel Duran** (C/Lasauca 5, 972 50 12 50, rates €59-€68, mains €10), was an old haunt of Dalí and exudes comfortable, battered elegance. The restaurant serves fine game and seafood. For clean and dull but well-equipped rooms, head for **La Barretina** (C/Lasauca 13, 972 67 34 25, www.hostalla barretina.com, closed Nov, rates €38). **President** (Ronda Firal 33, 972 50 17 00, closed Mon, set lunch €13) offers good, solid Catalan fare and excellent seafood. C/Jonquera is the main drag for cheap *menús del día*, with alfresco tables.

Tourist information

Oficina de Turisme de Cadaqués

C/Cotxe 2A (972 25 83 15/www.cadaques.org). **Open** *June-Sept* 10am-1pm, 4-7pm Mon-Sat; 10am-1pm Sun. *Oct-May* 10am-1pm, 4-7pm Mon-Sat.

Oficina de Turisme de L'Escala

Plaça de les Escoles 1 (972 77 06 03/www.lescala. org). **Open** *Mid June-mid Sept* 9am-8.30pm daily. *Mid Sept-mid June* 9am-1pm, 4-7pm Mon-Fri; 10am-4pm Sat; 10am-1pm Sun.

Oficina de Turisme de Figueres

Plaça del Sol (972 50 31 55). **Open** *Mar-June, Oct* 9am-2pm, 4-7pm Mon-Fri; 9.30am-2pm, 3.30-6.30pm Sat. *July-Sept* 9am-8pm Mon-Sat; 10am-3pm Sun. *Nov-Feb* 9am-2pm Mon-Fri.

Getting there

By bus

Barcelona Bus (93 232 04 59) has several buses daily to Figueres from Estació del Nord (2hrs 30mins). Sarfa (902 302 025) has 2 buses daily to Roses and Cadaqués (2hrs 15mins), and services to Roses, Port de la Selva, Cadaqués and L'Escala from Figueres.

By car

A7 or NII to Figueres (120km/74 miles). For Roses and Cadaqués, take the C260 from Figueres.

By train

RENFE from Sants or Passeig de Gràcia to Figueres (journey 2hrs). Trains leave every hour.

Trips Out of Town

Vic to the Pyrenees

The only way is up.

Vic & around

Very few tourists pass through **Vic**, despite its many buildings of historic importance. Life revolves around the impressive arcaded **Plaça Major**, and never more so than for its Saturday market, famed throughout the region and almost as old as the town itself. In one corner of the market square is the Modernista **Casa Comella**; sgraffiti depicts the four seasons designed by Gaietà Buïgas, who designed the Monument a Colom in Barcelona.

Vic began life as the capital of the Ausetian tribe, became a Roman city, and later fell briefly to the Moors, who lost it to Wilfred the Hairy, Count of Barcelona, in the ninth century. Since then, it's remained just an administrative, artistic and religious centre, with an amazing number of churches. The **Catedral de Sant Pere** contains Romanesque, Gothic and neo-classical elements, along with a set of dramatic 20th-century murals by Josep Lluís Sert, who is buried here. The **Museu Episcopal** (Plaça del Bisbe Oliva 3, 93 886 93 60, www.museu episcopalvic.com, closed Mon) is unmissable, with some magnificent 12th-century murals and a fascinating collection of Romanesque and Gothic art. The **Temple Romà** (Roman temple) was only discovered in 1882, when the 12th-century walls that surrounded it were knocked down. It's since been well restored, and now houses an art gallery.

The picturesque countryside around Vic is full of interesting villages, and the tourist offices have useful detailed maps of the many hiking routes. Following the C153 road towards Olot, **Rupit** makes a remarkably beautiful stop. An ancient village built on the side of a medieval castle, it has a precarious hanging bridge across a gorge. Later building in the town was done so sympathetically to the style that it's difficult to tell the old from the new. Almost as lovely, and not quite as touristy, is nearby **Tavertet**.

Where to stay & eat

In **Vic** itself, there's very little in the way of accommodation; its only *pensión* is **Hostal Osona** (C/Remei 3, 93 883 28 45, rates €27). It does, however, have some great restaurants. **Cardona 7** (C/Cardona 7, 93 886 38 15, closed Mon & lunch except Sat, closed 2wks Sept & Mar, mains €13) serves upmarket *platillos* – somewhere between a *tapa* and a main course. **La Taula** (C/Sant Marius 8, 93 417 28 48, closed lunch Sat, closed Aug, mains €12) offer a range of excellent-value set menus, or there's **Ca l'U** (Plaça Santa Teresa 4, 93 889 03 45, closed dinner Tue, Wed & Sun, all Mon and 3wks July-Aug, mains €15), a friendly, traditional inn that serves fish and game dishes. The small, colourful **La Creperia** (Plaça Sant Felip Neri 9, 93 886 37 81, closed dinner Tue, mains €4) is the budget option, with cheap crêpes, waffles and salads.

If you have transport (and a few quid), the nicest places to stay are outside Vic. The **Parador de Vic** is modern and comfortable, and sits in a fabulous location overlooking the Ter gorge (Paraje el Bac de Sau, 93 812 23 23, www.parador.es, rates €116-€127); take the C153 north and follow the signs (around 14km). In Tavèrnoles, just before it, **Mas Banús** (93 812 20 91, www.elbanus.com) is a giant old farmhouse, with self-contained cottages costing

Plaça Major in **Vic**.

from €230 for four people for a weekend. Also in Tavèrnoles is the **Fussimanya** (Ctra del Parador km 7, 93 812 21 88, closed dinner Wed & all day Thur, mains €9), a rambling old restaurant famous for its fine sausages. It's wildly popular at weekends. In Rupit, **Hotel Estrella** (Plaça Bisbe Font 1, 93 852 20 05, www.hotelestrella.com, rates incl breakfast €91, set lunch €14.50) is a *pensión* with a huge and popular restaurant.

Getting there

By bus
Empresa Sagalès (93 231 27 56) from the Fabra i Puig bus station (near metro of same name) to Vic. For Rupit, take a local bus from Vic.

By car
Take the C17, signed for Puigcerdà, to Vic (65km/40 miles). For Rupit, take the C153 out of Vic (signposted to Olot).

By train
RENFE from Sants or Plaça Catalunya to Vic. Trains leave about every 90mins. Journey time is 1hr 20mins.

Tourist information

Oficina de Turisme de Vic
C/Ciutat 4 (93 886 20 91/www.victurisme.com).
Open 10am-2pm, 4-8pm Mon-Sat; 10am-1pm Sun.

Berga to Puigcerdà

To the west, on the most popular approach to the Pyrenees from Barcelona, is **Berga**, famous for the frenzied festival of La Patum, held each May. Just north from there the giant cliffs of the **Serra del Cadí**, one of the ranges of the 'Pre-Pyrenees' or Pyrenees foothills, loom above the town. Berga has **Sant Ferran**, a medieval castle with a suitably storybook air, but the blight of endless holiday apartment blocks has taken its toll on the charm of its old centre.

Far prettier is the little town of **Bagà**, north of here along the C17. The town, with its partially preserved medieval walls around an atmospheric old quarter, marks the beginning of the **Parc Natural del Cadí-Moixeró**, a gigantic mountain park containing wildlife and forest reserves and some 20 or so ancient villages. All retain some medieval architecture, and many offer stunning views. Picasso stayed and painted in the village of **Gósol** in 1906.

Above Bagà, the C16 road enters the Túnel del Cadí to emerge into the wide, fertile plateau of the **Cerdanya**. Described by writer Josep Pla as a 'huge casserole', the area has an obvious geographical unity, but the French and Spanish border runs through the middle. **Puigcerdà**, the capital of the area (on the Spanish side), is a lively, pretty town with a French feel, populated mainly by skiing second-homers. It's a good

Trips Out of Town

base (and a memorable train journey from Barcelona) for exploring the area on foot: the tourist office has a decent selection of maps and itineraries. One of the more charming places to stay in the area is **Bellver de Cerdanya**, a lovely hilltop village with a lively market and Gothic church. The village has an information centre; all over town, noticeboards list hikes of varying degrees of difficulty.

Where to stay & eat

In Bagà, the **Hotel Ca L'Amagat** (C/Clota 4, 93 824 41 60, www.hotelcalamagat.com, rates €43) has rooms with large balconies and a

Rupit's medieval bridge. *See p298.*

restaurant serving dishes such as trout with almonds or veal with redcurrants (mains €11, closed Mon Oct-Apr). Puigcerdà has plenty of hotels in the town centre, including the small and charming **Avet Blau** (Plaça Santa Maria 14, 972 88 25 52, rates incl breakfast €70-€100). The **Hotel Rita-Belvedere** (C/Carmelites 6-8, 972 88 03 56, closed May-mid July, rates €50) has a small garden and terrace. The **Hotel del Lago** (Avda Doctor Piguillem 7, 972 88 10 00, www.hotellago.com, rates €86-€102), with its terracotta paintwork and green shutters, is not quite so pretty inside, but both staff and atmosphere are friendly, and there's a heated pool, a sauna and a jacuzzi. For modern French-Mediterranean food, try **La Col d'Hivern** (C/Baronia 7, 972 14 12 04, closed Mon-Wed, mains €17). A little further out in Bolvir, the sumptuous **Torre del Remei** (C/Camí Reial, 972 14 01 82, www.torredelremei.com, rates €214) also has one of the best (and most expensive) restaurants in the area (main courses €30). In Bellver, the **Fonda Bianya** (C/Sant Roc 11, 973 51 04 75, rates €70 incl breakfast) is utterly charming, with its sweet cornflower blue woodwork, a sunny bar and a lively feel. For sophisticated top-drawer dining, try **Picot Negre** (C/Camí Real 1, 973 51 11 98, mains €16.50), although a new owner and chef were taking over at the time of writing.

Getting there

By bus

Alsina Graëlls (93 265 68 66) runs five buses daily to Berga from the corner of C/Balmes and C/Pelai; journey time is about 2hrs. Same company has daily buses to Puigcerdà from Estació del Nord; journey time is 3hrs.

By car

Take the C16 to Berga (118km/73 miles) and Bagà. From Bagà continue on the C16 through Túnel del Cadí (toll), after which take the N260 east for Puigcerdà or west for Lles and Bellver. A scenic alternative is to take the C17 through Vic and Ripoll.

By train

RENFE from Sants or Plaça Catalunya to Puigcerdà. About one train every 2hrs, and the journey generally takes about 3hrs.

Tourist information

Oficina de Turisme de Berga

C/Angels 7 (93 821 13 84/www.ajberga.es). **Open** 10am-2pm Mon-Thur; 10am-2pm, 5-8pm Fri, Sat.

Oficina de Turisme de Puigcerdà

C/Querol (972 88 05 42). **Open** 9am-1pm, 4.30-8pm Mon-Sat; 10am-1pm Sun.

Ripoll to the Vall de Núria

Ripoll is best known for its extraordinary monastery, **Santa Maria de Ripoll**, founded in 879 by Wilfred the Hairy, who is buried here. The church has a superb 12th-century stone portal, its carvings among the finest examples of Romanesque art in Catalonia. The monastery museum, **Museu Etnogràfic** (972 70 31 44), due to reopen in 2005, traces the customs and history of the area with everyday objects. Wilfred also founded the monastery and town of **Sant Joan de les Abadesses**, ten kilometres (six miles) east up the C26, and worth a visit for its Gothic bridge as well as the 12th-century monastery. Neither town holds much charm outside its monasteries.

Ribes de Freser, the next town on the C-17 north of Ripoll, is an attractive base from which to travel to the pretty if slightly gentrified villages of **Campelles** and **Queralbs**. Ribes is also the starting point for the *cremallera*, or 'zipper train', a narrow-gauge cog railway that runs via Queralbs along the Freser river up to the sanctuary of **Núria**, affording incredible views. Many choose to walk back to Queralbs (around two hours), following the path through dramatic rock formations, crumbling scree, pine-wooded slopes and dramatic, crashing waterfalls.

Núria itself nestles by a lake on a plateau at over 2,000 metres (6,500 feet), and was the first ski resort on this side of the border. Home to the second most famous of Catalonia's patron virgins, a 12th-century wooden statue of the Madonna, Núria was a refuge and a place of pilgrimage long before then. The mostly 19th-century monastery that surrounds the shrine is nothing special, but its location is spectacular. You can bury your head in a pot to gain fertility or ring a bell to cure headaches, but most choose to hike, ski, row boats or ride horses. Get maps and information from the tourist office.

Where to stay & eat

In Ribes de Freser, the family-run **Hotel Els Caçadors** (C/Balandrau 24-26, 972 72 77 22, closed Nov, rates €61-€97 per person half-board) has good food and comfortable rooms. If it's full, try **Hostal Porta de Núria** (C/Nostra Senyora de Gràcia 3, 972 72 71 37, closed May, rates incl breakfast €45-€53.50). In Queralbs, try **Calamari Hostal l'Avet** (C/Major 5, 972 72 73 77, closed Mon-Thur Oct-May, rates €39 per person half-board). The one good place to eat in Queralbs is **De la Plaça** (Plaça de la Vila 2, 972 72 70 37, closed Tue, closed 2wks July-Oct, set menu €14), especially for regional specialities. In Núria is the three-star **Hotel**

Vall de Núria (Estación Vall de Sana, C/Santuari Mare de Deu de Núria, 972 73 20 20, www.valldenuria.com, closed Apr, rates €53-€77 half-board), with a two-night minimum.

Getting there

By bus
TEISA (972 20 48 68) from the corner of C/Pau Claris and C/Consell de Cent to Ripoll, Sant Joan de les Abadesses and Camprodon.

By car
Take the C17 direct to Ripoll (104km/65 miles). For Sant Joan de les Abadesses, Camprodon, take the C26 out of Ripoll.

By train
RENFE from Sants or Plaça Catalunya (journey time to Ripoll 2hrs). For Queralbs and Núria, change to the *cremallera* train in Ribes de Freser.

Tourist information

Oficina de Turisme de Núria
Estació de Montanya del Vall de Núria (972 73 20 20/www.valldenuria.com). **Open** *July-Sept* 8.30am-6.45pm daily. *Oct-June* 8.30am-6pm daily.

Oficina de Turisme de Ribes de Freser
Plaça del Ayuntamiento 3 (972 72 77 28). **Open** 10am-2pm, 5-8pm Tue-Sat; 11am-1pm Sun.

Besalú & Olot

The medieval fortified town of **Besalú** is one of the loveliest in Catalonia, its impressive 12th-century fortified bridge spanning the Fluvià river to mark its entrance. Once home to a sizeable Jewish community, it boasts the only remaining Jewish baths (*mikveh*) in Spain. These extraordinary structures date back to the 13th century but were only discovered in the 1960s. Charmingly, if the doors are locked when you arrive, the tourist office will give you a key so that you can let yourself in. Also worth visiting are the Romanesque church of Sant Pere and the arcaded Plaça de la Llibertat.

West from here the N260 runs to **Olot**, past a spectacular view of **Castellfollit de la Roca**, a village perched on the edge of a precipitous crag. The town is prettier from below than it is once you really get inside, but the old section still makes for an interesting stroll. **Olot** was destroyed in an earthquake in 1427, and so lost much of its oldest architecture, but it still has some impressive 18th-century and Modernista buildings. In the last century it was home to a school of landscape painters: the local **Museu de la Garrotxa** has works by them, along with

Ramon Casas, Santiago Rusiñol and other Modernista artists (C/Hospice 8, 972 27 91 30, closed Tue). The town is not especially interesting, however, and is mainly worth visiting because of its position amid the 30-odd inactive volcanoes and numerous lava flows of the volcanic region of **La Garrotxa**. Just south of town on the road to Vic is elegant **Casal dels Volcans** (Ctra Santa Coloma 43, 972 26 67 62, closed Tue), an information centre and museum where you can pick up maps detailing hikes.

Off the G1524 toward Banyoles is a delightful beech forest, the **Fageda d'en Jordà**, immortalised by Catalan poet Joan Maragall, and the pretty if touristy village **Santa Pau**, with an impressive castle and arcaded squares.

Where to stay & eat

In Besalú a 19th-century riverside inn, **Fonda Siqués** (Avda Lluís Companys 6-8, 972 59 01 10, rates incl breakfast €41-€65) offers clean if drab rooms and is located above a charming restaurant (closed Sun dinner and 3wks Jan, set lunch €9). For nicer, though still simple, rooms, try **Els Jardins de la Martana** (C/Pont 2, 972 59 00 09, www.lamartana.com, rates €86-€96). A couple of miles north of the town in Beuda, is a pretty *masia* with a pool, **Mas Salvanera** (972 59 09 75, www.salvanera.com, rates €120 incl breakfast). In Olot, **La Perla** (Avda Santa Coloma 97, 972 26 23 26, www.laperlahotels. com, rates €73-€79) is a large hotel with a good restaurant, or **Pensión La Vila** (C/Sant Roc 1, 972 26 98 07, rates incl breakfast €43) is modern and very central.

Restaurants in Besalú include the **Pont Vell** (C/Pont Vell 24, 972 59 10 27, closed dinner Mon & Tue, closed Jan, mains €11) for traditional cooking with a twist. The terrace of the **Cúria**

Reial (Plaça de la Llibertat 8-9, 972 59 02 63, closed dinner Mon & all day Tue, closed Feb, mains €14) is very popular, with good traditional cooking. In Olot, **Can Guix** (C/Mulleres 3-5, 972 26 10 40, closed dinner Wed & all day Sun, mains €4) has great, cheap local dishes. North of the town is the **Restaurant Les Cols** (Crta de la Canya, 972 26 92 09, closed Sun, dinner Mon & Tue, closed 3wks July-Aug, mains €19), set inside a picturesque *masia* with a terrace; try the house speciality of cabbage leaves stuffed with duck liver.

South of Olot, in La Pinya, is **Mas Garganta** (972 27 12 89, www.masgarganta.com, closed Jan & Feb, rates €50 per person half-board), an 18th-century *masia* with magnificent views that has walking tours with two *masies* nearby, so you can stay in one place and walk without bags to the next. In Banyoles, try the red mullet with tomato confit at the **Restaurant Fonda La Paz**, which also has rooms (C/Ponent 18, 972 57 04 32, closed dinner Sun & all day Mon, closed Jan & 2wks Sept, rates €37, mains €13).

Getting there

By bus
TEISA (972 20 48 68) to Besalú and Olot from the corner of C/Pau Claris and C/Consell de Cent.

By car
To Besalú, take the C66 from Girona, then N260 to Olot.

Tourist information

Oficina de Turisme de Olot
C/Hospici 8 (972 26 01 41/www.olot.org/turisme). **Open** *Mid Sept-mid June* 9am-2pm, 5-7pm Mon-Fri; 10am-2pm, 5-7pm Sat; 11am-2pm Sun. *Mid June-mid Sept* 10am-2pm, 5-8pm Mon-Sat; 11am-2pm Sun.

Rupit, old and new. *See p298.*

Directory

Getting Around   304
Resources A-Z   308
Spanish Vocabulary   323
Catalan Vocabulary   324
Further Reference   325
Index   326
Advertisers' Index   332

Features

Travel advice   309
Lost in translation   310
It's in the timing…   319
Average monthly climate   322

Directory

Arriving & Leaving

Barcelona's centre is compact and easily explored on foot. Bicycles are good for the Old City and port: there is a decent network of bike lanes across the city. The cheap, efficient metro and bus systems are best for longer journeys. Cars can be a hindrance: there's very little parking space, and most of the city is subject to one-way systems. Mopeds and motorbikes are popular among locals: they're ideal for zipping around in a generally dry climate. For transport outside Barcelona, *see p278*.

For transport outside Barcelona, *see p278*.

Arriving & leaving

By air

Barcelona's airport is at El Prat, just south-west of the city. Each airline works from one of the three main terminals (A, B or C) for all arrivals and departures. All terminals have cash machines, and there are tourist information desks and currency exchanges in terminals A and B.

For airport information, call 93 298 38 38 (operators speak English). Flight details and general information in English is online at www.aena.es.

Aerobús

The airport bus (information 93 415 60 20) runs from each terminal to Plaça Catalunya, with stops at Plaça d'Espanya, C/Urgell and Plaça Universitat. Buses to the airport go from Plaça Catalunya (in front of El Corte Inglés), stopping at Sants station and Plaça d'Espanya. Buses run every 12-13mins, leaving the airport from 6am-midnight Mon-Fri and 6.30am-midnight on weekends, returning from Plaça Catalunya 5.30am-11.15pm Mon-Fri and 6am-11.15pm at weekends. The trip takes 35-45mins, depending on traffic; a single ticket is €3.45. At night, a local bus, the 106, runs between the airport (from 10.15pm) and Plaça d'Espanya (from 10.55pm); it takes longer and only comes every 1hr15mins, but runs later (last airport departure 3.20am, from Plaça d'Espanya 3.50am).

Airport trains

The long overhead walkway between the terminals leads to the airport train station. Trains stop at Sants, Plaça Catalunya, Arc de Triomf and Clot-Aragó, all of which are also metro stops. Trains leave the airport at 13mins and 43mins past each hour, 6.13am-11.40pm Mon-Fri. Trains to the airport leave Plaça Catalunya at 8mins and 38mins past the hour, 5.38am-10.11pm Mon-Fri (5mins later from Sants). Weekend times vary slightly, but there are still usually trains every 30mins, mostly leaving Plaça Catalunya at 11mins and 41mins past the hour. The journey takes 17-30mins and costs €2.25 one way (there are no return tickets). Be aware that tickets are only valid for 2hrs after purchase.

Taxis from the airport

On weekdays, the taxi fare to central Barcelona should be €14-€26, including a €3 airport supplement. The current minimum fare for a taxi ride to or from the airport is €11.70. Fares are about 15% higher after 10pm and at weekends. There is a 90¢ supplement for each large piece of luggage placed in the car boot. All licensed cab drivers use the ranks outside the terminals.

Airlines

Terminals are shown in brackets.

Aer Lingus (B) 91 541 42 13/ www.aerlingus.com.
Air Europa (B) 93 478 47 63/ www.air-europa.com.
BMI Baby (A) 902 100 737/ www.bmibaby.com.
British Airways (B) 902 111 333/ www.british-airways.com.
Easyjet (A) 902 299 992/ www.easyjet.com.
Iberia (B or C) 902 400 500/ www.iberia.com.
Monarch Airlines (B) 902 502 737/ www.flymonarch.com.
Spanair (B) 902 131 415/ www.spanair.com.
Virgin Express (A) 902 888 459/ www.virgin-express.com.
Vueling (B) 902 333 933/ www.vueling.com.

Note that **Ryanair** (807 220 022, www.ryanair.com) does not fly to Barcelona. The closest destinations to which it flies are Girona, around 100km north of Barcelona, and Reus, which is approximately 100km south. There is a frequent train service from Girona to Barcelona, but the easiest way to travel is to take the Ryanair bus (902 36 15 50) from Girona airport to Barcelona city. Buses arrive and depart from Passeig Sant Joan 52, in Barcelona (near Girona or Tetuán metro stops) and are timed to coincide with Ryanair flight departure and arrival times. Call 902 361 550 or see www.ryanair.com for details. A 30-day return ticket costs €19 and a single is €11. Journey time is around 1hr 10mins. There's a similar bus connecting the less frequent Reus flights to Plaça Maria Cristina and Sants Estació in Barcelona (information 93 804 44 51). It costs €18 return and €11 one-way, and takes approximately 1hr 30mins.

By bus

Most long-distance coaches (national and international) stop or terminate at **Estació d'Autobusos Barcelona-Nord** at C/Ali Bei 80, next to Arc de Triomf rail and metro station (information 902 26 06 06, www.barcelonanord.com). The **Estació d'Autobusos Barcelona-Sants** at C/Viriat, between Sants mainline rail station and Sants-Estació metro stop, is only a secondary stop for many coaches, though some international Eurolines services (information 93 490 40 00, www.eurolines.es) both begin and end their journeys at Sants.

By car

The easiest way to central Barcelona from almost all directions is the Ronda Litoral, the coastal half of the ring road. Take exit 21 (Paral·lel) if you're coming from the south, or exit 22 (Via Laietana) from the north. Motorways also feed into Avda Diagonal, Avda Meridiana and Gran Via, which all lead to the city centre. Tolls are charged on most of the main approach routes, payable in cash (the lane marked 'manual'; motorbikes are charged half) or by credit card ('automatic'). For more on driving in Barcelona, *see p306*.

For more on driving in Barcelona, *see p306*.

By sea

Balearic Islands ferries dock at the **Moll de Barcelona** quay, at the bottom of Avda Paral·lel. **Trasmediterránea** (902 45 46 45, www.trasmediterranea.es) is the main operator. There are also other ferries running three times a week between Barcelona and Genoa in Italy, from the **Moll de Ponent**, a few hundred metres south (**Grimaldi Lines**; for information, phone agent Condeminas on 93 443 98 98 or see www.gnv.it). Cruise ships use several berths around the harbour. The **PortBus** shuttle service (information 93 415 60 20) runs between them and the bottom of the Rambla when ships are in port.

By train

Most long-distance services operated by the Spanish state railway company **RENFE** run from **Barcelona-Sants** station, easily reached by metro lines 3 (green) and 5 (blue). A few services from the French border terminate at the **Estació de França** in the Born, near the Barceloneta metro (line 4, yellow) but it's otherwise sparsely served these days. Many trains stop at **Passeig de Gràcia**, which can be the handiest for the city centre and also has a metro stop on lines 2 (purple), 3 (green) and 4 (yellow).

RENFE

National 902 24 02 02/international 902 24 34 02/www.renfe.es. **Open** *National* 5.30am-11.30pm daily. *International* 7am-11pm daily. **Credit** AmEx, DC, MC, V. Some English-speaking operators. RENFE tickets can be bought at train stations, travel agents or reserved over the phone and delivered to an address or hotel for a small extra fee.

Maps

For street, local train and metro maps, *see pp333-350*. Tourist offices provide a reasonable free street map, or a better quality map for €1.20. Metro maps (ask for '*una guia del metro*') are available free at all metro stations; bus maps can be obtained from city transport information offices (*see below*). There is an excellent interactive street map at www.bcn.es/guia.

Public transport

Although it's run by different organisations, Barcelona public transport is now highly integrated, with the same tickets valid for up to four changes of transport on bus, tram, local train and metro lines as long as you do it within 75 minutes.

The **metro** is generally the quickest, cheapest and easiest way of getting around the city; **buses** run throughout the night and to areas not covered by the metro system. Local buses and the metro are run by the city transport authority (**TMB**).

Two underground train lines connect with the metro but are run by Catalan government railways: the **FGC**, or **Ferrocarrils de la Generalitat de Catalunya**. One runs from Plaça Catalunya to Les Planes or Avda Tibidabo (and, beyond the city, to Terrassa and Sabadell); the other runs from Plaça Espanya to Cornellà (and Manresa and Igualada further out). Four new-ish tramlines connect the city with towns just outside it.

TMB information

Main vestibule, Metro Universitat, Eixample (93 318 70 74/www.tmb.net). **Open** 8am-8pm Mon-Fri. **Map** p344 A1. **Branches**: vestibule, Metro Sants Estació and Sagrada Família (both 7am-9pm Mon-Fri; Sants open 9am-7pm Sat & 9am-2pm Sun); vestibule, Metro Diagonal (8am-8pm Mon-Fri).

Fares & tickets

Travel in the Barcelona urban area has a flat fare of €1.15 per journey, but multi-journey tickets or *targetes* are better value. The basic ten-trip *targeta* is the **T-10** (*Te-Deu* in Catalan, *Te-Diez* in Spanish), which can be shared by any number of people travelling simultaneously; the ticket is validated in the machines on the metro, train or bus once per person per journey.

Along with the more 'integrated' *targetes* listed below, the T-10 offers access to all five of the city's main transport systems (local RENFE and FGC trains within the main metropolitan area, the metro, the tram and buses). To transfer, insert your card into a machine a second time; unless 75 minutes have elapsed since your last journey, another unit will not be deducted. Single tickets do not allow free transfers.

You can buy T-10s in newsagents and Servi-Caixa cashpoints as well as on the metro and train systems (from machines or the ticket office), but not on buses. More expensive versions of all *targetes* take you to the outer zones of the metropolitan region, but the prices listed below will get you anywhere in central Barcelona, and to the key sights on the outskirts of the city itself.

Integrated *targetes*

T-10 Valid for ten trips; can be shared by two or more people. €6.30.
T-Familiar Gives 70 trips in any 30-day period; can be shared. €38.55.
T-50/30 Gives 50 trips in any 30-day period; but can only be used by one person. €26.25.
T-Dia A one-day travelcard. €4.80.

T-Mes Valid for any 30-day period. €40.75.
T-Trimestre Valid for three months. €112.
T-Jove Valid for three months; for under-21s only. €95.20.

Other *targetes*

2, 3, 4 & 5 Dies Two-, three-, four- and five-day travelcards on the metro, buses and FGC trains. Also sold at tourist offices. €8.40, €11.80, €15.20 and €18.20.
Aerobús + Bus + Metro Unlimited Travel for one person on the metro and buses (not FGC), including a return trip to the airport. Two-day (€13.50), three-day (€16.75) and five-day (€22.35) passes are available. Sold on board the Aerobús.
Barcelona Card A tourist discount scheme offering unlimited use of public transport, for up to five days. *See p83*.

Metro & FGC

The five metro lines are identified by a number and a colour on maps and station signs. At interchanges, lines are shown by the names of the station at the end of the line. Some suburban FGC trains do not stop at all stations.

All metro lines operate from 5am to midnight Monday to Thursday, Sunday and public holidays; 5am to 2am Friday, Saturday and nights before public holidays.

FGC information

Vestibule, Plaça Catalunya FGC station (93 205 15 15/www.fgc.net). **Open** 7am-9pm Mon-Fri. **Map** p344 A1. **Branches**: FGC Provença (open 9am-7pm Mon-Fri, closed Aug); FGC Plaça d'Espanya (open 9am-2pm, 4-7pm Mon-Fri).

Buses

Many city bus routes originate in or pass through the city centre, at Plaça Catalunya, Plaça Universitat and Plaça Urquinaona. However, they often run along different parallel streets, due to the city's one-way system. Not all stops are labelled and street signs are not easy to locate.

Most routes run 6am-10.30pm daily except Sundays; some begin earlier and finish later. There's usually a bus at least every 10-15mins, but they're less frequent before 8am, after 9pm and on Saturdays. On Sundays, buses are less frequent still; a few do not run at all.

Board at the front and disembark through the middle or rear doors. Only single tickets can be bought from the driver; if you have a *targeta*, insert it into the machine behind the driver as you board.

Useful routes

The following services connect Plaça Catalunya with popular parts of town:

22 via Gràcia to the Tramvia Blau up to Tibidabo and the Pedralbes monastery.
24 goes up Passeig de Gràcia and to Park Güell.
41, 59, 67 and **68** go to the Plaça Francesc Macià area, which is not served by the metro.
39 connects Gràcia, the town centre and the beach.
41 also goes to Ciutadella and the Vila Olímpica.
45 stops in Plaça Urquinaona and goes to the beach near Port Olímpic.

Three good crosstown routes:

50 goes from north-east Barcelona past Sagrada Família, along Gran Via and then climbs Montjuïc from Plaça d'Espanya to Miramar.
64 goes from Barceloneta beach, past Colom, Avda Paral·lel, Plaça Universitat to Sarrià and Pedralbes.
7 runs the length of Avda Diagonal, from the Zona Universitària to Diagonal-Mar and along Passeig de Gràcia and Gran Via to Glòries.

Night buses

There are 16 urban night bus ('Nitbus') routes, most of which run from around 10.30-11.30pm to 4.30-6am nightly, with buses every 20-30mins. Most pass through Plaça Catalunya. Fares and *targetes* are as for daytime buses. Plaça Catalunya is also the terminus for all-night bus services linking Barcelona with more distant parts of its metropolitan area.

TombBús

A special shoppers' bus.

Local trains

Regional trains to Sabadell, Terrassa and other towns beyond Tibidabo depart from FGC Plaça Catalunya, and those for Montserrat from FGC Plaça Espanya.

All trains on the RENFE local network ('Rodalies/Cercanías') stop at Sants, but can also be caught at either Plaça Catalunya and Arc de Triomf (for Vic and the Pyrenees, Manresa, the Penedès and Costa del Maresme) or Passeig de Gràcia (for the southern coastal line to Sitges and the Girona–Figueres line north).

Trams

Barcelona's four tramlines run from central-ish parts of the city to towns on its outskirts. Lines **T1**, **T2** and **T3** go from Plaça Francesc Macià, Zona Alta. T1 goes to Cornellà via Hospitalet and Esplugues de Llobregat; T2 goes the same way, but

contines further to Sant Joan Despi; and though part of T3 is still under construction, it will eventually run to Sant Just Desvern. The fourth line runs from Ciutadella-Vila Olímpica (also a metro stop), via Glòries and El Maresme, on to Sant Adrià (also a RENFE train station).

All trams are fully accessible for wheelchair-users and are part of the integrated TMB *targeta* system: simply insert the ticket into the machine as you board. You can buy integrated tickets and single tickets from the machines at tram stops.

Tram information

Trambaix (902 19 32 75/www. trambcn.com). **Open** 9am-2pm, 4-7pm Mon-Thur; 9am-2pm Fri.

Taxis

It's usually easy to find one of Barcelona's 10,300 black and yellow taxis at any time of day and most of the night (*see p319* **It's all in the timing**). There are ranks at railway and bus stations, in main squares and throughout the city, but taxis can also be hailed on the street when they show a green light on the roof and a sign saying *'lliure/libre'* (free) behind the windscreen. Information on taxi fares, ranks and regulations can be found at www.emt-amb.com.

Fares

Current rates and supplements are shown inside cabs on a sticker in the rear side window (in English). The basic fare for a taxi hailed in the street to pick you up is €1.30 (or €1.40 at nights, weekends and holidays), which is what the meter should register when you set off. The basic rates (eg 74¢ per km) apply 7am-9pm Mon-Fri; at other times, including midweek public holidays, the rate is 20-30% higher. There are supplements for luggage (90¢), for trips to the airport (€3) and to the port (€2), and for 'special nights' such as New Year's Eve (€3), as well as a waiting charge. Taxi drivers are not required to carry more than €20 in change; few accept credit cards.

Receipts & complaints

To get a receipt, ask for *'un rebut/un recibo'*. It should include the fare, the taxi number, the driver's NIF (tax) number, the licence plate, the driver's signature and the date; if you have a complaint about a driver, insist on all these, and the more details the better (time, route). Complaints must be filed in writing to the Institut Metropolità del Taxi (93 223 51 51, www.emt-amb.com).

Radio cabs

These companies take bookings 24 hours daily. Phone cabs start the meter when a call is answered, but by the time it picks you up, it should not display more than €2.93 during weekdays and €3.66 at night, on weekends or at public holidays.

Autotaxi Mercedes Barcelona 93 303 32 66.
Barnataxi 93 357 77 55.
Fono-Taxi 93 300 11 00.
Ràdio Taxi '033' 93 303 30 33.
Servi-Taxi 93 330 03 00.
Taxi Groc 93 322 22 22.
Taxi Miramar 93 433 10 20.

Driving

For information (in Catalan or Spanish) on driving in Catalonia, call the **Servei Català de Trànsit** on 93 567 40 00 (open mid Sept-May 8.30am-2pm, 4-6pm; June-mid Sept 8.30am-2pm).

Driving in Barcelona can be tiring, intimidating and time-consuming. It's only out in the country that a car becomes an asset. If you do drive in town, bear these points in mind:

● Keep your driving licence, vehicle registration and insurance documents with you at all times.
● Do not leave anything of value, including car radios, in your car. Foreign plates can attract thieves.
● Be on your guard at motorway service areas, and take care to avoid thieves in the city who may try to make you stop, perhaps by indicating you have a flat tyre.

Breakdown services

If you're planning to take a car, join a motoring organisation such as the AA (www.theaa.co.uk) or the RAC (www.rac.co.uk) in the UK, which usually have reciprocal agreements.

RACE (Real Automóvil Club de España)

Information 902 40 45 45/24hr assistance 902 30 05 05/www.race.es. The RACE has English-speaking staff and offers 24-hour breakdown assistance in Spain. Repairs are carried out on the spot if possible; if not, your vehicle will be towed to a nearby garage. Members of affiliated organisations abroad are not charged for call-outs, but non-members will have to pay a fee (usually in cash).

Car & motorbike hire

Car hire is relatively pricey, but it's a competitive market so shop around. Check carefully what's included:

ideally, you want unlimited mileage, 16% VAT (IVA) included and full insurance cover (*seguro todo riesgo*) rather than the third-party minimum (*seguro obligatorio*). You'll need a credit card as a guarantee. Most companies require you to have had a licence for at least a year; many also enforce a minimum age limit.

EasyCar

C/Rivadeneyra, underground car park (807 21 21/www.easycar. com). Metro Catalunya. **Open** 7am-11pm daily. **Credit** AmEx, MC, V. **Map** p344 B1.
EasyCar Barcelona is largely run by www.pepecar.com; bookings can be made on the EasyCar website or Pepecar's helpline. Basic rates for its Mercedes A-Class hatchbacks can be low (for example, two days for €74), but check conditions (limited mileage, credit card supplements, insurance, etc). There are branches at Sants railway station (8am-8pm) and the Tryp Hotel near Barcelona airport (7am-11pm). Minimum rental age is 23. No cancellations or refunds.

Europcar

Plaça dels Països Catalans, Sants (93 491 48 22/reservations 902 10 50 30/www.europcar.com). Metro Sants Estació. **Open** 7am-11pm Mon-Fri; 8am-8pm Sat; 8am-10pm Sun. **Credit** AmEx, DC, MC, V. **Map** p341 A4.
A large international agency with several offices in Barcelona. Prices change daily: phone for details.
Other locations: Airport, terminals B & C (93 298 33 00); Gran Via de les Corts Catalanes 680, Eixample (93 302 05 43); C/Viladomat 214, Eixample (93 439 84 01).

Motissimo

C/Portbou 14-28, Sants (93 490 84 01/www.motissimo.es). Metro Badal. **Open** 9am-1.30pm, 4-8.30pm Mon-Fri; 10am-1pm Sat. **Credit** V.
Bike rental, from 50cc Honda mopeds to Suzuki and Honda motorbikes, as well as sale and repair of new and old models. For bigger bikes you must have had the A-class licence for at least two years. You'll need to call to reserve a bike; you can't just drop by.

Vanguard

C/Viladomat 297, Eixample (93 439 38 80/93 410 82 71/www.vanguard rent.com). Metro Hospital Clínic. **Open** 8am-1.30pm, 4-7.30pm Mon-Fri; 9am-1pm Sat, Sun. **Credit** AmEx, DC, MC, V. **Map** p337 B3.
Scooter, car and van hire. Bike prices start at €38/day for a 50cc Honda; a small car costs €58/day. You must be 21 to hire a small bike and have had a licence for a year; for cars, the age limit is 23, and the minimum licence requirement is two years.

Legal requirements

For full details of driving laws and regulations (in Spanish), see the Ministry of Interior's website (www. mir.es/trafico/trafico.htm).

● Tourists can drive in Spain with a valid driving licence from many other countries. Licences from EU states are all valid, though Spanish age restrictions prevail; older all-green UK licences are valid, but they may cause confusion.
● For bikes over 125cc, you need to be over 18 and have a bike licence.
● You must wear seatbelts in the front seats and the back if fitted, and to carry warning triangles, spares and tools to fit them. If you wear glasses, you must carry a spare pair.
● Helmets are compulsory on motorbikes and scooters.
● The speed limit is 50kmph (31mph) in built-up areas, 120kmph (75mph) on motorways and other major roads, and 90kmph (55mph) or 100kmph (62.5mph) on other roads. Most drivers ignore these limits.
● Children aged from 3 to 12 (and anyone measuring less than 150cm/5ft) cannot travel in the front except if a restraint system is fitted. Under-3s must travel in a child's car seat.
● Severe penalties may be enforced if the level of alcohol in your blood is found to be 0.05% or above.

Parking

Parking is fiendishly complicated, and municipal police are quick to hand out tickets or tow away cars. In some parts of the Old City, access is limited to residents for much of the day. In some Old City streets, time-controlled bollards appear, meaning your car may get stuck. Wherever you are, don't park in front of doors signed '*Gual Permanent*', indicating an entry with 24-hour right of access.

Pay & display areas

Many streets in the city centre and the Eixample are pay-and-display areas ('*zones blaves*', or blue zones), with parking spaces marked in blue on the street. Parking restrictions mostly apply 9am-2pm, 4-8pm Mon-Sat (check the machine for details); in the centre, the limit is 2hrs and the rate is €1.75/hr. If you overstay by no more than an hour, you can cancel the fine by paying an extra €6; to do so, press *Anul·lar denúncia* on the machine, insert €6, then press *Ticket*. In areas denoted with an orange hand, the limit is an hour and the rate is €2.50. Some machines accept credit cards (MC, V); none accepts notes or gives change. City hall plans to introduce a different system in April 2005: check www.bcn.es for details.

Car parks

Car parks ('*parkings*') are signalled by a white 'P' on a blue sign. **SABA** (Plaça Catalunya, Plaça Urquinaona, Rambla Catalunya, Avda Catedral, airport and elsewhere; 902 28 30 80, www.saba.es) costs around €2.25/hr, while **SMASSA** car parks (Plaça Catalunya 23, C/Hospital 25-29, Avda Francesc Cambó 10, Passeig de Gràcia 60, and elsewhere; 93 409 20 21, www.bsmsa.es/mobilitat) cost €1.60-€2.25/hr. The €4.80 fare at the **Metro-Park** park-and-ride facility (Plaça de les Glòries, Eixample, 93 265 10 47, open 4.30am-2.30am Mon-Sat) includes a day's unlimited travel on the metro and buses.

Towed vehicles

If the police have towed your car, they should leave a triangular sticker on the pavement where it was. The sticker should let you know to which pound it's been taken. If not, call 902 36 41 16; staff generally don't speak English. Recovering your vehicle within 4hrs costs €130, with each extra hour costing €1.70. On top of this, you'll have to pay a fine to the police, which varies. You'll need your passport and documentation, or the rental contract, to prove it's your car.

Petrol

Most *gasolineres* (petrol stations) have unleaded (*sense plom/sin plomo*), regular (*super*) and diesel (*gas-oil*).

Repsol

C/Provença 309, Eixample.. **Open** 24hrs. **Credit** AmEx, DC, MC, V. **Map** p339 E4.
Other locations: Avda Gaudí 1, Eixample and throughout the city.

Cycling

There's a network of bike lanes (*carrils bici*) along major avenues and by the seafront; local authorities are keen to promote cycling. However, weekday traffic can be risky, despite new legislation that states that drivers must slow down near cyclists. No more than two bikes may ride side by side. Rollerblading is popular along the seafront and the Diagonal and Rambla Catalunya. For information on cycling in Barcelona, see www.bcn.es/bicicleta.

Al punt de trobada (bicycle hire)

C/Badajoz 24, Poblenou (93 225 05 85/bicipuntrobada@hotmail.com). Metro Llacuna. **Open** *June-mid Sept* 9am-2pm, 4-8pm Mon-Fri; 9am-2pm Sat; 10am-3pm Sun. *Mid-May* 9am-2pm, 4-8pm Mon-Sat; 10am-3pm Sun. **Credit** AmEx, MC, V.

Directory

Resources A-Z

Addresses

Most apartment addresses consist of a street name followed by a street number, floor level and flat number, in that order. So, to go to C/València 246, 2° 3ª, find No.246, go to the second floor and find the door marked 3 or 3ª. Ground-floor flats are usually called *baixos* or *bajos* (often abbreviated 'bxs/bjos'); one floor up, the *entresol/entresuelo* ('entl'), and the next is often the *principal* ('pral'). Confusingly, numbered floors start here: first, second, up to the *àtic/ático* at the top.

Age restrictions

The minimum legal age for drinking or smoking is 16 (18 if your parents or guardian do not give permission), though it's not strictly enforced. The age of consent for both hetero- and homosexuals is just 13, one of the lowest in Europe. In Spain, you must be 18 to drive a car, motorbike or scooter above 125cc, 14 to drive a scooter up to 50cc and 16 to drive a scooter up to 125cc.

Business

Anyone wanting to set up shop in Barcelona needs to know the intricacies of local, Spanish and EU regulations. A visit to the **Cambra de Comerç** (*see p309*) is a must; some consulates can also refer you to professionals, and a *gestoria* (*see below*) will save you time and energy.

Admin services

The *gestoria* is a very Spanish institution, the main function of which is to lighten the weight of local bureaucracy by dealing with it for you. A combination of book-keeper, lawyer and business adviser, a good *gestor* can be helpful in handling all of the paperwork and advising on various shortcuts, although *gestoria* employees rarely speak English.

Martin Howard Associates

C/Londres 96, pral 1ª, Eixample (93 202 25 34/mobile 607 401 184/ www.mhasoc.com). **Open** by appointment. **Map** p338 C3.
British accountant Martin Howard and his Spanish associate offer business consultancy, accounting and tax services and advice on buying property for English-speaking expats in Spain.

Tutzo Assessors

C/Aribau 226, Eixample (93 209 67 88/tutzoass-juridic@infonegocio. com). Metro Diagonal/FGC Gràcia. **Open** 8.30am-2pm, 4-7pm Mon-Fri. Closed 2wks Aug, Fri pm July, Aug. **Map** p338 C3.
Lawyers and economists as well as a *gestoria*. Some English speakers.

Conventions & conferences

Barcelona Convention Bureau

Rambla Catalunya 123, pral, Eixample (93 368 97 00/www. barcelonaturisme.com). Metro Diagonal. **Open** Sept-June 9am-2.30pm, 3.30-6.30pm Mon-Thur; 9am-3pm Fri. July, Aug 8am-3pm Mon-Fri. **Map** p338 D4.
Specialist arm of the city tourist authority that assists organisations with conferences.

Fira de Barcelona

Avda Reina Maria Cristina, Montjuïc (93 233 20 00/www.firabcn.es). Metro Espanya. **Open** Mid Sept-mid June 9am-1.30pm, 3.30-5.30pm Mon-Fri. Mid June-mid Sept 9am-2pm Mon-Fri. **Map** p341 A5.
The Barcelona 'trade fair' is one of the largest exhibition complexes in Europe. In addition to the main area at Plaça d'Espanya, it includes a huge site, Montjuïc-2, towards the airport, and administers the Palau de Congressos conference hall in the Plaça d'Espanya site, which can be let separately.

World Trade Center

Moll de Barcelona, Port Vell (93 508 88 88/www.wtcbarcelona.es). Metro Drassanes. **Open** 9am-2pm, 4-7pm Mon-Thur; 9am-3pm Fri. **Map** p342 C7.
The WTC rents 130,000sq m of office space in a modern complex in the old port. Events and conferences can be arranged.

Courier services

Estació d'Autobusos Barcelona-Nord

C/Ali Bei 80, Eixample (93 232 43 29). Metro Arc de Triomf. **Open** 8am-9pm Mon-Fri; 8am-1pm Sat. **No credit cards**. **Map** p343 E5.
An inexpensive service available at the bus station for sending parcels on scheduled buses within Spain.

Missatgers Trèvol

C/Antonio Ricardos 14, La Sagrera (93 498 80 70/www.trevol.com). Metro Sagrera. **Open** Sept-July 8am-7pm Mon-Fri. Aug 8am-3pm Mon-Fri. **No credit cards**.
Courier firm serving central Barcelona. Check online for rates.

Seur

902 10 10 10/www.seur.es. **Open** 8am-8pm Mon-Fri; 9am-2pm Sat. **No credit cards**.
An efficient (though not always cheap) service for national and international deliveries. Call by 6pm during the week for same-day pick-up.

UPS

902 88 88 20/www.ups.com. **Open** 8am-8pm Mon-Fri. **Credit** AmEx, MC, V.
Next-day delivery to both Spanish and international destinations. There are some English-speaking operators.

Office & computer services

The area round Ronda Sant Antoni (Map p342 C5) is your best bet for PC hardware. **Life Informática** (C/Sepúlveda 173, 902 90 15 32, www.lifeinformatica.com) is good for components and consumables; **PC City** (C/Casanova 2, 902 10 03 02, www.pccity.es) is a reliable option for branded equipment. Shop around for the best bargain.

Centro de Negocios

C/Pau Claris 97, 4° 1ª, Eixample (93 304 38 58/www.centro-negocios. com). Metro Passeig de Gràcia. **Open** Sept-July 8am-9pm Mon-Fri. Aug 9am-3pm Mon-Fri. **No credit cards**. **Map** p342 D5.
Desks in shared offices, mailboxes, meeting rooms, secretarial services and administrative services.

GeoMac

Mobile 606 30 89 32/geomac@terra. es. **Open** by appointment. **No credit cards**.
Apple-certified US technician George Cowdery offers maintenance, trouble-shooting and tuition for Mac users.

K-Tuin

C/Muntaner 537, Zona Alta (93 418 02 03/www.k-tuin.es). FGC El Putxet. **Open** 10am-2pm, 4.30-8.30pm Mon-Fri; 10am-2.30pm Sat. **Credit** DC, MC, V.
As well as offering Mac repairs, K-Tuin also sells and rents equipment and accessories.

Microrent

C/Rosselló 35, Eixample (93 363 32 50/www.microrent.es). Metro Entença. **Open** 9am-6pm Mon-Fri. **No credit cards. Map** p341 B4.
Computer equipment for rent: PCs, Macs, laptops, printers, projectors.

Translators

For more translators, see www.act.es.

DUUAL

C/Ciutat 7, 2º 4ª, Barri Gòtic (93 302 29 85/www.duual.com). Metro Jaume I or Liceu. **Open** *Sept-June* 9am-2pm, 4-7pm Mon-Thur; 9am-2pm Fri. *July* 8.30am-3pm Mon-Fri. Closed 3wks Aug. **No credit cards. Map** p345 B3.
Services in many languages, along with desktop publishing.

Traduit

C/Ribera 6, 1º 2ª, Born (93 268 74 95/www.traduit.com). Metro Jaume I. **Open** 9am-2pm, 4-6.30pm Mon-Fri. **Map** p345 C4.
Different types of translations, including legally certified ones ('*traducciones juradas*'). Languages include English, French, German, Italian, Portuguese, Catalan and Spanish. You may need a *traducción jurada* for official transactions.

Useful organisations

Ajuntament de Barcelona

Plaça Sant Miquel 4-5, Barri Gòtic (93 402 70 00/www.bcn.es). Metro Jaume I. **Open** *Sept-June* 8.30am-5.30pm Mon-Fri. *July, Aug* 8.15am-2.15pm Mon-Fri. **Map** p345 B3.
The city council. Permits for new businesses are issued by the ten municipal districts.

Borsa de Valors de Barcelona

Passeig de Gràcia 19, Eixample (93 401 35 55/www.borsabcn.es). Metro Passeig de Gràcia. **Open** *Reception* 9am-5.30pm Mon-Fri. *Library* 9am-noon Mon-Fri. **Map** p342 D5.
The stock exchange.

British Society of Catalunya

Mailing address: Lloyds TSB Bank, Rambla Catalunya 123 (tel/fax 93 688 08 66).
This informal group for expats has been organising events since 1920. Most members are mature long-term residents, though everyone is welcome. Annual membership is €9.

Cambra de Comerç de Barcelona

Avda Diagonal 452-454, Eixample (902 448 448/www.cambrabcn.es). Metro Diagonal/FGC Provença. **Open** 9am-5pm Mon-Thur; 9am-2pm Fri. **Map** p338 D4.
The Chamber of Commerce offers information and advice.

Generalitat de Catalunya

Information 012/new businesses 902 20 15 20/www.gencat.net.
The Catalan government provides a range of consultancy services.

Complaints

If you have a complaint that can't be cleared up on the spot, ask for an official complaint form ('*hoja de reclamación/full de reclamació*'), which many businesses and all shops, bars and restaurants are required to have available (in English, Catalan and Spanish). Fill out the form, and leave one copy (marked as the establishment's) with the business. Take the others, along with any receipts, guarantees and so on, to the official consumer office. For complaints within Barcelona city, this is the office below; outside the city, each town has its own office.

Oficina Municipal d'Informació al Consumidor

Ronda de Sant Pau 43-45, Barri Gòtic (93 402 78 41/www.omic.bcn.es). Metro Paral·lel or Sant Antoni. **Open** 9am-2pm Mon-Fri. **Map** p342 C6.
A municipally run official centre for consumer advice and complaints follow-up. You can file complaints in English through the useful website.

Telèfon de Consulta del Consumidor

012. **Open** 9am-6pm Mon-Fri.
A phone line run by the Generalitat for consumer advice. Ask to speak to a consumer specialist.

Consulates

A full list of consulates is in the phone book under '*Ambaixades i consolats/Embajadas y consulados*'.

Australian Consulate *Gran Via Carles III 98, Zona Alta (93 490 90 13/fax 93 411 09 04/www.spain. embassy.gov.au). Metro Maria Cristina.* **Open** 10am-noon Mon-Fri. Closed Aug. **Map** p337 A3.
British Consulate *Avda Diagonal 477, Eixample (93 366 62 00/fax 93 366 62 21/www.ukinspain.com). Metro Hospital Clínic.* **Open** *Mid Sept-mid June* 9.30am-2pm Mon-Fri. *Mid June-mid Sept* 9am-1.30pm Mon-Fri. **Map** p338 C3.
Canadian Consulate *C/Elisenda de Pinós 10, Zona Alta (93 204 27 00/fax 93 204 27 01/www.canada-es.org). FGC Reina Elisenda.* **Open** 10am-1pm Mon-Fri.
Irish Consulate *Gran Via Carles III 94, Zona Alta (93 491 50 21/fax 93 490 09 86). Metro Maria Cristina.* **Open** 10am-1pm Mon-Fri. **Map** p337 A3.
New Zealand Consulate *Travessera de Gràcia 64, 2º, Gràcia (93 209 03 99/fax 93 202 08 90). Metro Diagonal.* **Open** *Sept-June* 9am-1pm, 4-6pm Mon-Fri. **Map** p338 C3.
South African Consulate *Travessera de Gràcia 43, Zona Alta (93 366 10 25/93 366 10 26). FGC Gràcia/14, 27, 32, 58, 64 bus.* **Open** 9am-noon Mon-Fri. **Map** p338 C3.
US Consulate *Passeig Reina Elisenda 23, Zona Alta (93 280 22 27/fax 93 205 52 06/www.embusa. es). FGC Reina Elisenda.* **Open** 9am-1pm Mon-Fri. **Map** p337 A1.

Travel advice

For up-to-date information on travelling to a specific country – including the latest news on safety and security, health issues, local laws and customs – contact your home country government's department of foreign affairs. Most have websites packed with useful advice for would-be travellers.

Australia
www.smartraveller.gov.au
Canada
www.voyage.gc.ca
New Zealand
www.mft.govt.nz/travel

Republic of Ireland
http://foreignaffairs.gov.ie
UK
www.fco.gov.uk/travel
USA
www.state.gov/travel

Directory

Lost in translation

For newcomers, one of the most bewildering aspects of Barcelona's bilingualism is its urban geography. All signs indicating street names are in Catalan, as are most current Barcelona maps, but some people use the Spanish (Castilian) translation, especially when addressing foreigners; speakers generally switch from Catalan to Castilian once they realise they're not talking to a local. Such well-meaning flexibility can cause confusion. With most foreigners using Castilian as their *lingua franca* and all *barcelonins* (including the majority who prefer to use Catalan) fluent in Spanish, the rift between the printed word and spoken street name has been the downfall of many an uninitiated visitor.

Taxi drivers, on the whole sticklers for linguistic consistency, are a major source of bemusement. Many were part of the wave of immigrants from other corners of Spain, who arrived in the 1960s to work as cheap labour in the flourishing Catalan capital. Their penchant for correcting and reprimanding passengers who use a Catalan place name when speaking Spanish foxes many an unwitting passenger.

While it doesn't take a great leap of imagination to work out that 'Passeig de Gràcia' and 'Paseo de Gràcia' are one and the same thing, other translations are not so obvious. A prime example is the area known as the 'Eixample', a term prevalent even among speakers who are more comfortable in Spanish than in Catalan. It's possible to live here for months or even years without cottoning on to the Spanish translation, 'Ensanche' ('urban expansion'). Yet this is one of the cabbies' bêtes noires.

You can't really blame them. Many got to know the town before 1980's '*normalització linguistica*', when they were all (re-)labelled in Catalan. Hence Calle Libertad became Carrer Llibertat, Ronda San Pedro turned into today's Ronda Sant Pere, and so on. To complicate matters further, several place names have changed over the years, reflecting the vicissitudes and outlooks of Barcelona's successive governing forces. And so, while the younger generation shops and parties near Plaça Francesc Macià (named in 1980, in honour of a renowned Catalan nationalist and erstwhile president of the Generalitat), their parents might still refer to it as Plaza Calvo Sotelo (named in 1939, as the fascist forces consolidated their power, after the extreme right-wing politician whose murder sparked the uprising led by Franco).

In practice, though, Catalan and Castilian are not far apart. Many homonyms often only differ by a letter or two (eg the Catalan for beach, '*platja*', becomes '*playa*' in Spanish), meaning that once you've got the hang of some basic vocabulary and the very existence of dual place names, the language of navigation is only a minor conundrum.

Below are listed some words that crop up often in addresses and place names; abbreviations are shown in brackets.

Catalan	Spanish	English
Carrer (C/)	Calle (C/)	Street
Avinguda (Avda)	Avenida (Avda)	Avenue
Passeig (Pg)	Paseo (Pº)	Boulevard
Passatge (Ptge)	Pasaje (Pje)	Alley/passageway
Plaça (Pl/Pça)	Plaza (Pl/Pza)	Square
Placeta	Plazuela	Small square
Palau	Palacio	Palace
Moll	Muelle	Dock
Port	Puerto	Port

Customs

Customs declarations are not usually necessary if you arrive in Spain from another EU country and are carrying only legal goods for personal use. The amounts given below are guidelines of amounts qualifying as for personal consumption. If you approach these maximums in several categories, you may still have to explain your personal habits; and if you import more than these amounts, you may be required to prove that the goods are solely for your use.

● 800 cigarettes, 400 small cigars, 200 cigars or 1kg loose tobacco
● 10 litres of spirits (over 22% alcohol), 90 litres of wine (under 22% alcohol) or 110 litres of beer

Coming from a non-EU country or the Canary Islands, you can bring:

● 200 cigarettes, 100 small cigars, 50 regular cigars or 250g (8.82oz) of tobacco
● 1 litre of spirits (over 22% alcohol) or 2 litres of wine or beer (under 22% alcohol)
● 50g (1.76oz) of perfume.
● 500g coffee; 100g tea

Non-EU residents can reclaim VAT (IVA) on some large purchases when they leave. For details, *see p189*.

Disabled

www.accessiblebarcelona.com, run by an American expat wheelchair-user living in Barcelona, is a useful resource.

Institut Municipal de Persones amb Disminució

Avda Diagonal 233, Eixample (93 413 27 75/www.bcn.es/imd). Metro Glòries or Monumental/56, 62 bus. **Open** 8.30am-2.30pm Mon-Fri. **Map** p343 F5.

The city's organisation for the disabled has information on access to venues, and can provide a map with wheelchair-friendly itineraries.

Access to sights

Newer museums such as **MACBA** (*see p101*) have good access (and occasionally also adapted toilets), but the process of converting older buildings is slow. Phoning ahead to check is always a good idea even if a place claims to be accessible.

Wheelchair-friendly museums and galleries include the following: CCCB; Col·lecció Thyssen-Bornemisza (Monestir de Pedralbes); Espai Gaudí – La Pedrera; Fundació Joan Miró; Fundacio Antoni Tàpies; MACBA; MNAC; Museu Barbier-Mueller d'Art Precolombi; Museu d'Arqueologia de Catalunya; Museu de les Arts Decoratives; Museu del Calçat; Museu de Cera de Barcelona; Museu del Temple Expiatori de la Sagrada Família; Museu d'Història de Catalunya; Museu d'Història de la Ciutat; Museu de la Ciència – CosmoCaixa; Museu de la Xocolata; Museu Egipci de Barcelona; Museu Frederic Marès; Museu Picasso; Museu Tèxtil i d'Indumentaria; Palau de la Música; Palau de la Virreina.

Transport

Access for disabled people to local transport still leaves quite a lot to be desired. For wheelchair-users, buses and taxis are usually the best bets. There is a transport information phone line (*see below*), and transport maps, which you can pick up from transport information offices (*see below*) and some metro stations, indicate wheelchair access points and adapted bus routes. For more, check www.tmb.net.

Centre d'Informació de Transport Adaptat

Information 93 486 07 52/fax 93 486 07 53. **Open** *Sept-July* 9am-9pm Mon-Fri; 9am-3pm Sat. *Aug* 9am-9pm Mon-Fri.

The TMB's disabled transport information department. English speakers are usually available. From 8.30am, staff have a list of how many buses on each route will be the type with ramps: call when planning your day's transport.

Buses

All the Aerobús airport buses, night buses and the open-topped tourist buses are fully accessible, though you may need assistance with the steep ramps. Adapted buses also alternate with standard buses on many daytime routes: call the transport authorities' helpline daily for details (*see above*). Press the blue button with the wheelchair symbol to alert the driver before you reach your stop. A sign saying *rampa sol·licitada* ('ramp requested') should light up, and a bleeping sound signals the ramp's deployment. Transport maps and bus stop signs indicate which routes use adapted vehicles.

Metro & FGC

Only L2 (purple) has lifts and ramps at all stations. On L1 and L3, a few stations have lifts, but may not always be on the correct line: several lines may intersect at one station, and the tunnels between them are not generally wheelchair-accessible. There is usually a step on to the train, the size of which varies; some assistance may be required.

The Montjuïc funicular railway is fully wheelchair-adapted. Accessible FGC stations include Provença, Muntaner and Avda Tibidabo. The FGC infrastructures at Catalunya and Espanya stations are accessible, but interchanges with metro lines are not.

RENFE trains

Sants and Plaça Catalunya stations are wheelchair-accessible, but trains are not. If you go to the *Atenció al viajero* office ahead of time, help on the platform can be arranged.

Taxis

All taxi drivers are officially required to transport wheelchairs and guide dogs for no extra charge, but cars can be small, and the willingness of drivers to co-operate varies widely. Special minibus taxis adapted for wheelchairs can be ordered from the Taxi Amic service, as well as from some general taxi services such as Servi-Taxi (93 330 03 00). You need to book at least 24-48 hours ahead.

Taxi Amic

93 420 80 88. **Open** 7am-11pm Mon-Fri; 9am-10pm Sat, Sun. Fares are the same as for regular cabs, but there is a minimum fare of €9.50 for Barcelona city (€10.50 on weekends), and more for surrounding

area. Numbers are limited, so call well in advance (two days if possible) to request a specific time.

Trams

All tram lines are fully accessible for wheelchair-users; there are ramps to access all platforms. A wheelchair symbol on the platform at each stop indicates where the accessible doors will be situated when the tram comes to a halt: the floor of the tram will be on a level with the platform.

Drugs

Many people smoke cannabis openly in Spain, but possession or consumption in public is illegal. In private, the law is contradictory: smoking is OK, but you can be nabbed for possession or distribution. Enforcement is often not the highest of police priorities, especially if it's just a matter of a few grams, but you could theoretically receive a fine. Larger amounts entail a fine, a possible court appearance and, in extreme cases, prison. Smoking in bars is also prohibited (and less common than in other parts of Spain); most proprietors are strict on this issue because it could cost them their licences. Having said that, it's not unheard of to catch a whiff of spliff on some terraces in summer.

If caught in possession of any other drugs, you are looking at hefty fines and a prison sentence.

Electricity

The standard current in Spain is 220V. Plugs are of the two-round-pin type. You'll need a plug adaptor to use British-bought electrical devices. If you have US (110V) equipment, you will need a current transformer as well as an adaptor.

Emergencies

The following are open 24 hours.

Emergency services 112. Police, fire or ambulance. **Ambulance/***Ambulància* 061. For hospitals and other health services, *see pp312-313.* **Fire/***Bombers/Bomberos* 080. **Policía Nacional** (first choice in a police emergency) 091. **Guàrdia Urbana** 092. The city police; for traffic but also general law and order. For more information on police forces, *see p316.* **Mossos d'Esquadra** 088. **Electricity/***Fecsa-Endesa* 900 77 00 77. **Gas/***Gas Natural* 900 75 07 50. **Water/***Aigües de Barcelona* 900 70 07 20.

Directory

Etiquette

The Catalans are less guarded about personal space than people in the UK or US. The common greeting between members of the opposite sex and between two women, even if it is the first time the two parties meet, is a kiss on both cheeks. Men usually greet each other by shaking hands. Don't be surprised if people bump into you on the street, or crowd or push brusquely past you on the bus or metro without saying sorry: it's not considered rude.

Gay & lesbian

Casal Lambda

C/Verdaguer i Callís 10, Barri Gòtic (93 319 55 50/www.lambdaweb.org). Metro Urquinaona. **Open** 6-9pm Mon-Sat. Closed 2wks Aug. **Map** p344 B2.
Gay cultural organisation that is the focus for a wide range of activities and publishes the magazine *Lambda* four times a year.

Coordinadora Gai-Lesbiana

C/Finlàndia 45, Sants (93 298 00 29/www.cogailes.org). Metro Plaça de Sants. **Open** 7-9pm Mon-Fri; 6-8pm Sat. **Map** p341A4.
This gay umbrella group works with the Ajuntament on issues of concern to the gay, bisexual and transexual communities. Its Telèfon Rosa service (900 601 601, open 6-10pm daily) gives help or advice on any gay or lesbian issue.

Front d'Alliberament Gai de Catalunya

C/Verdi 88, Gràcia (93 217 26 69). Metro Fontana. **Open** 7-9pm Tue, Wed, Fri. **Map** p339 E3.
A vocal multi-group that produces the *Debat Gai* information bulletin.

Health

Visitors can obtain emergency care through the public health service (**Servei Català de la Salut**, often referred to as the 'Seguretat Social/ Seguridad Social'). EU nationals are entitled to free basic medical attention if they have the European emergency health card, also known as the EU health insurance card. This electronic card recently replaced the E111 form and is valid for a year. Contact the health service in your country of residence for details. It's best to get the card in your home country before travelling. However, if you haven't done so but can get one sent or faxed within a few days, you will likely be exempt from charges.

Otherwise, you might be able to get reimbursed in your home country. Citizens of certain other countries that have a special agreement with Spain, among them several Latin American states, can also have access to free care. For details, call the Catalan government's 24-hour health information line on 902 11 14 44 or the Instituto Nacional de Seguridad Social on 900 16 65 65.

For non-emergencies, it's usually quicker to use private travel insurance rather than the state system. Similarly, non-EU nationals with private medical insurance can also make use of state health services on a paying basis, but it will usually be simpler to use a private clinic.

Accident & emergency

In a medical emergency, go to the casualty department (*Urgències*) of any of the main public hospitals. All are open 24 hours daily. The most central are the **Clínic**, which also has a first-aid centre for less serious emergencies two blocks away (C/València 184, 93 227 93 00, open 9am-9pm Mon-Fri, 9am-1pm Sat) and the **Perecamps**. If necessary, make an emergency call to 112 (ask the operator for the appropriate service) or 061 (ambulance).

Centre d'Urgències Perecamps
Avda Drassanes 13-15, Raval (93 441 06 00). Metro Drassanes or Paral.lel. **Map** p342 C6.
Hospital Clínic *C/Villarroel 170, Eixample (93 227 54 00). Metro Hospital Clínic.* **Map** p338 C4.
Hospital Dos de Maig *C/Dos de Maig 301, Eixample (93 507 27 00). Metro Hospital de Sant Pau.* **Map** p339 F4.
Hospital del Mar *Passeig Marítim 25-29, Barceloneta (93 248 30 00). Metro Ciutadella-Vila Olímpica.* **Map** p343 E7.
Hospital de la Santa Creu i Sant Pau *C/Sant Antoni Maria Claret 167, Eixample (93 291 90 00). Metro Hospital de Sant Pau.* **Map** p339 F3.

AIDS/HIV

According to UN statistics, Spain has the highest number of AIDS cases and deaths in the EU. Anti-retroviral drugs for HIV treatment are covered by social security in Spain, though. As a result, the death rate from AIDS is falling, but the HIV virus continues to spread in many groups, such as drug users and heterosexuals. There has also been a recent increase of HIV infections in the homosexual population, despite a dip in the previous few years.

Local chemists take part in a needle-exchange and condom-distribution programme for intravenous drug users. Free, anonymous blood tests for HIV and other STDs are given at the Unidad de Infección de Transmisión Sexual de Barcelona (93 441 46 12, open by appointment 8.30am-1pm, 2.30-7pm Mon Fri), at **CAP Drassanes** (*see p313*). HIV tests are also available at the **Coordinadora Gai-Lesbiana**'s (*see above*) Stop Sida centre, at the **Asocació Ciutadana Antisida de Catalunya** (C/Junta de Comerç 23, Raval, 93 317 05 05, open 10am-2pm, 4-7pm Mon-Fri) and at **Projecte dels Noms** (C/Escudellers Blancs 1, Barri Gòtic, 93 318 20 56).

Actua

C/Gomis 38, Zona Alta (93 418 50 00/www.interactua.net). Metro Vallcarca/bus 22, 27, 28, 73. **Open** 10am-2pm, 4-7pm Mon-Thur; 10am-2pm Fri.
Support group for people with HIV. Call to make an appointment.

AIDS Information Line

Freephone 900 21 22 22. **Open** *Mid Sept-May* 8am-5.30pm Mon-Thur; 8am-3pm Fri. *June-mid Sept* 8am-3pm Mon-Fri.
If you urgently require information outside the above times, contact the Generalitat's 24-hour health information line on 902 11 14 44.

Complementary medicine

Integral: Centre Mèdic i de Salut

C/Diputació 321, 1° 1°, Eixample (93 318 30 50/www.integralcentremedic. com). Metro Girona. **Open** (by appointment) 9am-9pm Mon-Fri. Closed Aug. **Map** p344 B1.
Acupuncture, homeopathy and other forms of complementary medicine are offered at this well-established clinic. A few speak English, including the osteopath.

Contraception & abortion

All pharmacies sell condoms (*condons/preservativos*) and other forms of contraception including pills (*la píndola/la píldora*), which can be bought without a prescription. You'll generally need a prescription to get the morning-after pill (*la píndola del día seguent/la píldora del día siguiente*) but some CAP health centres (*see p313*) will dispense it free themselves. Many bars and clubs have condom vending machines.

While abortion is decriminalised (the law is ambiguous in not using the term 'legal'), under certain circumstances (rape or possible physical or psychological damage to the mother), during the first 12 weeks of pregnancy, procedures usually take place in private clinics. Under-18s must have parental consent. The only time when abortions might be carried out in public hospitals is when there is foetal abnormality, in which case it's legal up to 22 weeks.

Centre Jove d'Anticoncepció i Sexualitat

C/La Granja 19-21, Gràcia (93 415 10 00/www.centrejove.org). Metro Lesseps. **Open** 12am-6.30pm Mon-Thur; 10am-2pm Fri. **Map** p339 E2. A family planning centre aimed at young people. Free AIDS tests are given to people under 30. There's a small fee for pregnancy tests.

Dentists

Most dentistry is not covered by the Spanish public health service (to which EU citizens have access; see p312). Check the classified ads in Barcelona Metropolitan (see p315) for English-speaking dentists.

Institut Odontològic Calàbria

C/Calàbria 251, Eixample (93 439 45 00/www.ioa.es). Metro Rocafort. **Open** Sept-July 9am-8pm Mon-Fri. Aug 9am-1pm, 3-8pm Mon-Fri. **Credit** DC, MC, V. **Map** p341 B4. Well-equipped clinics providing a complete range of dental services. Several of the staff speak English. **Other locations**: Institut Odontològic Sagrada Familia, C/Sardenya 319, Eixample (93 457 04 53); Institut Odontològic, C/Diputació 238, Eixample (93 342 64 00).

Doctors

A **Centre d'Assistència Primària** (CAP) is a local health centre (aka ambulatorio), where you can normally be seen fairly quickly by a doctor, although you usually do need to make an appointment. According to Catalan regulations, they should give emergency medical care to anyone (they may charge for it), and EU citizens with the European emergency health card should be entitled to it free from the Servei Català de la Salut (see p312). In practice, though, these centres are mainly for locals who are registered with a GP there. Below are some of the 40 or so in town; a full list is in the phone book. Alternatively, go private.

CAPs

CAP Casc Antic C/Rec Comtal 24, Barri Gòtic (93 310 14 21). Metro Arc de Triomf. **Open** 9am-8pm Mon-Fri; 9am-5pm Sat (emergencies only). **Map** p344 C2.
CAP Doctor Lluís Sayé C/Torres i Amat 8, Raval (93 301 24 82/emergencies 93 301 25 32). Metro Universitat. **Open** 9am-8pm Mon-Fri; 9am-5pm Sat (emergencies only). **Map** p344 A1.
CAP Drassanes Avda Drassanes 17-21, Raval (93 329 44 95). Metro Drassanes. **Open** 8am-8pm Mon-Fri. **Map** p342 C6.
CAP Vila Olímpica C/Joan Miró 17, Vila Olímpica (93 221 37 85). Metro Ciutadella-Vila Olímpica or Marina. **Open** 8am-8.30pm Mon-Fri. **Map** p343 F6.

Centre Mèdic Assistencial Catalonia

C/Provença 281, Eixample (93 215 37 93). Metro Diagonal. **Open** 8am-9pm Mon-Fri. **Map** p338 D4. Dr Lynd is a British doctor who has been practising in Barcelona for years. She can be seen at this surgery 3.50-7.10pm every Wednesday, but it is best to call beforehand.

Dr Mary McCarthy

C/Aribau 215, pral 1ª, Eixample (93 200 29 24/mobile 607 220 040). FGC Gràcia/14, 58, 64 bus. **Open** by appointment. **Credit** MC, V. **Map** p338 C3. Dr McCarthy is an internal medicine specialist from the US. She will also treat general patients at American healthcare (ie high) rates.

Opticians

See p211.

Pharmacies

Pharmacies (farmàcies/farmacias) are signalled by large green and red crosses, usually in flashing neon. Most are open 9am-1.30pm and 4.30-8pm weekdays, and 9am-1.30pm on Saturdays. About a dozen operate around the clock, while more have late opening hours; some of the most central are listed below. The full list of chemists that stay open late (usually until 10pm) and overnight on any given night is posted daily outside every pharmacy door and given in the day's newspapers. You can also call the 010 and 098 information lines (see p320). At night, duty pharmacies often appear to be closed, but knock on the shutters and you will be attended to.

The Spanish attitude to dispensing drugs is relaxed. You can legally obtain many things that are more tightly regulated in other countries, including contraceptive pills and some antibiotics, without a prescription. This state of affairs, coupled with the fact that they tend to be quite knowledgeable, means that pharmacists' advice is often sought in order to avoid a trip to the doctor. Some have even been known to dispense drugs that do require prescriptions over the counter. Those with the EU health insurance card will pay the same for prescriptions as Spaniards and foreign residents: 40% less than full price.

Farmàcia Alvarez Passeig de Gràcia 26, Eixample (93 302 11 24). Metro Passeig de Gràcia. **Open** 24hrs daily. **Credit** MC, V. **Map** p342 D5.
Farmàcia Cervera C/Muntaner 254, Eixample (93 200 09 96). Metro Diagonal/FGC Gràcia. **Open** 24hrs daily. **Credit** AmEx, MC, V. **Map** p338 C3.
Farmàcia Clapés La Rambla 98, Barri Gòtic (93 301 28 43). Metro Liceu. **Open** 24hrs daily. **Credit** AmEx, MC, V. **Map** p345 A3.
Farmàcia Vilar Vestíbule, Estació de Sants, Sants (93 490 92 07). Metro Sants Estació. **Open** 7am-10.30pm Mon-Fri; 8am-10.30pm Sat, Sun. **Credit** AmEx, MC, V. **Map** p341 A4.

Alcoholics Anonymous

93 317 77 77. **Open** 10am-1pm, 5-8pm Mon-Fri; 7-9pm Sat, Sun. Among the local AA groups several have dedicated English-speaking sections. Call for details.

Narcotics Anonymous

902 11 41 47/www.na-esp.org. **Open** hours vary. Check the website for details of twice-weekly meetings in English.

Telèfon de l'Esperança

93 414 48 48. **Open** 24hrs daily. Apart from 24-hour counselling, the staff at this local helpline service run by a private foundation can also consult an extensive database to put you in contact with other specialist help groups, from psychiatric to legal. English is occasionally spoken, but not guaranteed.

From the age of 14, Spaniards are legally obliged to carry their DNIs (identity cards). Foreigners are also meant to carry a national ID card or passport, and are in theory subject to a fine if stopped by the police and not carrying one. In practice, you're more likely to get a warning. If you don't

Directory

want to carry it around with you (a wise move, given the prevalence of petty crime), it's a good idea to carry a photocopy or a driver's licence instead: technically, it's not legal, but usually acceptable. Your passport will be essential when checking into a hotel, hiring a car, collecting post restante, paying with cards in shops and exchanging or paying with travellers' cheques. Foreign residents with NIEs (see p322) should carry this as well as their passport, while resident-cardholders can dispense with any other ID.

Insurance

For healthcare and EU nationals, see p312. Some non-EU countries have reciprocal healthcare agreements with Spain, but for most travellers it's usually more convenient to have private travel insurance, which will also, of course, cover you in case of theft and flight problems.

Internet

Broadband (ADSL), now more affordable than ever, is fast taking over from basic dial-up offered by ISPs such as **Wanadoo** (807 170 700, www.wanadoo.es). Ex-monopoly **Telefónica** (www.telefonicaonline. es) controls most of the infrastructure, but is obliged to rent its lines to other firms. Telefónica, Wanadoo, **Ya** (902 90 29 02, www.ya.com), **Auna** (902 50 00 60, www.auna.es) and **Terra** (902 15 20 25, www.terra.es) all offer high-speed connection with 24-hour access for a flat monthly rate. Many firms also offer discount 'package' deals for phone lines and high-speed internet (and, in some cases, cable TV).

Internet access

There are internet centres all over Barcelona. Some libraries (see below) have internet points.

Click Center

Ronda de Sant Antoni 32-34, Raval (93 324 80 79/www.click-center.net). Metro Sant Antoni. **Open** 9am-midnight Mon-Thur, Sun; 10am-1am Fri, Sat. **Credit** AmEx, MC, V. **Map** p342 C5.
Internet access and computer sales. **Other locations**: C/Verdi 9, Gràcia (93 415 88 39).

Cybermundo

C/Bergara 3, Eixample (93 317 71 42). Metro Catalunya. **Open** 9am-1am Mon-Thur; 9am-2am Fri; 10am-2am Sat; 11am-1am Sun. **No credit cards. Map** p344 A1.
Central, with some English/American keyboards. Time of day dictates price.

easyEverything

La Rambla 31, Barri Gòtic (93 318 24 35/www.easyeverything.com). Metro Drassanes or Liceu. **Open** 8am-2.30am daily. **No credit cards. Map** p345 A3.
There are 330 terminals here and 240 at Ronda Universitat 35 (open 8am-2am daily). Buy credit from the machines; price then increases with demand. Alternatively, buy passes that allow unlimited access during a set period (from 24hrs to 30 days).

Left luggage

Look for signs to the consigna.

Aeroport del Prat Terminal B. **Open** 24hrs daily. **Rates** €4/day.
Estació d'Autobusos Barcelona-Nord C/Ali Bei 80, Eixample. Metro Arc de Triomf. **Open** 24hrs daily. **Rates** €3-€4.50/day. **Map** p343 E5.
Train stations Sants-Estació & Estació de França, Born. **Open** 6am-11.45pm daily. **Rates** €3-€4.50/day. **Map** p341 A4 & p343 D6. Some smaller stations have lockers.

Legal help

Consulates (see p309) help tourists in emergencies, and recommend English-speaking lawyers/interpreters.

Marti & Associats

Avda Diagonal 584, pral, Eixample (93 201 62 66/www.martilawyers. com). Bus 6, 7, 15, 33, 34. **Open** 9am-2pm, 4-8pm Mon-Fri. **Map** p338 C3.
Australian John Rocklin is one of the lawyers at this Catalan firm. It also has native speakers of other languages on staff, and can help with work and residency permits.

Libraries

Some libraries offer novels in English and free internet access. Call 010 for library addresses.

Ateneu Barcelonès

C/Canuda 6, Barri Gòtic (93 343 61 21/www.ateneu-bcn.org). Metro Catalunya. **Open** 9am-11pm daily. **Map** p344 B2.
This venerable cultural and philosophical society has the city's best private library, plus a peaceful interior garden patio and a quiet bar. It also organises cultural events. Monthly membership costs €20.

Biblioteca de Catalunya

C/Hospital 56, Raval (93 270 23 00/www.gencat.es). Metro Liceu. **Open** 9am-8pm Mon-Fri; 9am-2pm Sat. **Map** p344 A2.

The Catalan national collection is housed in the medieval Hospital de la Santa Creu and has a wonderful stock reaching back centuries. Readers' cards are required, but free one-day research visits are allowed for over-18s (take your passport).

British Council/ Institut Britànic

C/Amigó 83, Zona Alta (93 241 97 11/www.britishcouncil.es). FGC Muntaner. **Open** Mid Sept-mid June 9.30am-12.30pm, 3.30-9pm Mon-Fri; 10.30am-2pm Sat. Mid June-July, 1st 2wks Sept 9.30am-12.30pm, 4-8.30pm Mon-Fri. **Map** p338 C2.
UK press, English books, satellite TV and a multimedia section oriented towards learning English. Access is free; borrowing costs €55 a year.

Mediateca

CaixaForum, Avda Marquès de Comillas 6-8, Montjuïc (902 22 30 40/93 476 86 51/www.mediateca online.net). Metro Espanya. **Open** Sept-July 10am-8pm Tue-Sat; 10am-2pm, 4-8pm Sun. Aug 4-8pm Tue, Thur-Sun; 4pm-midnight Wed. **Map** p341 A5.
A high-tech art, music and media library in the arts centre of Fundació la Caixa. Most materials are open-access; you can borrow books, magazines, CDs, etc. Membership is €6 (€3 concessions). The lending desk is open 10am-7.30pm Tue-Fri and 10am-2pm Sat (Sat closed Aug).

Lost property

If you lose something at the airport, report it to the lost property centre (Oficina de objetos perdidos, Bloque Técnico building, between terminals B and C, 93 298 33 49). If you have mislaid anything on a train, look for the Atención al Viajero desk or Jefe de Estació office at the nearest station to where your property went astray, call ahead to the destination station, or call station information and ask for objetos perdidos.

Municipal Lost Property Office

Oficina de Troballes, C/Ciutat 9, Barri Gòtic (lost property enquiries 010). Metro Jaume I. **Open** 9am-2pm Mon-Fri. **Map** p345 B3.
All items found on city public transport and taxis, or picked up by the police in the street, should eventually find their way to this office near the Ajuntament, within a few days. Call 010 for information. Within 24hrs of the loss, you can also try ringing the city transport authority on 93 318 70 74, or, for taxis, the Institut Metropolità del Taxi on 93 223 40 12.

Media

Spanish and Catalan newspapers tend to favour serious political commentary rather than the large snaps and easy-on-the-eye fonts of their British counterparts. There are no sensationalist tabloids in Spain: for scandal and salaciousness, the *prensa rosa* ('pink press', or gossip magazines) is the place to look. Television channels, though, go straight for the mass market, with *telebasura* junk television) prevalent. Catalan is the dominant language on both radio and TV, less so in print.

Daily newspapers

Free daily papers of reasonable quality, such as *20 Minutes* and *Metro*, are handed out in the city centre every morning. Articles in these papers jump between Spanish and Catalan with no apparent reason.

ABC

Heavyweight, reactionary reading.

Avui

A conservative, nationalist Catalan-language newspaper.

El Mundo

A decent centrist option.

El País

This serious, socialist-leaning paper is the most extensively read across Spain and provides the best foreign coverage and all-round political commentary. There is a daily Catalonia supplement.

El Periódico

Of the local press, this is the most akin to the British tabloid in terms of format, with bright colours and bold headlines, but it has serious content. There are two editions: one in Catalan and the other in Spanish.

La Vanguardia

The city's top-selling daily is conservative in tone, with a daily Barcelona supplement. Written in Spanish, it often includes the work of syndicated correspondents from around the world.

English language

Foreign newspapers are available at most kiosks on La Rambla and Passeig de Gràcia, and there is an international newsstand at FNAC (*see p193*).

Barcelona Connect

A free newspaper with tips for travellers to the city. .

b-guided

Quarterly style magazine in Spanish and English for bars, clubs, shops, restaurants and exhibitions; sold at hip venues and in FNAC.

Catalonia Today

English-language weekly paper launched in June 2004 by the publisher of Catalan-language daily *El Punt*; available from newsstands throughout the city.

Barcelona Metropolitan

A free monthly general interest magazine for English-speaking locals, distributed in bars, embassies and other anglophone hangouts.

Movin' BCN

A well-designed bilingual monthly covering concerts, movies, food, theatre, nightlife and cultural events.

Listings & classifieds

The main papers have daily 'what's on' listings, with entertainment supplements on Fridays (most run TV schedules on Saturdays). For monthly listings, see *Metropolitan* and freebies such as *Mondo Sonoro* and *AB* (found in bars and music shops). Of the dailies, *La Vanguardia* has the best classifieds, especially on Sundays; you can also consult it at www.los-clasificados.com. www. infojobs.net is a popular resource for job vacancies. *See also p322.*

Anuntis

The largest classified-ad publication, *Anuntis* (www.anuntis.es) emerges on Mondays, Wednesdays and Fridays.

Guía del Ocio

This weekly listings magazine (www.guiadelociobcn.es) is available at any kiosk, but its listings aren't always up to date.

Television

Spanish TV may come as something of a shock, with tedious variety shows, lame comedians, loads of gossip shows, appalling homegrown sitcoms and some trashy American films and series, all peppered with interminable ad breaks. Programme times are unreliable and films are mainly dubbed; undubbed films are shown by 'VO' in listings or, on 'dual' TVs, the dual symbol on screen.

TVE1

The Spanish state broadcaster, 'La Primera', is controlled by the government and has a corresponding bias. Do not expect cutting-edge TV.

TVE2

Also state-run, TVE 2, 'La Dos' offers more highbrow fare with some good late-night movies and documentaries.

TV3

Programmes are entirely in Catalan, with generally mainstream subject matter. OTV3 often has good films in original version or 'dual'.

Canal 33

Also regional and in Catalan, with documentaries, sports programmes and round-table discussions.

Antena 3

A private channel providing a mixture of chat and American films, as well as popular US programmes such as *The Simpsons* or *South Park*.

Tele 5

Also private, and part-owned by Silvio Berlusconi. Its main recent attraction has been *Gran Hermano* (*Big Brother*), as well as various celebrity gossip programmes.

Canal +

A subscription channel offering films, sport and US series. Some shows, such as the news, *Los 40 Principales* (Spain's top 40) and *Las Noticias de Guiñol* (an excellent daily news spoof using puppets) are shown unscrambled to whet your appetite.

BTV

The young staff of the Ajuntament's city channel produce Barcelona's most ground-breaking TV. The new focus for 2005 is to be programmes based on audience participation.

City TV

A private Catalan channel, cloned from a Toronto city station. The schedules are filled with magazine-style programmes and soft porn.

Satellite & cable

Satellite and cable are becoming increasingly popular in Barcelona. The leader is Digital+.

Radio

There are vast numbers of local, regional and national stations, with Catalan having a high profile. **Catalunya Música** (101.5 FM) is mainly classical and jazz, while **Flaix FM** (105.7 FM) provides news and music. For something a little more alternative, try **Radio Bronka** (99 FM), or **Radio 3** (98.7 FM), which has an eclectic music policy. You can listen to the **BBC World Service** on shortwave on 15485, 9410, 12095 and 6195 KHz, depending on the time of day.

Directory

Money

Spain's currency is the euro. Each euro (€) is divided into 100 cents (¢), known as *céntims/céntimos*. Notes come in denominations of €500, €200, €100, €50, €20, €10 and €5. Coins come in denominations of €2, €1, 50¢, 20¢, 10¢, 5¢, 2¢ and 1¢.

Banks & currency exchanges

Banks (*bancos*) and savings banks (*caixes d'estalvis/cajas de ahorros*) usually accept euro travellers' cheques for a commission, but tend to refuse any kind of personal cheque except one issued by that bank. Some foreign exchange bureaux (*cambios*) don't charge commission, but rates are worse. Obtaining money through an ATM (which are everywhere) with a debit or credit card is the easiest option, despite the fees often charged.

Bank hours

Banks are normally open 8.30am-2pm Monday to Friday. October to April, most branches open 8.30am-1pm on Saturdays. Hours vary a little between banks. Savings banks offer the same exchange facilities as banks and open the same hours; from October to May many are also open late on Thursdays, 4.30-7.45pm.

Out-of-hours banking

Foreign exchange offices at the airport (terminals A and B) are open 7am-11pm daily. Others in the centre open late: some on La Rambla open until midnight, later from July to September. At Sants, change money at La Caixa (8am-8pm daily). At the airport and outside some banks are automatic exchange machines that accept notes in major currencies. The **American Express** shop offers full AmEx card services, plus currency exchange, money transfers and a travel agency; **Western Union** is the quickest (but not the cheapest) way of sending money abroad.

American Express *La Rambla 74 (93 342 73 11). Metro Liceu.* **Open** 9am-9pm Mon-Sat. **Map** p345 A3.
Western Union Money Transfer *Loterias Manuel Martín, La Rambla 41 (93 412 70 41/www.western union.com). Metro Liceu.* **Open** 9.30am-11.30pm daily. **Map** p345 A3.
Other locations: Mail Boxes, C/València 214, Eixample (900 63 36 33); and throughout the city.

Credit and debit cards

Major credit cards are accepted in hotels, shops, restaurants and other places (including metro ticket

machines, and pay-and-display on-street parking machines). American Express and Diners Club cards are less accepted than MasterCard and Visa. Many debit cards from other European countries can also be used: check with your bank beforehand. You can withdraw cash with major cards from ATMs, and banks will advance cash against a credit card.

Note: you need photo ID (passport, driving licence or similar) when using a credit or debit card in a shop, but usually not in a restaurant.

Lost/stolen credit cards

All lines have English-speaking staff and are open 24hrs daily.

American Express 902 11 11 35.
Diners Club 901 10 10 11.
MasterCard 900 97 12 31.
Visa 900 99 11 24.

Tax

The standard rate for sales tax (IVA) is 16%; this drops to 7% in hotels and restaurants, and 4% on some books. IVA may or may not be included in listed prices at restaurants, and usually isn't included in rates quoted at hotels. If it's not, the expression *més/más* IVA (plus sales tax) or IVA *no inclòs/incluido* (sales tax not included) must appear after the price. Beware of this when getting quotes on expensive items. In shops displaying a 'Tax-Free Shopping' sticker, non-EU residents can reclaim tax on large purchases when leaving the country.

Opening times

Most shops open from 9am or 10am to 1pm or 2pm, and then 4pm or 5pm to 8pm or 9pm, Monday to Saturday. Many smaller businesses don't reopen on Saturday afternoons. All-day opening (10am to 8pm or 9pm) is becoming increasingly common, especially for larger and more central establishments.

Markets open at 7am or 8am; most stalls are shut by 2pm, although many open on Fridays until 8pm The Ajuntament encourages stallholders at each municipal market to remain open in the afternoons during the rest of the week in an effort to compete with supermarkets. Larger shops are allowed to open for Sundays and a few holidays, mostly near Christmas.

In summer, shops closing for weeks at a stretch is becoming less common, although many restaurants and shops still shut for all or part of August. Some businesses work a shortened day from June to September, from 8am or 9am until 3pm. Most museums close one day each week, usually Mondays.

Police

Barcelona has several police forces, whose respective functions are due to be reorganised during 2005. The **Guàrdia Urbana** (the municipal police) wear navy and pale blue, and are concerned with traffic and local regulations, but also help to keep general law and order, and deal with noise complaints. The **Policía Nacional**, in darker blue uniforms and white shirts (or blue, combat-style gear), patrol the streets, and are responsible for dealing with more serious crime, as well as paperwork concerning ID and passports.

However, as of the end of 2005, the Catalan government's police, the **Mossos d'Esquadra** (in navy and light blue with red trim), who have been working alongside the Policía Nacional in more touristy parts of the city and some towns outside it, will begin to take some responsibilities from the Guàrdia Urbana and Policía Nacional: patrolling the streets more and taking a leading role in dealing with lower-level crime and security.

The **Guàrdia Civil** is a paramilitary force with green uniforms, policing highways, customs posts, some government buildings and rural areas.

Reporting a crime

If you're robbed or attacked, report the incident as soon as possible at the nearest police station (*comisaría*), or dial 112. In the centre, the most convenient is the **Guàrdia Urbana** station on La Rambla, which often has English-speaking officers on duty; they may eventually transfer you to the **Policía Nacional** to formally report the crime.

To do this, you'll need to make an official statement (*denuncia*). It's highly improbable that you will recover your property, but you need the *denuncia* to make an insurance claim. You can also make this statement over the phone (902 10 21 12) in English, French, German, Arabic, Catalan and Spanish or online in Spanish (www.policia.es; except for crimes involving physical violence, or if the author has been identified). You'll still have to go to the *comisaría* within 72 hours to sign the *denuncia*, but you'll skip some queues. To contact the Policía Nacional, the 24-hour operator on 091 can connect you to the closest *comisaría*.

Guàrdia Urbana Ciutat Vella *La Rambla 43, Barri Gòtic (092/93 344 13 00). Metro Liceu or Drassanes.* **Open** 24hrs daily. **Map** p345 A3.
Policía Nacional Zona II *C/Nou de la Rambla 76, Raval (091/93 290 28 49). Metro Paral·lel.* **Open** 24hrs daily. **Map** p342 C6.

Postal services

Letters and postcards weighing up to 20g cost 28¢ within Spain; 53¢ to the rest of Europe; 78¢ to the rest of the world. It's usually easiest to buy stamps at *estancs (see below)*. Mail sent abroad is slow: 5-6 working days in Europe, 8-10 to the USA.

Postboxes in the street are yellow, sometimes with a white or blue horn insignia. Postal information is on 902 197 197 or at www.correos.es.

Correu Central

Plaça Antonio López, Barri Gòtic (93 486 80 50). Metro Jaume I or Barceloneta. **Open** 8.30am-9.30pm Mon-Sat. **Map** p342 D6.
Take a ticket from the machine as you enter and wait your turn. Apart from the typical services, fax sending and receiving is offered (with the option of courier delivery in Spain, using the Burofax option). To send something express, ask for *'urgente'*. Some post offices close in August. Many have painfully slow queues. **Other locations**: Ronda Universitat 23, Eixample; C/Aragó 282, Eixample (both 8.30am-8.30pm Mon-Fri, 9.30am-1pm Sat); and throughout the city.

Estancs/estancos

Government-run tobacco shops, known as an *estanc/estanco* (at times, just 'tabac') and identified by a brown and yellow sign, are very important institutions. As well as tobacco, they also supply postage stamps and envelopes, public transport *targetes* and phonecards.

Post boxes

A PO box *(apartado postal)* address costs €44.75 annually.

Postal Transfer

Plaça Urquinaona 6, Eixample (93 317 74 42). Metro Urquinaona. **Open** 10am-11pm Mon-Fri; 11am-midnight Sat: noon-11pm Sun.
The post office's national network of outlets aimed at Spain's immigrants. Apart from postal services, they offer Western Union money transfer, internet access, cheap international calls, fax, photocopying and some banking services.

Poste restante

Poste restante letters should be sent to Lista de Correos, 08080 Barcelona, Spain. Pick-up is from the main post office; you'll need your passport.

Queuing

Contrary to appearances, Catalans have an advanced queuing culture. They may not stand in an orderly line, but they're normally very aware of when it's their turn, particularly at market stalls and in small shops. The standard drill is to ask when you arrive, *'¿Qui es l'últim/la última?'* ('Who's last?') and get behind whoever answers. Say *'jo'* ('me') to the next person who asks.

Religion

Anglican: St George's Church

C/Horaci 38, Zona Alta (93 417 88 67/www.st-georges-church.com). FGC Avda Tibidabo. **Main service** 11am Sun.
An Anglican/Episcopalian church with a multicultural congregation. Activities include a weekly women's club, bridge and Sunday school.

Catholic mass in English: Parròquia Maria Reina

Carretera d'Esplugues 103, Zona Alta (93 203 41 15). Metro Maria Cristina/22, 63, 75 bus. **Mass** 10.30pm Sun. **Map** p337 A1.

Jewish Orthodox: Sinagoga de Barcelona & Comunitat Israelita de Barcelona

C/Avenir 24, Zona Alta (93 209 31 47/www.cibonline.org). **Prayers** call for times. **Map** p338 C3.
A Sephardic, Orthodox synagogue.

Jewish Reform: Comunitat Jueva Atid de Catalunya

C/Castanyer 27, Zona Alta (tel/fax 93 417 37 04/www.atid.es). FGC El Putxet. **Prayers** 8.15pm Fri. Call for other times.
You must give notice that you'll be attending: email or fax with your passport number by 2pm Fri.

Muslim: Mosque Tarik Bin Ziad

C/Hospital 91, Raval (93 441 91 49). Metro Liceu. **Prayers** 2pm Fri. Call for other times. **Map** p342 C6.

Renting a flat

Rental accommodation in Barcelona is pricier than ever. A room in a shared flat costs €300/month and up, while a one- to two-bed apartment in the centre goes for €550/month or more. Standards vary a great deal, so do shop around. Rental agreements generally cover a five-year period, within which the landlord can only raise the rent in line with inflation. Landlords usually ask for a month's rent as a *fianza* (deposit) and a month's rent in advance; some may also require an employment contract as proof of income. Details of contracts vary wildly: don't sign unless you're confident of your Spanish or Catalan and/or a local lawyer or *gestor* has seen it.

Classified ads in *La Vanguardia* and *Barcelona Metropolitan (see p315)* carry apartment ads. Also useful are *administradores de fincas*: these companies run buildings and sometimes have to find tenants for vacant apartments. Check www.coleadministradors.com for a list, but bear in mind that their classified ads are often out of date. Try calling instead. Also, while walking, look out for *Es lloga/Se alquila* or *En lloguer/En alquiler* ('for rent') signs: you do get lucky.

Safety

Pickpocketing and bag-snatching are epidemic in Barcelona, with tourists a prime target. Be especially careful around the Old City, particularly La Rambla, as well as at stations and on public transport. However, thieves go anywhere tourists go, including parks, beaches and – the latest hotspot – internet cafés. Most street crime is aimed at the inattentive, and can be avoided by taking a few simple common-sense precautions:

● Avoid giving invitations: don't keep wallets in accessible pockets, keep your bags closed and in front of you. When you stop, put your bags down beside you (or hold them on your lap), where you can see them.
● Don't flash about wads of cash or fancy cameras.
● In busy streets or crowded places, keep an eye on what is happening around you. If you're suspicious of someone, move somewhere else.
● As a rule, Barcelona street thieves tend to use stealth and surprise rather than violence. However, muggings and knife threats do sometimes occur. Avoid deserted streets in the city centre if you're on your own at night, and offer no resistance when threatened.
● Despite precautions, sometimes you can just be unlucky. Don't carry more money and valuables than you need: use your hotel's safe deposit facilities, and take travel insurance.

Smoking

Despite the odd sign telling them not to do so, people in Barcelona still seem to smoke wherever they want: banks, shops, offices and restaurants. Only a few of the latter have non-smoking areas; there are whispers of it being made a legal requirement in the next few years, but it will be quite a while before the concept is assimilated. Usually only upmarket hotels have non-smoking rooms or floors; if you ask for a non-smoking room, some hotels may just give you a room that has had the ashtray removed. (To our knowledge, this doesn't apply to hotels listed in the Where to Stay chapter as having non-smoking rooms.) Smoking bans in cinemas, in theatres and on trains are generally respected, though smoking on station platforms (but not on trains) is still quite common.

Study

Catalonia is pro-European, and the vast majority of foreign students in Spain under the EU's Erasmus scheme are studying at Catalan universities or colleges. Catalan is usually spoken in these universities, although some lecturers are relaxed about use of Castilian in class for the first few months.

Accommodation & advice

Barcelona Allotjament

C/Pelai 12, pral B, Eixample (93 268 43 57/www.barcelona-allotjament. com). Metro Catalunya or Universitat. **Open** 10am-2pm, 5-7pm Mon-Thur; 10am-2pm Fri. Closed Aug. **No credit cards. Map** p344 A1.
Rooms with local families, in shared student flats and in B&Bs, can be booked through this agency, aimed mainly at students. Rooms in shared apartments cost €150 and up per month, plus a €250 agency fee. It can also rent whole flats.

Centre d'Informació i Assessorament per a Joves (CIAJ)

C/Sant Oleguer 6, Raval (93 442 29 39/www.bcn.es/ciaj). Metro Liceu or Paral·lel. **Open** Sept-July 10am-2pm, 4-8pm Mon-Fri. *Aug* 10am-3pm Mon-Fri. **Map** p345 B3.
Youth information centre run by the city council, with information on work, study, accommodation (classifieds are online, not in the centre itself) and more. There are free web terminals (not for email).

Secretaria General de Joventut – Punt d'Informació Juvenil

C/Calabria 147-C/Rocafort 116, Eixample (reception 93 483 83 83/ information 93 483 83 84/www.bcu. cesca.es). Metro Rocafort. **Open** *Oct-May* 9am-2pm, 3-7pm Mon-Fri. *June-Sept* 8am-3pm Mon-Fri. **Map** p341 B5.

Generalitat-run centre with a number of services: information for young people on travel, work and study and internet access. Other Secretaria General de Joventut services include Borsa Jove d'Habitatge (93 483 83 92, www.habitatgejove.com), an accommodation service for 18-35s; it's mostly for whole flats, but there are some single rooms available.

Language classes

If you plan to stay in bilingual Barcelona for a while, you may want (or need) to learn some Catalan. The city is also a popular location for studying Spanish. For full course lists, try the youth information centres above. See www.cervantes.es for schools recommended by Spain's official language institute, the Instituto Cervantes.

Babylon Idiomas

C/Bruc 65, Eixample (93 488 15 85/ www.babylon-idiomas.com). Metro Girona. **Open** 9am-8pm Mon-Fri. **Credit** MC, V. **Map** p343 E5.
Small groups (eight people tops) run at all levels of Spanish in this school, which also has business courses. Staff can arrange accommodation.

Consorci per a la Normalització Lingüística

C/Quintana 11, 1° 1ª, Barri Gòtic (93 412 72 24/www.cpnl.org). Metro Liceu. **Open** 9am-1pm, 4-5.30pm Mon-Thur; 9am-2pm Fri. **No credit cards. Map** p345 A3.
The Generalitat organisation for the promotion of the Catalan language has centres around the city offering Catalan courses for non-Spanish speakers at very low prices or for free. Courses start in September and February; classes are very big and queues to enrol are long. There are also free monthly intensive courses and multimedia classes for beginners all year. Places are limited; call or arrive early when it's time to sign up. **Other locations:** C/Mallorca 115, entl 1ª, Eixample (93 451 24 45); and throughout the city.

Escola Oficial d'Idiomes de Barcelona – Drassanes

Avda Drassanes, Raval (93 324 93 30/www.eoibd.es). Metro Drassanes. **Open** *Sept-Jan* 8.30am-9pm Mon-Fri. *Feb-June* 8.30am-9pm Mon-Thur; 8.30am-2pm Fri. **Map** p342 C6.
This state-run school has semi-intensive four-month courses, starting in September and February, at all levels in Catalan, Spanish, French, German and English. From September to January, there are also

courses in ten other languages. It's cheap and has a good reputation; demand is high and classes are big. There's also a self-study centre and a good library. There are several other *Escolas Oficials* in Barcelona where it may be easier to get a place, although they do not offer such a wide range as the Drassanes one. Call 012 or see www.gencat.net/educacio for details.
Other locations: Escola Oficial, Avda del Jordà 18, Vall d'Hebrón (93 418 74 85); and throughout the city.

International House

C/Trafalgar 14, Eixample (93 268 45 11/www.ihes.com/bcn). Metro Urquinaona. **Open** 8am-9pm Mon-Fri; 10am-1.30pm Sat. **Map** p344 C2.
Intensive Spanish courses all year round. IH is also a leading TEFL teacher training centre.

Estudios Hispánicos de la Universitat de Barcelona

Gran Via de les Corts Catalanes 585, Eixample (information 93 403 55 19/www.eh.ub.es). Metro Universitat. **Open** *Information* (Pati de Ciències entrance) 9am-2pm, 4-5.30pm Mon-Thur; 9am-2pm Fri. Closed pm in Aug. **Map** p342 C-D5.
Intensive three-month and year-long Spanish language and culture courses. Enrolment runs year round.

Universities

The Erasmus student exchange scheme is part of the EU's Socrates programme to help students move between member states. Interested students should contact the Erasmus co-ordinator at their home college. Information is available in Britain from the UK Socrates-Erasmus Council, R&D Building, The University, Canterbury, Kent CT2 7PD (01227 762712/fax 01227 762711/ www.erasmus.ac.uk). See also http://europa.eu.int for an overview.

Universitat Autònoma de Barcelona

Campus de Bellaterra (93 581 10 00/ information 93 581 11 11/www.uab. es). FGC or RENFE Universidad Autonoma/by car A58 to Cerdanyola del Valles. **Open** *Information* 10am-1.30pm, 3.30-4.30pm Mon-Fri.
A 1960s campus outside the city at Bellaterra, near Sabadell. Frequent FGC train connections to the centre.

Universitat de Barcelona

Gran Via de les Corts Catalanes 585, Eixample (information 93 403 54 17/ www.ub.es). Metro Universitat. **Open** *Information* 9am-2pm Mon-Fri. Closed 1wk Aug. **Map** p342 C-D5.

It's in the timing...

Whether because they're slaves to an innate mob mentality or have oddly synchronised body-clocks, the vast majority of Barcelonans eat, sleep, work and play within a rigid schedule. It pays to familiarise yourself with the city's timing, and to organise your own activities around it.

Working. For most, the working day starts at 9am or 9.30am and ends at 7pm or 7.30pm, with a lunch break from 2pm to 4pm, when professional interaction is unceremoniously put on hold. Many shops that close for lunch push afternoon opening back to 4.30pm, 5pm or even 5.30pm. *See also p316.*

Eating out. You'll be lucky to get a restaurant to serve you dinner before 9pm; many are deserted even then. However, restaurants suddenly fill up between 10pm and 10.30pm on Fridays and Saturdays, and between 9.30pm and 10pm on other days. Beware of going for a drink to kill time before dinner, dallying over another and turning up at a restaurant at 10.15pm on a weekend without a reservation. You may find yourself traipsing the streets in search of a vacant table, or waiting until 11.30pm for one to become available. Likewise, many restaurants pack out for lunch by 2.30pm daily.

Taking in a movie. Turn up at least 30 minutes before the start of the show. Get there less than 25 minutes early, especially on weekends and on *día del espectador* (cheap ticket night; *see p231*), and you risk a wait. With fewer than 15 minutes to spare, and you're guaranteed a seat in the front three rows and 115 minutes of neck-craning.

Grabbing a cab. Barcelona generally has a healthy supply of taxis, but at weekends, at the stroke of 3am, the city centre turns into a cab-free zone. As bars close, huge queues materialise at taxi ranks. Common trouble spots include the rank at Plaça Catalunya, at the top of La Rambla, and at the bottom, the one in front of the Monument a Colom. When it rains, things get worse. If you're far from your next port of call, it might be wise to slip out early to avoid a soggy schlep back.

Shopping. The only day that most people indulge their urge to splurge is Saturday, when downtown shopping streets are oppressively swamped, especially in the afternoon. Steer clear of C/Portal de l'Àngel and C/Portaferrissa in particular.

Hitting the town. Bars don't get going until about 11.30pm and clubs don't start filling up until 2.30am or 3am: don't be surprised if you're having a solitary boogie at midnight, or if you're stuck in a queue at 3am.

We're all going on a (summer) holiday. You can almost hear them call 'ready, steady, go ...' As in other Spanish cities, '*operación salida*', when vast hordes leave town by car, and '*operación retorno*', when they come back, sparks major chaos. This happens on major *puentes* (bank holiday weekends) and other holidays – particularly August, when half the city drains away, countless businesses lower their shutters, and urban life comes to a virtual standstill. Note the monster traffic jams that build up around the start and end of these periods if you're planning to hit the roads yourself.

Barcelona's oldest, biggest university has faculties in the main building on Plaça Universitat, and elsewhere. For Spanish courses, *see p318.*

Universitat Pompeu Fabra

Information 93 542 22 28/www.upf. edu. Information points: La Rambla 30-32, Barri Gòtic; C/Ramon Trias Fargas 25-27, Vila Olímpica; Passeig Circumval·lació 8, Born. **Open** 9am-9pm Mon-Fri.
Faculties in various parts of central Barcelona, many in the Old City.

Universitat Ramon Llull

Main offices: C/Claravall 1-3, Zona Alta (902 50 20 50/93 602 22 00/www.url.es). FGC Avda Tibidabo. **Open** *Information* 9am-2pm, 4-6.30pm Mon-Fri. Closed 2wks Aug.

A private university bringing together a number of once-separate institutions, including the prestigious ESADE business school (93 280 61 62/29 95, www.esade.edu).

Telephones

Recent liberalisation of the phone market has led to the dissolution of former state operator **Telefónica**'s monopoly. However, while several new operators have emerged, the market is still very dependent on Telefónica's infrastructure, and rates remain high compared to other European countries.

Competitors survive either by renting (copper wire) lines from Telefónica at rates fixed by the government and reselling them or setting up their own cable network. The latter is the only way to compete, but requires major investment. The company that has most successfully managed this in Barcelona is **Auna** (902 50 00 60, www.auna.es), which has an optic fibre network in the city. If you plan to get an internet connection as well, it may work out cheapest to go for a combined phone and ADSL deal; *see p314.* **Tele2** (901 10 73 66, www. tele2.com) resells minutes of traffic on other companies' networks at competitive rates.

One outcome of diversification has been confusion among users, exemplified by the profusion of numbers for directory enquiries. There are now over 20 numbers (operated by various companies) for information; their cost fluctuates wildly. Telefónica itself has several, and is severely criticised for its massive advertising of the more expensive ones. It is, however, forced to offer a cheap number (free from pay phones); *see below*. Phone cards, and the phone centres that sell them, generally give cheaper rates, especially for international calls.

Dialling & codes

Normal Spanish phone numbers have nine digits; the area code (93 in the province of Barcelona) must be dialled with all calls, both local and long-distance. Spanish mobile numbers always begin with 6. Numbers starting 900 are freephone lines, while other 90 numbers are special-rate services.

International & long-distance calls from Barcelona

To make an international call, dial 00 and then the country code, followed by the area code (omitting the first zero in UK numbers), and then the number. Country codes are as follows:

Australia 61.
Canada 1.
Irish Republic 353.
New Zealand 64.
South Africa 27.
United Kingdom 44.
USA 1.

To phone Spain from abroad, dial the international access code (0011 from Australia; 00 from Ireland, New Zealand and the UK; 011 from the USA and Canada), followed by the country code for Spain (34), followed by the area code and the number.

Mobile phones

The mobile phone, or *móvil*, is omnipresent in Spain. Calls are paid for either through direct debit or by using prepaid phones, topped up with vouchers. Most mobile phones from other European countries can be used in Spain, but you may need to set this up before you leave. You may be charged international roaming rates even when making a local call, and will be charged for incoming calls. Not all US handsets are GSM-compatible; check with your service provider before you leave.

If you're staying more than a few weeks, it may work out cheaper to buy a pay-as-you-go package when you arrive. At places such as FNAC (*see p193*), buy a new handset and SIM card (or just the SIM card for your old handset, provided it's not blocked from using other service providers' SIM cards; check before leaving). Handsets usually include a

little credit, which you can then top up with pre-pay vouchers (from newsagents, cash machines and *estancs*). Firms include Amena (1474, www.amena.es), Movistar (1485, www.movistar.es) and Vodafone (607 123 000, www.vodafone.es).

Public phones

The most common type of payphone accepts coins (5¢ up), phonecards and credit cards. There is a multilingual digital display (press 'L' to change language) and written instructions in English and other languages.

For the first minute of a daytime local call, you'll be charged around 8¢; to a mobile phone around 12¢; and to a 902 number, around 20¢. Calls to directory enquiries on 11818 are free from payphones, but you'll usually have to insert a coin to make the call (it will be returned when you hang up). If you're still in credit at the end of your call, you can make further calls by pushing the 'R' button under where the handset rests and dialling again. Bars and cafés often have payphones, but these can be more expensive than street booths.

Telefónica phonecards (*tarjetas telefónica/targetes telefónica*) are sold at newsstands and *estancs* (*see p317*). Other cards sold at phone centres, shops and newsstands give cheaper rates on all but local calls. This latter type of card contains a toll-free number to call from any phone. You're told how many minutes you have (time varies according to where you are calling) and then connected with the number you want.

Operator services & useful phone numbers

Operators normally speak Catalan and Spanish only, except for international operators, most of whom speak English.

General information (Barcelona) 010 (8am-10pm Mon-Sat).
International directory enquiries 11825.
International operator for reverse charge calls Europe 1008; rest of world 1005.
National directory enquiries 11818 (Telefónica, the cheapest) or 11888 (*Yellow Pages*, more expensive), among others.
National operator for reverse charge calls 1009. After the recorded message, press the asterisk key twice, and then 4.
Pharmacies, postcodes, lottery 098.
Telephone faults service (Telefónica) 1002.
Time 093.

Wake-up calls 096. After the message, key in the time at which you wish to be woken, in the 24hr clock, in four figures: for example, 0830 for 8.30am, 2030 for 8.30pm.
Weather 807 170 308.

Phone centres

Phone centres (*locutorios*) are full of small booths where you can sit down and pay at the end. They offer cheap calls, and avoid the need for change. Concentrated particularly in streets such as C/Sant Pau and C/Hospital in the Raval, and along C/Carders-C/Corders in Sant Pere, they generally offer other services, including international money transfer, currency exchange and internet access.

Oftelcom *C/Canuda 7, Barri Gòtic (93 342 73 70). Metro Catalunya.* **Open** 9am-midnight daily. **Map** p344 B2.
Locutorio *C/Hospital 17, Barri Gòtic (93 318 97 39). Metro Liceu.* **Open** 10am-11pm daily. **Map** p344 A2.

Time

Local time is one hour ahead of GMT, six hours ahead of US Eastern Standard Time and nine ahead of Pacific Standard Time. Daylight saving time runs concurrently with the UK: clocks go back in the last week of October and forward in the last week of March.

Tipping

There are no fixed rules for tipping in Barcelona, but locals generally don't tip much. It's fair to leave 5-10% in restaurants, but if you think the service has been bad, don't feel you have to. People sometimes leave a little change in bars: not expected, but appreciated. In taxis, tipping is not standard, but if the fare works out at a few cents below a euro, many people will round up. It's usual to tip hotel porters.

Toilets

Public toilets are not common in Barcelona, although the Ajuntament may introduce more of them, as the problem of people urinating alfresco in the Old City becomes more acute. Most of the main railway stations have clean toilets. The beach at Barceloneta has a couple of (heavily in demand) Portaloos; there are toilets open in season under the boardwalk, up the beach towards the Port Olímpic. Most bar and café owners do not mind if you use their toilets (you may have to ask for the

Directory

key), although some in the centre and at the beach are less amenable. Fast-food restaurants are good standbys.

Toilets are known as *serveis*, *banys* or *lavabos* (Catalan) or *servicios*, *aseos*, *baños* or *lavabos* (Spanish). In bars or restaurants, the ladies' is generally denoted by a D (*dones/ damas*), and occasionally by an M (*mujeres*) or S (*señoras*) on the door; while the men's mostly say H (*homes/hombres*) or C (*caballeros*). Smaller establishments may have just one unisex toilet.

Tourist information

The city council (Ajuntament) and Catalan government (Generalitat) both run tourist offices. Information about what's on can be found in local papers as well as listings magazines.

Oficines d'Informació Turística

Plaça Catalunya, Eixample (information 807 11 72 22/from outside Spain +34 93 285 38 34/ www.bcn.es/www.barcelonaturisme. com). Metro Catalunya. **Open** *Office* 9am-9pm daily. *Call centre* 9am-8pm Mon-Fri. **Map** p344 B1.
The main office of the city tourist board is underground on the Corte Inglés side of the square: look for big red signs with 'i' in white. It has information, money exchange, a shop and a hotel booking service, and sells phonecards, tickets for shows, sights and public transport. Opening times for other offices and booths vary: smaller ones may close for the afternoon on Sundays and Oct-June. There may be temporary booths near cruise ship terminals in season.
Other locations: C/Ciutat 2 (ground floor of Ajuntament building, just off Plaça Sant Jaume), Barri Gòtic; C/Sardenya (opposite the Sagrada Familia), Eixample; Plaça Portal Pau (opposite Monument a Colom), Port Vell; Sants station; La Rambla; cnr of Plaça d'Espanya and Avda Maria Cristina; airport (terminals A & B).

Palau Robert

Passeig de Gràcia 107, Eixample (93 238 40 00/80 91/www.gencat.net/ probert). Metro Diagonal. **Open** 10am-7pm Mon-Sat; 10am-2.30pm Sun. **Map** p338 D4.
The Generalitat's lavishly equipped centre is at the junction of Passeig de Gràcia and the Diagonal. It has maps and other essentials for Barcelona, but its speciality is a huge range of information in different media for elsewhere in Catalonia. It sometimes hosts interesting exhibitions on local art, culture, gastronomy and nature.

Other locations: Airport terminals A (93 478 47 04) and B (93 478 05 65), open 9am-9pm daily.

Centre d'Informació de la Virreina

Palau de la Virreina, La Rambla 99, Barri Gòtic (93 301 77 75/ information 93 316 10 00/www. bcn.es/cultura). Metro Liceu. **Open** 10am-8pm Mon-Sat; 11am-3pm Sun. **Ticket sales** 11am-8pm Tue-Sun. **Map** p344 A2.
The information office of the city's culture department, with details of shows, exhibitions and special events. The good bookstore specialises in Barcelona.

010 phoneline

Open 8am-10pm Mon-Sat.
This city-run information line is aimed mainly at locals, but it does an impeccable job of answering all kinds of queries. There are sometimes English-speaking operators.

Visas & immigration

Spain is one of the EU countries covered by the Schengen agreement, which led to common visa regulations and limited border controls. However, neither the UK nor the Republic of Ireland are signatories; nationals of those countries will need their passports. Most EU citizens, as well as Norwegian and Icelandic nationals, only need a national identity card.

Visas are not required for US, Canadian, Australian and New Zealand citizens for stays of up to 90 days that are not for work or study. Citizens of South Africa and many other countries need visas to enter Spain; approach Spanish consulates and embassies in other countries (or from those of other Schengen countries you're planning to visit). Visa regulations are subject to change; check before leaving home.

Water

Tap water is drinkable, but tastes of chlorine. Bottled water is what you will be served if you ask for '*un aigua/agua*' in a bar or restaurant.

When to go

Barcelona is marvellous all year round, and the weather is usually very agreeable. The humidity in summer can be debilitating, however, and the city is definitely not running at full steam, with many shops, bars and restaurants closed (especially during August).

Climate

Spring in Barcelona is unpredictable: warm sunny days can alternate, dramatically at times, with cold winds and showers. Temperatures in May and June are pretty much perfect; the city is especially lively around 23 June, when locals celebrate the beginning of summer with all kinds of fireworks and fiestas. July and August can be decidedly unpleasant, as the summer heat and humidity kick in and make many locals leave town. Autumn weather is generally warm and fresh, with heavy downpours common around October. Crisp, cool sunshine is normal from December to February. Snow is very rare.

Public holidays

Almost all shops, banks and offices, and many bars and restaurants, close on public holidays (*festius/festivos*), and public transport runs a limited service. Many locals take long weekends whenever a major holiday comes along. If the holiday coincides with, say, a Tuesday or a Thursday, many people will take the Monday or Friday off: this is what is known as a *pont/puente*. The city's official holidays are as follows:

New Year's Day/*Any Nou***
1 Jan
Three Kings/*Reis Mags* 6 Jan
Good Friday/*Divendres Sant*
Easter Monday/*Dilluns de Pasqua*
May (Labour) Day/*Festa del Treball* 1 May
Segona Pascua (Whitsun) 31 May
Sant Joan 24 June
Verge de l'Assumpció 15 Aug
Diada de Catalunya 11 Sept
La Mercè 24 Sept
Dia de la Hispanitat 12 Oct
All Saints' Day/*Tots Sants*
1 Nov
Constitution Day/*Dia de la Constitución* 6 Dec
La Immaculada 8 Dec
Christmas Day/*Nadal* 25 Dec
Boxing Day/*Sant Esteve* 26 Dec.

Working & living

Common recourses for English speakers in Barcelona are to find work in the tourist sector (often seasonal and outside the city), work in a bar or teach English. For the latter it helps to have relevant TEFL qualifications. Bear in mind that teaching work dries up in summer. The amount of jobs in call centres for English speakers and other foreigners has also rocketed of late.

Queries regarding residency and legal requirements for foreigners working in Spain can be addressed to the Ministry of Interior's helpline on 900 150 000 (there are English-speaking operators). Its website (www.mir.es) lays out the regulations in force on these matters, but makes dense reading. *See also p313* **ID**.

EU citizens

New rules introduced in March 2003 exempt many EU citizens living in Spain from the obligation to apply for and carry a resident's card (*tarjeta de residencia*). Students, contracted workers, freelancers, business owners or retired people who have made Spanish social security contributions are entitled to live here and use their own country's ID card or passport for all dealings.

However, in order to get a work contract or a resident's bank account, to make tax declarations or for other official bureaucracy, you will need a *Número de Identificación del Extranjero* (foreigner's identity number), otherwise known as NIE. To do this, head to the Oficina de Comunitarios (*see below*).

To obtain a residency card, you may apply for one at the Delegación de Gobierno's Oficina de Extranjería (*see below*). First, though, you must get an NIE.

Delegación de Gobierno – Oficina de Expedición de Tarjetas Comunitarias y de Estudiantes

Passeig Joan de Borbó 32, Barceloneta (93 244 06 10/02/ www.mir.es). **Open** 9am-2pm Mon-Fri. **Map** p342 D7.

Queue here for your NIE application. Remember to bring your passport along with a photocopy of its main pages, two passport photos and a letter from whoever requested you to have an NIE explaining that they want you to have it. You can download the form at www.mir.es/extranje/modelos/ex14.pdf, but you will still have to bring it in person.

Once you've submitted the paperwork, staff will send your NIE by post within 30-40 days. Note, however, that they won't deliver NIEs to unmarked letterboxes: your name must appear on it for you to receive the letter. It consists of an unimpressive-looking piece of paper with a number printed on it, but this is the legal document that backs up your identification number: you may need to quote it on paperwork in various situations, such as receiving a registered letter.

Delegación del Gobierno – Oficina de Extranjería (EU citizens)

Avda Marquès de l'Argentera 2, 2°, Barceloneta (information 93 482 05 44/appointments 93 520 95 30). Metro Barceloneta. **Open** *information & appointment lines* 9am-2pm Mon-Fri. *Office* 9am-5.30pm Mon-Thur; 9am-2pm Fri. **Map** p345 C4.

You need an appointment here before you can make your residency card application. In theory, appointments can be made over the phone, but the line is constantly engaged; it works out quicker to come, queue up make an appointment and then come back. You'll need three passport photos, your passport and photocopies of the important passport pages. The application can be downloaded

from www.mir.es/extranje/modelos/ex16.pdf. Expect to wait three to four months for your appointment.

Non-EU citizens

Thanks to the soaring levels of immigration, the legal situation is tougher than ever for people from the rest of the world. While in Spain on a tourist visa, you are not legally allowed to work (though, of course, many do). First-time applicants officially need a special visa, obtained from a Spanish consulate in their home country. Even if you are made a job offer while in Spain, you must still make the trip home to apply for this *visado de residencia* residence visa. Without it, you may not enter Spain to work. The process can be lengthy and not all applications are successful.

Once the visa has been issued, you can travel to Spain, take the job and begin the protracted application process for a resident's card and work permit (*permiso de trabajo*) at the Oficina de Extranjería (*see below*). Getting good legal advice is important, given the length of the process and possible rule changes.

Delegación del Gobierno – Oficina de Extranjería (Non-EU citizens)

Avda Marquès de l'Argentera 4, sala A, Barceloneta (information 93 482 05 44/appointments 93 520 14 10). Metro Barceloneta. **Open** *information & appointment lines* 9am-2pm Mon-Fri. *Office* 9.30am-5.30pm Mon-Thur; 9am-2pm Fri. **Map** p345 C4.

On making the application for your residency card and work permit, you will need to submit the following documents, along with the completed application form (available at www.mir.es/extranje/modelos/ex01.pdf): a photocopy of a valid passport; a police certificate from your home city stating you don't have a criminal record (translated into Spanish by a sworn translator; *see p309*); an official medical certificate (obtained on arrival in Spain); three identical passport photographs; where applicable, documents proving why you are more capable of performing the job than an EU citizen, and, where necessary, proof that you have the qualifications or training required for the job.

Work permits and residency cards are valid for a year when first issued; the second for two; the third for three. After five years, you are granted a permanent work permit that, though valid indefinitely, must be renewed every five years.

Average monthly climate

	Max temp (C°/F°)	Min temp (C°/F°)	Rainfall (mm/in)
Jan	13/56	6/43	44/1.7
Feb	15/59	7/45	36/1.4
Mar	16/61	8/47	48/1.9
Apr	18/64	10/50	51/2
May	21/70	14/57	57/2.2
June	24/76	17/63	38/1.5
July	27/81	20/67	22/0.9
Aug	29/84	20/67	66/2.6
Sept	25/78	18/64	79/3.1
Oct	22/71	14/57	94/3.7
Nov	17/63	9/49	74/2.9
Dec	15/59	7/45	50/2.5

Directory

Spanish Vocabulary

Spanish is generally referred to as *castellano* (Castilian) rather than *español*. Although many locals prefer to speak Catalan, everyone in the city can speak Spanish, and will switch to it if visitors show signs of linguistic jitters. The Spanish familiar for 'you' – *tú* – is used very freely, but it's safer to use the more formal *usted* with older people and strangers (verbs below are given in the *usted* form).

For menu terms and for street names, *see p167*.

Spanish pronunciation

c before an **i** or an **e** and **z** are like **th** in **th**in
c in all other cases is as in **c**at
g before an **i** or an **e** and **j** are pronounced with a guttural **h**-sound that doesn't exist in English – like **ch** in Scottish loch, but much harder;
g in all other cases is as in **g**et
h at the beginning of a word is normally silent
ll is pronounced almost like a **y**
ñ is like **ny** in ca**ny**on
a single **r** at the beginning of a word and **rr** elsewhere are heavily rolled

Stress rules

In words ending with a vowel, **n** or **s**, the penultimate syllable is stressed: eg *barato, viven, habitaciones.* In words ending with any other consonant, the last syllable is stressed: eg *exterior, universidad.* An accent marks the stressed syllable in words that depart from these rules: eg *estación, tónica.*

Useful expressions

hello *hola*; hello (when answering the phone) *hola, diga*
good morning, good day *buenos días*; good afternoon, good evening *buenas tardes*; good evening (after dark), good night *buenas noches*
goodbye/see you later *adiós/hasta luego*
please *por favor*; thank you (very much) *(muchas) gracias*; you're welcome *de nada*
do you speak English? *¿habla*

inglés?; **I don't speak Spanish** *no hablo castellano*
I don't understand *no entiendo*
can you say that to me in Catalan, please? *¿me lo puede decir en catalán, por favor?*
what's your name? *¿cómo se llama?*
speak more slowly, please *hable más despacio, por favor*, **wait a moment** *espere un momento*
Sir/Mr *señor (sr)*; **Madam/Mrs** *señora (sra)*; **Miss** *señorita (srta)*
excuse me/sorry *perdón*;
excuse me, please *oiga* (the standard way to attract someone's attention, politely; literally, 'hear me')
OK/fine/(to a waiter) **that's enough** *vale*
where is...? *¿dónde está...?*
why? *¿porqué?*; **when?** *¿cuándo?*;
who? *¿quién?*; **what?** *¿qué?*;
where? *¿dónde?*; **how?** *¿cómo?*
who is it? *¿quién es?*; **is/are there any...?** *¿hay...?*
very *muy*; **and** *y*; **or** *o*; **with** *con*;
without *sin*
open *abierto*; **closed** *cerrado*;
what time does it open/close? *¿a qué hora abre/cierra?*
pull (on signs) *tirar*; **push** *empujar*
I would like *quiero*; **how many would you like?** *¿cuántos quiere?*;
how much is it *¿cuánto es?*
I like *me gusta*; **I don't like** *no me gusta*
good *bueno/a*; **bad** *malo/a*; **well/badly** *bien/mal*; **small** *pequeño/a*;
big *gran, grande*; **expensive** *caro/a*; **cheap** *barato/a*; **hot** (food, drink) *caliente*; **cold** *frío/a*;
something *algo*; **nothing** *nada*
more/less *más/menos*; **more or less** *más o menos*
do you have any change? *¿tiene cambio?*
price *precio*; **free** *gratis*; **discount** *descuento*; **bank** *banco*; **to rent** *alquilar*, **(for) rent, rental** *(en) alquiler*; **post office** *correos*; **stamp** *sello*; **postcard** *postal*; **toilet** *los servicios*

Getting around

airport *aeropuerto*; railway station *estación de ferrocarril/estación de RENFE* (Spanish railways); metro station *estación de metro*
entrance *entrada*; exit *salida*
car *coche*; bus *autobús*; train *tren*; a ticket *un billete*; return *de ida y vuelta*; bus stop *parada de autobús*; the next stop *la próxima parada*
excuse me, do you know the way to...? *¿oiga, señor/señora/etc, sabe cómo llegar a...?*
left *izquierda*; right *derecha*
here *aquí*; there *allí*; straight on

recto; to the end of the street *al final de la calle*; as far as *hasta*; towards *hacia*; near *cerca*; far *lejos*

Accommodation

do you have a double/single room for tonight/one week? *¿tiene una habitación doble/para una persona/para esta noche/una semana?*
we have a reservation *tenemos reserva*; an inside/outside room *una habitación interior/exterior*
with/without bathroom *con/sin baño*; shower *ducha*; double bed *cama de matrimonio*; with twin beds *con dos camas*; breakfast included *desayuno incluido*; air-conditioning *aire acondicionado*; lift *ascensor*; pool *piscina*

Time

now *ahora*; later *más tarde*;
yesterday *ayer*; today *hoy*;
tomorrow *mañana*; tomorrow morning *mañana por la mañana*; morning *la mañana*; midday *mediodía*; afternoon/evening *la tarde*; night *la noche*; late night (roughly 1-6am) *la madrugada*
at what time...? *¿a qué hora...?*; at 2 *a las dos*; at 8pm *a las ocho de la tarde*; at 1.30 *a la una y media*; at 5.15 *a las cinco y cuarto*; in an hour *en una hora*

Numbers

0 *cero*; 1 *un, uno, una*; 2 *dos*; 3 *tres*;
4 *cuatro*; 5 *cinco*; 6 *seis*; 7 *siete*;
8 *ocho*; 9 *nueve*; 10 *diez*; 11 *once*;
12 *doce*; 13 *trece*; 14 *catorce*; 15 *quince*; 16 *dieciséis*; 17 *diecisiete*;
18 *dieciocho*; 19 *diecinueve*; 20 *veinte*; 21 *veintiuno*; 22 *veintidós*;
30 *treinta*; 40 *cuarenta*; 50 *cincuenta*; 60 *sesenta*; 70 *setenta*;
80 *ochenta*; 90 *noventa*; 100 *cien*;
200 *doscientos*; 1,000 *mil*;
1,000,000 *un millón*

Date & season

Monday *lunes*; Tuesday *martes*;
Wednesday *miércoles*; Thursday *jueves*; Friday *viernes*; Saturday *sábado*; Sunday *domingo*
January *enero*; February *febrero*;
March *marzo*; April *abril*; May *mayo*; June *junio*; July *julio*;
August *agosto*; September *septiembre*; October *octubre*;
November *noviembre*; December *diciembre*
spring *primavera*; summer *verano*;
autumn/fall *otoño*; winter *invierno*

Catalan Vocabulary

Over a third of Barcelona residents use Catalan as their predominant everyday language, around 70 per cent speak it fluently, and more than 90 per cent understand it. If you take an interest and learn a few phrases, it is likely to be appreciated.

Catalan phonetics are significantly different from those of Spanish, with a wider range of vowel sounds and soft consonants. Catalans use the familiar (*tu*) rather than the polite (*vostè*) forms of the second person very freely, but for convenience verbs are given here in the polite form.

For menu terms and for street names, *see p167*.

Pronunciation

In Catalan, as in French but unlike in Spanish, words are run together, so *si us plau* (please) is more like *sees-plow*.

à at the end of a word (as in Francesc Macià) is an open **a** rather like *ah*, but very clipped
ç, and **c** before an **i** or an **e**, are like a soft **s**, as in sit; **c** in all other cases is as in cat
e, when unstressed as in *cerveses* (beers), or Jaume I, is a weak sound like centre or comfortable
g before **i** or **e** and **j** are pronounced like the **s** in plea*s*ure; **tg** and **tj** are similar to the **dg** in ba**dg**e
g after an **i** at the end of a word (Puig) is a hard ch sound, as in wat**ch**; **g** in all other cases is as in get
h is silent
ll is somewhere between the **y** in yes and the **lli** in mi**lli**on
l·l, the most unusual feature of Catalan spelling, has a slightly stronger stress on a single **l** sound, so paral·lel sounds similar to the English para**ll**el
o at the end of a word is like the **u** sound in fl**u**; **ó** at the end of a word is similar to the **o** in tomato; **ò** is like the **o** in h**o**t
r beginning a word and **rr** are heavily rolled; but at the end of many words is almost silent, so carrer (street) sounds like carr-ay
s at the beginning of words and **ss** between vowels are soft, as in sit; a single **s** between two vowels is

a **z** sound, as in la**z**y
t after **l** or **n** at the end of a word is almost silent
x at the beginning of a word, or after a consonant or the letter **i**, is like the **sh** in **sh**oe, at other times like the English e**x**pert
y after an **n** at the end of a word or in **nys** is not a vowel but adds a nasal stress and a y-sound to the n

Basics

please *si us plau*; **very good/ great/OK** *molt bé*
hello *hola*; **goodbye** *adéu*
open *obert*; **closed** *tancat*
entrance *entrada*; **exit** *sortida*
nothing at all/*zilch res de res* (said with both s silent)
price *preu*; **free** *gratuit/de franc*; **change, exchange** *canvi*
to rent *llogar*; **(for) rent, rental** *(de) lloguer*

More expressions

hello (when answering the phone) *hola, digui'm*
good morning, good day *bon dia*; **good afternoon, good evening** *bona tarda*; **good night** *bona nit*
thank you (very much) *(moltes) gràcies*; **you're welcome** *de res*
do you speak English? *parla anglès?*; **I'm sorry, I don't speak Catalan** *ho sento, no parlo català*
I don't understand *no entenc*
can you say it to me in Spanish, please? *m'ho pot dir en castellà, si us plau?*
how do you say that in Catalan? *com se diu això en català?*
what's your name? *com se diu?*
Sir/Mr *senyor (sr)*; **Madam/Mrs** *senyora (sra)*; **Miss** *senyoreta (srta)*
excuse me/sorry *perdoni/disculpi*; **excuse me, please** *escolti* (literally, 'listen to me'); **OK/fine** *val/d'acord*
how much is it? *quant és?*
why? *perquè?*; **when?** *quan?*; **who?** *qui?*; **what?** *què?*; **where?** *on?*; **how?** *com?*; **where is…?** *on és…?*; **who is it?** *qui és?*; **is/are there any…?** *hi ha…?/n'hi ha de…?*
very *molt*; **and** *i* or *o*; **with** *amb*; **without** *sense*; **enough** *prou*
I would like… *vull…* (literally, 'I want'); **how many would you like?** *quants en vol?*; **I don't want** *no vull*; **I like** *m'agrada*; **I don't like** *no m'agrada*
good *bo/bona*; **bad** *dolent/a*; **well/badly** *bé/malament*; **small** *petit/a*; **big** *gran*; **expensive** *car/a*; **cheap** *barat/a*; **hot** (food, drink) *calent/a*; **cold** *fred/a*
something *alguna cosa*; **nothing**

res; **more** *més*; **less** *menys*; **more or less** *més o menys*
toilet *el bany/els serveis/el lavabo*

Getting around

a ticket *un bitllet*; **return** *d'anada i tornada*; **card expired** (on metro) *títol esgotat*
left *esquerra*; **right** *dreta*; **here** *aquí*; **there** *allí*; **straight on** *recte*; **at the corner** *a la cantonada*; **as far as** *fins a*; **towards** *cap a*; **near** *a prop*; **far** *lluny*; **is it far?** *és lluny?*

Time

In Catalan, quarter- and half-hours can be referred to as quarters of the next hour (so, 1.30 is two quarters of 2).

now *ara*; **later** *més tard*; **yesterday** *ahir*; **today** *avui*; **tomorrow** *demà*; **tomorrow morning** *demà pel matí*; **midday** *migdia*; **morning** *el matí*; **afternoon** *la tarda*; **evening** *el vespre*; **night** *la nit*; **late night** (roughly, 1-6am) *la matinada*
at what time…? *a quina hora…?*; **in an hour** *en una hora*
at 2 *a les dues*; **at 8pm** *a les vuit del vespre*; **at 1.30** *a dos quarts de dues/a la una i mitja*; **at 5.15** *a un quart de sis/a las cinc i quart*; **at 22.30** *a vint-i-dos-trenta*

Numbers

0 *zero*; **1** *u, un, una*; **2** *dos, dues*; **3** *tres*; **4** *quatre*; **5** *cinc*; **6** *sis*; **7** *set*; **8** *vuit*; **9** *nou*; **10** *deu*; **11** *onze*; **12** *dotze*; **13** *tretze*; **14** *catorze*; **15** *quinze*; **16** *setze*; **17** *disset*; **18** *divuit*; **19** *dinou*; **20** *vint*; **21** *vint-i-u*; **22** *vint-i-dos, vint-i-dues*; **30** *trenta*; **40** *quaranta*; **50** *cinquanta*; **60** *seixanta*; **70** *setanta*; **80** *vuitanta*; **90** *noranta*; **100** *cent*; **200** *dos-cents, dues-centes*; **1,000** *mil*; **1,000,000** *un milló*

Date & season

Monday *dilluns*; **Tuesday** *dimarts*; **Wednesday** *dimecres*; **Thursday** *dijous*; **Friday** *divendres*; **Saturday** *dissabte*; **Sunday** *diumenge*
January *gener*; **February** *febrer*; **March** *març*; **April** *abril*; **May** *maig*; **June** *juny*; **July** *juliol*; **August** *agost*; **September** *setembre*; **October** *octobre*; **November** *novembre*; **December** *desembre*
spring *primavera*; **summer** *estiu*; **autumn/fall** *tardor*; **winter** *hivern*

Directory

Further Reference

Food & drink

Andrews, Colman *Catalan Cuisine*
A mine of information on food and much else (also with usable recipes).
Davidson, Alan *Tio Pepe Guide to the Seafood of Spain and Portugal*
An excellent pocket-sized guide with illustrations of Spain's fishy delights.

Guides & walks

Amelang, J, Gil, X & McDonogh, GW *Twelve Walks through Barcelona's Past*
(Ajuntament de Barcelona) Well-thought-out walks by historical theme. Original, and better informed than many walking guides.
Güell, Xavier *Gaudí Guide* A handy guide, with good background on all the architect's work.
Pomés Leiz, Juliet, & Feriche, Ricardo *Barcelona Design Guide*
An eccentrically wide-ranging but engaging listing of everything ever considered 'designer' in BCN.

History, architecture, art & culture

Burns, Jimmy *Barça: A People's Passion* The first full-scale history in English of one of the world's most overblown football clubs.
Elliott, JH *The Revolt of the Catalans* Fascinating, detailed account of the Guerra dels Segadors and the Catalan revolt of the 1640s.
Fernández Armesto, Felipe *Barcelona: A Thousand Years of the City's Past* A solid history.
Fraser, Ronald *Blood of Spain* A vivid oral history of the Spanish Civil War and the tensions that preceded it. It is especially good on the events of July 1936 in Barcelona.
Hooper, John *The New Spaniards* An incisive and very readable survey of the changes in Spanish society since the death of Franco.
Hughes, Robert *Barcelona* The most comprehensive single book about Barcelona: tendentious at times, erratic, but beautifully written, and covering every aspect of the city up to the 1992 Olympics.
Kaplan, Temma *Red City, Blue Period: Social Movements in Picasso's Barcelona*
An interesting book, tracing the interplay of avant-garde art and avant-garde politics in the 1900s.
Orwell, George *Homage to Catalonia* The classic account of

Barcelona in revolution, as written by an often bewildered, but always perceptive observer.
Paz, Abel *Durruti, The People Armed* A biography of the most legendary of Barcelona's anarchists.
Solà-Morales, Ignasi *Fin de Siècle Architecture in Barcelona*
Large-scale and wide-ranging description of the city's Modernista heritage.
Tóibín, Colm *Homage to Barcelona* Evocative and perceptive journey around the city: good on the booming Barcelona of the 1980s.
van Hensbergen, Gijs *Gaudí* A thorough account of the life of the architect.
Vázquez Montalbán, Manuel *Barcelonas* Idiosyncratic but insightful reflections on the city by one of its most prominent modern writers.
Zerbst, Rainer *Antoni Gaudí* Lavishly illustrated and comprehensive survey.

Literature

Calders, Pere *The Virgin of the Railway and Other Stories*
Ironic, engaging, quirky stories by a Catalan writer who spent many years in exile in Mexico.
Català, Victor *Solitude*
This masterpiece by female novelist Caterina Albert shocked readers in 1905 with its open, modern treatment of female sexuality.
Marsé, Juan *The Fallen* Classic novel of survival in Barcelona during the long *posguerra* after the Civil War.
Martorell, Joanot, & Martí de Gualba, Joan *Tirant lo Blanc*
The first European prose novel, from 1490, a rambling, bawdy, shaggy-dog story of travels, romances and chivalric adventures.
Mendoza, Eduardo *City of Marvels*; *Year of the Flood*
A sweeping saga of the city between its great Exhibitions in 1888 and 1929; and a more recent novel of passions in the city of the 1950s.
Oliver, Maria-Antònia *Antipodes*; *Study in Lilac*
Two adventures of Barcelona's first feminist detective.
Rodoreda, Mercè *The Time of the Doves*; *My Cristina and Other Stories*
A translation of *Plaça del Diamant*, most widely read of all Catalan novels; plus a collection of similarly bittersweet short tales.
Ruiz Zafón, Carlos *Shadow of the Wind* Required beach reading of recent years; enjoyable neo-Gothic melodrama set in post-war Barcelona.

Vázquez Montalbán, Manuel *The Angst-Ridden Executive*; *An Olympic Death*; *Southern Seas*
Three thrillers starring detective and gourmet Pepe Carvalho.

Angel Molina Leading Barcelona DJ with an international reputation and various remix albums released.
Barcelona Raval Sessions Dance/funk compilation of local artists, famous and unknown, conceived as a soundtrack to the city's most dynamic and multicultural *barrio*.
Lluís Llach An icon of the 1960s and early '70s protest against the fascist regime combines a melancholic tone with brilliant musicianship. One of the first to experiment with electronic music.
Maria del Mar Bonet Though from Mallorca, del Mar Bonet always sings in Catalan and specialises in her own compositions, North African music and traditional Mallorcan music.
Ojos de Brujo Current darlings of world music awards everywhere and leading proponents of *rumba catalana* fused with flamenco.
Pep Sala Excellent musician and survivor of the extremely successful Catalan group Sau. Sala now produces his own music, much of which shows a rockabilly and country influence.

www.barcelonarocks.com
Music listings and news.
www.barcelonaturisme.com
Information from the city's official tourist authority.
www.bcn.es The city council's information-packed website.
www.catalanencyclopaedia.com
Comprehensive English-language reference work covering Catalan history, geography and 'who's who'.
www.diaridebarcelona.com
Local online newspaper with good English content.
www.lecool.com Excellent weekly round-up of offbeat and interesting cultural events in the city.
www.mobilitat.net Generalitat's website getting from A to B in Catalonia, by bus, car or train.
www.renfe.es Spanish railways' website, with online booking.
www.timeout.com/barcelona
The online city guide, with a select monthly agenda.
www.vilaweb.com Catalan web portal and links page; in Catalan.

Directory

Index

Note: Page numbers in **bold**
indicate section(s) giving key
information on a topic; *italics*
indicate photographs.

a

Abellan, Carles 157
abortion 312
accident & emergency 312
accommodation 50-80
by price:
    budget 55-59, 61, 63, 64,
    73-75, 77
    expensive 53, 59, 63-64,
    65-70, 74, 77
    mid-range 53-55, 59-61, 63,
    64, 70-73, 75, 77, 79
apartment hotels 79
apartment & room rentals
    79-80
booking agencies 51
campsites 80
hotels 50-79
    the best 51
    for students 318
    suites, the best 56
    youth hostels 80
addresses 308
Adrià, Ferran 144, **171**
Aerobús 304
age restrictions 308
AIDS 312
Aiguablava 292
Aiguafreda 292
Aiguamolls de l'Empordà 297
air, arriving & leaving by 304
airlines 304
airport 304
Ajuntament 28, 29, 34, 36, 82, 86,
    87, **88**
albergues 51
Alella 286
Alfaro, Andreu 110
Alfonso XII, King 19
Alfonso XIII, King 21-22
Almirall, Valentí 19
Almodóvar, Pedro 230
Almogàvers, the 12
Altafulla 287
ambiente 238
Amenábar, Alejandro 230
Amics de l'Art Nou (ADLAN) 22
anarchism 21
Anella Olímpica 117
Antic Hospital de la Santa Creu
    & La Capella 98, **99**, *99*
Antich, Puig 28
antiques
    markets 191, **212**
    shops 191-192
apartment hotels 79
apartment & room rentals 79-80
Aqua Brava 228
Aquadiver 228
Aquàrium, L' 110, **226**
architecture **35-44**
Arenas, Las 44, **116**, *116*
Aribau, Bonaventura Carles 19
Arnau, Eusebi 39
Arola, Sergi 167
art galleries *see* galleries *and*
    museums & galleries
Articket 83
arts & entertainment **215-276**
arts, performing 262-270
ass, the 32
Ataülf 11
Auditori Winterthur 262, **263**

Auditori, L' 262
Aulenti, Gae 44
Autonomy Statute 29
AvuiMúsica 265, *265*
Azaña, Manuel 22
Aznar, José María 34

b

babysitting 229
Badalona 141
Bagà 299
Bagdad, the 121
Baixador de Vallvidrera 135
Baja Beach Club 250-251
banks 316
'Barrio Chino' 21, 110, 128
bars *see* cafés, tapas & bars
Bases de Manresa, the 19
basketball 271
Bassa, Ferrer 138
Baumgarten, Lothar 114
beaches
    in Barcelona 111
    in Catalonia 292
'Bears' 240
beauty treatments 210-211
beer 173
Begur 291, 292
Begutti, Domenico 142
Bellesguard *see* Torre Figueres
Bellver de Cerdanya 300
Berenguer, Francesc 133
Berenguer, General 22
Berga 299
Besalú 36, **301**
Betlem church 37, **99**
bicycles 307
    hire 307
    tours 85
birdwatching 289, 297
Bisbal, La 291
Black Death, the 15
Blanes 281, **292**
Blay, Miquel 39
Bofill, Ricard 110, 114, 117
Bohigas, Oriol 29, 42, **44**
Bonell, Esteve 44
Book & Coin Market 212
booking agencies,
    accommodation 51
books 325
    shops 192
Boqueria, La 37, 95, 98, **212**
Born 82, **103-109**

cafés, tapas & bars 179-184
    galleries 235
    music & nightlife 254-255
    restaurants 157-159
    shops 205
    where to stay 63
Borrell II, Count 11
boutiques, fashion 197-198
bowling 274
breakdown services 306
Bruno Quadros building 95
budget fashion shops 198
bullfighting **116**, 272
Bulli, El 144, **171**, 295
Burra, Violeta La 187
bus
    getting around Barcelona by
    306
    getting to and from the airport
    by 304
    tours 85
    travelling around Catalonia
    by 278
business services 308
busking 264

c

Cabet, Étienne 23
cable car 83, 110, **113**, 117, 121
Cabre, Mario 116
Caçamentides 229
Cadaqués 295
cafés, tapas & bars 173-188
    best bars in hotels 71
    best places 173
    for children 228
    displaying art 236
    gay & lesbian 238-239
CaixaForum 109, **117**, 225
Calafell 286
Calatrava, Santiago 117, 141
Caldes d'Estrac 281
Caldetes 281
Calella 280, **281**, 292
Calella de Palafrugell 292
Cambó, Francesc 21
Camí de Ronda 292
Campana de Gràcia, La 131, 134
Campelles 301
campsites 80
Can Batlló 133
Can Cortada 141
Can Dragó 142
Can Mariner 141
Can Ricart 97
Canadença, La 121
Canet 280
Cap d'Any (New Year's Eve) 224
Cap de Creus 295
Capella, La 99
Capella d'en Marcús 36, **104**,
    108
Capella Reial de Catalunya, La
    264
Capitania General 88
car 306-307
    arriving and leaving by 304
    hire 307
    travelling around Catalonia
    by 278
Carbonell, Guillem 37
Cardapeçois 229
Carlist Wars 17
Carnestoltes (king of carnival)
    224, 227
Carod Rivera, Josep 34
Carrero Blanco, Admiral 28
Casa de les Altures 142

Casa Amatller 39, 43, **123**
Casa de l'Ardiaca 86
Casa Batlló 41, 43, 46, *47*, **48**,
    122, **123**, *123*
Casa Bloc 43, **142**
Casa Boada 130
Casa Calvet 48, 125, **161**
Casa dels Canonges 86
Casa de la Caritat **98**, 99
Casa Casas 123
Casa Comalat 124
Casa Dolors Xiró 124
Casa Fargas 128
Casa Fuster **74-75**, 133
Casa Golferichs 130
Casa Isabel Pomar 124
Casa Jacinta Ruiz 124
Casa Jaume Forn 124
Casa Josep Thomas 124
Casa Juncadella 128
Casa Lleó Morera 43, **123**
Casa Llorenç Camprubí 125
Casa Macaya 41
Casa Manuel Felip 125
Casa Manuel Llopis i Bofill 124
Casa Milà *see* Pedrera, La
Casa Navàs, Reus 41
Casa de les Punxes 41, **124**, *125*
Casa de les Rajoles, La 121
Casa Ramon Oller 125
Casa Rull, Reus 41
Casa Serra 128
Casa Terrades *see* Casa de les
    Punxes
Casa Vicens 40, **133**, *138*
Casa Vidua Marfà 123
Casa de la Vila 133
Casa Villanueva 124
Casa-Museu Gaudí 133
Casa-Museu de Port Lligat 297
Casas, Ramon 21, 39, 123
Cases Pons i Pascual 123
Cases Tomàs Roger 125
Castanyada, La 222
Castell de Montgrí 294
Castell de Montjuïc 10, **115**
Castell de Púbol **291**, 292, *296*
Castell de Sant Salvador 296
Castell dels Tres Dragons 41
Castelldefels 279
Castellers 221, 272
Castellfollit de la Roca 301
Catalan Gothic architecture 13,
    36
Catalan National Day 16
'Catalan Republic', the 25
Catalan Romanesque art 11
Catalunya en Miniatura 228
catamaran cruises 110, **113**, 279
Cathedral 36, 83, **89**
Cavalcada dels Reis 224
Caves Codorníu 12
CCCB (Centre de Cultura
    Contemporània de Barcelona)
    44, 83, **98**, **99**, *101*, 267
Cellar Capçanes 286
Cellar de Garraf 279
Cellers Scala Dei 286
Cementiri de l'Est 141
Cementiri del Sud-Oest 118
Centre d'Art Santa Mònica 95
Centre de Cultura
    Contemporània de Barcelona
    see CCCB
Centre d'Informació de la
    Virreina 83
Centre de Modernisme 123
Cerdà, Ildefons 19, 23, **37-38**,

122, 141
Cerdanya 299
Cervantes, Miguel de 18
Charles II, King 16
Charles V, Holy Roman Emperor
15, *17*
Charles of Austria, Archduke 16
charnego 33
childcare 229
Chillida, Eduardo 140
Chino, Barrio *see* Barrio Chino
Chupa Chups 207
churrerias 166
cinema, outdoor 232
cinemas 231-232
Cistercian Route, the 287
City Hall *see* Ajuntament
Ciutat Sanitària 142
Ciutat del Teatre 117
Civil War *24-25*, **25-27**, 87, 92
Claris, Pau 16
Catalan language 11, 19, 34, 310,
324
classes 318
children 225-229
shops 195
chocolate
museum 107
shops 208
classical music *see* music,
classical & opera
Clàssics als Parcs **220**, 263
Clavé, Josep Anselm 23
cleaning services 195
climate 321, 322
Clos, Joan 29, 34, 42
Clos, Jordi 129
clothes shops 197-205
clubs *see* nightclubs
CNT (Confederación Nacional del
Trabajo) **21-22**, 25, 26, 27, 97
Coco, El 229
Codorniu 286
coffee 173
Coixet, Isabel 231
Col·legi d'Arquitectes 86
Col·legi de les Teresianes 40, 48,
137
Collserola 135-136
Colònia Güell 40, 46, **48**, **282**,
282
Columbus, Christopher 87, 89,
110, 113
communications tower 117
Companys, Lluís **25**, 115
complaints 309
complementary medicine 312
computer services 308
Comunitat Israelita de Barcelona
317
Comunitat Jueva Atid de
Catalunya 317
Concert des Nations, Le 264
Consell de Cent 12
consulates 309
contraception 312
Convent dels Àngels 98
Convent de Sant Agustí 104
Convent de Santa Caterina 104
conventions & conferences 308
Convergència i Unió 28
Corbusier, Le 43
Correa, Federico 117
Corte Inglés, El 189, **191**, 195,
212
Corts, Les 12, 134
cosmetics & perfume shops 211
CosmoCaixa 44, *132*, **137**, 225,
226
Costa Brava 292-295
Costa Daurada 286-287
Count-Duke of Olivares 15
Counts of Barcelona 11
courier services 308
credit and debit cards 316
Culés 273

currency exchanges 316
Cursa del Corte Inglés, La 272
customs allowances 310
cycling 274

d

Dagoll Dagom 269
Dalí, Salvador 22, 291, 295, 296
dance 266-270
festivals 220, 267
see also flamenco
Decadència, the 15
Deltebre 289
Demano 199, *199*
dentists 313
department stores 189-191
design & homeware shops 195
Design Museum *see* Museu de
Desseny
designer fashion shops 198-200
Desmortización, the 17
Dia del Treball (May Day) 217
Diada Nacional de Catalunya 16,
221
Diagonal Mar 141, 189, **191**
Dies de Dansa **220**, 267
disabled travellers 311
discount schemes 83
doctors 313
Domènech i Muntaner, Lluís
38, **41**, 43, 74-75, 86, 102, 105,
107, 108, 122, 123, 124, 127,
133, 263
Don Juan de Austria 112
Don Quixote 18
Dragon Gate, Pedralbes 48
Drassanes, the 13, 37, 110, 102
Dreta, the 122-129
driving *see* car
drugs 311
Durutti 25

e

Ebre Delta 289
Edifici Fòrum 44, **141**
Edifici de Gas Natural 42
Eixample, the 19, 23, 37-39, 82,
122-130
cafés, tapas & bars 185-186
galleries 235-237
gay & lesbian
cafés & bars 238-239
nightclubs 240-241
music & nightlife 257-260
restaurants 159-163
shops 205
where to stay 65-75
electricity 311
emergencies 311
Empúries 295
Encants, Els 212
entertainment *see* arts &
entertainment
ERC (Esquerra Republicana) **29**,
34, 134
Escala, L' 295
Escola Industrial 130
Espai, L' 267
Espai Gaudí
Espanya Industrial, L' 133
Espanyol Football Club *see* RCD
Espanyol
Espriu, Salvador 74
Esquerra, the 130
Esquerra Republicana 22
Estació d'Autobusos Barcelona-
Nord 304
Estació d'Autobusos Barcelona-
Sants 304
Estació de França 22, 305
Estadi Olímpic de Montjuïc 83,
117, 272
Estartit, L' 292
ETA 28

etiquette 312
Eulàlia (saint) 10, 89, **91**
events *see* festivals & events

f

Fabra, Pompeu 21
Fábrica Casaramona 41
FAD 98
Fageda d'en Jordà 302
Falqués, Pere 122
Falset 286
Fanelli, Giuseppe 19
Farmàcia Argelaguet 124
Farmàcia Nordbeck 125
Farmàcia Vilardell 125
fashion & accessories shops
197-207
fast food 166
FC Barcelona 28, **134**, 271, **272**,
273
febre d'or 19
Ferdinand of Aragon & Isabella
of Castile **15**, *16*, 87, 89
Ferdinand VII, King 17
Feria de Abril de Catalunya 217
Fernández i Janot 125
Fernando de Antequera 15
Ferrer, Francesc 21
ferries 304
Festa dels Cors de la Barceloneta
219
Festa dels Tres Tombs 224
Festa Major de la Barceloneta
222
Festa Major de Gràcia 131, **220**
Festa Major de Sants 220
Festa de la Música 219
Festes de la Mercè 222
Festes de Sant Medir de Gràcia
217, 227
Festival de Flamenco de Ciutat
Vella 217
Festival del Grec 220
Festival L'Hora del Jazz,
Memòria Tete Montollu 221
Festival Internacional de Cinema
de Catalunya, Sitges **233**, 280
Festival International de Jazz de
Barcelona 222
Festival de Música Antiga **217**,
262, 263
Festival de Músiques del Món
223
Festival d'Òpera de Butxaca i
Noves Creacions 266
Festival de Tardor Ribermúsica
222
festivals & events **216-224**
children's 227
dance 220, 267
film 233
flamenco 217
jazz 221, 222
music 217, 219, 220, 222, 223,
266
poetry 217
theatre 220, 266
wine 222
Feu, Modest 134
Figueras, Jean Luc 165
Figueres 296-297
film **230-233**
for children 227
Filmoteca de la Generalitat de
Catalunya 98, 128, 227, **232**
Fira de Barcelona 115, **308**
Fira de Santa Llúcia **212**, 224
fitness *see* sport & fitness
flag, origin of Catalan 11
flamenco 270
festival 217
Floresta, La 31
flower shops & stalls 95,
207-208
Font de Canaletes 95

Font del Gat information centre
117
Font Màgica de Montjuïc 117,
118, 225
Fontseré, Josep 108
food & drink
fairs 212
shops 208-209
football **272**, 275
Forestier, JCN 117
Fornells 292
Fòrum Universal de les Cultures
of 2004 26, 31, 42, 44, 141
Fossar de les Moreres 16, **105**
Fossas i Martínez 124
Foster, Norman 42, 44, 135, 137
Franco, General Francisco 27-28
Franks, the 11
Fraternidad, La 23
Freixenet 286
Fundació Antoni Tàpies 123,
125
Fundació Foto Colectània 133
Fundació Francisco Godia 123,
127
Fundació Joan Miró 43, 83, 115,
118, 185, 228, 262, 266
funfair 135, **226**
Funicular de Tibidabo 117, **135**

g

'Gaixample' 238-239
Galería Olímpica 118
galleries **234-237**
see also museums & galleries
Gallissà i Soqué 124
Gandules 232
García Oliver 25
gargoyles 39, *39*
Garraf 279, 279
Garriga, La 43
Garrotxa, La 278, **302**
GATCPAC 22, 43
Gaudí, Antoni 26, 39, 40-41, 43,
45-48, 82, 88, 89, 99, 122,
123, 124, 125, 129, 133, 161,
279, 282
don't miss Gaudí creations 46
Bellesguard *see* Torre
Figueres
Casa Batlló 41, 43, 46, *47*, **48**,
122, **123**, *123*
Casa Calvet 48, 125, **161**
Casa Milà *see* Pedrera, La
Casa-Museu Gaudí 133
Casa Vicens 40, **133**, *138*
Cellar de Garraf 279
Col·legi de les Teresianes 40,
48, **137**
Colònia Güell 40, 46, **48**, **282**,
282
Dragon Gate, Pedralbes 48
Espai Gaudí
Palau Güell 40, 46, **48**, 95, 102
Parc de la Ciutadella 40, 108
Park Güell 41, *45*, 46, *47*, **48**,
48, 82, 83, **133**, 227
Pavellons de la Finca Güell
137
Pedrera, La (Casa Milà) *35*, 41,
45-46, 46, *47*, 48, 82, 83,
122, **129**, 263
Plaça Reial 40, 88
Sagrada Família, La 39, 40,
40-41, 46, *47*, **48**, 82, 83,
123, **129**, *130*
Torre Figueres 137
gay & lesbian Barcelona 238-245
organisations 312
Gegants 223
Gehry, Frank 31, 42, 114
Generalitat 12, 22, 25, 29, 82, 86,
88, **93**, *93* *see also* Palau de
la Generalitat
gift shops 210

Girona **290-291**, *293*, 294
Godia, Francisco 127
Golden Age, the Catalan 13-15
golf 275
Golondrinas, Las 110, **113**
de Gómina, Erasme 16
Gósol 299
Gothic Quarter *see* Barri Gòtic
Gràcia 82, **131-133**
  cafés, tapas & bars 186-188
  galleries 237
  music & nightlife 260
  restaurants 163-167
  shops 205
  where to stay 75-77
Gran Teatre del Liceu *see* Liceu
Gran Trobada d'Havaneres 220
Granyer, Josep 128
Grec Festival **220**, 266
Gremial dels Velers 37
Grupo Prisa 34
Guëll, Eusebi 40, 48, 102, 133, 282
Guerin, José Luis 102
Guerra dels Segadors, the 16
Guifré el Pilós, Count *see* Wilfred the Hairy, Count
Guinardó 142
Guinjoan, Joan 262
gyms 275

h

Hadid, Zaha 42
hair & beauty 210-211
hairdressers 211
  gay & lesbian 244
handball 272
Hangar 234, **237**
health 312-313
helplines 313
Herzog and de Meuron 44, 141
Hespèrion XXI 264
history **10-29**
HIV 312
hockey 272
holidays, public 321
Homa, Gaspar 39
Homage to Catalonia 27, **92**, 116
Homar, Gaspar 129
Home del Sac, L' 229
homeware shops 195-197
Homilies d'Organyà 15
Horn, Rebecca 114
Horta 141-142
  restaurants 171
Hospital Clínic 130
Hospital de Llobregat, L' 142
Hospital de la Santa Creu i Sant Pau 41, 82, 83, 123, **127**
Hospitalet, L' 31
hostels, youth 80
Hotel Colón 25
hotels *see* accommodation

i

Icaria 23
ice skating 275
Ictíneo, the 23, *23*
ICV 29
ID 313
de la Iglesia, Alex 231
Illa, L' 189, **191**
Illa de Fantasia 228
Illa Pangea 141
Illa de la Rambla de Raval, L' 98
Illa Roja 292
Illes Medes 292
IMAX Port Vell 110, **227**, **232**
immigration 33, 97-98, **321**
Institut d'Estudis Catalans 21
Institut Pere Mata 41
Institut de Teatre 266
insurance 314

International Exhibition of 1929 **22**, 43, 115, 120
internet 314
Isabel II, Queen 17-19
Isabella of Castile *see* Ferdinand of Aragon & Isabella of Castile
Isozaki, Arata 44, 117
IVA 189
Izquierda Unida 29

j

Jan del Gel 229
Jardí Botànic 83, 117, **118**
Jardins de Cervantes *135*, 137
Jardins Cinto Verdaguer 117
Jardins Joan Brossa 117
Jardins Laribal 117
Jardins del Mirador 117
Jardins Mossèn Costa i Llobera 117, **118**
Jardins de la Tamarita **137**, 227
Jaume I 'the Conqueror', Count-King 12
Jaume II 'the Just', Count-King 12
jazz festivals 221, 222
jewellery shops 204-206
Jewish Barcelona 87, 115
jogging 272, **275**
Juan Carlos, King 28
Jujol, Josep Maria 41, 124, 129, 133

l

Laetani, the 10
language
  Catalan 11, 19, 34, 310, **324**
  classes 318
  Spanish 323
Lanz, Alfredo 114
leather & luggage shops 206-207
left luggage 314
legal help 314
LEM Festival **222**, 266
Lennon, John 133
León, Jean 284
León de Aranca, Fernando 230
Lepanto of 1571, Battle of 112
lesbian *see* gay & lesbian Barcelona
libraries 314
Lichtenstein, Roy 113
lingerie shops 203
living in Barcelona 321-322
Llafranc 292
Llena, Antoni 114
Llibre del Consolat de Mar 13
Llibre dels Feits 15
Lliga Anticolonial 32
Lliga Regionalista, the 21-22
Llimona, Josep 39
Lloret de Mar 292
Llotja, La 13, 36, **105**
Llull, Ramon 15
Loop 234
lost property 314
Louis XIII of France, King 16
Louis XIV of France, King 16
Louis the Pious 11
Lower Raval 101-102

m

MACBA (Museu d'Art Contemporani de Barcelona) 44, 83, 97, 98, **101**, 225
Macià, Francesc 22
Mackay, David 44, 140
Magic Fountain see Font Màgica de Montjuïc
malls 189-191
Mancomunitat 21

Manzana de la Discòrdia 43, 83, **122**
maps 305
Maragall, Joan 302
Maragall, Pasqual 29, 34
Marató de l'Espectacle 219
Marca Hispanica 11
Marcús, Bernat 104
Maremàgnum 44, 110, *113*, **191**
Marès, Frederic 93
Maria Cristina, Queen 17
Marineland 228
Mariscal, Javier 110
markets 98, 104, **211-212**
  antiques 191
Marquès de la Mina 17
Marquès de Santa Coloma 16
Martí I 'the Humane', Count-King 15
Martí i Alsina, Ramón 23
Martinell, Cèsar 43
Martorell, Francesc 105
Martorell, Joanot 15
Martorell, Josep 44, 140
'Martyrs of Montjuïc' 21
Masnou, El 281
MBM architects 42, **44**
Medem, Julio 231
media 315
Meier, Richard 42, 44, 101
Meller, Raquel 121
menu glossary 154-155
Mercat de la Boqueria *see* Boqueria, La
Mercat de la Concepció 123
Mercat de les Flors 267
Mercat de la Llibertat 133
Mercat de Sant Antoni 130
Mercat de Santa Caterina **104**, 211
Mercè (saint) 91, 222
Mercè, La 37, **88**
Mercè, festival of La 227
Metro, the 305
Metrònom 105, **266**, 267
Mies van der Rohe, Ludwig 22, 43, 115, 120
Milà, Alfonso 117
Mina, La 141
Mirador del Rei Martí 87
Miralles, Enric 42, 44, 114, 141
Miramar 117
Miró, Joan 22, 95, **118**, 130
MNAC (Museu Nacional d'Art de Catalunya) 44, 117, **119**
mobile phones 320
Model, La 130
Modernisme 19-21, **38-43**, 85, 123, 133, 134
Molina, Francesc Daniel 37
Moll d'Espanya 110
Moll de la Fusta 110
Món Raval 98
monasteries in Catalonia 287-289
Monastir de Pedralbes 48, 137, **138**, 263
Monastir de Poblet **287**, 288
Monastir de Santes Creus **287**, 288
Monastir de Vallbona de les Monges 287, **288**
Moncunill, Lluís 43
Moneo, Rafael 263
money 316
Mons Taber 10, 12, 36
Montblanc 287
Montcada, C/ 15, 37, **104**, 108
Montcada, Guillem Ramon de 104
Montjuïc 44, 83, **115-121**
  music & nightlife 256-257
  restaurants 170
Montjuïc Card 83
'Montjuïc Processes', the 107
Montsant 286
Montserrat 278, **282**

Monturiol, Narcis 23
Monument a Colom 95, 110, **113**
Moreneta, La 282
Moreno, Pedro 187
Mosque Tarik Bin Ziad 317
Mostra de Teatre 266
Mostra de Vins I Caves de Catalunya 222
motor sports 272
motorbike hire 306
Muñoz, Juan 114
Muntaner, Ramon 15
Muret of 1213, Battle of 11
Museu d'Arqueologia de Catalunya 117, **118**
Museu d'Art Contemporani de Barcelona *see* MACBA
Museu de les Arts Decoratives 137, **138**
Museu d'Automates 135
Museu Barbier-Mueller d'Art Precolombí 104, **105**, 262
Museu del Calçat 87, **91**
Museu de Carrosses Fúnebres 123, **127**
Museu Cau Ferrat, Sitges 279
Museu de Cera 95, **226**
Museu de Ceràmica 137, **138**
Museu de Ciències Naturals de la Ciutadella 117
Museu de Dessenv 42, 140
Museu Diocesà 86, **91**
Museu Egipci de Barcelona 123, **129**
Museu de l'Eròtica 96
Museu Etnològic 117, **119**
Museu del FC Barcelona **134**, 225
Museu Frederic Marès 86, **93**
Museu d'Història de Catalunya 12, **113**, 225
Museu d'Història de la Ciutat 87, **92**
Museu de la Màgia 226
Museu Marítim 37, 102, 110, **112**, 262
Museu Militar 115, **120**
Museu Nacional Arqueològic de Tarragona 283, **284**
Museu Nacional d'Art de Catalunya *see* MNAC
Museu del Perfum 127
Museu Picasso 83, 104, **105**, 108
Museu Tèxtil 104, **107**, 108
Museu Verdaguer 135
Museu de la Xocolata **107**, 225, **226**
Museu de Zoologia 41
museums & galleries
  archaeology: Museu d'Arqueologia de Catalunya 117, **118**
  art: CCCB (Centre de Cultura Contemporània de Barcelona) 44, 83, 98, **99**, *101*, 267; Fundació Antoni Tàpies 123, 125; Fundació Francisco Godia 123, **127**; Fundació Joan Miró 83, 115, **118**, 185, 228, 262, 266; MACBA (Museu d'Art Contemporani de Barcelona) 44, 83, 97, 98, **101**, 225; Metrònom 105; MNAC (Museu Nacional d'Art de Catalunya) 44, 117, **119**; Museu Barbier-Mueller d'Art Precolombí 104, **105**, 262; Museu Diocesà 86, **91**; Museu Picasso 83, 104, **105**, 108; Palau de la Virreina 95, **96**; Thyssen-Bornemisza collection **119**, 137
  ceramics: Museu de Ceràmica 137, **138**

chocolate: Museu de la Xocolata 107, 225, **226**
coin-operated machines: Museu d'Automates 135
decorative arts: Museu de les Arts Decoratives 137, **138**
design: Museu de Dessigny 42, 140
Egyptology: Museu Egipci de Barcelona 123, **129**
erotica: Museu de l'Eròtica 96
ethnology: Museu Etnològic 117, **119**
football: Museu del FC Barcelona **134**, 225
funeral carriages: Museu de Carrosses Fúnebres 123, **127**
Gaudí: Casa-Museu Gaudí 133
history: Museu d'Història de Catalunya 12, **113**, 225; Museu d'Història de la Ciutat 87, **92**
literature: Museu Verdaguer 135
magic: Museu de la Màgia 226
maritime: Museu Marítim 37, 102, 110, **112**, 262
military: Museu Militar 115, **120**
miscellaneous: Museu Frederic Marès 86, **93**
music: Metrònom 105
natural history: Museu de Ciències Naturals de la Ciutadella 105; Museu de Zoologia 41
perfume: Museu del Perfum 127
photography: Fundació Foto Colectània 133
science: CosmoCaixa *132*, **137**, 225, **226**
shoes: Museu del Calçat 87, **91**
textiles: Museu Tèxtil 104, **107**, 108
waxworks: Museu de Cera 95, **226**
music
  classical & opera 262-266
  festivals 217, 219, 220, 222, 223, 266
  further reference 325
  rock, roots & dance 246-261
  shops 212-213
Muslims (Moors), the 11-12

Nadal & Sant Esteve (Christmas Day & Boxing Day) 224
Napoleon 17
Natural Gas headquarters 114
Negrin, Juan 27
newspapers 315
nightlife & clubs 246-261
  gay 240-241
  lesbian 243
Ninot, the 130
Nonell, Isidre 39
Nou Barris 142
Nou Camp **134**, 272
Noucentisme 22, **43**
Nous Sons – Músiques Contemporànies 262, **266**
Nouvel, Jean 42, 141
Nova Bocana 110
Nova Planta, decree of 16
Núria 301

OBC (Orquestra Simfònica de Barcelona Nacional de Catalunya) 262

Oda a la Pàtria 19
Off Loop 234
office services 308
Oficines d'Informació Turística 321
Okupas 139
Olot 301
Olympic Stadium *see* Estadi Olímpic
Olympic Village *see* Vila Olímpica
Olympics of 1992 29, 44, 114, 117, 118, 271
one-stop shops 189-191
opening times 316
opera *see* music, classical & opera
opticians 211
orchestras & ensembles 264
Orfeó Català 264
Orquesta Simfònica i Cor del Gran Teatre del Liceu 265
Orquestra Simfònica del Vallès 265
Orwell, George 27, 87, 88, **92**, 116, 123, 129
Ou Com Balla, L' 219

Palacios, Alvaro 286
Palafrugell 292
Palamós 292
Palau Baró de Quadras 124
Palau Berenguer d'Aguilar 108
Palau de la Generalitat 36, 37, 86, 88, **93**, *93*
Palau Güell 40, 46, 48, 95, 102
Palau de Lloctinent 37, **86**, 115
Palau Macaya 123
Palau de Mar 113
Palau dels Marquesos de Lliò 108
Palau Moja 37
Palau de la Música Catalana 41, 83, 103, *104*, **107**, 262, **263**
Palau Nacional 43, 44, **117**
Palau Ramón de Montaner 124
Palau Reial 36, **87**, 137
Palau Robert 321
Palau Sant Jordi 44, **117**
Palau de la Virreina 95, **96**
Palauet de les Heures 142
Pals 291
Paral·lel 121
Parc Central 142
Parc de les Aigües 142
Parc de les Aus 228
Parc del Castell de l'Oreneta 228, *228*
Parc de la Ciutadella 19, 37, 40, 103, *103*, **108**, 225, 227
Parc del Clot 141
Parc de Collserola **135**, 278
Parc de la Creueta del Coll 137, **140**, 227
Parc Diagonal-Mar 44, **141**
Parc de l'Escorxador *see* Parc Joan Miró
Parc de l'Espanya Industrial 134
Parc de l'Estació del Nord 123, **129**
Parc de la Font de Racó 137
Parc del Garraf 279
Parc del Guinardó 142
Parc Joan Miró 130
Parc del Laberint **142**, 227
Parc Natural del Cadí-Moixeró 299
Parc Natural del Delta de l'Ebre 289
Parc de la Pegaso 141
Parc Sol i Ombra *see* Parc de l'Estació del Nord
Parc de les Tres Xemeneies 121
Park Güell 41, *45*, 46, *47*, **48**, *48*, 82, 83, **133**, 227

parking 307
parks for children 227
Parròquia Maria Reina 317
Passatge de les Manufactures 103
Passatge Permanyer 122
Passeig del Born **104**, 108
Passeig de Colom 88
Passeig de Gràcia 83, **122**
Pati Llimona 13
patisseries 208
Pavelló Mies van der Rohe (Pavelló Barcelona) 22, 43, *43*, 115, **120**
Pavelló de la República 43, **142**
Pavellons de la Finca Güell 137
Pedralbes (area) 137
Pedralbes Monastery *see* Monastir de Pedralbes
Pedrera, La (Casa Milà) 35, 41, **45-46**, 46, *47*, 48, 82, 83, 122, **129**, 263
Peña Ganchegui, Luis 134
Penedès 284
pensiones 51
Peratallada 291
Pere I 'the Catholic', Count-King 11
Pere II 'the Great', Count-King **12**, 13
Pere III, Count-King 13
  performing arts **262-270**
Pesanta, La 229
petrol 307
Petronella of Aragon 11
pharmacies 313
Philip II, King 15
Philip IV, King 15-16
Philip V, King 16
photography shops 213
Picasso, Pablo 21, 86, 87, 99, 105, 146, 279, 295
Pijos 194
Piñón, Helio 44
Pinós, Carme 114
Piscina Bernat Picornell 117, 232, **276**
Pla Macià 43
Pla de l'Os 95
Pla del Palau 105
Plaça de l'Àngel 103
Plaça de les Arts 42
Plaça de Braus Monumental 123
Plaça Catalunya 122
Plaça de la Concòrdia 134
Plaça del Diamant 133
Plaça Espanya 115
Plaça Duc de Medinaceli 88
Plaça Francesc Macià 130
Plaça George Orwell 87, **88**
Plaça de les Glòries 141
Plaça Joaquim Xirau 88
Plaça John Lennon 133
Plaça de la Llana 108
Plaça de la Mercè 88
Plaça de les Olles 105
Plaça dels Països Catalans 44, **133**
Plaça del Pi 87, **88**
Plaça Ramon Berenguer el Gran 12
Plaça del Rei 89
Plaça Reial 37, 40, 83, **88**, *88*
Plaça Rius i Taulet 133, **134**
Plaça Rovira 133
Plaça Salvador Seguí 97
Plaça de Sant Felip Neri 87, **89**, *89*
Plaça Sant Iu 87
Plaça Sant Jaume 82, **86**
Plaça Sant Josep Oriol 87
Plaça Sant Just 87, **89**
Plaça Santa Maria 119
Plaça de Sants 134
Plaça del Sol 131
Plaça Traginers 13

'Plaça Trippy' 88
Plaça de Valenti Almirall 141
Plaça Vila de Madrid 12, *86*, **87**
Plaça de la Virreina 131
Plan de Establización 28
Platja d'Aro 292
Platja de Barceloneta 111
Platja de Bogatell 111
Platja de Mar Bella 111
Platja de Nova Icària 111
Platja de Nova Mar Bella 111
Platja del Raco, La 292
Platja de Sant Miquel 111
Platja de Sant Sebastià 111
playgrounds 227
Plaza de Toros Monumental 272
Poble Espanyol 117, *120*, **121**, 225, 232
Poble Sec 121
  cafés, tapas & bars 185
  music & nightlife 256-257
  restaurants 170
  where to stay 64
Poblenou 19, **140-141**
  music & nightlife 261
  restaurants 171
Poblet **287**, 288
poetry festival 217
police 316
Pont de Calatrava *140*, 141
Popular Front 25
Porcioles, José Maria de 28
Port Aventura 228, 284, **287**
Port Lligat 295
Port Olímpic
  music & nightlife 255-256
Port de la Selva 295
Port Vell 44, 83, **110-113**
  music & nightlife 255-256
Porta d'Europa 110
Ports & shoreline *see* Barceloneta & the Ports
Porxos d'en Xifré 37
postal services 317
POUM (Partit Obrer d'Unificació Marxista) 27, 92
PP (Partido Popular) 29, 33-34
Prat airport, El 304
Prat de la Riba, Enric 21
Primavera Sound **219**, 227
Primo de Rivera, Miguel 22
Priorat 286
ProEixample 122
PSC (Catalan Socialist Party) 29
public holidays 321
public transport 305-306
Púbol castle **291**, 292, *296*
Puig i Cadafalch, Josep 21, 22, **41**, 87, 117, 122, 123, 124, 128, 286
Puigcerdà 299
Pujol, Jordi 28, 29
Punta de la Banya 289
Putxet 137

Quadrat d'Or 122
Quatre Barres, the 11
Queralbs 301
queuing 317
Queviures Murrià 124

radio 315
Rambla, La 17, 82, 83, **95-96**, *96*, 225
  where to stay 51-59
Rambla de Catalunya **128**
Rambla de les Flores 95
Rambla de Poblenou 128, 140
Rambla de Raval 98, **128**
Rambla de Santa Mònica 95
Ramon Berenguer II, Count 11
Ramon Berenguer IV, Count-King 11

Raspall, MJ 43
Raval 17, 21, 44, 82, **97-102**
  cafés, tapas & bars 177-179
  galleries 235
  music & nightlife 250-254
  restaurants 149-157
  shops 205
  where to stay 59-61
RCD Espanyol 272
Recha, Marc 231
redevelopment 22@ 31
Redoreda, Mercè 133
reference 325
Refugi Antiaeri del Poble Sec 121
religion 317
Renaixença, the 19, **37**, 46
RENFE 305
renting a flat 317
repairs 316
resources A-Z 308-322
restaurants 144-171
  the best 145
  for children 228
  fast food 166
  gay & lesbian 243-244
  international 147-149, 154-155,
    158-159, 163, 165-167, 169,
    170
  menu glossary 154-155
  vegetarian 149, 155-157
Reus 46
Revolta de les Quintes, La 134
Ribera, La 13, **103**
Ribes de Freser 301
rickshaws 83
Ripoll 11, **301**
Rius i Taulet, Francesc 19
Rogers, Richard 44, 115, 116
roller hockey 272
rollerblading 275
Roman Barcelona **10-11**,
  12-13, 130
Roses 295
Rovira, Joan 23
Rovira i Trias, Antoni 122, 123,
  133
Rubio i Bellver, Joan 43, 124, 130
rugby 272
running 272, **275**
Rupit *298, 300, 302*
Rusiñol, Santiago 21, 39, 279
Ruta del Cister, La 287
Ruta del Modernisme 85

Sa Riera 292
Sabaté brothers 27
safety 317
Sagnier, Enric 123, 125, 128
Sagrada Familia, La 39, 40,
  40-41, 46, *47*, **48**, 82, 83, 123,
  129, *130*
Sagrat Cor 135
Sagrera, La 42
sailing 276
St George's Church 317
Sala Beckett 268
Sala Montcada 109
Sala Parés 87, **235**
sales tax 189
Saló de Cent 89
Saló de Tinell 13, 36, 37, 87, **93**
Salou 287
Salvat i Espasa 125
Sant Adrià de Besòs 141
Sant Andreu 142
Sant Felip Neri 37, **87**, 263
Sant Feliu de Guixols 292
Sant Ferran 299
Sant Gervasi 137
Sant Jeroni 282
Sant Joan 220
Sant Joan de les Abadesses 36,
  301
Sant Joan festival **220**, 227

Sant Joan hermitage 282
Sant Jordi 217
Sant Llàtzer 98
Sant Pacià 142
Sant Pau del Camp 36, *36*, **102**
Sant Pere 82, **103-109**
  cafés, tapas & bars 179-184
  music & nightlife 254-255
  restaurants 157-159
  where to stay 63
Sant Pere de les Puelles 103
Sant Pere de Rodes 11, 36, **295**,
  297
Sant Pol de Mar 280, **281**, *281*,
  292
Sant Sadurní d'Anoia 286
Sant Salvador 287
Santa Àgata 87
Santa Anna 36, **87**
Santa Cova 282
Santa Eulàlia (festival) 224
Santa Llúcia 36
Santa Llúcia market 227
Santa Maria de Gràcia 131
Santa Maria de Ripoll 301
Santa Maria del Mar 13, 37, *38*,
  83, 105, **109**, 263
Santa Maria del Pi 13, 37, **87**,
  263
Santa Pau 302
Santes Creus **287**, 288
Santos, Carles 262
Sants 19, 82, **133-134**
  where to stay 77
Sants Just i Pastor 87
Barcelona-Sants station 305
Sarrià 82, 137
saunas, gay 244
Second Spanish Republic 22
second-hand & vintage clothes
  shops 201-203
Segadors, Els 16
Segimon, Roser 129
Segui, Salvador 97
Serra, Narcis 28
Serra del Cadi 299
Serrano de Casanova, Eugenio
  19
Sert, Josep Lluís 43, 89, 118, 142
services *see* shops & services
Setmana Santa (Holy Week) 217,
  220
Setmana Tràgica (Tragic Week)
  21
Seu de Nou Barris 142
sex shops, gay 245
shoe shops 203-204
shops & services **189-214**
  the best 189
  gay & lesbian 244-245
sightseeing **81-142**
Sinagoga de Barcelona 317
Sinagoga Shlomo Ben Adret 93
Sitges 233, **279-281**
  gay & lesbian scene **245**, 279
Sitges Teatre Internacional 266
skiing 276
smoking 317
Socialist Party 28
Sónar 219
Sotoo, Etsuro 130
Spanish Civil War *see* Civil War
Spanish language 323
speciality shops 213-214
sport & fitness **271-276**
  shops 214
squatters 139
stamp and coin market 212
street fashion shops 201
studying in Barcelona 318
Suárez, Adolfo 28
Subirachs, Josep Maria 130
supermarkets 208
sweet shops 206
swimming 276
synagogues 87, 93, 317

Tamarit castle 287
Tamariu 292
tapas *see* cafés, tapas & bars
Tàpies, Antoni 27, 123, **125**
tardofranquisme 28
Tarraco 10
Tarradellas, Josep 24
Tarragona 10, **283-284**
tax 316
  sales 189
taxis 306
  getting to and from the airport
    by 304
Teatre Grec 117
Teatre Joventut 142
Teatre Lliure 266, **268**
Teatre Nacional de Catalunya
  (TNC) 266, 267, *267*, **268**
Teatre Poliorama 268
Teatre Roma 268
Teatre-Museu Dali, Figueres
  296, 297
Tecla Sala Centre Cultural 142
Teléferic de Montjuic 117, **121**
telephones 319
television 315
Temple Romà d'Augusti 12, 86,
  95
tennis 273, 276
Terra Alta 286
Terrassa 43
theatre 266-269
  for children 227
  festivals 220, 266
Thyssen-Bornemisza collection
  119, 137
Tibidabo 135-136
  cafés, tapas & bars 188
  funfair 226, *227*
ticket agents 214
time 320
Tinyosa, La 229
tipping 320
Tirant lo Blanc 15
toilets 320
Torre Agbar 42, **141**
Torre de les Aigües 122
Torre de Collserola 44, 135, **137**
Torre Figueres 137
Torres, Miguel 285
Torres winery 284, **285**
Tortosa 289
tourist information 321
tours 85
toy shops 195
train
  arriving and leaving by 305
  getting around Barcelona by
    306
  getting to and from the airport
    by 304
  travelling around Catalonia
    by 278
trams 26, **306**
Tramvia Blau *131*, 140
Transbordador Aeri 83, 110,
  113, 117, 225
translators 309
transport, public 305-306
Trastámaras, the 15
travel advice 309
travel services 214
Tren Montjuic 121
Tres Gràcies 130
tribes, urban
  Bears 240
  Castellers 221
  Culés 273
  Gegants 223
  Okupas 139
  Pijos 194
Trueta, Josep 128

Turó Parc 137
Tusquets, Oscar 141

UCD (Union de Centro
  Democratico 28
UGT (Union General de
  Trabajadores) 21
Ullastret 291
underwear shops 203
Universal Exhibition of 1888
  19, 41
Universal Forum of Cultures
  see Forum Universal de les
  Cultures of 2004
Universal Mediterránea 287
Universitat Autònoma de
  Barcelona 318
Universitat de Barcelona 130,
  318
Universitat Pompeu Fabra 319
Universitat Ramon Llull 319
universities 318
Upper Raval 98-101

Valeri, Salvador 43
Valeri i Pupurull 124
Vall d'Hebron 44, **142**
Vallbona de les Monges 287,
  288
Vapor Vell 133
Vázquez Montalbán, Manuel 102
Velódrom 44, **142**
Verboom, Prosper 114
Verdaguer, Jacint 135
Verges 291
Via Laietana 22
Viaplana, Albert 44
Vic 298-299, *298-299*
Vila Olimpica 44, **114**
Vil·la Joana 135
Vilafranca del Penedès **284**, 286
Vilanova del Mar 37
Vilaseca, Josep 43
Viñolas i Llosas 124
Virreina, La 37
visas 321
Visigoths, the 11
vocabulary
  Catalan 324
  Spanish 323

walks
  in Catalonia 278
  Medieval trading 108-109
  Modernisme 124-125
  Roman remains 12-13
  tours 85
War of the Spanish Succession
  16
water 321
water parks 228
Water World 228
watersports 294
weather 321, 322
websites 325
Wilfred the Hairy, Count *10*, **11**,
  301
wine 173
  festival 222
  shops 209
Wine Country 284-286
Wintercase Barcelona 223
working in Barcelona 321-322
World Trade Center **110**, 308
World War I 21
World War II 28

xiringuitos 111, 114

y

youth hostels 80

z

Zapatero, Captain-General 19, 115, 134
Zapatero, José Luis Rodriguez 34
Zona Alta 137-140
    galleries 237
    where to stay 77-79
Zoo de Barcelona 226

Where to stay

Acropolis Guest House 77
Alberg Mare de Déu de
    Montserrat 80
Barcelona Mar Youth Hostel 80
Camping Masnou 80
Casa Camper 59
Casa Fuster **74-75**, 133
Center Ramblas Youth Hostel 80
Citadines 51, **79**
Duc de la Victòria 55
Estrella de Mar 80
Gothic Point 80
Gran Hotel La Florida 51, 56, 71, **77**
H10 Racó del Pi 53, *55*
Hispanos Siete Suiza 79
Hostal Central Barcelona 73
Hostal Eden 73
Hostal Fontanella 55
Hostal Gat Raval 59
Hostal Gat Xino 51, *57*, **59**
Hostal Girona 51, **74**
Hostal Goya Principal 70
Hostal Jardi 53
Hostal Lausanne 56
Hostal Maldà 56
Hostal Noya 57
Hostal Opera 61
Hostal Orleans 51, **63**
Hostal La Palmera 61
Hostal Parisien 57
Hostal Rembrandt 57
Hostal Restaurante Oliveta 64
Hostal de Ribagorza 74
Hostal San Remo 74
Hostal Sofia 77
Hostal La Terrassa 61
Hostal d'Uxelles **70**, 73
Hostal-Residencia Ramos 60
Hosteria Grau 61
Hotel Actual 51, **70**
Hotel Ambassador 51, **59**
Hotel Arts 51, 56, *56*, **63**, 71
Hotel Astoria 65
Hotel Atrium Palace 65
Hotel Axel 51, *60*, **65**, 71
Hotel Balmes 67
Hotel Banys Orientals 51, **63**
Hotel Barcelona House 53
Hotel Catalonia Barcelona Plaza 77
Hotel Catalonia Berna 67
Hotel Catalonia Princesa 61
Hotel Claris 67
Hotel Colón 53
Hotel Condes de Barcelona 67, *69*
Hotel Confort 75
Hotel Constanza 51, **70**
Hotel Duques de Cardona 51, **64**
Hotel España **60**, 102
Hotel Gaudi 60
Hotel Ginebra 73
Hotel Gran Via 73
Hotel Guillermo Tell 79
Hotel Inglaterra 67
Hotel Jazz 51, **67**, 71
Hotel Majestic 51, 56, **69**
Hotel Le Meridien Barcelona 53
Hotel Mesón Castilla 60
Hotel Neri 51, **53**, 56, 71
Hotel Nouvel 53

Hotel Nuevo Triunfo 64
Hotel Omm *64-65*, **69**, 71
Hotel Onix Fira 77
Hotel Onix Rambla Catalunya 69
Hotel Oriente 55
Hotel Peninsular 61
Hotel Podium 69
Hotel Princesa 141
Hotel Principal 61
Hotel Pulitzer 51, **69**, 71
Hotel Rivoli Ramblas 53
Hotel Sant Agusti 61
Hotel Toledano 57
Itaca Alberg-Hostel 80
Marina Folch 64
Pensió 2000 51, **63**
Pensión Francia 61
Pensión Hostal Mari-Luz 57
Pensión Portugal 59
Pensión Segre 59
Petit Hotel 79, *79*
Podium 51, **69**
Prestige Paseo de Gràcia 70
Residencia Australia 75
Residencia Victoria 59
Ritz Hotel 70

Restaurants

Agua 145, **167**, *169*
Al Passatore 228
Alkimia 159
Ànima 149
Arola 145, **167**
Astoria 145, **159**
Bar Salvador 157
Bella Napoli, La 170
Bestial 145, **169**
Biblioteca 145, **149**
Big Sur 236
Blanc i Negre 163
Botafumeiro 163
Bulli, El 144, **171**, 295
Bunga Raya 158
Café de l'Acadèmia 145
Cafeti, El 145, **150**
Cal Pep 157
Can Culleretes 145
Can Maño 167
Can Solé 169
Can Travi Nou 145, **171**
Cantina Machito 165
Caracoles, Los 145
Casa de Andalucia 151
Casa Calvet 145, **161**
Casa Gallega 151
Casa de la Rioja 151
Castro 243
Cata 1.81 161
Centre Cultural Euskal Etxea 151
Cinc Sentits 145, *159*, **161**
Comerç 24 145, **157**
Cua Curta, La 158
Cubaneo 244
Dionisus 158
Dos Trece 150
Drassanes 150
Econòmic, L' 145, **157**
Elisabets 145, *147*, **150**
Emu 165
Envalira 163
Fernández, Las 150
Fil Manila 154
Foc, El 170
Folquer 163
Font del Gat, La 170
FoodBall *146*, 150
Gaig 145, **161**
Gallo Kiriko, El 13
Gran Café, El 145, **146**
Habana Vieja 159
Himali 165
Hofmann 157
Iurantia 244
Jean Luc Figueras 165, *167*
Juicy Jones 149

Laurak 165
Locanda, La 147
Lupino 145, **153**
Mama Café 153
Mastroqué 146
Matsuri 147
Mercè Vins 146
Mesón David 145, **153**
Mesón Jesús 146
Mesopotamia 167
Moo 161
Moti Mahal 154
Mundial Bar 157
Noti 145, **161**, *162-163*
Octubre 145, **165**
Organic 155
Ot 165
Oven 232
Paradeta, La 145, **158**
Paraguayo, El 149
Passatore, Al 159
Pebre Blau, El 145, **158**
Peimong 149
Pescadors, Els 145, **171**
Pla de la Garsa 145, **158**
Pla dels Àngels 153
Pollo Rico 145, **153**
Principal 162
Quatre Gats, Els 87, **146**, 174, 236
Quinze Nits, Les *144*, 145, **146**
Re-Pla 145, *150*, **158**
Salón, El 147
San Kil 167
Semproniana 162
Sésamo 157
Set Portes 145, **169**
Shojiro 167
Shunka 149
Silenus 145, **153**
Suquet de l'Almirall 145, **169**
Taberna Santa Maria 158
Taxidermista 147
Thai Lounge 163
Tokyo 149
Tomaquera, La 170
Tragaluz 162
Ty-Bihan 163
Venta, La 171
Verònica, La 145, **150**, 243
Vivanda *170-171*, 171
Windsor 145, **162**
Zarabanda 153

Cafés, tapas & bars

Al Limón Negro 236
Antic Teatre, L' 173, **180**
Arc Café 173, **174**
Arquer, L' 181
Atelier, L' 181
Átame 238
Baignoire, La 187
Bar Bodega Teo 189
Bar Celta 173, **175**
Bar Colombo 173, **184**, 228
Bar Kabara 177
Bar Kasparo 228
Bar Manolo 181
Bar Mendizábal **177**, 228
Bar Pastis 178
Bar Pinotxo 175
Bar Primavera 185
Barcelonina de Vins i Esperits, La 186
Bàscula, La 179
Bauma 185
Boadas 178
Bodega Kenobi 178
Bodega Manolo 186
Bodegueta, La 186
Born Cooking 180
Bosc de les Fades, El 229
Buenas Migas 177
Burdel 74u 229, *239*
Café Berlin 185

Café de l'Acàdemia 89, **145**
Café de les Delicies *177*, 179
Café de l'Opera 95, **174**
Café Miranda 243
Can Paixano 184
Canódromo, El 181
Caribbean Club 178
Casa Alfonso 186
Casa Paco 189
Casa Quimet 187
Caseta del Migdia, La 117, 173, **185**
Cerveseria Catalana 186
Clandestina, La 184
Col·lectiu Gai de Barcelona 238
Concha, La 239, **250**
Cova Fumada, La 173, **184**, *184*
Crazy's 238
Daguiri 173, **184**
Dietrich 238
Dry Martini **186**, 187
Escandalus 238
Espai Barroc 189
Espai Mallorca 151
Euskal Etxea 189
Fènix 238
Fianna, La 173, **180**, *183*
Filferro 184
Fira, La 181, *181*
Flash Flash 186
Fundació Joan Miró 185
Gimlet 183
Ginger 175
Granja, La 174
Granja M Viader 173, **177**
Hivernacle, L' **180**, 228
I Què? 236
Iposa 173, **178**, 236, *236*
Kahiki 181
Leticia 236
London Bar 178
Luz de Gas – Port Vell 185
Mam i Teca 173, **178**
Marsella 173, **179**
Merbeyé 173, **188**
Merry Ant **179**, 236
Mi Madre! 238
Miranda del Museu, La 173, **184**, 228
Mosquito 180
Mudanzas 183
Noise i Art 188
Oddland 178
Onofre 175
Oui Café 238
Palma, La 177
Planeta Rai 183
Portalón, El 173, **175**
Premier 185
Primitiva, La 181
Puku Café 188
Punto BCN 238
Quatre Gats, Els 87, **174**, 236
Quiet Man, The 178
Quimet i Quimet 173, **185**
Saint-Germain 188
Sal i Pebre 238
Salambó 186
Samsara 188
Schilling **175**, 239
Spiritual Café 173, *178*, **179**
Sureny 186
Sweet 239
Taller de Tapas 173, **175**
Tèxtil Café 173, **180**
Tio Ché, El 128
Tres Tombs, Els 178
24, El 236
Va de Vi 183
Vaso de Oro, El 185
Venus Delicatessen 243
Vinissim 173
Vinya del Senyor 183
Xampanyet, El 184
Xocoa 173, *174*, **175**
Zeltas Club 239
Zelig 178

Advertisers' Index

Please refer to the relevant pages for contact details

Pizza Marzano	IFC

In Context

Europerator	8
Vivebarcelona	8
Hotel Triunfo	8
Hispanos Siete Suiza	14
La Cupula	14
Grand Hotel Central	20
Piso Barcelona	30
Guest House Acropolis	30

Where to Stay

CitySiesta	52
Oh-Barcelona.com	52
Apartments BCN	54
Barcelona On-line	54
Rent A Flat in Barcelona	58
Apartments Ramblas	58
MH Apartments	62
Prestige Paseo de Gracia	62
Apartime	66
Friendly Rentals	66
House Family B&B	68
Lodging Barcelona	68
Lofts & Apartments	68
Zoom Mundi	68
Barcelona For Rent	72
Chic & Basic	72
Home Hostels	72
Les Trois B	72
Barcelona 30 Per Night	76
Allnice Apartments	76
BCN Apart	76
Silver Aparthotel	78
NivellMar	78
BarcelonaPoint	78
BCN-Rentals	78

Sightseeing

Universitat de Barcelona	84
Generalitat de Catalunya	90
Amigo Autos	94
Bike & Walk Tours	94
Book & Rent	94
Speakeasy Language School	94
Articket/MACBA	100
Outlet Spain	106
Palau de la Música Catalana	106
Version Original	106
International House	126
Barcelona Tours	136
Bike Tours	136
Museu de la Xocolata	136

Restaurants

Taxidermista	148
La Locanda	152
Barcelona Metropolitan	152
Fresc Co	156
La Fianna	156
Rita Blue	160
Out of China	160
Soba	160
Hello Sushi	164
Little Italy	168
Rubí	168
Catalunya Classified	168

Cafés & Bars

The Fastnet	172
Milk Bar & Bistro	172
The Michael Collins	172
BCN-Nightlife.com	176
The Clansman	176
The Queen Vic	176
Kennedy Group	182

Shops & Services

La Roca Village	190
Noténom	196
Desigual	202
Monkeybiz	202

Festivals & Events

HotelConnect	218
Spain Ticket Bureau	218

Gay & Lesbian

Gay Travel Barcelona	242
Hotel Axel	242
Hostal Que Tal	242

Nightlife

Corto Club	252
La Birreria	252
La Paloma	252

Maps

Maremagnum	340
Apartments By Day	IBC

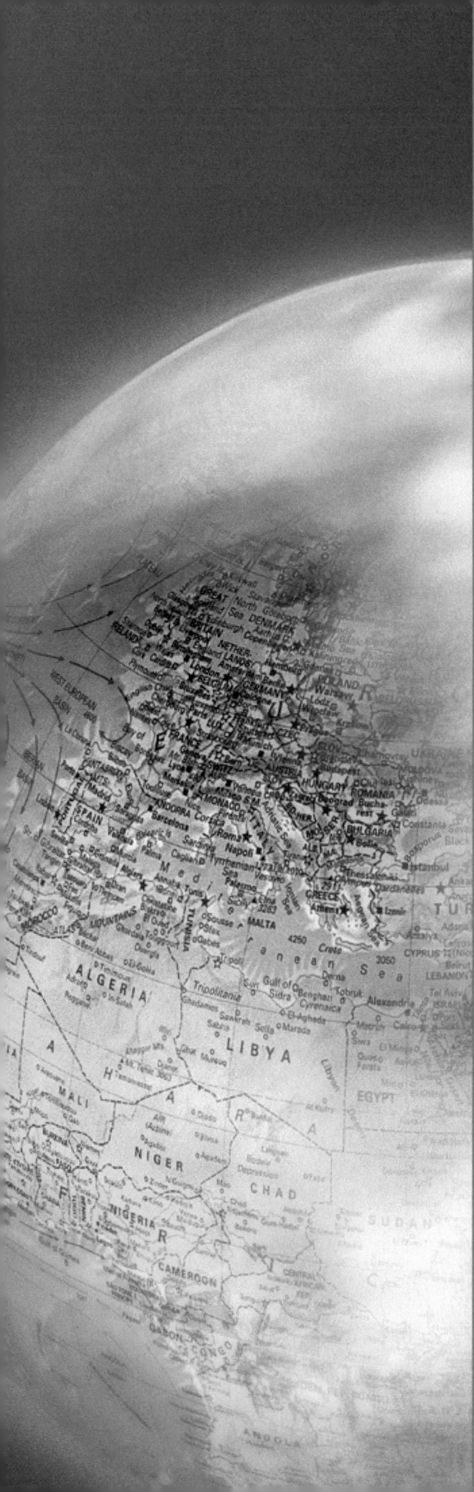

Place of interest and/or entertainment	
Hospital or college	
Pedestrianised zone	
Railway station	
Metro station, FGC station	Ⓜ
Area name	BARRI GÒTIC

Maps

Trips Out of Town	334
Around Barcelona	335
Barcelona Areas	336
Street Maps	337
Street Index	346
RENFE Local Trains	349
Metro	350

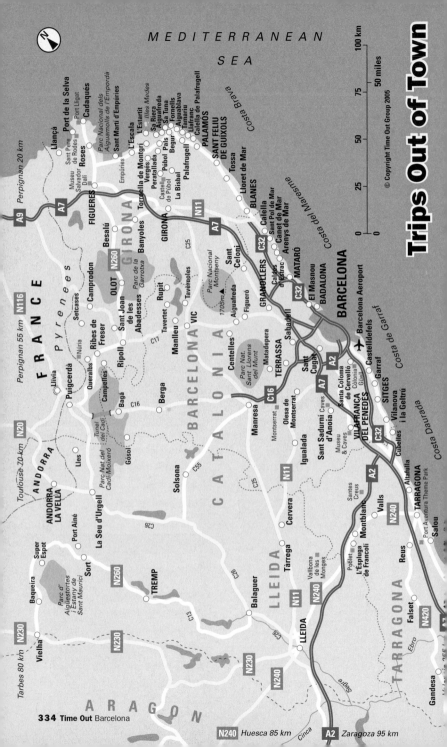

Trips Out of Town

MEDITERRANEAN SEA

© Copyright Time Out Group 2005

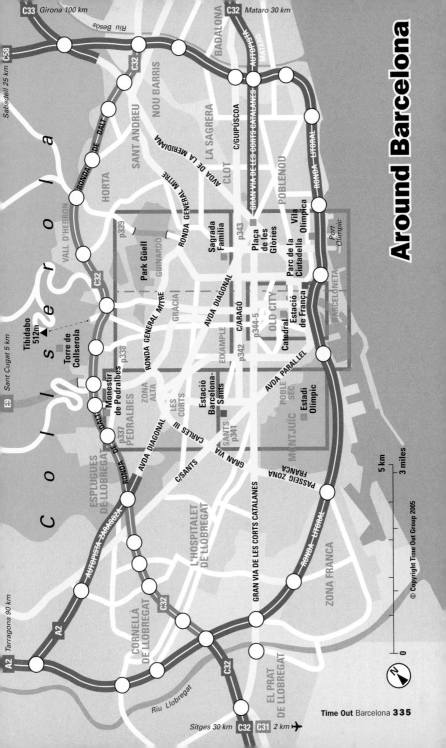

Around Barcelona

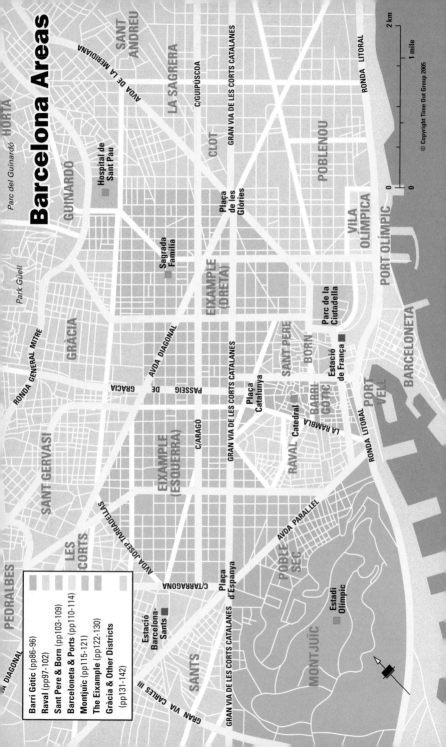

Barcelona Areas

Barri Gòtic (pp86-96)
Raval (pp97-102)
Sant Pere & Born (pp103-109)
Barceloneta & Ports (pp110-114)
Montjuïc (pp115-121)
The Eixample (pp122-130)
Gràcia & Other Districts
(pp131-142)

© Copyright Time Out Group 2005

PEDRALBES

A DIAGONAL

LES CORTS

SANT GERVASI

RONDA GENERAL MITRE

GRÀCIA

Parc del Guinardó

Park Güell

HORTA

GUINARDÓ

SANT ANDREU

AVDA DE LA MERIDIANA

LA SAGRERA

C/GUIPÚSCOA

CLOT

GRAN VIA DE LES CORTS CATALANES

Hospital de Sant Pau

Sagrada Família

AVDA DIAGONAL

EIXAMPLE (DRETA)

Plaça de les Glòries

POBLENOU

VILA OLÍMPICA

PORT OLÍMPIC

PASSEIG DE GRÀCIA

C/ARAGÓ

EIXAMPLE (ESQUERRA)

GRAN VIA DE LES CORTS CATALANES

Plaça Catalunya

SANT PERE

BORN

Parc de la Ciutadella

Estació de França

BARRI GÒTIC

Catedral

LA RAMBLA

RAVAL

BARCELONETA

AVDA JOSEP TARRADELLAS

AVDA PARAL·LEL

POBLE SEC

PORT VELL

RONDA LITORAL

Plaça d'Espanya

C/TARRAGONA

Estació Barcelona-Sants

SANTS

GRAN VIA DE LES CORTS CATALANES

GRAN VIA CARLES III

MONTJUÏC

Estadi Olímpic

RONDA LITORAL

0   1 mile

0   2 km

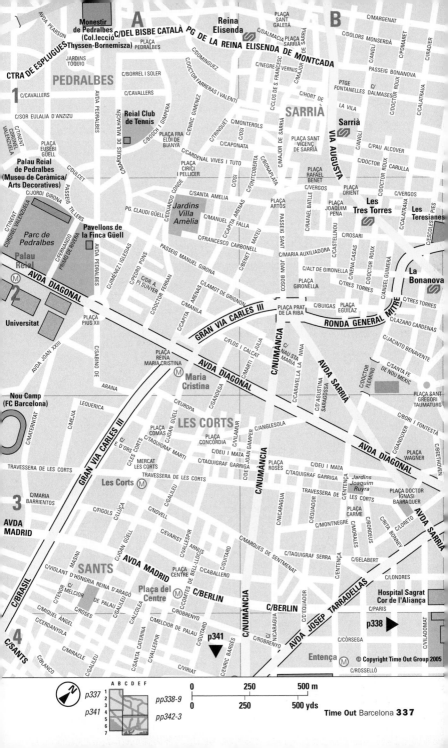

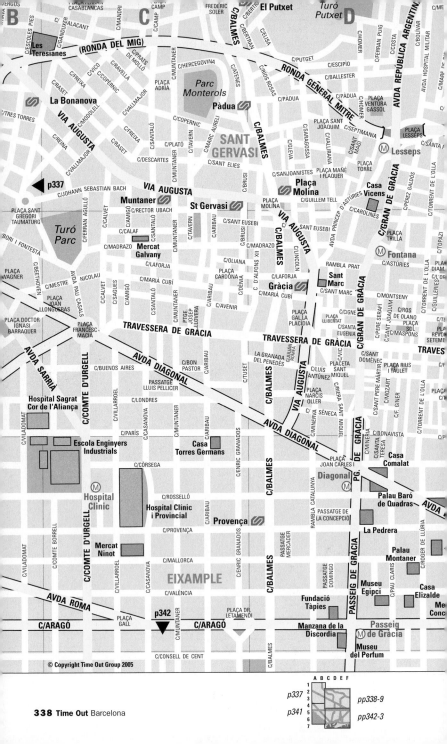

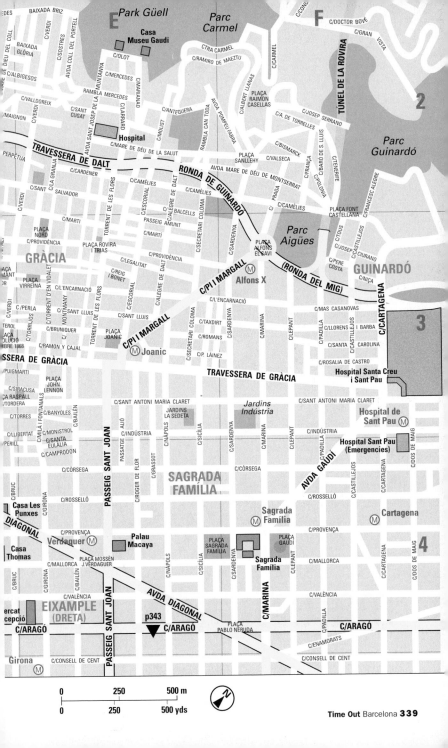

Park Güell

Parc Carmel

E

F

C/CONDE

C/DOCTOR BOVÉ

C/GRAN VISTA

BAIXADA BRIZ

C/VERDI

C/SOSTRES

Casa
Museu Gaudí

C/OLOT

C/DE DÉU DEL COLL

BAIXADA
GLÒRIA

AVDA COLL DEL PORTELL

C/ALBIGESOS

C/VALLDOREIX

C/MERCEDES

C/MARIANAO

CTRA CARMEL

C/RAMIRO DE MAEZTU

C/CARMEL

TÚNEL DE LA ROVIRA

2

/MAIGNON

C/VERDI

RAMBLA MERCEDES

MUNTANYA

C/SANT
CUGAT

AVDA SANT JOSEP DE LA

C/LARRARD

C/ANTEQUERA

RAMBLA CAN TODA

AVDA POMPEU FABRA

PLAÇA
RAIMON
CASELLAS

C/ALBERT LLANAS

C/JOSEP SERRANO

Parc
Guinardó

PERPÈTUA

TRAVESSERA DE DALT

Hospital

C/MARE DE DÉU DE LA SALUT

C/MOLIST

PLAÇA
SANLLEHY

C/BISMARCK

C/A. DE TORRELLES

C/BARÓ DE S. LLUÍS

C/TENERIFE

C/LA GRANJA

C/CARDENER

C/CAMÉLIES

RONDA DE GUINARDO

C/VALSECA

C/FRANÇA

C/PODOLIA

C/SANT SALVADOR

C/CAMÉLIES

AVDA MARE DE DÉU DE MONTSERRAT

C/PRAGA

PLAÇA FONT
CASTELLANA

C/FRANCESC ALEGRE

C/VERDI

C/ESCORIAL

C/ALEGRE DE DALT

C/CAMÉLIES

C/SECRETARI COLOMA

C/CAMÉLIES

C/TOUS

C/JOSEP SERRANO

C/CASTILLEJOS

C/SANT

PLAÇA
NORD

C/PROVIDÈNCIA

PLAÇA ROVIRA
I TRIAS

PASSEIG AMUNT

C/MARTÍ

PLAÇA
ALFONS
EL SAVI

C/JOSEP CIURANO

GUINARDÓ

GRÀCIA

C/MARTI

C/LEGALITAT

C/PROVIDÈNCIA

C/PERE
COSTA

C/PI I MARGALL

Alfons X

PLAÇA
VIRREINA

REIG
I BONET

C/ALEGRE DE DALT

C/L'ENCARNACIÓ

(RONDA DEL MIG)

C/NIÇA

C/CARTAGENA

3

C/VERDI

C/PERLA

C/L'ENCARNACIÓ

C/TORRENT D'EN VIDALET

C/ESCORIAL

C/L'ENCARNACIÓ

C/TAXDIRT

C/SARDENYA

C/MARINA

C/LLEPANT

C/MAS CASANOVAS

C/PADILLA

C/TEROL

C/TORRIJOS

MONTMANY

C/SANT LLUÍS

C/SANT LLUIS

TORRENT DE LES FLORS

C/ROMANS

C/LLORENS I BARBA

C/SANTA
CAROLINA

C/CASTILLEJOS

C/BRUNIQUER

PLAÇA
JOANIC

C/P. LÁINEZ

SSERA DE GRÀCIA

C/RAMON Y CAJAL

Joanic

C/SECRETARI COLOMA

C/ROSALIA DE CASTRO

/PUIGMARTÍ

C/SIRACUSA

PLAÇA
JOHN
LENNON

TRAVESSERA DE GRÀCIA

Hospital Santa Creu
i Sant Pau

ÇA RASPALL

/TORDERA

C/BANYOLES

C/BAILÉN

C/SANT ANTONI MARIA CLARET

C/SANT ANTONI MARIA CLARET

Hospital de
Sant Pau

C/TORRES

C/MILA I FONTANALS

ALIÓ

Jardins
Indústria

C/INDÚSTRIA

Hospital Sant Pau
(Emergencies)

C/DOS DE MAIG

C/LLIBERTAT

C/MONISTROL

PASSATGE

JARDINS
LA SEDETA

C/NÀPOLS

C/SICILIA

C/SARDENYA

C/MARINA

C/LLEPANT

C/PADILLA

C/CASTILLEJOS

C/CARTAGENA

/PERILL

C/SANTA
EULALIA

C/INDÚSTRIA

C/INDÚSTRIA

C/CAMPRODON

C/CÓRSEGA

ROGER DE FLOR

GRASSOT

C/CÓRSEGA

C/CÓRSEGA

C/ROSSELLÓ

C/BRUC

C/GIRONA

C/ROSSELLÓ

SAGRADA
FAMÍLIA

AVDA GAUDÍ

C/ROSSELLÓ

Casa Les
Punxes

C/PROVENÇA

PASSEIG SANT JOAN

Sagrada
Família

C/PROVENÇA

DIAGONAL

C/PROVENÇA

Cartagena

Casa
Thomas

Verdaguer

Palau
Macaya

PLAÇA
SAGRADA
FAMÍLIA

PLAÇA
GAUDÍ

C/MALLORCA

C/DOS DE MAIG

4

C/BRUC

C/GIRONA

C/BAILÉN

PLAÇA MOSSÈN
J. VERDAGUER

C/MALLORCA

C/NÀPOLS

C/SICILIA

C/SARDENYA

Sagrada
Família

C/LLEPANT

C/CARTAGENA

C/VALÈNCIA

C/BAILÉN

AVDA DIAGONAL

C/VALÈNCIA

C/PADILLA

ercat
cepció

EIXAMPLE
(DRETA)

p343

C/MARINA

C/ARAGÓ

C/ARAGÓ

PASSEIG SANT JOAN

C/ARAGÓ

PLAÇA
PABLO NERUDA

C/ARAGÓ

C/ENAMORATS

Girona

C/CONSELL DE CENT

C/CONSELL DE CENT

C/CONSELL DE CENT

0   250   500 m

0   250   500 yds

N

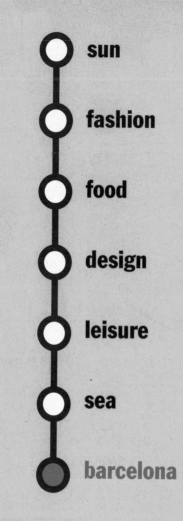

mare**magnum**

Moll d'Espanya, s/n
08039 Barcelona
932 258 100

www.maremagnum.es

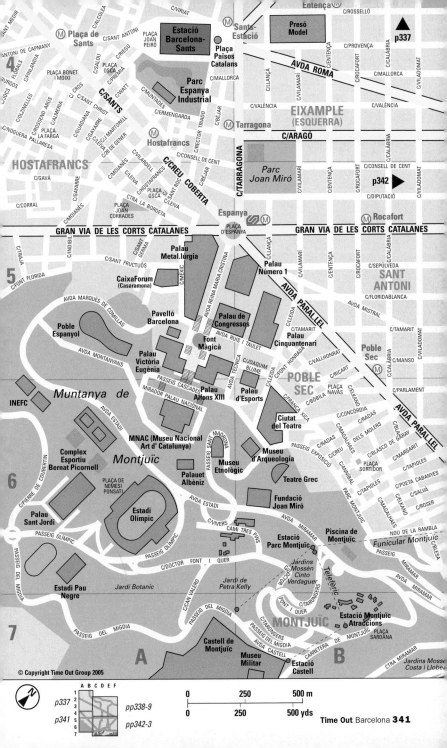

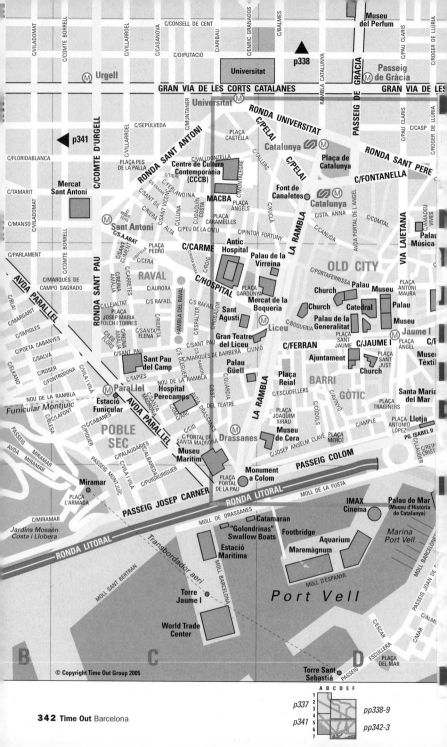

Museu
del Perfum

p338

Passeig
de Gràcia

Urgell

Universitat

GRAN VIA DE LES CORTS CATALANES
GRAN VIA DE LES

Universitat

RONDA UNIVERSITAT

PASSEIG DE

RONDA SANT PERE

p341

Catalunya
Plaça de
Catalunya

Centre de Cultura
Contemporània
(CCCB)

Mercat
Sant Antoni

MACBA

Font de
Canaletes

Catalunya

Sant Antoni

OLD CITY

Antic
Hospital

RAVAL

C/CARME

Palau de la
Virreina

Church

Palau

Museu

Palau

Mercat de la
Boqueria

C/HOSPITAL

Church

Catedral

Sant
Agustí

Museu

Palau de la
Generalitat

Gran Teatre
del Liceu

Liceu

Jaume I

C/FERRAN

C/JAUME I

Sant Pau
del Camp

Palau
Güell

Ajuntament

Museu
Tèxtil

Church

Hospital
Perecamps

Paral.lel

Estació
Funicular

Plaça
Reial

BARRI

Santa Maria
del Mar

Funicular Montjuïc

GÒTIC

POBLE
SEC

Llotja

Drassanes

Museu
de Cera

Museu
Marítim

PG. ISABEL II

Miramar

Monument
a Colom

PASSEIG COLOM

IMAX
Cinema

Palau de Mar
(Museu d'Història
de Catalunya)

PASSEIG JOSEP CARNER
RONDA LITORAL
MOLL DE LA FUSTA

RONDA LITORAL

MOLL DE DRASSANES

Catamaran

Marina
Port Vell

Transbordador aeri

"Golondrinas"
Swallow Boats

Footbridge

Aquarium

Jardins Mossèn
Costa i Llobera

Estació
Marítima

Maremàgnum

Torre
Jaume I

Port Vell

World Trade
Center

B

C

D

Torre Sant
Sebastià

A B C D E F
1
2   p337
3
4   p341
5
6
7

pp338-9

pp342-3

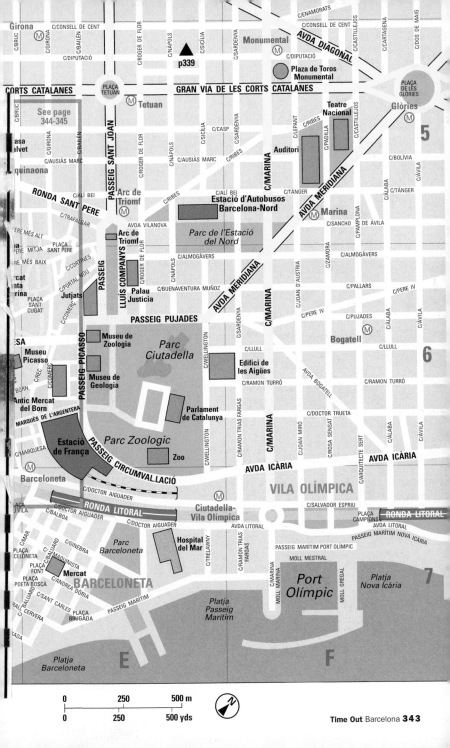

Girona

C/CONSELL DE CENT

C/ENAMORATS

C/CONSELL DE CENT

AVDA DIAGONAL

C/BRUC

C/GIRONA Ⓜ

C/BAILÉN

C/ROGER DE FLOR

C/NÀPOLS

C/SICÍLIA

C/SARDENYA

Monumental Ⓜ

C/CASTILLEJOS

C/CARTAGENA

C/DOS DE MAIG

C/DIPUTACIÓ

▲
p339

Plaza de Toros
Monumental ●

PLAÇA
DE LES
GLÒRIES

C/DIPUTACIÓ

CORTS CATALANES

PLAÇA
TETUAN

GRAN VIA DE LES CORTS CATALANES

Glòries

Ⓜ

5

See page
344-345

Tetuan Ⓜ

Teatre
Nacional

C/CASTILLEJOS

C/BRUC

C/GIRONA

C/BAILÉN

PASSEIG SANT JOAN

C/ROGER DE FLOR

C/NÀPOLS

C/SICÍLIA

C/CASP

C/SARDENYA

C/LLEPANT

C/RIBES

C/PADILLA

asa
alvet

Auditori

C/BOLÍVIA

C/ÀVILA

quinaona

C/AUSIÀS MARC

C/AUSIÀS MARC

C/MARINA

AVDA MERIDIANA

C/ALABA

C/TÀNGER

RONDA SANT PERE

C/ALÍ BEI

Arc de
Triomf Ⓜ

C/RIBES

C/ALÍ BEI

Estació d'Autobusos
Barcelona-Nord

C/TÀNGER

Marina

C/PAMPLONA

DE ÀVILA

Ⓜ

C/SANCHO

a
ere MÉS ALT

C/TRAFALGAR

AVDA VILANOVA

Parc de l'Estació
del Nord

C/ZAMORA

C/ALMOGÀVERS

a
ere MÉS BAIX

PLAÇA
SANT PERE

Arc de
Triomf

C/ROGER DE FLOR

C/CORTINES

C/PORTAL NOU

C/NÀPOLS

C/ALMOGÀVERS

C/JOAN D'ÀUSTRIA

C/PALLARS

C/PERE IV

C/ÀLABA

C/PERE IV

C/ÀVILA

cat
nta
rina

PASSEIG

LLUÍS COMPANYS

C/BUENAVENTURA MUÑOZ

C/COMERÇ

PLAÇA
SANT
CUGAT

Jutjats

Palau
Justícia

AVDA MERIDIANA

C/SARDENYA

C/PUJADES

Bogatell

Ⓜ

PASSEIG PUJADES

6

SA

Museu
Picasso

Museu de
Zoologia

PASSEIG PICASSO

Parc
Ciutadella

C/WELLINGTON

Edifici de
les Aigües

C/LLULL

C/MARINA

C/LLULL

C/REC

C/COMERÇ

Museu de
Geologia

C/RAMON TURRÓ

AVDA BOGATELL

C/RAMON TURRÓ

BORN

Antic Mercat
del Born

MARQUÈS DE L'ARGENTERA

Parlament
de Catalunya

C/DOCTOR TRUETA

C/ÀLABA

C/ÀVILA

C/MARQUESA

Parc Zoologic

Zoo

C/WELLINGTON

C/RAMON TRIAS FARGAS

C/MARINA

C/JOAN MIRÓ

C/ROSA SENSAT

AVDA ICÀRIA

Estació
de França

PASSEIG CIRCUMVAL.LACIÓ

AVDA ICÀRIA

C/ARQUITECTE SERT

Barceloneta

VILA OLÍMPICA

ACA
VILA

C/DOCTOR AIGUADER

RONDA LITORAL

C/DOCTOR AIGUADER

Ⓜ

Ciutadella-
Vila Olímpica

C/SALVADOR ESPRIU

PLAÇA
CAMPIONS

RONDA LITORAL

C/BALBOA

AVDA LITORAL

AVDA LITORAL

PASSEIG MARÍTIM NOVA ICÀRIA

C/MAR

C/GINEBRA

Parc
Barceloneta

Hospital
del Mar

C/TRELAWNY

C/RAMON TRIAS FARGAS

PASSEIG MARÍTIM PORT OLÍMPIC

MOLL MESTRAL

PLAÇA
CELONETA

C/BALUARD

C/MAQUINISTA

Mercat

C/ANDREA DÒRIA

MOLL MARINA

C/MARINA

Port
Olímpic

MOLL GREGAL

Platja
Nova Icària

7

PLAÇA
FONT

BARCELONETA

PLAÇA
POETA BOSCÀ

C/SANT CARLES

PLAÇA
BRUGADA

PASSEIG MARÍTIM

Platja
Passeig
Marítim

AL CERVERA

ADA

Platja
Barceloneta

E

F

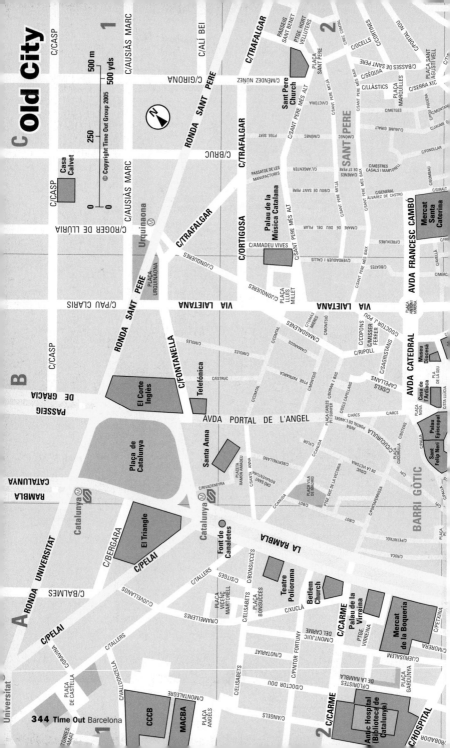

Street Index

26 de Gener, C. – p341 A4
Abaixadors, C. – p345 B3
Adrià, Plaça – p338 C2
Aglà, C. – p345 A3
Agullers, C. – p345 B4
Agustina Saragossa, C. – p337 B3
Àlaba, C. – p343 F5-6
Alacant, C. – p338 C2
Albareda, C. – p342 C6
Albert Llanas, C. – p339 F2
Albigesos, C. – p339 E2
Alcolea, C. – p337 A4
Alegre de Dalt – p339 E2-3
Alfons el Savi, Plaça – p339 F3
Alfons XII, C. d' – p338 D3
Alí Bei, C. – p343 E5/p344 C1
Alió, Passatge – p339 E4
Allada-Vermell, C. – p345 C3
Almeria, C. – p341 A4
Almirall Aixada, C. – p342 D7
Almirall Cervera, C. – p342 D7
Almogàvers, C. – p343 E6-F6
Alt de Gironella, C. – p337 B2
Amadeu Vives, C. – p342 D5/p344 C2
Amargós, C. – p344 B2
Amigó, C. – p338 C3
Ample, C. – p342 D6/p345 B4
Amunt, Passeig – p339 E3
Andrea Dòria, C. – p343 E7
Àngel Baixeras, C. – p345 B4
Àngel Guimerà – p337 B2
Àngel, Plaça – p342 D6/p345 B3
Àngels, C. – p344 A2
Àngels, Plaça – p342 C5/p344 A1
Anglesola, C. – p337 B3
Anglí, C. – p337 B1
Anníbal, C. – p341 B6
Antequera, C. – p339 E2
Antic de Sant Joan, C. – p345 C3
Antoni de Capmany, C. – p341 A4
Antoni Maura, Plaça – p342 D6/p344 B2
Antonio López, Plaça – p342 D6/p345 B4
Aragó, C. – p341-338 B4-F4
Arai, C. – p345 B3
Arc de Sant Agustí, C. – p345 A3
Arc de Sant Ramon del Call, C. – p345 B3
Arc del Teatre, C. – p342 C6/p345 A4
Arcs, C. – p344 B2
Arenes de St Pere, C. – p344 C2
Argenter, C. L' – p344 C2
Argentería, C. – p345 B3
Aribau, C. – p338-342 C3-F5
Arlet, C. – p345 B3
Armada, Plaça – p342 C7
Aroles, C. – p345 A3
Arquitecte Sert, C. – p343 F7
Artos, Plaça – p337 B2
Ases, C. – p345 C4
Assaonadors, C. – p345 C3
Astúries, C. – p338 D3
Ataülf, C. – p345 B3-4
Atenes, C. – p338 C2
Augusta, Via – p337-338 B1-D3
Aurora, C. – p342 C6
Ausiàs Marc, C. – p343 E5/p344 C1
Avellà, C. – p344 B2
Avenir, C. – p338 C3
Àvila, C. – p343 F5-6
Avinyó, C. – p342 D6/p345 B3-4
Bacardí, Passatge – p345 A3
Bailèn, C. – p339-343 E3-5
Balboa, C. – p343 E7
Balcells, C. – p339 E2
Ballester, C. – p338 D2
Balmes, C. – p338 C2-D4
Baluard, C. – p343 E7
Banca, Passatge de la – p345 A4
Banyoles, C. – p339 E3
Banys Nous, C. – p345 B3
Banys Vells, C. – p345 C3
Barceloneta, Plaça – p342 D7
Baró de S. Lluis, C. – p339 F2

Barra de Ferro, C. – p345 C3
Basea, C. – p345 B3
Basses de Sant Pere, C. – p344 C2
Beates, C. – p344 B2
Beethoven, C. – p337 B3
Béjar, C. – p341 A4-5
Bellafila, C. – p345 B3
Benet Mateu, C. – p337 B2
Bergara, C. – p344 A1
Berlín, C. – p337 A3-B3
Berlines, C. – p338 C2
Bertran, C. – p338 C2
Bertrellans, C. – p344 B2
Bisbe Català, C. – p337 A1
Bisbe, C. – p345 B3
Bismarck, C. – p339 F2
Blai, C. – p341 B6
Blanco, C. – p337 A4
Blanquería, C. – p345 C3
Blasco de Garay, C. – p341 B6
Blesa, C. – p341 B6
Bòbila, C. – p341 B6
Bogatell, Avda – p343 F6
Bolívar, C. – p338 D2
Bolívia, C. – p343 F5
Bon Pastor, C. – p338 C3
Bonaire, C. – p345 C4
Bonanova, Passeig – p337 B1
Bonaplata, C. – p337 B1
Bonavista, C. – p338 D3
Bonet i Moixi, Plaça – p341 A4
Bonsuccés, C. – p344 A2
Bonsuccés, Plaça – p344 A2
Boquer, C. – p345 C3
Boqueria, C. – p342 D6/p345 A3
Boqueria, Plaça – p345 A3
Bordeta, Ctra la – p341 A5
Bordeus, C. – p337 B3
Bori i Fontestà, C. – p337 B3
Bòria, C. – p345 B3
Born, Passeig del – p345 C3
Bosch i Gimpera, C. – p337 A1
Bot, C. – p344 A2
Botella, C. – p342 C6
Boters, C. – p344 B2
Bou de Sant Pere, C. – p344 C2
Brasil, C. – p337 A3
Brosolí, C. – p345 C4
Bruc, C. – p339-342 D4-5/p344 C1
Brugada, Plaça – p343 E7
Bruniquer, C. – p339 E3
Brusi, C. – p338 C2-3
Buenaventura Muñoz, C. – p343 E6
Buenos Aires, C. – p338 C3
Buïgas, C. – p337 B2
Burgos, C. – p341 A4
Caballero, C. – p337 A3
Cabanes, C. – p342 C6
Caçador, Baixada – p345 B3
Calàbria, C. – p341 B4-5
Calaf, C. – p338 C3
Calatrava, C. – p337 B1-2
Calders, C. – p345 C3
Call, C. – p345 B3
Calvet, C. – p338 C3
Camèlies, C. – p339 E2-F2
Camp, C. – p338 C2
Campions, Plaça – p343 F7
Camprodon, C. – p339 E4
Can Toda, Riera – p339 E2
Can Valero, C. de – p341 A7
Canuda, C. – p342 D5/p344 B2
Canvis Nous, C. – p345 B4
Canvis Vells, C. – p345 C4
Capellans, C. dels – p344 B2
Capità Arenas, C. – p337 A2
Caponata, C. – p337 A1
Carabassa, C. – p345 B4
Caramelles, Plaça – p342 C5
Caravel.la La Niña, C. – p337 B2
Cardenal Casañas – p345 A3
Cardenal Vives i Tutó, C. – p337 A1
Cardener, C. – p339 E2

Carders, C. – p345 C3
Cardona, Plaça – p338 C3
Carles Pi i Sunyer, Plaça – p344 B2
Carme, C. – p342 C6/p344 A2
Carme, Plaça – p337 B3
Carmel, Crta – p339 E2-F2
Carolines, C. – p338 D3
Carretes, C. – p342 C6
Cartagena, C. – p339-343 F3-5
Casanova, C. – p338-342 C3-5
Cascades, Passeig – p341 A6
Casp, C. – p342-343 D5-E5/p344 B1-C1
Castell, Avda – p341 B7
Castella, Plaça de – p342 C5/p344 A1
Castellnou, C. – p337 B2
Castillejos, C. – p339-343 F3-5
Catedral, Avda – p344 B2
Cavallers, C. – p337 A1
Cecs Boqueria, C. – p345 A3
Cecs Sant Cugat, C. – p345 C3
Centre, Plaça – p337 A3
Cera, C. – p342 C6
Cerdanyola, C. – p337 A4
Cervantes, C. – p345 B3
Cid, C. – p342 C6
Cigne, C. – p338 D3
Circumval.lació, Passeig – p343 E6
Cirera, C. – p345 C4
Cirici Pellicer, Plaça – p337 A1
Ciutat, C. – p345 B3
Claudi Güell, Passeig – p337 A2
Clos de S. Francesc, C. – p337 B2
Còdols, C. – p342 D6/p345 A4
Coll del Portell, Avda – p339 E2
Colom, C. – p345 A3
Colom, Passeig – p342 D6/p345 A4-B4
Colomines, C. – p345 C3
Comas, Plaça – p337 A3
Comerç, C. – p343 E6/p345 C3-4
Comercial, C. – p345 C3
Comercial, Plaça – p345 C3
Cometa, C. – p345 B3
Comtal, C. – p342 D5/p344 B2
Comte Borrell, C. – p338-342 C4-6
Comte d'Urgell, C. – p338-342 C3-5
Comtes de Bell-lloc, C. – p337 A3
Comtes, C. – p345 B3
Comtessa de Sobradiel, C. – p345 B3
Concepció, Ptge de la – p338 D4
Concòrdia, C. – p341 B6
Concòrdia, Plaça – p337 A3
Consell de Cent, C. – p341-343 A4-F4
Consellers, C. – p345 B4
Consolat de Mar, C. – p345 B4
Copèrnic, C. – p338 C2
Copons, C. – p344 B2
Corders, C. – p345 C3
Corral, C. – p341 A5
Corretger, C. – p345 C3
Correu Vell, C. – p345 B4
Còrsega, C. – p337-339 B4-F4
Cortines, C. – p343 E6/p344 C2
Costa, C. – p338 D2
Cotoners, C. – p345 B3
Crèdit, Passatge – p345 B3
Cremat Gran, C. – p345 C3
Cremat Xic, C. – p345 C3
Creu Coberta, C. – p341 A5
Creu dels Molers, C. – p341 B6
Cros, C. – p341 A4
Cucurulla, C. – p344 B2
Cucurulla, C. – p344 B2
Daguería, C. – p345 B3
Dalmàcia, C. – p337 B3
Dalmases, C. – p337 B1
Dalt, Travessera de – p339 E2
Dènia, C. – p338 C3
Descartes, C. – p338 C2
Deu i Mata, C. – p337 A3-B3
Diagonal, Avda – p337-343 A2-F5
Diamant, Plaça – p338 D3
Diputació, C. – p341-343 B5-F5

Doctor A. Pi Sunyer – p337 A2
Doctor Aiguader, C. – p343 E7/p345 C4
Doctor Bové, C. – p339 F2
Doctor Carulla, C. – p337 B1
Doctor Dou, C. – p344 A2
Doctor Farreras i Valentí, C. – p337 A1
Doctor Ferran, C. – p337 A2
Doctor Fleming, C. – p337 B2
Doctor Font i Quer, C. del – p341 A6/B6
Doctor Ignasi Barraquer, Plaça – p337 B3
Doctor J. Pou, C. – p344 B2
Doctor Letamendi, Plaça – p338 C4
Doctor Roux, C. – p337 B1-2
Doctor Trueta, C. – p343 F6
Domingo, Ptge – p338 D4
Domínguez, C. – p337 A1
Dormitori Sant Francesc, Ptge – p345 A4
Dos de Maig, C. – p339-343 F4-F5
Drassanes, Avda – p342 C6
Duc de la Victòria, C. – p344 B2
Duc de la Victòria, Plaça – p344 B2
Duc de Medinaceli, Plaça – p345 A4
Dulcet, C. – p337 A1
Duran i Bas, C. – p344 B2
Eduardo Conde, C. – p337 A2
Eguilaz, Plaça – p337 B2
Elisa, C. – p338 D2
Elisabets, C. – p344 A2
Elkano, C. – p341 B6
Enamorats, C. – p339 F4
Encarnació, C. – p339 E3-F3
Enric Bargés, C. – p337 A4
Enric Giménez, C. – p337 A1
Enric Granados, C. – p338 C4-C4-5
Ensenyança, C. – p338 D3
Entença, C. – p337-341 B3-5
Equador, C. – p337 B3-4
Ermengarda, C. – p341 A4
Escar, C. – p342 D7
Escipió, C. – p338 D2
Escoles Pies, C. – p337 B2
Escorial, C. – p339 E2-3
Escudellers Blancs, C. – p345 A3-B3
Escudellers, C. – p342 D6/p345 A3-B3
Escudellers, Ptge – p345 A4
Escullera, Passeig – p342 D7
Espalter, C. – p342 C6
Espanya, Plaça d' – p341 A5
Esparteria, C. – p345 C4
Esplugues, C. de – p337 A1
Est, C. – p342 C6
Estadi, Avda – p341 A6
Estruc, C. – p344 B2
Eugeni d'Ors, C. – p337 A3
Europa, C. – p337 A3
Eusebi Güell, Plaça – p337 A1
Evarist Arnús, C. – p337 A3
Exposició, Passeig – p341 B6
Farga, Plaça la – p341 A4
Ferlandina, C. – p342 C5
Fernando Primo de Rivera, C. – p337 A2
Ferran Agulló, C. – p338 C3
Ferran Puig, C. – p338 D2
Ferran, C. – p342 D6/p345 A3-B3
Figols, C. – p337 A3
Finlàndia, C. – p341 A4
Flassaders, C. – p345 C3
Flor de Lliri, C. – p345 C3
Flor, C. – p344 B2
Floridablanca, C. – p341 B5
Floristes de la Rambla, C. – p344 A2
Flors, C. – p342 C6
Flos i Calcat – p337 A2
Fonollar, C. – p344 C2
Font Castellana, Plaça – p339 F2
Font Florida, C. – p341 A5

346 Time Out Barcelona

Font Honrada, C. – p341 B5
Font, Plaça – p343 E7
Fontanella, C. – p342 D5/p344 B1
Fontanelles, Ptge – p337 B1
Fontcoberta, C. – p337 B2
Fontrodona, C. – p342 C6
Formatgeria, C. – p345 C3
Fossar de les Moreres – p345 C3
Fra Eloi de Bianya, Plaça – p337 A1
França Xica, C. – p341 B6
França, C. – p339 F2
Francesc Alegre, C. – p339 F2
Francesc Cambó, Avda – p344 B2
Francesc Carbonell, C. – p337 A2
Francesc Macià, Plaça – p338 C3
Francisco Giner, C. – p338 D3
Freixa, C. – p338 C2
Freixures, C. – p344-3 C2-3
Freneria, C. – p345 B3
Fruita, C. – p345 B3
Fusina, C. – p345 C3
Fusteria, C. – p345 B4
Gal.la Placidia, Plaça – p338 D3
Galileu, C. – p337 A3-4
Gall, Plaça – p338 C4
Gandesa, C. – p337 A3
Ganduxer, C. – p337-8 B3-C2
Gardunya, Plaça – p342 C6/p344 A2
Gaudí, Avda – p339 F4
Gaudí, Plaça – p339 F4
Gavà, C. – p341 A5
Gayarre, C. – p341 A4
Gegants, C. – p345 B3
Gelabert, C. – p337 B3
General Alvarez de Castro, C. – p344 C2
General Castaños, C. – p345 C4
George Orwell, Plaça – p345 B3
Gignàs, C. – p345 B4
Ginebra, C. – p343 E7
Giralt el pellisser, C. – p344 C2
Giriti, C. – p345 B3
Girona, C. – p339-343 E4-5/p344 C1
Gironella, Plaça – p337 B2
Gleva, C. – p338 D2
Glòria, Baixada – p339 E2
Glòries, Plaça de les – p343 F5
Gombau, C. – p344 C2
Gràcia, Passeig de – p338-342 D3-5/p344 B1
Gràcia, Travessera de – p338-9 C3-F3
Gran de Gràcia, C. – p338 D3
Gran Via Carles III – p337 A2-3
Gran Via de les Corts Catalanes – p341-343 A5-F5
Gran Vista, C. – p339 F2
Granada del Penedès – p338 D3
Granja, C. – p339 E2
Grassot, C. – p339 E4
Gravina, C. – p344 A1
Groc, C. – p345 B4
Grunyí, C. – p345 C3
Guadiana, C. – p341 A4
Guàrdia, C. – p342 C6/p345 A3
Guillem Tell, C. – p338 D2
Guilleries, C. – p339 D3
Guitard, C. – p337 A3-4
Hercegovina, C. – p338 C2
Hèrcules, C. – p345 B3
Heures, C. – p345 A3
Homer, C. – p338 D2
Hort de la Vila, C. – p337 B1
Hort Velluters, Passatge – p344 C2
Hospital Militar, Avda – p338 D2
Hospital, C. – p342 C6/p344-5 A2-3
Hostafrancs, C. – p341 A5
Hostal d'en Sol, C. – p345 B4
Icària, Avda – p343 F6-7
Indíbil, C. – p341 A5
Indústria, C. – p339 E3-F3
Iradier, C. – p337 B1
Isabel II, Passeig – p343 D6/p345 B4
Jacinto Benavente, C. – p337 B2
Jaume Giralt, C. – p344 C2
Jaume I, C. – p342 D6/p345 B3
Jerusalem, C. – p344 A2
Jiménez i Iglesias, C. – p337 A2
Joan Carles I, Plaça – p338 D4
Joan Corrades, Plaça – p341 A5

Joan d'Austria, C. – p343 F6
Joan de Borbó, Passeig – p342 D7/p345 C4
Joan Gamper, C. de – p337 B3
Joan Güell, C. – p337 A3
Joan Llongueras, Plaça – p338 C3
Joan Massana, C. – p345 B4
Joan Miró, C. – p343 F6
Joan Peiró, Plaça – p341 A4
Joan XXIII, Avda – p337 A2
Joanic, Plaça – p339 E3
Joanot Martorell, C. – p341 A4
Joaquim Blume, C. – p341 B5
Joaquim Pena, Plaça – p337 B2
Joaquim Xirau, Plaça – p342 D6/p345 A4
Joaquín Costa, C. – p342 C5
Jocs Florals, C. – p341 A4
Johann Sebastian Bach, C. – p338 C2
John Lennon, Plaça – p339 E3
Jonqueres, C. – p344 B1-2
Jordi Girona, C. – p337 A2
Josep Anselm Clavé, C. – p342 D6/p345 A4
Josep Carner, Passeig – p342 C7
Josep Ciurano, C. – p339 F3
Josep Llovera, Passatge – p338 C3
Josep Maria Folch i Torres, Plaça – p342 C6
Josep Serrano, C. – p339 F2
Josep Tarradellas, Avda – p337 B4
Jovellanos, C. – p344 A1
Julián Romea, C. – p338 D3
Junta de Comerç – p345 A3
Lafont, C. – p342 C6
Laforja, C. – p338 C3-D3
Laietana, Via – p342 D5-6/p344-5 B2-3
Lamote de Grignon, C. – p337 A2
Lancaster, C. – p345 A3
Larrard, C. – p339 E2
Lázaro Cárdenas, C. – p337 B2
Legalitat, C. – p339 E3
Leiva, C. – p341 A4-5
Lepant, C. – p339-343 F3-5
Les Corts, C. – p337 A3
Les Corts,Travessera de – p337 A3-B3
Lesseps, Plaça – p338 D2
Lincoln, C. – p338 D3
Litoral, Avda – p343 F7
Llana, Plaça – p345 C3
Llançà, C. – p341 B4-5
Llàstics, C. – p344 C2
Llauder, C. – p342 D6/p345 B4
Lledó, C. – p345 B3
Lleialtat, C. – p342 C6
Lleona, C. – p345 A3
Llibertat, C. – p338 D3
Llibertat, Plaça – p338 D3
Llibreteria, C. – p345 B3
Llorens i Barba, C. – p339 F3
Lluçà, C. – p337 A3
Lluís Companys, Passeig – p343 E6
Lluís Millet, Plaça – p344 B2
Lluís Pellicer, Passatge – p338 C3
Llull, C. – p343 F6
Lluna, C. – p342 C5
Londres, C. – p337-8 B3-C3
Loreto, C. – p337 B3
Luis Antúnez, C. – p338 D3
Madoz, Passatge – p345 A3
Madrazo, C. – p338 C3-D3
Madrid, Avda – p337 A3
Magalhães, C. – p341 B6
Magdalenes, C. – p344 B2
Maignon, C. – p338 D2
Major de Sarrià – p337 B1
Malcuinat, C. – p345 C4
Mallorca, C. – p341-339 A4-F4
Mandri, C. – p338 C2
Mañé i Flaquer, Plaça – p338 D3
Manila, C. – p337 A2
Manresa, C. – p345 B3
Manso, C. – p341 B5
Manuel Falla, C. – p337 A2
Manuel Girona, Passeig – p337 A2
Manuel Ribé, Placeta – p345 B3
Manufactures, Pgte de les – p344 C2
Maquinista, C. – p343 E7

Mar, C. – p342-343 D7-E7
Mar, Plaça del – p342 D7
Marc Aureli, C. – p338 C2
Marcús, Placeta – p345 C3
Mare de Déu de la Salut – p339 E2
Mare de Déu de Montserrat, Avda – p339 F2
Mare de Déu del Coll, C. – p338 D2
Mare de Déu del Pilar, C. – p344 C2
Margarit, C. – p341 B6
Margenat, C. – p337 B1
Maria Auxiliadora, C. – p337 B2
Maria Barrientos, C. – p337 A3
Marià Cubí, C. – p338 C3-D3
Marianao, C. – p339 E2
Marina, C. – p339-343 F3-7
Marítim Nova Icària, Passeig – p343 F7
Marítim Port Olímpic, Passeig – p343 F7
Marítim, Passeig – p343 E7
Marlet, C. – p345 B3
Marquès de Barberà, C. – p342 C6/p345 A3
Marquès de Campo Sagrado, C. – p341 B6
Marquès de Comillas, Avda – p341 A5
Marquès de l'Argentera, Avda – p343 E6/p345 C4
Marquès de Mulhacén, C. – p337 A1
Marquès de Sentmenat, C. – p337 B3
Marquesa, C. – p343 E6/p345 C4
Marquet, C. – p345 B4
Marquilles, Plaça – p344 C2
Martí i Julià, C. – p337 B2
Martí, C. – p339 E3
Mas Casanovas, C. – p339 F3
Maspons, C. – p338 D3
Massanet, C. – p345 B3
Maternitat, C. – p337 A3
Mejía Lequerica, C. – p337 A3-4
Melcior de Palau, C. – p337 A3-4
Méndez Núñez, C. – p344 B2
Mercader, Passatge – p338 D4
Mercaders, C. – p344-5 B2-3
Mercantil, Passeig – p345 C3
Mercè, C. – p345 B4
Mercè, Plaça – p342 D6/p345 B4
Mercedes, C. – p339 E2
Meridiana, Avda – p343 F5-6
Mestre Nicolau – p338 C3
Mestres Casals i Martorell, C. – p344 C2
Metges, C. – p344 C2
Mèxic, C. – p341 A5
Migdia, Passeig del – p341 A6-7
Milà i Fontanals, C. – p339 E3
Milans, Plaça – p345 B4
Mineria, C. – p338 D4
Minerva, C. – p338 D3
Miquel Àngel, C. – p337 A3
Miracle, C. – p337 A4
Mirador Palau Nacional – p341 A6
Mirallers, C. – p345 C3
Miramar, Avda – p341 B6
Miramar, Ctra – p341 B7
Miramar, Passeig – p341 B6
Misser Ferrer, C. – p344 B2
Mistral, Avda – p341 B5
Modolell, C. – p338 C2
Moianès, C. – p341 A5
Moles, C. – p344 B1-2
Molina, Plaça – p338 D2
Molist, C. – p339 E2
Moll Barceloneta – p342 C7
Moll Barceloneta – p342 D7
Moll d'Espanya – p342 D7/p345 B4
Moll de Drassanes – p342 C7
Moll de la Fusta – p342 D7/p345 B4
Moll Gregal – p343 F7
Moll Marina – p343 F7
Moll Mestral – p343 F7
Moll Sant Bertran – p342 C7
Mònec, C. – p344 C2
Monistrol, C. – p339 E3
Montalegre, C. – p342 C5/p344 A1
Montanyans, Avda – p341 A5

Montanyans, C. – p344 C2
Montcada, Placeta – p345 C3
Monterols, C. – p337 B1
Montjuïc del Carme, C. – p344 A2
Montjuïc, Carretera – p341 B7
Montjuïc, Passeig – p342 C7
Montmany, C. – p339 E3
Montnegre, C. – p337 B3
Montseny, C. – p338 D3
Montserrat, C. – p345 A4
Montsió, C. – p344 B2
Morales, C. – p337 B3
Morera, C. – p344 A2
Mosques, C. – p345 C4
Mossèn J. Verdaguer, Plaça – p339 E4
Mozart, C. – p338 D3
Muntades, C. – p341 A4
Muntaner, C. – p338-342 C2-5
Nàpols, C. – p339-343 E3-6
Narcis Oller, Plaça – p338 D3
Nau Santa Maria, C. – p337 B2
Nau, C. – p345 B3
Navas, Plaça de – p341 B6
Negrevernis, C. – p337 B1
Nemesi Ponsati, Plaça de – p341 A6
Nena Casas, C. – p337 B2
Niça, C. – p339 F3
Nicaragua, C. – p337 B3-4
Noguera Pallaresa, C. – p341 A4
Nord, Plaça – p339 E3
Notariat, C. – p344 A2
Nou de la Rambla, C. – p341-342 B6-C6/p345 A3
Nou de Sant Francesc, C. – p345 A4
Nou de Zurbano, C. – p345 A3
Nova, Plaça – p344 B2
Novell, C. – p337 A3
Numància, C. – p337 B2-4
Obradors, C. – p345 A3
Ocells, C. – p344 C2
Oli, C. – p345 B3
Oliana, C. – p338 C3
Olímpic, Passeig – p341 A6
Olles, Plaça – p345 C4
Olot, C. – p339 E2
Olzinelles, C. – p341 A4
Om, C. – p342 C6
Or, C. – p338 D3
Orient, Plaça – p337 B2
Ortigosa, C. – p344 C2
Osca, Plaça – p341 A5
Osi, C. – p337 A2-B1
Pablo Neruda, Plaça – p339 F4
Padilla, C. – p339-343 F3-5
Pàdua, C. – p338 D2
Paisos Catalans, Plaça – p341 A4
Palau, C. – p345 B3
Palau, Passatge – p345 C4
Palau, Pla de – p342 D6/p345 C4
Palaudàries, C. – p342 C6
Palla, C. – p344-5 B2-C3
Pallars, C. – p343 F6
Palma de Sant Just, C. – p345 B3
Pamplona, C. – p343 F5
Panses, C. – p345 C4
Paradís, C. – p345 B3
Paral.lel, Avda – p341-342 B5-C6
Parc Montjuïc – p341 B6
Parc, C. – p345 A4
Pare Laínez, C. – p339 E3
París, C. – p337-8 B3-C3
Parlament, C. – p341 B6
Patriarca, Passatge – p344 B2
Pau Alcover, C. – p337 B1
Pau Casals, Avda – p338 C3
Pau Claris, C. – p338-342 D4-5/p344 B1
Pau Vila, Plaça de – p342 D7/p345 C4
Pau, Passatge – p345 A4
Pearson, Avda – p337 A1
Pedralbes, Avda – p337 A1-2
Pedralbes, Plaça – p337 A1
Pedro i Pons, C. – p337 A2
Pedró, Plaça – p342 C6
Pelai, C. – p342 D5/p344 A1
Penedides, C. – p345 A3
Pere Costa, C. – p339 F3
Pere Gallifa, C. – p345 B3
Pere IV, C. – p343 F6
Pere Serafí, C. – p338 D3
Pérez Galdós, C. – p338 D2
Perill, C. – p338 D3

Perla, C. – p339 E3
Pes de la Palla, Plaça – p342 C5
Pescateria, C. – p345 C4
Petritxol, C. – p344 A2
Petxina, C. – p344 A2
Peu de la Creu, C. – p342 C5
Pi i Margall, C. – p339 E3-F3
Pi, C. – p344 B2
Pi, Plaça – p344 A2
Pi, Placeta – p345 A3
Picasso, Passeig – p343 E6
Pierre de Coubertin, C. de – p341
  A6
Pietat, C. – p345 B3
Pintor Fortuny, C. – p342
  C5/p344 A2
Piquer, C. – p342 C6
Pius XII, Plaça – p337 A2
Plata, C. – p345 B4
Plató, C. – p338 C2
Plegamans, C. – p345 C4
Poeta Bosçà, Plaça – p343 E7
Poeta Cabanyes, C. – p341 B6
Polònia, C. – p339 F2
Pomaret, C. – p337 B1
Pompeu Fabra, Avda – p339 F2
Pons i Clerch, Plaça – p345 C3
Portaferrissa, C. – p342 D6/p344
  A2
Portal de l'Àngel, Avda – p342
  D5/p344 B1-2
Portal de la Pau, Plaça – p342
  C7/p345 A4
Portal de Santa Madrona, C.
  – p342 C6
Portal Nou, C. – p343 E6/p344
  C2
Pou Dolç, C. – p345 B3
Pou Figuera, C. – p344 C2
Praga, C. – p339 F2
Prat de la Riba, Plaça – p337 B2
Prats de Molló, C. – p338 C2
Premià, C. – p341 A4
Príncep d'Astúries, Avda – p338
  D3
Princesa, C. – p343 D6/p345 C3
Provença, C. – p341-339 B4-F4
Providència, C. – p339 E3
Puigmartí, C. – p338 D3
Puigxuriguer, C. – p342 C7
Pujades, C. – p343 F6
Pujades, Passeig – p343 E6
Putget, C. – p338 D2
Quintana, C. – p345 A3
Radas, C. – p341 B6
Rafael Batlle, C. – p337 B2
Rafael Benet, Plaça – p337 B1
Raimon Casellas, Plaça – p339
  E3
Rambla Catalunya – p338-342
  D4-5/p344 B1
Rambla del Raval – p342 C6
Rambla Mercedes – p338 C2
Rambla Prat – p338 D3
Rambla, La – p342 D5-6/p344-5
  A2-4
Ramelleres, C. – p344 A1
Ramiro de Maeztu, C. – p339 E2
Ramon Amadeu, Placeta – p344 B2
Ramon Berenguer el Gran, Plaça –
  p345 B3
Ramon Trias Fargas, C. – p343
  F6-7
Ramon Turró, C. – p343 F6
Ramón y Cajal, C. – p339 E3
Raset, C. – p338 C2
Raspall, Plaça – p338 D3
Rauric, C. – p344 A2
Ravella, C. – p338 C2
Rec Comtal, C. – p344 C2
Rec, C. – p343 E6/p345 C3-4
Rector Tradó, C. – p341 A4
Rector Ubach, C. – p338 C3
Regomir, C. – p345 B3
Regomir, Plaça – p345 B3
Rei, Plaça de – p345 B3
Reial, Plaça – p342 D6/p345 A3
Reig i Bonet, C. – p339 E3
Reina Amàlia, C. – p342 C6
Reina Cristina, C. – p342
  D6/p345 C4
Reina Elisenda de Montcada,
  Passeig – p337 A1-B1
Reina Maria Cristina, Avda – p341
  A5
Reina Maria Cristina, Plaça –
  p337 A2

Reina Victòria, C. – p338 C2
República Argentina, Avda – p338
  D2
Requesens, C. – p342 C5
Rera Palau, C. – p345 C4
Revolució Setembre 1868, Plaça
  – p338 D3
Ribera, C. – p345 C4
Ribes, C. – p343 E5-F5
Ricart, C. – p341 B5
Riego, C. – p341 A4
Riera Alta, C. – p342 C5
Riera Baixa, C. – p342 C6
Riera Sant Miquel, C. – p338 D3
Riereta, C. – p342 C6
Ríos Rosas, C. – p338 D2
Ripoll, C. – p344 A2
Rita Bonnat, C. – p337 B3
Rius i Taulet, Avda – p341 A5
Rius i Taulet, Plaça – p338 D3
Rivadeneyra, C. – p344 B1
Robador, C. – p342 C6
Robrenyo, C. – p337 A3-B4
Roca, C. – p344 A2
Rocafort, C. – p341 B4-5
Roger de Flor, C. – p339-343 E4-6
Roger de Llúria, C. – p338-342
  D4-5/p344 C1
Roig, C. – p342 C6
Roma, Avda – p341-338 B4-C4
Romans, C. – p339 E3
Ronda del Mig – p338-9 C2-F3
Ronda General Mitre – p338 B2-D2
Ronda Guinardó – p339 E2
Ronda Litoral – p342-3 C7-
  F7/p345 A4-C4
Ronda Sant Antoni – p342 C5
Ronda Sant Pau – p342 C6
Ronda Sant Pere – p342-3 D5-
  E5/p344 B1-C1
Ronda Universitat – p342
  D5/p344 A1
Ros de Olano, C. – p338 D3
Rosa Sensat, C. – p343 F6
Rosa, C. – p345 B4
Rosalía de Castro, C. – p339 F3
Rosari, C. – p337 B2
Roser, C. – p341 B6
Rosés, C. – p337 A3
Rosés, Plaça – p337 B3
Rosic, C. – p345 C4
Rosselló, C. – p337-9 B4-F4
Rossend Arús, C. – p341 A4
Rovira i Trias, Plaça – p339 E3
Rovira, Túnel de la – p339 F2
Ruis i Taulet, Plaça – p338 D3
Rull, C. – p345 A4
Sabateret, C. – p345 C3
Sabino de Arana, C. – p337 A2
Sagrada Família, Plaça – p339 E4
Sagristans, C. – p344 B2
Sagüés, C. – p338 C3
Salou, C. – p341 A4
Salvà, C. – p341 B6
Salvador Espriu, C. – p343 F7
Sancho de Ávila, C. – p343 F5
Sanllehy, Plaça – p339 E2
Sant Agustí Vell, Plaça – p344 C2
Sant Agustí, Plaça – p345 A3
Sant Antoni Abat, C. – p342 C5
Sant Antoni dels Sombrerers, C. –
  p345 C3
Sant Antoni Maria Claret, C. –
  p339 E3-F3
Sant Antoni, C. – p341 A4
Sant Benet, Ptge – p344 C2
Sant Bonaventura, Cró – p344 B2
Sant Carles, C. – p343 E7
Sant Climent, C. – p342 C6
Sant Crist, C. – p341 A4
Sant Cugat, C. – p339 E2
Sant Cugat, Plaça – p343
  E6/p345 C3
Sant Domènec del Call, C. – p345
  B3
Sant Domènec, C. – p338 D3
Sant Elies, C. – p338 C2
Sant Erasme, C. – p342 C5
Sant Eusebi, C. – p338 C3-D3
Sant Felip Neri, Plaça – p345 B3
Sant Francesc, Placeta – p345 A3
Sant Fructuós, C. – p341 A5
Sant Gaietà, Plaça – p337 B1
Sant Germà, C. – p341 A5
Sant Gil, C. – p342 C5
Sant Gregori Taumaturg, Plaça –
  p337 B3

Sant Honorat, C. – p345 B3
Sant Iu, Plaça – p345 B3
Sant Jacint, C. – p345 C3
Sant Jaume, Plaça – p342
  D6/p345 B3
Sant Joan Bosco, Passeig – p337
  B2
Sant Joan, Passeig – p339-343
  E4-5
Sant Joaquim, C. – p338 D3
Sant Joaquim, Plaça – p338 D2
Sant Josep Oriol, Plaça – p345 A3
Sant Just, Plaça – p342 D6/p345
  B3
Sant Lluís, C. – p339 E3
Sant Magí, C. – p338 D2
Sant Marc, C. – p338 D3
Sant Medir, C. – p341 A4
Sant Miquel, Baixada – p345 B3
Sant Miquel, Plaça – p345 B3
Sant Miquel, Plaçeta – p338 D3
Sant Oleguer, C. – p342 C6
Sant Pau, C. – p342 C6/p345 A3
Sant Pere Màrtir, C. – p338 D3
Sant Pere Més Alt, C. – p342
  D5/p344 C2
Sant Pere Més Baix, C. – p342
  D6/p344 B2-C2
Sant Pere Mitjà, C. – p342
  D6/p344 C2
Sant Pere, C. – p344 C2
Sant Pere, Plaça – p343 E6/p344
  C2
Sant Rafael, C. – p342 C6
Sant Ramon, C. – p342 C6
Sant Roc, C. – p341 A5
Sant Salvador, C. – p339 E2
Sant Sever, C. – p345 B3
Sant Vicenç de Sarrià, Plaça –
  p337 B1
Sant Vicenç, C. – p342 C5
Santa Amèlia, C. – p337 A2
Santa Anna, C. – p342 D5/p344
  B2
Santa Carolina, C. – p339 F3
Santa Caterina, C. – p345 A4
Santa Caterina, Plaça – p338 C3
Santa Elena, C. – p342 C6
Santa Eugènia, C. – p338 D3
Santa Eulàlia, Baixada – p345 B3
Santa Eulàlia, C. – p339 E4
Santa Fe de Nou Mèxic – p337 B2
Santa Llúcia, C. – p345 B3
Santa Madrona, C. – p342 C6
Santa Madrona, Passeig – p341 A6
Santa Maria, C. – p345 C3
Santa Maria, Plaça – p345 C3
Santa Mònica, C. – p345 A4
Santa Perpètua, C. – p338 D2
Santa Teresa, C. – p338 D4
Santaló, C. – p338 C2-3
Santjoanistes, C. – p338 D2
Sants, C. – p341 A4
Santuari de Sant Josep de la
  Muntanya, Avda – p339 E2
Saragossa, C. – p338 D2
Sardana, Plaça – p341 B7
Sardenya, C. – p339-343 F3-6
Sarrià, Avda – p337 B2-3
Sarrià, Plaça – p337 B1
Seca, C. – p345 C4
Secretari Coloma, C. – p339 E3
Semoleres, C. – p345 C3
Sèneca, C. – p338 D3
Septimania, C. – p338 D2
Sepúlveda, C. – p341-342 B5-C5
Sèquia, C. – p344 C2
Serra Xic, C. – p344 C2
Serra, C. – p345 B4
Sert, Passatge – p344 C2
Seu, Plaça de la – p344 B2
Sicília, C. – p339-343 E3-5
Sidé, C. – p345 C3
Sils, C. – p345 A4
Simó Oller, C. – p345 B4
Siracusa, C. – p338 D3
Sitges, C. – p344 A2
Sol, Plaça – p338 D3
Sombrerers, C. – p345 C3
Sor Eulalia d'Anzizu, C. – p337 A1
Sortidor, Plaça – p341 B6
Sostres, C. – p339 E2
Sota Muralla, Passeig – p345 B4
Sots-tinent Navarro, C. – p345 B3
**Tallers, C. – p342 C5-D5/p344
  A1**
Tamarit, C. – p341 B5

Tànger, C. – p343 F5
Tantarantana, C. – p345 C3
Tàpies, C. – p342 C6
Tapineria, C. – p345 B3
Tapioles, C. – p341 B6
Taquígraf Garriga – p337 A3-B3
Taquígraf Martí, C. – p337 A3
Taquígraf Serra, C. – p337 B3
Tarongers, C. dels – p341 B6
Tarongeta, C. – p345 B3
Tarragona, C. – p341 B5
Tarròs, C. – p345 C3
Tavern, C. – p338 C2-3
Taxdirt, C. – p339 E3
Teatre, Plaça de – p345 A4
Tècnica, Avda – p341 A6
Templers, C. – p345 B3
Tenerife, C. – p339 F2
Tenor Masini, C. – p337 A3
Terol, C. – p338 D3
Tetuan, Plaça – p343 E5
Tigre, C. – p342 C5
Til.lers, Passeig – p337 A2
Tinent Coronel Valenzuela, C. –
  p337 A1-2
Tiradors, C. – p345 C3
Tomàs Mieres, C. – p344 B2
Topazi, C. – p338 D3
Tordera, C. – p338 D3
Torre, Plaça – p338 D2
Torrent de l'Olla, C. – p338 D2-3
Torrent de les Flors – p339 E3
Torrent d'en Vidalet, C. – p339 E3
Torres i Amat – p344 A1
Torres, C. – p338 D3
Torrijos, C. – p339 E3
Tous, C. – p339 F3
Trafalgar, C. – p342-3 D5-
  E5/p344 C1-2
Traginers, Plaça – p342 D6/p345
  B3
Trajà, C. – p341 A5
Trelawny, C. – p343 E7
Tres Pins, Camí – p341 A6
Tres Torres, C. – p337 B2
Trilla, Plaça – p338 D3
Trinitat, C. – p345 A3
Trinquet, C. – p337 A1
Tuset, C. – p338 C3
Unió, C. – p342 C6/p345 A3
Urquinaona, Plaça – p344 B1
València, C. – p341-339 B4-F4
Valldonzella, C. – p342 C5/p344
  A1
Valldoreix, C. – p339 E3
Vallespir, C. – p337 A3-4
Vallhonrat, C. – p341 B5
Vallirana, C. – p338 D2
Vallmajor, C. – p338 C2
Valseca, C. – p339 F2
Veguer, C. – p345 B3
Ventura Gassol, Plaça – p338 D2
Verdaguer i Callís, C. – p344 B2
Verdi, C. – p339 D3-E2
Vergós, C. – p337 B2
Verònica, Plaça – p345 B3
Vic, C. – p338 D3
Vicenç Martorell, Plaça – p344 A2
Vico, C. – p338 C2
Víctor Balaguer, Plaça – p345 B3
Victòria, C. – p344 C2
Vidre, C. – p345 A3
Vidrieria, C. – p345 C3
Vigatans, C. – p345 B3
Vila de Madrid, Plaça – p344 B2
Vila i Vilà, C. – p342 C6-7
Viladecols, Baixada – p344 B2
Viladomat, C. – p337-341 B3-5
Vilamarí, C. – p341 B4-5
Vilamur, C. – p337 A3
Vilanova, Avda – p343 E5
Vilardell, C. – p341 A4
Villarroel, C. – p338-342 C3-5
Violant d'Hongria, Reina d'Aragó,
  C. – p337 A3
Viriat, C. – p337 A4
Virreina, Passatge – p344 A2
Virreina, Plaça – p339 E3
Vivers, C. – p341 A6
Wagner, Plaça – p337 B3
Watt, C. – p341 A4
Wellington, C. – p343 E6
Xuclà, C. – p342 D5/p344 A2
Zamora, C. – p343 F6

Where to Stay

⊙ Rodalies Barcelona ⑫

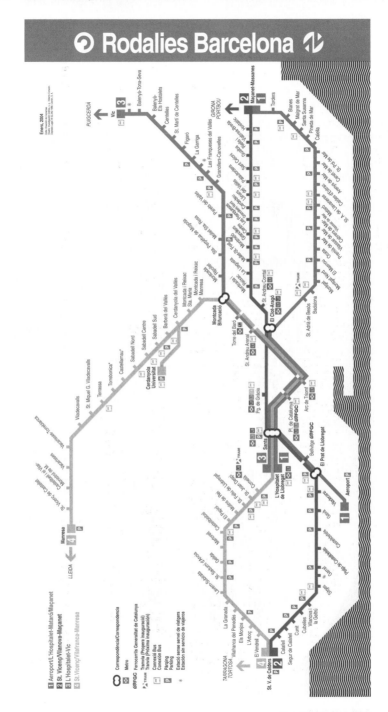

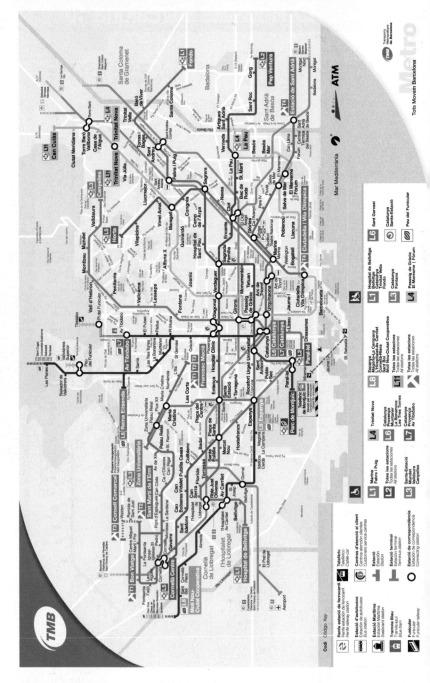